ORGANIZATIONAL CHANGE

Visit the *Organizational Change, third edition* Companion Website at
www.pearsoned.co.uk/senior to find valuable **student** learning
material including:

- Chapter overviews
- Case study feedback
- Annotated links to relevant sites on the web

PEARSON
Education

We work with leading authors to develop the strongest educational materials in business and management, bringing cutting-edge thinking and best learning practice to a global market.

Under a range of well-known imprints, including Financial Times Prentice Hall, we craft high quality print and electronic publications which help readers to understand and apply their content, whether studying or at work.

To find out more about the complete range of our publishing, please visit us on the World Wide Web at: www.pearsoned.co.uk

Third Edition

ORGANIZATIONAL CHANGE

Barbara Senior

Jocelyne Fleming

 Prentice Hall
FINANCIAL TIMES

An imprint of Pearson Education
Harlow, England • London • New York • Boston • San Francisco • Toronto
Sydney • Tokyo • Singapore • Hong Kong • Seoul • Taipei • New Delhi
Cape Town • Madrid • Mexico City • Amsterdam • Munich • Paris • Milan

Pearson Education Limited

Edinburgh Gate
Harlow
Essex CM20 2JE
England

and Associated Companies throughout the world

Visit us on the World Wide Web at:
www.pearsoned.co.uk

———————————

First published 1997
Second edition published 2002
Third edition published 2006

© Barbara Senior, 1997, 2002
© Barbara Senior and Jocelyne Fleming 2006

ISBN: 978-0-27369-598-1

British Library Cataloguing-in-Publication Data
A catalogue record for this book is available from the British Library

Library of Congress Cataloging-in-Publication Data
A catalog record for this book is available from the Library of Congress

10 9 8 7 6 5 4 3
10 09 08

Typeset in Stone Serif 9.5/13pt by 30
Printed and bound by Graficas Estella, Navarro, Spain

The publisher's policy is to use paper manufactured from sustainable forests.

Contents

Part One
THE CONTEXT AND MEANING OF CHANGE

Part Two
ORGANIZATIONS FOR CHANGE

List of illustrations, figures and tables

Illustrations

Figures

Tables

Supporting resources

Visit www.pearsoned.co.uk/senior to find valuable online resources

Companion Website for students
- Chapter overviews
- Case study feedback
- Annotated links to relevant sites on the web

For instructors
- Power Point slides of key learning points, objectives and activities
- Chapter overviews and synopsis
- Feedback on activities and key areas of discussion
- Case example notes
- Possible session structures

For more information please contact your local Pearson Education sales representative or visit www.pearsoned.co.uk/senior

About this book

Introduction

All people in all organizations are concerned with and involved with change, whether of the small-scale variety, such as adopting an updated version of a computer program, or on a larger scale, such as a change of strategy with subsequent changes in structure and operations. Consequently, no study of organizational life is complete without complementary studies of the way change affects an organization and how that change can be managed. In a world of constantly fluctuating demand and supply, of changing customer needs as well as the wider concerns brought about by the legitimate expectations of employees, change is essential. The impetus for writing this book comes from the belief that organizations and change must live comfortably together or they will perish. Its content derives from many years of experience in helping to meet the learning needs of students of business and management with respect to the way people in organizations approach and deal with change and with managing and working with change in a variety of organizations.

The aim of this book

The overall aim of this book is to provide a discussion of change in relation to the complexities of organizational life. The text takes both a theoretical and practical approach to the issue of organizational change in seeking to meet both the academic and applied aims of most business and management courses.

More specifically this text aims to be:

- *Comprehensive* in its coverage of the significant ideas and issues associated with change at all levels of organizational activity, from the strategic to the operational. Change is also examined in terms of its effects at the individual, group, organizational and societal levels.
- *Conceptual* in the way it explores and critiques theory and research in relation to organizations and change.
- *Practical* in its provision of descriptions and worked examples of different approaches to 'doing' change.
- *Challenging* through asking readers to undertake activities including responding to discussion questions. The text in each chapter is interspersed with activities intended to personalize ideas from the text and to reinforce learning. End of chapter discussion questions, assignments and case examples ask for longer and more detailed responses.

- *Balanced* in its use of case studies and examples, which are drawn from various types of organizations – public, private and voluntary sectors, small and large.

Who should use this book?

The book is intended for all those who are interested in exploring, in some detail, issues associated with organizational change and how to deal with it. Specifically:

- *Undergraduate students* on business studies, modular or joint degrees should find it sufficiently structured to provide an understandable route through the subject.
- *MBA students* should find the blend of theory and practice appropriate to the academic and applied demands of their courses. Requirements to relate theory and research to their own situations should prove useful in their day-to-day organizational activities. The case examples and longer case studies provide real-life instances of change.
- *Postgraduate students* on other specialist taught Master's programmes should find sufficient practical examples in the text, and through the case examples and case studies, to illustrate theory even if they have little practical experience of management and business themselves.
- *Students on professional courses* that include elements relating to the management of change.
- *Practising middle and senior managers* who wish to delve more deeply into theoretical discussions of change and its complexity in relation to organizational functioning. In addition, or alternatively, they could benefit from study of the various change models described in the book as they apply to different change situations.

Readers of the book will benefit if they have some prior knowledge of the subject area of organizational behaviour. However, the book is written so as to be understandable to those with no such/little prior knowledge.

Distinctive features

- **Clear structure.** The book is structured into three parts. The first considers the nature of organizations operating in complex environments and responding to the 'winds of change'. It includes some detailed discussion of the causes of change. Theoretical perspectives are introduced with a discussion of the nature of change. Part One of the book acts as an introduction to Part Two, which 'opens up' the organization to expand on a number of issues that are crucial to an understanding of organizational change and how it happens. Finally, Part Three moves firmly into addressing the more practical considerations of designing, planning and implementing change. It concludes with a chapter that broadens the other discussions by looking into the future to speculate on organizations beyond the year 2006 and the attitudes and behaviours to be expected of those who will work in them.

- **Chapter summaries and learning objectives.** Each chapter begins with a short summary of the chapter content. This is followed by a list of learning objectives. On completion of each chapter, readers can check their learning against these objectives. Chapter conclusions round off the chapter discussions.
- **Boxed illustrations and activities.** Illustrations that expand or give examples of points made in the text are used throughout. These might be quotations from writings referred to in the text or further explanations of theories, research or other points made. They include small case studies and extracts from relevant newspaper articles. The text in the illustration boxes is simply for reading. The activity boxes, however, typically ask the reader to carry out an activity or piece of research or actively apply some ideas from the text to their own experience.
- **End of chapter discussion questions and assignments.** Each chapter ends with questions that are intended to promote a more lengthy consideration of issues raised in the text. Many of the questions are set in 'examination'-type terms and can be used as preparation for such tests that might be associated with a particular course.
- **End of chapter case examples.** The chapters in Parts One and Two of the book include, at the end, a short case example and case exercise, which helps readers apply concepts, theories and ideas introduced in the chapter to a real example of change. The questions on these case examples are intended only as a guide to thinking about the different aspects of the situation described in relation to ideas and themes, not only in the chapter in which they appear, but elsewhere in the book.
- **Indicative resources for the reader.** Additional textbooks are offered to the reader to attain further perspectives on the subject areas of each of the chapters. Their full reference is included, along with a brief overview of how they might support further analysis.
- **Website addresses for readers.** This information is provided for the reader to obtain further information to support assignments or research in areas related to topics discussed in each of the chapters.
- **A two-part, longer case study.** This appears at the end of Parts One and Two. It tells the story of change at Orange, a major mobile telephone network provider. Researched by the authors, it provides an opportunity to apply theory, research of change as discussed throughout the book.
- **Academic sources and references.** In line with the academic requirements of most courses, discussion of issues is supported by numerous references to other people's work in this subject area. Full details of references in the text can be easily found by consulting the alphabetical listings in the author index at the end of the book.
- **Lecturer's Guide and PowerPoint slides.** A Lecturer's Guide is available, downloadable from **www.pearsoned.co.uk/senior**, to those lecturers adopting this textbook. It includes commentaries on each chapter, in particular how to use the activities and the kinds of responses to be expected from stu-

dents carrying out the activities and answering the discussion questions. Additional study work is suggested and PowerPoint slides are provided.

How to use this book

The book has a simple structure. Readers new to the subject of organizational change will find the chapters in Part One essential. If they have no knowledge of organizational behaviour, Part Two is especially important. For those who have already studied organizational theory and behaviour, Part Two offers some revision of these issues, but with additional discussion of how change interacts with these aspects of organizational life. Part Three provides advice on how to plan and implement change, for those who need it.

Some readers have found it useful to go through the chapters as they are laid out. Others say that, by skim reading the chapters in Part Three first, they have gained an idea of how change can be implemented before delving deeper into the many issues associated with it, which are discussed in Part Two. With regard to the large case study of Orange, which is positioned in two parts at the end of Parts One and Two of the book, it can be helpful to read this first and then attempt to apply learning as reading progresses through the chapters.

Distributed throughout all the chapters are a series of activities, which are intended to extend learning brought about by reading. Sometimes they ask for reflection of points made. At other times they ask for application of concepts and ideas to situations familiar to the reader. In the main, the activities are formulated to help readers apply knowledge to practice. A useful strategy is to read through a chapter quickly first then, on a second reading, to carry out the activities.

The discussion questions, assignments and case examples offer opportunities for readers to write at some length on issues associated with organizational change. They are particularly useful as preparation for completing qualification assignments and examinations. The large case study of Orange covers many aspects of change discussed in the book. The material covered there can be supplemented by readers' own experiences working in organizations and by obtaining information about Orange and other similar organizations from the Web.

About the authors

Barbara Senior

Barbara is Director of Highfield House Consultants and an Associate Lecturer with the Open University where she lectures on, and supervises doctoral students in managing and leading in organizations. She is a Chartered Occupational Psychologist and a Member of the Chartered Institute of Personnel and Development (CIPD).

Her past experience is varied. After working in administration and running her own dressmaking and tailoring business, she became Senior Lecturer in Human Resource Management at John Moores University, followed by working as Team Leader of the Work and Unemployment programme at the Open University. More recently she was Regional Manager for the Open College before becoming Director of the MA in Organizational Behaviour and Change Management at the University of Northampton and Director of the Postgraduate Modular Scheme.

She is the author (with John Naylor) of two previous books on the subjects of work and unemployment. She contributed a chapter entitled: 'Organisational Change and Development' to the book *Introduction to Work and Organisational Psychology*, edited by Nik Chmiel (Blackwell, 2000) and has published many articles and conference papers based on her research interests in the areas of teamworking and cross-cultural management. She has a particular interest in promoting creative thinking and innovation.

Jocelyne Fleming

Jocelyne is a Senior Lecturer at the University of Gloucestershire (Business School). She teaches on various programmes, in particular the undergraduate Managing Change Module, MBA, Master's in Human Resource Development and CIPD programmes. Most of her past experience lies with managing in the public sector. Particular areas of interest are in change management, organizational development, action research and action learning. Jocelyne works with a team of consultants at the university who work with organizations nationally to support change strategies in organizations.

Acknowledgements

Barbara

The first and second editions of this book would not have been possible without the practical and moral support of my late husband Gerry. I dedicate this third edition to his memory. My two children David and Jayne and my very good friends Vernabelle and Derek have given sound advice and kind words when needed. My apologies go to those friends and family who were neglected in the final stages of my completing the book.

I welcome Jocelyne as co-author and thank her for her significant contribution to the book. As always, the staff of Pearson – Jacqueline Senior (no relation!), Linda Dhondy, Ben Greshon and others – have been unfailingly supportive and patient.

Finally, Jocelyne and I have tried to be true to the large amount of reseach and work already accomplished in the subject area of organizational change. Every effort has been made to trace and acknowledge ownership of copyright.

Jocelyne

As this is the first publication for me with Pearson, I would like to thank Barbara for her kindness and encouragement; this is also true for Jacqueline. I have thoroughly enjoyed the co-author experience and it has challenged my research skills, analytical skills and, of course, my skills in time management!

For support closer to home, thanks to my husband Martin, my parents Kevin and Patricia, and my dear friend Darren.

Publisher's acknowledgements

We are grateful to the following for permission to reproduce copyright material:

Figure 1.2 and Table 1.1 from *Creative Management*, Prentice Hall (Goodman, M. 1995); Table 1.2 from *The changing structure of employment in Italy 1980–2010*, Working Paper, Interindustry Economic Research Fund, Inc. (IERF) (Almon, C. and Grassini, M. 2002); Unnumbered figure 1.1, Table 9.1, Figures 9.1, 9.2 and 9.3 from *Working Futures: New Projections of Employment by Sector 2002–2012*, vol. 1, The Sector Skills Development Agency (Wilson, R., Homenidou, K. and Dickerson, A. 2004), The Sector Skills Development Agency (SSDA) commissioned the Institute for Employment Research (IER) at the University of Warwick and Cambridge Econometrics to produce *Working Futures*. This comprises a series of reports presenting projections of UK employment (2002–2012) by occupation, sector, UK country and English region. The reports are available from SSDA's website: www.ssda.org.uk. Updated projections of employment (*Working Futures*, 2004–2014) are to be published by the SSDA in autumn 2005. A network of UK-wide Sector Skills Councils (SSCs) has been charged to lead the skills and productivity drive in industry or business sectors recognized by employers. The SSDA has been established to underpin the SSC network and promote effective working between sectors; Figure 2.1 from *Implementing Strategic Change*, Kogan Page (Grundy, T. 1993); Figure 2.2 from *Exploring Strategic Change*, FT Prentice Hall (Balogun, J. and Hailey,V.H. 2004); reprinted by permission of *Harvard Business Review* Figure 2.3 and Table 6.3 (derived). From 'Evolution and revolution as organizations grow' by Greiner, L.E., July–August 1972, copyright © 1972 by the Harvard Business School Publishing Corporation; all rights reserved; Table 2.1 from *The Essence of Change*, Prentice Hall (Clarke, L. 1994); Figure 3.1 from *Management and Organisational Behaviour*, 7th edn, FT Prentice Hall (Mullins, L. J. 2005); Unnumbered figures 3.3 and 3.4 from www.unilever.com/ourcompany/newsandmedia, Unilever Plc; Figure 3.6 from Morgan, G. (1989), *Creative Organization Theory. A Resource Book*, London, Sage, p.66; Figure 3.9 from 'The effective organization forces and forms' in *Sloan Management Review*, vol. 32, part 2, Winter (Mintzberg, H. 1991), copyright 1991 by Massachusetts Institute of Technology, all rights reserved, distributed by Tribune Media Services; Figure 4.2 from 'Measuring organizational cultures: a qualitative and quantitative study across twenty cases' in *Administrative Science Quarterly*, vol. 35, Cornell University (Hofstede, G., Neuijen, B., Ohayv, D. D. and Sanders, G. 1990); Illustration 4.3 (Unnumbered figure 4.1) from *Exploring Corporate Strategy, Texts and Cases*, 7th edn, Pearson Education Ltd (Johnson, G., Scholes, K. and Whittington, R. 2005); Figure 4.4 from *Managing Cultures: Making Strategic*

Relationships Work (Hall, W., 1995, p. 95), Chichester, Wiley, © 1995, copyright John Wiley & Sons Ltd, reproduced with permission; Figure 4.5 from *Managing Change Across Corporate Cultures* (Trompenaars, F. and Prud'homme, P., 2004, p. 67, figure 2.6), Chichester, Capstone Publishing, © 2004, copyright John Wiley & Sons Ltd, reproduced with permission of John Wiley & Sons Ltd on behalf of Capstone Publishing Ltd; Table 4.1 adapted with permission from 'Cultural constraints in management theories' in *Academy of Management Executive*, February (Hofstede, G. 1993), copyright © Geert Hofstede; Figure 4.7 adapted with permission from *Cultures and Organizations*, McGraw Hill (Hofstede, G. 1991), copyright © Geert Hofstede; Figure 4.8 from *A European Management Model Beyond Diversity*, Prentice Hall (Calori, R. and De Woot, P. 1994); Figures 4.10, 4.11 and 4.12 reprinted from *Organizational Dynamics*, Summer, Schwartz, H. and Davis, S.M., 'Matching corporate strategy and business strategy', pp. 36, 41 and 44, copyright 1981, with permission from Elsevier; Figure 5.1 from *Women's Empowerment: Measuring the Global Gender Gap*, World Economic Forum Gender Gap Index-Story from BBC News: http://www.newsvote.bbc.co.uk (World Economic Forum 2005); Illustration 6.3 adapted with the permission of The Free Press, a Division of Simon & Schuster Adult Publishing Group, from *Force for Change: How Leadership Differs From Management* by John P. Kotter, copyright © 1990 by John P. Kotter, Inc, all rights reserved; Figure 6.1 from *Leadership Dilemmas: Grid Solutions, Gulf Publishing* (Blake, R. and McCanse 1991), copyright © 1991 by Robert R. Blake and the Estate of Jane S. Mouton, Austin, Texas, used with permission, all rights reserved, The Grid® designation is the property of Scientific Methods Inc. and is used here with permission; Figure 6.7 reprinted by permission of Sage Publications Ltd from Dunphy, D. and Stace, D., 'The strategic management of corporate change' in *Human Relations*, vol. 46, no. 8, copyright (© The Tavistock Institute, 1993); Figure 8.4 from 'The Pugh Matrix', from Course P679 Planning and Managing Change, Block 4, Section 6, Copyright © The Open University; Illustration 9.2 (Figure UF 9.1) from National Statistics Website: http://www.statistics.gov.uk, Crown copyright material is reproduced with the permission of the Controller of HMSO; Figure 9.2 from Bulletin no. 73, p. 3, table 2 at http://www.warwick.ac.uk/fac/soc/ier/publications/bulletins, SSDA (Institute for Employment Research 2004), The Sector Skills Development Agency (SSDA) commissioned the Institute for Employment Research (IER) at the University of Warwick and Cambridge Econometrics to produce Working Futures. This comprises a series of reports presenting projections of UK employment (2002–2012) by occupation, sector, UK country and English region. The reports are available from SSDA's website: www.ssda.org.uk. Updated projections of employment (Working Futures, 2004–2014) are to be published by the SSDA in autumn 2005. A network of UK wide Sector Skills Councils (SSCs) has been charged to lead the skills and productivity drive in industry or business sectors recognized by employers. The SSDA has been established to underpin the SSC network and promote effective working between sectors.

In some instances we have been unable to trace the owners of copyright material, and we would appreciate any information that would enable us to do so.

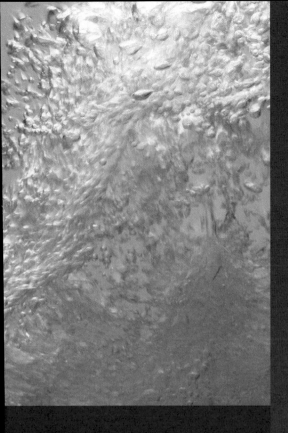

Part One

THE CONTEXT AND MEANING OF CHANGE

Change in organizations is really the norm today. Organizations are influenced by a multitude of factors, which are influenced by both the internal and external environment. Change in organizations does not happen in a vacuum. If nothing happened to disturb organizational life change would be very slow and, perhaps, merely accidental. However, commentators on organizational life have evidenced that the pace of change is accelerating and all organizations, if they are to benefit from continued survival, must be prepared not only to respond to, but to anticipate, change.

Part One of this book examines what is meant by organizational change and the reasons why it happens. Chapter 1 begins this process by proposing a model of organization which recognizes the fact that organizational life is influenced by many factors, mainly those originating outside the organization. A metaphor of the 'winds of change' is used to show how organizational activities are the outcomes of historical developments as well as the results of the day-by-day vagaries of political, economic, technological and sociocultural influences.

The second chapter of Part One investigates, in more detail, the nature of organizational change itself and introduces ways of working with it. Part One therefore sets the scene for the more detailed discussion of organizations and change in Part Two.

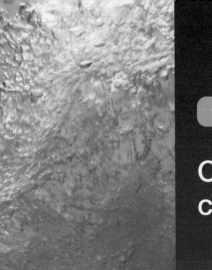

Chapter 1

Organizations and their changing environments

In this chapter, organizations are defined as systems comprising elements of formal organizational management and operations as well as elements of more informal aspects of organizational life. The organizational systems themselves are conceptualized as operating in three types of environment. These are the temporal, external and internal environments whose elements interact with each other to form the 'triggers' of change that are significant in bringing about organizational changes.

Learning objectives

By the end of this chapter you will be able to:

● describe the general characteristics of organizations and their essential components;

● say how different methods of wealth creation, viewed from a historical perspective, have influenced present-day organizational strategies and focus;

● discuss the concept of organizations as systems operating in multi-dimensional environments and its implications for understanding the causes of organizational change;

● recognize that change can be triggered from any number of directions: through historical influences, from the external environment and from within the organization itself – the internal environment.

●●●● A view of organizations

It is sometimes difficult to track down a comprehensive definition of what is meant by 'an organization'. Many books on management, decision making, even organizational design, do not give a straightforward definition of what organization means. Some definitions, however, have been attempted. The following is an attempt to describe some of the main elements associated with organizations:

> Individuals and groups interact within a formal structure. Structure is created by management to establish relationships between individuals and groups, to provide order and systems and to direct efforts to carry out goal seeking activities.
>
> (Mullins, 2005, p. 32)

> An organization: consists of people trying to influence others to achieve certain objectives that create wealth or well-being through a variety of processes, technologies, structures and cultures.   (wps.prenhall.com, 2004)

> An organization is a social arrangement for achieving controlled performance in pursuit of collective goals.   (Buchanan and Huczynski, 2004, p. 5)

> Organization: a group of people brought together for the purpose of achieving certain objectives. As the basic unit of an organization is the role rather than the person in it the organization is maintained in existence, sometimes over a long period of time, despite many changes of members.   (Statt, 1991, p. 102)

Although the last of these definitions appears more complex than the others, they all have similar themes – people interacting in some kind of structured or organized way to achieve some defined purpose or goal. However, as might be deduced, the interactions of people, as members of an organization, need some kind of managing, that is there will be elements of coordination and control of these activities. In organizations with more than ten or so people this implies some kind of structuring of their activities that picks up the idea of organizational roles mentioned in Statt's definition. In addition, the activities of individual organizational members and their interactions with one another imply a process through which work gets done in order to achieve the organization's purposes or goals. Above all, there is the requirement for decision taking about the processes (the means) by which the goals (the ends) are achieved. Illustration 1.1 encapsulates most of this but also adds the idea of a boundary that prescribes which people belong to the organization and which do not.

The example of the factory given by Butler (1991) draws attention to the fact that organizations cut across geographical boundaries and, therefore, organizational boundaries are, in Butler's words, also 'abstractions'. Yet the notion of an organizational boundary is very real in that it draws attention to the concept of an organization's environment. By this is meant all those influences that may act to disturb organizational life but are not considered directly part of it. The mention of capital provided by some kind of financial institution is a recognition that organizations are connected to wider systems which form part of the environment – such as those supplying finance and other resources, not least human resources.

Illustration 1.1

The meaning of organization

A typical working definition of an organization might say it is: (1) a social entity that (2) has a purpose, (3) has a boundary, so that some participants are considered inside while others are considered outside, and (4) patterns the activities of participants into a recognizable structure (Daft, 1989). Although organizations are real in their consequences, both for their participants and for their environments, they are essentially abstractions. ... The hospital, the firm or the school will have physical aspects to them, the buildings, the plant and equipment and so on, but to understand how organizations work we need to go further than this. The factory has something real and physical about it but this is not the organization; people are doing tasks to which there is a pattern, raw materials are taken in, converted and distributed to markets; capital is provided by banks and other financial institutions; systems provide information for decision making and coordination; people are talking about matters that do not necessarily appear to have anything to do with the job, some people remote from the physical plant, perhaps a continent away, are making decisions critical to our factory.

Source: Butler, R. (1991), *Designing Organizations. A Decision-Making Perspective* (London, Routledge, pp. 1–2).

This view of organizations draws on the concept of an organization as a system of interacting subsystems and components set within wider systems and environments that provide inputs to the system and which receive its outputs.

This is shown in Figure 1.1, which identifies the main elements of most organizations and their functioning. These are grouped into two main subsystems – the formal and informal. Thus elements of the formal subsystem include the organization's strategy, whether this is devised by a single person, as in the case of a very small owner–manager company, or by the board of directors and top management group in a large multi-divisional organization. Other components include the organization's goals and the means of achieving these through operational activities such as the production of goods or provision of services. In addition, there is a service component, which is that set of activities which help and facilitate the core operational activities to happen. Examples are the personnel departments, accounting and finance, information technology services and clerical and administrative support. Management, as the formal decision-making and control element, is also evident in all organizations, whether this involves a few people or is spread throughout the organization.

It is clear from any examination of complex systems such as organizations that some kind of structuring of activities is required if chaos is not to ensue. Thus the concept of organizational structure is central to that of organizational systems. However, over 20 years ago Child (1973) drew attention to other, more intangible elements of organizational life such as the political behaviour of organizational members. A more recent example is Nadler's (1988) inclusion of the informal organization (patterns of communication, power and influence, values and norms) in his systems model of organizational behaviour. Stacey (2003) has

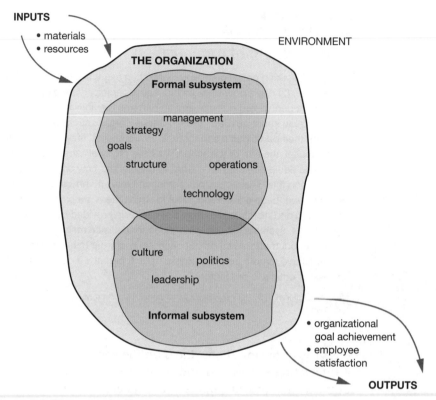

Figure 1.1 The organization as a system

coined the phrase 'shadow system' to describe these less predictable and more intangible aspects of organizational life. Thus the idea of the 'informal subsystem' encapsulates the more hidden elements of organizational culture and politics and the rather less hidden element of leadership – including those who are led.

These relatively stable subsystems and elements of organizational functioning interact with each other in some kind of transformation process. This means taking inputs such as materials and other resources from the organization's environment and transforming them into outputs, which are received back into the environment by customers and clients. However, while these outputs can be thought of as the legitimate reason for the organization's existence, an output that is relevant, in particular, to the informal subsystem is employees' behaviour and their satisfaction with their jobs. This is reinforced by Storey, Edwards and Sisson's (1997, p. 1) statement that: 'Given that technology and finance are increasingly internationally mobile and that innovations can be copied rapidly, it is the unique use of human resources, which is especially critical to long-term organizational success.'

However, the concept of organizational systems as open systems has not gone without criticism. As long ago as 1970 Silverman challenged the idea of organizations as systems, in that this notion rests on an assumption that defining an organization's goals is uncontentious and that, within the organization, there is consensus as to what its goals might be. A contrasting view of organizations, as being composed of individuals and groups with multiple different interests – who construe their actions in many different ways – came to the fore. Known as the 'social action' approach to understanding organizations, this became recognized as an alternative view to the idea of organizations as systems. More recently, with the development of the concepts of *modernism* and, particularly, *postmodernism*, which are discussed further in Chapter 9, there is the assumption that the world is unpredictable and frequently chaotic in that change can occur in any direction at any time – witness the weekly pronouncements in the media of the latest Internet-based company to come into being and, nearly as frequently, their fading and in some cases their demise.

Stacey's (2003) ideas on organizations as *complex* systems take the notion of unpredictability even further through emphasizing the multitude of interactions in the individual (psychological), social, organizational and environmental domains and between any and all of them. He also stresses the difficulties or, as he sees them, impossibilities in trying to understand organizations and the people within them from the point of view of an objective outsider as some open systems theorists have done. Having said this, the concept of organizational systems as *open* systems is an important one. As already mentioned, all organizations receive inputs from their environments and provide outputs back into that environment. The boundaries of organizational systems are, therefore, permeable. This means that they are also significantly influenced in their strategies and activities by both historical and contemporary environmental demands, opportunities and constraints. The next section traces some historical trends, which have influenced organizational strategies and processes through time. This tracing of history acts as a prelude to a consideration of the more immediate environment of organizations today and as they might present themselves in the future.

The historical context for change

The forces that operate to bring about change in organizations can be thought of as winds which are many and varied – from small summer breezes that merely disturb a few papers to mighty howling gales which cause devastation to structures and operations causing consequent reorientation of purpose and rebuilding. Sometimes, however, the winds die down to give periods of relative calm, periods of relative organizational stability. Such a period was the agricultural age, which Goodman (1995) maintains prevailed in Europe and western societies as a whole until the early 1700s. During this period, wealth was created in the context of an agriculturally based society influenced mainly by local markets (both customer and labour) and factors outside people's control such as the weather. During this time people could fairly well predict the cycle of activities required to maintain life, even if that life might be at little more than subsistence level.

To maintain the meteorological metaphor, stronger winds of change blew to bring in the Industrial Revolution and the industrial age. Again according to Goodman, this lasted until around 1945. It was characterized by a series of inventions and innovations that reduced the number of people needed to work the land and, in turn, provided the means of mass production of hitherto rarely obtainable artefacts; for organizations, supplying these in ever increasing numbers became the aim. To a large extent demand and supply were predictable, enabling companies to structure their organizations along what Burns and Stalker (1966) described as mechanistic lines, that is as systems of strict hierarchical structures and firm means of control.

This situation prevailed for some time after the Second World War, with demand still coming mainly from the domestic market and organizations striving to fill the 'supply gap'. Thus the most disturbing environmental influence on organizations of this time was the demand for products, which outstripped supply. The (supposed) saying by Henry Ford that 'You can have any colour of car so long as it is black', gives a flavour of the supply-led state of the market. Apart from any technical difficulties of producing different colours of car, Ford did not have to worry about customers' colour preferences: he could sell all that he made.

Figure 1.2 characterizes organizations of this period as 'task oriented', with effort being put into increasing production through more effective and efficient production processes.

The push, during this period, for ever-increasing efficiency of production supported the continuing application of the earlier ideas of Taylor (1911) and scientific management allied to Fordism that was derived from Henry Ford's ideas on assembly-line production (see Wood, 1989). This was a period mainly of command and control, of bureaucratic structures and the belief that there was 'one best way' of structuring organizations for efficient production. However, as time passed, this favourable period for organizations began to wane as people became more discriminating in the goods and services they wished to buy and as technological advancements brought about increased productivity so

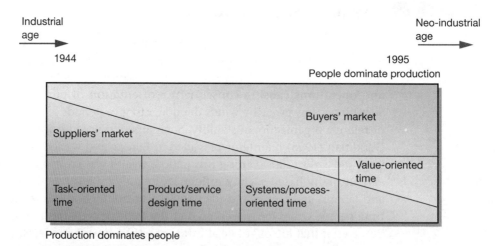

Figure 1.2 Market factors impacting on operations of western organizations
Source: Goodman, M. (1995), *Creative Management* (Hemel Hempstead, Prentice Hall, p. 38).

that supply overtook demand. In addition, companies began, increasingly, to look abroad for additional markets.

At the same time, organizations faced more intensive competition from abroad for their own products and services. In the West, this development has been accompanied by a shift in focus from manufacturing to service, whether this merely adds value to manufactured products or whether it is service in its own right; for instance financial services, help in selling houses, the services of doctors and solicitors or taking part in education and training. In the neo-industrial age of the advanced countries, the emphasis is moving towards adding value to goods and services – what Goodman calls the value-oriented time (see Illustration 1.2) as contrasted with the task-oriented, products/services-oriented and systems-oriented times of the past and current periods. Table 1.1 lists the organizational responses, in terms of marketing, production and people, to the different time periods.

Illustration 1.2

Value-oriented time

Customers

As competition becomes more severe and markets oversupplied, organizations must find products and services that are differentiated not only by purpose and form but also by the 'added value' which attaches to them. This means identifying potential customer expectations and then exceeding them. In other words, organizations must constantly increase customers' perceived value for money.

As the life cycle of a product shortens, organizations are under constant pressure to introduce new product offerings. This implies a continuing striving for innovation in terms of both products and the services associated with them. Innovation is, however, not only associated with the product itself but also with ways of supplying and marketing it. What may differentiate one product offering from another is not the product itself but the innovative production techniques, quality and relationship marketing – skills that are difficult for the competition to copy.

Production

Of the production processes of the future, Goodman (1995, p. 49) says:

On the supply side, production will continue to get leaner and more responsive to customer demand. Lean production appears to do the impossible. It delivers the great product variety once associated with craft production at costs that are often less than

those associated with mass production. Furthermore these benefits are provided together with products of high quality by sophisticated networking processes.

Human brainpower

The economies of the West can no longer rely on mass production processes. Ideas and brainpower have become an increasingly important component of modern product and service packages. It is through people's intelligence and creative thinking that organizations will improve competitiveness. Information technology and information systems are of more importance than mass production systems, which gave competitive advantage in the past. People will become an organization's most important asset, as it is only people who have the brainpower to focus on identifying and solving complex problems. To quote Goodman again (1995, pp. 49–50):

The successful product packages of the future will result from the exposure of creativity to complex, curvilinear, messy, fuzzy logic-type problems. As demand grows for such value packages, so individuals will respond by having ingenious ideas. This will challenge organisations, with their liking for structure and order, as intensive creativity usually arises out of chaos and disorder conditions. ... Thus, old mind-sets and rule books will have to give way to new organisational patterns that continuously encourage individuals to have ideas.

Table 1.1 Key organizational responses in the UK, 1994–5

Key organizational responses	Task-oriented time	Product/service design time	Systems/process-oriented time	Value-oriented time
Marketing	• Seller's market • Focus on increasing sales	• Development of market segments • Positioning and targeting • Niche marketing	• Strategic marketing • Increasing importance of single customer focus	• Relationship marketing • Value-added marketing
Production	• Supplying volume • Reducing costs	• Automation • Work study	• Statistical process control • Quality/service chain • Just in time	• Lean systems • Information management • Autonomous units • Improving response times • Networking
People	• Compliance • Work study • Problems caused by growth and functionalisms	• Manpower planning • Human resources management • Teamworking	• Quality (systems) • Kaizen • Problem solving	• Task/project-focused teams • Cross-functional teams • Information management • Proliferation of messy problems

Source: Goodman, M. (1995), *Creative Management* (Hemel Hempstead, Prentice Hall, p. 40).

Change throughout the ages is encapsulated in the comments of Jones, Palmer, Osterweil and Whitehead (1996) when they say:

> As we approach the 21st century the pace and scale of the change demanded of organizations and those who work within them are enormous. Global competition and the advent of the information age, where knowledge is the key resource, have thrown the world of work into disarray. Just as we had to shed the processes, skills and systems of the agricultural era to meet the demands of the industrial era, so we are now having to shed ways of working honed for the industrial era to take advantage of the opportunities offered by the information age. ... Organizations are attempting to recreate themselves and move from the traditional structure to a dynamic new model where people can contribute their creativity, energy and foresight in return for being nurtured, developed and enthused.

Jones *et al.* (1996) are probably being realistic as they predict these developments for western advanced societies. However, it must be remembered that not all parts of the world are at this stage of development in terms of the move from agriculture to industry to services. Table 1.2 illustrates the numbers of people work-

Table 1.2 The changing structure of employment: Europe, the United States, Japan and China 1980–2010 (%)

Country	Agriculture 1980	Agriculture 2010	Industry 1980	Industry 2010	Services 1980	Services 2010
Italy	16	6	42	31	40	62
Germany	2	1	58	45	40	56
France	11	5	47	32	41	63
Spain	22	5	40	42	38	52
USA	4	3	62	21	62	76
Japan	13	6	38	38	49	58
China	70	44	19	26	12	30

Source: Almon, C and Grassini, M. (2002), *The Changing Structure of Employment in Italy 1980–2010. Working Paper.*

ing in the agricultural, industrial and service sectors of the economies in Europe, the United States and Japan compared to China (Almon and Grassini, 2002).

In the past, China and Russia were considered to be countries that were predominantly agriculturally based and lagging behind western countries and Japan, which had moved fairly rapidly after the Second World War towards more predominantly product and service industries. The information in Table 1.2 offers a comparison of a cross-section of countries and compares their development over a 30-year period. The data suggests that China is still predominantly an agricultural society, particularly when compared to the European countries in this illustration.

Yet the statistics given in Table 1.2 indicate that China is quickly moving towards an industry and services-dominated period. Since 1978, China's economy has been growing at a rate of 9.4 per cent annually and its foreign trade has also expanded in recent years to 15 per cent (Adhikarianu Yang, 2002). The countries now considered to be developing from a predominantly agriculturally based economy to a more developed service industry are Russia (and the countries that have derived from Russia's subsequent division) and India (*BBC*, News, 2004b). China is still predominantly an agricultural society, particularly when compared to the United Kingdom where only 3.5 per cent of people work in the primary and utilities sector – which includes workers in the gas, electric and water industries as well as agriculture (Wilson, Homenidou and Dickerson 2004).

Even so, the winds of change are blowing strongly for countries such as China, Russia and India. The BBC reported (BBC News, 2004b) that India's economy grew at over 8 per cent during the first quarter of the year (April–June 2004), one of the highest growth rates in the world and 'just a shade lower than its rival Asian economic giant, China'. Their progress through the agricultural, industrial and services periods will be swift in comparison with the time it took the more advanced western countries to reach the same stage.

Activity 1.1

Consider how you would describe an organization with which you are familiar in terms of its wealth-creating capacity. For instance, try answering the following questions:

- *With which sector of the economy (agricultural, manufacturing, services) are its outputs mainly associated?*

- *Does the organization operate at a local, regional, national or international level?*

- *What type of market does it have? Use the categories given in Table 1.1 as a guide.*

- *Does it supply domestic or foreign markets – or both?*

- *Is it into volume production, automation of products/services or group/autonomous unit production?*

- *Does it practise just-in-time (JIT) delivery with an emphasis on quality service?*

- *What type of people does it employ – unskilled, skilled, professional?*

- *Are people easily attracted to work in the organization?*

- *How much autonomy do employees have with regard to the work they choose to do and the way they do it?*

- *Is decision taking devolved to the lowest level possible or kept within the hands of top management?*

An uncertain future

Some responses to Activity 1.1 may give a sense of an organization operating in a fairly predictable environment, with a sense of security for the future – that is, where the winds of change are moderate and fairly constant. Other responses may suggest a sense of uncertainty about markets, demand, the ability to attract the type of labour required and whether employment will increase or decrease – an environment where the winds of change come in short, unpredictable gusts. If creativity and innovation, and working in teams to solve complex problems are indicative of the organization analyzed in Activity 1.1, it has quite likely already moved into value-oriented time.

Most people asked about organizational life today agree that it is becoming ever more uncertain as the pace of change quickens and the future becomes more unpredictable. Academics and business people alike echo this. For instance, looking ahead to the future, Drucker, writing in 1988, maintained that 20 years hence (i.e. about the year 2008) organizations would be almost wholly information based and that they would resemble more a symphony orchestra than the command and control, managed structures prevalent in the last decade (see Illustration 1.3).

Organizations as symphony orchestras

Writing about the way that information technology is transforming business enterprises, Drucker says:

> A large symphony orchestra is even more instructive, since for some works there may be a few hundred musicians on stage playing together. According to organization theory then, there should be several group vice president conductors and perhaps a half-dozen division VP conductors. But that's not how it works. There is only the conductor-CEO – and every one of the musicians plays directly to that person without an intermediary. And each is a high-grade specialist, indeed an artist.

Source: Drucker (1988, p. 48).

With this as one example of the way organizations might change in the future, Drucker predicted the demise of middle management and the rise of organizations staffed almost exclusively with high-grade, specialist staff. The view that middle management will no longer be required is debatable and would certainly not be subscribed to by everyone (e.g. Eccles, 1996). However, for the United Kingdom, the projected growth in the numbers of professionals and knowledge-based workers and the decrease in numbers of lower-skilled workers is supported by the latest figures and trends, published by the Institute for Employment Research (see Illustration 1.4).

Since the industrialization of production, the more recent rise of ever more service industries and the information technology explosion, the pace of change in the environment in which organizations operate has quickened to such an extent that, twelve years ago, writers such as Clarke (1994, p. 1) were maintaining that: 'The last decade has brought with it a time of totally unprecedented change. In every direction businesses are in turmoil, from computing to financial services, from telecommunications to health care. Change is an accelerating constant.' This view was broadly confirmed by Dawson (2003, pp. 1–2) in his discussion of a 'new bias for organizational action', by which he means the need for managers to be leaders of change or else, in an increasingly competitive environment, their organizations will cease to exist.

The somewhat dramatic tone of these pronouncements appears to be supported, more recently, by two US academics turned consultants, Nadler and Tushman (1999, p. 45), who say: 'Poised on the eve of the next century, we are witnessing a profound transformation in the very nature of our business organizations. Historic forces have converged to fundamentally reshape the scope, strategies, and structures of large, multi-business enterprises.' At a less macro level of analysis, an article by Merope Mills in the *Guardian* (2000) refers to Graeme Leach, chief economist at the Institute of Directors, who claims that: 'By 2020, the nine-to-five rat race will be extinct and present levels of self-employment, commuting and technology use, as well as age and sex gaps, will

Illustration 1.4

Projected employment changes: 2002–12

There are likely to be some important underlying changes in terms of which occupational groups are expanding or declining. This has important implications for the numbers of people required, in each category, to replace any projected expansion and people who leave (mainly for retirement reasons). Expanding occupational groups include: caring service occupations, corporate managers and most professional occupations (e.g. teaching, health, science).

In comparison, employment demand in other occupations, for example elementary clerical occupations or in skilled trades associated with metal, plant and machinery, are in structural decline.

Source: Wlson, R., Homenidou, K. and Dickerson, A. (2004) *Working Futures: New Projections of Employment by Sector 2002 – 2012 (Published 2004) Volume 1*. Institute for Employment Research, University of Warwick, Coventry CV4 7AL. See also Bulletin Number 73, 2004 http://www2.warwick.ac.uk/fac/soc/ier/publications/bulletins

The Sector Skills Development Agency (SSDA) commissioned the Institute for Employment Research (IER) at the University of Warwick and Cambridge Econometrics to produce *Working Futures*. This comprises a series of reports presenting projections of UK employment (2002–2012) by occupation, sector, UK country and English region. The reports are available from the SSDA's website: www.ssda.org. Updated projections of employment (*Working Futures, 2004–2014*) are to be published by the SSDA in autumn 2005. A network of UK-wide Sector Skills Councils (SSCs) has been charged to lead the productivity drive in industry or business sectors recognised by employers. The SSDA has been established to underpin the SSC network and promote effective working between sectors.

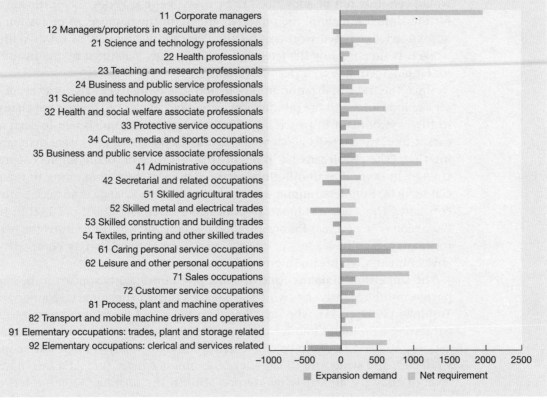

UK: All industries

Expansion demand   Net requirement

have changed beyond recognition.' According to the article, Leach anticipates that: 'In 20 years time, 20–25% of the workforce will be temporary workers and many more will be flexible, ... 25% of people will no longer work in a traditional office and ... 50% will work from home in some form.' Continuing to use the 'winds of change' metaphor, the expectation is of damaging gale-force winds bringing the need for rebuilding that takes the opportunity to incorporate new ideas and ways of doing things.

Whether all this will come to pass is arguable. Predicting the future is always fraught with difficulties. For instance, Furnham (2000) refers to Mannermann (1998, p. 427), who sees future studies as part art and part science and who notes: 'The future is full of surprises, uncertainty, trends and trend breaks, irrationality and rationality, and it is changing and escaping from our hands as time goes by. It is also the result of actions made by innumerable more or less powerful forces.' What seems uncontestable is that the organizational world is changing at a fast rate – even if the direction of change is not always predictable. Consequently, it is crucial that organizational managers and decision makers are aware of, and understand, more about the environmental winds that are blowing to disturb organizational life; in other words to be able to analyze the factors which trigger organizational change.

Organizations today – environmental triggers of change

So far we have considered elements that help make up an organization. There has also been some discussion relating to the environment in which an organization operates.

Activity 1.2

1 List factors that you can think of which could affect what or how an organization chooses to produce or sell, how the goods and services might be marketed, and the way in which the work might get done.

2 Has your organization, or one with which you are familiar, changed in the areas highlighted above?

3 Have you personally changed how you choose or buy your products and services over the last few years? If so, identify some examples and think why this might be the case.

Figure 1.1 depicts an organization as a system receiving inputs from its environment and releasing outputs back into it. The previous section discussed how social and technological changes have, in the past, impacted on the products and services offered by organizations and the way they operate. A number of writers have been mentioned, who predict ever more 'turbulent' (Emery and Trist, 1967) environments – ever more stormy winds.

The view of organizations existing as systems of interrelated elements operating in multi-dimensional environments has a number of supporters. The work of Checkland (1972), for instance, is well known for the development of the soft systems model – an approach designed specifically for analyzing and designing change in what Checkland terms 'human activity systems', most frequently, organizational systems. Nadler (1988) has proposed a systems model applied to organizational behaviour and other authors such as Stacey (2003) use systems concepts in their discussion of organizations and change. Most writers on organizations stress the importance of the nature of the environment for organizational management and decision making. The following lists some of the elements of an organization's environment that might have emerged from completing Activity 1.2:

- an organization's markets (clients or customers)
- suppliers
- governmental and regulatory bodies
- trade union organizations
- competitors
- financial institutions
- labour supply
- levels of unemployment
- economic climate
- technological advances
- marketing techniques
- price of goods: change of location for factories, change of distribution, change of location, i.e. call centres, Amazon, Egg etc.
- computing and information systems developments
- the growth of e-commerce and use of the Internet.

An organization's environment will also include broader influences such as the internationalization of trade, influences from the political environment, the prevailing political ideology, attitudes to trade unions, changes from public to private ownership or vice versa, demographic changes and changes in family structure and differences between the rich and the poor. Thus Nadler and Tushman (1988, p. 152) summarize the environment as: 'All factors, including institutions, groups, individuals, events and so on, that are outside the organization being analyzed, but that have a potential impact on that organization.' The remainder of this section considers, more closely, examples of these and draws attention to the way changes in one or more elements of the organizational environment are likely to trigger consequent changes in some or all the ways an organization and its constituent components operate.

The impact of PEST

Some analysts have found it useful to group different environmental factors into categories under the mnemonics PEST (Johnson and Scholes, 1999) and STEP (Goodman, 1995), both of which refer to the political, economic, technological

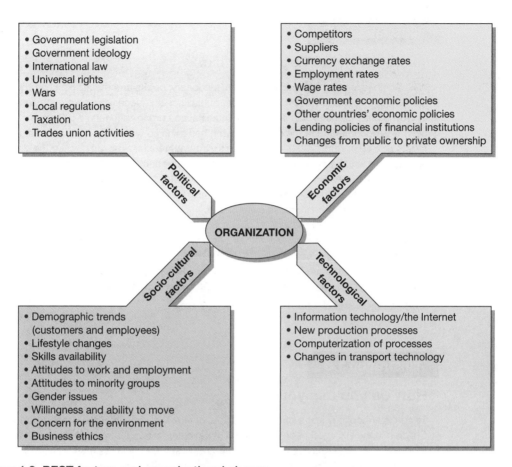

- Government legislation
- Government ideology
- International law
- Universal rights
- Wars
- Local regulations
- Taxation
- Trades union activities

- Competitors
- Suppliers
- Currency exchange rates
- Employment rates
- Wage rates
- Government economic policies
- Other countries' economic policies
- Lending policies of financial institutions
- Changes from public to private ownership

Political factors

Economic factors

ORGANIZATION

Socio-cultural factors

Technological factors

- Demographic trends
  (customers and employees)
- Lifestyle changes
- Skills availability
- Attitudes to work and employment
- Attitudes to minority groups
- Gender issues
- Willingness and ability to move
- Concern for the environment
- Business ethics

- Information technology/the Internet
- New production processes
- Computerization of processes
- Changes in transport technology

Figure 1.3 PEST factors and organizational change

and socio-cultural factors that influence organizations, their strategies, structures and means of operating, including their human resource practices. In addition, it is a useful metaphor to distinguish different aspects of the organizational environment and their specific relationship to organizations as triggers of change. Figure 1.3 illustrates the PEST factors that exist as part of an organization's environment. All, at some time, will impact upon an organization's formal and informal subsystems and their components as well as which products or services it offers and in which markets.

Triggers for change from the technological environment

Examples of triggers for change emanating from changes in technology and the economic environment are many and varied. Illustration 1.5 gives us an example of how changes in the technological and economic environment, which were ignored as triggers for change, forced a well-known UK retailer to re-evaluate its market sustainability for the future. The massive use of mobile phones by such a young consumer group (see Illustration 1.6) might not have

Illustration 1.5

Teaching an old dog new tricks

W.H. Smith (a leading UK retailer of cards, stationery, books and magazines) has been renowned for its speciality niche in books, magazines and accessories for quite a number of years. It has certainly had a variety of financial and organizational difficulties that have been well documented in the press. So what has gone so wrong? In stark contrast to the results posted in April (2004) for W.H. Smith, Internet retailer Amazon bucked the dotcom disaster scenario by announcing profits up by 141 per cent on the back of a rise in sales of 41 per cent. In April 2004 Amazon's worldwide sales stood at $5.26 billion (£2.97 billion) and allowed the company to make its first full-year profit since it began trading, and it expects profits to increase even further.

The issue being debated at W.H. Smith was exactly what the retail store was – a bookseller, music retailer, newsagent etc. Amazon appears to be all of that. W.H. Smith will need to focus on a 'core business' to survive in the future; however it is a good example of the fast pace of change and how quickly competitors, who once may have learned from you, pass you in the ever-ongoing race of competition.

Source: Based on data available at www.news.bbc.co.uk 2004

Illustration 1.6

How do you use yours?

To adults a mobile is just a phone but to youngsters it represents a life-support system. Children in the UK aged between 10 and 14 have not known life without mobile phones. … The 10–14-year-olds use far more value-added services such as music, sports and offers than adults: 55 per cent of them compared with only 36 per cent of adults. 'The research showed that this group has an extreme familiarity with the device. The relationship with the mobile phones is very different from that of older groups'.

Mobile manufacturer by age of consumer

Manufacturer	Age categories				
	15–18	19–21	22–25	26–30	31–35
			Percentage of market		
Nokia	53	43	53	59	61
Samsung	8	15	20	15	10
Motorola	5	8	6	7	8
Siemens	4	6	4	4	5
Sony Ericsson	13	9	6	4	5
Sagem	8	7	3	3	2
Panasonic	3	3	2	3	2
Sharp	4	5	2	3	2
Other	2	3	2	1	2

Source: www.teleconomy.com, Emiko Terazono; based on 'Creative Business', *Financial Times*, 22 June 2004 (p. 7).

been predicted. Advertisements seen nowadays denouncing 'old-fashioned'-looking mobiles in favour of the latest designs (i.e. looks rather than technology) are aimed at younger people who have made mobile phones a fashion accessory.

An article by Roy Westbrook, in the 16 October 2000 *Financial Times* 'Mastering Management' series has the sub-heading 'Production techniques have revolutionized product manufacturing'. Westbrook describes the way that, through devising very speedy production machine changes, customized 'one-off' products can be made using automated processes previously used only for mass production. An example of linking processes to information technology is in the increasing use of robots to perform human tasks. Westbrook gives statistics for what he calls 'robot density' (the number of robots for every 10,000 people employed). In 1998 the robot density for the United Kingdom was 19, that for the United States was 42 and for Japan 277. The relative differences in the use of robots between countries might be a function of the different spread of industries among them. However, Illustration 1.7 shows that the opportunity to use robots in increasing numbers is a matter of choice. If the choice to increase the use of robots is taken this will inevitably have an impact on employment rates and the organization of work for those far fewer workers retained in the new operations environment.

Illustration 1.7

Robots or people

Both cost and quality benefits are offered by robotics and the latter is critical in electronics. Certain areas of a semiconductor plant need to be 1000 times cleaner than a hospital operating theatre, so some tasks are carried out by robots in a vacuum. In disk drive assembly, the work is easier for robots than people. Matsushita Kotobuki Electronics (MKE) make Quantum's disk drives at an automated facility where 400 people and 150 robots produce 50,000 units a day. Quantum's main competitor is Seagate, which makes a similar number in Singapore and Taiwan, with few robots and 25,000 people.

Source: Based on Westbrook, R. (2000), 'Look to the process for a better product', *Financial Times Mastering Management*, 16 October, pp. 6–7.

An extremely important and far-reaching influence on organizations, in almost everything they do, is the increasing power of Internet-based communications. Consider the following quotations:

Will the Internet cafés survive 10 more years? The first UK cyber café is believed to have been opened in London's West End in 1994. As it celebrates its 10th Birthday, the future is uncertain as access at home is an everyday reality.

(*BBC News*, 9 September 2004)

EasyJet automates check-in desks as a latest cost cutting exercise. Passengers will check themselves in through a computerized system.

(*Financial Times*, Monday, 31 May 2004)

The generation of young Chinese is embracing the Internet as part of daily life. The Earth has become a village.   (*BBC News*, World Edition, 27 August 2004)

The Internet bank that never sleeps is winning many converts. The premium savings rates and cheap loans seem too good to miss – until, that is, the system crashes and there is no one to shout at.   (*FT* Life on the net, 5 September 2000, p. 1)

E-government drive boosts jobs. Tony Blair plans to drag the government kicking and screaming into the virtual world. His plans include the idea that the government should be e-enabled by the end of next year. This will include patients being able to choose times of hospital appointments with their GP, and all Inland Revenue customers ... able to access all tax returns online.
          (*Financial Times*, Monday, 28 June 2004)

A morbid set of Cassandra dotcoms has emerged, gloating about business-to-customer start-ups headed for liquidation not liquidity. The irony of this gloom is that online retailing is growing exponentially, as consumers lose their fear of buying over the Internet.   (*FT* Life on the net, 13 September 2000, p. 1)

Your airline will know you are gridlocked on the M25 thanks to the positioning system in your Internet-enabled mobile phone. No need to panic. It will automatically book you on to a later flight, while emailing the details to your office and your spouse.   (*FT* Life on the net, 14 September 2000, p. 1)

The Internet is a creative tool for learning. It is not about doing what we have always done in the classroom. It is not about replacing books or televisions or teachers or even parents. And it is not just about delivering knowledge. It is about adding to a child's most basic equipment.
          (*FT* Life on the net, 15 September 2000, p. 1)

From club websites to event intranets, from stadium ticketing systems to computational fluid dynamics, and from virtual advertising to interactive television,

Illustration 1.8

Log on for banking and shopping

Internet usage has risen steadily over the past decade, and is still showing growth in the United Kingdom. This results largely from the continued growth in the number of Internet users at work, with email and searching for information on products leading the way.

Banking and shopping have been among the fastest in growth over the past 12 months. Participation in online banking has increased by 26 per cent to almost 11 million people. In the past year Lloyds TSB has overtaken Barclays as the most popular online bank.

Online shopping has grown by 29 per cent and now attracts around 15.5 million adults. These shoppers are each spending an average of around £110 per month, totalling over £20 billion per year.

Related to the rise in Internet use is the increasing take-up of broadband, which has played a significant role in the rising popularity of online activities.

Source: www.bmrb.co.uk; 'Creative Business', *Financial Times* 25 May 2004

the applications of information technology in modern-day sport seem almost limitless.   (Haverson, 2000, p. 10)

A glance through the quotations above illustrates how the increasing ability to communicate through the Internet is significantly influencing the way we work as well as the way we shop, bank, how we organize travel and how we use technology available to us for entertainment. The list is endless. It is useful to note, as parts of some of these quotations show, that Internet use is not without problems and organizations which wish to reach markets, customers and clients need to remain alert to the fact that not everyone has access to computers or the new generation of Internet-linkable mobile phones – or has the ability and motivation to use them.

This remains an important consideration, particularly for those working and using education and health services (see Applebee, Clayton, Pascoe and Bruce's (2000) study of Australian academic use of the Internet; and Howcroft and Mitev's (2000) study of the UK National Health Service's NHSnet). In the United Kingdom, however, the Department for Education and Skills (2002) document, 'A Profile of the UK Higher Education Sector 2000/2001', following on from the document 'Opportunity for All' (2000b) stated that 'Annual admissions of UK students to computer studies courses in our universities rose four-fold in the ten years to 1998, reaching over 16,500. ... *UK on-line computer skills training*, launched in May, offers ICT employability training for up to 50,000 unemployed people at a cost of £25m.'

Looking to the East, Dan Roberts writing in the *Financial Times* (2000, p. 1) says: 'China now buys more mobile telecoms equipment from multinational suppliers than any market outside the US. These suppliers are investing at breakneck speed to meet the demand.' For markets still wishing to penetrate the product market, China is an obvious choice to turn to due to its population; it is hard to rival an audience so large anywhere else in the world. In contrast, statistics from the World Bank (2005) show that only 10 in 1,000 people in the South Asian region (with 20 per cent of the world population) have access to the Internet, compared to 160 per 1,000 in Europe and central Asia.

The rapid rise and fall of what have become known as 'dotcom' companies does not appear to have diminished the enthusiasm for the Web among European executives. The number and range of companies, new and existing, that are devising innovative ways of harnessing the Internet to their purposes is too great to detail here. A publication that gives much of this information, including a frequently updated 'E-index' of PC, Internet and mobile phone penetration and access is *Connectis*, which bills itself as 'Europe's e-business magazine'. (Information on the English version can be found at **http://specials.ft.com/connectis/**.) Illustration 1.9 contrasts with the account in Illustration 1.6 to demonstrate how changes in the technological environment impact on the behaviour of (in this case) older people and what this means for organizations using IT for selling and other purposes.

Illustration 1.9

Wrinkles and all

By Christine Ryll in Munich and Philippe Collier in Paris

'Will you marry me?' We can't be sure whether Pegasus actually asked for Hilde's hand online. One thing we do know, however, is that this 'young' couple met last January in the www.feier@bend.com chat-room. By the following June, wedding bells were ringing. To joyful cries from their chat-room chums, Hilde, now 58, and her seven-years-younger partner were married in the small German town of Ingolstadt, on the Danube.

Older people constitute the fastest-growing group of web surfers worldwide. They have time and money, and their interests are many and varied. They are the most powerful consumer group of our time. So why have European advertisers ignored them for so long?

'The older generation is a critical and demanding segment of the population. They have time to read. They are keen to get in-depth information. And when you approach them in the right way, they are extremely appreciative,' insists Alexander Wild, managing director of Feier@bend.

'Unfortunately, retired people are still overlooked by advertisers,' laments Conrad Schfer, marketing director of the Senior Snid network. 'Advertising money floods towards younger people, whereas senior citizens have half of all spending power and they are open to offers. All you have to do is approach them in the right way.'

According to Jutta Rosenbach, who started the gateway www.senioren-zentrale.de, 'Elderly people today feel up to 15 years younger than the previous generation did. Bear this in mind when you approach them.'

A study carried out by Jupiter MMXI in March this year showed that throughout Europe people over 55 already make up 10 per cent of all web surfers. Meanwhile, investigations by the French consultancy NetValue among home-based Internet users revealed major differences from country to country.

In December 2000, over-50s accounted for 19.3 per cent of surfers in the United Kingdom, 17.2 per cent in Germany, 15.7 per cent in France and 7.5 per cent in Spain.

In March this year NetValue further observed that, in France, surfers aged over 50 made up 23.7 per cent of heavy users – those who go online an average of 20.1 days a month and who spend an average of 14 hours a month surfing (as opposed to 6.4 hours for the whole of the French Internet community).

According to a survey of British users by the consultancy firm NetPoll, 44 per cent of British users aged 55 or over have already made purchases online. And last year Forrester Research forecast that by the end of 2003 more than 5 million British over-55s would be connected to the Internet. A study by Age Concern and Microsoft published in July 2000 showed that surfing the net ranked fourth among the 10 favourite pastimes of the over-50s.

Americans are leading the way. In the United States the over-50s, of whom more than 20 million are Internet users, are among the most frequently targeted consumers. According to Charles Schwab, the largest US brokerage firm, 40 per cent of them have their own computers and 70 per cent surf the net. Of these surfers, 81 per cent use the Internet for shopping or to look for goods and services.

What's more, this age group can afford it. According to the Deutsches Institut für Wirtschaftsforschung (German Institute for Economic Research), over-65s, who make up only 16.27 per cent of the German population, hold over 30 per cent of the national wealth. Documents from the Senioren Marketing per Internet conference show that every year they have a total purchasing power of about €20.5 billion (£12.8 billion).

Of older surfers questioned by the marketing consultancy GfK, 60 per cent have already shopped online. And, according to Senioren Marketing per Internet, they spent around three times more money on online purchases than the average user.

Source: http://specials.ft.com/connectis/Published: 19 September 2001

The explosive nature of the spread of Internet use and the opportunities brought about by advances in information technology generally clearly impact not only on organizations and those who work in them but also on other parts of the organizational environment. As employees use email and the Internet much more frequently through their workplace connections, employers have become increasingly anxious to monitor activity that is not work related. This is supported by a *Financial Times* article (2004). The Internet's popularity as a marketing medium has been overwhelming, but the added value of this format is being questioned due to the time-consuming nature of the explosion of 'spam' and other marketing formats. Clearly guidelines in line with 'best practice' will need to be developed for both organizational and individual use.

This has caught the attention of the UK trade unions to the extent that it was debated at the 2000 annual Trades Union Congress. Government legislation regarding the degree to which employers have investigatory powers of this nature is causing concern, along with the degree to which these might impinge on employees' human rights in the light of the incorporation into law, in October 2000, of the European Union Human Rights Convention. Without employer monitoring, managers may have little sense of how much time an employee is spending on non-work-related emails and Internet surfing. With surveillance, a climate of distrust can be created.

The discussion so far illustrates the power of increased opportunities for technological communications to influence organizational life. It is instructive to look also at other triggers for change that at various times, emanate from the PEST environment.

Triggers for change from the political environment

Whether countries are governed dictatorially or according to Marxist or democratic principles their policies, laws and actions have a profound effect on the world of business, whether it is publicly or privately operated. A plethora of national and international bodies, elected and unelected, influence organizational life to a greater or lesser degree. Consequently, not only do changes in the political environment influence organizations directly, they also interact with changes in the economic environment – for instance, the government-inspired privatization of previously publicly owned institutions (e.g. in the United Kingdom electricity, gas, the railways), or the cooperation of different countries to form economic trading blocs (e.g. the European Union or the ASEAN-4 Group). As Illustration 1.10 shows, changes coming from one sector of the environment are compounded by their interaction with influencing factors from other sectors of the environment – a clear demonstration that environmental triggers for change rarely act as single influences.

Perhaps the most important role for governments is the bringing of economic prosperity to their countries. However, they also act as lawmakers at more micro levels. The socialist government of the United Kingdom at the time of writing

Illustration 1.10

UK 'Not ready yet for the euro'

BBC News reported on 2 June 2003 that the key economic tests (which were set in 1997) for ditching the pound and joining the euro had not yet been met. In 2005, there is no indication that this time has come. The Chancellor of the Exchequer, when asked in 2002: 'Would joining the EMU create better conditions for firms making long-term decisions to invest in Britain?' indicated that a successful single currency would achieve the following:

● create an attractive area – with low inflation and stability – for firms to invest in;
● be a complement to the Single Market, boosting competition and providing new opportunities for companies.

With regard to employment and growth, he said that: 'Joining the euro could enhance both growth and employment prospects'.

On the other hand, the Chancellor warned that joining at the wrong time could see unemployment rise, see cuts in public service spending and stall economic growth. If the UK did join the euro, the economy (says the Treasury) must have the ability to 'adjust to change … because of the inevitable loss of domestic control over monetary policy' and the risk of future economic turbulence.

Source: BBC News (2002); BBC News (2004c).

has pushed legislation relating to the 1995 Pensions Act, changing the official retirement age for women from 60 to 65 years. Between 2010 and 2020 we will see the equalization of the pensionable age. This could produce further changes in the future due to the demands of the economy and the future lack of skilled workers. The Office for National Statistics has forecast some figures relating to the numbers of adults over the age of 80 – growing from 2.5 million in 2002 to 4.9 million by 2031. The focus for governments in the past was to set policies and legislation for the future of the young, and adults over the age of 65 are often seen as the invisible population. From studies over the years, the focus of government policy will now be on how to manage an increasingly older population, and how the younger population will support this. Those older people will have an increased political and economic voice, which will have to be considered when delivering services both in the United Kingdom and its economic partners.

September 2000 saw French and British workers from the transport and oil industries, supported by farmers, taking action to protest at the price of fuel, saying that this negatively affected their ability to compete with similar organizations from other countries. However, reductions in the price of petrol and diesel would reduce both governments' tax revenues, which would, presumably, have knock-on effects on their ability to make money available for other purposes and industries such as education and health, thus affecting the organizations operating within these and the people working within them. If the governments acted to reduce the tax rates on fuel, and thus the price of it, this would clearly impact on the cost of travelling, not only for business purposes but also for domestic and leisure purposes, which might in turn change people's lifestyles. This is an important debate because, now more than ever, oil prices have been set at an all-time high and consumers in Europe have already been experiencing an increased price level for services related to travel.

Illustration 1.11 is a good example of a government intervening directly in what in other countries might be considered a purely commercial decision. In addition, it illustrates how decisions by one country's government influence organizational decisions not only in the same country, but in others across the globe, with further repercussions for the way they will operate.

Illustration 1.11

Hong Kong eyes policy change on arts complex

The Hong Kong government is preparing to reverse its single-developer policy on a controversial waterfront arts complex, fuelling uncertainty about commitments to participate by some of the world's leading architects and arts institutions.

Officials have been sounding out local property developers about dropping the government's insistence that the 40-hectare project – known as the West Kowloon Cultural District and situated in a prime location on Hong Kong's harbour – be developed by a single group, according to people familiar with the situation.

Donald Tsang, the leading contender to be the territory's next chief executive, said: 'Ordinary people would realise now that if the project is to go ahead, and if we don't want to start from scratch again, then there is no way we can insist on a single-bidder approach.'

Abandoning the current arrangement would be a conciliatory gesture by Mr Tsang, who launched his campaign for the July 10 leadership race this week. Many local property moguls, politicians and members of the arts community have also criticised the single-tender plan.

They say a single tender would allow the government to release a huge piece of land to one of the city's property developers without sufficient input from the public and local artists. Many contend the land should be put up for auction.

'This is the first issue that Donald Tsang has to tackle [as chief executive],' said Anthony Cheung,

professor at City University of Hong Kong. 'I don't think he would like to see this issue destroy his honeymoon as chief executive.'

But the change would raise questions about the involvement of international groups such as Andrew Lloyd Webber's Really Useful Group, the Pompidou Centre and the Solomon R. Guggenheim Foundation.

Each of these reached separate agreements with one of the three bidders shortlisted for the waterfront project last year. The Pompidou Centre, which agreed to work with Cheung Kong and Sun Hung Kai Properties, declined to comment yesterday.

Tadao Ando, the Japanese architect, Lord Rogers, the UK architect, and Herzog de Meuron, designers of London's Tate Modern Gallery, have signed on with Sunny Development, a consortium led by Sino Land.

Because these architects and museum groups signed on to a particular design for the complex, they might pull out if their developer was not able to realise the agreed plan. However, people involved in the bidding process said given the enormous size of the project, interest from international museums and architects was likely to be strong regardless of the developers.

The current plan calls for three theatres, four museums, a 10,000-seat performance venue, and a theatre for water performances.

'Everybody in America and Britain is very, very interested,' said a person who worked on the project.

How Mr Tsang would proceed with the scheme if it did not use the single-developer approach is not clear.

▶

Illustration 1.11 *continued*

As chief secretary for administration under Tung Chee-hwa, who resigned as chief executive in March, Mr Tsang was an ardent advocate of the current scheme.

The government's website for the complex says: 'Splitting the contract could cause problems in aligning the design, construction and schedule of the infrastructure. ... Split tendering would also create additional costs and delays by forcing the government to sell separate parcels of land, which could take years, and by increasing the risk of litigation over separate land leases.'

Analysts and industry executives expect the government to keep the design feature, by Sir Norman Foster, of a canopy covering the district.

They added that the government might have to appoint a statutory body to oversee the project.

The government declined to comment on its plans, except to say: 'The public consultation on the West Kowloon Cultural District project is still in progress. We shall consider carefully all public views received before deciding the way forward.'

The public consultation on the project is due to continue until June 30.

Source: Alexandra Harney, *Financial Times*, Asia (3 June 2005)

At a more domestic level, nearly all governments have something to say or control with respect to their healthcare systems. Consequently they influence significantly their countries' health policies and practices and the health of their populations. Illustration 1.12 demonstrates the complexity of issues arising from what some might regard as a change in health delivery policy.

The earlier description and the situation described in Illustration 1.11 demonstrate the multiplicity of cause and effect of actions by government that, in turn, influence factors within the economic environment and which impact on different business and public sectors and the attitudes and behaviour of people within and outside them.

Illustration 1.12

Health reforms approved in France

The French parliament has approved controversial healthcare changes aimed at cutting the debt burden. Changes include the following:

- a new charge of one euro for seeing a doctor;
- an increase in the levy payable by pensioners and companies;
- a new reimbursement system to reward patients who use a doctor rather than going straight to a specialist;
- incentives for patients to choose generic drugs over more expensive branded varieties;
- cracking down on fraudulent sick leave;
- new health 'ID' cards to stop abuse of prescriptions.

The moves are a key part of President Chirac's attempt to trim the budget deficit, which has exceeded EU limits for three years in a row. The deficit is estimated at running to €13 billion (£8.5 billion pounds).

An official report said the standard of care provided by French doctors was among the best in the world, but the system was badly regulated and badly governed. Some of the reforms have been criticised by health workers, who accuse the government of creeping privatisation.

Source: BBC News (2004c)

Activity 1.3

Look back at Figure 1.3 and your answer to Activity 1.2.

How many PEST factors, listed by you and in Figure 1.3, appear in the account of the UK government's role in relation to the following:

- *issues raised in the UK's five tests of readiness to adopt the euro (see Illustration 1.10);*
- *issues raised by the change of population make-up in the future;*
- *the results of the French health reforms described in Illustration 1.12?*

What do your conclusions tell you about the interconnections between the various aspects of the PEST environment?

What interconnections can be made about decisions made in other countries that may impact on decisions in the United Kingdom?

Having read Illustrations 1.11 and 1.12 and completed Activity 1.3, it is interesting to note that although the illustrations were political/economic issues that originate in two different countries, undertaking a PEST analysis and identifying triggers for change might highlight some commonalities.

Undoubtedly the political environment has enormous influence on the type of change, and also the speed of change and how the triggers/influences might be managed. The speed of change for these two governments is certainly different, the influence of public opinion is managed differently in the decision-making process, and possibly one political environment is more radical than the other.

Triggers for change from the socio-cultural environment

As government policies, laws and actions affect organizations and people's everyday lives, so do the attitudes and expectations of people towards work, in the context of other aspects of their lives. All the factors listed as socio-cultural in Figure 1.3 influence the way organizations are set up, run and managed as well as their capacity to attract people to work within them.

Examples of how changes in the socio-cultural environment influence people's attitudes to work, and trigger other changes elsewhere, are listed here:

- social expectations for continuous increases in the standard of living, which must, however, be set against fewer opportunities for permanent secure employment;
- demographic changes causing 'gluts' or shortages in the numbers of young people coming into the labour market;
- changes in family structures where men as well as, or instead of, women may wish to stay home to look after children;
- demographic changes influencing the numbers of people in different age groups and therefore the numbers of people of working age compared to those of retirement age.

An article in the *Financial Times* by Kate Bevan (1996) comments on the increase in the numbers of single men and women living alone (from 933,000 in 1971 to 1,705,000 in 1991, projected to 3,154,000 in 2011) in addition to the increase in single widowed people (from 1.6 million in 1971 to a projected 2.5 million in 2011) in the context of the changing role of housing associations that currently provide social housing for more than 900,000 tenants. The Housing Act of 1988 requires housing associations to seek funds from the private sector to replace partially funds that were hitherto provided through government. The ability to raise money in this way has meant that, as well as providing social housing, associations have moved into provision of accommodation for other groups such as medical staff (on behalf of health authorities) and students, thus encompassing profit and not-for-profit activities.

This widening of their scope also extends beyond the provision of housing (for which they were originally set up) to provision of community facilities such as meals on wheels and community alarm systems. However, a statement at the end of the article shows how the changes they have made in response to a change in the law and their funding base is beginning to distort their fundamental purpose of care and support of people who could be termed 'disadvantaged'.

Scase (1999), looking into the future, confirms the growth of single-person households and an increase, in particular, of women living alone. Overall, according to the UK Government Actuaries Department (2004), the UK population will increase by 6.1 million to 2031. This is the equivalent of an average annual growth rate of 0.35 per cent. Nearly half of this increase will come from an increase of births over deaths, with the remainder the result of inward migration. In Britain, the population will age. However, the current trend towards earlier retirement could be slowed in the context of the increase in the official retirement age of women. These trends will have implications for the way advertising is oriented – towards the leisure and entertainment industries and from younger to what he calls 'time-rich, cash-rich, middle age consumers'. In addition, the rising costs of care for increased numbers of over 75s will drive developments in information computer technology in healthcare and welfare functions. Scase also comments that the increase in single-person households will require the building of increased numbers of new homes (designed specifically for single-person living), encourage the rejuvenation of inner city, urban areas and influence the development of interactive communication technologies including video surveillance systems against crime.

At least one implication of all this for many organizations is the requirement to increase investment in the creativity of their workers and systems to encourage innovation. This in turn has implications for the way organizations are structured (with hierarchical structures less evident) and for more flexible ways of working, frequently cooperating across organizations while still retaining a competitive edge – issues that are dealt with in more detail in Chapter 3 in particular and in other chapters in this book.

Activity 1.4

Take the list you made as a result of carrying out Activity 1.2 and categorize each factor identified there according to whether you consider it to stem from the political, economic, technological or socio-cultural sectors of the environment. Are there any factors that do not necessarily fit into these categories neatly?

This example illustrates how housing associations are being significantly affected, not only by democratic changes but also by a combination of legislative, economic and other socio-cultural changes in the environment.

Triggers for change from the economic environment

Carrying out Activity 1.4 may show that some factors can be categorized in more than one way. This is not unusual and simply illustrates the fact that aspects of the organizational environment are interrelated and operate in a complex way to trigger change within organizations. However, because organizations operate in the main to make money or, in the case of public sector organizations (e.g. hospitals, schools, some railway systems) operate within budgets, some of their more serious concerns are with triggers for change in the economic environment. This includes a concern for competitors and other issues, such as exchange rates, corporation tax, wage rates and skills availability, which determine their ability to compete (or, in the case of many publicly owned organizations, operate within budgets) (see Illustration 1.13).

The European Union (EU) tends to be promoted as an economic union and, as such, its policies and requirements impinge on organizations in all its constituent countries. At the time of writing, in the context of the UK having agreed to a minimum wage for its own citizens, some other countries are suggesting that the EU should set a common minimum wage for workers in all its constituent countries. Some of these factors may increase with the addition of 10 further countries being accepted into the European community fold. Examples such as this illustrate how organizations do not operate in their own clearly defined competitive environment. The capacity to compete is the result of a myriad of different forces, which come from a range of different directions. What is more, at some time in an organization's life it will seek merely to survive, at other times to reduce profits in order to invest and at other times to push strongly for high profits in order to satisfy shareholders. Some organizations will, for a limited time, run at a loss or over budget – calculating that better times are in the future.

What is clear is that there is no one rationale for the way in which organizations react or interact with triggers for change coming from the PEST environment and perhaps constraints coming from their own histories and the influences of their temporal environments. External and internal politics play a

Illustration 1.13

Tesco jobs go east

The transfer of work to India reached the retail sector today as Tesco, Britain's leading supermarket, announced it was moving 420 jobs to Bangalore.

The jobs, in the area of business support, will go from offices in Cardiff, Dundee and Welwyn Garden City. The supermarket giant said its UK employees would be offered new jobs within Tesco if they were willing to be flexible.

'Everybody will be offered an alternative role at Tesco. Last year we had 350 roles that were moved, and 70% of the staff that were affected took up alternative positions at Tesco,' the company said.

By moving jobs to India, Tesco is following in the footsteps of financial services and telecommunications giants such as HSBC and BT, which have been drawn by the pool of English-speaking, skilled and cheap labour available in India.

Now that Tesco has decided to adopt the same tactic, other companies in the retail sector – a growth area for jobs in the UK – may well follow the company's lead.

Even the public sector is jumping on the outsourcing bandwagon. The government is considering shipping blood and urine samples from NHS patients to India for clinical tests, in order to cut costs.

Indian laboratory technicians can be hired for as little as £4,000 a year; the savings would more than make up for the cost of flying samples across the world. Test results could be emailed back to UK hospitals. Private sector hospitals are already conducting trials of the service, which could reduce costs by as much as one-third.

Babcock, the engineering conglomerate, is to cut 290 jobs at its dockyard in Fife, Scotland, as part of a drive to cut costs. Babcock, which is transforming itself into a support services firm, said restructuring its Rosyth dockyard had helped it to win contracts to refit four British Navy warships and secure work on the new Terminal 5, to be built at Heathrow airport. The cuts will reduce the Rosyth workforce to just more than 1,500 people.

Source: Mark Tran, 'Tesco jobs to go east', Guardian Unlimited, Guardian Newspapers Limited July 23 (2004).

part in decisions to change and in what way. While rational decision making may seem attractive, and many persuade themselves that this is what they are involved in, personal circumstances, attitudes and emotions also come into play. In addition, not only do triggers for change come from organizations' PEST environment, there are also forces for change operating within organizations themselves – and these also need to be managed. A number of writers (e.g. Stewart, 1991; Paton and McCalman, 2000; Buchanan and Huczynski, 2004; Johnson, Scholes and Whittington, 2005) are in agreement in identifying these as internal triggers or sources of change. Consequently, organizations must cope with not only a plethora of external forces for change, but also internal forces for change.

Internal triggers for change

Drawing on the views of writers such as those listed previously, the following is an indicative list of what might be categorized as internal triggers for change:

- an organization becoming unionized or de-unionized
- a new chief executive or other senior manager
- a revision of administrative structures

- the redesign of a group of jobs
- the redesign of a factory or office layout
- the purchase of new IT equipment
- a new marketing strategy
- a cut in overtime working
- staff redundancies
- strengthening of specific departments such as research and development.

A glance through this list will show that almost all can be conceptualized as changes in response to influences external to the organization. It is, therefore, difficult in reality to separate completely internal from external triggers for change. Many writers suggest that changes in structure and ways of working should be aligned to changes in strategy that, in their turn, should be aligned to changes in the political, economic, technological and socio-economic environments.

This argument is taken up in more detail in Chapter 3. Meanwhile, as the next section shows, there are other ways of categorizing organizational environments that are more focused on organizations and change.

Organizational responses to change

Thus far the discussion suggests that organizations operate in at least three types of environment, which together make up the total 'operating environment' (Sadler, 1989, p. 174) of an organization. The first consists of the historical developments bringing changes over time. These range from those activities that are mainly industry focused to those which rely more on knowledge and brainpower – what Handy (1994) calls 'focused intelligence', that is the ability to acquire and apply knowledge and know-how. These can be categorized as the *temporal environment*. This is an environment that influences organizations in at least two ways. The first is in a general way, through the cycles of industry-based innovation, which move organizations through major series of developments such as shown in Figure 1.2. The second is in a more specific way through the life cycle of the organization itself. This includes its particular history built up from its founder days through periods of expansion and decline, all of which are instrumental in helping to explain an organization's 'idiosyncrasies' of strategy and structure, culture, politics and leadership style.

The second type of environment is the *external environment*, which includes the political (including legal), economic, technological and socio-cultural environment as well as those factors pushing for globalization and an increasing concern with the physical environment (the PEST environment). The third environment is the organization's *internal environment*, which, to some extent, consists of those organizational changes that are the first-line responses to changes in the external and temporal environments. Figure 1.4 is a stylized depiction of the concept of organizations as systems operating in multi-dimensional environments, with all that this means for organizations and change. However, this way of conceptualizing the

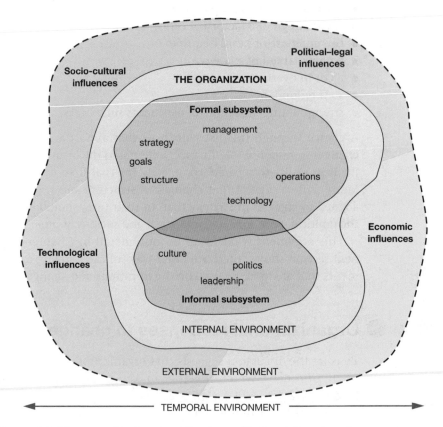

Figure 1.4 The organizational system in multi-dimensional environments

organizational environment to some extent misses its dynamic nature and the degree of *strength* of the wind of change.

Environmental turbulence

The dynamics of any organization's environment have also been described in terms of the degree of environmental turbulence. Ansoff and McDonnell (1990) state that a firm's performance is optimized when its aggressiveness and responsiveness match its environment. They propose five levels of environmental turbulence:

- *Level 1: Predictable.* A repetitive environment characterized by stability of markets; where the challenges repeat themselves; change is slower than the organization's ability to respond; the future is expected to be the same as the past.
- *Level 2: Forecastable by extrapolation.* Complexity increases but managers can still extrapolate from the past and forecast the future with confidence.
- *Level 3: Predictable threats and opportunities.* Complexity increases further when the organization's ability to respond becomes more problematic; however, the future can still be predicted with some degree of confidence.

- *Level 4: Partially predictable opportunities*. Turbulence increases with the addition of global and socio-political changes. The future is only partly predictable.
- *Level 5: Unpredictable surprises*. Turbulence increases further with unexpected events and situations occurring more quickly than the organization can respond.

These levels can be compared to three different kinds of change situation proposed by Stacey (1996), namely: closed change, contained change and open-ended change – a description of which can be found in Illustration 1.14.

Illustration 1.14

Closed, contained and open-ended change

Closed change

When we look back at the history of an organisation there are some sequences of events that we can clearly recount in a manner commanding the widespread agreement of the members involved. We are able to say what happened, why it happened, and what the consequences are. We are also able to explain in a widely accepted way that such a sequence of events and actions will continue to affect the future course of the business. We will call this a closed change situation.

Such closed change would normally apply to the continuing operation of an existing business. For example, consider a business that supplies pop records and tapes to the teenage market. Managers in that business are able to say with some precision how the number of customers in that market has changed over the past and furthermore how it will change for the next 15 years or so. Those customers already exist. The managers can establish fairly clear-cut relationships between the number of customers and the number of records and tapes they have bought and will buy.

Contained change

Other sequences of events and actions flowing from the past are less clear-cut. Here we find that we are able to say only what probably happened why it probably happened, and what its probable consequences were. The impact of such a sequence of events upon the future course of the business has similarly to be qualified by probability statements.

For example, the supplier of records and tapes will find it harder to explain why particular kinds of records and tapes sold better than others. That supplier will find it somewhat difficult to forecast what kinds of tapes and records will sell better in the future; but market research, lifestyle studies and statistical projections will enable reasonably helpful forecasts for at least the short term.

Open-ended change

There are yet other sequences of events and actions arising from the past and continuing to impact on the future where explanations do not command anything like widespread acceptance by those involved.

The company supplying records and tapes may have decided in the past to diversify into video film distribution, by acquiring another company already in that business. That acquisition may then become unprofitable and the managers involved could well subscribe to conflicting explanations of why this is so. Some may claim that the market for video films is too competitive. Others that the diversification was a wrong move because it meant operating in a different market with which they were not familiar. Others may say that it is due to a temporary decline in demand and that the market will pick up in the future. Yet others may ascribe it to poor management of the acquisition, or to a failure to integrate it properly into the business, or to a clash of cultures between the two businesses. What that team of managers does next to deal with low profitability obviously depends upon the explanation of past failure they subscribe to.

Source: Stacey, R. D. (1996), *Strategic Management and Organisational Dynamics*, 2nd edn (London, Pitman, pp. 23–4).

Both Ansoff and McDonnell's levels of environmental turbulence and Stacey's closed, contained and open-ended kinds of change situation can also be related to Stacey's (1996, p. 26) concepts of 'close to certainty' and 'far from certainty'. Thus, close to certainty describes a situation where organizational members face closed and contained change or, in Ansoff and McDonnell's terms, when the environment resembles Levels 1 to 3. As the degree of environmental turbulence moves from Level 4 to Level 5 or, in Stacey's terms, to a situation of open-ended change, organizations can be said to be far from certainty. These changing situations have significant implications for the actions of managers as they attempt to choose appropriate strategies to deal with them.

Activity 1.5 offers the opportunity to carry out a simple environmental assessment of one or more organizations. It is a challenging activity and you will almost certainly say you need further information. However, organizations always exist in situations of imperfect knowledge and managers have to do their best in the circumstances. A start may be made by (simply?) identifying whether the forces for change are strong, moderate or weak. Strebel (1996) describes a strong change force as one causing a substantial decline or a substantial improvement in performance. He identifies a moderate force for change as one causing only a minor impact on performance, while a weak force is one whose nature and direction are difficult to discern.

Activity 1.5

Think about two or three organizations with which you are familiar. Carry out a simple environmental assessment for each organization. To help you with this, consider the following:

- *the PEST factors and the organizations' internal environments;*

- *whether past historical developments (either in societal or organizational terms) have an influence on the organizations' strategies and operations.*

Using Ansoff and McDonnell's (1990) framework, make a judgement about the level of environmental turbulence prevailing for each organization.

Match these levels to Stacey's (1996) types of change situations.

Identify the similarities and differences in the three organizations' environments.

What lessons can you draw about the probability of each organization responding to future environmental triggers for change?

The strength of the forces for change can be related to the degree of turbulence in the environment: the stronger the force the more probable it is that the environment is moving to Ansoff and McDonnell's (1990) Level 5. What this implies is that the ability to plan and manage change becomes ever more difficult as the forces and levels of turbulence increase. This is related to, but complicated further by, the different types of change that can be experienced by organizations.

●●●● Comment and conclusions

Organizations operate in multiple environments (temporal, external and internal). It is not difficult, therefore, to speculate on the effects that the many, and interacting, influences referred to in this chapter can have on organizational life. The key task, for organizations, is to work with and try to manage these – in Schein's (1988, p. 94) words, organizations have continually to achieve 'external adaption and internal integration'. In addition, they need to be 'quick on their feet' to anticipate, where possible, opportunities and threats and react with knowledge to the 'unpredictable surprises' that Ansoff and McDonnell (1990) speak of. The purpose and focus of efforts to do so are, essentially, what managing organizational change is all about. This means understanding more fully how the formal aspects of organizational life respond to pressures from the internal, external and temporal environments – that is how change is leveraged through strategy, structure and operational processes. In addition, it means understanding the more informal processes such as power, politics and conflict, culture and leadership.

Having said this, in reality it can be argued that all scanning tools are limited in some way. It is difficult to identify all the determinants of change, which will make it difficult to always prescribe appropriate strategies. It could also be argued that the information gathered is subjective and personal to the researcher at any one moment in time.

Albright (2004) argues, however, that if managed effectively and applied progressively a continuous process of identifying, collecting and translating progressive information about external influences will benefit strategic decision making towards establishing a preparative stance to environmental factors.

This chapter has commented on the winds of change as they blow variably and, to a degree, unpredictably. Having set the organizational environmental 'scene' in this chapter, Chapter 2 looks in more detail at the impact of these winds of change upon organizations with a more detailed examination of the nature of change itself.

Discussion questions and assignments

1 To what extent do you think the open systems concept is helpful in understanding how organizational change might happen?

2 Give examples of environmental forces for change that are likely to affect, significantly, the way organizations operate in ten years' time. Justify your choices.

3 How realistic do you think it is to categorize types of change within an organization? What might be the advantages and disadvantages of doing this?

Discussion questions and assignments *continued*

4 Carry out an 'environmental scan' of an organization you know well. The following steps should help:

(a) Using the PEST framework, the results from Activities 1.2 and 1.3, and the suggestions in Figure 1.3, list those factors you consider could affect the future performance of the organization and/or the way it operates. Concentrate on those factors external to the organization.

(b) Indicate on your list where there are linkages between the various factors. Doing this diagrammatically, using lines and arrows, helps. You could use a plus sign to show where the effects combine to reinforce each other and a minus sign to indicate where one factor might help negate another.

(c) Mark with a star those factors that are critically important to the organization. Consider whether these originate mostly in the political–legal, economic, technological or socio-cultural parts of the PEST environment. Are they also linked to the general movement of organizations into value-oriented time?

(d) Finally, list the starred factors and rank them according to the volatility of the external environment. Consider whether this volatility provides an opportunity or a threat to the organization and its future performance.

Through carrying out this process you may have realized how much you know about the organization's environment but also how much you do not know! The outcome of this activity may be, therefore, not only an increased understanding of the environmental forces facing the organization, but also a realization that environmental scanning requires continuous vigilance and collection of information that must then be used creatively to help predict necessary changes within the organization itself.

Case example ●●●

Not so Mobile: will Nokia now get the message of changing consumer tastes, new technology and stronger rivals?

This Finnish company has dominated mobile telecoms but has been slow to recognize recent challenges to its market share. A customer who has used Nokia products for over 10 years broke his Nokia allegiance and bought an updated camera phone from a competitor. The Nokia product portfolio does not seem to have changed its look over the past 10 years. Its European share in the market is beginning to decline, and even in the company's native Finland (where loyalty is very high), the share is down from 93 per cent to 80 per cent.

A Finnish retail mobile phone chain commented that other brands, such as Samsung and Sony

Ericsson, have colour screens that are so sharp, and the clam shell (folding design) is extremely handy. Nokia appears to be facing its greatest challenge since it transformed itself from a sprawling conglomerate to a highly focused telecommunications group in the early 1990s. The US share is also thought to have gone down due to competition from Motorola and LG of South Korea.

Nokia is also suffering because of a desire by mobile phone operators to launch a 'look and feel' over that of the handset maker. Vodafone and T-Mobile are large operators looking for differentiation in the market. Exclusivity has never been a Nokia strategy. Co-branding is becoming more common, again a strategy not yet taken by Nokia.

If Nokia were to continue to lose its share in the market, the 'tremor would be felt throughout Finland'. This company has helped put Finland on the map as a technological leader, and due to its size the employee numbers are considerable.

Source: Based on Christopher Brown-Humes and Robert Budden (2004). 'Not so Mobile: will Nokia now get the message of changing consumer tastes, new technology and stronger rivals?' *Financial Times*, 7 May 2004.

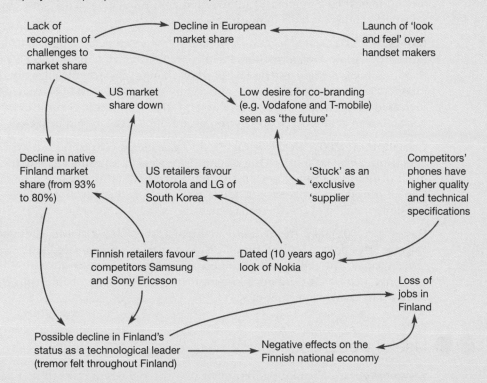

Case exercise   Analyzing the causes of change

Situations of change, such as the ones just described, draw attention to the complexity of the change environment. However, it is not sufficient merely to *identify* these triggers for change. Analyzing the relationships between them – in other words, their systemic nature – is even more important. The multiple-cause diagram in the case example is an attempt to do this.

Such diagrams have the power to capture the complex dynamics of change situations. They help bring about a deeper understanding of how interventions in one variable can have far-reaching effects in other parts of the situation. They act, therefore, not only in a descriptive mode, but also as an analytical tool for understanding and managing change.

1 Write a brief account of how different elements of the temporal and PEST environments interact to influence the situation described in the case.

2 Consider how you could use multiple-cause diagrams to 'picture' the multiple and interacting causes that bring pressure for change in your own organization or one you know well.

Indicative resources

Brooks, I., Weatherston, J. and Wilkinson G. (2004) *The International Business Environment*, Harlow: Pearson Education. This text is specifically written for university students studying in the business fields. It provides additional theoretical perspectives on the 'modern' business environment. The first part of the text focuses on and identifies a number of interrelated environmental factors and how they might affect different types of organizations.

Burnes, B. (2004) *Managing Change: A Strategic Approach to Organizational Dynamics* (4th edn), Harlow: Financial Times Prentice Hall. Although a more strategic perspective, this book recognizes the fast pace of change and acknowledges that local markets are becoming much more affected by globalization. It also recognizes the increased competition and pressure organizations are faced with to survive. The book offers an additional perspective on organizational theory and behaviour.

Carnall, C. A. (2003) *Managing Change in Organizations* (4th edn), Harlow: Pearson Education. This text looks at the diagnostic process of assessing change, the likelihood of success, and focuses on the 'implementability' of change programmes. Carnall considers a range of individual, team and organizational issues relevant to any understanding of change management.

Hayes, J. (2002) *The Theory and Practice of Change Management*, Chippenham: Palgrave. This book is written for practising managers who are faced with organizational change. The initial part of the book considers the nature of change and the challenge it poses for organizations, but in particular the people who have to manage any change interventions.

Useful websites

www.dfes.gov.uk Useful for government statistics and recent research that has been undertaken relating to employment, education and future national trends.

www.guardian.co.uk Useful for current affairs articles relating to IT, politics and business.

www.ft.com Useful for business updates at a national UK level, European level and also worldwide.

www.statistics.gov.uk Useful for information relating to current UK and some European comparisons.

www.pearsoned.co.uk Offers alternative books relating to change and some additional online resources.

www.amazon.co.uk Offers new and used books related to this topic area.

www.worldbank.com (2005) Statistics for access to the Internet.

To click straight to these links and other resources go to
www.pearsoned.co.uk/senior

 References

Adhikari, R. and Yang, Y. (2002) 'What will WTO membership mean for China and its trading partners?', *Finance and Development*, September, vol. 39, no. 3

Albright, K. (2004) 'Environmental Scanning: radar for success', *The Information Management Journal*, May/June, pp. 38–45

Almon, C. and Grassini, M. (2002) *The Changing Structure of Employment in Italy 1980–2010*. Working Paper.

Ansoff, I. H. and McDonnell, E. J. (1990) *Implanting Strategic Management*, Englewood Cliffs, NJ: Prentice Hall.

Applebee, A., Clayton, P., Pascoe, C. and Bruce, H. (2000) 'Australian academic use of the Internet: implications for university adminstrators', *Internet Research: Electronic Networking Applications and Policy*, vol. 5, no. 2, pp. 141–9. http://www.emerald-library.com.

Arnold, W. (2004) 'E-mail becomes a victim of its own instant success', *Financial Times*, 27 May.

BBC News (2002) The UK's five tests. www.news.bbc.co.uk, 30 September.

BBC News (2004a) India's economy continues to grow. www.news.bbc.co.uk

BBC News (2004b) UK not ready for the euro. www.news.bbc.co.uk.

BBC News (2004c) 'Health reforms approved in France' www.news.bbc.co.uk.2/hi/Europe/3940609.stm, 30 July.

Bevan, K. (1996) 'The challenge of coping with change', *Financial Times*, 20 September.

Brooks, I. Weatherspoon, J. and Wilkinson, G. (2004) *The International Business Environment*, Harlow: Pearson Education.

Brown-Humes, C. and Budden, R. (2004) 'Not so mobile: will Nokia now get the message of changing consumer tastes, new technology and stronger rivals?', *Financial Times*, 7 May.

Buchanan, D. and Huczynski, A. (2004) *Organizational Behaviour* (5th edn), Hemel Hempstead: FT Prentice Hall.

Burnes, B. (2004) *Managing Change* (4th edn), Harlow: Pearson Education.

Burns, T. and Stalker, G. M. (1966) *The Management of Innovation*, London: Tavistock.

Butler, R. (1991) *Designing Organizations: A Decision-making Perspective*, London: Routledge.

Carnall, C.A. (2003) *Managing Change in Organisations* (4th edn), Harlow: Pearson Education.

Checkland, P. B. (1972) 'Towards a system-based methodology for real-world problem solving', *Journal of Systems Engineering*, vol. 3, no. 2.

Child, J. (1973) 'Organization: a choice for man', in Child, J. (ed.) *Man and Organization*, London: Allen & Unwin.

Clarke, L. (1994) *The Essence of Change*, Hemel Hempstead: Prentice Hall.

Daft, R. L. (1989) *Organization Theory and Design* (2nd edn), St. Paul, MN: West Publishing.

Dawson, P. (2003) *Reshaping Change: A Processual Perspective*, London: Routledge.

Department of Education and Employment (2000) *Opportunity for All: Skills for the New Economy: Initial Response to the National Skills Force Final Report from the Secretary of State for Education and Employment*, London: The Stationery Office, Crown Copyright.

Department for Education and Skills (2002) *A Profile of the UK Higher Education Sector 2000/2001*, London: HMSO.

Drucker, P. F. (1988) 'The coming of the new organization', *Harvard Business Review*, January–February, pp. 45–53.

Eccles, T. (1996) 'Management power and strategic change', *Financial Times*, 12 July.

Emery, F. E. and Trist, E. L. (1967) 'The next 30 years: concepts, methods and anticipations', *Human Relations*, vol. 20, pp. 199–237.

Financial Times (2004) 'Email becomes a victim of its own success', 27 May, p. 13.

FT (2004) 'Creative Business', *Financial Times*, 25 May.

FT Life on the net (2000) *Financial Times*, 5 September, p. 1. www.ft.com/lifeonthenet

FT Life on the net (2000) *Financial Times*, 13 September, p. 1. www.ft.com/lifeonthenet.

FT Life on the net (2000) *Financial Times*, 14 September, p. 1. www.ft.com/lifeonthenet.

FT Life on the net (2000) *Financial Times*, 15 September, p. 1. www.ft.com/lifeonthenet.

Furnham, A. (2000) 'Work in 2020: prognostications about the world of work 20 years into the millennium', *Journal of Managerial Psychology*, vol. 15, no. 3, pp. 242–54.

Goodman, M. (1995) *Creative Management*, Hemel Hempstead: Prentice Hall.

Government Actuaries Department (2004) London, www.gad.gov.uk/.

Handy, C. (1994) *The Empty Raincoat*, London: Hutchinson.

Harney, A. (2005) 'Hong Kong eyes policy change on arts complex', *Financial Times*, Asia, 3 June.

Haverson, P. (2000) 'A key player in the sports team', *Financial Times*, 2 August, p. 10.

Hayes, J. (2002) *The Theory and Practice of Change Management*, Chippenham: Palgrave.

Howcroft, D. and Mitev, N. (2000) 'An empirical study of Internet usage and difficulties among medical practice management in the UK', *Internet Research: Electronic Networking Applications and Policy*, vol. 10, no. 2, pp. 170–81. http://www.emerald-library.com.

Johnson, G. and Scholes, K. (1999) *Exploring Corporate Strategy: Text and Cases* (5th edn), Hemel Hempstead: Prentice Hall.

Johnson, G., Scholes, K. and Whittington, R. (2005) *Exploring Corporate Strategy: Text and Cases* (7th edn), Hemel Hempstead: FT Prentice Hall.

Jones, P., Palmer, J., Osterweil, C. and Whitehead, D. (1996) *Delivering Exceptional Performance: Aligning the Potential of Organisations, Teams and Individuals*, London: Pitman.

Mannermann, M. (1998) 'Politics and science = futures studies', *American Behavioral Scientist*, vol. 42, pp. 427–35.

Mullins, L. (2005) *Management and Organisational Behaviour* (7th edn), Harlow: Pearson Education.

Nadler, D. A. (1988) 'Concepts for the management of organizational change', in Tushman, M. L. and Moore, W. L. (eds) *Readings in the Management of Innovation*, New York: Ballinger, pp. 718–32.

Nadler, D. A. and Tushman, M. L. (1988) 'A model for diagnosing organizational behavior', in Tushman, M. L. and Moore, W. L. (eds) *Readings in the Management of Innovation*, New York: Ballinger, pp. 148–63.

Nadler, D. A. and Tushman, M. L. (1999) 'The organization of the future: strategic imperatives and core competencies for the 21st century', *Organizational Dynamics*, vol. 28, no. 1, pp. 71–80.

Paton, R. A. and McCalman, J. (2000) *Change Management: Guide to Effective Implementation* (2nd edn), London: PCP.

Roberts, D. (2000) 'A dragon with plenty of good connections', FT Telecoms, *Financial Times*, 20 September.

Roberts, S. P. and Coulter, M. (2005) *Management* (8th edn), Englewood Cliffs, NJ: Pearson/ Prentice-Hall.

Ryll, C. and Collier, P. (2001) 'Wrinkles and all', *Financial Times*, 19 September.

Sadler, P. (1989), 'Management development', in Sisson, K. (ed.) *Personnel Management in Britain* (2nd edn), Oxford: Blackwell, p. 174.

Scase, R. (1999) *Britain Towards 2010: The Changing Business Environment*, Office of Science and Technology, Department of Trade and Industry, Crown Copyright.

Schein, E. H. (1988) 'Coming to a new awareness of organisational culture', *Sloan Management Review*, vol. 25, no. 1, p. 94.

Silverman, D. (1970) *The Theory of Organisations*, London: Heinemann Educational.

Stacey, R. D. (1996) *Strategic Management and Organisational Dynamics* (2nd edn), London: Pitman.

Stacey, R.D. (2003) *Strategic Management and Organisational Dynamics* (4th edn), Harlow: FT Prentice Hall.

Statt, D. A. (1991) *The Concise Dictionary of Management*, London: Routledge.

Stewart, J. (1991) *Managing Change Through Training and Development*, London: Kogan Page.

Storey, J., Edwards, P. and Sisson, K. (1997) *Managers in the Making: Careers, Development and Control in Corporate Britain and Japan*, London: Sage.

Strebel, P. (1996) 'Choosing the right path', *Mastering Management*, Part 14, *Financial Times*.

Taylor, F. W. (1911) *Principles of Scientific Management*, New York: Harper & Row.

Terazono, E. (2004) *Financial Times*, 22 June, p. 7.

Tran, M. (2004) 'Tesco jobs go East', Guardian Unlimited, Guardian Newspapers Limited, 23 July.

Westbrook, R. (2000) 'Look to the process for a better product', Mastering Management, *Financial Times*, 16 October.

*Wiley, J. (2004) www.johnwiley.com.

Wilson, R., Homenidou, K. and Dickerson, A. (2004) *Working Futures: New Projections of Employment by Sector 2002–2012, Volume 1,* University of Warwick: Institute for Employment Research.

Wood, S. (1989) 'The transformation of work?' in Wood, S. (ed.) *The Transformation of Work*, London: Unwin Hyman, Chapter 1.

*www.aspexint.com/information/glossary_of_terms. html 2004

www.teleconomy.com (2004)

www.worldbank.org (2005)

* wps.prenhall.com. 2004

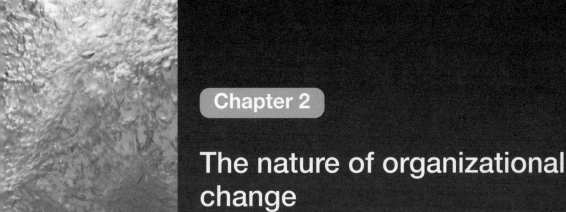

Chapter 2

The nature of organizational change

This chapter introduces the idea that organizational change has many faces, that is that there are many different types of change. A basic distinction is made between convergent types of change and transformational change that is organization wide and is characterized by radical shifts in strategy, mission and values as well as associated changes of structures and systems. There is consideration, also, of the idea that some change *emerges* while at other times change can be *planned*. The chapter concludes with an examination of the different change situations that organizations experience and provides an appreciation of their relationship to the way change might be designed and implemented – thus looking forward to the chapters in Part Three, where different methodologies for designing and implementing change are discussed in more detail.

Learning objectives

By the end of this chapter, you will be able to:

● emphasize the complex nature of organizational change;

● describe and discuss the multi-dimensional nature of organizational change;

● analyze change situations in order to choose appropriate methods of managing and implementing change;

● recognize that there are limitations to the 'common-sense' approach to managing change because of cultural, political and leadership influences;

● critically evaluate the theoretical perspectives relating to the types of change that organizations may experience.

 # The changing faces of change

Consider the statements in Illustration 2.1.

Illustration 2.1

Changing organizations

Eastern promise

Tesco (a leading UK supermarket chain) outsources jobs to India. Following the lead of several financial and telecommunications companies, Tesco has plans to make its first move to India. The plans include shifting job roles from Tesco's three UK centres to Bangalore, which means closure of UK-based sites in Dundee, Cardiff and Welwyn Garden City. Tesco moved 350 jobs last year and says that 70 per cent of the staff who were affected took up alternative roles at Tesco. This could have a long-term effect on employment in the United Kingdom. There is increasing trade union opposition, as they claim that the increasing transfer of work to India could cost up to 200,000 jobs in the United Kingdom.

[At the time of going to print, Tesco has 730 UK stores, 26 per cent of the UK market share and employs 200,000 people.]

Source: http://news.bbc.co.uk, 2004; http://www.guardian.co.uk, 2004.

Xenos, a world leader

Xenos, a world leader in the development and implementation of software solutions that transform documents and data into e-content, today announced a restructuring of its organisation. The changes will help fast-track new product development, enhance customer support and enable the forging of new strategic alliances to fuel the company's future growth. Key elements of the restructure include: the consolidation of the company's product development; the merger of implementation services and pre-sales activities; a new customer support operation; the establishment of a new global marketing organization, and the streamlining of finance, human resources and administration departments. The restructure involves a reduction in staff of 12 per cent across the organization globally and one-time costs of approximately $1 million.

Source: M2 Communications Ltd (Wednesday, 30 August 2000).

Novell to cut 900 jobs and restructure

Novell, a leading software company, yesterday announced a restructuring of its operations that included cutting 900 jobs, or 16 per cent of its workforce. The job losses had been expected as the company focused on e-business applications and moved beyond its core network operating system business.

Source: Tom Foremski, *Financial Times* (Thursday, 7 September 2000).

United Utilities embraces the benefits of eBusiness

Moving forward, our single business managing the group's own licensed assets will be focused on cost cutting and greater efficiency. The group's other core businesses – customer sales, contract asset management and business process outsourcing – will be focused on growth, controlling costs and being genuinely profitable. Across them all, we will embrace the benefits of e-Business – investing in ideas and pushing new boundaries, a very different and exciting approach from anything the group has done before. Business as usual is not an option for us. There are opportunities to seize. We will reorganize the group, effective from October 2000, and make progress on the firm base of the group's two core skills, and we will play to our strengths in our initiatives to exploit the opportunities of competition and e-Business.

Source: John Roberts, Chief Executive, the United Utilities Shareholders' Review (2000, p.1).

Adaptability furnishes key to craftsmen's long survival

As an example of the changing face of industrial Britain, High Wycombe in Buckinghamshire is hard to beat. ... Due to intense competition from furniture makers in lower-cost countries, High Wycombe's companies in this field have dwindled to about 20. But the survivors ... are far from downbeat. [For instance] Peter Head, managing director, says the company [Hands of Wycombe] has had to introduce new designs to keep up with the competition. It makes up-market office furniture – including 'pods' that combine a desk, chair and computer workstation and are directed towards the needs of high-technology businesses. These can sell for thousands of pounds.

Source: Peter Marsh, *Financial Times* (Wednesday, 6 September 2000, p. 32).

Deal reduces low-cost flights to two main carriers

Low-cost airline company (Irish-based) Ryanair intensified low-cost airline competition in early 2003 by buying the ailing airline company BUZZ. The planned takeover marks a further reduction in choice for customers on the 'no-frills' sector of the market. BUZZ was originally set up in 1999 by the Dutch airline company KLM. It has been looking for a partner for a few months after the Dutch company decided it could no longer continue to finance the business.

This takeover has increased the number of routes that Ryanair will operate and on the strength of this business development Ryanair has increased its order for an additional 100 Boeing aircraft.

Source: Geoffrey Gibbs, the *Guardian* (3 February 2003).

A good year for 'patient protection' laws

Mark 1996 as the year of the managed-care customer. Mandated 48-hour maternity stays, bans on gag clauses imposed on physicians by HMOs, and other 'patient protection' measures sailed through state legislatures this year, each passing in at least 16 states. Portions of the Patient Protection Act, drafted by the American Medical Association, passed in at least 20 states. It was considered in another 15. ... The flurry of incremental reforms caught the managed-care industry off guard, said Joy Johnson Wilson, director of the health committee at the Denver-based National Conference of State Legislatures. She predicted managed-care organizations will change their practices to head off further legislation in 1997.

Source: Modern Healthcare (18 October 1996, p. 22).

NHS revolution breathes new life into private sector

The UK government is turning to outside (private both within the UK and possibly worldwide) health providers in its plan to cut hospital waiting times. It is a large move for the government to work in conjunction with the private health sector. The government has decided to turn the NHS less into a direct service provider, and more into a purchaser of care. It has been considering providers in various bases in Europe and as far afield as South Africa. This will have a knock-on effect for UK service providers as the NHS is prepared to go further afield to other countries that can offer competitive prices.

Source: Timmins, *Financial Times* (3 May 2004).

All the statements in Illustration 2.1 identify actual or predicted organizational change. However, a cursory reading of these statements indicates that change in one organization is not the same as change in another. For instance, at Tesco, moving services to another country will penetrate the whole future of this business. In addition it may set precedents for similar businesses to follow suit. These changes are clearly part of an overall planned strategy, which could ultimately affect the number of contracted employees within the United Kingdom. The changes have been instigated by the competitive nature of the

industry, which includes a changing political, economic and technological environment in which businesses operate today.

Ryanair's plans to expand will initially cost in excess of £15 million; however,
additional aircraft and increased routes will also affect employee numbers and
the cost of the service. In the external environment, cost and service may be
affected as competition has reduced, and airline regulatory bodies may increase
their European requirements. The strategy for Micheal O'Leary (CEO of Ryanair)
appears to be at present: 'do more of the same', and take advantages of the
increased use of technology to reduce labour costs and increase use of services.

Tesco and Ryanair provide examples of a planned approach to change to
remain competitive. The strategies employed respond to the increased competitive environment. Both companies are, at present, market leaders in their field
and are creating strategies to maintain the market advantage. They are clearly
adapting to the changing environment in which they operate. Part of the strategy is to exploit the use of telecommunication and Internet developments,
attempting to meet customer demands on response times and cost.

It is arguable whether the term 'adaptability' should be applied to the
changes being planned for the UK National Health Service illustration. This
public sector organization has had to respond to and create a strategy to try and
resolve issues related to increased stress being placed on the current service.
Population trends in the United Kingdom mean that people live longer, and our
expectations of services increase. Therefore alternative systems need to be
explored to resolve some of the urgent supply and demand issues faced by the
NHS. For instance, at Xenos, it seems that there is very little left untouched in
the changes that are planned. Change is proposed right across the organization,
including a significant reduction in the number of staff. The article from which
this extract is taken indicates that all these changes are a result of a change in
Xenos's strategy which is, in turn, a reaction to the changing commercial, technological and economic environment in which the company operates.

Novell's restructuring is reported to be costing $40–$50 million but it expects
to set $25 million of savings against this. The report on Novell again indicates
that the changes are large scale and are in response to changes in market
demand for the software products supplied by Novell. By contrast, while United
Utilities' chief executive's statement in the annual report indicates that 'business
as usual is not an option', he goes on to say that, in seeking to deliver growth
(while at the same time delivering cost reductions) the intention is to do it in a
way that aligns with the group's core skills, that is not doing 'things we do not
understand'. Consequently United Utilities gives the impression that, while
changes must occur in response to government regulatory requirements and the
increasing possibilities of e-commerce, some parts of the group's businesses,
while striving for growth, will do this using what they know rather than ventur-
ing into unknown territory.

It is arguable whether the term 'adaptability' should be applied to the
changes being made at United Utilities. This is, however, an appropriate term to

describe how the fifth organization mentioned – Hands of Wycombe – has responded to changing demands for its product. Continuing to serve a market it knows well, it has, even so, had to keep up with the changing demands for its products brought about by changing requirements resulting from the advent of computer-based office systems. The penultimate example of change features the many ways in which new legislation impacts on, in this case, part of the health services in the United States. However, as the article implies, the changes required from this particular group of care providers would seem to be well within its capabilities without radical restructuring or wholesale reorganization.

Strebel (1996a, p. 5), in an article in the *Financial Times*, says 'Change may be a constant but it is not always the same' and this is well exemplified by the examples given in Illustration 2.1. Building on this notion, what follows in this chapter is a discussion of a number of frameworks for categorizing change and why it is necessary to do so if organizational change is to be successful. The discussion starts with a broad generalization of the concept of change.

Varieties of change

A starting point for considering the nature of organizational change is Grundy's (1993) three 'varieties of change' as shown in Figure 2.1. As a background to proposing these, Grundy states that many managers perceive change as a homogeneous concept, while others describe change as being primarily the enemy of stability. However, he maintains that it is possible to differentiate a number of characteristic types of change.

The first of these Grundy defines as 'smooth incremental change'. Smooth incremental change is change that evolves slowly in a systematic and predictable way. Grundy maintains that this type of change is mainly reminiscent of the UK and the US situation from the 1950s to early 1970s, but that this situation would

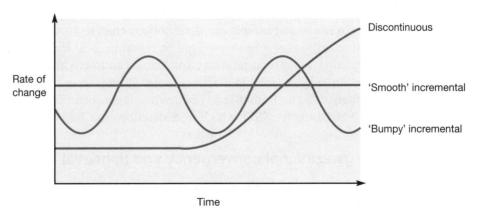

Figure 2.1 Grundy's major types of change

Source: Grundy, T. (1993), *Implementing Strategic Change* (London, Kogan Page, p. 25).

be relatively exceptional in the 1990s and the future. It is important to note that, in Figure 2.1, the vertical axis represents *rate* of change, not *amount* of change. Thus, smooth incremental change does involve an amount of change but this happens at a constant rate.

The second variety of change Grundy terms 'bumpy incremental change'. This is characterized by periods of relative tranquillity punctuated by accelera- tion in the pace of change. He likens the 'bumps' to 'the movement of continental land masses where the 'fault' enables periodic readjustment to occur without cataclysmic effect' (Grundy, 1993, p. 24). He says that the triggers for this type of change are likely to include those from both the environment in which organizations operate and internal changes such as those instigated to improve efficiency and ways of working. An example given is the periodic re- organization that organizations go through. One way of categorizing both types of incremental change is to see them as change that is associated more with the *means* by which organizations achieve their goals rather than as a change in the goals themselves. Two of the examples of change described earlier (at Hands of Wycombe and in the managed-care sector of US health care generally) could be categorized as instances of this type of change.

Grundy's third variety of change is 'discontinuous change', which he defines as 'change which is marked by rapid shifts in strategy, structure or culture, or in all three' (p. 26). An example given is that of the privatization of previously publicly owned utilities, for instance electricity generation and distribution. Another example is what Strebel (1996b) calls a 'divergent breakpoint', that is change which results from the discovery of a new business opportunity, and he instances the first Apple computer, the arrival of the Macintosh and, most recently, the new chips and software. The opportunities offered by the develop- ment of the Internet and being able to access this, not only through computers but also through television sets and mobile telephones, are most likely to lead to forms of discontinuous change in many organizations.

The change involving strategy, structure (and almost certainly culture and the relative influence held by different individuals and groups) being undertaken by Xenos is a good example of discontinuous change. However, not all instances of discontinuous change are linked to technological innovations. Health scares rendering some food products unsaleable can have cataclysmic effects through- out an industry. Thus discontinuous change can be likened to change in response to the higher levels of environmental turbulence detailed by Ansoff and McDonnell (1990), which were described in Chapter 1.

Organizational convergence and upheaval

Grundy's three types of change are somewhat simplistic and appear to be based on observation rather than investigation and research. While this appears also to be the case with Balogun and Hope Hailey's (2004) identification of change 'paths', they go one step further in suggesting four types of change. These are:

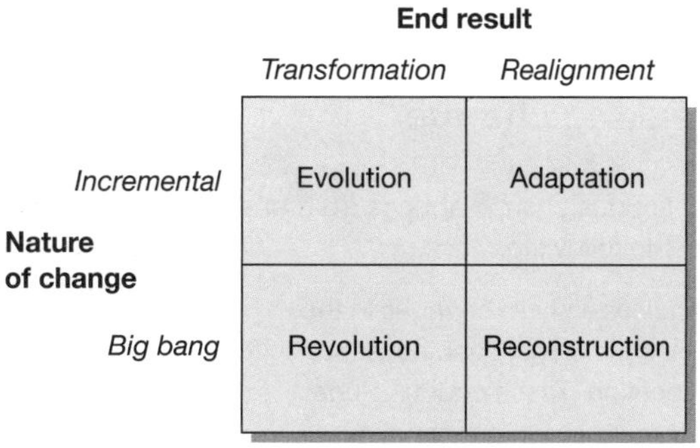

End result

	Transformation	Realignment
Incremental	Evolution	Adaptation
Big bang	Revolution	Reconstruction

Nature of change

Figure 2.2 Types of change
Source: Balogun, J. and Hope Hailey, V. H. (2004), *Exploring Strategic Change* (Harlow, FT Prentice Hall).

incremental change divided into adaptive and evolutionary change; and 'big bang' change divided into reconstruction and revolution. The end result of these varieties of change is either realignment or transformation (see Figure 2.2).

There is a different basis for the framework for describing change proposed by Tushman, Newman and Romanelli (1988) – even though it is similar to that of Grundy in some respects. On the basis of an examination of numerous organizational studies and case histories, these writers propose a model of organizational life that consists of 'periods of incremental change, or convergence, punctuated by discontinuous changes' (p. 707).

They suggest there are two types of converging change: fine-tuning and incremental adaptations. Both these types of change have the common aim of maintaining the fit between organizational strategy, structure and processes. However, whereas fine-tuning is aimed at doing better what is already done well, incremental adaptation involves small changes in response to minor shifts in the environment in which organizations operate – what the authors popularly call the 'ten-percent change'.

Both fine-tuning and incremental adjustments to environmental shifts allow organizations to perform more effectively and optimize the consistencies between strategy, structure, people and processes. Yet Tushman *et al.* show how, as organizations grow, become more successful and develop internal forces for stability, these same forces eventually produce resistance when, for whatever reason, an organization's strategy must change. Thus at times of major change in an organization's environment incremental adjustment will not bring about the major changes in strategy, structure, people and processes that might be required. At times such as these Tushman *et al.* maintain that most organizations will be required to undergo discontinuous or frame-breaking change. Thus, in any organization's life cycle, periods of relative tranquillity will be punctuated with (probably shorter) periods of frame-breaking change.

Illustration 2.2 summarizes the definition of frame-breaking change advanced by Tushman *et al.*

Illustration 2.2

On frame-breaking change

The need for discontinuous change springs from one or a combination of the following:

- *Industry discontinuities* – sharp changes in the legal, political or technological conditions that shift the basis of competition. These could include: deregulation, substitute product technologies, substitute process technologies, the emergence of industry standards or dominant designs, major economic changes (e.g. oil crises), legal shifts (e.g. patent protection, trade/regulator barriers).
- *Product/life cycle shifts* – changes in strategy from the emergence of a product to its establishment in the market, the effects of international competition.
- *Internal company dynamics* – the implications of size for new management design, new management style as inventor–entrepreneurs give way to the need for more steady state management, revised corporate portfolio strategy that can sharply alter the role and resources assigned to business units or functional areas.

The scope of frame-breaking change includes discontinuous change throughout the organization. Frame-breaking change is usually implemented rapidly. Frame-breaking changes are revolutionary changes of the system as opposed to incremental changes in the system. Frame-breaking change usually involves the following features:

- *reformed mission and core values* – new definition of company mission;
- *altered power and status* – reflecting shifts in the bases of competition and resource allocation;
- *reorganization* – new strategy requires a modification in structure, systems and procedures, change of organization form;
- *revised interaction patterns* – new procedures, work flows, communication networks, decision-making patterns;
- *new executives* – usually from outside the organisation;

Frame-breaking change is revolutionary in that the shifts reshape the entire nature of the organization. It requires discontinuous shifts in strategy, structure, people and processes concurrently. Reasons for the rapid, simultaneous implementation of frame-breaking change include the following:

- *synergy* – the need for all pieces of the organization to pull together;
- *pockets of resistance* – have a chance to grow and develop when frame-breaking change is implemented slowly;
- *pent-up need for change* – when constraints are relaxed, change is in fashion;
- *riskiness and uncertainty* – the longer the implementation period, the greater the period of uncertainty and instability.

Source: Based on Tushman, M. L., Newman, W. H. and Romanelli, E. (1988), 'Convergence and upheaval: managing the unsteady pace of organizational evolution', in Tushman, M. L. and Moore, W. L. (eds) (1988), *Readings in the Management of Innovation* (New York, Ballinger Publishing Company, pp. 712–13)

An example of frame-breaking change springing from the changes in the political conditions in Europe is Nato (North Atlantic Treaty Organization). This organization was founded in 1949 (post-World War II), in an atmosphere of anxiety, largely to block Soviet expansion into Europe. The first frame-breaking change for this organization, testing its longevity, was the collapse of the Soviet Union in 1991. This created the subsequent demise of the Warsaw Pact, which left Nato with no obvious purpose. It had to reconfigure to include new countries, in particular those countries that were once part of the eastern bloc. Nato also changed its strategy, attempting to foster a more proactive approach to 'out of area' activities – arguing that instability in any part of Europe would constitute a threat to its members.

The Nato Permanent Joint Council was established in May 1997 to give Russia a consultative role for discussion in matters of mutual interest. There have been other political incidents that have forced Nato to re-evaluate their role, for today and in the future. The 11 September 2001 incident (when a terrorist attack on the World Trade Center and the Pentagon killed 3,000 people) was seen as a pivotal moment as the United States did not involve the Nato alliance in the international campaign that followed.

Russia's supportive reaction following the attacks proved to be a catalyst for a thaw in relations and saw yet again a change in direction for the organization. Russia is now a member of the decision-making team on policies to counter terrorism and other security threats.

Once again a change was to take place as there were disputes between Germany, France and the United States over the invasion of Iraq in March, 2003. Nato's leadership was tested. Since the invasion, analysts perceive Nato to be shaping a new role for itself. There have been joint plans relating to the rapid reaction team that was jointly designed for swift deployment to anywhere in the world. The first test of this partnership is the role the alliance is playing in Afghanistan. Troops numbering 9,000 have currently been agreed and there are plans to expand this number to 21,000 by 2006.

This is a useful example of various types of change that will be discussed within this chapter, in particular frame-breaking change. NATO is clearly an organization which would like to be proactive, however, political and environmental factors often happen at such a fast pace that there is a constant need for it to evaluate its role as an effective and responsive organization (Longescu, 2004).

Fine-tuning to corporate transformation

Grundy (1993) does not claim any particular status for his typology of change; he states specifically that it is not an empirically tested model. The power of the Tushman *et al.* (1988) typology is its claim to be based on research and investigation. This is also the case with the typology put forward by Australian academics Dunphy and Stace (1993). What is more, they claim the status of a model when their typology of change, on the one hand, is combined with a typology of styles of change management, on the other. The full Dunphy and Stace model is discussed further in Chapter 6. What is interesting here is the four descriptions that represent their scale of change. Illustration 2.3 reproduces these descriptions.

A simple correspondence between Grundy's and Dunphy and Stace's categorizations of change is not possible. However, it is reasonable to suggest that Dunphy and Stace's scale types 1 and 2 are typical of Grundy's concept of smooth incremental change, while their scale types 3 and 4 are reminiscent of Grundy's bumpy incremental and discontinuous types of change respectively. The benefit of the Dunphy and Stace model, though, is in the detailed descriptions of each scale type and its testing with the executives, managers and supervisors of 13 Australian organizations from the service sector. Interestingly, organizations operating scale 1 and 2 type changes were in the minority, leading

Illustration 2.3

Defining the scale of change

Scale Type 1: Fine tuning

Organizational change that is an ongoing process characterized by fine-tuning of the 'fit' or match between the organization's strategy, structure, people and processes. Such effort is typically manifested at departmental/divisional levels and deals with one or more of the following:

- refining policies, methods and procedures;
- creating specialist units and linking mechanisms to permit increased volume and increased attention to unit quality and cost;
- developing personnel especially suited to the present strategy (improved training and development; tailoring award systems to match strategic thrusts);
- fostering individual and group commitment to the company mission and the excellence of one's own department;
- promoting confidence in the accepted norms, beliefs and myths;
- clarifying established roles (with their associated authorities and posers), and the mechanisms for allocating resources.

Scale Type 2: Incremental adjustment

Organizational change that is characterized by incremental adjustments to the changing environment. Such change involves distinct modifications (but not radical change) to corporate business strategies, structures and management processes, for example:

- expanding sales territory;
- shifting the emphasis among products;
- improved production process technology;
- articulating a modified statement of mission to employees;
- adjustments to organizational structures within or across divisional boundaries to achieve better links in product/service delivery.

Scale Type 3: Modular transformation

Organizational change that is characterized by major realignment of one or more departments/divisions. The process of radical change is focused on these subparts rather than on the organization as a whole, for example:

- major restructuring of particular departments/divisions;
- changes in key executives and managerial appointments in these areas;
- work and productivity studies resulting in significantly reduced or increased workforce numbers;
- reformed departmental/divisional goals;
- introduction of significantly new process technologies affecting key departments or divisions.

Scale Type 4: Corporate transformation

Organizational change that is corporation wide, characterized by radical shifts in business strategy and revolutionary changes throughout the whole organization involving many of the following features:

- reformed organizational mission and core values;
- altered power and status affecting the distribution of power in the organization;
- reorganization – major changes in structures, systems and procedures across the organization;
- revised interaction patterns – new procedures, work flows, communication networks and decision-making patterns across the organization;
- new executives in key managerial positions from outside the organization.

Source: Dunphy, D. and Stace, D. (1993), 'The strategic management of corporate change', *Human Relations*, vol. 45, no. 8, pp. 917–18.

the researchers to conclude that modular and corporate transformations had become the norm rather than the exception.

However, care must be taken with conclusions such as this based on a small sample of 13 organizations from one sector of industry only. For instance, Abrahamson (2000) in an article entitled 'Change WITHOUT pain' challenges the need for organizations to rush headlong into change as fast as they can, following each change with another one as the first seems not to work. What he recommends is a process of 'painless tinkering with existing business practices and alternating a few bigger changes with a lot of incremental ones', which seems very much like Grundy's bumpy incremental change with quite long periods of incremental change between the bumps.

Having said this, Dunphy and Stace are not on their own in suggesting the types of change they do. For instance, there is a great deal of correspondence between the typology of Tushman *et al.* and that of Dunphy and Stace. It is fairly clear that Dunphy and Stace found the same two types of change as are grouped by Tushman *et al.* under the concept of converging change. Both sets of researchers use identical names – 'fine-tuning' and 'incremental adjustment'. Where Dunphy and Stace go beyond Tushman *et al.* is in, apparently, splitting what Tushman *et al.* termed 'frame-*breaking*' change into two types – 'modular transformation' and 'corporate transformation'. This is a useful development in detailing more clearly the different levels at which frame-breaking change can take place. It still recognizes the implications of these types of change for goals and purposes, but identifies the fact that these may have different meanings at the departmental/divisional level than at the corporate/organizational level.

Activity 2.1

Look again at Dunphy and Stace's scale types of change (see Illustration 2.3). Position an organization with which you are familiar on the following scale:

Fine-tuning   Incremental adjustment   Modular transformation   Corporate transformation

◀───▶

Tushman et al. *(1988) say:*

> *The most effective firms take advantage of relatively long convergent periods. These periods of incremental change build on and take advantage of organization inertia. Frame-breaking change is quite dysfunctional if the organization is successful and the environment is stable. If, however, the organization is performing poorly and/or if the environment changes substantially, frame-breaking change is the only way to realign the organization with its competitive environment (pp. 713–14).*

Form a view as to whether the type of change now being experienced by your organization fits the environment in which it is currently operating and that is likely to prevail in the foreseeable future.

The types of change discussed earlier are helpful for a number of reasons that are discussed later in this chapter. However, they indicate little about the way change comes about, other than to say it occurs, generally, in response to changes in the organizational environment. Writers about types of change such as those identified above assume, perhaps, that change can be *planned*. However, as the next section shows, this is not always the case.

Planned and emergent change

Fine-tuning and incremental change are features of all organizational life and, while they can be planned, are frequently associated with change as it *emerges*. The idea of emergent change has been linked by Wilson (1992) with the concept of organizations as open systems. Writers such as Kast and Rosenzweig (1970), von Bertanlanfy (1971), Checkland (1972) and McAleer (1982) have produced detailed discussions of the concept of a system that includes organizational systems. Briefly, these discussions include the idea of organizations striving to maintain a state of equilibrium where the forces for change are balanced by the forces for stability. Therefore, organizations viewed as systems will always strive to restore equilibrium whenever they are disturbed. According to this view, the organizational system is constantly sensing its environment in order continuously to adjust to maintain its purpose and optimum state.

It could be speculated that, in an ideal world, organizational sensing of the environment would be so effective as to render frame-breaking change unnecessary. If organizations responded continuously to the need for change, they would have no need for the periodic upheavals that sometimes seem inevitable. In other words, through their assessing continuously the environments in which they operate, change should emerge almost 'naturally'.

However, writers such as Tushman *et al.* (1988), Johnson (1988) and Johnson, Scholes and Whittington (2005) describe a phenomenon whereby managers and other organizational personnel become so comfortable with 'how we work here' and 'what we hold important here' that they also become impervious to warning signs of impending difficulties from the environment. According to Tushman *et al.*, this is the effect of what they call the 'double-edged sword' of converging periods of change. Thus the habits, patterns of behaviour, finding out the best way to do things and commitment to values that have been built up during periods of converging change can contribute significantly to the success of the organization. However, the organizational history built up during this period can also be counterproductive in restricting the vigilance needed towards the environment and may become a source of resistance to the need for more radical forms of change.

Johnson (1988, p. 44) refers to the organizational 'paradigm' to describe the core set of beliefs and assumptions held commonly by the managers of an organization. He says:

> This set of beliefs, which evolves over time, might embrace assumptions about the nature of the organizational environment, the managerial style in the organization, the nature of its leaders, and the operational routines seen as important to ensure the success of the organization.

The fact that the paradigm is held relatively commonly is taken for granted and is not, therefore, seen as problematical means that signals from the environment are filtered through it. These signals are only made sense of in terms of what Johnson (1988, p. 44) calls 'the way we do things around here'. Therefore, when signals for change come from the environment, he says:

[Their] relevance is determined, not by the competitive activity, but by the constructs of the paradigm [and] in these circumstances it is likely that, over time, the phenomenon of 'strategic drift' will occur: that is gradually, probably imperceptibly, the strategy of the organization will become less and less in tune with the environment in which the organization exists. (Johnson, 1988, p. 44)

As the process of strategic drift continues, an organization's strategy, structure and processes gradually move further away from a path that would take account of the triggers for change coming from the environment. It is at these points that more frame-breaking or revolutionary change becomes necessary to realign the organization's purposes and operations with environmental imperatives.

From the discussion so far, it is clear that the process of strategic drift forces organizations into a more conscious deliberate *planning* of change, for instance the four-stage (exploration, planning, action and integration phases) process discussed by Burnes (2004). However, the distinction between emergent and planned change is not clear-cut. Criticisms of the idea that change can be planned logically and systematically have been made by Wilson (1992). He argues that planned change is a management concept which relies heavily on a single view of the way change ought to be done. This view assumes that the environment is known and, therefore, that a logical process of environmental analysis can be harnessed in the service of planning any change. Wilson says this view emphasizes the role of human agency, that is, that chief executives and managers are able to invoke the changes they feel are necessary and that this process is not problematic. His argument is that this view does not take account of the context in which change must take place; for instance, the cultural and political components that influence most, if not all, implementations of any planned change.

Quinn (1980) has also criticized the idea of planned change as something that is deliberately and carefully thought through and then implemented. His research into the decision-making processes of a number of organizations demonstrated that most strategic decisions are made in spite of formal planning systems rather than because of them. As reinforcement of this idea, Stacey (2000, p. 92) summarizes the key points made by Quinn as follows:

1. Effective managers do not manage strategically in a piecemeal manner. They have a clear view of what they want to achieve, where they are trying to take the business. The destination is thus intended.
2. But the route to that destination, the strategy itself, is not intended from the start in any comprehensive way. Effective managers know that the environment they have to operate in is uncertain and ambiguous. They therefore sustain flexibility by holding open the method of reaching the goal.
3. The strategy itself then emerges from the interaction between different groupings of people in the organization, different groupings with different amounts of power, different requirements for and access to information, different time spans and parochial interest. These different pressures are orchestrated by senior managers. The top is always reassessing, integrating and organizing.
4. The strategy emerges or evolves in small incremental, opportunistic steps. But such evolution is not piecemeal or haphazard because of the agreed purpose

and the role of top management in reassessing what is happening. It is this that provides the logic in the incremental action.

5. The result is an organization that is feeling its way to a known goal, opportunistically learning as it goes.

Quinn terms this process 'logical incrementalism' in that it is based in a certain logic of thinking but is incremental in its ability to change in the light of new information and the results of ongoing action. Opportunism plays an important part in this process (see Illustration 2.4).

Illustration 2.4

Proactively managing incrementalism in the development of corporate strategies

Quinn (1979) makes the following statement to illustrate how executives proactively manage incrementalism in the development of corporate strategies.

Typically you start with general concerns, vaguely felt. Next you roll an issue around in your mind until you think you have a conclusion that makes sense for the company. You then go out and sort of post the idea without being too wedded to its details. You then start hearing the arguments pro and con, and some very good refinements of the idea usually emerge. Then you pull the idea in and put some resources together to study it so it can be put forward as more of a formal presentation. You wait for 'stimuli occurrences' or 'crises', and launch pieces of the idea to help in these situations. But they lead toward your ultimate aim. You know where you want to get to. You would like to get there in six months. But it may take three years, or you may not get there. And when you do get there, you do not know whether it was originally your own idea – or somebody else had reached the same conclusion before you and just got you on board for it. You never know. The president would follow the same basic process, but he could drive it much faster than an executive lower in the organization.

Source: Quinn, J. B. (1979), 'Xerox Corporation (B)', copyrighted case, Amos Tuck School of Business Administration, Dartmouth College, Hanover, NH.

Predictable change

In some respects change could be viewed as neither wholly emergent nor planned. As cycles of growth and activity are an essential part of living, so the concept of an organizational life cycle (Greiner, 1972; Kimberley and Miles, 1980) has been used to describe the stages through which organizations go as they grow and develop. Figure 2.3 illustrates these in terms of the size and maturity of organizations.

Greiner maintains that, as organizations grow in size and mature, their activities go through five phases, each of which is associated with a different growth period in an organization's life. In addition, as each growth period moves into the next, the organization goes through a shorter-lived crisis period. These are, respectively, the evolution and revolution stages shown in Figure 2.3. Illustration 2.5 is a brief description of a typical life cycle pattern that is complemented by Clarke's (1994) useful categorization of the characteristics and crisis points associated with each phase of growth (see Table 2.1).

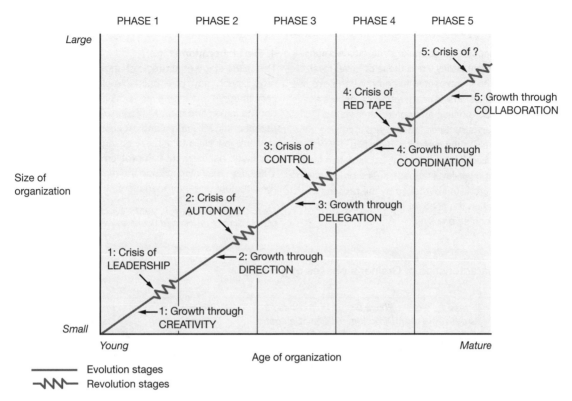

Figure 2.3 The organizational life cycle

Illustration 2.5

A typical life cycle pattern

1. The entrepreneurial stage
In this first (often entrepreneurial) stage, the first task to be achieved is to provide a service or manufacture a product. Survival is the key strategy. Organizational culture is fashioned by the founders of the organization. It may be a brand-new organization, a new subsidiary or part of an established, larger organization. Success brings growth and the need to recruit more staff. Staff need managing, and the question of future organizational strategy becomes more complex. The alternatives are to limit growth and remain small (but risk being unable to sustain competition) or to grow and recruit professional managers.

2. The collective stage
The organization begins to take 'shape'. Departments and functions begin to be defined and the division of labour is the dominant theme. The professional managers recruited tend to be strong leaders who share the same vision as the founders. Further growth brings the need for management control and delegation. The organization has begun to establish its position; internal tasks are allocated and who has responsibility and autonomy to carry them out become pre-eminent.

3. The formalization stage
Systems of communication and control become more formal. There is a need to differentiate between the

▶

Illustration 2.5 *continued*

tasks of management – to make strategic decisions and to implement policy – and those of lower-level managers, who are expected to carry out and oversee operational decisions. Bureaucratization occurs as systems of coordination and control emerge, including salary structures, reward and incentive schemes, levels in the hierarchy, reporting relationships and formalized areas of discretion and autonomy for lower-level managers. The organization continues to grow, but burdened by the process of bureaucratization the need for the structure to be 'freed up' becomes pressing.

4. The elaboration stage
This is the stage of strategic change. The organization may have reached a plateau in its growth curve and may even show the first stages of decline in performance. Managers used to handling bureaucratic structures and processes usually have to learn new skills to achieve change, such as team work, self-assessment and problem confrontation. This stage may also include the rapid turnover and replacement of senior managers.

Source: Based on Greiner, L. (1972), 'Evolution and revolution as organizations grow', *Harvard Business Review*, July–August.

Table 2.1 Characteristics of Greiner's phases of growth

	Phase 1 Creativity	Phase 2 Direction	Phase 3 Delegation	Phase 4 Coordination	Phase 5 Collaboration
Structure	• Informal	• Functional • Centralized • Hierarchical • Top down	• Decentralized • Bottom up	• Staff functions • Strategic business units (SBUs) • Decentralized • Units merged into product groups	• Matrix-type structure
Systems	• Immediate response to customer feedback	• Standards • Cost centres • Budget • Salary systems	• Profit centres • Bonuses • Management by exception	• Formal planning procedures • Investment centres • Tight expenditure controls	• Simplified and integrated information systems
Styles/people	• Individualistic • Creative • Entrepreneurial • Ownership	• Strong directive	• Full delegation of autonomy	• Watchdog	• Team oriented • Interpersonal skills at a premium • Innovative • Educational bias
Strengths	• Fun • Market response	• Efficient	• High management motivation	• More efficient allocation of corporate and local resources	• Greater spontaneity • Flexible and behavioural approach
Crisis point	• Crisis of leadership	• Crisis of autonomy	• Crisis of control	• Crisis of red tape	?
Weaknesses	• Founder often temperamentally unsuited to managing • Boss overload	• Unsuited to diversity • Cumbersome • Hierarchical • Doesn't grow people	• Top managers lose control as freedom breeds parochial attitudes	• Bureaucratic divisions between line/staff, headquarters/field, etc.	• Psychological saturation

Source: Clarke, L. (1994), *The Essence of Change* (Hemel Hempstead, Prentice Hall, p. 12).

Activity 2.2

Consider an organization you know well.

Using the descriptions in Illustration 2.5 and Table 2.1, position the organization on the Greiner graph in Figure 2.3

The Greiner model is useful for identifying an organization's situation, thus providing warning of the next crisis point it may have to face. It therefore helps in the planning of necessary change. It also assists managers and other organizational personnel to realize that change is, to some extent, inevitable; organizations must of necessity change as they grow and mature. It therefore helps legitimize the need for change and may be useful in discussions to bring about a reduction in resistance to change. However, while it may be possible to predict the next crisis point (through application of the concept of the organizational life cycle), more needs to be done to develop ways of bringing about the necessary changes from one stage to another. It therefore becomes necessary to have some models and techniques for diagnosing the type of change situation prevailing at any one time in order to determine what kind of change approach to take.

Diagnosing change situations

> Those who pretend that the same kind of change medicine can be applied no matter what the context are either naive or charlatans. (Strebel, 1996a, p. 5)

Strebel begins an article entitled 'Choosing the right path' with these words. He goes on to say, 'Thus, change leaders cannot afford the risk of blindly applying a standard change recipe and hoping it will work. Successful change takes place on a path that is appropriate to the right situation' (p. 5). Pettigrew and Whipp (1993, p. 108), reporting on their study of a range of UK companies across four industry sectors, said: 'One of the central characteristics of the firms under study, therefore, is that the management of strategic and operational change for competitive success is an uncertain and emergent process.'

Being able to diagnose change situations is, therefore, important if organizations are going to have any chance of responding to and managing change successfully. However, diagnosing any organizational situation is not an exact science. There are, though, some tools and techniques that can help. For instance, the Greiner model of the organizational life cycle is useful for drawing attention to periods when organizational change is likely to be needed. In addition, there are a number of techniques for strategic planning (e.g. stakeholder, SWOT and PEST analyses), the application of which can lead to consciously planned change. In particular, an analysis of an organization's strengths and weaknesses and the opportunities and threats (SWOT) presented by changes in its environments can increase awareness of the need for continuous incremental type change and, hopefully, avoid the process of strategic drift already discussed. Using multiple-cause diagrams assists a greater understanding of the interactions between the many different and often simultaneous causes of change.

There are, however, a number of other methods that can be used for anticipating when change is imminent and for deciding an appropriate approach to use for its management and implementation.

Looking for breakpoints

The discussion thus far has focused on the requirement to scan the organizational environment for signals that could trigger change within organizations. To help with this Strebel (1996b) has suggested a model of industry behaviour. This model is similar to that of Greiner in the concept of a cycle of behaviour. However, while Greiner links his model mainly to changes in the structure and management of organizations, Strebel links his model more to an organization's competitive environment (see Figure 2.4). He uses the concept of the 'evolutionary cycle of competitive behaviour' to introduce the idea of 'breakpoints', that is those times when organizations must change their strategies in response to changes in competitors' behaviour.

The cycle of competitive behaviour involves two main phases. One is the innovation phase when someone discovers a new business opportunity, whatever its source. This triggers a breakpoint to introduce a phase in the evolutionary

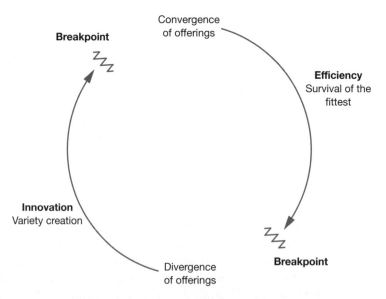

Figure 2.4 Evolutionary cycle of competitive behaviour

Source: Strebel, P. (1996b), 'Breakpoint: how to stay in the game', *Mastering Management*, Part 17, *Financial Times*.

cycle that causes a *divergence* in competitors' behaviour as they attempt to exploit the new opportunity with innovative new offerings. Strebel (1996b) says this phase corresponds to variety creation in the evolutionary cycle and he gives examples of the first Apple computer, the arrival of the Macintosh and, most recently, the new chips and software, all of which triggered breakpoints. He goes on (p. 13) to say:

> Divergent competitive behaviour aimed at enhancing the value of offerings continues until it becomes impossible to differentiate offerings because value innovation has run its course and imitation of the competitors' best features has taken over. As the offerings converge and the returns to value innovation decline, someone sees the advantage of trying to reduce delivered cost. Competitors converge on total quality management, continual improvement, and re-engineering or restructuring of the business system in an attempt to cut costs and maintain market share.

This brings about the other of the two phases – that of *convergence*. During this phase, the least efficient leave the scene and only the fittest survive. This is a phase of cost cutting and consolidation until the returns from cost reduction decline and people see the advantage of looking for a new business opportunity – bringing a new breakpoint with the cycle starting all over again. In summary Strebel (1996b, p. 5) says:

> The competitive cycle suggests that there are two basic types of breakpoint:
>
> ● Divergent Breakpoints associated with sharply increasing variety in the competitive offerings, resulting in more value for the customer.
> ● Convergent Breakpoints associated with sharp improvements in the systems and processes used to deliver the offerings, resulting in lower delivered cost.

It should be noted that although the competitive cycle repeats itself, the industry continues to evolve and Strebel presents this in diagram form with respect to the computer industry (see Figure 2.5).

The vertical axis in Figure 2.5 represents the innovation–variety creation phase of the cycle of competitive behaviour; the horizontal axis represents the efficiency–survival phase. The vertical arrows denote periods of innovation (following divergence breakpoint) while the horizontal arrows denote periods of efficiency seeking and cost cutting (following convergence breakpoint). Strebel stresses that the diagram is not to scale. However he says that, over time, industries move up the diagonal with increasing customer value and lower delivered cost. Clearly some industries (e.g. those based on commodities) offer less opportunity for innovation and customer-value creation. Others (e.g. clothing and fashion) offer fewer opportunities for cost reduction. They evolve mainly through innovation in the direction of customer value.

Strebel's model is very useful in explaining the external environment in which organizations operate, in particular the economic and technological aspects. What is as useful is his advice on how to detect patterns in the environment that indicate a breakpoint might be imminent. Illustration 2.6 details this advice.

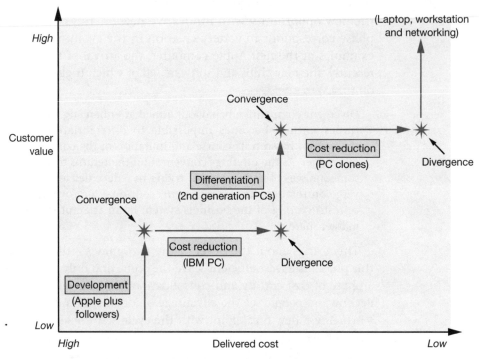

Figure 2.5 Breakpoint evolution of personal computer industry

Source: Strebel, P. (1996b), 'Breakpoint: how to stay in the game', *Mastering Management,* Part 17, *Financial Times*.

Illustration 2.6

Looking for breakpoints, with leading indicators

The timing of breakpoints is impossible to predict because they might be triggered by many different factors and because they require both a latent market and a supplier with the right business system. However, with an understanding of an industry's evolution it is possible to look for patterns indicating that a breakpoint may be imminent. Specifically, the competitive cycle can be used to look for leading indicators of a potential breakpoint.

The tendency of the competitive cycle to oscillate between divergence (variety creation) on the one hand, and convergence (survival of the fittest) on the other hand, provides the framework.

Convergence is usually easier to anticipate, because it is built on an offering that already exists.

Typical indicators are contained in the following list. When several of these are in place, all that is needed is a player, or event, to trigger the breakpoint:

- *Competitors*: Convergence is visible in increasingly similar products, service and image.
- *Customers*: The differentiation between offerings looks increasingly artificial to customers and the segmentation in the market starts breaking down.
- *Distributors*: The bargaining power in the industry often shifts downstream to distributors who play competitors off against each other.
- *Suppliers*: They cannot provide a source of competitive advantage because everyone knows how to use their inputs.

Divergence is more difficult to anticipate because it is based on a new offering that does not yet exist. However, if the following are in place, the industry is ready for a new offering that breaks with the past.

- *Customers*: An increasingly saturated market is accompanied by declining growth rates and restless customers.
- *New entrants*: Restless customers are attracting new entrants.

- *Competitors*: Declining returns may force them to experiment with new offerings or look elsewhere for profits.
- *Suppliers*: New resources and, especially, new technology are frequently the source of a divergent breakpoint.
- *Distributors*: They lag behind because they have to adapt to the new offering.

Source: Strebel, P. (1996), 'Breakpoint: how to stay in the game', *Mastering Management*, Part 17, *Financial Times*, p. 14.

It is clear there are a number of issues associated with the identification of breakpoints. First, organizations need to have both formal and informal systems attuned to searching for indicators from the environment. The formal systems will probably include those involved with environmental scanning, benchmarking and data collection and interpretation. In addition, the way in which organizations are structured must help, rather than hinder, these activities.

As important are the more informal aspects of organizations, such as open attitudes on the part of managers and personnel, a degree of cooperation rather than destructive competition between divisions and departments, and a culture supportive of innovation and change. Part Two of the book discusses these and other factors in more detail. Before moving on to these, the final section of this chapter describes another way of assessing both the impact and the magnitude of impending change as an essential tool in determining the most appropriate methodology for carrying out the change management process. However, rather than diagnosing change by scanning the organization's competitive environment (as Strebel recommends), this approach characterizes organizational problems (and therefore the need for change) in terms of their complexity, variability, people involvement and how much consensus there is on what constitutes the problem and what might bring a solution.

Hard (difficult) and soft (messy) problems

The discussion so far shows how situations forcing change vary in complexity and seriousness. Thus a minor upset in some part of an organization's environment (most likely to be the internal environment) can bring about small-scale, incremental change. Other disturbances (more likely to come from the external environment) will have a much more wide-ranging impact on an organization's strategy, structure and processes.

In the preceding section, reference was made to Strebel's advice on identifying industry breakpoints. Sometimes, however, the signals arriving on managers' desks are not as clearly categorized as Strebel implies, neither can they always be separated easily into those concerned with competitors, customers, suppliers and distributors. These signals are frequently confused and diffuse and it is not easy to see clearly just what type of situation prevails – the only thing managers perceive are 'problems'. These problems may vary in complexity and seriousness, ranging from minor upsets to major catastrophes, from temporary hitches to gnawing 'tangles'. Paton and McCalman (2000) use the terms 'hard' and 'soft' to describe, respectively, these two types of problems. Alternatively, the Open University (1985) uses the terms 'difficulties' and 'messes', the latter term based on Ackoff's (1993) article entitled 'The art and science of mess management'.

Illustration 2.7 demonstrates some differences between difficulties and messes and shows how difficulties are simply more limited sorts of problems while messes are larger and much more taxing for those who want some kind of change to 'solve' the problem. However, messes are not just bigger problems, they are qualitatively different from difficulties.

In distinguishing between these two types of problem the Open University authors use the concepts of 'hard complexity' as characteristic of difficulties and 'soft complexity' as characteristic of messes. In beginning an explanation of these they say:

> Complexity is not just a matter of there being many different factors and interactions to bear in mind, of uncertainty concerning some of them, of a multitude of combinations and permutations of possible decisions and events to allow for, evaluate and select. It is not only a computational matter – such as operational researchers deal with. Complexity is also generated by the very different constructions that can be placed on those factors, decisions and events.
>
> (Open University, 1985, p. 18)

Illustration 2.7

Difficulties and messes

Difficulties are bounded in that they:
- tend to be smaller scale;
- are less serious in their implications;
- can be considered in relative isolation from their organizational context;
- have clear priorities as to what might need to be done;
- generally have quantifiable objectives and performance indicators;
- have a systems/technical orientation;
- generally involve relatively few people;
- have facts that are known and which can contribute to the solution;
- have agreement by the people involved on what constitutes the problem;
- tend to have solutions of which the type at least is known;
- have known timescales;
- are 'bounded' in that they can be considered separately from the wider organizational context and have minimal interactions with the environment.

Messes are unbounded in that they:
- tend to be larger scale;
- have serious and worrying implications for all concerned;
- are an interrelated complex of problems that cannot be separated from their context;
- have many people of different persuasions and attitudes involved in the problem;
- have subjective and at best semi-quantifiable objectives;
- have an absence of knowledge of factors and uncertainty as to what needs be known;
- have little agreement on what constitutes the problem let alone what might be possible solutions;
- have usually been around for some time and will not be solved quickly, if at all; bringing about an improvement may be all that can be hoped for;
- have fuzzy timescales;
- are 'unbounded' in that they spread throughout the organization and, sometimes, beyond.

The consequence of these different interpretations of complexity is to describe hard complexity as characteristic of those problems that lend themselves to quantification and an optimal solution – an example is working out the best timetables for workers on production lines to achieve the most output. Soft complexity, by way of contrast, is indicative of situations where the description of events is ambiguous and there is a 'tantalizing multiplicity of different interpretations and reconstructions' (Open University, 1985, p. 18) that can be put upon a problem, let alone its possible solution.

The introduction of new working practices is an example of a messy problem involving soft complexity. For instance, not everyone will agree there is a problem and a need for new working practices. Some will interpret this action as a wish to reduce numbers of staff. Others may see it as an attempt to split up possibly troublesome groups. Yet others may even view this optimistically in terms of getting extra experience and, perhaps, new responsibilities. Management is likely to think it a 'good thing' while any trade union will want to know what is in it for the other employees. What is more, if the changes have implications for pay and status, the possible 'losers' will see the world very differently from the possible 'winners'.

Activity 2.3

1 *Note three difficulties you have faced at work or in similar situations elsewhere.*
2 *Note two (if possible three) messes you have ever faced or been involved in.*
3 *Using Illustration 2.7, list the ways in which the difficulties differ from the messes. What might this tell you about ways of dealing with them?*

The change spectrum

Asking a number of questions about a change situation may help to identify whether it is likely to involve hard or soft complexity and whether it can, therefore, be seen to be more of a difficulty or more of a mess. Using the terms 'hard' and 'soft' to distinguish these two types of problem, Paton and McCalman (2000) have devised what they call the 'TROPICS' test to help locate a change situation on a continuum from hard to soft. Illustration 2.8 presents the TROPICS factors as dimensions on which a change situation can be positioned, according to whether it is further towards the hard or soft end of each factor.

The TROPICS test, as with any analysis of problems according to the lists in Illustration 2.7 and Illustration 2.8, can only be a guide to the nature of the problem. What is important is to have undertaken exercises such as these in order to understand more clearly the type of change situation faced, in order to guide the design, planning and implementation of any change. This is because problem solving and managing subsequent change is not simply an intellectual problem. As situations move away from being difficulties and towards what has been termed a mess, they encompass not only issues that can be addressed

Illustration 2.8

The TROPICS factors

Hard		Soft
Timescales clearly defined/ short to medium term	_____	Timescales ill-defined/ medium to long term
Resources needed for the change clearly identified	_____	Resources needed for the change uncertain
Objectives clearly stated and could be quantified	_____	Change objectives subjective and ambiguous
Perceptions of the problem and its possible solution shared by all	_____	No consensus on what constitutes the problem/ conflicts of interest
Interest in the problem is limited and defined	_____	Interest in the problem is widespread and ill-defined
Control Is maintained by the managing group	_____	Control is shared with people outside the managing group
Source of the problem originates from within the organization	_____	The source of the problem originates from outside the organization

through the application of intellect, but also issues which have emotional and social dimensions requiring different kinds of approaches for their solution. Simplistically, these approaches can be categorized as hard and soft and there are a number of models of change that, in broad terms, attach to these different approaches. These are considered further and in much more detail in Part Three, when the issues of 'doing' change are addressed.

Activity 2.4

Take each example you thought of in answer to Activity 2.3 and apply the TROPICS test to it. To do this, put a cross on each line according to whether your example is nearer to one end or the other of the factor. When you have done this for all factors for each example, make a judgement as to whether your example is, overall, a hard or soft problem/change situation.

Did the TROPICS test confirm or refute your judgement of what is a difficulty and what is a mess in terms of your answer to Activity 2.3?

●●●● Comment and conclusions

Organizational change can be conceptualized in simple terms, as Grundy's three types of change show. However, the nature of organizational change is much more complex than this, as other typologies of change demonstrate. Not only are there different types of change, which manifest themselves in different organizations, change also appears differently at different levels of an organization and in its various functions. The discussion in this chapter has demonstrated the multi-dimensional nature of organizational change.

However, change does not happen in a vacuum and should not always be unexpected, as illustrated by Greiner's description of the life cycles that organizations go through as they are born and develop. As a complement to models such as Greiner's, which consider change at the organizational level, Strebel's model of change at the industry level is useful in looking to the wider environment for triggers for change. This model, together with the TROPICS test, can be used to analyze situations where change is considered desirable in order to understand which approach might be adopted in order to bring it about.

Chapter 1 examined the different environments in which organizational life takes place and how changes in an organization's environment can trigger changes in the organization itself. This chapter discussed the nature of organizational change. Table 2.2 summarizes the similarities and congruences between the theories and research discussed in these chapters. Finally, these two chapters, which form Part One of the book, set the scene for the more detailed discussion of issues of change in Part Two and approaches to implementing change in Part Three.

Table 2.2 Environmental conditions and types of change

Environmental forces for change			Types of change					
Ansoff and McDonnell (1990)	Strebel (1996a)	Stacey (1996)	Tushman et al. (1988)	Dunphy and Stace (1993)	Balogun and Hope Hailey (2004)	Grundy (1993)	Stacey (1996)
Predictable	Weak	Close to certainty	Converging (fine-tuning)	Fine-tuning	Adaptation	Smooth incremental	Closed
Forecastable by extrapolation	Moderate	Close to certainty	Converging (incremental)	Incremental adjustment	Evolution		Contained
Predictable threats and opportunities				Modular transformation	Reconstruction	Bumpy incremental	
Partially predictable opportunities	Strong			Corporate transformation	Revolution		
Unpredictable surprises		Far from certainty	Discontinuous or frame breaking			Discontinuous	Open ended

Discussion questions and assignments

1 Discuss the proposition that: 'All change can be categorized as either incremental or radical.' Use examples from your own experience to support points made.

2 To what extent are Dunphy and Stace's four types of change helpful in working with 'real-life' change in organizations? Illustrate your answer with examples from organizations you know well.

3 Discuss Quinn's (1979) contention that change occurs through a process of 'logical incrementalism'. Give examples to support your argument.

4 To what extent do organizational messes get treated as if they were difficulties? What are the organizational consequences of this? Does it matter how change situations are classified?

5 To what extent do you think the environmental scanning tools are effective in diagnosing the environment for organizations? Are there situations when they might not be effective?

Case example ●●●

NHS revolution breathes new life into private sector

The government is turning to outside health providers in its determination to cut hospital waiting times, explains Nicholas Timmins.

A revolution is taking place in the private health sector that could see its hospital activity double in less than 10 years. Ironically, it is the determination of the government and the National Health Service to secure big cuts in waiting times for its own patients that has breathed new life into the industry. But the remarkable shake-up taking place in the private sector is not unalloyed good news for those companies established in the market. Expansion will come at a price as consultants see their fees squeezed and could even threaten some of the main medical insurers' business. William Laing, who for 25 years has been the leading analyst of the private sector and its relationship with the NHS, says: 'It is the biggest change in the sector that there has ever been. And it is a real change if they [the government] go through with it.'

The government's decision to turn the NHS less into a direct provider of services, and more into a purchaser of care has big implications for the private hospital groups as overseas providers are brought in to supply waiting list operations and diagnostic procedures. It is also changing the NHS itself as elective, waiting list care is increasingly separated from more urgent work. NHS consultants, whose rates for private work are the highest in the world, are beginning to see their fees squeezed. And for private patients there is the potential for the cost of treatment to fall, at least in real terms, as the government begins to create a genuine market in healthcare supply. In the longer term, however, the market could threaten the business of Bupa, Axa PPP, Norwich Union, and the other private medical insurers. According to David Mobbs, chief executive of Nuffield Hospitals, and Tim Elsigood, chief executive of Capio – two of Britain's big four private hospital suppliers – the market is being transformed by the arrival of the NHS as a bulk purchaser of care from the private sector.

The change has come in two stages. The first was the government's decision to bring in overseas suppliers to compete for chains of fast-track treatment centres to provide 250,000 operations a year for NHS patients. When the deals were announced, almost all the preferred bidders came from overseas – from South Africa, Canada and the US – on the grounds of price and innovation. Home-grown operators, which include Bupa and General Healthcare's BMI hospitals, lost out. The second breakthrough came last month, when the private sector reacted to the threat to their business. Capio, which is Swedish owned, and Nuffield won the deal to provide 25,000 operations this year by offering prices that neither they nor the NHS would disclose in detail. However, John Reid, Health Secretary, said they were 'on a par with equivalent NHS prices' while Capio described them as 'very, very close to NHS costs'. That compares with the premium of 20 per cent to 46 per cent over NHS costs that the service has been paying for the 60,000 to 80,000 procedures a year that it has bought from UK private hospitals. The competition is starting to make private treatment affordable for the NHS.

Direct comparison of private sector and NHS prices is fraught with difficulty; and NHS prices are expected to rise as they become more accurate as a result of being used internally to pay hospitals. But with contracts for a second wave of treatment centres expected to be announced in the summer, by 2008 the private sector looks set to be treating a minimum of 600,000 NHS patients a year – approaching a ten-fold increase on the numbers last year. Mr Reid has said perhaps 15 per cent of NHS operations could be privately provided – that would amount to 1m a year out of the 7m-plus that the NHS is projected to provide towards the end of the decade. And that figure would match the current total size of the private sector.

There is an undoubted irony that it is a Labour government presiding over the biggest expansion in privately provided care since the NHS was founded in 1948. Some doubt it will last. Not all the overseas contracts have been signed. Some providers have been dumped and swapped for others. These are either teething troubles as the NHS seeks the best price going, or a sign of more fundamental problems. Among the sceptics is Charles Auld, chief executive of General Healthcare. Last week he said: 'The big question is sustainability' – an issue that worries other private hospital executives.

His company has undertaken significant cardiac work for the NHS but has yet to win one of the big contracts. The treatment centre deals run for five years. But he queried whether the money would be there to pay for them when the current period of 7 per cent real terms growth for the NHS ended in 2008. In addition, to achieve its current cuts in waiting times 'the NHS is sprinting. But this is a marathon. And you can't keep sprinting over a marathon.' However, William Laing, of Laing and Buisson, said that while NHS spending growth might well slow after 2008, growth was bound to continue.

Source: Nicholas Timmins (2004), 'NHS revolution breathes new life into private sector', *Financial Times*, May 3.

Case exercise   Is this 'frame-breaking' change?

1 To what extent do you consider this change to be 'frame-breaking' change? Justify your view.

2 In your opinion, which sectors and elements of the environment do you consider to have had the most influence on the decisions detailed in the case? Justify your conclusions.

3 From your knowledge and experience of the NHS and private healthcare providers, analyze the effects that will be felt by doctors, other medical staff and administrators in the NHS and other healthcare providers.

4 What effects, if any, over the longer term might these changes have for patients?

Indicative resources

Balogun, J. and Hope Hailey, V. (2004) *Exploring Strategic Change (2nd edn)*, Harlow: Financial Times Prentice Hall. This book offers a view of change processes that builds on the ideas put forward by Johnson *et al.* (2005) in their book on corporate strategy. It focuses on what they term the 'transition' – that is the change process itself. It is a good text for considering change at the strategic level.

Thompson, P. and McHugh, D. (2002) *Work Organisation* (3rd edn), Chippenham: Palgrave. This text has been organized so the reader does not have to start at the beginning and read it like a novel. Each chapter is quite individual, dealing with various aspects of the work environment. The book focuses on the organization and how it operates, both in terms of small and large scale. A particularly useful chapter and one that would link well with this chapter is organizations and environments.

Useful websites

www.ctg.albany.edu This site is useful for those working in the public sector and interested in using scanning tools to plan future change. There is an article under the section 'publications' that promotes environmental scanning and offers areas of benefits to those who use it. This focus is within the public sector, but a useful supplement to work discussed in this chapter.

www.informationr.net In 1997 C. Zita and T. D. Wilson wrote an article based on a theoretical approach to environmental scanning. It can be found on this website 1997 – Vol. 2, no. 4. This was updated in April 2000, and is interesting for those who wish to do additional reading in relation to assessing the internal and external business environment.

www.ft.com The *Financial Times* website and the newspaper itself are useful for examples of organizations that are having to respond to change similar to those that can be found in this chapter.

> To click straight to these links and for other resources go to
> **www.pearsoned.co.uk/senior**

References

Abrahamson, E. (2000) 'Change WITHOUT pain', *Harvard Business Review*, vol. 78, Issue 4, July–August, pp. 75–80.

Ackoff, R. L. (1993) 'The art and science of mess management', in Mabey, C. and Mayon-White, B. (eds) *Managing Change* (2nd edn), London: PCP.

Ansoff, I. H. and McDonnell, E. J. (1990) *Implanting Strategic Management*, Englewood Cliffs, NJ: Prentice-Hall.

Balogun, J. and Hope Hailey, V. (2004) *Exploring Strategic Change* (2nd edn), Harlow: Financial Times Prentice Hall.

Burnes, B. (2004) *Managing Change: A Strategic Approach to Organisational Dynamics* (4th edn), Harlow: Financial Times Prentice Hall.

Checkland, P. B. (1972) 'Towards a systems based methodology for real world problem solving', *Journal of Systems Engineering*, vol. 3, no. 2, pp. 87–116.

Clarke, L. (1994) *The Essence of Change*, Hemel Hempstead: Prentice Hall.

Corzine, R. and Adams, P. (1996) 'Shell may face fresh pressure over Nigerian oil discovery', *Financial Times*, 8 March, p. 1.

Dawson, P. (1994) *Organizational Change: A Processual Approach*, London: PCP.

Dunphy, D. and Stace, D. (1993) 'The strategic management of corporate change', *Human Relations*, vol. 46, no. 8, pp. 905–20.

Foremski, T. (2000) 'Novell to cut 900 jobs and restructure', *Financial Times*, 7 September, p. 32.

Gibbs, G. (2003) 'Ryanair swallows up ailing rival', the *Guardian*, 3 February

Greiner, L. E. (1972) 'Evolution and revolution as organizations grow', *Harvard Business Review*, July–August, vol. 50, pp. 37–46.

Grundy, T. (1993) *Managing Strategic Change*, London: Kogan Page.

Johnson, G. (1988) 'Processes of managing strategic change', *Management Research News*, vol. 11, no. 4/5, pp. 43–6. This article can also be found in Mabey, C. and Mayon-White, B. (eds) *Managing Change* (2nd edn), London: PCP.

Johnson, G. Scholes, K. and Whittington, R. (2005) *Exploring Corporate Strategy Texts and Cases*, Harlow: Financial Times Prentice Hall.

Kast, F. E. and Rosenzweig, J. E. (1970) *Organization and Management: A Systems Approach*, New York: McGraw-Hill.

Kimberley, J. R. and Miles, R. H. (1980) *The Organizational Life-cycle*, San Francisco, CA: Jossey-Bass.

Longescu, O. (2004) 'Nato sets date for big expansion', www.bbc.co.uk/world/news March.

McAleer, W. E. (1982) 'Systems: a concept for business and management', *Journal of Applied Systems Analysis*, vol. 9, pp. 99–129.

Marsh, P. (2000) 'Adaptability furnishes key to craftsmen's long survival', *Financial Times*, 6 September, p. 7.

Modern Healthcare (1996) 'A good year for "patient protection" laws', *Modern Healthcare*, 28 October, p. 22.

M2 Communications Ltd (2000) 'Xenos restructures to fuel future growth: Organisational changes will benefit new product development, customer support and future alliance strategy', 30 August. http://ebb.onesource.com.

Open University (1985) Block 1, 'Managing and messy problems', Course T244, *Managing in Organizations*, Milton Keynes: Open University.

Paton, R. A. and McCalman, J. (2000) *Change Management: Guide to Effective Implementation* (2nd edn), London: Sage.

Pettigrew, A. and Whipp, R. (1993) *Managing Change for Competitive Success*, Oxford: Blackwell.

Quinn, J. B. (1979) 'Xerox Corporation (B)', copyrighted case, Hanover, NH: Amos Tuck School of Business Administration, Dartmouth College.

Quinn, J. B. (1980) 'Managing strategic change', *Sloan Management Review*, Summer, pp. 3–20.

Roberts, J. (2000) 'Business as usual', *United Utilities Shareholders' Annual Review*, Warrington, United Utilities plc, p. 1.

Stacey, R. (1996) *Strategic Management and Organisational Dynamics: The Challenge of Complexity* (3rd edn), Harlow: Financial Times Prentice Hall.

Strebel, P. (1996a) 'Choosing the right path', *Mastering Management*, Part 14, *Financial Times*.

Strebel, P. (1996b) 'Breakpoint: how to stay in the game', *Mastering Management*, Part 17, *Financial Times*.

Timmins, N. (2004) 'NHS revolution breathes new life into private sector', *Financial Times*, 3 May, p.

Tushman, M. L., Newman, W. H. and Romanelli, E. (1988) 'Convergence and upheaval: managing the unsteady pace of organizational evolution', in Tushman, M. L. and Moore, W. L. (eds) *Readings in the Management of Innovation*, New York: Ballinger.

von Bertanlanfy, L. (1971) *General Systems Theory*, Harmondsworth: Penguin.

Wilson, D. C. (1992) *A Strategy of Change*, New York: Routledge.

Orange, a study of change: part 1

The brand new brand

'The future is bright, the future is orange' sounds somewhat perplexing without any context. Audiences in older age brackets around the world would certainly find it strange. These people would probably not have a mobile phone and would not be frequent visitors to the cinema to see the latest advertising release. By contrast, in the last few years anyone using a mobile network or visiting a cinema (certainly in the United Kingdom) will have been aware of the advertising slogan 'The future is bright, the future is orange'. They might even have read it as: 'the future is Orange'.

In 1994 a new brand arrived: Orange. Back then, nobody knew what it was – in French and English it meant a citrus fruit, and perhaps, a colour in the rainbow. The new logo, a square coloured orange with the word orange picked out in white along the bottom of the square, was designed to encourage consumers to forget the fruit and go for the colour – and ask a question: 'What is orange?' – or more accurately: 'What is Orange?' Thus a teaser campaign opened until everyone finally realised: 'Ah. A mobile phone.' Well, yes and no. Orange was not meant to communicate, first and foremost, that it was a mobile phone company. It was much more aspirational than that; and, as it turns out, much more savvy about the mobile phone market when viewed both as a set of providers and products and, even more importantly, as a large number of customers.

The idea was that this brand was about the future; a future where individuals could use communications when and where they wanted. Consequently, the brand positioned itself as less a provider of a service and more a facilitator of personal communications, and hence, personal identity. Of interest is: 'Where did Orange (Panatone colour patented) spring from at its launch?' Well, it sprang from a past labelled Hutchison and as a subsidiary of France Telecom, the former monopolistic provider of telephony in France, but long since privatized.

It is hard to remember a time without mobile phones. Many people will have had one from their secondary schooldays. Now they are prevalent among primary school pupils. Today they can be used to contact a friend for a real-time conversation ('How quaint' some might say!), to give a text-free message suspended in time – to be read at the recipient's convenience, to look something up on the Internet and even to chat online with a series of friends; and all in real time, but not in shared space. Anyone aged over 50, by contrast, thought a mobile phone was for phone calls, preferably outgoing ones only, preferably for emergency use only, such that the quiet scene of picnickers on a midsummer's day might not be ruined by bleepers and alarms (personalized for free, just the effort required). Now mobile phones are not even just one more fashion accessory (although size matters and it has to be small), but are an everyday artefact basic to life.

Could all this have happened to a mobile phone launch labelled Hutchinson Telecom UK and known as French? Perhaps not. The very youthful energy, the zaniness of 'Orange' as a brand name, the enthusiasm of the values of this brand: 'Orange has a very strong vision of a wirefree future' are what has made it successful.

These factors have enabled Orange to be an aspirational brand, with a concept retail unit available for real-time visits by those in Birmingham, the UK's second largest city, or for virtual visits with anyone on the Internet. The changes embraced at launch and feted in the ten-year anniversary celebrations that started in spring 2004 and lasted a year are a necessary part of the success story of this new brand.

Orange's pre-history

France Telecom was spun out of the Postes, Télégraphes et Télécommunications (PTT) organization, the state-owned monopoly that had provided postal and telephone services in France for decades. Not regulated in the way that British Telecom was as it underwent similar processes, France Télécom developed 'Itineris', which became in 1994 its very successful subsidiary, Orange PCS. The simultaneous launch of Orange in the United Kingdom led to a doubling of the customer base from 379,000 to 785,000 by the end of 1995.

The new executive vice-president, Bernard Ghillebaert, appointed at the end of October 2004 but announced the previous July, has a long pre-history with Orange. He joined in 1976 as a recent graduate of the highly prestigious Ecole Polytechnique et de Télécom de Paris (an elite French university specializing in telecommunications), when the company was France Télécom, and later moved into the new France Télécom Mobile, which in turn became Orange. In this way Bernard Ghillebaud is typical of Orange's executive team: French and steeped in French telecommunications. The global reach of Orange reflects this pre-history as countries strongly connected to France have given it the edge in sub-Saharan Africa. In addition, its English strength has led to compelling positions in English-speaking countries across the world – in the Caribbean and in Australasia.

Orange's history

In 1997 Orange reached the milestone of 1 million customers in the United Kingdom. In June 1999 Orange won the NatWest/*Sunday Times* Business Enterprise Award, which described Orange as 'one of the outstanding business success stories of the past few years'. By the end of March 2004 Orange controlled companies that had over 50 million customers worldwide. It was the largest mobile operator in the United Kingdom, with 13.8 million active customers and 20.4 million registered customers in France. It is a global operator: the jobs website proudly proclaims: 'A job at Orange could be anywhere in the world', but more specifically, in any of the following countries:

Australia	Dominican Republic
Botswana	France
Cameroon	India
Caribbean	Israel

Ivory Coast	Slovakia
Madagascar	Switzerland
Netherlands	Thailand
Réunion	UK
Romania	

However, to imagine that this is an organization definable in this way is perhaps to miss a point about organizations and organizing. What it has avoided is defining itself as a manufacturer or provider of a particular product or service. The confident slogan that the future is Orange masks an uncomfortable fact of life: the future is unknown. Even so, for a high-tech company at the cutting edge of personal communications, this unknown future approaches rapidly.

In order to compete in such a fast-changing environment Orange needs to attract flexible, adaptable talent to work for it. On its website Orange lists the benefits of working for the company. The first is time off. In terms of values, Orange advertises itself as an organization committed to customer service, and therefore to providing a responsive, flexible service, staffed by flexible, responsive graduates, whose needs for flexible working conditions are in turn met by the organization. In touch with current culture in its recruitment as in its advertising Orange positions itself to its aspiring, recruitment market as a social entity. Its purpose is to increase individuals' personal communications possibilities, and so, with Orange, the future is bright. The organization has a pattern to it, and that pattern is upbeat, personal and liberating.

In an industry not known for its customer focus, this emphasis on values permeating the organization has paid off. In June 2003 the sixth annual J. D. Power UK Mobile Customer Satisfaction Survey ranked Orange no.1 in the contract sector for the sixth consecutive time.

The strategic vision

At its launch, and in the preceding branding exercise, Orange had the vision which intended to embody an attitude to the future rather than to sell mobile phones. The corporate identity firm involved in the launch, Wolff Olins, chose from four names – all abstract and unconnected to mobile telephony or even to personal communications. This has led to Orange's story, its meteoric rise in customer base, revenues and significance, being described as 'courageous vision and commitment to the long-running potential of mobile communications'. Orange always focused on the purpose of mobile communications, not the paraphernalia of the product itself.

Its history page on the website: **http://www.orange.co.uk/about/history.html**, states it has 'a vision for a brighter future, where people can communicate wherever, whenever and however they wish'. Orange's latest challenge is to develop strategic networks: in August 2003 it became a founding member of an alliance, along with TIM (Telefonica and T-Mobile). This was branded FreeMove a year later. This alliance had 170 million existing customers across 15 countries. One month later it agreed to let Alcatel, Nokia and Nortel Networks provide their 3G radio access network (RAN) technology infrastructure across its 'footprint', or area of operations.

A fast-changing and increasingly competitive environment

Providers in the market for mobile phones divide into manufacturers and network providers, and the industry is mirroring the car industry's move from vertical integration as the key competitive tactic to fragmentation and increasing competition in each stage of the value chain, from primary components through design, manufacture, fashion creation and network distribution. In 2002 Orange launched the world's first Windows®-powered 'Smartphone', which combined high-resolution colour, speed and applications such as full web access, easy-to-use, wire-free email and instant messaging, all on a small, stylish handset. Yet two years later it was third to launch the 3G or Third Generation phone, which cost the companies so much to get licences to operate, at least in the United Kingdom. Nokia became the no.1 player in the vertical integration game and approached 40 per cent of the market with share hovering in that range for some years. It then sank to some 28 per cent in 2004 and is not thought likely to recover this lost market share. As a consequence, not only innovating rapidly but keeping to the fore competitively in a changing market is the name of the strategy into the future. Meanwhile Orange was again first to market with the 'Talk Now' service, becoming the first operator globally to launch an international service of this kind.

Case exercises   Orange (part 1)

1 Using the Internet and other sources, as well as the information given in the case study, summarize the elements in Orange's temporal and external environments in terms of the influence it had on the opportunity for this new brand to succeed, 1994–2006.

2 What type of change do you think Orange was pursuing? In terms of the concepts and ideas put forward, particularly in Chapter 2, justify your views.

3 How far do you think the changes made have been appropriate to the environments in which Orange was operating?

The second part of the Orange story can be found at the end of Part Two of the book.

Part Two

ORGANIZATIONS FOR CHANGE

Everything exists in the context of a wider environment. This is true for entities such as organizations. The idea of organizations as systems operating in a wider environment was developed in Part One, where there was some discussion of the environmental triggers for change and their potential for influencing organizational policy and practices. However, organizations are not simply the hapless recipients of the winds of change blowing from this external environment. They, in turn, form an environment – the internal environment – for the activities that take place within them. Thus the strategy an organization pursues and the way in which it is structured will be significant for its capacity to respond to and initiate change.

Strategy and structure can be thought of as the more formal, overt aspects of an organization's functioning. As important, however, are the more informal, covert aspects of organizational life such as organizational culture (set in the context of its national culture), organizational politics and issues of power, cooperation and conflict, as well as the way the organization is led.

Part Two of the book extends the discussion in Part One, to investigate the internal life of the organization in terms of its relations with the external environment and the opportunities and constraints for change. The four chapters in Part Two reflect this focus and, with the discussion from Part One, prepare the ground for the more practically oriented material on the designing and implementing of change to be presented in Part Three.

Chapter 3 is oriented to the more formal structural aspects of organizational life while Chapters 4 and 5 concentrate on the more informal contexts of organizational culture and politics and their significance for the success or otherwise of any change process. The final chapter discusses the role of leadership in the change process as a lead into Part Three of the book, which is oriented towards the more practical issues of designing and implementing change.

Chapter 3

Organizational structure, design and change

This chapter discusses the characteristics of different types of organizational structures and design. It provides details of the advantages and disadvantages of each in relation to organizational performance and the ability of organizations to introduce and implement change. More recent examples of network and 'virtual' organizational forms are examined as having the potential to respond more quickly to changes in organizations' internal and external environments. Factors such as an organization's strategy, its size and the technology used are examined as to the degree of influence they may have on choice of structure. There is recognition that there is still ample 'room' for managers to exercise personal choice and style in these matters.

Learning objectives

At the end of this chapter you will be able to:

- define what is meant by organizational structure and the organizational forms through which it manifests itself;

- discuss the relationship between an organization's strategy and its structure;

- evaluate the contingency relationships between organizational structure, size, technology and the external environment;

- assess the extent to which different types of organizational structure and form can cope with and adapt to a variety of change processes.

●●●● The meaning of organization structure

The introduction to this part of the book states that everything exists in a wider environment. This is true for entities such as organizations, as discussed in Part One. However, organizations as systems are, in particular, social systems. They are social because, in most organizations, to get work done requires the grouping of individuals and the activities they do into some type of divisions or sections. Thus, in order to achieve its goals and objectives, an organization needs to have some way of dividing work up so that it can be allocated to members of the organization for its execution. In other words, the work and the people who will manage and do it must be structured if chaos is not to ensue. The allocation of responsibilities, the grouping of workers' activities and the coordination and control of these are all basic elements of what is called an organization's structure, which is in essence the social structuring of people and processes. Wilson and Rosenfeld (1990, p. 215) offer the following definition of organization structure:

> The established pattern of relationships between the component parts of an organization, outlining both communication, control and authority patterns. Structure distinguishes the parts of an organization and delineates the relationship between them.

Bartol and Martin (1994, p. 283) include the additional element of 'designed by management' in their definition of structure, which is:

> The formal pattern of interactions and coordination designed by management to link the tasks of individuals and groups in achieving organizational goals.

Activity 3.1

What other elements do Bartol and Martin give in their definition of organization structure that do not appear in Wilson and Rosenfeld's definition?

These two definitions taken together give a sense of the objectives that any structure must serve (meeting the goals of the organization) as well as the process through which these objectives can be met (the effective and efficient ordering of activities and delineation of the relationships between them). Note, however, the emphasis in Bartol and Martin's definition on individuals *and* groups. In addition, the word 'formal' in Bartol and Martin's definition draws attention to the fact that organizational structures are typically created by management for specific purposes. This is well exemplified in Stacey's (2003, p. 62) definition:

> The structure of an organisation is the formal way of identifying who is to take responsibility for what; who is to exercise authority over whom; and who is to be answerable to whom. The structure is a hierarchy of managers and is the source of authority, as well as the legitimacy of decisions and actions.

From these perspectives, therefore, an organization's structure could be regarded as the official definition of the way that a particular organization functions. However, organizational life is never as neat as this. Organizational structures are not 'objective' in the sense that they can be understood by reference simply to some organization chart or description of formal power and status relationships between individuals and groups.

Organizations also have what has become known as 'informal' structures that are not designed by management but are the outcome of friendship and interest groupings as well as those which serve political purposes, sometimes not related to the organization's goals. These issues are not ignored in this chapter but arise in more detail in the discussions of organizational cultures, power and politics and the leadership of change associated with the other chapters in this part of the book.

The dimensions of structure

Organization structure can vary along a number of dimensions. An early, but influential, piece of research by Pugh, Hickson, Hinings and Turner (1969) identified the following six primary dimensions of organization structure:

1 *Specialization*: the number of different specialist roles in an organization and their distribution.
2 *Standardization*: the number of regularly occurring procedures that are supported by bureaucratic procedures of invariable rules and processes.
3 *Formalization*: the number of written rules, procedures, instructions and communications.
4 *Centralization*: where authority lies in the hierarchy to make decisions that have an impact for the whole organization.
5 *Configuration*: the width and the height of the role structure, i.e. the 'shape' of the organization, how many layers there are and the number of people who, typically, report to any one person.
6 *Traditionalism*: how many procedures are 'understood' rather than having to be written down, how commonly accepted is the notion of 'the way things are done around this organization'.

As a result of the research done to confirm these dimensions, Pugh *et al.* established four underlying dimensions that they described as:

1 *Structuring of activities*: the extent to which there is formal regulation of employee behaviour through the processes of specialization, standardization and formalization.
2 *Concentration of authority*: the extent to which decision making is centralized at the top of the organization or at some other headquarters.
3 *Line control of workflow*: the extent to which control of the work is exercised directly by line management rather than through more impersonal procedures.
4 *Support component*: the relative size of the administrative and other non-workflow personnel performing activities auxiliary to the main workflow.

In another large study, Child (1988) found general confirmation of the dimensions established by Pugh *et al.* and made some additions of his own. These were:

- the way sections, departments, divisions and other units are grouped together;
- systems for communication, the integration of effort and participation;
- systems for motivating employees, for instance performance appraisal and reward.

It is clear from this that structure, applied to organizations, is a multi-dimensional concept and the assumption is that organizations can be structured in many different ways according to where they might be placed on any of the dimensions mentioned. Thus, in theory, there could be a limitless number of different combinations of these variables. However, most people would agree that some categorizing of organization structures is possible. What is more, there is some evidence to show that some types of structures are more appropriate to some types of organizational situations than others. This is discussed later in the chapter. First it is necessary to understand the broad range of structures that are possible.

Models of structure

Bureaucratic structure

One of the best-known forms or organization structure is the bureaucratic form. Morgan (1989) states that the term bureaucracy was coined in the eighteenth century by the French economist Vincent de Gournay. However, it was the German sociologist Max Weber, in the early twentieth century, who defined and expanded its meaning and indeed maintained that it was the only effective way to organize work. An account of Henderson and Parsons's translation of Weber's (1947) writing on 'Legitimate authority and bureaucracy' can be found in Pugh (1990). This identifies three ideas that are central to the concept of bureaucracy:

1 the idea of rational legal authority
2 the idea of 'office'
3 the idea of 'impersonal order'.

There are a number of fundamental elements to these ideas:

- a continuous organization of official functions bound by rules;
- a specified sphere of competence, i.e. differentiation of function;
- the organization of offices (i.e. positions) follows the principle of hierarchy;
- the separation of members of the administrative staff from ownership of production or administration;
- no appropriation of his/her official position by the incumbent;
- administrative acts, decisions and rules are formulated and recorded in writing, even in cases where oral discussion is the rule or is even mandatory.

Illustration 3.1 summarizes the characteristics of the pure form of bureaucratic structure.

Illustration 3.1

Bureaucracy

Weber specified several characteristics of his ideal organization structure. The four major ones are the following:

1 Specialization and division of labour. Work is finely divided between well-defined and highly specialized jobs or roles.
2 Hierarchical arrangement of positions. Roles are hierarchically arranged with a single chain of command from the top of the organization to the bottom.
3 A system of impersonal rules. The incumbents of roles (or positions) carry out their duties impersonally in accordance with clearly defined rules.
4 Impersonal relationships. Coordination of activities relies heavily on the use of rules, procedures and written records and on the decision of the lowest common superior to the people concerned.

Other characteristics of a bureaucracy identified by Weber are: the selection of officials solely on the basis of technical qualifications; appointment not election; remuneration by fixed salaries with a right to pensions; only under certain conditions can the employing authority terminate an employment; the employee can leave at any time; a system of promotion according to seniority or achievement or both.

Source: Based on Weber, M. (1947), *The Theory of Social and Economic Organisation*, Free Press, translated and edited by Henderson, A. M. and Parsons, T. in Pugh, D. (1990), *Organization Theory. Selected Readings*, Penguin. (German original published in 1924.)

The endurance of the bureaucratic form of organization structure is evident in many organizations. In particular it typified, until recently, most if not all large public sector UK organizations. For instance, McHugh and Bennett's (1999, p. 81) account of an attempt to bring about change in a large public sector agency describes organizations such as the one they studied in the following way:

> A rigid bureaucratic maze typified structural formation within many such organizations with the majority of members having narrowly defined and highly specialized jobs, and being protected from making decisions through their constant deference to authority and reference to their rule books.

The difficulties expressed by McHugh and Bennett regarding the significant problems foreseen in changing such a structure could well support Weber, who was convinced of the case for the prevalence and endurance of the bureaucratic form. For instance, he says (Pugh, 1990, p. 12):

> It would be sheer illusion to think for a moment that continuous administrative work can be carried out in any field except by the means of officials working in offices. ... For bureaucratic administration is, other things being equal, always, from a formal, technical point of view, the most rational type. For the needs of mass administration today, it is completely indispensable.

Illustration 3.2 is a brief description of a construction company called the Beautiful Buildings Company (known as the BB Company). The organization chart illustrates its current bureaucratic structure. The BB Company will be used in later parts of the chapter to illustrate other types of organizational structures, when it will be seen that Weber's commitment to the bureaucratic form is not shared by everyone.

Illustration 3.2

The Beautiful Buildings Company

The Beautiful Buildings Company is a construction company involved in the design and building of a variety of different types of structure. For instance, it prides itself on having won contracts to build a new civic hall in one of the world's leading cities. It is known for its imaginative designs and the construction of a range of factory and other industrial-type buildings. Just over 12 months ago it took over a smaller building company specializing in home building for middle- to higher-income families. It would like to develop further into the area of commercial office buildings.

During the past 20 years the company has grown from operating solely in the United Kingdom to securing contracts in Australia and North America, and it has footholds in a number of mainland European countries.

The BB Company is headed by Gillian Lambeth, the daughter of the previous owner. There are a number of directors reporting to Gillian who are each in charge of one of the company's main functions. Marcos Davidson, the Marketing Director, has been

the person most involved in promoting the company's activities outside the United Kingdom.

Currently the company is structured on typical bureaucratic lines as illustrated in the simplified chart shown here.

Activity 3.2

● If you are currently working in an organization, draw an organization chart for it. Otherwise, draw one for an organization with which you are familiar.

● After you have produced your own chart, try to obtain an official chart or description of the organization.

● Compare your version with the official version.

● To what extent would you regard your organization's structure as reminiscent of a bureaucratic one? How much of a match is there between either of these versions and the BB Company's bureaucratic structure? To what extent does the organization of work conform to Weber's bureaucratic principles?

● What barriers might exist for an organization, structured as a bureaucracy, to be able to adapt to strong 'winds of change' blowing from its environment?

An examination of readers' responses to Activity 3.2 shows them to be many and varied. Of particular interest are the differences between individuals' perceptions of their organizations' structures and (where they exist) the formal statements of these provided by senior management. This is not surprising, according to Jackson and Carter (2000), who offer a strong argument for the view that structure, although just as necessary for organizations as for (say) buildings, is not, in the case of organizations, something *concrete* and *objective*, but essentially *abstract*. Adopting what they term 'a poststructuralism' approach to explaining structure, they maintain (in contradiction to Weber) that there is no obvious and *natural* way of ordering the management of organizational activities. What is more, they maintain that what one person perceives or experiences as (say) an authoritarian, oppressive structure, another person perceives as a structure that is democratic and which treats everyone fairly according to the rules.

It is certainly the latter of these two views of bureaucracies that was part of Weber's thinking. The bureaucratic form of organization, as conceived by Weber, was intended to imply neutrality and fairness in the way people in organizations were treated. However, the term *bureaucratic* has, more recently, taken on negative connotations with notions of undesirable and burdensome rules and regulations, and an overwhelming feeling of control. The phrase 'too much bureaucracy' is often heard, particularly in large public sector organizations, such as the one studied by McHugh and Bennett (1999). Their study illustrates graphically the difficulties faced by such organizations in instituting change (see the case example at the end of Chapter 6). However, bureaucratic forms of structure are in themselves varied and, as such, can have different effects on those working in them.

Tall and flat bureaucracies

Figures 3.1 and 3.2 illustrate the difference between tall and flat structures. Figure 3.1 is of interest in demonstrating how widening the span of control (the number of people reporting to any one superior) reduces the number of levels in the structure, while retaining all the staff. By contrast, Figure 3.2 shows how flattening the structure through doubling the span of control can 'save' 780 managers, that is 57 per cent of the number of management positions, while retaining the number of lower-level positions. Knowing this, however, does not reveal how many levels an organization should have (how vertically differentiated it should be) or what the span of control (horizontal differentiation) should be at each level.

One rule of thumb is that the more similar are the jobs to be done by individuals at any one level (the standardization of jobs), the more people a manager can coordinate and control. Managing many people doing very different kinds of jobs occupies a manager's attention far more than when all are doing the same. Butler (1991) says that as task ambiguity increases (the extent to which the task is ill-defined) there is an increase in the number of problems a manager

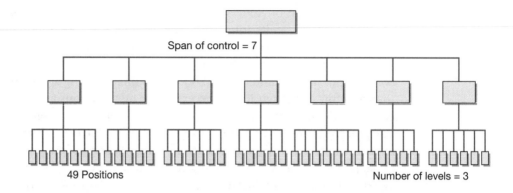

Span of control = 7

49 Positions   Number of levels = 3

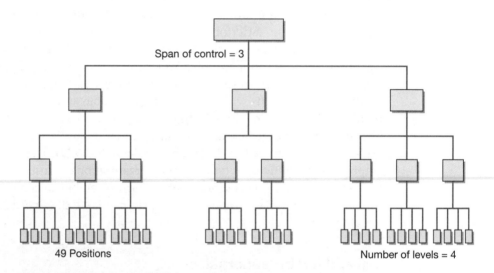

Span of control = 3

49 Positions   Number of levels = 4

Figure 3.1 Flattening the structure but retaining the people

Source: Mullins, L. J. (2005), *Management and Organisational Behaviour,* 7th edn (Harlow, Financial Times/Prentice Hall, p. 612).

has to solve and these add to managerial overload. Another rule of thumb is that the more decentralized the decision making is and, therefore, the fewer decisions which have to be made by the manager (and it is difficult to tell this from simply looking at an organization chart), the broader the span of control. Where most decisions have to be made by managers, then the larger the number being managed (the greater the span of control) the more overloaded is the manager. Mullins (2005) mentions other factors that affect the span of control such as the physical location or geographical spread of subordinates, the abilities of subordinate staff and the ability and personal qualities of the manager concerned.

With regard to the number of levels in the structure of the organization (often referred to as the 'scalar chain' or 'chain of command'), Drucker (1999) suggests that these should be as few as possible. Too many levels bring difficul-

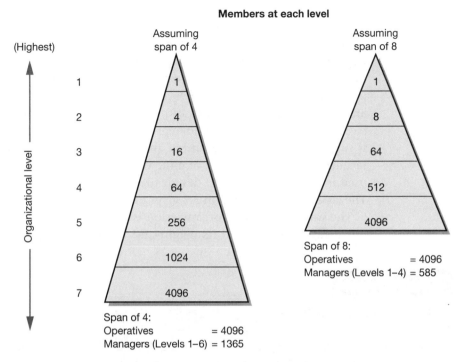

Figure 3.2 Flattening the structure but saving the people

Source: Robbins, S. P. (2003), *Organizational Behavior*, 10th edn (Englewood Cliffs, NJ, Pearson Education Limited, pp. 433, 419).

ties in understanding of objectives and communicating both up and down the hierarchy. The current desire in many organizations for flatter structures follows this principle. However, a more precise method of calculating the number of levels for an organization has been devised by Jacques (1990). He claimed to have identified time-span boundaries that can be drawn around an individual's role.

Jacques used the term 'the time-span of discretion' to refer to the target completion time of the most complex tasks that make up any job role. He makes clear that this target completion time is not always made explicit, but is inevitably always there – otherwise the carrying out of the task could not be planned. For example, someone labouring on one of the BB Company's building sites will see (or others will see) the results of his or her work in a very short time from carrying it out. For instance, the results of mixing concrete (a typical task for a building labourer), well or otherwise, will show within a few hours and certainly within days. By the same token, the results of the work that Gillian Lambeth, head of the BB Company, does – such as devising strategy for the next five years or formulating policy regarding moves into additional areas – will not show up as successful or otherwise for many years. Thus Gillian Lambeth might have a time span of discretion of five years or more while the labourer will have a time span of discretion of no more than the time it takes to check whether the concrete mix is right or not.

Illustration 3.3 shows how different time spans are mapped to different levels (stratum in Jacques's terms) in the organizational hierarchy. Of note is the geometric progression of the time-span differences compared to the arithmetic progression of the bureaucratic levels, a pattern Jacques says became observable after very many investigations of his theory. He claims this progression has its basis in the operation of a fundamental psychological process. If this is the case, it suggests a certain 'naturalness' in the way the time-span theory operates. Jacques's theory is, however, of more than academic interest. He claims it can be used in a practical sense to design the number of levels for any organization. The latter part of Illustration 3.3 gives the details of how this can be done.

The way in which an organization is configured, that is, the 'shape' of the organization in terms of its height and width, is one consideration for those

Illustration 3.3

Elliot Jacques and the time span of discretion

This regularity – and it has so far appeared constantly in over 100 studies – points to the existence of a structure underlying bureaucratic organization, a sub-structure in depth, composed of managerial strata with consistent boundaries measured in time span as illustrated.

The data suggest that this apparently general depth structure of bureaucratic stratification is universally applicable and that it gives a formula for the design of bureaucratic organization. The formula is easily applied. Measure the level of work in time span of any role, managerial or not, and that time span will give the stratum in which that role should be placed. For example, if the time span is 18 months, that makes it a Str-3 role; or 9 months, a Str-2 role.

If the role is a managerial role, not only can the stratum of the role be ascertained, but also how many strata of organization there should requisitely be, including shop or office floor Str-1 roles if any. Measure the level of work in time span of the top role of the bureaucratic hierarchy – say, chief executive of the hierarchy, or departmental head of a department within the hierarchy – and that time span will give the stratum in which the role will fall and therefore the number of organizational strata required below that role. For example, if the role has a time span of three years, it makes the bureaucracy

a Str-4 institution and calls for four levels of work organization, including the top role and the shop or office floor if the work roles go down to that level. If the bottom work role, however, is above the three-month time span – say, for example, six months, as may be the case in some types of professional institution – then the institution will require only three levels of work organization, namely, Str-4, an intermediate Str-3 and the bottom professional Str-2.

Source: Jacques, E. (1990), 'The stratified depth-structure of bureaucracy', in Pugh, D. S. (ed.), *Organization Theory* (London, Penguin, pp. 23–4).

Note: The chapter by Jaques from which this is taken, and which is reproduced in Pugh (1990), comes from Jacques, E. (1976), *A General Theory of Bureaucracy* (Oxford, Heinemann).

Time span	Stratum
(?) 20 yrs	Str-7
10 yrs	Str-6
5 yrs	Str-5
2 yrs	Str-4
1 yr	Str-3
3 months	Str-2
	Str-1

(*Note*: Later work by Jacques and Clement (1994) gives an additional stratum level 8, of 50 years time span.)

who are charged with formally designing its structure. However, managers in different organizations choose different ways of defining 'specialization' of tasks. Thus the division of tasks horizontally across the organization can be done in a number of different ways.

Horizontal differentiation – the departmentalization of work

The decision on which way to departmentalize frequently relies on the characteristics of the work to be done, the size of the organization, the physical location(s) of its activities and the need to maintain a balance between high-level strategic decision making and lower-level operational imperatives. There are also issues as to who has the power to decide and the consequences for gain or loss of power and influence, given one type of structure against another. Some people argue for departmentalization by function, others argue for departmentalization by product, by customer or by geographical location. Each method of structuring has its advantages and disadvantages, which may not be the same, of course, for some employees compared to others. In the main, the comments on the advantages and disadvantages of each type, as given in the following, represent a management, 'organizational' view. Activity 3.3 (on page 94) addresses the issue of advantages and disadvantages from other people's points of view.

Departmentalization by function

This is one of the most frequently found ways of structuring, particularly in the stages of an organization's development when the early entrepreneurial phase is giving way to a more settled phase of sustained growth guided by able and directive leaders, what Greiner (1972) calls the 'growth through direction' phase (see Figure 2.2 in Chapter 2). The US 'large integrated corporations' resulting from the Industrial Revolution of the late nineteenth century and into the 1990s, referred to by Cohen and Agrawal (2000) (see Chapter 1) were almost certainly structured on these lines, which Cummings and Worley (2005) identify as originating from early management theories in relation to specialization, span of control, relationships, authority and responsibility.

Cohen and Agrawal mention that manufacturing, distribution and retail as conforming to today's frequently found functions, including finance, production (whether goods or services), marketing/sales, distribution and human resource management. Some types of organizations such as the National Health Service will have hospitals that self-manage at a more localized level which includes medical services, domestic and ancillary services as well as finance and perhaps research and development. Depending on the culture of the hospital, customer services might be managed at a localized level as well.

Retailers will have buying and selling departments, customer care and finance. Any of these types of organization could also have human resource management departments that might include training and development and health and safety. The organization chart of the BB Company in Illustration 3.2 shows the BB Company restructured along functional lines. This is a simplified example of a functional structure – only the operations department is developed below level 3.

Illustration 3.4

Advantages and disadvantages of functional structures

Advantages

Departmentalization by function has advantages in its logical mirroring of the basic functions of business. Each function has its high-level representative to guard its interests. Tight control is possible at the top. It encourages the development of specialist skills and expertise and provides a career structure within the function. Training can be organized relatively easily along specialist lines. In organizations where technical skill gives competitive advantage, the functional structure can enhance this.

Disadvantages

The advantages of a functional structure to small and medium-sized organizations become disadvantages as organizations grow and diversify products or services or locate in geographically distant places. There can be delays as one function waits for another to complete its work and coordination of activities across functions can be difficult. Functionalism sometimes encourages narrowness of viewpoint and works against the development of innovation, which requires cooperation from a number of sources. Functional structures limit the opportunity for the development of general managers.

Contingency factors

Based on the factors suggested by Cummings and Worley (2005)

- stable and certain environment
- small to medium size
- routine technology, interdependence with functions
- goals of efficiency and technical quality.

Associated with departmentalization by function is the degree of specialization of departments. The example of the operations function of the BB Company shows it splitting up into separate projects, each managed by a different project manager. Each project includes sections dealing with work scheduling, site management and plant and materials procurement. All the different specialist building crafts (joinery, bricklaying, roofing, electrical works, heating/plumbing, etc.) are found at the lower levels of the hierarchy.

A functional structure serves organizations well as they move from what Greiner (1972) termed the 'growth by creativity' stage in a company's development to the 'growth by direction' stage (see Figure 2.3 in Chapter 2). However, as they grow and diversify in customer and product markets – as Unilever did in early 2004 (see Illustration 3.5, page 90) – they pass through what Greiner calls a 'crisis of autonomy'. This is characterized by demands for greater autonomy on the part of lower-level managers who frequently possess greater knowledge about markets and operations than do top management. Situations likely to arise are those in which each different class of product experiences a different level of turbulence in its environment. This may, therefore, signal that the time has come to departmentalize by product rather than by function. Illustration 3.4 lists advantages and disadvantages of functional structures together with the factors that provide the forces for moving towards this type of structure.

Departmentalization by product or service

It is not difficult to imagine the problems that the BB Company might have, given a functional structure. Its current and hoped-for activities cross at least four product areas (public buildings, industrial buildings, houses/homes, office and other commercial-type accommodation). Each of these product areas is governed by different sets of customer expectations, research and design problems and building regulations. Each is prey to different political, economic, technological and sociocultural influences.

Departmentalizing by product might then be a sensible move for the BB Company. Figure 3.3 shows a product-based structural grouping for the BB Company.

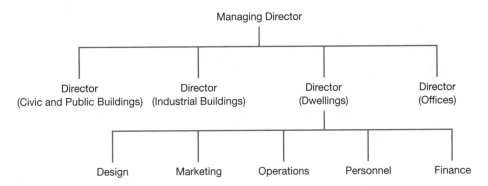

Figure 3.3 The BB Company – departmentalization by product

For the BB Company, the division of work into groupings based on its four main categories of building projects enables staff with expertise in a particular area to share it with others working on the same products. The people working in each department have collective responsibility for the business processes and cycles of activity for that department's products. Departmentalization by product or service becomes more effective as an organization grows and begins to diversify its activities into a number of differentiated product/service areas. This was, apparently, the reason for Unilever's restructuring, which took place in the early part of 2004 and was due to be complete by the latter part of 2005 (see Illustration 3.5).

Unilever clearly saw advantages in restructuring on a product combined with a location basis (see the next section for a discussion of this). As might be expected, however, there are disadvantages as well as advantages in structuring on a product/service basis as Illustration 3.6 shows.

Illustration 3.5

Structural transformation at Unilever

Unilever, a Dutch-owned company that has trademarks for such products as Birds Eye, Domestos, Flora, Cif, Marmite, Hellmann's and Ben & Jerry's, has plans to create a new operating company. This was in response to environmental factors such as competition and performance results for the previous year. Unilever has been established under the Lever Brothers Brand since 1890.

Unilever will combine its present (three) operating companies to create a new and more efficient structure that will concentrate on product sales specific to individual countries in which it operates. The reasoning for this restructuring is to simplify current management to enable faster local decision making and improve agility in the marketplace in the future. The company has operated from the dual sites of Rotterdam and London since 1930. The base will now be located in Rotterdam and will work worldwide, however it will form one operating company per country, adopting an economy of scale approach to match its product portfolio to each country it operates in.

The rationale for this approach is to support the reorganization, which will aim to achieve the following:

● single point responsibility
● faster decision making
● clear accountability for delivery
● leadership close to customer and consumer
● balance between market focus and scale.

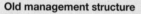

Old management structure

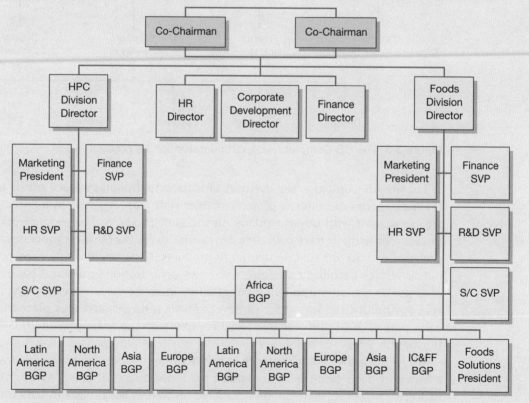

Structural transformation at Unilever *continued*

The new structure

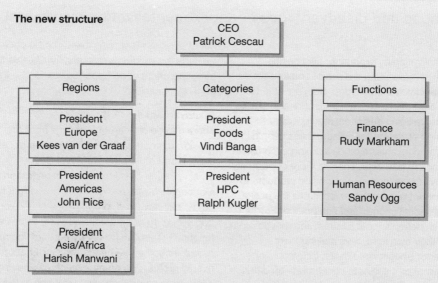

Source: www.unliver.com/ourcompany/news and media

The main features of the announced plans are as follows:

- Moving to a simpler structure by integrating all existing operating companies into one operating company per country presenting 'one face' to the market. These companies will be supported by regional shared services and common Unilever processes for finance, HR, IT and other supporting processes.
- Retaining the focus on product portfolios that are currently selling and those with planned future developments. On a local level, each business unit will have its own dedicated marketing and service teams.

- Further simplifying Unilever's international corporate and divisional structure to ensure seamless management of Unilever's strategic direction and allocation of resources.
- Providing more fuel for growth through savings to ensure the brands have the resources they need to grow.

Unilever's changes were not new to the business world and were adopted by other competitors long before. It does show the responsiveness this organization has demonstrated to ensure market competitiveness. Their success has spanned over three centuries!

Source: BBC News (2005); Unilever (2004).

It appears, from looking at the BB Company's product-based structure and the freedom for Unilever's business units to organize differently, that once a pure functional structure has been rejected functionalism could still have a place. This will be either in centralized functions before product departmentalization takes place, or within product/service divisions. However, increased use of computer-based programmes and communications networks, such as intranets as well as the Internet, is shifting the balance of importance of some 'departments' against others.

Illustration 3.6

Advantages and disadvantages of departmentalization by product

Advantages

Departmentalization by product or service has advantages of maximizing the use of employees' skills and specialized knowledge. Staff are able to specialize more than with a strict functional structure. For instance, building designers may specialize in factory design or design for homes. Sales people in particular can concentrate on developing expertise in just one range of products. There is more opportunity for innovative ideas for new or modified products to flourish. Product differentiation facilitates the use of specialized capital (money and equipment). Product divisions can be made cost centres, and maybe profit centres, in their own right, thus making them responsible for budgets and sales. Differentiation by product makes it easier to concentrate on different classes of customer, particularly when different products coincide with different customer groupings. Where a product division has its own set of business functions these can be coordinated towards the product's markets. Finally, this type of structure offers good opportunities for the training of general managers.

Disadvantages

There can be overlap of functions from one product division to another, that is, duplication of central service and other staff activities. Overall administration costs tend to be higher than in pure functional structures. Where business functions are not wholly devolved, product-based divisions are 'top sliced' to provide resources for more centralized functions. This can be felt by product line managers as burdensome overheads, which detract from their overall profits. Top management may have more difficulty in controlling what happens at the product divisional level. Coordinating policy and practice across product areas can be complex.

Departmentalization by location

The description of the BB Company indicates that its operations span more than one country, although it might be stretching a point to say it is becoming multinational. However, the company might be advised to structure on the basis of its being located in different geographical places in order to develop further its operations outside the United Kingdom (see Figure 3.4).

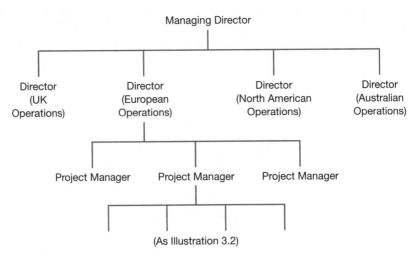

Figure 3.4 The BB Company structured on a geographical basis

Departmentalization by location is common where organizations operate over a wide geographical area, whether this involves a number of different countries, areas within the same country or very widespread sites. It is attractive to large organizations whose activities are physically dispersed. Thus managers may be put in charge of geographical regions, each of which is further differentiated on a functional or product/service basis. Although not shown in Figure 3.4, further differentiation of product or function could occur at the next level down. Interestingly, some territorial differentiation might occur within other structure types. For example, in hotels, housekeeping staff may be allocated to particular floors and bar staff to particular bars. Some government organizations (e.g. the National Health Service), which operate on a national basis, structure themselves geographically. This enables them to offer a similar service across the nation but, where necessary, modify this service to suit more localized geographical requirements. For instance, different monopolistic companies supply water to different areas of the United Kingdom. Unlike the National Health Service, however, which sets common targets across the country, the water companies operate a differential pricing structure according to the geographical location of their customers, the rateable value of properties to be charged and whether a water meter is installed or not. Illustration 3.7 identifies the advantages for this form of structure and its disadvantages.

Illustration 3.7

Advantages and disadvantages of departmentalization by geographic area or territory

Advantages

Departmentalization by geographic area/territory offers the advantage of being close to conditions in a division's locality and can clearly offer the opportunity to coordinate activities in a region. The employment of locally based staff means that travelling time is reduced. Local staff are more likely to know the conditions prevailing in a region. The establishment of manufacturing or service operations in the region reduces transportation costs. In some cases labour costs may be lower in one region than another and it may, therefore, be advantageous for organizations to set up a division in that region. Structures based on geography provide good training grounds for general managers.

Disadvantages

The more geographically differentiated the structure, the more the requirement for management and administration. For example, with a head office in Belgium and regional divisions in Hong Kong and San Francisco, it would be difficult to offer personnel services wholly from the centre. Each location would need to develop its own human resource functions, not least because of different employment laws prevailing across the different locations. This duplication of services can be costly. Control from top management can be a problem, particularly where headquarters is very far from some areas. In some areas, it may be difficult to recruit the skills required. This may be for reasons of culture or that the local population has not had the level of general education deemed sufficient for the purposes of the work they would have to do.

An overall advantage of differentiation by any means other than purely by function is that it offers the opportunity for variations in structure to occur in different parts of the organization. For instance, a geographically based structure can be differentiated on the basis of product, or indeed customer, at other levels. Similarly, a product-based structure could incorporate aspects of differentiation by geography and/or customer.

Activity 3.3

Consider the three different ways of horizontally structuring organizations as already discussed.

From your own experience and that of others known to you, what advantages and disadvantages are there, in each of these types, for the following groups of workers?

- *Professional 'experts' who specialize in a narrow field of work (e.g. nurses working in operating theatres; writers of distance learning materials concerned with the training of staff in human resources departments).*
- *Unskilled workers on factory assembly lines.*
- *Marketing managers.*
- *Call centre advisors, located in one place, but taking calls from anywhere in the world.*

How similar/different are the advantages and disadvantages for one group of workers compared to another? How far do your findings demonstrate the argument that different individuals and groups will perceive the 'same' organizational structures in different ways?

Through the discussion thus far it seems that, despite Weber's arguments in support of the strict, functionally based bureaucratic form, there are many complex and different ways of structuring organizations, each of which has its advantages and disadvantages, which might be very different for one group of employees to another. For instance, those at the top of organizations generally experience 'structure' of whatever form rather differently from those at lower levels. In functionally structured organizations marketing departments frequently operate to different rules and time scales to production departments. Employees working in the East Asian division of an organization are likely to experience organizational life differently to those working in the US division.

However, the examples of the BB Company have all shown a similar adherence to the principles of hierarchy and a single chain of command. This goes against the view of Morgan (1989), who maintains that most hierarchically structured organizations are being reshaped in response to the changing demands and challenges of the world around them. He says some of these changes are marginal but others are more radical and result in significant transformations in organizational form. This category of new organizational form can be loosely termed a *network* structure, of which the matrix or grid organization is a forerunner.

Matrix organization

The essence of a matrix structure is that a set of departments or divisions is superimposed, horizontally, across a traditional hierarchically organized structure. Thus the structure is (normally) functionally designed in terms of its vertical axis, but designed on some other principle (product, customer, region) in terms of its horizontal axis. There are, therefore, two chains of command, one vertical and one horizontal, which operate at the same time.

Figure 3.5 shows a hypothetical matrix structure for an advertising agency. In this case, the heads of marketing, finance, personnel, and research and development form the vertical lines of reporting while the different customer bases represent the divisions that operate horizontally across the structure.

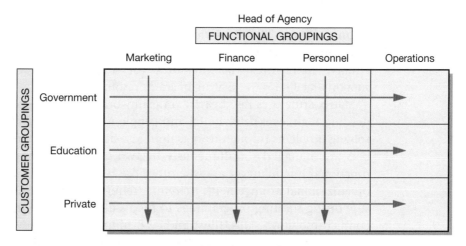

Figure 3.5 Matrix structure for an advertising agency

According to Greiner (1972), organizations move to a matrix form of structure through a 'crisis of red tape' brought about as they mature in the 'coordination' phase of the organizational life cycle (see Figure 2.3, Chapter 2). Thus staff begin to resist the control systems that centralized managers impose on decentralized product/customer or geographical groupings. He says this is particularly the case as organizations become too large and complex to be managed through formal programmes and bureaucratic paper systems. A move to a matrix structure emphasizes interpersonal collaboration in an attempt to overcome the red tape crisis.

Drawing on Davis and Lawrence's (1977) work, Bartol and Martin (1994) maintain that organizations which ultimately adopt a matrix structure usually go through four identifiable stages. These are:

Stage 1 is a *traditional structure*, usually a functional structure, which follows the unity-of-command principle.

Stage 2 is a *temporary overlay*, in which managerial integrator positions are created to take charge of particular projects (e.g. project managers), oversee product launches (e.g. product managers), or handle some other issue of finite duration that involves co-ordination across functional departments. These managers often lead or work with temporary interdepartmental teams created to address the issue.

Stage 3 is a *permanent overlay* in which the managerial integrators operate on a permanent basis (e.g. a brand manager coordinates issues related to a brand on an ongoing basis), often through permanent interdepartmental teams.

Stage 4 is a *mature matrix*, in which matrix bosses have equal power.

(Barton and Martin, 1994, pp. 321–2)

More recently, Cummings and Worley (2005) using the same source (Davis and Lawrence, 1977) suggest that matrix structures are appropriate under three important conditions. In the first instance there needs to be pressure from the external environment for a dual focus: for instance an organization providing products and/or services to many customers with unique demands. Second, a matrix structure is of benefit when an organization must process a large amount of information. This is particularly useful when organizations operate in an environment of unpredictability or need to produce information quickly. Finally, there must be pressures for shared resources. This structure supports/facilitates the sharing of scarce resources.

Matrix structures rely heavily on teamwork for their success, with managers needing high-level behavioural and people management skills. The focus is on solving problems through team action. In a mature matrix structure, team members are managed simultaneously by two different managers – one is their functional line manager and the other the team or project leader. This type of organizational arrangement, therefore, requires a culture of cooperation, with supporting training programmes to help staff develop their teamworking and conflict-resolution skills. Illustration 3.8 summarizes the advantages and disadvantages of matrix structures, together with the factors that provide the forces for moving towards this type of structure.

The ideas presented above support the ideas of Wilson and Rosenfeld (1991), who say it is usually not worth investing in a matrix structure unless the tasks to be performed are complex, unpredictable and highly interdependent. While many organizations continue to operate in stable, predictable environments, many others are required to innovate in the face of environmental turbulence. The matrix form of organization, which emphasized working in teams, will help in this objective. However, some organizations have gone beyond a matrix structure to devise structures that Morgan (1989) calls 'loosely coupled networks', but which can be (more generally) called 'network organizations' (Snow, Miles and Coleman, 1992).

Illustration 3.8

Advantages and disadvantages of matrix structures

Advantages

With a matrix organizational design decisions can be decentralized to the functional and divisional/ project-level managers. This facilitates speed of operation and decision making. There is increased flexibility in being able to form and re-form cross-functional teams according to business priorities. These teams can monitor their own localized business environments and move quickly to adapt to changes in them. Staff belonging to particular functional departments have the opportunity of working with staff from other functional departments, yet maintain their alliance and information sharing with their own professional grouping. Through allocating functional staff to one or more projects on a permanent or semi-permanent basis, loyalties to the projects are built. Matrix structures allow for flexible use of human resources and the efficient use of support systems.

Disadvantages

Matrix structures are complex and, because they add a layer of project managers, can be administratively expensive. There can be confusion over who is ultimately responsible for staff and project outcomes, particularly if things go wrong. The dual arrangement and need for enhanced communications between the 'arms' of the matrix can increase the potential for conflict, particularly between the functional and project managers. Staff may have to juggle their time between different projects or divisions and project managers may make competing demands on staff, who work across more than one team. The emphasis on group decision making could increase the time to respond to change.

Contingencies

● dual focus on unique product demands and technical specialization
● pressure for high information-processing capacity
● pressure for shared resources
● divided loyalties between two or more managers.

Source: Adapted by Cummings and Worley (2005) from McCann and Galbraith (1981)

Activity 3.4

Koontz and Weihrich (1990) say that matrix-type organizations occur frequently in construction, aerospace, marketing and management consulting firms in which professionals work together on a project.

Figure 3.5 shows a matrix structure for an advertising agency, which is an example of the last of the instances just mentioned. The BB Company, as a building construction firm, is an example of the first of Koontz and Weihrich's examples.

Using any general knowledge you may have of the building industry (see also Illustration 4.17 in Chapter 4) to embellish the description of the BB Company, design a matrix structure for the way the organization, as a whole, might operate. Then design a matrix structure for a division or department that deals only with the building of homes.

Compare your results with those of anyone else who can be persuaded to do this. Argue the pros and cons for any differences.

Network organizations

The process through which organizations go as they reshape themselves from being rigidly structured bureaucracies to what might be termed 'loosely coupled or organic networks' has been set out by Morgan (1989). Figure 3.6 is a pictorial representation of the transition from the rigid bureaucracy to the loosely coupled organic network.

The discussion so far has already set out the characteristics of models 1 to 4 in Figure 3.6, that is, the three bureaucratic types and the matrix organization. Of interest here is what Morgan calls the 'project organization' and the 'loosely coupled organic network'.

According to Morgan, the project organization carries out most of its activities through project teams. Although there are, notionally, still functional departments, they are there only to play a supporting role. The main work of the organization is done wholly through the work of teams that rely for their

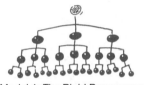

Model 1: The Rigid Bureaucracy

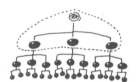

Model 2: The Bureaucracy with a senior 'management' team

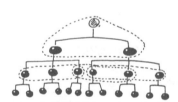

Model 3: The Bureaucracy with Project Teams and Task Forces

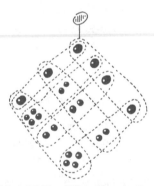

Model 4: The Matrix Organization

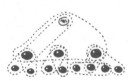

Model 5: The Project Organization

Model 6: The Loosely coupled Organic Network

Figure 3.6 From bureaucracies to matrix, project and network organizations

Source: Reprinted by permission of Sage Publications, Inc. Morgan, G. (1989), *Creative Organization Theory. A Resource Book* (London, Sage, p. 66). Copyright © 1989 by Sage.

success on being 'dynamic, innovative, powerful and exciting' and to which senior management tries to give free rein within what has been defined as the strategic direction of the organization. Morgan summarizes the nature of the project organization in the following way.

> The organization is much more like a network of interaction than a bureaucratic structure. The teams are powerful, exciting, and dynamic entities. Co-ordination is informal. There is frequent cross-fertilization of ideas, and a regular exchange of information, especially between team leaders and the senior management group. Much effort is devoted to creating shared appreciations and understandings of the nature and identity of the organization and its mission, but always within a context that encourages a learning-oriented approach. The organization is constantly trying to find and create the new initiatives, ideas, systems, and processes that will contribute to its success.
> (Morgan, 1989, p. 67)

The project organization has overlapping characteristics with what Mintzberg (1983, p. 262) calls 'The Adhocracy'. The adhocracy, as its name suggests, is an ad hoc group of people (mainly professionals) who are brought together for a single purpose associated with a particular project. The team may be together for a few months or, in rarer cases, for several years. Once the project is complete or moves into a different stage of its life the team will disband. An example is that of a group of professionals coming together to make a film. Adhocracies are characterized by having few formal rules and regulations or standardized routines – in terms of the dimensions of structure advanced by Pugh *et al.* (1969), they are low on standardization and formalization. The shape of the organization is flat, but with horizontal differentiation generally high because adhocracies are staffed mainly by professionals, each with his/her own specialism.

The project organization usually employs its own staff. The adhocracy may also do this but may additionally have staff who, for the time the adhocracy exists, work on a contract basis. This contrasts with Morgan's (1989) description of the loosely coupled organic network. In terms of a continuum of organizational forms, this type of network organization might be said to be at the end furthest from the rigid bureaucracy. The loosely coupled organic network describes a form of structure that, rather than employing large numbers of people directly, operates in a subcontracting mode. The small number of permanent staff set the strategic direction and provide the necessary operational support to sustain the network. However, while project teams and adhocracies have limited lives, the loosely coupled network can be a permanent structure. Figure 3.7 depicts three types of network.

Internal networks

According to Snow *et al.* (1992, p. 11), the internal network 'typically arises to capture entrepreneurial and market benefits without having the company engage in much outsourcing'. Hinterhuber and Levin (1994), by way of contrast, depict internal networks as collections of profit centres or semi-independent strategic business units.

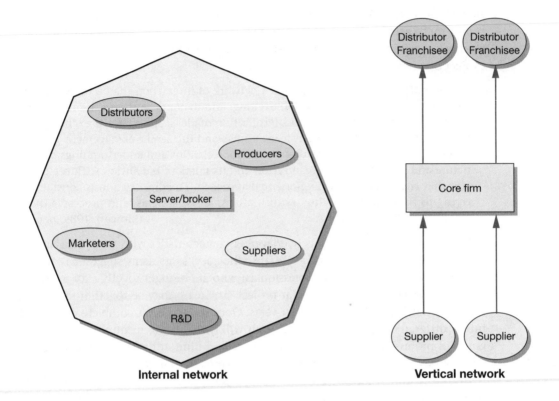

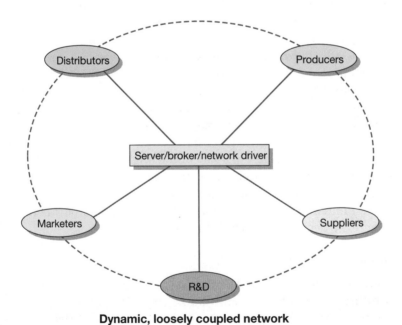

Figure 3.7 Common types of network

Internal networks are typical of situations where an organization owns most or all of the assets associated with its business. However, it has usually created 'businesses within the business' that, although still owned by the organization as a whole, operate independently in terms of the discipline of the market. The argument is that, if they are subject to market forces, they will constantly seek innovations which improve performance. What is interesting is that these quasi-independent units are encouraged to sell their output to buyers outside the organization to which they belong.

A typical example would be the training and development unit that, on the one hand, 'sells' its services to its parent organization and, on the other, seeks to sell its services to other organizations. The internal network is not dissimilar to Morgan's (1989) description of a project organization.

Vertical networks

A second network type is the vertical network (Hinterhuber and Levin, 1994). This is typical of the situation where the assets are owned by several firms but are dedicated to a particular business. This is similar to what Snow *et al.* call a 'stable' network that consists of 'a set of vendors ... nestled around a large "core" firm, either providing inputs to the firm or distributing its outputs' (Snow *et al.*, 1992, p. 13). Thus the core organization spreads asset ownership and risk across a number of other independent organizations and, additionally, gains the benefits of dependability of supply and/or distribution. The distributors can be franchisees. Toyota in Japan could be perceived as the core firm within a stable network of organizations. Clegg (1990), referring to Cusamano (1985), notes that Toyota has some 220 primary subcontractors, of which 80 per cent had plants within the production complex surrounding Toyota in Toyota City. Handy's (1989, p. 110) description of what he terms the 'federal organization' is reminiscent of the Toyota example. He says:

> [Federalism] allows individuals to work in organization villages with the advantages of big city facilities. Organizational cities no longer work unless they are broken down into villages. In their big city mode they cannot cope with the variety needed in their products, their processes, and their people. On the other hand, the villages on their own have not the resources nor the imagination to grow. Some villages, of course, will be content to survive happy in their niche, but global markets need global products and large confederations to make them or do them.

Dynamic, loosely coupled networks

For Snow *et al.* (1992), the dynamic network organization is the one that has 'pushed the network form to the apparent limit of its capabilities' (p. 14). This form operates with a lead firm (sometimes called the 'server', 'broker' or 'network driver') that identifies and assembles assets which are owned by other companies. The lead firm may, itself, provide a core skill such as manufacturing or design. However, in some cases the lead firm may merely act as broker. The dynamic network is probably the form nearest to Morgan's loosely coupled organic network.

Illustration 3.9 describes TFW Images, a communications and image design organization where the lead firm provides the core skill of design and 'brokers' other activities such as photography and illustration, printing, translations into other languages, and marketing.

If TFW Images also chose to outsource the design and writing process and the invoicing of clients and collection of payments, it would be as far along the network continuum as is apparently possible.

However, whether dynamic networks operate in a partial or pure broker capacity, they are unlikely to function effectively without good and effective

Illustration 3.9

TFW Images

TFW Images was formed in 1989 by two ex-employees of IBM who became the managing director and creative director of the company. They were very soon joined by a sales director with experience from a range of companies, mainly manufacturing. The main business of TFW Images is communications in its widest sense. Examples of its activities are designing corporate brochures that might include annual reports as well as advertising material, designing and organizing conferences and all the material that goes with them and creating company logos and other symbols of corporate identity.

TFW Images' main client was, and still is, IBM. In fact, the rise of the company coincided with the large-scale changes IBM went through as it refocused its efforts away from the mainframe computer market towards that of the personal computer market. As technology began to replace people, TFW Images was able to take advantage of the willingness of companies such as IBM to outsource some of their design requirements.

From a high point of directly employing 17 people (two of whom were in Paris), TFW Images now has 7 direct employees. Of the original three directors, one remains, the creative director, although he does not currently carry a particular title.

In a volatile market – there are other competitors and the fortunes of IBM are less certain nowadays – one reason for the company's success is its ability to maintain a flexible structure that can be tailored to the demands of the market. Essentially, TFW Images is an organization that 'brokers' services from other organizations to bring its products to the market. Thus, rather than employing printers, photographers, illustrators, market researchers and additional writers and designers directly, it closely associates with other companies and independent consultants who offer these services. The use of sophisticated computer systems facilitates the transfer of the part-finished products from one sector of the network to another, wherever it might be in the world.

Most recently, TFW Images has joined in partnership with Omni-Graphics, a well-established design company operating mainly in the publishing and arts spheres. Examples of Omni-Graphics' activities are the design of calendars, brochures for and layout of art galleries and the design of news magazines.

Given the equality of skills and size of the two organizations, the benefits of the partnership will come from their complementary activities (TFW Images is business oriented while Omni-Graphics is arts oriented) and the financial advantages that will flow from this. The management of the two partner organizations will remain separate and both will keep their own names. Thus, to any client, nothing will have changed. Yet, conceptually and financially, a new overarching organization has been 'virtually' created.

communications between their 'parts'. This is what is likely to distinguish dynamic or loosely coupled organic networks from the more 'in-house' internal and stable networks. For instance, TFW Images could not operate without fast and effective information technology links to the other organizations with which it associates. The power of the computer allied to telecommunication links enables TFW Images' design team to send its output anywhere in the world to be modified or added to by other writers and illustrators, to be marketed appropriately and, where in keeping, printed or manufactured to the specification for the finished product. Except for its relatively permanent status, the company might be likened to what some are now calling the 'virtual organization', particularly given its current situation of joining together in partnership with Omni-Graphics.

The virtual organization

The concept of the virtual organization can be allied to that of the network organization. The virtual organization (Davidow and Malone, 1992, referred to in Luthans, 1995) comes from the idea of 'virtual memory' rather than 'virtual reality' – virtual memory being a way of making a computer's memory capacity appear greater than it is. Simply put:

> The virtual organization is a temporary network of companies that come together quickly to exploit fast-changing opportunities. Different from traditional mergers and acquisitions, the partners in the virtual organization share costs, skills, and access to international markets. Each partner contributes to the virtual organization what it is best at.
> (Luthans, 1995, p. 487)

Illustration 3.10

Advantages and disadvantages of network organizations

Advantages

It enables a highly flexible and adaptive response to dynamic environments. It has the potential to create 'the best of the best' organization to focus resources on customer and market needs. Due to the fast pace and flexible nature, it enables each organization to leverage a distinctive competency. This structure also allows/permits rapid global expansion if needed. And finally, it can produce synergistic results.

Disadvantages

Managing lateral relations across autonomous organizations is difficult. It is also difficult motivating members to relinquish autonomy to join the network. There are also issues relating to sustaining membership, and benefits can be problematic. Finally, this structure has the opportunity to give partners access to knowledge and technology that one may not wish to part with.

Contingency factors
- highly complex and uncertain environments
- organizations of all sizes
- goals and organizational specialization and innovation
- highly uncertain technologies
- worldwide operations.

Source: Cummings and Worley (2005, p. 287)

Illustration 3.11 summarizes the key attributes of the virtual organization.

Illustration 3.11

Key attributes of the virtual organization

- **Technology**. Informational networks will help far-flung companies and entrepreneurs link up and work together from start to finish. The partnerships will be based on electronic contracts to keep the lawyers away and speed the linkups.
- **Opportunism.** Partnerships will be less permanent, less formal and more opportunistic. Companies will band together to meet all specific market opportunities and, more often than not, fall apart once the need evaporates.
- **No borders.** This new organizational model redefines the traditional boundaries of the company. More cooperation among competitors, suppliers and customers makes it harder to determine where one company ends and another begins.
- **Trust.** These relationships make companies far more reliant on each other and require far more trust than ever before. They will share a sense of 'co-destiny', meaning that the fate of each partner is dependent on the other.
- **Excellence.** Because each partner brings its 'core competencies' to the effort, it may be possible to create a 'best-of-everything' organization. Every function and process could be world class – something that no single company could achieve.

Source: Business Week, 'The virtual corporation', *Business Week*, 8 February 1993, pp. 98–102.

It seems clear from Illustration 3.11 that network (particularly dynamic network) and virtual organizations are suited to organizational environments that are themselves dynamic. The emphasis in these forms of organization is on horizontal rather than vertical structuring and the concept of partnership rather than command and control. However, organizations structured on these principles have implications for employment and the reward expectations of employees, whether full time, part time, contract or in other kinds of relationships with the organization. Network and virtual organizations are only able to offer stable, secure employment to a few, from whom they expect commitment and loyalty. The idea of the ultra-flexible firm is attractive for the owners and core staff, but can bring a sense of being used to those who are employed on a short-term contract basis, particularly if these people are employed in temporary, perhaps part-time, less skilled, lower-paid jobs. Lack of commitment may not be restricted to the lower paid. More highly paid consultants and contractors will give service as long as it suits them, but may desert as soon as something more attractive comes along.

On the other hand, Geisler (2002) suggests that advances in communication infrastructures globally have dramatically changed the nature of teamwork and, subsequently, organizational structures. Traditional groupings are gradually being replaced with virtual teams, distributed across boundaries of time, space and existing organizational structures.

Luthans (1995) uses the term 'horizontal organizations' to cover the more recent matrix and network type of organizational design. He maintains that, in these organizations, teams are used to manage everything, with team performance, rather than individual performance, being rewarded. Yet teamworking does not always come naturally to people; they frequently require training for this form of working. The emphasis on empowerment and more democratic ways of working, which comes with these 'modern organization designs' (Luthans, 1995, p. 458), does not happen without planned human resource development. What is more, the move away from classical ways of organizing may not suit every organizational situation. The main issue for organizations is not whether one form of structure is any better than another. It is whether the structure currently adopted is one that is able to facilitate the achievement of the organization's purpose and respond to the need for organizational change in the particular environmental circumstances prevailing for particular organizations.

● ● ● ● Influences on structure

Choosing how to structure is not straightforward. The way an organization is structured is closely linked to many factors as Figure 3.8 shows.

As identified at the beginning of this chapter, one of the most important links is the relationship between organizational strategy and organizational structure – as an organization changes its strategy to respond to political, economic, technological or sociocultural changes in its external environment, so should its structure change to maintain the strategy–structure relationship. However, apart from technological advances from outside the organization, which may force changes in production methods or in the way that services are delivered, the organization's own use of technology, particularly information technology, will affect the way in which it is structured. The earlier discussion shows also how organizational structure is likely to change as organizational size increases.

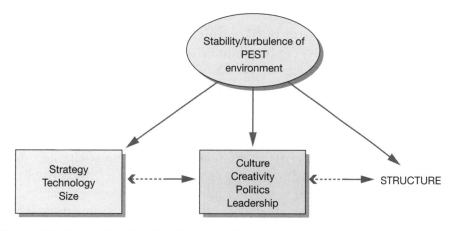

Figure 3.8 The determinants of organizational structure

What is less tangible is the role that organizational culture and politics have on decisions to structure one way rather than another. That is why, in Figure 3.8, these two factors are shown as mediating variables rather than as direct influences. There is nothing set, however, in the way all these variables should be regarded. Figure 3.8 is offered as a helpful descriptive device for summarizing the factors that influence organizational forms rather than as a tried and tested model of how they work in practice. Even so, there is a body of literature that is of help in deciding which organizational structure is most appropriate to which set of circumstances. Before moving to this, it is salutary to stop and think why 'good' or appropriate organizational structure is so important to the efficient and effective operation of organizations.

The consequences of deficient organizational structures

An example of the consequences, for the organizational functioning of a deficient organizational structure, is a list produced by Child (1988) (see Illustration 3.12). What is interesting about this list is that some of the main 'dysfunctions' listed (e.g. 'Motivation and morale may be depressed') could be regarded as having little to do with structure. Yet, as the other points make clear, structural deficiencies could very well be major contributing causes.

Activity 3.5

1 *Consider your own organization, or one you know well or, if the organization is large, a particular section of it. Do any of the five proposed consequences of structural deficiencies listed in Illustration 3.12 apply to the prevailing situation?*

2 *If the answer is yes to any of the points, what does this imply for the way the organization is structured? What changes could be made? Justify your conclusions by reference to the discussions of different structural forms discussed.*

A well-structured organization (i.e. one that is functioning effectively and efficiently) can be compared to a healthy human being. For instance, a healthy human being will have a fully functioning brain that controls what the body does; the nervous system carries messages from the brain to all parts of the body. The body, in turn, has a skeletal structure that, if damaged, will severely hamper its movements and the ability to respond to the brain's messages. Without the skeleton the body will collapse. Blood is needed to feed the brain and other parts of the body. Muscles help strengthen the skeleton and the whole body in order to help it operate more efficiently. Thus, all components are required to ensure a fully operating, effective organism. However, the skeletal structure is that part of the person which supports the rest. It is not sufficient

Illustration 3.12

Consequences of deficient organizational structures

There are a number of problems that so often mark the struggling organization and which even at the best of times are dangers that have to be looked for. Child suggests the following list, which he says structural deficiencies will exacerbate.

1 *Motivation and morale may be depressed because*:
   (a) Decisions appear to be inconsistent and arbitrary in the absence of standardized rules.
   (b) People perceive that they have little responsibility, opportunity for achievement and recognition of their worth because there is insufficient delegation of decision making. This may be connected with narrow spans of control.
   (c) There is a lack of clarity as to what is expected of people and how their performance is assessed. This could be due to inadequate job definition.
   (d) People are subject to competing pressures from different parts of the organization due to absence of clearly defined priorities, decision rules or work programmes.
   (e) People are overloaded because their support systems are not adequate. Supervisors, for instance, have to leave the job to chase up materials, parts and tools as there is no adequate system for communicating forthcoming requirements to stores and tool room.

2 *Decision making may be delayed and lacking in quality because*:
   (a) Necessary information is not transmitted on time to the appropriate people. This may be due to an over-extended hierarchy.
   (b) Decision makers are too segmented into separate units and there is inadequate provision to coordinate them.
   (c) Decision makers are overloaded due to insufficient delegation on their part.
   (d) There are no adequate procedures for evaluating the results of similar decisions made in the past.

3 *There may be conflict and a lack of coordination because*:

(a) There are conflicting goals that have not been structured into a single set of objectives and priorities. People are acting at cross-purposes. They may, for example, be put under pressure to follow departmental priorities at the expense of product or project goals.
(b) People are working out of step with each other because they are not brought together into teams or because mechanisms for liaison have not been laid down.
(c) The people who are actually carrying out operational work and who are in touch with changing contingencies are not permitted to participate in the planning of the work. There is therefore a breakdown between planning and operations.

4 *An organization may not respond innovatively to changing circumstances because*:
   (a) It has not established specialized jobs concerned with forecasting and scanning the environment.
   (b) There is a failure to ensure that innovation and planning of change are mainstream activities backed up by top management through appropriate procedures to provide them with adequate priority, programming and resources.
   (c) There is inadequate coordination between the part of an organization identifying changing market needs and the research area working on possible technological solutions.

5 *Costs may be rising rapidly, particularly in the administrative area, because*:
   (a) The organization has a long hierarchy with a high ratio of 'chiefs' to 'Indians'.
   (b) There is an excess of procedure and paperwork distracting people's attention away from productive work and requiring additional staff personnel to administer.
   (c) Some or all of the other organization problems are present.

Source: Child (1988), *Organizations: A Guide to Problems and Practice* (London, Paul Chapman).

to ensure effective functioning of the person, but it is a necessary precondition upon which the other parts depend.

In such a way does an organization work. The analogy here is that the brain is the organization's strategy, the skeleton the structure, the blood supply the financial resources, the nervous system and the muscles, the people and the technology and information systems. So, however intelligent the *strategic* 'brain' and developed the nervous system and the muscles (the people, technology and information systems) without an appropriate structure – the 'skeleton' – to provide the basic support, the organization will at the least wobble and even, possibly, collapse. Conversely, without a strategy (a brain) to direct it, the structure (the skeleton) will become misaligned to its purpose. The first contingency factor to be considered is, therefore, the relationship between strategy and structure.

The strategy–structure 'fit'

As always when considering concepts associated with the behaviour of people, there is rarely one accepted and clear definition. According to Burnes (2004) this is also true of any attempt to define strategy and strategic management. It is not the purpose here to rehearse all the arguments for one definition against another. For the purpose of this discussion, the definition given by Johnson, Scholes and Whittington (2005, p. 9) will suffice for a start. They say:

> Strategy is the *direction* and *scope* of an organisation over the *long term*: which achieves *advantage* for the organization through its configuration of *resources* within a changing *environment*, to meet the needs of *markets* and to fulfill *stakeholder* expectations.

The term stakeholder is taken to represent anyone who has an interest in the organization that is affected by the policies and practices of that organization. This includes not only shareholders, suppliers, financiers and customers – that is, interested parties outside the organization – but also employees.

To accompany this definition, Johnson *et al.* list six characteristics they say are associated with the words 'strategy' and 'strategic decisions'. Essentially this list elaborates the notion that strategy and strategic decisions encompass all the organization's activities; that they are concerned with the organization's internal and external environments; that they are influenced by the values and expectations of those who have power in the organization; and that they affect the long-term direction of the organization.

They take this idea further, suggesting that strategic decisions are likely to (p. 10):

- be complex in nature
- be made in situations of uncertainty
- affect operational decisions

- require an integrated approach (both inside and outside the organization)
- involve considerable change.

Mintzberg, Quinn and James (1988), in asking the question, 'Is strategy a process or the outcome of a process?' draw attention to the issue of whether strategy should be regarded as being amenable to rational planning or whether it is the emergent result of a social and political process. Mintzberg's (1994) own view is that effective strategies are a mixture of both deliberate and emergent strategies. It is clear that, sometimes, strategy can be thought about and planned prior to the process of its implementation. The organizational changes that follow will be incremental or more radical, depending on the nature of the process of implementing the strategy. Such changes most frequently involve changes in the organization's structure, because it is the structure that must provide the framework within which the strategic process must operate to achieve the organization's objectives. According to Robbins (2003) structure should follow strategy, a statement which confirms Miles and Snow's (1984a, p. 10) statement that:

> It is becoming increasingly evident that a simple though profound core concept is at the heart of many organisation and management research findings as well as many of the proposed remedies for industrial and organisational renewal. The concept is that of fit among an organisation's strategy, structure, and management processes.

The implications of this are that different types of strategy can be identified and consideration given to the most appropriate structure for each type. A number of scholars and researchers have discussed this proposition. The first to be considered is Chandler (1962).

Chandler's strategy–structure thesis

Chandler's strategy–structure thesis has been summarized by Miles and Snow (1984b). This summary shows that Chandler developed his thesis from an extensive study of nearly 100 large US companies, whose history he traced from around the mid-1800s. What Chandler found was that owner-managed companies were predominant during the 1800s. These organizations usually started simply with a single product line and a structure where the owner–manager took all major decisions as well as attempting to monitor the activities of the employees. Miles and Snow refer to this type of organization as having an 'agency' structure, given that key subordinates would act as agents of the owner–manager to ensure his/her wishes. The term 'agent' was used to imply that these subordinates did not occupy specialized functional roles as might be found in today's organizations.

As companies grew, they became more complex and were then more likely to employ professional managers who began the process of dividing the organization into different functional areas. The appearance of the functional organization (around the turn of the century) enabled some growth to occur, particularly through acquiring suppliers, to ensure guaranteed inputs, and through market penetration. The strategy of these organizations was to supply a limited number of standardized products, with the aim of supplying a national rather than a purely regional market. The structure of these functional organizations provided the means of standardized production on a high-volume basis to a limited number of markets. This structure proved cost effective and delivered profits accordingly. The disadvantages of this type of structure were, first, that it did not allow ease of movement into new products and markets and, second, it produced specialists rather than generalists, with few managers able to look at the overall picture of the company activities and its prospects. In Miles and Snow's (1984b, p. 40) words:

> Each succeeding product or market innovation became increasingly difficult to administer within the confines of the specialized functional structure. It was against this backdrop – the desire to diversify thwarted by administrative complexity – that the search for another organizational form began.

This new form turned out to be the divisional structure, which, according to Chandler, appeared simultaneously in four pioneering firms during the 1920s and 1930s: General Motors, Du Pont, Standard Oil of New Jersey and Sears, Roebuck. The divisional structure could take the form of departmentalization by product or region. However, whatever the basis of this move to horizontal differentiation, each division was most likely to become its own cost and profit centre, which was seen as essential if control was to be maintained and growth encouraged. What is more, each division would be able to develop its own strategy in line with its products, markets and (if organized into geographical divisions) its cultural environment. These different strategies might well produce their own types of structure.

According to Miles and Snow (1984b), during the 1960s and 1970s two competing strategies were pushing companies into a new form of structure. These strategies were, first, the pressure for functionally structured organizations to improve their capacity for product development – which sometimes resulted in project groupings being added to the basic structure. The second strategy was the pressure for organizations structured into product-differentiated divisions to take advantage of cost savings by centralizing some functions such as manufacturing that would, for instance, allow economies of scale. These two apparently competing strategies came together in the form of the organization that has been discussed above as the matrix form. Table 3.1 illustrates the evolution of these organizational forms, together with their associated mechanisms and means of control. It includes the dynamic network structure already described

Table 3.1 Evolution of organizational forms

	Product/market strategy	Organization structure	Core activating and control mechanisms
1800	• Single product or service • Local/regional markets	• Agency	• Personal direction and control
1850	• Limited, standardized product or service line • Regional/national markets	• Functional	• Centre plan and budgets
1900	• Diversified, changing product or service line • National/ international markets	• Divisional	• Corporate policies and division profit centres
1950	• Standard and innovative products or services • Stable and changing markets	• Matrix	• Temporary teams and lateral allocation devices such as internal markets, joint planning systems, etc.
2000	• Product or service design • Global, changing markets	• Dynamic network	• Broker-assembled temporary structures with shared information systems as basis for trust and coordination

Source: Based on Miles, R. E. and Snow, C. C. (1984a), 'Fit, failure and the hall of fame', *California Management*. Copyright © 1984, by The Regents of the University of California. Reprinted from the *California Management Review*. Vol.26, No.3. By permission of the Regents.

and that, at the time of writing (1984) and in the later paper by Snow *et al.* (1992), was held to be the structure for the year 2000 onwards.

Miles and Snow's strategic types

Miles and Snow (1984b) have developed a categorization of business strategies that can also be likened to Chandler's typology, as Miles and Snow themselves discuss. Illustration 3.13 describes Miles and Snow's three basic types of strategic behaviour, together with a fourth strategy which is really not a strategy at all in that organizations described as 'reactors' might be said to have no clear strategy of their own.

Miles and Snow liken their strategy types to Chandler's historical discussion of strategy and structure, saying that today's organizations are the products of their ancestors. For instance, they associate *Defenders* with the organizations which were typical of the period before the 1920s, that is, those with limited product/service lines, functional structures and centralized planning and control systems focused on cost efficiency.

Prospectors are likened to the divisionalized organizations of the 1920s and 1930s that proliferated in the 1950s. They seek to develop diversified products and structure themselves into product groups organized into decentralized operating divisions. *Analyzers* are said to have the characteristics of the most recent of

Illustration 3.13

Miles and Snow's typology of strategic behaviour

On the basis of their research and observations of many hundreds of companies in a wide range of industries, Miles and Snow claim to have identified four types of strategic behaviour with associated organizational characteristics. The types are as follows:

- **Defenders** have narrow and relatively stable product-market domains. As a result of this they seldom need to make major adjustments in their technology, structure or methods of operation. They focus on improving the efficiency of their existing operations. Defenders' characteristics include a limited product line; single, capital-intensive technology; a functional structure; and skills in production efficiency, process engineering and cost control.
- **Prospectors** continually search for product and market opportunities and regularly experiment with potential responses to emerging environmental trends. They are often the creators of change and uncertainty to which their competitors must respond. Because of this, they are usually not completely efficient. Prospectors' characteristics include a diverse product line; multiple technologies; a product or geographically divisionalized structure; and skills in product

research and development, market research and development engineering.
- **Analyzers** operate in two types of product-market domains – one relatively stable, the other changing. In their stable areas, these organizations operate routinely and efficiently through use of formalized structures and processes. In their more innovative areas, key managers watch their competitors closely for new ideas and then they rapidly adopt those that appear to be the most promising. Analyzers' characteristics include a limited basic product line; search for a small number of related product and/or market opportunities; cost-efficient technology for stable products and project technologies for new products; mixed (frequently matrix) structure; and skills in production efficiency, process engineering and marketing.
- **Reactors** are those organizations in which strategy–environment inconsistency exists or in which strategy, structure and process are poorly aligned. There is some evidence that, in highly regulated industries, Reactors perform less well than the other three types.

Source: Based on Miles, R. E. and Snow, C. C. (1984b), 'Designing strategic human resource systems', *Organisational Dynamics*, vol. 13, part 8, pp. 37–8.

Chandler's organization forms. Thus, small Analyzers 'are alert to diversification opportunities but tend to limit their expansion activities to those that can be handled by the present production technology and organization structure (typically functional)' (Miles and Snow, 1984b, p. 41). Of large Analyzers, Miles and Snow (ibid.) say:

> Larger Analyzers create semiautonomous divisions to handle major diversification efforts but tend to do so only when those products and markets are viewed as relatively stable and manageable. Typically, large Analyzers use matrix structures to handle market and product innovations until these can be incorporated into the established production system.

Mintzberg's forces and forms

A more recent paper by Mintzberg (1991) offers the concepts 'forces' and 'forms'

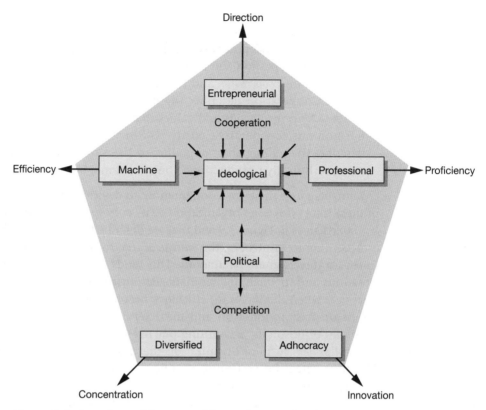

Figure 3.9 A system of forces and forms in organizations

Source: Mintzberg, H. (1991), 'The effective organization forces and forms', *Sloan Management Review*, Winter 1991, vol. 32, part 2, p. 55. Copyright © 1991 by Massachusetts Institute of Technology. All rights reserved. Distributed by Tribune Media Services.

that can be loosely translated as strategy and structure, although Mintzberg himself uses these terms sparingly. However, his descriptions of the forces that drive organizations to adopt particular forms are similar to the strategies which Chandler, and Miles and Snow, identify. Figure 3.9 illustrates the seven forces, each of which is associated with a particular form.

The seven forces which drive the organization can be described briefly as follows:

- The force for *direction*, which can be likened to having a 'strategic vision'. This gives a sense of where the organization must go as an integrated entity.
- The force for *efficiency*, which balances the costs and benefits – the lower the ratio of costs to benefits the higher the efficiency. The force for efficiency tends to encourage standardization and formalization, focusing on rationalization and restructuring for economy.
- The force for *proficiency*, that is for carrying out tasks with high levels of knowledge and skills.
- The force for *concentration*, which means the opportunity for particular units to concentrate their efforts on serving particular markets. This is necessary in

organizations that are diversified in structure.

- The force for *innovation*, which encourages the search for new products or services or for different ways of delivering them. The force for innovation encourages adaptation and learning.
- The forces for *cooperation* and *competition* are the forces Mintzberg calls 'catalytic'. Cooperation describes the pulling together of ideology, that is, the culture of norms, beliefs and values that 'knit a disparate set of people into a harmonious, cooperative entity' (Mintzberg, 1991, p. 55). Competition describes the pulling apart of politics in the sense of politics as the non-legitimate, technically not sanctioned organizational behaviour.

Mintzberg uses the term 'configuration' to describe the situation when any one of these forces drives an organization to its corresponding form – as evidenced by the boxed areas in Figure 3.9 and that are described in Illustration 3.14.

According to Mintzberg, the *entrepreneurial* form tends to dominate when the forces for direction are paramount. This tends to be in start-up and turnaround situations and in small, owner-managed organizations. The *machine* form tends to appear when the forces for efficiency become paramount, for instance in situations of mass production and mass service organizations. Mintzberg gives examples of hospitals, accounting practices and engineering offices to illustrate the *professional* form of organization that results from the force for proficiency. The drive here is for perfecting existing skills and knowledge rather than inventing new ones. This is different from the force for innovation that pushes organizations into an *adhocracy* form, which is characterized by independent

---

Illustration 3.14

Mintzberg's (1979, 1983) organizational forms

- **Entrepreneurial form** – tends to be low in formalization and standardization, but high in centralization with authority located in a single person.
- **Machine form** – high formalization and standardization, centralized authority vested in rules and regulations, functional departments.
- **Professional form** – high in complexity and formalization, but low in centralization; allows the employment of trained specialist staff for the core work of the organization.
- **The adhocracy form** – very low in standardization and formalization, little hierarchy, much use of project teams that may well be temporary.
- **Diversified form** – a combination of functions and products, with products dominating; they can be of matrix form or organized as divisions on the basis of products/markets.

These five forms are based on descriptions given by Mintzberg in his 1979 and 1983 books. In his 1991 paper, on which much of this section is based, he added the *ideological* and *political* forms, giving as examples the Israeli kibbutz and a conflictual regulatory agency respectively. However, he says these two forms are not common and restricts his discussion to the five forms described here.

project teams with fluid structures. Finally, the *diversified* form arises as a result of the force for an organization to concentrate on more than one distinct product or market. Each division will have a different structure and enjoy considerable autonomy from the small central headquarters.

Mintzberg calls the fit between the forces and forms that organizations take 'configuration': 'My basic point about configuration is simple: when the form fits, the organization may be well advised to wear it, at least for a time' (Mintzberg, 1991, p. 58). This argument supports those of Chandler and Miles and Snow that organizational structure should align itself with organizational strategy. The implications of this are that, as an organization's strategy changes, so must its structure if tensions, contradictions and, eventually, crises are not to ensue. However, strategy is not the only factor upon which structure is contingent.

The influence of size on structure

One of the outcomes of the large research projects carried out by Pugh and his associates (1969), mentioned earlier in this chapter, was that size of organization (measured by numbers employed) is positively correlated with overall role specialization and formalization (measured by the amount of paperwork procedures and usage). However, as Pugh (1973) points out, there are organizations whose size suggests particular structural configurations, but which confound the predictions. Even so, he suggests that the degree of constraint on organizational form imposed by variables such as size and technology is substantial, possibly accounting for some 50 per cent of the variability.

The work of Pugh and his associates does not have much to say about the relationship between organizational size, structure and economic performance. However, Child (1988) did carry out a study of the effects of size on organizational performance. His findings were that, for large organizations, the more bureaucratically structured they were, the better they performed. Smaller organizations performed better if they were less bureaucratically structured. The significant size appeared to be around 2,000 employees. Thus, in organizations below this size, performance is assumed to be better in those that have little formal structure whereas in organizations with more than 2,000 employees the association between more bureaucracy and superior performance was greater.

Both Pugh's and Child's research was done some time ago and might be assumed to precede the prevalence of the more 'modern' types of structure such as the matrix or the network. Thus the use of number of employees as a measure of size might not be as useful a measure for organizations with either of these types of structure. In highly divisionalized organizations, the size of the divisions is more likely to influence structure than is the size of the organization as a whole. In network structures, it is perhaps not size in its relation to structure that is significant in determining performance, but the type of relationship existing between core and other parts of the network and between permanent and temporary or contract staff.

Illustration 3.15 is an account of the way one division of a medium-sized multinational organization was able to radically change its structure independently of the structure of other divisions in the organization – with good results. What must be noted about this change, however, is the very careful way it was planned with the total involvement of the workers, foremen, managers and

---

Illustration 3.15

From hierarchy to self-managed teams

In 1994 a factory of some 200 employees, which was part of a division of a US organization manufacturing ceramics, took a deliberate decision to move from a hierarchically structured organization to one based on self-managed teams. The factory, based in Scotland, was one of 74 manufacturing plants employing a total of 8,500 people in 21 countries. As the company started operating new plants, employees were often sent for training or retraining to the Scottish factory, which, by that time, was the oldest in the company. However, the management realized that the factory's status as a 'master plant' could not be taken for granted. In the words of the operations manager: 'Here we are, a successful company in the west of Scotland. But the head office is in Brussels and we have no customers nearer than the north of England and no raw materials near by.' Having no natural advantages other than themselves, the concern was that, if they were not seen as being as good as the rest they would 'wither on the vine'.

Consequently a change programme was put into place under the banner of what is known as the business excellence model developed by the European Foundation for Quality Management (EFQM). The programme centred on the introduction of self-managed teams. Elements of the programme included the institution of new work practices for which all staff received training. All facilitators gained NVQs at level 3 with all 185 shop floor workers gaining an NVQ level 1. Every employee had an individual development plan linked to team targets, which in turn linked to wider business objectives. The factory's time clock was removed to symbolize

management's trust in the workforce. People no longer had to clock in. Consultations and negotiations with trade union representatives overcame their initial resistance, particularly in the context of no loss of jobs.

Over the period 1994 to 1997 the differential pay rates for different production jobs were replaced by a single wage structure and complete labour flexibility across jobs and departments. At an average age of 51, the plant's foremen underwent an extensive development programme designed to equip them for their new roles as facilitators rather than supervisors.

Indicators of the success of the new structure came from the results of employee opinion surveys. These indicated significantly increased levels of overall satisfaction and satisfaction with quality and productivity, company image, employee involvement and career development. Satisfaction with health and safety 'a dismal 53 per cent in 1993' went up to 90 per cent. At the time of this account (1999), all aspects of the business – including HR, purchasing, accounts and senior management – were self-managing teams. However, the ultimate measure of success comes from the company's results. The Scottish plant's turnover rose from £37 million in 1993 to £55 million in 1998 – a result the company attributes to the competitive edge gained from empowering the employees and giving them responsibility for quality. Cost savings amount to £500,000 a year. Most significantly, the company's market share has grown.

Source: Based on Arkin, A. (1999), 'Peak practice', *People Management*, 11 November, pp. 57–9.

Activity 3.6

1 *Refer back to Chapter 1 and the discussion of external and internal environmental triggers for change. Drawing on your own speculations and intuition, as well as what you can glean from the account, consider where you think the triggers for change were coming from for the organization in Illustration 3.15. How might some triggers have interacted with others?*

2 *If your organization (or your particular part of it) is structured into self-managing teams, what, if any, are the issues that cause most concern? What benefits are there for managers and others?*

3 *If your situation is one of individualized working or managed teams, what benefits and barriers could you envisage in moving to a structure of self-managed teams?*

trade union in its implementation.

The influence of changing technology

Two major studies are usually referred to in any discussion of the relationship of technology to organizational structure. These are, first, the work of Woodward (1965) and, second, the work of Perrow (1967).

Woodward studied 100 manufacturing firms in the south-east of England to investigate the relationship between organizational performance and elements of organizational structure such as unity of command and span of control. The companies were divided into three categories according to their methods of production, that is, the type of technology used: unit or small batch production; large batch and mass production; and process production.

Woodward found that there was a definite relationship between the types of technology used and aspects of organizational structure – in particular, the number of levels of management authority and the span of control of first-line supervisors. In addition, she concluded that the effectiveness of organizations was related to the 'fit' between technology and structure. In her words, 'not only was the system of production an important variable in the determination of organizational structure, but also that one particular form of organization was most appropriate to each system of production' (p. 69). For instance, firms falling within the large-batch/mass-production category were more likely to be successful if they had adopted a more mechanistic type of structure (e.g. similar to Mintzberg's machine form). Firms falling into either of the other two categories were more likely to be successful if they adopted a more organic structure (e.g. more flexible, decentralized with low standardization and formalization).

One criticism of Woodward's study is that it was done using only manufacturing organizations and, therefore, defined technology in a particular kind of way. The work of Perrow (1967) defined technology in a more general way which was more concerned with knowledge technology (that is, with both the ends and the means of achieving an output) than production technology. He suggested that technology could be viewed as a combination of two variables. The first of these he called 'task variability' and the second 'problem analyzability'. Thus a task that is highly routine would be low in task variability and vice versa; in other words, variability refers to the number of exceptional or unpredictable cases which have to be dealt with. Problem analyzability refers to the extent to which problems are clearly defined and can be solved by using recognized routines and procedures, in other words, whether a task is clearly defined or whether it is ambiguous in terms of the task itself and how it might be completed. Where task completion requires innovative thinking, it is likely to be low on problem analyzability.

Perrow used these two dimensions to construct a two-by-two matrix that provided a continuum of technology ranging from the routine to the non-routine as shown in Figure 3.10. The cells in the matrix represent four types of technology: routine, engineering, craft and non-routine.

In line with Woodward, Perrow argued that each type of technology would produce the best organizational performance if linked to an appropriate structure. Consequently, technologies such as are described in cell 1 are most likely to fit well with mechanistic structures. Cell 2 technologies require mechanistic structures but with aspects of organic organizational forms. It is proposed that cell 4 technologies link most closely to much 'looser' organic structures (perhaps of the matrix, project or network type) while cell 3 technologies require mainly organic structures with aspects of mechanistic bureaucracies.

Butler (1991, p. 100) says that, 'in complex organizations technologies cannot be operated by individuals acting singly', which leads to his discussion of Thompson's (1967) identification of an additional dimension of technology interdependence. According to Butler, interdependence applies to the ways that

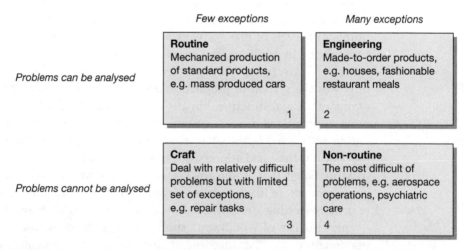

Figure 3.10 Perrow's technology classification
Source: Based on summaries by Robbins (2003) and Mullins (2005)

Technological interdependence

Pooled interdependence
This is the lowest degree of interdependence, which occurs when units operate independently but their individual efforts are still significant for the overall success of the organization. There is no flow of products or services between the different units, but they are all dependent on a central headquarters for resources and are responsible to it for outputs. Thompson called this form of interdependence a mediating technology. An example would be a bank, which mediates resources between lenders and borrowers.

Sequential interdependence
This involves a higher degree of interdependence between units in that one unit must complete its work before another takes over. Sequential interdependence is typified by the traditional assembly line type of production. Thompson called this type of technological interdependence long-linked technology.

Reciprocal interdependence
This is the most complex situation, with the highest degree of interdependence among units. For example, one unit's inputs to another are reciprocated by that unit's outputs becoming inputs to the first unit. This is further complicated where a network of units operates in this way. Examples might be the work of a hospital in looking after patients or a university in educating students. Thompson called this form of technological interdependence intensive technology.

work activities flow from one unit, group or department to another. Thompson suggests three types of technological interdependence: pooled, sequential and reciprocal (see Illustration 3.16).

It is not difficult to speculate on the different organizational structures that would support one form of technological interdependence rather than another. Butler (1991) uses the concept of decision-making capacity to differentiate between those situations where the capacity for decision making would need to be large and others where it would need to be small. Situations where mediating technology prevailed would be examples of the former and those of intensive technology examples of the latter. Long-linked technology would require something in between. Thus, intensive technologies are likely to require more horizontal linkages throughout the organization, with mediating and long-linked technologies requiring more vertical integration.

From this discussion, in particular of the work of Woodward, Perrow and Thompson, it appears that there is a link between organization structure and technology, and the hypothesis that organizational structure is contingent upon type of technology predominating in organizations is upheld. Robbins (2003) summarizes the evidence for this. He divides the evidence up in terms of its relationship to different aspects of structure. Thus he finds that technologies involving more routine work are moderately associated with structures that are highly differentiated both horizontally and vertically and vice versa. As regards formalization of processes and procedures, the more routine the technology the more formalized the structure. However, although routine technologies might be related to centralization of decision making, where highly developed formalized rules and regulations exist, decision making might be devolved but in line with the requirements of the formalized documentation.

While Robbins's summary is useful, it tends to assume a single technology for a single organization. Although this might be true, there are many cases where large organizations in particular have multiple technologies. Butler (1991, p. 110) asks the question: 'From an organizational design viewpoint what basis is there for deciding about the hierarchical priority to be given to particular units?' Drawing on Thompson's (1967) findings, he suggests that intensive technologies, as the most costly to operate, should first of all be identified and units organized around these. The implication is that these units would be structured into more organic forms than those based on mediating and long-linked technologies. However, where there are a number of units using intensive technologies these, in turn, would need to be linked together through some form of sequential or pooled interdependence. Thus, for the multi-divisional organization, there may be a variety of technologies and associated structures in the divisions, with each division linked to the central hub of the organization through pooled interdependence.

Woodward's, Perrow's and Thompson's research was done some time ago, before the widespread increase in the use of more advanced communications technologies including those using intranets and the Internet. For instance, many manufacturing organizations now work much more closely with suppliers and distributors – with either or both linking directly into the information systems of the manufacturers. In this way suppliers, for instance, know just when additional components are required and where. Of the 'old' systems, Ody (2000, p. 1) says: 'The supply chain used to be simple, serial and linear, with raw materials moving slowly through manufacturing production and onward via the distribution system to retailers and end-consumers' – in other words like Woodward's mass production or Thompson's long-linked technology. She goes on to say: 'Today, talk is of "supply networks", "parallel chains", "enhanced concurrent activities", and "synchronized models", with information technology set to cut both inventory and lead times throughout the pipeline still further' – a mixture of pooled, sequential and reciprocal interdependence, with perhaps more of the first two than the third. In this kind of scenario, the need for people to carry out the tasks of integrating one process with another reduces the numbers of staff employed, but demands more of those who are left.

This would appear to be somewhat in line with what has become known as 'business process re-engineering'. BPR, as it has become known, concentrates on reorganizing the core processes of an organization to eliminate those that do not contribute directly to what can be defined as an organization's 'core competencies'. BPR requires management to reorganize around horizontal processes including the institution of cross-functional and self-managed teams. Hammer and Champy (1993), the academics who coined the term 're-engineering' emphasize the need for radical, all-encompassing change (frame-breaking or discontinuous change – see Chapter 2) which is driven from the top of the organization – a process that in itself is contentious given the amount of resistance it is likely to cause. (This issue is debated further in Chapter 6.)

Not everyone has been convinced of the benefits of BPR, the implementation of which has resulted in reductions in people employed – especially middle managers. In some instances working on the re-engineered processes is very much like working on a complex production line. The team philosophy appears liberating but the work processes are still regimented and are carried out in regulated form. How far BPR can be applied to organizational processes as complex as, say, looking after elderly people in residential homes or educating children is uncertain. How far BPR can be applied in organizations where processes are not standardized and where creativity and innovation are the means of survival is also uncertain. It seems hard to imagine in organizations where the goals are not constant and where the boundaries are 'fuzzy' and diffuse.

Robbins (2003) talks of the 'boundaryless' organization where both internal and external boundaries are eliminated. He refers to Lucas's (1996) use of the term 'the T-form (or technology-based) organization'. The removal of internal vertical boundaries flattens the hierarchy with status and rank minimized. This type of organization uses cross-hierarchical teams, which are used to coordinating their own work. The removal of external barriers against suppliers has been mentioned already. With regard to customers, the increasing use of what Hollinger (2000) refers to as e-tailing makes the buying of goods from a wide range of producers and retailers much easier for those linked up to the Internet. In the United Kingdom, even the post offices have entered this field through offering home shoppers the opportunity to collect goods bought over the Internet at post offices.

The breaking down of organizational barriers extends also to the home/work boundary. Lyons (2000, p. 60) says: 'For many people, the division between work and life is becoming blurred ... people now live and work in the post-farm, post-factory setting. They travel, they work at home. They even work while they travel – in hotels, planes, cyber cafés, and at "touch down spaces".' This division is becoming blurred mainly because of the ability of workers to maintain contact with their offices and organizations through the use of email and mobile phones, which can also be used to send and accept emails and other telecommunications. Cooper (2000, p. 32) remarks: 'The future of employment seems to lie either in small and medium-sized businesses or in outsourced and portfolio working for virtual organizations.' This type of working is only made possible by the increased accessibility and use of telecommunications.

Not everyone, however, is convinced of the conclusions of a survey of 1,500 workers and 150 companies by the Institute of Directors which claims that, by 2020, the nine-to-five rat race will be extinct and present levels of self-employment, commuting and technology use will have changed beyond all recognition. According to Mills (2000, p. 2) in her reporting of comments made by Graeme Leach, Chief Economist of the UK Institute of Directors:

> The labour market of 2000 is far more traditional than perceived. It is not dominated by part-time employment, flexible working, home-working, teleworking or portfolio workers. But by 2010, I think that's all going to be different. There's going to be a huge sea-change in the labour market.

Mills quotes other people such as the director of the Helen Hamlyn Research Centre who support this view on the basis of an ageing population and the relative shortage of young workers who, it is said, will demand more family-friendly policies. According to Mills, Clare Lees, an associate director of the Henley Centre, which forecasts work trends, is not convinced by the homeworking habit when she comments: 'Right now, only 1 per cent of the working population are formally contracted home workers – it's hardly a mass market.' By contrast with the work-to-home proponents, Lees highlights the home-to-work trend, where lengthening working hours encourage people to do home shopping and Internet surfing at the office, which is seen by employers as a treat, that if not condoned would mean low retention of staff.

In spite of the arguments for and against homeworking, *flexible working* is certainly part of the present-day organizational world. The consequences for management of the many different forms of working and the ways tasks are organized are complex. In many cases organizations must operate different structures in different parts of their operations. There are, as yet, unknown ways that more sophisticated and complex management, operational and information technologies could be used to change the way work is done and how it is managed. The virtual organization is a reality made possible by developments in information technology. Woodward, Perrow and Thompson concentrated on the links between operational technologies and organizational structures with varied implications for the dimensions of structure identified by Pugh *et al.*, discussed at the beginning of this chapter. In the world of virtuality, managing staff and operations 'at a (real and virtual) distance' could well increase the need for centralized decision making and/or formalization in terms of written rules, procedures, instructions and communications. It is clear that, along with size, technology, in its broadest sense, must take its place as one of the determinants of organizational structure – changes in technology quite frequently lead to changes in structure. In addition, the fact that organizations operate in environments external to them means that these also will influence the form they take.

The influence of the external environment

Environmental stability and turbulence

The nature and components of any organization's external environment have been discussed in previous chapters. The use of the PEST mnemonic drew attention to the political, economic, socio-cultural and technological components of the external environment. Ansoff and McDonnell's (1990) categorization of levels of environmental turbulence was used to warn about the need for organizations to maintain a state of appropriate responsiveness to changes from one level to another (see Chapter 1). A conclusion from these discussions is that an organization's structure will be affected by its external environment because of environmental uncertainty.

One of the best-known studies on the effects of the environment on organizational structure is that of Burns and Stalker (1961). In studying some 20 British industrial organizations, these researchers concluded that organizations had different structures depending on whether they operated in more stable environments that changed little over time or in more dynamic, changeable environments which were unpredictable in their instability. They claim to have identified two main types of structure – mechanistic structures that they main-

Illustration 3.17

Organic structures

The organic form is appropriate to changing conditions, which give rise constantly to fresh problems and unforeseen requirements for action that cannot be broken down or distributed automatically arising from the functional roles defined within a hierarchic structure. It is characterized by:

(a) The contributive nature of special knowledge and experience to the common task of the concern.
(b) The 'realistic' nature of the individual task, which is seen as set by the total situation of the concern.
(c) The adjustment and continual redefinition of individual tasks through interaction with others.
(d) The shedding of 'responsibility' as a limited field of rights, obligations and methods. (Problems may not be posted upwards, downwards or sideways as being someone else's responsibility.)
(e) The spread of commitment to the concern beyond any technical definition.
(f) A network structure of control, authority, and communication. The sanctions that apply to the individual's conduct in his working role derive more from presumed community of interest with the rest of the working organization in the survival and growth of the firm and less from a contractual relationship between himself and a non-personal corporation, represented for him by an immediate superior.
(g) Omniscience no longer imputed to the head of the concern; knowledge about the technical or commercial nature of the task may be located anywhere in the network; this location becoming an ad hoc centre of control authority and communication.
(h) A lateral rather than a vertical direction of communication through the organization, communication between people of different rank, also, resembling consultation rather than command.
(i) A content of communication that consists of information and advice rather than instructions and decisions.
(j) Commitment to the concern's tasks and to the 'technological ethos' of material progress and expansion is more highly valued than loyalty and obedience.
(k) Importance and prestige attached to affiliations and expertise valid in the industrial, technical and commercial milieux external to the firm.

Source: Burns, T. and Stalker, G. M. (1961), 'Mechanistic and organic systems', in *Management of Innovation* (London, Tavistock, p. 120).

tain were more suited to the more stable unchanging environments and organic structures (see Illustration 3.17) which were more suited to the unpredictable, more dynamic environments.

Mechanistic structures conform to Morgan's models 1 and 2, shown in Figure 3.6 (rigid bureaucracies and bureaucracies with a senior management team) and Mintzberg's 'machine' form of organization (see Illustration 3.14). Organic structures resemble Morgan's models 4, 5 and 6 and Mintzberg's 'adhocracy' and 'diversified' forms of organization. Illustration 3.17 describes the way Burns and Stalker perceived organic structures.

Lawrence and Lorsch (1967) went further than Burns and Stalker in suggesting that different departments within organizations face different environments and that, in successful organizations, each department would structure itself in line with its specific sub-environment. Thus in organizations operating in fairly stable environments, there would be less need for departments to be differentiated one from another. However, to ensure success, those organizations operating in highly uncertain environments would need to differentiate those departments most exposed to the environment (e.g. research and development) from those that were less exposed (e.g. production). In addition, where differentiation of departments was required, an organization would need to ensure appropriate integrating mechanisms between departments to avoid the negative effects of different structures and operating procedures for different departments. This was confirmed by the results of their research which showed that the successful organizations, in the three industries they studied, were the ones with a high degree of integration between departments.

Robbins (2003) also addresses the issue of environments specific to different parts of organizations. Drawing on other research (see Robbins, p. 472), he suggests that environments can be characterized in terms of three key dimensions. The first is the *capacity* of the environment, which refers to the degree to which it can support growth. The second is the degree of *stability* in the environment; stable environments are low in volatility whereas unstable environments are characterized by a high degree of unpredictable change. The third is environmental *complexity*, that is the degree of homogeneity or heterogeneity among environmental elements. Given this three-dimensional definition of environment, Robbins concludes that the scarcer the capacity and the greater the degree of instability and complexity, the more organic a structure should be; the more abundant, stable and simple the environment, the more mechanistic a structure should be.

Socio-cultural influences

The discussion so far has concentrated on what can be termed 'macro' influences on organizational structure: size of organizations, as they grow or shrink, the effects of changing technologies and the degree of turbulence that in general reflects changes in the political and economic environments.

Conclusions can be drawn that increasing size pushes organizations towards increasingly bureaucratic structures, which Robbins (2001, pp. 443–4) concludes is still the most efficient way to organize large-scale activities. By the same token, the desire of employees for more flexible ways of organizing their home/leisure/work relationships, coupled with the opportunities for self-employment and/or virtual forms of working may force organizational structures into forms that are as yet little understood.

Regardless of the size of organizations and type of technology used, more flexible working patterns and ways of structuring the work appear to be increasing. An interesting issue, however, is whether this trend is a result of initiatives taken by employers for the sole benefit of business or in response to the changing expectations of those they wish to employ. For instance, Cooper (2000, p. 32), an academic specializing in research concerned with stress, says:

> The future of employment seems to lie either in small and medium-sized businesses or in outsourced and portfolio working for virtual organizations. Since the industrial revolution, managerial and professional workers have not experienced high levels of job insecurity, so will people be able to cope with permanent job insecurity without the security of organizational structure?

By way of contrast, Bevan (2000, p. 20), in an article entitled: 'Flexible designs on domestic harmony', reports on a UK government initiative that pays for advice to employers on implementing a better work/life balance. Examples of employees who have benefited from more flexible work arrangements imply few difficulties as they choose arrangements to suit their particular home and life circumstances. The benefits to employers and businesses seem to outweigh the disadvantages.

It is difficult to know whether most people would prefer not to work on production lines, doing repetitive work, supermarket checkouts or as labourers in the winter on building sites if they had the choice of interesting work that they could arrange to suit their personal circumstances. Work serves many purposes besides being a source of earnings. According to Robbins (2003), however: 'While more people today are undoubtedly turned off by overly specialized jobs than were their parents and grandparents, it would be naïve to ignore the reality that there is still a segment of the workforce that prefers the routine and repetitiveness of highly specialized jobs.' Not everyone is suited to working in highly organic or loosely structured networks, let alone working in virtual reality.

People choose organizations as much as organizations choose people. Those working in organizations are more likely to remain in organizations whose structures, with their particular degrees of centralization, formalization, specialization and traditionalism, suit their individual and group preferences and needs. Designing organizational structures that satisfy the needs of those working in and associated with them is not straightforward. Indeed, designing organizational structures for change, while at the same time ensuring that the needs of the market and of employees are met, is as much an art as a science.

Organizational structure and change

The discussion in this chapter has led to the conclusion that there are many influences on the way an organization might structure for successful performance and to cope with change. What is apparent is that there is no one best way to design organizational structures or any particular form that will guarantee successful performance. Depending on factors such as strategy, size, technology used, the degree of predictability of the environment and the expectations and lifestyle of employees, an organization could well be successful and respond to the need for change whether it was structured along strict bureaucratic, mechanistic lines or as one of the newer network forms.

Care must be taken, however, not to assume that these contingency relationships are straightforward and that, provided the 'formula' is learned and applied, success will result. Robbins (1993, p. 528), drawing on the work of Child (1972) and Pugh (1973), states that: 'Strategy, size, technology and environment – even when combined – can at best explain only fifty percent of the variability in structure.' In addition, the idea that there is a one-way causal relationship between an organization's environment and its structure is open to question.

Organizations are not only influenced by their environments, they may, in turn, be able, themselves, to influence certain parts of their environments. For instance, the political environment can be influenced through lobbying, customers in the economic environment influenced through advertising and people's expectations of employment influenced by the way groups of organizations design jobs. The existence of monopoly conditions clearly helps organizations modify their environments. In times of high unemployment, the introduction of technology that significantly changes working practices will be easier.

If organizations are able, to some extent, to manipulate their environments to suit their strategies and structures, this will enable them to preserve existing structures and operational arrangements. The pressure to do this is evident from Mullins's (2005, p. 648) statement that: 'Developing organizations cannot, without difficulty, change their formal structure at too frequent an interval. There must be a significant change in contingency factors before an organisation will respond.' This implies a considerable time lag between situational change and changes in structure. Therefore, even if changes in strategy, size, technology and environmental factors do build forces for changes in organizational structure, there are other factors that may accelerate or, more likely, impede this process.

One of these factors is associated with the concept of 'strategic choice' (Child, 1972) and draws attention to the power of senior managers to choose which criteria they will use in assessing what organizational changes should take place.

Managers who may lose power and/or position are unlikely to choose those alternatives that, from a logical–rational point of view, maximize the organization's interest. Robbins (1993, p. 528) summarizes this view of structure as the 'power–control' explanation of organizational structure, that is, 'an organization's structure is the result of a power struggle by internal constituencies who are seeking to further their interests'. Thus, given the discretion available to management, rather than changes in organizational structure being logically planned and implemented, what results will be a structure that 'emerges' to satisfy not only the imperatives of the internal and external environments, but the personalities and power needs of dominant stakeholders.

Organizational politics and the issue of power balance are not the only factors influencing structural change in organizations. Neither does the mere process of changing an organization's structure necessarily bring about permanent change in management strategy, style of operating and other employees' attitudes and behaviours. The pervasiveness of organizational and national cultures can be strong enough to work against change. Thus the mechanisms for managing any kind of organizational change must take account of what French and Bell (1990) call the informal, 'covert' aspects of organizational life such as people's values and feelings, the informal, as opposed to formal, groupings and the norms of behaviours that become part of any organization but which are rarely 'spelt out'. Johnson (1990) puts emphasis on the role of symbols, rituals, stories and myths as being important parts of an organization's culture. He says that organizational change cannot be brought about simply by changing strategy and structure. The organizational culture has a significant and maybe even dominant role to play if anything more than incremental change is to happen. This is the subject of the next chapter.

Comment and conclusions

Organizational structure can be likened to the skeleton of the organization supporting the implementation of strategic decision making and operational processes. This chapter has focused on issues associated with the strategy, size, technology, environment and structure 'fit'. Structural change is seen to be influenced by changes in these situational factors. A number of different organizational forms have been described and the appropriateness of them to different situations in which organizations find themselves discussed. Of particular interest, in environments that push for organizational change, are the newer project and network forms of organization. The significant development of communications technologies has increased the possibilities for virtual working in what can be called virtual organizations. However, it is not feasible to think that organizations can constantly restructure as their environments move and change. Redesigning an organization's structure has to be carefully planned with change taking place as current business performance has to be sustained. This implies a mixture of incremental and transformational change.

Chapter 1 showed how organizations are, to some extent, a product of their history. In addition, organizations have existing structures, workforces, who are used to working in them, existing cultures, current businesses to sustain and, in many cases, trades unions to satisfy. Given this context, it is interesting to note the examples of highly structured organizations that have managed to adapt their formalized structures and developed matrix and virtual organizations layered over their existing structures to ensure responsiveness in the fast-paced economic environment in which they operate.

It is also important to remember that many businesses do not operate within formalized structures. Over 70 per cent of UK businesses employ 200 people or fewer, therefore the traditional approaches to structure that can create barriers may not be appropriate for these companies. What is important, for these and other organizations, is the need to be vigilant about changes in the environment to ensure, where possible, that the organizational structure reflects the demands put upon them by these external forces.

Redesigning an organization's structure has to be carefully planned with change taking place as current business performance is sustained. This implies a mixture of incremental and transformational change.

Having said all this, focusing on the formal aspects of organizational life, such as structure, can furnish only part of the explanation of why and how organizations choose to change and, if they do so, what form that change might take.

Discussion questions and assignments

1 Consider the following statement:

Starting from scratch underplays the fact that significant redesign has to be planned and implemented in a real-life context that won't go away. Hospitals' re-engineering projects run into the problems of physician power. Government projects are often stifled by a context where people can't see the need for fundamental change. In manufacturing and service organizations, plans to implement a new way of doing business are often undermined by the thinking and mindsets of the old way. These realities have to be actively managed and changed if new initiatives are to succeed.
(Morgan, 1994)

To what extent do these or similar issues apply to your own organization or one you know well? Anticipating what has still to be discussed in the chapters to come, put forward ideas for how managers and other relevant people might address them.

2 'In spite of the talk about network and virtual organizations, most organizations conform to more traditional structure types.' Discuss this in relation to your own organization and others you know well, using in addition any information you can gain from articles, the media and the Internet.

Case example ●●●

Mitsubishi Motors revises organization

22 June 2004

Mitsubishi Motors Corporation (MMC) today announced plans to revise its organizational structure. The changes will see the company's structure slim down from 230 departments to 131, which will hopefully speed up the decision-making process and clarify responsibilities.

The MMC affirms the following guiding principles in conducting business, which are the same since the company began in the 1930s. It has recognized that there have been dramatic shifts in values, the structure of society and environment since its first values were announced, and therefore some revisions are necessary to bring it up to date.

'Shoki Hoko' – Strive to enrich society, both materially and spiritually, while contributing towards the preservation of the global environment.

'Shoji Komei' – Maintain principles of transparency and openness, conducting business with integrity and fairness.

'Ritsugyo Boeki' – Expand business, based on an all-encompassing global perspective.

To support its desire to restore consumer trust in the company and a belief in how employees should be treated, MMC has created a number of restructuring initiatives.

Restoring trust, implementing reform

- A Business Ethics Committee consisting mainly of experts from outside the company will be established to supervise the company's efforts to comply with its pledge to place the utmost importance on customers, safety and quality.
- A new Quality Affairs Office will handle issues related to quality assurance and management, while a new Corporate Social Responsibility (CSR) Promotion Office, directly under the CEO, will promote and improve quality auditing and compliance issues throughout the company.
- A Corporate Restructuring Committee (CRC), headed by a Corporate Restructuring Office appointed from among outside investors, will be set up directly under the CEO for one year and

cross-functional teams created for all issues related to the revitalization plan. The teams will reach through the entire organization and make bold proposals to the CRC.

Organizations directly under the CEO (Chairman of the Board) and COO (President)

- The CEO will supervise departments related to overall management while the COO will supervise departments involved in executing business operations. Newly established departments reporting to the CEO include the CSR Promotion Office, Finance Group Headquarters, Group Corporate Strategy Office and the secretariat of the CRC.
- Newly established departments reporting directly to the COO include the Quality Affairs Office, Corporate Staff Office, Product Operations Group Headquarters, Domestic Operations Controlling and Accounting Department, and Produce Controlling and Accounting Department.

Other departments to be set or re-organized

- CSR Promotion Office, which also includes the Business Ethics Committee
- Finance Group Headquarters will include the Group, Overseas, Domestic and product Controlling and Accounting Departments
- Group Corporate Strategy Office
- Quality Affairs Office
- Corporate Staff Office
- Product Operations Group Headquarters
- Production and Logistics Office
- Global Aftersales Office
- Domestic Operations Group Headquarters
- Overseas Operations Group Headquarters.

In short, all functions will fall under the CEO or the COO. The aim is to clarify the roles and responsibilities for each part of the business. More detailed information can be found at:

http://media.mitsubishi-motors.com/
pressrelease/e/corporate/detail1069.html

The organization chart on pages 130–132 shows lower levels of the structure in more detail.

Mitsubishi Motors Corporation Organization Chart (29 June 2004)

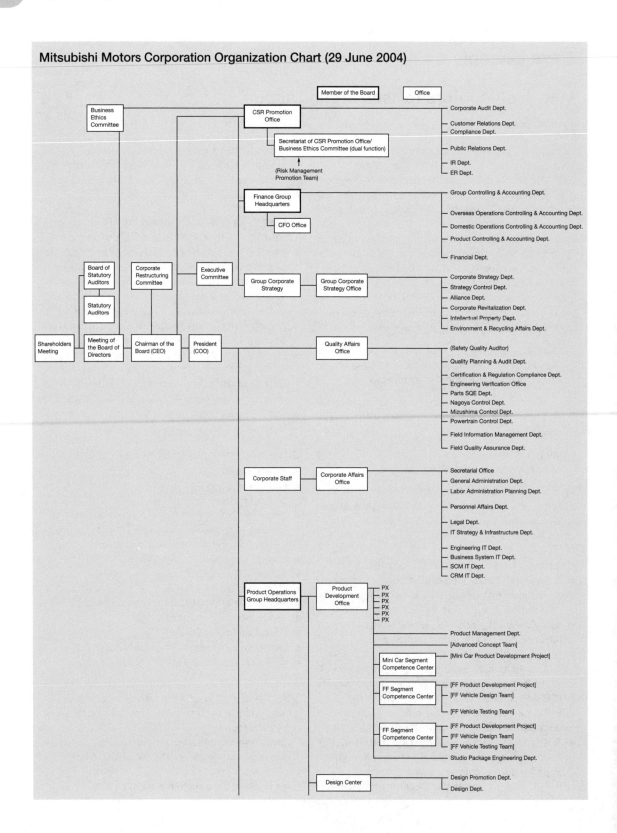

Mitsubishi Motors Corporation Organization Chart (29 June 2004) *continued*

Development Engineering Center
- Development Planning Dept.
- Cost Engineering Office
- Digital Engineering Office
- [Motor Sports Team]
- Vehicle Engineering Dept.
- Electronics Engineering Dept.
- Vehicle Proving Dept.
- Safety Testing Dept.
- Designing Dept.
- Engine Testing Dept.
- Drivetrain Engineering Dept.
- Performance Testing Dept.
- Powertrain Control Engineering Dept.
- Advanced Powertrain Development Dept.
- Material Engineering Dept.
- Prototype Dept.

Global Procurement Office
- Administration Dept.
- Strategy Dept.
- Cost Reduction Promotion Team
- Global Integation Team
- [Product Purchasing Project]
- Engine Parts Purchasing Dept.
- Drivetrain Parts Purchasing Dept.
- Raw Materials & Exterior Parts Purchasing Dept.
- Interior Parts Purchasing Dept.
- Electrical Parts Purchasing Dept.
- Chassis Parts & Complete Vehicle Purchasing Dept.
- Indirect Materials Purchasing Dept.

Production & Logistics Office
- Planning & Production Cost Control Dept.
- Production Engineering Control Dept
- Production Engineering Body Dept
- Production Engineering Paint Dept
- Production Engineering Final Assembly Dept
- Production Engineering Powertrain Dept
- [Production Project]
- Production Scheduling Dept.
- Production Parts Logistics Dept.
- Vehicles & KD Logistics Dept.

Nagoya Plant
- Control Dept.
- Plant Logistics Dept.
- Production Dept.

Mizushima Plant
- Control Dept.
- Plant Logistics Dept.
- Passenger Car Assembling Production Dept.
- Mini & Commercial Car Assembling Production Dept.
- Hospital

Powertrain Plant
- Control Dept.
- Plant Logistics Dept.
- Kyoto Production Dept.
- Shiga Production Dept.
- Mizushima Production Dept.
- Hospital

Global Aftersales Office
- Aftersales Marketing Dept.
- Distributor Business Support Dept.
- Service Information Management Dept.
- Technical Service Dept.
- Parts & Accessories Planning & Sales Dept.
- Parts & Accessories Development Dept.
- Parts & Accessories Logistics Dept.

Continued overleaf ▶

Mitsubishi Motors Corporation Organization Chart (29 June 2004) *continued*

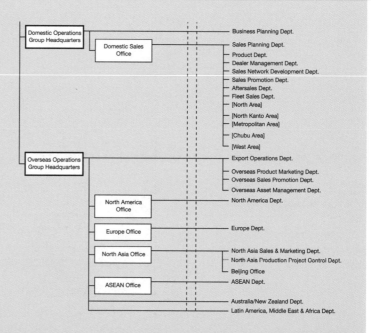

Case exercise   Questions

1 How would you categorize these changes in terms of the types of change discussed in Chapter 1?

2 Attempt to match the proposals and the structure shown in Illustration 3.18 to any, or a mixture, of the types of organizational structure discussed in this chapter.

3 What might be the advantages and disadvantages of Mitsubishi's proposed structural changes?

The next two chapters, therefore, extend this discussion further by addressing the more informal, 'covert' aspects of organizational life; that is, the prevailing values, attitudes and beliefs about what should be done and how – the culture which is part of, and surrounds, organizations – and the politics that are equally important in any examination of organizations and change.

●●●● Indicative resources

Butler, R. (1991) *Designing Organizations: A Decision-making Perspective*, London: Routledge. Although this text might appear dated, it presents useful arguments relating to the idea that structure is central to an organization's performance. This book focuses on structure and strategy and presents concepts key to an organization's flexibility and adaptability, and in particular links external factors that influence its effectiveness.

Drucker, P. F. (1999) *The Practice of Management*, Oxford: Butterworth Heinemann. This text has been written by a management 'guru'. Drucker provides an accurate contribution to the study of business effectiveness. The book has a chapter on 'the structure of management', which will complement this chapter.

Watson, T. (2002) *Organising and Managing Work*. Harlow: Pearson Education. The aim of this text is to provide a resource for understanding present-day work activities and how they are managed. It evaluates knowledge about organizational activities. It has particular relevance in supporting this chapter in the areas focused upon in Chapters 7 and 8 relating to structure and culture.

Useful websites

www.amazon.com Useful for students/professionals who would like the history of the network structure that Amazon has adopted. Launched as the 'earth's biggest bookstore' in 1995 and using state of the art technology, Amazon offers a useful example of success in the world of dotcom organizations.

www.businesslink.gov.uk Useful for attaining information relating to best practice in organizations, in particular there are publications in relation to organizations that employ people who work from home, and also publications in relation to practical

To click straight to these links and for other resources go to
www.pearsoned.co.uk/senior

References

Ansoff, I. H. and McDonnell, E. J. (1990) *Implanting Strategic Management*, Englewood Cliffs, NJ: Prentice-Hall.

Arkin, A. (1999) 'Peak practice', *People Management*, 11 November, pp. 57–9.

Bartol, K. M. and Martin, D. C. (1994) *Management* (2nd edn), Maidenhead: McGraw-Hill.

BBC News (2005) Unilever Shakeup as Profit Slips, www.bbc.co.uk, 10 February.

Bevan, S. (2000) 'Flexible designs on domestic harmony', *Financial Times*, 5 October, p. 5.

Burnes, B. (2004) *Managing Change* (4th edn), Harlow: Pearson Education.

Burns, T. and Stalker, G. M. (1961) *The Management of Innovation*, London: Tavistock.

Business Week (1993) 'The virtual corporation', *Business Week*, 8 February, pp. 98–102.

Butler, R. (1991) *Designing Organizations: A Decision-making Perspective*, London: Routledge.

Chandler, A. D., Jr (1962) *Strategy and Structure: Chapters in the History of the Industrial Enterprise*, Cambridge, MA: MIT Press.

Child, J. (1972) 'Organization structure, environment and performance: the role of strategic choice', *Sociology*, January, pp. 1–22.

Child, J. (1988) *Organizations: A Guide to Problems and Practice* (2nd edn), London: Paul Chapman.

Clegg, S. R. (1990) *Modern Organizations: Organization Studies in the Postmodern World*, London: Sage.

Cohen, M. and Agrawal, V. (2000) 'All change in the second supply chain revolution', *Mastering Management, Financial Times*, 2 October, pp. 8–10.

Cooper, C. (2000) 'Rolling with it', *People Management*, 28 September, pp. 32–4.

Cummings, T. and Worley, C (2005) *Organization Development and Change* (8th edn), Mason, OH: Thomson South-Western.

Cusamano, M. (1985) *The Japanese Automobile Industry: Technology and Management at Nissan and Toyota*, Cambridge, MA: Harvard Industry Press.

Davidow, W. H. and Malone, M. S. (1992) *The Virtual Corporation*, New York: Harper Business.

Davis, S. M. and Lawrence, P. R. (1977) *Matrix*, Reading, MA: Addison-Wesley.

Drucker, P. F. (1999) *The Practice of Management*, Oxford: Butterworth Heinemann.

French, W. L. and Bell, C. H., Jr (1999) *Organization Development: Behavioral Science Interventions for Organization Improvement*, Englewood Cliffs, NJ: Prentice-Hall.

Geisler, B. (2002) Virtual Teams. Newfoundations.com

Greiner, L. (1972) 'Evolution and revolution as organizations grow', *Harvard Business Review*, July–August, pp. 37–46.

Hammer, M. and Champy, J. (1993) *Reengineering the Corporation: A Manifesto for Business Revolution*, New York: Harper Business.

Handy, C. B. (1989) *The Age of Unreason*, London: Business Books.

Hinterhuber, H. H. and Levin, B. M. (1994) 'Strategic networks: the organization of the future', *Long Range Planning*, vol. 27, no. 3, pp. 43–53.

Hollinger, P. (2000) 'Festive internet rush may surprise retailers', *Financial Times*, 30 October, p. 6.

Jackson, N. and Carter, P. (2000) *Rethinking Organisational Behaviour*, Harlow: Financial Times Prentice Hall Pearson Education.

Jacques, E. (1976) *A General Theory of Bureaucracy*, Oxford: Heinemann.

Jacques, E. (1990) 'The stratified depth-structure of bureaucracy', Chapter 2 in Pugh, D. S. (ed.) *Organization Theory*, London: Penguin.

Jacques, E. and Clement, S. D. (1994) *Executive Leadership*, Oxford: Blackwell.

Johnson, G. (1990) 'Managing strategic action; the role of symbolic action', *British Journal of Management*, vol. 1, pp. 183–200.

Johnson, G., Scholes, K. and Whittington, R. (2005) *Exploring Corporate Strategy* (7th edn), Harlow: Pearson Education.

Koontz, H. and Weihrich, H. (eds) (1990) *Essentials of Management*, New York: McGraw-Hill.

Lawrence, P. R. and Lorsch, J. W. (1967) *Organization and Environment: Managing Differentiation and Integration*, Boston, MA: Harvard Business School.

Lucas, H. C., Jr (1996) *The T-Form Organization: Using Technology to Design Organizations for the 21st Century*, San Francisco, CA: Jossey-Bass.

Luthans, F. (1995) *Organizational Behavior* (7th edn), New York: McGraw-Hill.

Lyons, L. (2000) 'Management is dead', *People Management*, 26 October, pp. 60–4.

McCann, J. and Galbraith, J. R. (1981) 'Interdepartmental relations' in Nystrom, P. C. and Starbuck, W. H. (eds) *Handbook of Organizational Design: Remodelling Organizations and Their Environment*, vol. 2, New York: Oxford University Press.

McHugh, M. and Bennett, H. (1999) 'Introducing teamwork within a bureaucratic maze', *The Leadership and Organization Development Journal*, vol. 20, no. 2, pp. 81–93.

Miles, R. E. and Snow, C. C. (1984a) 'Fit, failure and the hall of fame', *California Management Review*, vol. 26, no. 3, pp. 10–28.

Miles, R. E. and Snow, C. C. (1984b) 'Designing strategic human resource systems', *Organisational Dynamics*, vol. 13, part 8, pp. 36–52.

Mills, M. (2000) 'Coming to a screen near you ...', Office Hours, the *Guardian*, 18 September, p. 2.

Mintzberg, H. (1979) *The Structuring of Organizations*, Englewood Cliffs, NJ: Prentice-Hall.

Mintzberg, H. (1983) *Structure in Fives: Designing Effective Organizations*, Englewood Cliffs, NJ: Prentice-Hall.

Mintzberg, H. (1991) 'The effective organization forces and forms', *Sloan Management Review*, winter, vol. 32, part 2, pp. 54–67.

Mintzberg, H. (1994) 'Rethinking strategic planning. Part I: pitfalls and fallacies', *Long Range Planning*, vol. 27, no. 3, pp. 12–21.

Mintzberg, H., Quinn, J. B. and James, R. M. (1988) *The Strategy Process: Concepts, Contexts and Cases*, Hemel Hempstead: Prentice Hall.

Morgan, G. (1989) *Creative Organization Theory: A Resource Book*, London: Sage.

Morgan, G. (1994) 'Quantum leaps ... step by step', *The Globe and Mail* Canada's national newspaper, 28 June. Also available at http://www.imaginiz.com/ leaps.html

Mullins, L. (2005) *Management and Organizational Behaviour* (7th edn), Harlow: Financial Times Prentice Hall.

Ody, P. (2000) 'Working towards a total, visible network', *Financial Times* Survey Supply Chain Management, 25 October, p. 1.

Perrow, C. (1967) *Organizational Analysis: A Sociological View*, London: Tavistock.

Pugh, D. S. (1973) 'The measurement of organisation structures: does context determine form?' *Organisational Dynamics*, spring, pp. 19–34.

Pugh, D. (1990) *Organization Theory: Selected Readings*, Harmondsworth: Penguin.

Pugh, D. S., Hickson, D. J., Hinings, C. R. and Turner, C. (1969) 'Dimensions of organization structure', *Administrative Science Quarterly*, vol. 17, pp. 163–76.

Robbins, S. P. (1993) *Organizational Behavior*, Englewood Cliffs, NJ: Prentice-Hall.

Robbins, S. P. (2003) *Organizational Behavior* (10th edn), Englewood Cliffs, NJ: Prentice-Hall.

Snow, C. C., Miles, R. E. and Coleman, H. J., Jr (1992) 'Managing 21st century network organizations', *Organizational Dynamics*, winter, pp. 5–19.

Stacey, R.D. (2003) *Strategic Management and Organisational Dynamics: The Challenge of Complexity*, Harlow: Financial Times Prentice Hall Pearson Education.

Thompson, J. D. (1967) *Organizations in Action*, New York: McGraw-Hill.

Unilever (2004) www.unilever.com/ourcompany/newsandmedia, 19 August.

Weber, M. (1947) *The Theory of Social and Economic Organization*, Free Press, trans. and ed. by Henderson, A. M. and Parsons, T., in Pugh, D. S. (1990), *Organization Theory: Selected Readings*, Harmondsworth: Penguin. (German original published in 1924.)

Wilson, D. C. and Rosenfeld, R. H. (1990) *Managing Organizations: Text, Readings and Cases*, Maidenhead: McGraw-Hill.

Wilson, D. C. and Rosenfeld, R. H. (1991) *Managing Organizations: Text, Readings and Cases: Instructor's Resource Book*, Maidenhead: McGraw-Hill.

Woodward, J. (1965) *Industrial Organization: Theory and Practice*, London: Oxford University Press.

Chapter 4

Cultures for change

This chapter complements Chapter 2. In contrast to the emphasis in that chapter on the formal aspects of organizational functioning, this chapter begins the process of addressing the informal aspects of organizational functioning with an exploration of the concept of culture as it influences organizational life and organizational change processes. The meaning of culture at both the organizational and national levels is discussed and different models and typologies are compared. Methods for diagnosing and identifying organizational culture are discussed together with the different sources from which organizational culture derives. The links between organizational strategy, structure and culture are explored in order to understand the issues associated with and possibilities for changing organizational culture. The chapter ends with a discussion of the feasibility of changing an organization's culture according to the strategy and context prevailing at the time. Much of what is said in this chapter relates to issues of organizational politics and power discussed in Chapter 5 and approaches to designing and implementing change in Chapters 7 and 8, but Chapter 8 in particular.

Learning objectives

By the end of this chapter you will be able to:

- recognize the importance of the informal organization and its role in relation to organizations and change;

- explain the meaning of culture in the context of a range of perspectives offered by researchers in the field;

- compare and contrast different cultural models and typologies;

- diagnose organizational culture as the first step in the process of culture change;

- identify the sources, including those of the wider society, from which an organization derives its culture in order to understand how culture pervades all aspects of organizational life;

- examine different cultures in terms of their capacity to help or hinder organizational change;

- investigate degrees of strategy–culture compatibility and their implications for large-scale strategic change.

The informal organization

It is clear from the discussion in the previous chapters that organizations are composed of formal elements such as structure, strategy and technology. In addition there is, apparently, little that is contentious in describing their size, whether this is measured by number of employees or by one or more financial indicators. The goals of an organization and its financial resources might also be regarded as fairly understood and explicit elements of organizational life. These aspects of organizational functioning can be termed the formal organization. Thus the determination of an organization's goals, its strategy and structure, the technology it will use and its need for financial resources can, legitimately, be associated with logical thinking and rational methods of decision making. In addition, because these more formal organizational features can be reasonably understood by most people, they are, in the main, susceptible to the process of *planned* change (see Chapter 2).

However, as the comments at the end of Chapter 2 showed, organizational life is not nearly as neat and tidy as this implies. This has been well expressed by French and Bell (1990, 1999) in their use of the concept of the informal organization and the metaphor of the 'organizational iceberg'. Figure 4.1 illustrates this idea pictorially.

The iceberg metaphor can be used to depict two contrasting aspects of organizational life. The first is that part of the iceberg which is visible above the water and is composed of the more easy-to-see and formal aspects of an organization; that is those issues that are based on agreed, measurable ouputs/outcomes relating to how organizational goals and objectives will be met. The second is the hidden part of the iceberg that is composed of the more covert aspects of organizational life. These include the values, beliefs and attitudes held by management and other employees, the emergent informal groupings that occur in every organization, the norms of behaviour which direct how things are done but which are rarely talked about and the politics of organizational life that are mainly hidden but which, for all that, are a powerful driver of decisions and actions.

It is significant that the metaphor of an iceberg not only points to the overt and covert aspects of organizations but draws attention to the proposition that the informal systems, as well as being hidden, are the greater part of the organizational iceberg. For those who have seen icebergs, whatever is seen above the

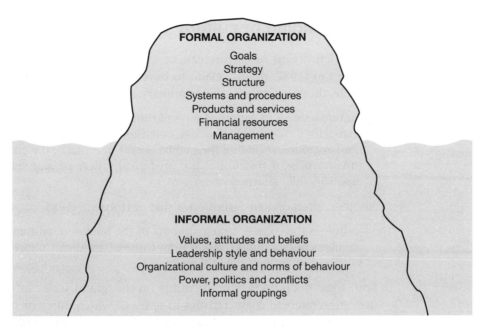

Figure 4.1 The organizational iceberg

water, underneath is at least 10 times this mass. However, as with unseen parts of icebergs, organizational cultures may not become apparent until one collides with them unwittingly. Thus the difficulties in detecting the extent and characteristics of the hidden part of the iceberg are analogous to the difficulties encountered in examining and understanding the more informal, hidden aspects of organizational behaviour. Indeed, French and Bell (1990, p. 18) go so far as to say: 'Traditionally, this hidden domain either is not examined at all or is only partially examined.' The truth of this comment is debatable. However, whether it is wholly true or not, the acceptance that the informal organization exists and can act powerfully to influence organizational activity is reason enough to examine how it impinges upon the extent to which organizations can deal with change.

The concepts of culture, politics and power have come to embrace much of what is included in the hidden part of the organization. What is more, they play an important role in helping or hindering the process of change, as Morgan (1989) confirms in his statement: 'The culture and politics of many organizations constrain the degree of change and transformation in which they can successfully engage, even though such change may be highly desirable for meeting the challenges and demands of the wider environment.' Regardless of how well change might be planned in terms of the more formal organizational characteristics, it is the hidden informal aspects of organizational life that will ultimately help or hinder an organization's success. The discussion that follows, in this chapter and the next, explores the nature and influence of culture and politics in terms of their significance for organizations in times of change.

●●●● The meaning of culture

Many definitions of culture can be found in the literature and Kroeber and Kluckhohn (1952, p. 181) claim to have examined well over 100. It seems reasonable, therefore, to give their summary definition, which is:

> Culture consists in patterned ways of thinking, feeling and reacting, acquired and transmitted mainly by symbols, constituting the distinctive achievements of human groups, including their embodiment in artifacts; the essential core of culture consists of traditional (i.e. historically derived and selected) ideas and especially their attached values.

Another, often quoted definition is that of Hofstede (1981, p. 24):

> Culture is the collective programming of the human mind that distinguishes the members of one human group from those of another. Culture in this sense is a system of collectively held values.

Both these definitions refer to culture on the 'grand scale'. In the first case, the definition refers to characteristics in terms of which different *societies* differ one from another. In the second case, Hofstede uses his definition to delineate one *national* culture from another. For instance, his reference to 'human groups' is taken to mean groupings based on nationality.

These definitions can be compared to those that are used more specifically to describe organizational cultures. The first three are chosen from a list given by Brown (1995) in his book entitled *Organisational Culture*. They span the years from 1952 to the early 1990s. The final three definitions have incorporated the initial ideas and have built on them.

> The culture of the factory is its customary and traditional way of thinking and of doing things, which is shared to a greater or lesser degree by all its members, and which new members must learn, and at least partially accept, in order to be accepted into service in the firm. Culture in this sense covers a wide range of behaviour: the methods of production; job skills and technical knowledge; attitudes towards discipline and punishment; the customs and habits of managerial behaviour; the objectives of the concern; its way of doing business; the methods of payment; the values placed on different types of work; beliefs in democratic living and joint consultation; and the less conscious conventions and taboos.
>
> (Jaques, 1952, p. 251)

> A set of understandings or meanings shared by a group of people. The meanings are largely tacit among members, are clearly relevant to the particular group, and are distinctive to the group. Meanings are passed on to new group members.
>
> (Louis, 1980)

> Culture is 'how things are done around here'. It is what is typical of the organization, the habits, the prevailing attitudes, the grown-up pattern of accepted and expected behaviour.   (Drennan, 1992, p. 3)

Organization or corporate culture is the pattern of values, norms, beliefs, attitudes and assumptions that may not have been articulated but shape the ways in which people behave and get things done.   (Armstrong, 2003, p. 263)

A pattern by which a company connects different value orientations, such as rules versus exceptions, people focus versus focus on reaching goals and targets, decisiveness versus consensus, controlling the environment versus adapting to it, in such a way that they work together in a mutually enhancing way.

(Trompenaars and Prud'homme, 2004, p. 9)

An organization's culture is the pattern of assumptions, values and norms that are more or less shared by an organization's members. A growing body of research has shown that culture can affect strategy formulation and implementation as well as a firm's ability to achieve high levels of excellence.

(Cummings and Worley, 2005, p. 509)

An examination of all these definitions illustrates a degree of overlap. Thus, in general, people are seen as being from different cultures if their ways of life as a group (whether societal or organizational) differ significantly, one from another.

Collectively, these definitions imply that culture is an objective entity which can be identified and which delineates one human grouping from another. It is clear that culture has cognitive (to do with thinking), affective (to do with feeling) and behavioural characteristics. However, this tends to give the impression that different cultures are easily identified and, on the whole, this is not so. Schein (1992, p. 6) sums this up by referring to organizational culture as:

The deeper level of basic assumptions and beliefs that are shared by members of an organization, that operate unconsciously and define in a basic 'taken for granted' fashion an organization's view of its self and its environment.

The fact that these elements of culture operate 'tacitly' as Louis says, 'unconsciously' as Schein says, or unarticulated as Armstrong says, reinforces the metaphor of the hidden part of the iceberg. What is also implicit in the use of this metaphor and these definitions is that culture is 'deep-seated' and is, therefore, likely to be resistant to change. However, as Bate (1996, p. 28) points out: 'Culture can be changed, in fact it is changing all the time.' The issue is the degree of change to which culture can be submitted over the short and long term and the process for doing this. Much depends on the perspective adopted and the type of change proposed. Three perspectives can be identified (see Ogbonna and Harris, 1998). These are: that culture *can* be managed; that culture *may* be manipulated; and that culture *cannot* be consciously changed. Most of the writing and research concerned with culture change subscribes to the first two of these perspectives. The last of these might be true if, for culture change to take place, some external (and perhaps unpredictable) forces are required to make it. However, even in these circumstances, the situation emerging from such events will need to be managed. This discussion, therefore, concentrates on issues associated with the first two of these perspectives on the assumption that much of what is said would apply if culture change occurs spontaneously rather than as a result of a more planned process.

Advice on how to *plan* culture change is not in short supply (for some examples see Eccles, 1994; Carnall, 1995, 2003; Bate, 1996; Ogbonna and Harris, 1998). There is general agreement that there is a need to: (i) assess the current situation; (ii) have some idea of what the aimed-for situation looks like; and (iii) work out the 'what' and 'how' of moving the organization, or section of it, away from its current culture to what is perceived to be a more desirable one. Of major importance is the need, before any attempt is made to alter the culture, to know more about the culture to be changed. Some ways of doing this are discussed in the next section.

Describing organizational culture

Methods for describing organizational culture are varied. Some simply list what are seen to be the characteristics of culture. For instance, Brown (1995, p. 8) lists the following:

- artefacts
- language in the form of jokes, metaphors, stories, myths and legends
- behaviour patterns in the form of rites, rituals, ceremonies and celebrations
- norms of behaviour
- heroes
- symbols and symbolic action
- beliefs, values and attitudes
- ethical codes
- basic assumptions
- history.

It is then left to those attempting to describe a culture to frame their descriptions in terms of these characteristics. This is more or less easily done according to the precision with which the general characteristics are set out. In addition, not all writers are agreed on what should or should not be included in any list. For instance, a comparison of Brown's list with that of Robbins (2003, p. 525 – see Illustration 4.1) illustrates well the two parts of the organizational iceberg in that Brown emphasizes more strongly the more informal aspects of organizational life while Robbins includes some of the more formal elements.

Identifying an organization's culture using Brown's list could be done qualitatively or by constructing some kind of questionnaire type instrument. Activity 4.1 shows how a more quantitative method of identification can be used. The questionnaire there is based on Robbins's rather more precise culture characteristics.

Models of organizational culture such as those of Brown and Robbins do not make any attempt to link one culture characteristic with another. By contrast other writers suggest that different cultural characteristics *are* linked to one

Illustration 4.1

The characteristics of organizational culture

1 **Innovation and risk taking.** The degree to which employees are encouraged to be innovative and take risks.

2 **Attention to detail.** The degree to which employees are expected to exhibit precision, analysis and attention to detail.

3 **Outcome orientation.** The degree to which management focuses on results or outcomes rather than on the techniques and processes used to achieve those outcomes.

4 **People orientation.** The degree to which management decisions take into consideration the effect of outcomes on people within the organization.

5 **Team orientation.** The degree to which work activities are organized around groups rather than individuals.

6 **Aggression.** The degree to which people are aggressive and competitive rather than easygoing.

7 **Stability.** The degree to which organizational activities emphasize maintaining the status quo in contrast to growth.

Source: Robbins, S. P. (2005) *Organisational Behaviour,* 11th edn (Pearson Education, New Jersey, p. 485)

Activity 4.1 *Appraising your own organization*

The scales relate to the organizational culture characteristics listed in Illustration 4.1. Put a cross on each scale according to how you rate your own organization (or one with which you are familiar). If possible, ask colleagues in different parts of the organization to your own to carry out this rating process. This will help analyze their perspective of the organization and how they perceive these characteristics of culture.

Organizational culture characteristics

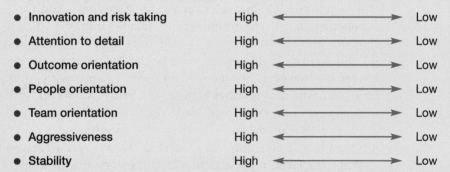

- Innovation and risk taking   High ⟷ Low
- Attention to detail   High ⟷ Low
- Outcome orientation   High ⟷ Low
- People orientation   High ⟷ Low
- Team orientation   High ⟷ Low
- Aggressiveness   High ⟷ Low
- Stability   High ⟷ Low

Upon completion of your analysis of your organization's culture and that of your colleagues, analyze where there are any differences; consider why their views might be different from your own.

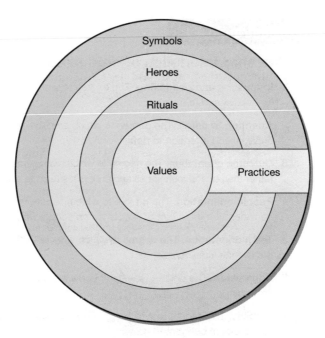

Figure 4.2 Different levels of culture

Source: Hofstede, G., Neuijen, B., Ohayv, D. D. and Sanders, G. (1990), 'Measuring organizational cultures: a qualitative and quantitative study across twenty cases', *Administrative Science Quarterly*, vol. 35, p. 291.

another through a hierarchy of 'levels' of culture. An example is shown in Figure 4.2. This illustrates the suggestions of Hofstede *et al.* (1990) that culture manifests itself at the deepest level through people's values and at the shallowest level in terms of the things that symbolize those values.

Other 'levels' models are those of Schein (1992, 2004) and Dyer (1985). Schein suggests three levels that are from the shallowest to the deepest: the *artefacts* level (the visible organizational structures and processes such as language, environment, rituals, ceremonies, myths and stories); the *espoused values* level (the organization's strategies, goals, philosophies); and the *basic underlying assumptions* level (the unconscious, taken-for-granted beliefs, perceptions, thoughts and feelings that are the ultimate source of values and actions). Thus the rituals, heroes and symbols level of Hofstede *et al.* equate with Schein's artefacts level. However, Hofstede's values level is, apparently, split into two levels by Schein, who distinguishes between the beliefs, values and attitudes associated with the espoused values level and the deeper level of basic assumptions. As far as Dyer's (1985) model goes, the only difference from that of Schein is that Dyer proposes four levels – *artefacts*, *perspectives*, *values* and *tacit assumptions*.

While the levels models have much in common with Brown's list of the elements of organizational culture, on initial analysis, it seems that the seven characteristics of organizational culture identified by Robbins have little to do with them, yet Robbins's list appears much more amenable to being *used* to describe an organization's culture in practical terms. However, it is possible to use the levels model to get some understanding of an organization's culture. In this case, the process requires interpretation of signs and symbols, as well as language used, to assess the prevailing values and underlying assumptions about how the organization should operate. Illustration 4.2 shows how a combination of Schein's and Dyer's models might be applied to the Beautiful Buildings Company, whose structure was described in Chapter 3.

Illustration 4.2

Levels of culture in the BB Company

1 **Artefacts.** The annual report of the company includes policies concerned with employees as well as customers and shareholders. Building sites have well-kept, clean facilities for the workers. Gillian Lambeth is frequently referred to by her first name.

2 **Perspective.** It is acceptable for the trade union representatives to know what volume of work might be expected in the future, but the directors are not expected to talk about details of the proposed expansion until it becomes a well-established fact.

3 **Values.** Although there is a clear distinction between directors/managers and site workers, pay and conditions for workers should be fair and their views taken into account on matters pertaining to them. However, gaining contracts and satisfying customers is a priority.

4 **Basic/tacit assumptions.** All people should be treated with dignity whatever their level and function.

Objectivist and interpretive views of culture

Attempts to build models of organizational culture, such as those represented by Robbins's list and the levels models, throw up the issue of how to bring meaning to the concept of culture itself. In pursuit of this Alvesson (1993), Bate (1996) and Brown (1995) all draw attention to the distinction between two classifications of culture. The first, of which Robbins's list and the levels models might be considered examples, treat culture as a critical variable that forms a partial explanation for differences in organizational operations. This can be termed the objectivist or functional view of culture (Alvesson, 1993). Alternatively, culture can be defined as a set of behavioural and/or cognitive characteristics (Brown, 1995). This view places culture alongside structure, technology and the environment (for instance) as one of the variables that influence organizational life and performance. In summary, this view of culture implies that organizations *have* cultures (see Brooks and Bate, 1994) and further implies that changing cultures is not that difficult given the correct way of going about it.

There is, however, a second view of culture, which interprets the meaning of culture as a metaphor for the concept of organization itself. Thus, Pacanowsky and O'Donnell-Trujillo (1982, p. 126) say: 'Organizational culture is not just another piece of the puzzle. From our point of view, a culture is not something an organization *has*; a culture is something an organization *is*' [authors' emphasis]. This view is echoed by Morgan (1986), who uses the metaphor 'organizations as cultures' as one of a range of metaphors that present different images of organization. Morgan's definition of culture gives some sense of this. He says:

> Shared meaning, shared understanding and shared sense making are all different ways of describing culture. In talking about culture we are really talking about a process of reality construction that allows people to see and understand particular events, actions, objects, utterances, or situations in distinctive ways. These patterns of understanding also provide a basis for making one's own behaviour sensible and meaningful.   (p. 128)

Morgan maintains that, in doing this, members of organizations are, in fact, creating the organization itself. In essence this means that organizations are *socially* constructed realities and that, rather than being defined by their structures, rules and regulations, they are constructed as much in the heads and minds of their members and are strongly related to members' self-concepts and identity. Taking this view of culture implies that, if understanding of an organization's culture is to be reached, it is necessary to look at the routine aspects of everyday life as well as at the more obvious and more public signs, symbols and ceremonies, which are more frequently associated with organizational leaders. It also implies a requirement to examine how culture is created and sustained. This means recognizing that culture is part of a much bigger historical pattern, and therefore that 'more often it is a *recurrence* rather than just an occurrence' (see Bate, 1996, p. 29). A model of organizational culture which appears to bring together the idea of culture as congruent with everything that happens in an organization is Johnson, Scholes and Whittington's (2005, pp. 201–5) 'cultural web' as described in Illustration 4.3.

The cultural web

It can be seen from Illustration 4.3 that the cultural web is all-encompassing in the organizational elements that it includes. Johnson (1990), Johnson and Scholes (1999) and Johnson *et al.* (2005) draw attention to the influence of prevailing organizational paradigms (i.e. the beliefs and assumptions of the people making up the organization) in any attempt to bring about strategic change. The link between the beliefs and assumptions making up the paradigm and other aspects of organizational functioning is exemplified in the statement by Johnson *et al.* (2005, pp. 47–8) that: 'It would be a mistake to conceive of the paradigm as merely a set of beliefs and assumptions removed from organizational action. They lie within a cultural web which bonds them to the day-to-day action of organizational life.'

These authors probably do not go as far as Morgan in equating culture fully with organization, but neither do they completely objectify culture as separate

Illustration 4.3

The cultural web

Johnson *et al.* explain the different elements of the cultural web as follows:

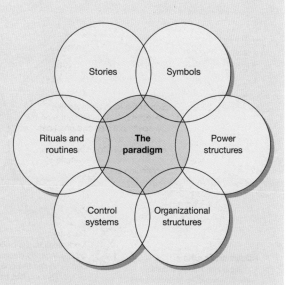

- The *routine* ways that members of the organization behave towards each other and that link different parts of the organization comprise 'the way we do things around here', which at their best lubricate the working of the organization and may provide a distinctive and beneficial organizational competency. However, they can also represent a taken-for-grantedness about how things should happen that is extremely difficult to change and highly protective of core assumptions in the paradigm.
- The *rituals* of organizational life, such as training programmes, promotion and assessment, point to what is important in the organization, reinforce 'the way we do things around here' and signal what is important and valued.
- The *stories* told by members of the organization to each other, to outsiders, to new recruits and so on, embed the present in its organizational history and flag up important events and personalities, as well as mavericks who 'deviate from the norm'.
- The more *symbolic* aspects of organizations, such as logos, offices, cars and titles or the type of language and terminology commonly used, become a shorthand representation of the nature of the organization.
- The *control systems*, measurements and reward systems emphasize what it is important to monitor in the organization and to focus attention and activity on.

- *Power structures* are also likely to be associated with the key constructs of the paradigm. The most powerful managerial groupings in the organization are likely to be the ones most associated with core assumptions and beliefs about what is important.
- The *formal organizational structure* or the more informal ways in which the organizations work are likely to reflect power structures and, again, to delineate important relationships and emphasize what is important in the organization.

Source: Based on Johnson, G., Scholes, K., and Whittington, R. (2005) *Exploring Corporate Strategy, Texts and Cases*, 7th edn (Pearson Education, Harlow, pp. 201–5).

from other aspects of organizational life. In addition, the subtitle of Johnson's (1990) article, 'the role of symbolic action', illustrates the emphasis put upon the rituals or routines, stories or myths, and symbols elements of the cultural web in any attempt to bring about change resulting in a shift in the organizational paradigm. For Johnson (1996), changing organizational structures, control systems and even power structures will not necessarily bring about a paradigm shift. He argues that, for this to happen, a much greater effort must be put into bringing about changes in the other elements of the cultural web.

Illustration 4.4

A cultural web of Paper Unlimited, a large UK-based paper distributor

Stories
- Son of the founder (recently deceased) and his influence on the company policies and practices – a people-oriented company
- Frequent need to expand paper stacking space as example of continuing success

Symbols
- New building and warehouses
- Swimming pool and leisure facilities for employees and families
- IIP award
- Quality award
- Award for excellence in the use of IT

Rituals and routines
- Walk-about management – always available to employees
- Management can be interrupted
- Lots of talking
- Yearly employee/family outing

Paradigm
Dedicated to the philosophy laid down by the recently deceased original owner's son, who ran the company for over 40 years. This implies being:
- A people-oriented organization also dedicated to high task performance
- Provider of long-term employment
- Aware of success while also aware of the need continuously to analyze the environment to detect new markets
- Committed to incremental rather than radical changes

Power structures
- Long-serving managers and workforce
- Can 'work your way up'
- Positions based on expertise in the business rather than on qualifications
- Paternalistic style of management
- Emphasis on continuity
- Relaxed attitudes
- Cooperation at head office, competition between the branches where selling occurs

Controls
- IT controls most operations
- Error measurement
- Help given to improve

Organization structure
- Hierarchical at head office – bureaucracy with a human face
- Teamworking in the branches with team-based rewards
- Profit-related pay
- Responsibilities clearly defined

Activity 4.2 *Creating a cultural web for your organization*

Illustration 4.4 shows the cultural web for an organization involved in buying paper in bulk and then cutting and preparing it for sale to large-scale paper users.*

Using this as a guide, construct a cultural web for an organization you know well (or if it is large, one particular division or department).

If you wished to institute change at the strategic level, how would you go about changing the rituals or routines, stories and symbols elements of your cultural web?

*Additional examples of the use of the cultural web can be found in Johnson and Scholes (1997, pp. 70 and 460–1), and Johnson, Scholes and Whittington (2005, pp. 201–5).

Johnson and Scholes's cultural web has been applied mainly to organizational cultures. In contrast, Morgan's proposal that organizations *are* cultures discusses (among other things) differences in national cultures, including the way these have formed through historical processes. The notion of culture as a metaphor for organization also encompasses the concept of sub-cultures. This is reinforced by Alvesson (1993), who recommends combining perspectives at three levels. These are:

1 the organization as a culture (unitary and unique);
2 the organization as a meeting place for great cultures (which includes national ethnic and class cultures);
3 local perspectives on organizational sub-cultures.

From this point of view, in order to analyze organizational culture, it is necessary to understand the mixture of cultural manifestations at all three levels. The methods for describing culture just discussed can be used to describe culture at the organizational and sub-organizational levels. However, the results of Hall's (1995) research offer a model that appears to accommodate descriptions of culture at all levels. Hall's compass model of culture and its associated culture typologies have been developed through an apparent interest in cultural differences in 'partnerships', by which she means inter-company relationships that may be in the form of alliances, mergers, acquisitions or some other form. From her research, she claims to have identified two components of behaviour or cultural styles of behaviour.

The first of these is *assertiveness*, which is the degree to which a company's behaviours are seen by others as being forceful or directive. She says:

Companies which behave in high assertive ways are seen to be decisive, quick and firm. There is little hesitation in their action. If they introduce a new product or enter a new market they do so with full force. ... Low assertive companies behave in more slow and steady ways. They are careful to consider what they do before they take firm action. They introduce a new product or enter a new market step by step, keeping their options open. Unlike the one-track mind of the high assertive company, the low assertive company has a 'multi-track mind'.

(Hall, 1995, p. 52)

The second behavioural component of culture is *responsiveness*, which is the degree to which a company's behaviours are seen by others as being emotionally expressed. Thus:

> Companies which behave in high responsive ways are seen to be employee friendly, relaxed or spontaneous. These companies give the impression that they compete on feelings more than on facts. In industry gatherings, high responsive companies tend to be very 'likable'. They seem more open than other companies. Low responsive companies behave in more reserved or closed ways. They are not so much liked as 'respected'. They tend to be more rigid, their employees serious. Low responsive companies compete more on facts than on feelings.
>
> (Hall, 1995, pp. 54–5)

Illustration 4.5 lists the behaviours that indicate high and low assertiveness and responsiveness. An example of a moderately assertive but more highly responsive organization is given in Illustration 4.6.

Illustration 4.5

Assertive and responsive behaviours

Behaviours that indicate high and (low) assertiveness are:
- individualistic
- demanding rather than obliging
- taking control
- pushy
- authoritative
- charging ahead
- challenging
- hardworking
- quick moving
- (low) cautious (indecisive).

Behaviours that indicate high and (low) responsiveness are:
- sensitive
- loyal
- compromising
- trusting
- team players
- value harmony
- unpredictable
- (low) quantitative rather than qualitative
- (low) factual rather than emotional
- (low) precise rather than inexact
- (low) task rather than people oriented
- (low) consistent (methodological).

Source: Hall, W. (1995), *Managing Cultures. Making Strategic Relationships Work* (Chichester, Wiley, pp. 54–5).

Hall maintains that the four different combinations of the two behavioural components she has identified result in four different cultural styles. Figure 4.3 illustrates why this model is called the compass model in that each of the four styles is labelled as one of the four points of the compass.

Hall claims, on the basis of her research, that the compass model with its four culture styles can be used to analyze culture, not only across a single organization, but also with respect to individuals, departments and the industry and nation within which an organization operates. Consequently she claims that the model can be used to compare cultural relationships between organizations,

RS Components – a moderately assertive but more highly responsive organization

RS Components is a Corby-based company that supplies, from a mail order catalogue, a range of components varying from capacitors, bearings, bushes and seals to cleaning agents, fastenings and power tools to trade organizations and organizations and members of the public. However, as one of the product buyers says: 'The company sells just one thing and that is service to the customer.'

Visiting the company, one is struck by the quiet efficiency with which orders are taken by around 100 staff, working in specially designed open-plan environments. Orders are taken at the rate of some 20,000 a day and a customer service standard of answering any telephone call within 5 seconds is maintained. In the order-taking areas overhead displays give continuous information on the number of orders taken that day, the number of customers waiting and the number of staff available and waiting to take calls.

Within 15 minutes of an order being taken it is received in the huge warehouse where product-collecting containers travel on rail-type tracks around the shelves holding the products to take the quickest route past 'pickers' who fill them to satisfy the order, before continuing to the packing and despatch areas. The company guarantees delivery the day after the order is taken or the same day if required. The complete operation, from a customer requesting a product to its despatch, is computer controlled. At any time, computer displays give up-to-the-second information about any part of the process.

RS Components is not, however, just a distributor of products that are required in a hurry. It also offers technical advice and support on the range of products it sells, thus increasing the probability of achieving nearly 100 per cent satisfied customers.

Through its large, on-the-road sales staff and other market intelligence-gathering activities, it is successful in keeping up with projected market demands. Yet it does not act hastily in offering a full service for the latest emerging products. If a new product appears to fit the company's selling policy, buyers will proceed cautiously in holding small stocks of the item until the demand can be more clearly discerned. As the demand becomes more established the item will be stocked in quantities appropriate to meet customers' needs and the 'boast' to be able to supply the day after order.

Given the high level of computerization that also allows almost every employee to be monitored, it might be thought that care for employees comes some distance after attention to the task. It is clear, however, to anyone spending time in the company, that care for employees is important. Every employee is identified by name, either by a name 'tag' attached to his or her computer (if one of the staff taking orders) or attached to their workstation (if in the 'pick and pack' warehouse). With a fairly large workforce, this enables everyone, whether known to each other or not, to address others by their name. The majority of staff work in teams that, although led by a team leader, are to a large extent self-managing.

Wages are slightly above the average for the type of work and pleasant restaurant facilities are available. The site the company occupies includes garden areas where staff can sit or walk in break times. A series of different start and finish times are available to suit the demands of the business, but these also provide flexible working hours to suit the different needs of different employees.

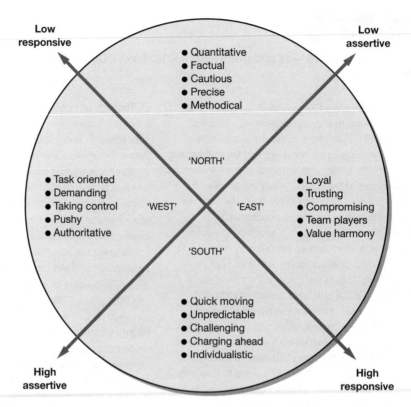

Figure 4.3 The compass model: characteristics of each style

Source: Reprinted by permission of John Wiley and Sons Ltd. Hall, W. (1995), *Managing Cultures: Making Strategic Relationships Work* (Chichester, Wiley, p. 58).

nations and between one part of a multinational corporation and another. The choice of the 'compass' analogy seems to be derived from the identification of different national cultures and the positioning of these in terms of the points of a compass. As illustration of this, Figure 4.4 plots seven different countries on the assertiveness–responsiveness cultural style dimensions.

It should be noted that, in Figure 4.4, the further to the edge of the plot, the more extreme the cultural style. For instance, West Germany has a very high assertive, very low responsive cultural style, while Italy is more moderately placed on both of the cultural style dimensions. France is almost in the middle of the responsiveness dimension, but higher on the assertiveness scale. These results were based on a total of 211 responses from executives with experience of living and working in the seven countries represented. However, it should be noted that the executives were not, necessarily, of the nationalities on which they gave their views. These views were mainly those of executives who had, through their own work across national boundaries, experience of managers from the countries in the sample. It is not clear, therefore, how much the executives who were questioned were working from stereotypes of the managers on whom they were giving their views. In addition, the research used a sample of

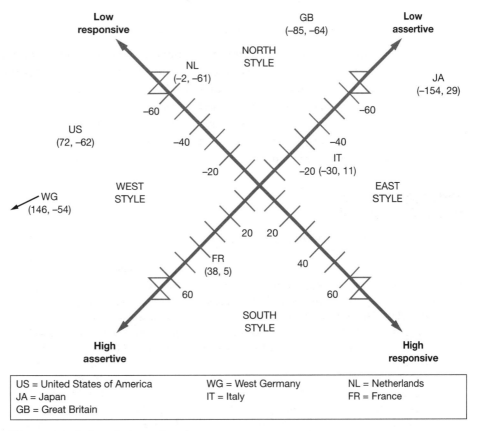

US = United States of America	WG = West Germany	NL = Netherlands
JA = Japan	IT = Italy	FR = France
GB = Great Britain		

Figure 4.4 Cultural plots of nations

Source: Reprinted by permission of John Wiley & Sons Ltd. Hall, W. (1995), *Managing Cultures: Making Strategic Relationships Work* (Chichester, Wiley, p. 95).

executives from two industries only – the automobile industry and the high-technology industry. Given these reservations, Hall's typology is detailed and comprehensive. It attempts to link Alvesson's (1993) three levels of culture and more. In addition, it points at one of the influences on organizational culture through its focus on differences between national cultures.

It is clear however that, in line with models of culture such as Robbins's discussed earlier, Hall's model is an example of an attempt to 'objectify', and so measure, culture. The result is to identify a number of different types of culture. Regardless of whether an objectivist or interpretive perspective on organizational culture is adopted, forming a 'typology' of cultures in this kind of way is useful as a device for describing organizational culture – even if it does not capture the richness of description that more qualitative, ethnographic studies of culture do. Consequently, it is useful to consider other organizational culture typologies that, as Hall's model does, allow a relatively easy comparison of one culture with another. These can, for the purpose of the discussion, be posed as 'dimensions' of organizational culture.

Dimensions of organizational culture

The structural view of culture

Structural views of culture inevitably draw on descriptions of different structural forms for their expression. One of the leading proponents of this view is Handy (1993) who draws on Harrison's (1972) studies in this respect. Handy refers to organizational culture as atmosphere, ways of doing things, levels of energy and levels of individual freedom – or collectively, the 'sets of values and norms and beliefs – reflected in different structures and systems' (p. 180). On the basis of Harrison's studies, he suggests four organizational culture types. Illustration 4.7 describes these.

Illustration 4.7

A structural view of organizational culture

The power culture

Power cultures are those in which a single person or group tends to dominate. Handy refers to this culture as a web in the sense that the spider in the middle controls what happens throughout the organization. Decision making is centralized. This type of culture is seen as, essentially, political in that decisions are taken on the basis of influence rather than through a logical rational process. Power is held by the centre by virtue of personal charisma or the control of resources. Family businesses, small entrepreneurial companies and occasionally trade unions are likely to have this type of culture. The strength of this type of culture depends on the strength of the centre and the willingness of other organizational members to defer to this power source. Handy likens this culture to the Greek god Zeus who ruled by whim and impulse, by thunderbolt and shower of gold from Mount Olympus.

The role culture

Handy likens role cultures to a *Greek temple*. The patron god here is Apollo, the god of reason, the argument being that role cultures work by logic and rationality. The pillars of the temple are strong in their own right and activity is controlled more by rules and regulations than by personal directive from the top. The pediment of the temple is seen as coordinating activity rather than overtly controlling it. Emphasis is on defined roles and occupants are expected to fulfil these but not overstep them. Role cultures flourish in stable situations and a sellers' market.

The task culture

The task culture is represented by a *net*. The dominant concept in a task culture is project work associated with matrix-type structures. Handy pushes the Greek god association somewhat here in suggesting Athena, whose emphasis was on getting the job done. The task culture, therefore, is not particularly concerned with personal power or hierarchy, but with marshalling the required resources to complete work efficiently and effectively. Decision making is devolved to the project groups to enhance flexibility of working method and speed the outcomes. The task culture is said to flourish where creativity and innovation are desirable, particularly in organizations concerned with such activities as research and development, marketing, advertising and new ventures.

The person culture

According to Handy, this culture is an unusual one. It exists only to service the needs of the participating members. It does not have an overarching objective such as is found in more conventionally structured organizations. Examples of person cultures are barristers' chambers, doctors' centres, hippy communes and small consultancy firms. Person cultures have minimal structures and can be likened to a cluster or galaxy of individual stars. Handy proposes Dionysus as its patron deity – the god of the self-oriented individual.

Source: Based on Handy, C. (1993). *Understanding Organizations* (London, Penguin, pp. 183–91).

Handy does not claim high levels of rigour for the descriptions given in Illustration 4.7, saying that a culture cannot be defined precisely. However, these descriptions could be used to determine a particular organization's way of doing things. Pheysey (1993) builds on Handy's and Harrison's typologies to propose a categorization of role, power, support and achievement cultures. The definitions of role and power cultures are those used by Handy, with support and achievement cultures having similar characteristics to Handy's task and person cultures. However Pheysey goes beyond Handy in linking her four types of culture not only to organizational structure (i.e. the design of organizations) but also to control systems, employee motivation, leadership styles and organization development.

Activity 4.3 *The strategy/structure–culture link*

Look back at the discussion of Miles and Snow's typologies of strategic behaviour and Mintzberg's organizational forms in Chapter 3 and assess how well or poorly they fit with the types of culture proposed by Handy and Pheysey.

Organizational culture and the external environment

It is hoped that the results of Activity 4.3 show how a view of culture, such as those of Handy and Pheysey, link closely to organizational structure and, by extension, to the strategies that organizations pursue. These culture typologies are mainly concerned with the internal environment of organizations (see the discussion in Chapter 1). By contrast, Deal and Kennedy's (1982) four culture types of the tough-guy, macho culture, the work-hard/play-hard culture, the bet-your-company culture and the process culture, link more closely to the external environment (the marketplace) of the organization. Illustration 4.8 gives a detailed description of these.

Illustration 4.8

The Deal and Kennedy typology

From their examination of hundreds of companies Deal and Kennedy (1982) claim to have identified four generic cultures.

The tough-guy, macho culture
These organizations are peopled with individuals who regularly take high risks and receive rapid feedback on the outcomes of their actions. Examples cited are police departments, surgeons, publishing, sports and the entertainment industry. In

tough-guy, macho cultures the stakes are high and there is a focus on speed rather than endurance. Staff in these cultures tend to be young and financial rewards come early, but failure is punished severely through 'the sack'. Burnout is likely before middle age is reached. Internal competition and conflict are normal and this means tantrums are tolerated and everyone tries to score points off each other. However, while tough-guy cultures can be highly

Illustration 4.8 *continued*

successful in high-risk, quick-return environments they are less suited to making long-term investments. Being unable to benefit from cooperative activity, these organizations tend to have a high turnover of staff and thus often fail to develop a strong and cohesive culture.

The work-hard/play-hard culture

This culture exists in organizations where there is low risk but quick feedback on actions – the world of sales organizations that incorporate hard work and fun. Examples are Avon, Mary Kay cosmetics and encyclopedia companies as well as companies such as McDonald's. Persistence, keeping at it and working to recognized procedures are typical of work-hard/play-hard cultures. In these cultures, the risks are small because no individual sale will severely damage the salesperson. In addition production systems are built to withstand temporary hitches or deviations from normal. However, being selling oriented, all employees gain quick feedback on their performance. Heroes in these organizations are the super salespeople who turn in volume sales. Contests, conventions and other means of encouraging intense selling are used. Yet the culture emphasizes the team because it is the team that makes the difference, not the achievements of single individuals. However, although work/play cultures can achieve sales volumes, this can be at the expense of quality – they frequently forget that success may be 'one shot' only.

Bet-your-company culture

These cultures are typical of organizations where the risks are high and the feedback on actions and decisions takes a long time. Bet-your-company organizations are those that invest millions or billions in projects which take years to come to fruition. Examples include large aircraft manufacturers such as Boeing, oil companies such as Mobil and large-systems businesses. In contrast to tough-guy cultures, people working in bet-your-company cultures bet the company rather than themselves. Consequently there is a sense of deliberateness that

manifests itself in ritualized business meetings. All decisions are carefully weighed and based on considered research. Decision making tends to be top down, reflecting the hierarchical nature of the organization. The survivors in these organizations respect authority and technical competence and have the stamina to endure long-term ambiguity with limited feedback. They will act cooperatively, and have proved themselves over a number of years – immaturity is not tolerated in this culture. Bet-your-company cultures lead to high-quality inventions and major scientific breakthroughs, but their slow response times make them vulnerable to short-term economic fluctuations in the economy. However, it is said that these companies may be those that the economy most needs.

The process culture

This culture is typical of organizations where there is low risk and slow feedback on actions and decisions. Examples are banks, insurance companies, public and government organizations and other heavily regulated industries. Working with little feedback, employees have no sense of their own effectiveness or otherwise.

Consequently they tend to concentrate on the means by which things are done rather than what should be done. Values tend to focus on technical perfection, working out the risks and getting the process right. Protecting one's back is what most employees will do, so the people who prosper are those who are orderly and punctual and who attend to detail. The ability to weather political storms and changes becomes a desirable trait. In process cultures there is considerable emphasis on job titles and status and the signs that symbolize them, such as style of office furniture. Position power is desired. Staying with the organization is revered by the institution of long-service awards. Process cultures are effective when dealing with a stable and predictable environment, but find it difficult to react quickly to changing circumstances. On a positive note, they offer a counterpoint to the other three cultures just described

Deal and Kennedy's typology was constructed in the early 1980s. While the cultural types may still be relevant and can be found in today's organizations, it is arguable whether the examples of each type that Deal and Kennedy give still hold today. In later writings (Deal and Kennedy, 2000, p. 169), they also agree that assumptions from the previous decade needed to be revised. For instance, banks (as examples of process cultures) have evolved more into sales-type organizations but do not, perhaps, yet fit the work-hard/play-hard culture suggested for sales-oriented companies. Figure 4.5 shows Trompenaars and Prud'homme's (2004, p. 67) depiction of these four types with more up-to-date examples of each culture.

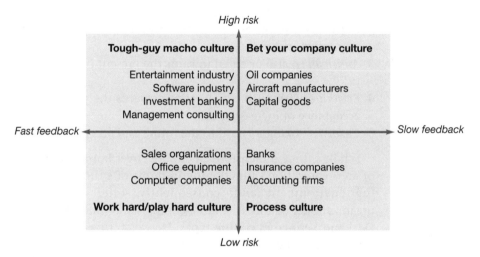

Figure 4.5 Deal and Kennedy model for corporate culture

Source: Reprinted by permission of John Wiley & Sons Ltd on behalf of Capstone Publishing Ltd. Trompenaars, F. and Prud'homme, P. (2004), *Managing change across corporate cultures* (Chichester, Capstone Publishing).

Many government agencies in the United Kingdom have become 'privatized' in the way they operate and are moving away from the process-oriented culture of old. It is also clear that organizations do not always fit neatly into one typology or another. Through discussions in Chapter 3 it was evident that organizations may sustain more than one structure at any given time. This, inevitably, gives rise to difficulties in describing a particular organization's culture and in choosing which framework of typologies to use.

Organizational culture, structure, strategy and the external environment

The discussion so far has addressed perspectives on organizational culture that link it, separately, to the internal and external environments of the organization in terms of organizational structure and the marketplace in which organizations operate. Someone who brings these two dimensions together along with a third is Scholz (1987), who uses the terms evolution-induced, internal-induced and external-induced culture dimensions. The external-induced dimension of organizational culture draws directly on the work of Deal and Kennedy and Scholz uses Deal and Kennedy's four culture types to represent this dimension. The internal-induced dimension identifies three culture types (production, bureaucratic and professional) that are derived from organizational structure characteristics. The final cultural dimension, which is where Scholz goes beyond the earlier models, is the evolution-induced dimension. This dimension is related to the strategic orientation of the organization. Five possible culture types are identified as follows:

1 *Stable*, with a time orientation towards the past and an aversion to risk.
2 *Reactive*, with a time orientation towards the present and an acceptance of 'minimum' risk.
3 *Anticipating*, also oriented towards the present but more accepting of 'familiar' risks.
4 *Exploring*, with a time orientation towards the present and the future and an acceptance of increasing risk.
5 *Creative*, looking forward to the future and accepting risk as normal.

Scholz's three dimensions of culture cover both internal and external aspects of an organization's functioning in terms of structure, strategy and the operating environment and, consequently, offer a possibility of describing organizational culture in a more complex way than that offered by Handy's and Deal and Kennedy's culture types. However, there is no suggestion of how cultures of one type rather than another can be identified. This is in contrast with Robbins's and Hall's methods of describing culture, which can be done using questionnaire-based, quantitative techniques.

By the same token some researchers, particularly those who subscribe to the interpretive view of culture, would say that organizational culture is much too complex a phenomenon to be measured through questionnaire and other similar quantitative-based methods. They suggest the need to use more qualitative techniques such as observation, interviews, focus groups and an ethnographic approach, as exemplified in Brooks and Bate's (1994, p. 178) study of a UK government agency through '(immersion) in the minutiae of everyday life' of the organization.

What is more, qualitative techniques for identifying culture are more likely to reveal something of the sources from which current cultures spring.

Activity 4.4

Critically evaluate Scholz's evolution-induced dimension with Miles and Snow's identification of the evolution of organizational forms in Table 3.1 in Chapter 3. How far can you 'map' each of Scholz's evolution-induced types of culture to each of Miles and Snow's corporate strategies and forms?

The sources of organizational culture

The influence of organizational history

Illustrations 4.9 and 4.10 are summaries of the attempts of two multinational organizations (from quite different industries) to introduce overall company cultures from disparate sub-cultures prevailing among their varied product and geographical divisions. Later sections of this chapter discuss the issues associated with attempts such as these to bring about culture change.

Illustration 4.9

The making of a modern HSBC Group

When the Hong Kong and Shanghai Banking Corporation acquired the Mercantile Bank and the British Bank of the Middle East in 1959, it laid the foundations of today's HSBC Group. The first part of this historic story begins in 1865, when the founder opened a bank to finance the growing trade between Europe, India and China.

Over the course of time there have been numerous milestones with this diverse company. There have been a series of takeovers and acquisitions and the company has grown through these subsidiary companies, however it has continued to use their expertise and experience in whatever country the acquisitions were located in. Late in the 1980s there was the acquisition of Midlands Bank Canada, and Midland Bank in 1992. By 2003 there were in excess of 20 companies/subsidiaries. At this stage most of the interests were operating individually in their respective countries and it was not until 1991 that HSBC Holdings created this name as an umbrella for all of its businesses.

Further developments in 1993 meant that the Head Office, which was originally in Hong Kong, had moved to London due to UK regulatory requirements. Although the Bank of England became the lead regulator for HSBC Holdings the banking subsidiaries continued to be regulated locally in their own country of operation.

It is at this stage that the strategy of the Group progressed with positive work to create a corporate culture by integrating and consolidating all of the businesses. It standardized the offices of New York and Tokyo by integrating technology. HSBC began to draw together key business areas, so the larger groups as a whole benefited from a greater level of coordination and commitment to effective technology and training. In April 2003 the Group relocated to London's Docklands, which furthered the effectiveness relating to logistics and working conditions for over 8,000 staff. The number of countries HSBC was trading in by 2003 was 79.

Once the move was completed, it updated the corporate strategy that included a slogan used worldwide: 'The World's Local Bank', emphasizing and celebrating the Group's experience and understanding of a great variety of markets and cultures. The adoption of a single Group identity had simplified the task of consolidating and developing HSBC's role in the community.

HSBC currently occupies a leading position in the world of banking and finance. Its international network now spans six continents and serves almost 100 million customers worldwide. The group is truly international and reflects the long history of its member companies throughout the world. The history and development of HSBC has put it in a strong position to meet the challenges of the continually changing environment of the twenty-first century.

Source: www.hsbc.com

Illustration 4.10

Driving change: an interview with Ford Motor Company's Jacques Nasser

In an interview for the *Harvard Business Review* (1999) Jacques Nasser, Chief Executive Officer of Ford Motor Company, speaks of his attempt to bring about radical change in the company 'mind-set' of everyone working there. According to the interview account, Nasser is asking his employees (apparently all 340,000 in 200 countries) 'to think and act as if they own the company'. (In fact they do, to the extent of 20 per cent of the outstanding stock.) 'To adopt, in other words, the capital markets' view of Ford – to look at the company in its entirety, as shareholders do.' Nasser says that this is 'a radically different mentality for Ford'. This mentality (or culture as it might be termed in the context of this discussion) is very different from the one that has, apparently, prevailed for much of the time since the company was formed 95 years ago – one Nasser describes as: 'A collection of fiercely independent fiefdoms united under the flag of their functional or regional expertise'. Each division in this 'collection' appears to have its own organizational sub-culture for which, as Nasser comments, there were 'legitimate historical reasons'.

Elaborating on this he says: 'Think about Ford's history in three chunks: from its founding in 1905 to the early 1920s, the late 1920s through to the 1950s, and the 1960s through the 1980s.' The first period was one of 'colonization' and the opening of assembly plants (which were smaller versions of the original company in Detroit) in other countries, but with very little competition from other automotive companies. The second period was one of 'intense nationalism' with large automotive companies growing up in the United Kingdom, France, Germany, Australia, all making their own vehicles and exporting them to others – but in their own regions. The third period saw the rise of regionalism and the emergence of the European common market and the North American Free Trade Association (NAFTA). It was this period that saw the entrenchment of the regional and functional fiefdoms.

Nasser comments that, given the prevailing environment at that time, this arrangement worked very well: squeezing 'every last ounce of efficiency out of the regional model'. However, he goes on to say that this model does not work any more in the current environment of increasing globalization of capital, communications, economic policy, trade policy, human resources, marketing, advertising, brands – and so on. Consequently there is a perceived need to 'reinvent' Ford as a global organization with a single focus on consumers and shareholder value.

Nasser talks of striving for some kind of DNA that drives how Ford does things everywhere. This includes a global mind-set, an intuitive knowledge of customers and a strong belief in leaders as teachers. However, this does not mean that the same products are produced and sold everywhere. What it does mean is that, although Ford cars have many common systems that bring scale efficiencies, they can also be tailored to individual local markets. What is more, although Ford would like to see common reward systems for staff wherever they work, Nasser recognizes that different cultures have different attitudes to pay and rewards, for instance about the balance between fixed and variable rewards. What is also clear is that in some countries (with Australia as an example) the tax and other laws require different attitudes to employment, stock purchase and so on.

Having said all this, it is clear that Nasser is looking for a significant cultural shift from one suited to the conditions of the past to one that recognizes the conditions of the present and the future. The article describes, in some detail, the approach being taken to help this to happen – an approach based on a multi-faceted teaching initiative, led by senior and middle managers and aimed, eventually, at all Ford employees wherever they are located. Nasser says: 'The Ford you see today has no resemblance to the Ford of five years ago. If you dissected us and inspected every blood vessel, we're different; our DNA has changed. I don't think we'll go back.'

Source: Based on Nasser, J. and Wetlaufer, S. (1999). 'Driving change: an interview with Ford Motor Company's Jacques Nasser', *Harvard Business Review*, March–April, pp. 76–88.

Other accounts, for instance the cultural barriers to change associated with the incorporation of a college, which provided pre- and post-registration nursing and midwifery education, into a much larger institution, within the university sector (see Hill and McNulty, 1998); a newly semi-privatized British Civil Service department (see Brookes and Bate, 1994) and Ogbonna and Harris's (1998) description of changes in a major retailing organization tell similar tales of the large influences that historical factors and the long-standing cultures of each institution had on the process of the change.

All these accounts confirm the views of a well-known academic researcher in this field who commented, back in 1981, that: 'The subculture of an organization reflects national culture, professional subculture, and the organization's own history' (Hofstede, 1981, p. 27).

Regarding the last of these, Robbins (2001) emphasizes how the philosophy of the organization's founder and, as time passes, the top management define acceptable behaviour. The importance of leadership as a source of organizational culture is discussed by Brown (1995), who cites the example of Henry Ford (who started the Ford Motor Company), as well as Ken Olsen at Digital Equipment Corporation and Gerard and Anton Philips at Philips. Sir John Harvey-Jones is well known for his influence at ICI and is an example of a leader continuing, through his writings, to influence the business scene with his views beyond his retirement. The cultural web of Paper Unlimited (see Illustration 4.4) is almost wholly derived from the way the company founder's son and long-time managing director established an organizational philosophy while setting up the organization's structure, operating systems and procedures, criteria for recruitment and promotion and the style of management to be observed. Through his own behaviour, he was an example of how he wanted the company managed and run.

The influence of history is not, however, limited to the influence of particular people of importance to an organization. A broader influence is referred to by Hofstede (1981, p. 27) who says: 'The rules of behaviour in industrial workshops in the nineteenth century were modelled after those in armies and monasteries. The structure and functioning of organizations are determined not merely by rationality, or, if they are, by rationality that varies according to the cultural environment.' Goodman's (1995) discussion of the different ages of wealth creation described in Chapter 1 is evidence of the way historical processes influence all aspects of organizational functioning including an organization's culture. Even so, these processes and their timing are not the same for every society. They will be modified to some extent by the national culture in which they take place.

The influence of national culture

A survey of the literature on the cultural similarities and differences between nations identifies a long-standing debate known popularly as the convergence–divergence debate. In summary, those who support the convergence view argue that the forces of industrialization (for instance, see Kerr, Dunlop, Harbison and Myers, 1960) and the use of similar technologies (see Castells, 1989; Woodward, 1965) as well as increasing size (see Chandler, 1962; Pugh and Hickson, 1976; Hickson and MacMillan, 1981) will push organizations, whatever their location, towards particular configurations with respect to strategy, structure and management. In addition, the growth of international organizations and those who trade abroad increases the need for 'international managers' who bring common management practices to all parts of their organizations wherever they are in the world. In support of this view, Ohmae (1991) puts forward the concept of the 'global organization', which has no national allegiance, only an international common purpose. Furthermore, Ohmae argues for 'getting rid of the headquarters mentality', implying the possibility that an organization's national cultural base will have no influence on the culture of the organization itself. While not directly advocating what Ohmae says, the account of Jacques Nasser's change programme at Ford Motor Company (see Illustration 4.10) is an example of Nasser's vision to eliminate the regional 'fiefdoms' built up over a long period of time. He speaks of the markets valuing a global approach to business – 'an approach in which a company's units, divisions, teams, functions, and regions are all tightly integrated and synchronized across borders' (p. 78).

In contrast to this view is the notion that differences in countries' languages, religions, social organization, laws, politics, education systems, and values and attitudes (Hofstede, 1980; Tayeb, 1989; Wilson, 1992) will, of necessity, mean that one nation's culture will diverge significantly from another's. For instance, Knightley (2000) in his book *Australia: Biography of a Nation* maintains that the geographic isolation of the country brought populations and cultures (Aboriginals, British and Irish convicts and their overseers, post-war refugees and Asian boat people) together into interaction that created a society with its own peculiar ways of doing things. It is interesting to note that Jacques Nasser (see Illustration 4.10) had to make separate arrangements for Australia regarding his Ford Motor Company-wide policy to roll out a worldwide employee stock-purchase programme because of the different tax regime there. It is still too early to know what influence e-commerce (both business to customer and business to business) and the increasing pressures on organizations to operate globally will have on the convergence or continuing divergence of national cultures. However, there is sufficient evidence of national cultural differences for the influence of national culture on organizational culture to be taken seriously.

The diversity of national cultures

There is an expanding body of research that claims to have identified *how* cultures vary. Illustration 4.11 summarizes a frequently referenced framework – that of Kluckhohn and Strodtbeck (1961) – who claim there are six basic dimensions that describe the cultural orientation of societies.

Illustration 4.11

Six different cultural orientations of societies

1 *People's qualities as individuals in terms of whether people are seen as basically good or basically bad*. Societies that consider people good tend to trust people, while those that consider people bad tend to start from a premise of mistrust and suspicion.

2 *People's relationship to their world*. Some societies believe they can dominate their environment while others believe the environment and themselves to be inseparable and, therefore, that they must live in harmony with it.

3 *People's personal relationships in terms of individualism or collectivism*. Some societies encourage individualism and the notion of being self-supporting with achievement being based on individual worth; while others are more group-oriented, where people define themselves as members of clans or communities (which might be the work organization) and consider the group's welfare to be more important than the individual.

4 *An orientation to either doing or being*. Societies that are doing and action-oriented stress accomplishments which are measurable by standards believed to be external to the individual; societies oriented to being are more passive, believing that work should be enjoyed and they should live more for the moment.

5 *People's orientation to time*. Some societies are past-oriented, believing that current plans and actions should fit with the customs and traditions of the past, while future-oriented societies justify innovation and change in terms of future pay-offs, believing radical change to be desirable as well as acceptable.

6 *People's use of space*. Societies differ on such matters as offices in relation to status, the designation of public space compared to private space, the separation of managers from subordinates.

Both Adler (1997) and Robbins (1996) draw on Kluckhohn and Strodtbeck's framework in their discussions of societal and national cultures. In her book, Adler gives many examples of differences between societies and nations on these cultural dimensions. Regarding the good–evil dimension or trust–mistrust dimension, the way one group of people regards another will differ according to whether they set off with the assumption that people are trustworthy or that all people will cheat if given the opportunity. This translates, for instance, into whether things are kept locked up or not, whether information is freely available and how one group's actions are interpreted by another. Adler contrasts the North Americans with the Chinese and Navaho in terms of the former's belief that they can dominate nature and the latter's belief that they must live in harmony with nature.

She describes Americans' strong individualistic tendencies as evidenced in their language, such as 'trounced the opposition', and their recruitment and promotion practices based on criteria relating to individual knowledge and skills. This contrasts with more group-oriented societies such as Japan, China, Indonesia and Malaysia that put more stress on assignments, responsibilities and reporting relationships in collective terms. People in these societies are more likely to gain employment through personal contacts who can vouch for their trustworthiness and ability to work with others. Finding jobs for family and friends is not seen as unusual or nepotism as it might be in more individualistic societies. Adler makes an interesting comparison between doers and 'be'ers' in their typically different reactions to a salary rise. The doers react to higher pay rates by working more hours because they can earn more. The be'ers react to higher pay rates by working fewer hours, arguing that they can earn the same money in less time, so leaving more time for enjoying life. Offering overtime bonuses may work in 'doing' societies but will not work in 'being' societies.

Adler points out that different time orientations can impact significantly on people's attitudes to timekeeping and punctuality. Different time orientations also bring differences in the length of time someone might be given to show his or her worth in a job. If employees are recruited with the expectation of staying many years with an organization they will not have to show achievement in the short time expected in societies that recruit in the knowledge that the person may move on before very long. Finally, Adler uses the examples of North Americans and Japanese to contrast different societies' attitudes to the use of space. The former prefer closed offices and meetings behind closed doors while the latter prefer open-plan working areas that include managers as well as subordinates. Other interesting differences can be seen in how close one desk is to another and whether an office can be entered without ceremony or whether people must wait outside for permission to enter.

Figure 4.6 is based on Robbins's summary of the Kluckhohn–Strodtbeck framework with a profile for the United States plotted on it. It is obvious, from a reading of these descriptions, that variations will occur within societies as well as between societies. However, evidence from a series of well-known pieces of research (Hofstede, 1980, 1981, 1993, 1994; Hofstede, Neuijen, Ohayv and

Dimensions	Variations		
Nature of people	Good	Mixed	Bad
Relationship to the environment	Domination	Harmony	Subjugation
Focus of responsibility	Individualistic	Group	Hierarchical
Activity orientation	Being	Controlling	Doing
Time orientation	Past	Present	Future
Conception of space	Private	Mixed	Public

Figure 4.6 Variations in Kluckhohn and Strodtbeck's cultural dimensions

Source: Based on Robbins, S. P. (1996), *Organizational Behavior, Concepts, Controversies, Applications* (Englewood Cliffs, NJ, Prentice Hall, p. 56).

Sanders, 1990) appears to support the concept of geographically identifiable, culturally differentiated regions that are based on national boundaries. The major piece of research referred to was carried out in IBM and involved the analysis of questionnaires from some 116,000 employees in 50 different countries. This analysis resulted in the identification of four dimensions, which were found to differentiate national cultural groups. A fifth dimension based on the philosophy of Confucianism (which Hofstede categorized as virtue versus truth or, more simply, long-term versus short-term orientation) was identified by Bond working with a team of 24 Chinese researchers (see Chinese Culture Connection, 1987). Illustration 4.12 describes these.

Illustration 4.12

Hofstede's dimensions of national culture

Power distance

Power distance refers to how a society deals with the fact that people are unequal, for instance in physical and intellectual abilities. Some societies let these inequalities grow over time into inequalities in power and wealth. Other societies try to play down inequalities in power and wealth. In high power distance societies, inequalities of power and wealth are accepted not only by the leaders but also by those at the bottom of the power hierarchy, with corresponding large differences in status and salaries. In low power distance societies, inequalities among people will tend to be minimized, with subordinates expecting to be consulted by superiors over decisions that affect them, and to be treated more as equals of those with the power.

Individualism/collectivism

Individualism/collectivism refers to relationships between an individual and his or her fellow individuals. In an individualistic society, the ties between individuals are very loose. Everybody is expected to look after self-interest and perhaps that of their immediate family. Individuals in these societies have a large amount of freedom of action. In collectivist societies the ties between individuals are very tight. The concept of the extended family is important and can reach work groups and organizations. Everybody is supposed to look after the interests of their in-group, which will protect them when they are in trouble.

Masculinity/femininity

Masculinity/femininity refers to the degree to which social gender roles are clearly distinct. In high-masculinity societies, the social division between the sexes is maximized, with traditional masculine social values permeating the society. These values include the importance of showing off, of making money and of 'big is beautiful'. In more feminine societies, the dominant values – for both men and women – are those more traditionally associated with the feminine role of nurturing and caring, putting relationships before money, minding the quality of life and 'small is beautiful'.

Uncertainty avoidance

Uncertainly avoidance refers to how a society deals with the fact that time runs only one way – from the past to the future – and that the future is unknown and, therefore, uncertain. Some societies accept this uncertainty and do not get upset about it; others seek to reduce the uncertainty as much as possible. People in weak uncertainty-avoidance societies tend to accept each day as it comes and are comfortable with a higher degree of risk taking. Societies demonstrating strong uncertainty-avoidance characteristics socialize their people into trying to beat the future. Precision and punctuality are important in a context of fear of ambiguous situations and unfamiliar risks.

Long-term/short-term orientation

This dimension is about virtue versus truth. Societies with a long-term orientation look to the past and present

Illustration 4.12 *continued*

for their value systems. People living in these societies have a respect for traditions and fulfilling social obligations. It is important that they 'save face'. They do not believe in absolute truths. Societies with a short-term orientation look towards the future cultivating habits of thrift and perseverance. People living in these societies value analytical thinking and the search for truths. This dimension is not as developed as the other four, not having been subjected to the amount of follow-up research since Hofstede's original study.

Based on information given in an article written by Hofstede in 1993, and elaborated by Burnes (2004, p.175), Table 4.1 gives the results of research for a selected number of countries.

Table 4.1 Culture dimension scores for ten countries

Country	Power distance	Individualism*	Masculine**	Uncertainty avoidance	Long-term orientation***
China	High	Low	Moderate	Moderate	High
France	High	High	Moderate	High	Low
Germany	Low	High	High	Moderate	Moderate
Hong Kong	High	Low	High	Low	High
Indonesia	High	Low	Moderate	Low	Low
Japan	Moderate	Moderate	High	High	High
Netherlands	Low	High	Low	Moderate	Moderate
Russia	High	Moderate	Low	Low	Low
United States	Low	High	High	Low	Low
West Africa	High	Low	Moderate	Moderate	Low

* A low score implies collectivism. ** A low score implies feminine. *** A low score implies short-term orientation.

Source: Adapted with permission from Hofstede, G. (1993), 'Cultural constraints in management theories', *Academy of Management Executive*, February, p. 91. Copyright © Geert Hofstede.

Figure 4.7 illustrates four possible organizational models that, according to Hofstede (1991), refer to empirically derived relationships between a country's position on the power distance/uncertainty avoidance matrix and models of organizations implicit in the minds of people from the countries concerned.

From this it can be seen how Hofstede uses the metaphors of a village market, a well-oiled machine, a pyramid and a family to describe different approaches to organizing. Thus, people from countries with a 'village market' culture do not appear to have the same need for hierarchy and certainty as those from a pyramid type culture. These contrast with people from cultures reminiscent of 'well-oiled machines' – such as West Germany – where hierarchy is not particularly required because there are established procedures and rules to which everyone works. People who live in countries located in the 'family' quadrant – such as India, West

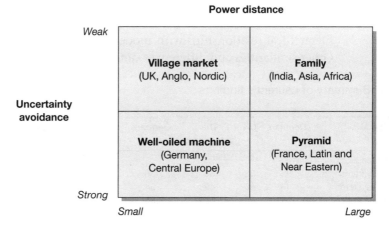

Figure 4.7 Implicit models of organization

Source: Adapted with permission from Hofstede, G. (1991), *Cultures and Organizations* (Maidenhead, McGraw Hill). Copyright © Geert Hofstede.

Africa and Malaysia – are said to have an implicit model of organization that resembles a family in which the owner–manager is the omnipotent (grand)father.

It is clear that if, as Hofstede maintains, these differences between cultural groupings exist and any convergence across them will be very slow, then there is a good chance that they will influence organizational cultures in correspondingly different ways. It should not be forgotten, however, that Hofstede's research was carried out some time ago and mainly within a single multinational organization. The clustering of countries into the four models depicted in Figure 4.7 is a simplification of the complexity of distinguishing one country's culture from another, let alone differences within countries.

There is, however, support for Hofstede's views on national cultural differences from research carried out by Laurent (1983). In contrast to Hofstede's research, which sampled the views of employees at all levels of a single organization, Laurent's research focused on the views of upper- and middle-level managers in a large number of different organizations, spread across nine European countries and the United States. Laurent's hypothesis was that the national origin of managers significantly affects their views of what proper management should be. The focus was, perhaps, slightly narrower than that of Hofstede, but had the advantage of sampling across several different organizations.

From his survey of 817 managers across the ten countries, Laurent identified four dimensions, which he labelled: organizations as political systems, organizations as authority systems, organizations as role-formalization systems and organizations as hierarchical-relationship systems. Table 4.2 summarizes the relative position of the ten countries on each of Laurent's dimensions. The results show France and Italy at the high end of the scores for all dimensions – meaning that they were politicized, hierarchical, had high degrees of role formalization and believed in the authority of individuals. Denmark and the United Kingdom are positioned similarly to each other with low levels of hierarchy and politicization, moderate degrees of belief in individual authority and high levels of role formalization. Sweden had the lowest score in terms of hierarchical relationships with moderate scores on the other three dimensions. Other similarities and differences can be seen from the table.

Table 4.2 Summary of Laurent's findings

Dimension	Denmark	UK	The Netherlands	Germany	Sweden	USA	Switzerland	France	Italy	Belgium
Organizations as:										
Political systems	26	32	36	36	42	43	51	62	66	missing
Authority systems	46	48	49	34	46	30	32	65	61	61
Role-formalization systems	80	80	67	85	57	66	85	81	84	81
Hierarchical-relationship systems	37	36	33	47	25	28	43	50	66	50

Source: Summarized from Laurent, A. (1983), 'The cultural diversity of Western conceptions of management', *International Studies of Management and Organisation*, Vol. XIII, Nos. 1–2, pp. 75–96.

In contrast to the identification of national cultural characteristics typified by quantified data on defined dimensions, Illustration 4.13 is an example of a qualitative account of Danish managers and how to do business with them. However, as can be seen by Activity 4.5, it is possible to validate one set of results, obtained using one type of data collection technique, with another set of results using a different technique.

Illustration 4.13

On a wavelength with the Danes

**'Language is not a problem – but doing business with the "Italians of the north" requires tact',
argues Sergey Frank**

At first sight, doing business in Denmark may seem straightforward. The country is prosperous and an important trade partner in the European Union. Its people communicate in a friendly and direct way. Negotiators tend to be to the point, relaxed and informal. And the whole process is accompanied with a sense of humour. But do not fall into the trap of thinking you need only be yourself.

Throughout Scandinavia, communication is characterised by calmness and understatement. This applies to Danes, too, although they are known for being more temperamental than Swedes and Norwegians and are sometimes described as the 'Italians of the north'.

That does not make Copenhagen the same as Rome. Extrovert rhetoric and exaggeration are poorly regarded in Denmark. The body language of Danes underlines this – especially on a first meeting. To touch someone's arm or to pat someone on the back while shaking hands is not appropriate when dealing with a Danish business partner. You should also keep enough distance from your counterpart for him or her to feel comfortable.

Danes tend to be open-minded when they deal with foreign business partners. A formal introduction from an international bank or sales representative, for example, is not absolutely necessary. Most Danish people speak and read English fluently. There is no need for an interpreter.

▶

At the start of the negotiations, your Danish counterpart will tend to understate his or her own achievements, much as the English would. It is good to be punctual and to structure the agenda. To display the sort of self-confidence that would strike extrovert cultures as quite normal would be inappropriate in Denmark.

One general principle of communication applies throughout Scandinavia: less is more. It is in your interest to provide a realistic initial offer with enough room for concessions. You should also avoid giving the impression that you think you are more successful than other people.

It is unwise to 'oversell' yourself and to reveal everything about yourself and your company. Instead, try to let your Danish business partner seek out the relevant information about a potential match with your company, your products and services. The same applies for presentations: a properly documented presentation aligned with a consistent argument goes down better than a hard sell.

Your Danish counterparts will be open, polite, flexible and ready to provide you with insights into their point of view. In brainstorming sessions they will be prepared to think up imaginative solutions and to evaluate them with you afterwards. In all this you should deploy humour, especially of the understated English variety.

However, you should be cautious in some respects. Danes do not start negotiations as quickly as, for example, Americans. They consider it rude for anyone to be interrupted in mid-sentence, especially if it is not to clarify something that has just been said. Be patient with the decision-making process: Danish executives do not like to be rushed.

The notion of 'fair play' counts for a lot in Denmark. It is reflected in social welfare and culture. Thus, your partner will usually try to find win–win solutions where both parties will receive a fair amount of profit – though Danes can drive a hard bargain.

The concern for fair play can be seen in Danish management culture: managers do not place much emphasis on hierarchy. Women have done well in Denmark, too. The country has the highest percentage of women in business in the European Union.

Most Danes are friendly, generous hosts. Entertaining is done at lunch or dinner, mostly in restaurants. An invitation to someone's home is a great honour. Wherever you are dining, you should arrive on time. Evening meals take place early but, unlike many east Asian business people, your Danish counterpart will expect you to stay and chat at the hotel bar.

Source: Frank, S. (2000), 'On a wavelength with the Danes', *Financial Times*, 23 October, p. 15.

Activity 4.5

Compare and contrast the account in Illustration 4.13 with Laurent's findings with respect to the orientations of Danish managers in Table 4.2. Hofstede's results, in Table 4.1, show Danish workers as having low power distance, low uncertainty avoidance, high feminine, and moderately high individualism characteristics and British managers as having low power distance, low uncertainty avoidance, high masculine and very high individualism characteristics. Does this accord with what is said about Danish managers and implied about British managers in the account in Illustration 4.13?

Compare the brief reference to American managers in this account with their positions on Hofstede's and Laurent's scales (as shown in Tables 4.1 and 4.2). How do you think American managers would fare doing business with Danish managers? In addition to using Hofstede's and Laurent's findings, use the profile for the United States in Figure 4.6 (Kluckhohn and Strodtbeck's cultural dimensions) to help you.

Hofstede's and Laurent's research are only two of many possible national culture models derived from the administration of questionnaires. However, they exemplify the way questionnaires can be used to demonstrate national cultural similarities and differences. Having said this, their methods can be criticized in terms of their attempts to 'objectivize' culture compared to more qualitative methods referred to in the previous discussion of organizational cultures. This criticism can, however, be balanced by other studies (e.g. Maurice, Sorge and Warner, 1980; d'Iribarne, 1989) that have found differences between national cultures, but which were based on in-depth, comprehensive examinations of similar organizations or organizational units in a limited number of countries.

A third method was employed by Calori and De Woot (1994) when they used non-directive interviews with 51 human resource directors in 40 large international companies with headquarters or major operating units in Europe. On the basis of the results of these interviews, Calori and De Woot claim to have found country clusters that suggest a typology of management systems (see Figure 4.8). Illustration 4.14 summarizes Calori and De Woot's conclusions on the characteristics typical of the first two levels of segmentation, that is the Anglo-Saxon, Latin and Northern Europe (using the German model as an example) groupings.

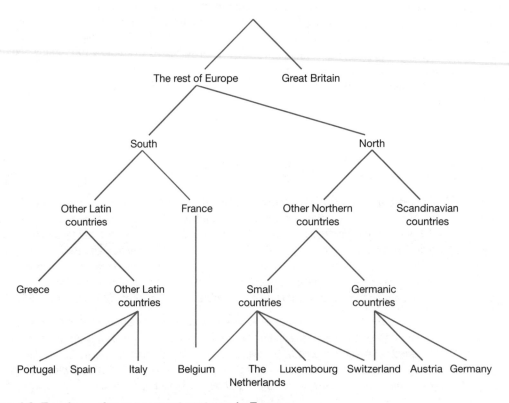

Figure 4.8 Typology of management systems in Europe

Source: Calori, R. and De Woot, P. (1994), *A European Management Model Beyond Diversity* (Hemel Hempstead, Prentice Hall, p. 20).

Illustration 4.14

Differences between Great Britain, Southern Europe (including France) and Northern Europe (typified by Germany – pre-unification)

The United Kingdom, an exception in Europe

Management in the United Kingdom has more in common with the United States than the rest of Europe. It has:

- a short-term orientation (more than continental Europe);
- a shareholder orientation (whereas the rest of Europe has more of a stakeholder orientation);
- an orientation towards trading and finance (the importance of the stock market is more developed than in continental Europe);
- a higher turnover of managers;
- a greater liberalism towards foreigners (e.g. the Japanese);
- more freedom for top management vis-à-vis the workers and government;
- more direct and pragmatic relationships between people;
- more variable remuneration.

However, different from the United States, it additionally has:

- adversarial relationships with labour;
- the tradition of the manager as a 'gifted amateur' (as opposed to the professionalism of US managers);
- the influence of class differences in the firm.

The Latin way of doing business

Southern Europe (including France) differs from the rest of Europe in that it has:

- more state intervention;
- more protectionism;

- more hierarchy in the firm;
- more intuitive management;
- more family business (especially in Italy);
- more reliance on an elite (especially in France).

The German model

Characteristic of Germany, Austria and, to some extent, Switzerland as well as the Benelux countries, the German model is based on three cultural and structural characteristics:

- strong links between banks and industry;
- a balance between a sense of national collectivity and the *Länder* (regional) system;
- a system of training and development of managers.

It has the following five components:

- the system of co-determination with workers' representatives present on the board;
- the loyalty of managers (and employees in general) who spend their career in a single firm, which then gives priority to in-house training;
- the collective orientation of the workforce, which includes dedication to the company, team spirit and a sense of discipline;
- the long-term orientation that appears in planning, in the seriousness and stability of supplier–client relationships and in the priority of industrial goals over short-term financial objectives;
- the reliability and stability of shareholders, influenced by a strong involvement of banks in industry.

Source: Based on Calori, R. and De Woot, P. (1994), *A European Management Model Beyond Diversity* (Hemel Hempstead, Prentice Hall, pp. 22–9).

Activity 4.6

Compare and contrast Calori and De Woot's country groupings and characteristics with the countries' positions on Laurent's cultural dimensions and the models presented in Figure 4.7. To what extent do any of these characterizations agree with your own experience, either through business dealings or as a tourist?

National culture and organizational culture

The result of carrying out Activity 4.6 illustrates the complexity of attempting to build tight categories into which different national cultures can be put. It would be difficult to argue, however, that these differences do not occur. In addition, the evidence points to close relationships between national culture and organizational culture. For instance, a study by Furnham and Gunter (1993) provides examples of organizations in countries such as Australia, Israel and Denmark that had low scores on Hofstede's power distance dimension also having common organizational structures. Their structures incorporated low centralization of decision making and flatter pyramids of control, reminiscent of Handy's task organizational culture (Handy, 1993). These organizations' structures contrasted with those in countries such as the Philippines, Mexico and India, which scored highly on Hofstede's power distance dimension of culture. These latter organizations were typified by strict hierarchical structures and centralized decision making, reminiscent of Handy's role organizational culture.

Activity 4.7

Look back at Figure 4.7, which positions four implicit models of organization on Hofstede's power distance and uncertainty avoidance dimensions. Consider Deal and Kennedy's four culture types described in Illustration 4.8 and decide how far each can be related to one or more of Hofstede's organizational models. What conclusions can you derive from this?

It is not difficult to link Deal and Kennedy's 'bet-your-company' culture with countries that score similarly to Germany on Laurent's dimensions of culture (see Table 4.1). In fact, because Laurent focused his questions on managers and their perceptions of organizational life, it is not surprising that there is a large overlap between his dimensions of national culture and others' dimensions of organizational culture. Both Hofstede (1994) and Adler (1991) draw attention to the way organizational theory (e.g. as it relates to motivation, decision making, leadership, etc.) is culturally determined. Because most management and organizational theory derives from the work of scholars based in western academic institutions, caution is advised about applying it indiscriminately to organizations in other parts of the world. For instance, organizational cultures that imply an adherence to participative styles of leadership and decision making and which are part of western national cultures may not be welcomed in societies that see consultation on the part of leaders as a weakness and where workers would be embarrassed if consulted by their managers. Chambers (1996), in an article entitled 'Russia's different problems', points out a number of elements in western guides to management that are of little practical use to Russian managers. For instance, the concepts of 'just-in-time' and 'lean production' make little sense in a situation of uncertainties of supply of both raw materials and components. In an environment of minimal structures for data collection and market intelligence and no framework of commercial law, western sales and marketing strategies are of little use. Organizations in Russia are a product of a previous non-commercial culture and the infrastructure of business still reflects this.

It must not be forgotten, however, that, even though influenced to a smaller or larger extent by national culture, organizational cultures can change, although change is not easy. Conversely, some organizational cultures are more conducive than others to supporting organizational change.

Organizational culture and change

Wilson and Rosenfeld (1990, p. 237) say: 'The pervasive nature of organizational culture cannot be stressed too much. It is likely to affect virtually all aspects of organizational life.' According to Schwartz and Davis (1981, p. 35): 'Culture is capable of blunting or significantly altering the intended impact of even well-thought-out changes in an organization.' This is a popular view of culture and its implications for instigating any kind of change are clear. However, as the preceding discussion shows, organizational culture comes in many forms and, therefore, can be more or less supportive of change.

There are a number of different views on the relationship between culture and change. Figure 4.9 depicts various elements of organizational culture as they might influence organizational change.

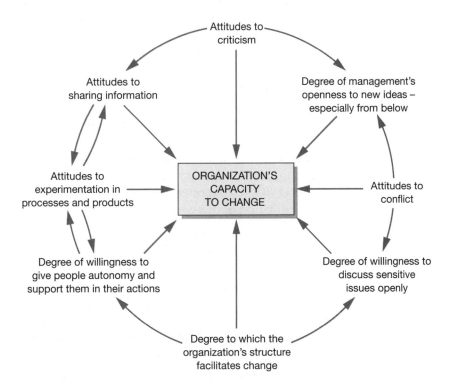

Figure 4.9 Organizational culture and change

Cultures in defence against, or supportive of, change

Figure 4.9 depicts the way some elements of organizational culture might support change while, at the same time, work against it – in other words how they might put up a defence against change. One element of organizational design that is particularly relevant to the ease with which change comes about is that of an organization's structure. Some of the typologies of organizational culture (e.g. Handy, Harrison and Pheysey) discussed earlier in the chapter are related closely to types of organization structure. Indeed, in these cases, culture and structure seem almost to be interchangeable. A similar case can be made for the mechanistic and organic organizational structures identified by Burns and Stalker (1961) and that were discussed in Chapter 3. Burns and Stalker's research is a good example of the merger of the concepts of structure and culture, as is seen in their argument that organic types of organization are much more likely to be able to respond to the need for change than are mechanistic ones. However, it could be going too far to say that Burns and Stalker would have regarded mechanistic-type organizations to be *defensive* against change, because all organizations change, to some extent, incrementally, all the time. The use of the term 'defensive against change' is not, therefore, intended to imply, necessarily, that mechanistic and role-type organizational cultures will not support change. They are, however, unlikely to support, without serious trauma, the frame-breaking (see Tushman *et al.*, 1988), transformational (see Dunphy and Stace, 1993) or revolutionary types of change (see Johnson, 1987) discussed in Chapter 2. This is likely to be the case because of their structural characteristics, but might also be because of the attitudes, beliefs and values held by the people who work in them.

Kanter (1983) gives detailed descriptions of two extremes of organizational culture that are not only different in structural characteristics but also differ in the underlying attitudes and beliefs of the people working in them. The first she calls a 'segmentalist' culture and the other an 'integrative' culture. Illustration 4.15 summarizes the characteristics of these two cultures.

In addition to the summary of a segmentalist culture given in Illustration 4.15, Kanter (1983, p. 101) offers the following ten 'rules for stifling innovation' as further elucidation of this concept:

1 Regard any new idea from below with suspicion – because it is new, and because it is from below.
2 Insist that people who need your approval to act first go through several other levels of management to get their signatures.
3 Ask departments or individuals to challenge and criticize each other's proposals. (That saves you the task of deciding; you just pick the survivor.)
4 Express your criticisms freely and withhold your praise. (That keeps people on their toes.) Let them know they can be fired at any time.
5 Treat identification of problems as signs of failure, to discourage people from letting you know when something in their area isn't working.

Illustration 4.15

Segmentalist and integrative cultures

Segmentalist cultures:
- compartmentalize actions, events and problems;
- see problems as narrowly as possible;
- have segmented structures with large numbers of departments walled off from one another;
- assume problems can be solved by carving them up into pieces that are then assigned to specialists who work in isolation;
- divide resources up among the many departments;
- avoid experimentation;
- avoid conflict and confrontation;
- have weak coordinating mechanisms;
- stress precedent and procedures.

Integrative cultures:
- are willing to move beyond received wisdom;
- combine ideas from unconnected sources;
- see problems as wholes, related to larger wholes;
- challenge established practices;
- operate at the edge of competencies;
- measure themselves by looking to visions of the future rather than by referring to the standards of the past;
- create mechanisms for exchange of information and new ideas;
- recognize and even encourage differences, but then are prepared to cooperate;
- are outward looking;
- look for novel solutions to problems.

Source: Based on the discussion in Kanter, R. M. (1983), *The Change Masters* (London, Routledge, Chapter 1).

6 Control everything carefully. Make sure people count anything that can be counted, frequently.

7 Make decisions to reorganize or change policies in secret, and spring them on people unexpectedly. (That also keeps people on their toes.)

8 Make sure that requests for information are fully justified and make sure that it is not given out to managers freely. (You don't want data to fall into the wrong hands.)

9 Assign to lower-level managers, in the name of delegation and participation, responsibility for figuring out how to cut back, lay off, move people around or otherwise implement threatening decisions you have made. And get them to do it quickly.

10 And above all, never forget that you, the higher-ups, already know everything important about this business.

The Open University course *Managing in organizations* (1985) discusses Argyris and Schon's (1978) identification of what appear to be the 'unwritten rules' governing some organizational relationships that mirror Kanter's rules for stifling change. These are as follows:

1 Keep your views of sensitive issues private; enforce the taboo against their public discussion.

2 Do not surface and test differences in views of organizational problems.

3 Avoid seeing the whole picture; allow maps of the problem to remain scattered, vague and ambiguous.

4 Protect yourself unilaterally – by avoiding both direct interpersonal confrontation and public discussion of sensitive issues that might expose you to blame.

5 Protect others unilaterally – by avoiding the testing of assumptions where that testing might evoke negative feelings and by keeping others from exposure to blame.

6 Control the situation and the task – by making up your own mind about the problem and acting on your view, by keeping your view private and by avoiding the public inquiry that might refute your view.

The Open University material (pp. 47–9) contrasts this set of rules, which it says typifies what it calls a 'defensive climate', with the following rules that it says are more typical of a 'supportive' climate:

1 Surface sensitive issues and encourage others to do so.

2 Ensure differences of view are publicly tested and that statements are made in ways that can be tested.

3 Bring together dispersed information and clarify vague and ambiguous data.

4 Do not avoid interpersonal confrontation even if it involves negative feelings.

5 Make protection of oneself and others a joint task oriented towards growth.

6 Control the task jointly.

It is clear from both Kanter, and Argyris and Schon's writings that a segmentalist or defensive culture will militate against organizational change, while a supportive culture will do much to help the change process. Of additional interest is that many of the items in all the lists of rules frequently become the 'symbols' and 'symbolic acts' that Johnson (1990) says are so important to the maintenance or changing of organizational paradigms. They form the basis on which organizational learning and therefore organizational change may or may not take place.

Organizational learning and types of change

Argyris (1964) was one of the first people to point out the difference between two kinds of learning. The first, called *single-loop learning*, is indicative of a situation where an objective or goal is defined and an individual works out the most favoured way of reaching the goal. In single-loop learning, while many different possibilities for achieving personal or organizational goals might be considered, the goal itself is not questioned. Single-loop learning is also referred to as individual learning, that is, learning which an individual achieves but that seldom passes throughout the organization in any coherent way.

This type of learning is contrasted by Argyris with *double-loop learning* where questions are asked not only about the *means* by which goals can be achieved, but about the *ends*, that is, the goals themselves. Johnson (1990) refers to this type of learning as *organizational relearning*, which he says is a 'process in which that which is taken for granted and which is the basis of strategic direction – the paradigm – is re-formulated' (p. 189). Given that the organizational paradigm contains all the elements of Johnson *et al.*'s (2005) cultural web, this implies change throughout the organization in all aspects of its behaviour.

Individual or single-loop learning is most likely to be the dominant type of learning to take place within a segmentalist or defensive culture. The characteristics of this type of culture militate, significantly, against the sharing of information and openness that is required for organizational learning to take place. Therefore, while it could be said to be sufficient for the types of change which Dunphy and Stace (1993) define as 'fine-tuning' and 'incremental adjustment', it will be blind to the need for the kind of radical thinking required to bring about change in the organization's direction, that is, strategic change. In addition, the inability of an organization to operate double-loop learning contributes to the process of 'strategic drift' (Johnson 1987), which was discussed in Chapter 2, a process that can lead to change being forced upon an organization.

Strong and weak cultures

'Organizational cultures differ markedly in terms of their relative strengths' (Brown, 1995, p. 74). Whether defensive or supportive, intuitively, the existence of a strong culture implies a commonly understood perspective on how organizational life should happen, with most organizational members subscribing to it. Conversely, a weak culture implies no dominant pervasive culture but an organization made up of many different cultures, some of which will be in conflict with each other. Payne (1990) has suggested that the strength of an organization's culture can be measured by, first, the degree to which it is shared by all members and, second, by the intensity with which organizational members believe in it. The greater the intensity of an organization's culture, the greater the degree to which it pervades all levels at which culture manifests itself, that is, in influencing not only people's attitudes, but also their values, basic assumptions and beliefs.

The strength or weakness of organizational cultures is important in that it performs a number of functions for the organization. A popular view is that it is the glue which holds the organization together. Brown (1995) suggests the following functions at the organizational level.

Conflict resolution

As organizations can be characterized as grounds for disagreement and conflict, culture can be a force for integration and consensus. Knowing 'how things are done around here' can help avoid conflict.

Coordination and control

If a strong organizational culture helps avoid conflict it will, conversely, facilitate the processes of coordination and control. Strongly held values and beliefs will ensure that all concerned will pull together in the same direction.

Reduction of uncertainty

For new recruits to an organization, the more quickly they 'learn' the norms of behaviour, the more confident they will become in their assumptions about how others will behave and the way in which organizational processes are carried out. This has the advantage of reducing the complexity of the organizational world, neutralizing uncertainties so that any actions taken are in tune with organizational rationalities as seen by the majority of organizational members.

Motivation

While extrinsic rewards such as pay, bonuses and promotions can motivate employees to perform well, a culture that can offer employees a means of identification with their work, which can foster loyalty and assist their belief that they are valued, will add to their motivation and presumably the overall organizational performance.

Competitive advantage

A strong culture is said to improve organizational performance. Peters and Waterman (1982) and Kanter (1983) are just three well-known writers and consultants who claim to have found recipes for cultures that are presumed to link to performance. Their arguments are that the more closely an organization sticks to their particular recipe, the greater the probability that it will be a high performer. It is debatable, however, whether a strong culture, even of the supportive kind, necessarily links to increased competitive advantage. For instance, Kotter and Heskett's (1992) research during the period 1977–88 identified ten large and well-known organizations (including Sears, Procter & Gamble and Goodyear), all of which had exceptionally strong cultures, but all of which had weak performances.

In some organizations the existence of a weak dominant culture with multiple sub-cultures may be an advantage. Strong, all-pervasive cultures can be a disadvantage when they become so controlling that there is little potential for the nonconformity which brings innovation and the capacity to adapt to change.

Changing organizational culture to bring about organizational change

The discussion in this chapter shows that it is difficult to deny the importance of culture as a dominant influence on the whole of organizational life. From this it could be deduced that, in order to bring about any kind of significant organizational change, the organization's culture must be managed accordingly. This view is subscribed to by scholars such as Johnson and Scholes (1993) in their depiction of the cultural web. It is also evident in the arguments that recommend organizations to take on the characteristics of a supportive (integrative) culture (see Kanter, 1983) linked to an organic structure (Burns and Stalker, 1961) or those which will bring excellence in performance (see Peters and Waterman, 1982). From these points of view, permanent organizational change will only be brought about by first changing people's attitudes and values – in other words changing the culture at the deeper levels of its meaning as was illustrated in Figure 4.2.

However, changing an organization's culture is not easy, as Schwartz and Davis (1981) point out from their observations of change at companies they researched. In relation to one of these – AT&T, which, in the late 1970s, undertook a large-scale corporate and organizational reorientation – Schwartz and Davis (1981, p. 31) say:

> Despite the major changes in structure, in human resources, and in support systems, there is a general consensus both inside and outside AT&T that its greatest task in making its strategy succeed will be its ability to transform the AT&T culture. *It will probably be a decade before direct judgements should be made as to its success.* [authors' emphasis]

Yet another example they quote is the case where the president of an engineering company resigned after six years of trying to change the company's culture from being production-oriented to being market-oriented. At this point he reckoned he had managed to dent but not change the culture.

Given this background, some means of measuring organizational culture and its relationship to organizational change appears desirable.

Assessing cultural risk

Activity 4.1 is one way of measuring organizational culture and this method can obviously be applied to any list of culture characteristics. For instance, Furnham and Gunter (1993) suggest this in relation to Schein's (1985) list of dimensions of corporate culture – a list not dissimilar to that of Robbins – and in addition give a list of various quantitative measures of culture. However, measuring organizational culture is, of itself, only a means to an end. The end is to determine how culture should be managed as part of the process of organizational change.

It was, therefore, in pursuit of this end that Schwartz and Davis devised a means of measuring culture in terms of descriptions of the way management tasks are typically handled in company-wide, boss–subordinate, peer and interdepartment relationships so as to assess the degree of cultural compatibility with any proposed strategic change. Figure 4.10 is an example of Schwartz and Davis's corporate culture matrix that they designed to carry out the first part of this process. It has been completed for the UK-based division of a company in the computer services industry.

Once you have carried out Activity 4.8 you can use the results of this analysis to assess the compatibility of the culture of this organization to any proposed changes in the organization's approach to its strategy, structure and operations. The framework for this comparative assessment is shown in Figure 4.11 as a

Tasks	Relationships				
	Companywide	Boss-subordinate	Peer	Inter-department	Summary of culture in relation to tasks
Innovating	Innovation if part of the mission	Bosses open to suggestions	Teamwork	Teamwork	Encourage creativity and innovation
Decision making	Has to fit in with strategy	Input from subordinates encouraged – boss has final word	Collective decisions	Work together to produce an integrated package	Collaborative decision making but boss has the final word; corporate strategy rules
Communicating	Easy, use of E-mail and phone	Friendly	Face to face and open	Easy, use of E-mail and phone	Easy, informal and friendly communications
Organizing	Market focus	Democratic	Professional relationships	Collaborative	Organized on the basis of skills and professional relationships
Monitoring	Shareholder-led organization	Meet short-term profit targets and deadlines	Project management	Project management	Need to meet short-term profit goals
Appraising and rewarding	Encourage performers	Hard work = good rewards	Results important	Results important	Meritocracy
Summary of culture in relation to relationships	Allow freedom to managers as long as they operate within the strategy and meet profit targets; output-oriented	Friendly, rely on each other for success	Highly skilled professionals who help each other out	Work together	Overall performance and profit matter in a culture that welcomes dynamic and performance-related individuals

Figure 4.10 Corporate culture matrix

Source: Matrix adapted from Schwartz, H. and Davis, S. M. (1981), 'Matching corporate strategy and business strategy', *Organizational Dynamics*, Summer, p. 36; example from the author's own experience. Copyright (1981), with permission from Elsevier.

Activity 4.8

For any organization you know well, use the basic matrix in Figure 4.10 to do the following:

1 *Insert, in each cell of the main body of the matrix, words and/or phrases that encapsulate the different relationships (listed horizontally) according to the management of the tasks (listed vertically).*

2 *In the final column on the right, summarize the corporate culture for each task.*

3 *In the final row, summarize the corporate culture for each of the relationships.*

What do the summaries tell you about this organization's overall culture?

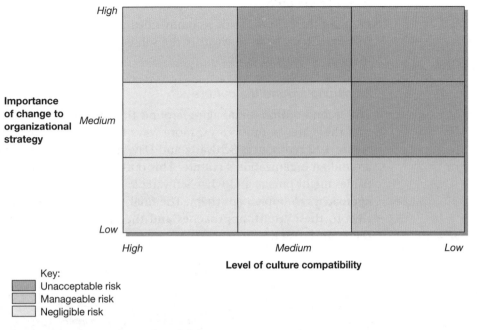

Figure 4.11 Assessing cultural risk

Source: Matrix adapted from Schwartz, H. and Davis, S. M. (1981), 'Matching corporate strategy and business strategy', *Organizational Dynamics*, Summer, p. 41. Copyright (1981), with permission from Elsevier.

matrix that allows elements of the proposed strategy changes to be plotted against their importance to that strategy and the degree to which they are compatible with the culture. From this matrix, it can be seen that the nearer the elements of any proposed strategic change are to the top right-hand corner, the lower the chance that they will be accepted, given the prevailing culture. For instance, if a change to a matrix structure is of the utmost importance to a proposed strategic change, yet the culture is one that is reminiscent of Handy's (1993) 'role-oriented' culture or of Hall's (1995) 'north' culture, the need for a matrix structure would be positioned in the top right cell of the matrix in Figure 4.10. Other elements of the proposed change might still be low in level of culture compatibility but of low importance in the overall change strategy. They would, therefore, be positioned towards the lower right-hand part of the matrix.

The relevance of culture change to organizational change

Assessing cultural risk helps management pinpoint where they are likely to meet resistance to change because of incompatibility between strategy and culture. This further allows them to make choices regarding whether to: (a) ignore the culture; (b) manage around the culture; (c) try to change the culture to fit the strategy; or (d) change the strategy to fit the culture, perhaps by reducing performance expectations.

Ignoring the culture

Ignoring the culture is not recommended unless the organization has sufficient resources to draw on to weather the subsequent storm and the possibility of an initial downturn in business.

Managing around the culture

The second option – managing around the culture – is a real possibility given that there are, in most cases, more ways than one of achieving desired goals. Figure 4.12 reproduces Schwartz and Davis's (1981) example of how to manage around an organization's culture. This outlines four typical strategies that companies might pursue and what Schwartz and Davis call the 'right' organizational approaches to implement them. The final two columns set out the cultural barriers to these 'right' approaches and the alternative approaches that could, therefore, be used.

	Strategy	'Right' approach	Cultural barriers	Alternative approaches
Company A	Diversify product and market	Divisionalize	Centralized power One-man rule Functional focus Hierarchical structure	Use business teams Use explicit strategic planning Change business measures
Company B	Focus marketing on most profitable segments	Fine-tune reward system. Adjust management information system	Diffused power Highly individualized operations	Dedicate full-time personnel to each key market
Company C	Extend technology to new markets	Set up matrix organization	Multiple power centres Functional focus	Use programme coordinators Set up planning committees Get top management more involved
Company D	Withdraw gradually from declining market and maximize cash throw-offs	Focus organization specifically Fine-tune rewards Ensure top management visibility	New-business driven Innovators rewarded State-of-the-art operation	Sell out

Figure 4.12 How to manage around company culture

Source: Matrix adapted from Schwartz, H. and Davis, S. M. (1981), 'Matching corporate strategy and business strategy', *Organizational Dynamics*, Summer, p. 44. Copyright (1981), with permission from Elsevier.

Changing the culture

The third option, deliberately changing the culture to fit the desired strategic changes, is also a possibility and, according to Ogbonna and Harris (2002, p. 33) is still a popular form of management intervention. However, as much of the literature cautions, this can be an extremely difficult and lengthy process, particularly if the culture is a strong one (Scholz, 1987; Furnham and Gunter, 1993). Furthermore, there are strong arguments (e.g. Hope and Hendry, 1995) against cultural change as a concept for present-day organizations given what Hope and Hendry (p. 62) describe as the move away from the large-scale hierarchies characteristic of the multinationals of the 1970s and 1980s towards the much leaner and more focused units of the 1990s and 2000s.

According to Hope and Hendry, this move has been accompanied by an increase in the employment of what Drucker (1992) calls 'professional knowledge workers' but also by an erosion of security of employment and predictable career paths, with consequent difficulties of employee control. Two problems are said to arise from this. The first is that the 'knowledge workers' who are likely to flourish in these new types of organization are least likely to be open to cultural manipulation. Second, any new managerial practice must allow for a degree of cynicism in the context of the downsizing that has removed several layers of middle management and therefore removed the opportunity for steady advancement once assumed as almost everyone's right. As a consequence of all this, it is still the case that: 'employees in general may be less receptive to evangelical calls for shared cultural values' (Hope and Hendry, 1995, p. 62).

Beer, Eisenstat and Spector's (1993) view that trying to change attitudes and values directly is futile is still relevant; particularly their comment that the way to bring about organizational change is first to change behaviour. The behavioural change will then lead to the desired changes in attitudes and values.

Thus Beer *et al.* argue for changing the organizational context (people's roles, responsibilities and the relationships between them) first, which will then result in changed behaviour and associated attitudes. This view of change rests on the assumption that changing organizational structures, systems and role relationships, which comprise, in the main, the formal aspects of organizational life, will bring about desired cultural changes incorporating organizational members' attitudes and beliefs. Many models of planned change subscribe to this view and the 'Six steps to effective change' propounded by Beer *et al.* are an example of this (see Illustration 4.16).

Both Beer *et al.* and Hope and Hendry can be said to have their views supported by Hofstede (1981, p. 26) who quotes Bem (1970, p. 60) as saying: 'One of the most effective ways of changing mental programmes of individuals is changing behavior first'. He continues: 'That value change has to precede behavior change is a naive (idealistic) assumption that neglects the contribution of the *situation* to actual behaviour.'

The literature does not help in deciding whether cultural change is a real possibility or whether managers requiring organizational change should work

Illustration 4.16

Six steps to effective change propounded by Beer *et al.*

1 Mobilize commitment to change through joint diagnosis of business problems.

2 Develop a shared vision of how to organize and manage for competitiveness.

3 Foster consensus for the new vision, competence to enact it and cohesion to move it along.

4 Spread revitalization to all departments without pushing it from the top.

5 Institutionalize revitalization through formal policies, systems and structures.

6 Monitor and adjust strategies in response to problems in the revitalization process.

Source: Beer, M., Eisenstat, R. A. and Spector, B. (1993), 'Why change programs don't produce change', in Mabey, C. and Mayon-White, B. (eds) *Managing Change* (London, PCP, pp. 99–107).

around the culture. Some methods of bringing about culture change depend upon education and persuasion or, in some cases, coercion, to help bring about changes in attitudes (Anthony, 1994). Others rely more on changing recruitment, selection, promotion, reward and redundancy policies to alter the composition of the workforce and so retain those who have the desired beliefs, values and attitudes associated with the desired culture (Dobson, 1988). It seems that a combination of approaches would be most effective unless the organizational changes proposed can themselves be changed to be more compatible with the existing culture.

Illustration 4.17 gives an example of a company that was able to manage around its culture for a number of years, and during that time still succeeded in growing and developing in the global market. However, to achieve longer-term success, the company decided to create a strategy that would ultimately attempt to change the culture.

Changing the strategy to match the culture

Schwartz and Davis (1981) give the merging of two organizations as an example of changing the strategy to be more compatible with the existing cultures. This choice for an organization is similar to that of managing around the culture and further emphasizes the possibilities inherent in the idea that organizations are able to choose the means by which they achieve their ends. In addition, those who view culture as a metaphor for organizations (Morgan, 1986) would find it difficult to preach wholesale cultural change. Some accommodation between changing the culture and adapting the strategy is more likely to be accepted.

Overall, compromise between these different approaches to managing organizational culture within a context of organizational change is counselled. Using a process that combines education and persuasion (to bring about attitude and value change) with changes in structures and systems (to bring about changes in

Illustration 4.17

Found in translation

Christian Herrault recalls what a professor of organizational development once told him: 'Change doesn't happen when it's necessary, it happens when it is possible'. For Herrault, HR Director of the French building company Lafarge, this is a significant statement, because over the past decade the French-owned building materials company has come under pressure to change. Until recently the company has been managing around the culture of the core historical business, but with the acquisition of companies from outside its borders, most notably two large British companies, its ways of working have come under intense scrutiny. According to Herrault, it needed to adapt its Gallic style to suit its new status as an international company. Within the company the new, non-French blood at times struggled with the Gallic management style, with external expectations also changing. Before 1997 Lafarge had almost a sense of partnership with its shareholders, who were mostly French. Now the big financial institutions are looking closely at the company and expect considerable improvements in performance to justify the acquisitions.

Some Anglo-Saxon colleagues told Herrault that if he wanted to change the organization he needed to create a crisis. But Herrault says: 'it was clear that Lafarge didn't and still doesn't have any real problems'. Therefore he felt it was inappropriate to create one, indicating that a first crisis would have to be followed by a bigger second one and so on. Changes needed to be made in more subtle ways. There were some issues that needed to be resolved in relation to the structure. A management consultant identified that 'there were four people at the top of the organization, all French, all powerful, with a lot of influence, but it wasn't clear how the group was organized or run on divisional lines'. This was due to the fact that, historically, the group had been working in an implicit, informal environment; now the challenge was to make the rules more explicit for the newcomer. So, in 1998,

Lafarge was organized by division for the first time, with a corporate level above and business unit levels below.

Other changes involved the introduction of an integrated HR system that Harrault says: 'was completely counter-cultural' given the small size of the operating units with staff feeling they did not need an information system. He refers to this as 'a painful process'. The Lafarge website gives the goals of the company as: first, to ensure total cohesion within a major multinational Group present in 75 different countries; and second, to encourage the exchange of best practices yet leave operating units with a high degree of autonomy.

With respect to its management, and led by the chief executive, Lafarge has developed a 'leader for tomorrow' programme, which aims to create a performance culture and engage the workforce; and to put people management and organizational capability at the top of the corporate agenda. 'The rule of the game is that each level has to teach the next one down, and so to teach the next one, you have to engage yourself'. Another initiative Herrault pioneered was to work with his senior HR team to develop a global HR network that meets regularly and pools its ideas.

For a global company, the focus is local, with the original French culture and ways of working having to be adapted to other countries' markets, customers and employees. When asked: 'With hindsight would you have done anything differently over the past six years', Herrault says: It's a question of speed. When you are keen to change its always, "Can I go faster?" Some people think we have lost time; that we should have been tougher. But we're in the long-term business, and we don't like to manage people by fear. With our businesses being local, people need to be creative and autonomous to manage well.' It all appears to be working!

Source: Smethurst (2005), *People Management*, CIPD, 05 May 2005, pp. 34–36. www.lafarge.com (accessed 2005).

behaviour) will help modify organizational culture as it is linked to organizational change on a broader scale. However, Pettigrew (1990) offers a timely reminder that cultural and strategic change is associated with organizational politics as well as with the core beliefs of the top decision makers. The next two chapters address these issues.

Comment and conclusions

The concept of culture is complex given its application to societies, organizations and groups, all of which interact one with another. The literature reviewed in this chapter has shown, to a considerable extent, the enduring differences between national or societal cultures; although there is evidence that some organizations can operate in very similar ways, regardless of where their different parts are located. The concept of national culture is, of course, not precise, when there are clearly differences in attitudes and norms of behaviour from one place to another within the same country. Even so, there are some generalizations which can be made and managers and others must be aware that what they consider the norm might turn out to be something very different as national boundaries are crossed. Furthermore, in identifying key elements of culture, it cannot be assumed that there is an optimum culture for an organization.

For instance, although some might suggest that stable organizations with strong cultures are what organizations should strive for, there is always a risk that these organizations will not be able to respond well in the face of having to change due to factors in the external environment. There is also evidence that, with even the strongest of cultures, sub-cultures inevitably exist within them. These also need to be considered, managed or, perhaps, changed.

Regarding the concept of organizational culture, it is possible that when individuals join and work within particular organizations they learn how to behave according to the expectations and norms of behaviour expected from them in that situation, even though outside the organization they may behave rather differently. Organizational culture might, therefore, be considered rather less enduring than national culture, particularly when, according to Robbins (2005), something dramatic happens where the organization has little choice but to change the way of working, or the leadership style changes in line with changing leaders. Even so, the evidence shows that attempts to change organizational or sub-organizational cultures frequently run into difficulties. Given that the more organic and integrative organizational cultures are said to support change and, in particular, the increasing requirement for creativity and innovation in order for organizations to remain forward looking and competitive, it seems reasonable for many organizations to attempt to change their cultures in these directions.

It was seen in Chapter 3 that changing structures is not always easy, even though organizational structures are to a large extent visible and understood. By contrast, organizational culture, although allied to organizational structure, is much less visible and, with its many layers, dimensions and types, that much more difficult to change. Indeed, many writers have considerable reservations about even attempting to change an organization's culture.

Consequently, as the later parts of this chapter show, there are occasions when attempting to change cultures is too risky and consideration must, therefore, be given to managing around the current culture or even changing the strategy to take account of the culture. What is more, as anyone involved in organizational change knows, some resistance to change is ever present, not least because of perceived changes in position and therefore power base. Organizational politics and the politics of change are as embedded in organizations as are their structures and cultures. In recognition of this, the next chapter examines the issues of power, politics, conflict and change.

Discussion questions and assignments

1 Drawing on your experience or that of others, and with reference to the literature, critically discuss why, in some cases, culture change seems to have been possible while in others this was not so.

2 To what extent does an organization's structure influence its culture and its capacity to work with change? Justify your answer.

3 Review the evidence for and against the notion that, because of increasing globalization of business and people's increasing knowledge of the attitudes and behaviour of people in different countries, national cultures are converging. Provide evidence for your arguments.

4 Prepare a presentation to demonstrate the degree of appropriateness of different types of organizational culture to different types of organizational change

Case example ●●●

Wal-Mart and Germany has not exactly been a love affair made in heaven

Wal-Mart, started by Sam Walton, continues to build on their successful formula and develop businesses outside of the US where the company originated. Within the information they provide, their statement to Americans in relation to employment commitment is as follows:

'Wal-Mart is committed to customers and communities we serve. What better way to represent the personality of each community than to hire locally, representing the diversity and uniqueness of everyone's home town? As the demographics of the nation have changed, so has our family of Wal-Mart Associates. Our Associates represent every age and walk of life. More than 15% of Wal-Mart Associates in the US are over the age of 55, and Wal-Mart is the nation's largest employer of truly mosaic cultures,

Case example *continued*

lifestyles and heritage. ... Our culture fosters a creative environment that enables people of different backgrounds and abilities to succeed. The success of our Associates means the continued success and growth of our company.'

These values have been developed from the core values of the business that began in the 1960s. Since that time they have continued to develop their business and now operate in 9 countries: Argentina, Brazil, Canada, China, Germany, Korea, Mexico, Puerto Rico and the United Kingdom. Currently Wal-Mart has 1,500 units with 330,000 Associates (their term for their employees).

In 2004, the BBC reviewed the progress of Wal-Mart in relation to its shaky beginnings in Germany. When Wal-Mart purchased two local store chains in Germany in 1997, they were not welcomed with open arms; in fact 'they left a trail of red ink'. The main criticism at the time was that they failed to understand German culture, 'what worked in Arkansas has flopped in Aachen'. Wal-Mart's founder liked the idea of 'greeters' at the doors of his stores so the concept was instituted in America and then the rest of the world. The report says though: 'The Germans ... balked'. The German culture did not warm to the 'homely friendliness of an elderly

man or woman greeting them at the door of the store'. Consequently, the idea was dropped 'uniquely on the planet, in Germany'.

By contrast, what Wal-Mart calls 'Flirt points' were set up where 'singles shoppers' can pause for a glass of wine and 'take a peek at the potential'. The practice appears to be working, particularly with older single people who wouldn't have the nerve to date on the Internet.

However, although there are signs the relationship is warming, the Wal-Mart culture and German business culture do not mesh easily (in contrast to the British culture). There are heavy constraints to selling goods below cost price in German superstores so 'loss leaders' are banned. In 2000, Wal-Mart found itself in court for selling long-life milk at less than cost. Wal-Mart's non-union policy was also at odds with German union loyalty.

Wal-Mart is not, however, giving up. In spite of the fact that they have had a bumpy ride, they are trying to introduce new products and adapt to the norms of operating in Germany. To date they run 92 Supercentres and employ 13,000 Associates.

Source: Evans, S (2004); Wal-Mart Flirt points arouse German interest. BBC. 16/11/2004; based on information in www.walmartstores.com; www.walmartgermany.de

---

Case exercise   Analyzing the cultures of Wal-Mart and Germany

In general terms, there are real issues for organizations that have been operating and wish to operate on a global scale. This scenario is not special, in so much that very often organizations will begin operating in a different country that may not have the same value base as their own. How this is managed will ultimately affect the success of the business.

1 Using at least two of the ways of analyzing an organization's culture discussed in the chapter, 'paint a picture' of the different cultures that appear in this case study.

2 From your reading and other knowledge you might have, what key initial factors do you think exist between this clash of national and organizational cultures?

3 By carrying out further research, through journals, texts, the Internet and the media, what other facts/information can you gather to build a richer picture relating to this clash of cultures?

4 Through the research in question 3, can you find examples of organizations that have been able to integrate into other cultures? What were some of their key success indicators/factors?

Indicative resources

Hofstede, G. (1994) *Cultures and Organizations*, London: McGraw-Hill. This book is an essential read for any student or manager interested in work relating to culture, both at national and organizational level. The book is organized into four parts, initially laying the foundation in relation to the concepts of culture. Part two deals with the differences in national cultures, with part three concentrating on organizational cultures. The fourth part of the book deals with the practical implications of culture within organizations and beyond.

Schein, H. E. (2004) *Organizational Culture and Leadership* (3rd edn) San Francisco, CA: Jossey-Bass. This book does not focus on the basic details in relation to culture; it assumes the reader has this knowledge already. It goes into more depth in relation to national and organizational culture. There are also useful case examples of Schein's work with organizations that add insight into this area.

Trompenaars, F. and Prud'homme, P. (2004) *Managing Change Across Corporate Cultures*, Chichester: Capstone Publishing. Although this is not strictly a text, it does focus on corporate culture at company, national and international levels. It offers theoretical perspectives relating to corporate culture, and includes case studies and research conducted by the authors.

Useful websites

www.thtconsulting.com This site offers various articles and consultancy information in relation to cross-cultural issues. It has information relating to business challenges of today and ideas on problem solving. Several areas of this site can be accessed without charge.

www.new-paradigm.co.uk/resources.htm This site provides a link to various organizational activities, of which understanding culture is one. It has categorized culture into specific areas of interest. These topics have additional links to choose from if you want to pursue a particular aspect of culture.

www.mapnp.org This is a free management library service that supports all aspects of management. The particular address for culture is **www.mapnp.org/library/org_thry/culture/culture/htm**. This provides you an article on organizational culture with a series of links that start with a definition, a library link, and you are also able to participate in online discussions.

To click straight to these links and for other resources go to
www.pearsoned.co.uk/senior

References

Adler, N. J. (1991) *International Dimensions of Organizational Behavior* (2nd edn), Belmont, CA: Wadsworth Publishing Company.

Adler, N. J. (1997) *International Dimensions of Organizational Behavior* (3rd edn), Cincinnati, OH: South Western College Publishing, ITP.

Alvesson, M. (1993) *Cultural Perspectives on Organizations*, Cambridge: Cambridge University Press.

Anthony, P. (1994) *Managing Culture*, Milton Keynes: Open University Press.

Argyris, C. (1964) *Integrating the Individual and the Organization*, New York: Wiley.

Argyris, C. and Schon, D. A. (1978) *Organizational Learning: A Theory of Action Perspective*, Reading, MA: Addison-Wesley.

Armstrong, M. (2003) *The Handbook of Human Resource Management Practice* (9th edn), London: Kogan Page.

Bate, S. P. (1996) 'Towards a strategic framework for changing corporate culture', *Strategic Change*, vol. 5, pp. 27–42.

Beer, M., Eisenstat, R. A. and Spector, B. (1993) 'Why change programs don't produce change', in Mabey, C. and Mayon-White, B. (eds) *Managing Change* (2nd edn), London: PCP.

Bem, D. J. (1970) *Beliefs, Attitudes and Human Affairs*, Belmont, CA: Brooks/Cole.

Brooks, I. and Bate, S. P. (1994) 'The problems of effecting change within the British Civil Service: a cultural perspective', *British Journal of Management*, vol. 5, pp. 177–90.

Brown, A. (1995) *Organisational Culture*, London: Pitman.

Burnes, B. (2004) *Managing Change* (4th edn), Harlow: Financial Times Prentice Hall.

Burns, T. and Stalker, G. M. (1961) *The Management of Innovation*, London: Tavistock.

Calori, R. and De Woot, P. (1994) *A European Management Model Beyond Diversity*, Hemel Hempstead: Prentice Hall.

Carnall, C. (1995) *Managing Change in Organizations* (2nd edn), Hemel Hempstead: Prentice Hall.

Carnall, C. (2003) *Managing Change in Organizations* (4th edn), Harlow: Financial Times Prentice Hall.

Castells, M. (1989) 'High technology and the new international division of labour', *Labour and Society*, vol. 14, Special Issue, pp. 7–20.

Chambers, D. (1996) 'Russia's different problems', *Financial Times*, 23 February, pp. 9–10.

Chandler, A. D., Jr (1962) *Strategy and Structure: Chapters in the History of the Industrial Enterprise*, Cambridge, MA: MIT Press.

Chinese Culture Connection (1987) 'Chinese values and the search for culture-free dimensions of culture', *Journal of Cross-Cultural Psychology*, vol. 18, no. 2, pp. 143–64.

Cummings, T. G. and Worley, C. G. (2005) *Organization Development and Change* (8th edn), Mason, OH: Thompson South-Western.

Deal, T. E. and Kennedy, A. A. (1982) *Corporate Cultures: The Rites and Rituals of Corporate Life*, Reading, MA: Addison-Wesley.

Deal, T. and Kennedy, A. (2000) *The New Corporate Cultures*, London: Perseus Books.

D'Iribarne, P. (1989) *La Logique de l'Honneur: Gestion des Entreprises et Traditions Nationales*, Paris: Seuil.

Dobson, P. (1988) 'Changing culture', *Employment Gazette*, December, pp. 647–50.

Drennan, D. (1992) *Transforming Company Culture*, London: McGraw-Hill.

Drucker, P. (1992) 'The new society of organizations', *Harvard Business Review*, September–October, pp. 95–104.

Dunphy, D. and Stace, D. (1993) 'The strategic management of corporate change', *Human Relations*, vol. 46, no. 8, pp. 905–20.

Dyer, W. (1985) 'The cycle of cultural evolution in organizations', in Kilmann, R. H., Saxton, M. J. and Serpa, R. (eds) *Gaining Control of the Corporate Culture*, San Francisco, CA: Jossey-Bass.

Eccles, T. (1994) *Succeeding with Change Implementing Action-driven Strategies*, Maidenhead: McGraw Hill.

Evans, S. (2004) 'Wal-Mart Flirt points arouse German interest', BBC, 16 November.

Frank, S. (2000) 'On a wavelength with the Danes', *Financial Times*, October 23, p. 15.

French, W. L. and Bell, C. H., Jr (1990) *Organization Development: Behavioral Science Interventions for Organization Improvement* (4th edn), Englewood Cliffs, NJ: Prentice-Hall.

French, W. L. and Bell, C. H., Jr (1999) *Organizational Development* (6th edn), Englewood Cliffs, NJ: Prentice-Hall.

Furnham, A. and Gunter, B. (1993) 'Corporate culture: diagnosis and change', in Cooper, C. L. (ed.) *International Review of Industrial and Organisational Psychology*, Chichester: Wiley.

Goodman, M. (1995) *Creative Management*, Hemel Hempstead: Prentice Hall.

Hall, W. (1995) *Managing Cultures: Making Strategic Relationships Work*, Chichester: Wiley.

Handy, C. (1993) *Understanding Organizations*, Hamondsworth: Penguin.

Harrison, R. (1972) 'How to describe your organization', *Harvard Business Review*, September–October, pp. 119–28.

Hickson, D. J. and MacMillan, C. J. (1981) *Organization and Nation: The Aston Programme IV*, Aldershot: Gower.

Hill, S. and McNulty, D. (1998) 'Overcoming cultural barriers to change', *Health Manpower Mangement*, vol. 24, no. 1, pp. 6–12.

Hofstede, G. (1980) *Culture's Consequences: International Differences in Work-related Values*, London and Beverly Hills, CA: Sage, pp. 4–10.

Hofstede, G. (1981) 'Culture and organizations', *International Studies of Management and Organizations*, vol. X, no. 4, pp. 15–41.

Hofstede, G. (1991) *Cultures and Organizations: Software of the Mind*, Maidenhead: McGraw Hill.

Hofstede, G. (1993) 'Cultural constraints in management theories', *Academy of Management Executive*, February, pp. 81–94.

Hofstede, G. (1994) *Cultures and Organizations*, London: McGraw-Hill.

Hofstede, G. (1994) 'Management scientists are human', *Management Science*, vol. 40, no. 1, January.

Hofstede, G., Neuijen, B., Ohayv, D. and Sanders, G. (1990) 'Measuring organizational cultures: a qualitative and quantitative study across twenty cases', *Administrative Science Quarterly*, vol. 35, pp. 286–316.

Hope, V. and Hendry, J. (1995) 'Corporate cultural change: is it relevant for the organisations of the 1990s?', *Human Resource Management Journal*, vol. 5, no. 4, Summer, pp. 61–73.

Jaques, E. (1952) *The Changing Culture of a Factory*, New York: Dryden.

Johnson, G. (1987) *Strategic Change and the Management Process*, Oxford: Blackwell.

Johnson, G. (1990) 'Managing strategic action: the role of symbolic action', *British Journal of Management*, vol. 1, pp. 183–200.

Johnson, G. (1996) Lecture to Diploma in Management Studies students at Nene College of Higher Education, Northampton.

Johnson, G. and Scholes, K. (1997) *Exploring Corporate Strategy, Texts and Cases*, Hemel Hempstead: Prentice Hall.

Johnson, G. and Scholes, K. (1999) *Exploring Corporate Strategy, Texts and Cases* (5th edn), Hemel Hempstead: Prentice Hall.

Johnson, G., Scholes, K., and Whittington, R. (2005) *Exploring Strategic Change: Texts and Cases* (7th edn), Harlow: Pearson Education.

Kanter, R. M. (1983) *The Change Masters*, London: Routledge.

Kerr, C., Dunlop, J. T., Harbison, F. H. and Myers, C. A. (1960) *Industrialism and Industrial Man*, London: Heinemann.

Kluckhohn, F. and Strodtbeck, F. L. (1961) *Variations in Value Orientations*, Evanston, IL: Row, Peterson.

Knightley, P. (2000) *Australia: Biography of a Nation*, London: Cape.

Kotter, J. P. and Heskett, J. L. (1992) *Corporate Culture and Performance*, New York: Free Press.

Kroeber, A. L. and Kluckhohn, F. (1952) *Culture: A Critical Review of Concepts and Definitions*, New York: Vintage Books.

Laurent, A. (1983) 'The cultural diversity of Western conceptions of management', *International Studies of Management and Organisation*, vol. XIII, nos 1–2, pp. 75–96.

Louis, M. R. (1980) 'Organizations as culture-bearing milieux', in Pondy, L. R. *et al.* (eds) *Organizational Symbolism*, Greenwich, CT: JAI.

Maurice, M., Sorge, A. and Warner, M. (1980) 'Societal differences in organizing manufacturing units', *Organization Studies*, vol. 1, pp. 63–91.

Morgan, G. (1986) *Images of Organization*, London: Sage.

Morgan, G. (1989) *Creative Organization Theory*: A Resource Book, London: Sage.

Nasser, J. and Wetlaufer, S. (1999) 'Driving change: an interview with Jacques Nasser', *Harvard Business Review*, March–April, pp. 76–88.

Ogbonna, E. and Harris, L. C. (1998) 'Managing organizational culture: compliance or genuine change', *British Journal of Management*, vol. 9, pp. 273–88.

Ogbonna, E. and Harris, L. C. (2002) 'Managing organisational culture: insights from the hospitality industry', *Human Resource Management Journal*, vol. 12, no. 1, pp. 33–51.

Ohmae, K. (1991) 'Getting rid of headquarters mentality', in *The Borderless World: Power and Strategy in the Interlinked Economy*, London: Fontana, pp. 101–24.

Open University (1985) Block III, 'Organizations', Course T244, *Managing in Organizations*, Milton Keynes: Open University.

Pacanowsky, M. E. and O'Donnell-Trujillo, N. (1982) 'Communication and organizational culture', *The Western Journal of Speech Communication*, vol. 46, Spring, pp. 115–30.

Payne, R. L. (1990), 'The concepts of culture and climate', Working Paper 202, Manchester Business School.

Peters, T. J. and Waterman, R. H. (1982) *In Search of Excellence*, New York: Harper & Row.

Pettigrew, A. M. (1990) 'Is corporate culture manageable?', in Wilson, D. C. and Rosenfeld, R. H. (eds) *Managing Organizations: Text, Readings and Cases*, Maidenhead: McGraw-Hill, pp. 266–72.

Pheysey, D. C. (1993) *Organizational Cultures: Types and Transformations*, London: Routledge.

Pugh, D. S. and Hickson, D. J. (1976) *Organizational Structure in its Context: The Aston Programme 1*, Aldershot: Gower.

Robbins, S. P. (1996) *Organizational Behavior: Concepts, Controversies, Applications* (7th edn), Englewood Cliffs, NJ: Prentice-Hall.

Robbins, S. P. (2001) *Organizational Behavior: Concepts, Controversies, Applications* (9th edn), Englewood Cliffs, NJ: Prentice-Hall.

Robbins, S. P. (2003) *Organizational Behaviour* (10th edn), Englewood Cliffs, NJ: Pearson Education.

Robbins, S. P (2005) *Organizational Behaviour* (11th edn), Englewood Cliffs, NJ: Pearson Education.

Schein, E. H. (1985) *Organizational Culture and Leadership*, San Francisco, CA: Jossey-Bass.

Schein, E. H. (1992) *Organizational Culture and Leadership* (2nd edn), San Francisco, CA: Jossey-Bass.

Schein, E. H. (2004) *Organizational Culture and Leadership* (3rd edn), San Francisco, CA: Jossey-Bass.

Scholz, C. (1987) 'Corporate culture and strategy: the problem of strategic fit', *Long Range Planning*, vol. 20, no. 4, pp. 78–87.

Schwartz, H. and Davis, S. M. (1981) 'Matching corporate strategy and business strategy', *Organizational Dynamics*, Summer, pp. 30–48.

Smethurst, S. (2005) 'Found in translation', *People Management*, 5 May, pp. 34–6.

Tayeb, M. (1989) *Organizations and National Culture: A Comparative Analysis*, London: Sage.

Trompenaars, F. and Prud'homme, P. (2004) *Managing Change across Corporate Cultures*, Chichester: Capstone Publishing.

Tushman, M. L., Newman, W. H. and Romanelli, E. (1988) 'Convergence and upheaval: managing the unsteady pace of organizational evolution', in Tushman, M. L. and Moore, W. L. (eds) *Readings in the Management of Innovation*, New York: Ballinger Publishing.

Wilson, D. C. (1992) *A Strategy of Change: Concepts and Controversies in the Management of Change*, London: Routledge.

Wilson, D. C. and Rosenfeld, R. H. (1990) *Managing Organizations: Text, Readings and Cases*, Maidenhead: McGraw-Hill.

Woodward, J. (1965) *Industrial Organization: Theory and Practice*, London: Oxford University Press.

www.hsbc.com

www.lafarge.com

www.walmartstores.com

www.walmartgermany.de

Chapter 5

The politics of change

Issues of power, cooperation and conflict are part of the politics of organizational life. Their importance is recognized in this chapter through a discussion of the sources of power and the way political action, as an expression of power, can be used in the management of change. This discussion is extended to include issues of powerlessness, with particular attention being paid to the position of women and members of minority groupings. A debate about the role of conflict concludes that not all conflict is dysfunctional to organizational performance and the ability of organizations to change.

Learning objectives

By the end of this chapter, you will be able to:

● define the meaning of 'organizational politics';

● distinguish between different sources of power and ways of using power to influence people and events;

● define and discuss the link between power, politics and conflict;

● identify different types of conflict as a means of suggesting possible actions for conflict resolution;

● critically discuss the relationship between power, conflict and change and ways of managing these.

●●●● Organizational politics

Observation of small children left to their own devices shows a natural curiosity evidenced by a propensity to explore, experiment, form friendships with some children and not others and, quite frequently, thwart the intentions of their parents and other adults. These childlike characteristics do not disappear as children become adult and members of different organizations. In fact, learning how to thwart parents is probably good training for learning how to thwart the more formal aspects of organizational life such as rules and regulated procedures. Stacey (1996, p. 387) calls this type of activity 'self-organization', that is, the self-forming patterns and processes which 'shadow' the formal organization and that are endemic in all organizations. These patterns and processes are essentially political processes, which imply the exercise of power and the management of conflict. As such, they are of intrinsic interest in any discussion of organizational change.

The previous chapter discussed the culture of organizations as part of the informal or hidden part of organizational life; that is, part of the hidden section of the organizational iceberg. One conclusion about the nature of organizational culture is that it may be so all-pervasive that it is not so much hidden as not noticed until some kind of change occurs. The same might be said about the political processes, which appear to be an essential part of an organization's functioning. Yet the concepts of politics, power and conflict, particularly in the context of resistance to change, frequently appear in the role of the more undesirable aspects of organizational life. For instance, Robbins (2005, p. 390), drawing on the writings of Kanter (1979), says: 'Power has been described as the last dirty word. … People who have it deny it, people who want it try not to appear to be seeking it, and those who are good at getting it are secretive about how they got it.'

A survey of attitudes towards change management and organizational politics involving 90 English managers during 1997 found that politics was a distracting side issue compared to the issue of organizational performance (see Buchanan and Badham, 1999, p. 19). Of the respondents, 53 per cent agreed (against 24 per cent disagreement and 23 per cent neutral) that organizational politics is usually damaging, is a sign of incompetent management, and needs to be eradicated wherever possible. Contrariwise, 72 per cent agreed that, 'the more complex and wide-reaching the change, the more intense the politics become', with most agreeing that change agents (those facilitating or managing change) needed to be politically skilled. It seems that most managers would like to manage without the need to resort to political behaviour yet acknowledge the reality of it, particularly in the context of organizational change.

Defining power and politics

Defining 'power' and 'politics' is not straightforward. As Buchanan and Huczynski (2004, p. 828) say: 'These are broad and vague concepts that have proved difficult to define or to measure, with precision and without ambiguity.' For their purposes, in discussing power, politics and organizational change, they offer the following:

> Power concerns the capacity of individuals to exert their will over others. Political behaviour is the practical domain of power in action, worked out through the use of techniques of influence and other (more or less extreme) tactics.

Consequently, power is an ability to make things happen and to overcome resistance in order to achieve desired objectives or results. Political behaviour, according to Buchanan and Huczynski, is 'the observable, but often covert, actions by which executives (and others) enhance their power to influence decisions'.

The concept of 'power in action' is echoed by Robbins (2005, p. 390) who maintains that this happens whenever people get together in groups and where an individual or group seeks to influence the thoughts, attitudes or behaviours of another individual or group. Acting politically is also a part of negotiation, as a means to overcoming resistance and of resolving conflict. It can, however, be the cause of conflict in that an individual or group seeks to affect, negatively, another individual or group. Thus conflict may be the result of the use of power to affect others adversely. However, as Hardy (1994) points out, although power can be used to overcome conflict it can also be used to avert it. Therefore, as will be seen later in this discussion, political behaviour in organizations is not all bad.

Robbins divides the meaning of politics into 'legitimate' and illegitimate' political behaviour, the former being normal everyday politics such as bypassing the chain of command, forming coalitions, obstructing organization policies and so on; the latter being deliberate sabotage, whistle blowing and groups of employees reporting sick. Robbins's (pp. 400–1) viewpoint can be summarized in his formal definition of political behaviour as follows:

> For our purposes, we shall define political behaviour in organizations as those activities that are not required as part of one's formal role in the organization, but that influence, or attempt to influence, the distribution of advantages and disadvantages within the organization.

This definition seems to accord with the views of Buchanan and Badham's sample of managers, discussed earlier, in their aversion to political behaviour in the normal course of organizational life. Having said this, Robbins clearly recognizes the reality of politics when he refers to politics as a fact of life in organizations.

All these definitions appear to view political behaviour as one aspect of organizational life, which mirrors the 'objectivist' view of culture discussed in Chapter 4. Given Morgan's (1997) contrary views on organizational culture, it is not surprising that he poses organizations as political systems. As a consequence of this, he says that different types of organizations can be characterized as displaying different types of political rule. Illustration 5.1 describes the varieties of political rule that Morgan claims can be found in organizations.

Illustration 5.1

Organizations and modes of political rule

- **Autocracy**. Absolute government where power is held by an individual or small group and supported by control of critical resources, property or ownership rights, tradition, charisma and other claims to personal privilege.

- **Bureaucracy**. Rule exercised through use of the written word, which provides the basis for a rational–legal type of authority or 'rule of law'.

- **Technocracy**. Rule exercised through use of knowledge, expert power and the ability to solve relevant problems.

- **Co-determination**. The form of rule where opposing parties combine in the joint management of mutual interests, as in coalition government or corporatism, each party drawing on a specific power base.

- **Representative democracy**. Rule exercised through the election of officers mandated to act on behalf of the electorate and who hold office for a specified time period or so long as they command the support of the electorate, as in parliamentary government and forms of worker control and shareholder control in industry.

- **Direct democracy**. The system where everyone has an equal right to rule and is involved in all decision making, as in many communal organizations such as cooperatives and kibbutzim. This political principle encourages self-organization as a key mode of organizing.

Source: Morgan, G. (1997), *Images of Organizations* (London, Sage, p. 157).

In his discussion of different types of political rule, Morgan draws attention to how the suffix -*cracy*, which appears in these terms, is derived from *kratia* – a Greek term meaning power or rule. Thus the word autocracy implies the rule of one person, that is, the use of dictatorial power; the term bureaucracy is associated with people who sit at bureaux or desks making and administering rules; a technocracy is associated with the power of those with technical knowledge and skills; and democracy draws on the meaning of the prefix *demos* or populace, so that in democratic forms of organization power rests with the people as a whole or through their representatives.

Given these expressions of organizational politics, it is not difficult to conclude that politics are a part of everyday organizational life. That this is so becomes evident, most clearly, in the context of organizational change, particularly in the context of discontinuous, frame-breaking or transformational change discussed in Chapter 2. In order to understand, more thoroughly, the relationship between the political aspects of organizations and their ability to cope with change, some attention should be paid to power, conflict and resistance as component parts of organizational politics.

 **Power in organizations**

The characteristics of power

Buchanan and Huczynski's (2004) definition of power has been offered above. It is interesting to contrast this with a number of other definitions of power. For instance:

> Power influences who gets what, when and how.   (Morgan, 1997, p. 170)

> Power is the potential or actual ability to influence others in a desired direction. An individual, group, or other social unit has power if it controls information, knowledge, or resources desired by another individual, group, or social unit
> (Gordon, 1993, p. 392)

> Power is defined as the potential ability to influence behaviour, to change the course of events, to overcome resistance, and to get people to do things that they would otherwise not do.   (Pfeffer, 1993, pp. 204–5)

> Power refers to a capacity that A has to influence the behaviour of B, so that B acts in accordance with A's wishes.   (Robbins, 2005, p. 390)

All these definitions have one thing in common – having power means being able to influence someone else's behaviour. Pfeffer's and Robbins's definitions bring in the added dimension of influencing that behaviour in a direction which the person or group would not, otherwise, have chosen. Robbins, in relation to his own definition, says it implies: a potential that need not be actualized to be effective; a dependency relationship; and the assumption that B has some discretion over his or her own behaviour. Power, therefore, is a function of relationships. It is not something a person 'has' regardless of what other people are thinking or doing; it only becomes valid when one person has something that the other values. For instance, a bank's ability to lend money to businesses gives it power over those businesses only if they are in need of finance and cannot obtain it anywhere else on the same terms.

Power also derives from differences between people and groups. Some people have more knowledge, expertise or resources than others do and, if these are scarce and desired, that person or group will have greater amounts of power than others. This can be referred to as the 'elasticity of power', a term taken from economics. In the field of higher education, staff with good research records are more highly valued than those without. Therefore the power of staff to seek employment in many places is directly related to their publication records. The power of a head of department is inversely related to the strength of his or her staff's publication records.

Not all people in an organizational situation would agree on who has power, of whatever type, and who has not. Power exists, to a large extent, only in the eye of the beholder. It is not necessarily the resources or knowledge controlled that give someone power but the belief by others that he or she has that power of control. Many employees have not progressed in their organizations because they misjudged those who had the power to help them and those who did not. Others may potentially have power of one kind or another but perceive themselves to be powerless and thus miss the opportunity to exercise it on their own behalf. Handy (1993, p. 125) refers to the 'relativity of power' to describe the situation where one person or group perceives another to have power while a second person or group believes otherwise. As he says (*ibid.*): 'The group that overawes one person with its prestige and renown looks ludicrous to another. ... Bribes will sway some but repulse others.'

Handy also notes that power is rarely one-sided. Hitting back or saying no is an option open to those who are seemingly powerless. The dominance of one person over another depends on the power balance – how much one can put into the equation against the power of the other. One type of power can often be traded for another, for instance money for image, as in the case of a company giving money to a university to fund a professorial chair which is intended to improve that company's image in the eyes of the community.

In summary, power is about the potential to influence as well as the actuality of influence and it is a function of relationships and differences between people, people's beliefs about it and how much one person has it in relation to another.

The relationship between power and influence

Many writers separate what power is from the means by which it is used. Handy (1993) distinguishes the concept of power from that of influence as evidence of this. Illustration 5.2 summarizes Handy's descriptions.

Handy's classification of power and influence is useful, but life is not always as clear-cut as he suggests. For instance, a particular method of influence could be used in conjunction with several sources of power. In addition, the distinction between power and influence may, to some extent, be artificial – one shades into another. Morgan (1997), in his chapter entitled 'Organizations as political systems', does not differentiate between power and influence but discusses a list of 14 sources of power (see Illustration 5.3).

Paton (1994) discusses many of the sources of power found in Morgan's list but, usefully, divides them into what he calls 'visible' and 'invisible' sources of power. Many of these categorizations overlap with Hardy's (1994) identification of four 'dimensions' of power – decision-making power, non-decision-making power, symbolic power and the power of the system. Yet another example of a discussion of different types of power is that of Robbins (2005), shown in Illustration 5.4.

Illustration 5.2

Power and influence

The possible sources of individual power that give one the ability to influence others are as follows:

- *Physical power*: the power of superior force.
- *Resource power*: the possession of valued resources; the control of rewards.
- *Position power*: legitimate power; comes as a result of the role or position held in the organization.
- *Expert power*: vested in someone because of their acknowledged expertise.
- *Personal power*: charisma, popularity; resides in the person and in their personality.
- *Negative power*: illegitimate power; the ability to disrupt or stop things happening.

Methods of influence

Different types of power are used in different kinds of ways. Particular methods of influence attach themselves (more or less) to particular types of power. Some methods of influence draw on two or more sources of power:

- *Force*: derived from having physical power; physical bullying, hold-ups, loss of temper.
- *Rules and procedures*: derived from having position power, backed by resource power; devising rules and procedures to result in particular outcomes.
- *Exchange*: derived from having resource power; bargaining, negotiating, bribing.
- *Persuasion*: derived from having personal power; use of logic, the power of argument, evidence of facts.
- *Ecology*: derived from different power sources; manipulating the physical and psychological environment to achieve certain purposes.
- *Magnetism*: derives from personal and sometimes expert power; inspiring trust, respect; using charm, infectious enthusiasm.

Source: Based on Handy, C. (1993), *Understanding Organizations* (London, Penguin, pp. 126–41).

Illustration 5.3

Morgan's sources of power in organizations

1 Formal authority.
2 Control of scarce resources.
3 Use of organizational structure, rules and regulations.
4 Control of decision processes.
5 Control of knowledge and information.
6 Control of boundaries.
7 Ability to cope with uncertainty.
8 Control of technology.
9 Interpersonal alliances, networks, and control of 'informal organization'.
10 Control of counterorganizations.
11 Symbolism and the management of meaning.
12 Gender and the management of gender relations.
13 Structural factors that define the stage of action.
14 The power one already has.

Source: Morgan, G. (1997), *Images of Organizations* (London, Sage, p. 171).

Illustration 5.4

Formal and personal power

Formal power

- *Coercive power*. This is dependent on fear. One reacts to this power out of fear of the negative results that might occur if one failed to comply.
- *Reward power*. The opposite of coercive power. People comply with directives because doing so produces positive benefits; therefore one who can distribute rewards that others view as valuable will have power over others.
- *Legitimate power*. Formal groups that are part of a structure in an organization. It represents the formal authority to control and use organizational resources.
- *Information power*. This derives from the access to and control over information. People in organizations who have data or knowledge that others need can make those others dependent on them.

Personal power

- *Expert power*. Influence displayed in expertise, specialist skills and knowledge. Particularly relevant in a technological environment in which most of us now operate.
- *Referent power*. Identification with a person who has desirable resources or personal traits.
- *Charismatic power*. An extension of referent power that comes from an individual's personality and interpersonal style. These individuals may not be in formal positions of power or leadership, but may have influence over others.

Source: Robbins, S.P. (2005). *Organizational Behavior*, 11th edn, pp. 392–4.

Robbins suggests there are two broad categories of power: formal power and personal power. Formal power relates to the position of the individual within the organization and incorporates coercive, reward, legitimate and information power, all of which are particularly important in times of uncertainty and change. Personal power derives from the 'unique characteristics' of individuals such as their skills and expertise, their personalities and their favoured association with others from whom they gain status and other desirable resources.

However, regardless of whose account is read, a number of common themes occur. The first of these is the recognition that power comes with position and the ability to control resources.

Activity 5.1

1 *In relation to Robbins's descriptions of the sub-categories of formal power, identify individuals in your own organization who you consider 'fit' each of the four sub-categories.*

2 *In relation to Robbins's descriptions of the sub-categories of personal power, identify individuals inside and external to your organization. These might include individuals in the media, entertainment industry and other external organizations who use one or more personal power bases to influence others opinions and actions – and even your own!*

Position power and the control of resources

Almost all writers list position power or formal authority as an obvious source of power in organizations. Weber (1947), in his studies of organizations, drew attention to three types of authority. The first derives from tradition, that is, authority legitimized by custom and practice and a belief in the right of certain individuals to rule others. The second is charismatic authority, which is legitimized through the leader's particular qualities being valued and an inspiration to others. The third type of authority is what Weber called 'rational–legal authority'. It is this type of authority that characterizes the power held by people because of their position in some formal or understood hierarchy that has some independent standing with regard to the rules and procedures sustaining it. Position power, or as Robbins (see Illustration 5.4) terms it 'formal power' bestows certain rights on those who have it, for instance the right to order others to do things or to refuse other people's requests.

Handy (1993) links position power with resource power by arguing that if some control over resources does not come with the position, the source of this power will be invalid. This implies the backing of the organization for the decisions of the individual concerned. In most modern organizations some resource power accrues automatically to particular positions by virtue of the rational–legal basis on which the organization is structured.

Resource power

Resource power comes with the power to distribute valued rewards or to withhold or withdraw something that someone else values. Illustration 5.5 describes two different, but related, strategies associated with the ability to withdraw or bestow valued rewards. These are 'push' and 'pull' strategies.

Illustration 5.5

Influencing others through push and pull strategies

'Push' strategies

Push strategies attempt to influence people by imposing or threatening to impose 'costs' on the people or group concerned if they do not do what is required. This may be done either by *withdrawing* something that the 'target' of your influence values, for example your cooperation and support, or by threatening a sanction if your 'target' does not comply, for example disciplinary action, a poor appraisal, removal of a bonus or perk, or often it may be public criticism or shaming. The ability to impose such costs will depend largely on a person's *position* and the *resources* that she or he controls.

'Pull' or 'reward' strategies

If push strategies are the stick, then 'pull' or 'reward' strategies are the carrot. They are 'the stuff' of theories of motivation that emphasize material, social and other extrinsic rewards. Rewards are often used to influence people by a process of *exchange*: 'I will give you so and so if you will do this for me.' Pull strategies may follow from any of the power bases: resources, for example extra pay or extra staff may be offered; expertise or information may be traded; increased status may be conferred or access to valuable contacts given. Less obvious, but perhaps more common, there are friendship and favour, approval, and inclusion in a group.

Source: Based on Handy, C. (1993), *Understanding Organizations* (London, Penguin, pp. 126–41).

Activity 5.2

Describe some occasions when you have tried to use either a 'push' strategy or a 'pull' strategy to achieve an outcome you desired – perhaps to influence how other people acted.

Were the strategies successful? If so, why do you think they worked?

If any of the strategies were not successful, why do you think this was so?

Invisible power

Control over resources such as determining other people's budgets or rate of promotion are examples of what Paton (1994) calls *visible assets* of the power holder. However, both Handy (1993) and Paton draw attention to what they term *invisible assets*. These are, first, the power to control information, which is also referred to in Morgan's and Robbins's lists of sources of power. Handy (1993, p. 129) says:

> A flow of information often belongs as of right to a 'position' in the organization. If it does not already belong it can often be originated as a necessary input to that position. This can be horizontal information, i.e. information, often of a technical nature, from the same level of the organization; vertical information, from above or from below but potentially trapped in the particular 'position' and to be dispersed with the agreement of the occupant. Information, above all else in life, seems to display the essential features of synergy. The whole is so often much more meaningful than the parts. An informational jig-saw, even though all the pieces are separately available, is nothing until put together. A 'position' can be, or can be made to be, simply by function of its position, a junction-box for information.

Morgan (1997, p. 179) echoes this by saying:

> These (people) are often known as 'gatekeepers' who open and close channels of communication and filtering, summarizing, analyzing, and thus shaping knowledge in accordance with a view of the world that favours their interests.

The ability to slow down or accelerate the flow of information gives power to many people who probably do not occupy 'high' positions, but who simply act as messengers or copiers of information from one part of the organization to another. It is interesting that the advent of electronic mail and other means of electronic communication have become 'protected' by the use of personal passwords which control who gets what information and when. Illustration 5.6 is an example of invisible power that became visible only in one of its uses.

A second type of invisible asset (Handy, 1993) is that of right of access, which is similar to what Robbins calls referent power and what Morgan refers to as having access to interpersonal alliances, networks and the 'informal organization'. Certain positions in organizations give the right of entry to a variety of networks. While many of these are formal, there exist many informal networks

Illustration 5.6

Listening in at the Beautiful Buildings Company

Just recently, the BB Company has secured contracts for three large-scale office buildings in Manchester, Melbourne and New York. As a consequence of the need to maintain quick and reliable communications across the company, whose head office is currently in Milton Keynes, Gillian Lambeth, the Managing Director, and her co-directors have decided to install a technologically based information system to facilitate communications using systems such as electronic mail.

A few weeks after staff had been trained to use the email system, Marcos Davidson, the Marketing Director, sent messages to his project manager in New York asking for information on another company's building that was similar to the one the BB Company was erecting in Manchester.

Imagine his surprise when a message came back within an hour from Gillian Lambeth asking to be informed of the results of his enquiry. He thought that, with the use of his personal (secret) password, no one but himself and whoever else he designated had access to his messages. What he did not know, until then, was that Gillian had asked the system installers to place her in a position where she could 'listen in' to any messages sent by anyone to anyone else on the system.

Marcos decided there and then to take care, in the future, about the types of message he sent and to use other communication channels for information he did not yet want Gillian to know about. Furthermore, he thought it might be a good idea if he had the same 'rights' over his staff that his Managing Director had over him!

and groupings to which entry comes more easily because of a person's position. Morgan (1997, p. 186) says:

> The skilled organizational politician systematically builds and cultivates such informal alliances and networks, incorporating whenever possible the help and influence of all those with an important stake in the domain in which he or she is operating.

An invisible asset mentioned by both Paton (1994) and Handy (1993) is the right to organize, which tends to be part of position power. Here again, this is not unlike Morgan's (1997) statement that a source of power is being able to use the organization's structure, rules and regulations to suit one's own purposes. The right to organize is linked to methods of influence associated with ecology. An example is the power to say who occupies which organizational spaces or to waive certain rules according to convenience. Morgan and Paton both argue that organizational and work group structure can be used as a political instrument. Reorganization always means a redistribution of power. Therefore, the power to restructure an organization or part of it can be regarded as visible power. However, hidden agendas to use this process to accomplish other aims (e.g. reducing someone's access to certain information; changing someone else's committee memberships) are good examples of the use of invisible power.

Non-decision-making power

Position power almost always includes the right to make particular decisions. This is one of Hardy's (1994) dimensions of power – decision-making power.

Illustration 5.7

Controlling the decision agenda

The marketing manager of an insurance company was on the brink of launching a large product development campaign. At the next management meeting it had been decided to discuss poor profit performance in the previous two quarters. At issue was whether to deploy resources to expanding sales or to cutting costs by increasing automation (via electronic data processing). He knew that if this issue were to be raised at the meeting he would be outvoted by a small minority of peers who leaned toward investing the funds in automation. However, he was convinced that automation did not sell insurance! Therefore he needed to find an issue that would rearrange the coalition structure currently against him. He realized that the key issue he would prefer to have discussed was market share and not profits, so he did three things. First, he sent a report to all the management committee

members that showed how losses in market share could be regained by his proposal. Second, he sent to all members of the management committee a memo asking them to consider ways in which his proposed product development programme could be carried out effectively and at a lower cost. Third, he persuaded the chief executive to place his project proposal first on the agenda. When the meeting started, the issue was not whether the product launch should take place or not, but what funds would be required to launch the product; the automation proposal was postponed, because some marginal members of the automation coalition had become committed to the market share issue.

Source: Paton, R. (1994), 'Power in organizations', in Arson, R. and Paton, R., *Organizations, Cases, Issues, Concepts* (London, PCP, p. 194).

This power is frequently visible and unquestioned because of the power of the position. However, both Hardy (1994) and Paton (1994) show how issues that are not, strictly speaking, directly concerned with the decision itself can, even so, be presented in such a way as to influence the outcome (see Illustration 5.7).

Wilson (1992, p. 54) refers to the type of power described in Illustration 5.7 as 'covert' power, saying: 'Here power is exercised through "non-decision making" rather than by means of attempts to influence readily identifiable (and commonly known) decision topics.' Invisible or covert power associated with decision making takes many forms. For instance, as shown in Illustration 5.7, it may take the form of the power to 'set' the agenda under which something will be discussed, limiting who may or may not take part in the discussion or defining the scope of the discussion. Hardy (1994) discusses the notion of 'safe' agendas where some issues do not even get discussed. Thus some topics and people are deliberately excluded from the decision-making process. Exclusion from this process can also come about because participants do not have the knowledge or expertise to express a view or take part in any meaningful debate. The role of the 'expert' appears in many guises.

Personal power

Robbins (2005), as shown in Illustration 5.4, distinguishes personal power from formal power. While this distinction is not always clear-cut, it draws attention to sources of power that do not necessarily derive from the position a person occupies in an organization or the resources controlled. Three categories of personal power are suggested: expert or knowledge power; symbolic power; and individual power.

Expert or knowledge power

Paton (1994, p. 191) says: 'Organizations use specialist knowledge to cope with task and environmental uncertainty. This means that on certain issues they must rely on and accept the judgement of those who possess that knowledge.' Those who have specialist knowledge or expertise that is in scarce supply have resource power of a particular kind. Paton (ibid.) gives an example of this:

> The middle-ranking research chemist who calmly says 'it just can't be done' can stop the marketing director of a chemical firm dead in his or her tracks. If the director is unwise enough to press the point he or she simply invites a lecture on, say, some finer points of polymer chemistry, whereupon – whether he or she pretends to understand and agree, or instead admits to not understanding and refuses to agree – the point is irretrievably lost.

However, as Handy (1993, p. 130) says, 'expert power is hedged about by one major qualification; it can only be given by those over whom it will be exercised'. Therefore, unless someone's claim to expertise is recognized, it will not become a power source for that person.

Morgan (1997, p. 184) says: 'From the beginning of history, technology has served as an instrument of power, enhancing the ability of humans to manipulate, control, and impose themselves on their environment.' Knowledge of how to design and operate information technology systems is a special form of expert power. So many organizational functions and processes are dependent on information technology. Therefore, those who can solve the frequently recurring operating problems have power, often above their status. Many of these people are classed only as technicians, yet they have the power to reduce, instantly, the frustrations of others who are reduced to sitting impotently in front of a computer or prolong those frustrations through operating their own informal queuing system of those in need of help.

An interesting aspect of expert power (Handy, 1993) is that it is relative. To accumulate expert power, the expertise does not have to be very much greater than that of other people. A small amount of extra expertise can bring large amounts of power. However, as Handy points out, this power can easily be lost if someone comes along who has even a small degree of further expertise.

Symbolic power

In an article in the *Guardian* (26 July 1996) on the selling of copied computer software programs alongside religious amulets, John Ryle says:

> An amulet is an ally, a reminder of an exemplary life, but its deepest meaning is decipherable only by priests and scholars. Likewise with software: the programs promise power and knowledge, but can be fully exploited only by cognoscenti (especially if the manufacturers, anticipating piracy, have protected them from encryption devices).

He goes on to say that the pleasure found in CD-ROMs does not necessarily relate to their use. This pleasure and feeling of power-knowledge relates more to the 'mystical potency (ascribed) to the software inscribed – invisibly – on its surface'. Implicit in this story is the concept of expert or knowledge power. However, the CD-ROM is also spoken of as an icon or symbol of pure information that, although invisible, is perceived as incorruptible. Such is the power of symbols, in this case a physical symbol representing something more profound. Hardy (1994) draws attention to this aspect of symbols – that they stand for something other than themselves. The power that comes from the ability to manipulate symbols comes, therefore, from their capacity to signal to others the meaning, not of the symbol itself, but of what they stand for. This is implicit in Morgan's (1997) reference to symbolism as the management of meaning.

Symbolic power is, therefore, the power to manipulate and use symbols to create organizational environments and the beliefs and understandings of others to suit one's own purposes. Hardy includes the use of language, rituals and myths as examples of symbolic power. The use of phrases such as, 'all pulling in the same direction', 'we are a happy team', 'flatten the opposition' or 'argumentative (as opposed to conciliatory)' all give their own specific, covert messages about expected behaviour. The use of phrases such as, 'we are a happy team', negates the necessity to say, 'conflict and disagreement are not tolerated in this organization'. Rituals involving who sits where at meetings and how people greet each other are indications of who holds power in relation to whom. Leaving the chair at the head of the table free for the most senior person or addressing someone as 'boss' symbolizes one person's power in relation to another's. If a high-status person deliberately chooses to position her or himself next to a particular person, this could very well symbolize the chosen person's 'favourable' standing with regard to the other.

Morgan (1997) uses the term 'theatre' to describe the physical settings, appearances and styles of behaviour that can add to someone's power. He says (p. 189) of those who seek to add to their power in this way: 'Many deserve organizational Oscars for their performances.' Examples of the use of theatre are the size and furnishing of offices, the seating of visitors and the (unspoken) rules of dress. Morgan says (p. 190):

> Style also counts. It's amazing how you can symbolize power by being a couple of minutes late for that all-important meeting where everyone depends on your presence, or how visibility in certain situations can enhance your status.

He gives an example of how some people visiting the US president in the White House turn up early so as to be seen by as many people as possible while waiting for their appointment, thus dramatizing their supposed importance.

As discussed in the previous chapter, Johnson, Scholes and Whittington (2005, pp. 202–3) include symbols, rituals and routines, and stories as elements of their cultural web. They present these as representative of the dominant culture of an organization, thus providing clear evidence that symbols of power are inevitably intertwined with an organization's culture and are, frequently, an outward expression of it. In summary, therefore, any analysis of power in organizations must take account of not only the types of power which are exercised over the content of decisions, but also the types of power that influence attitudes and behaviour, frequently in ways that those influenced are hardly aware of. Activity 5.3 presents some questions, the answers to which can be used to increase understanding of how symbolic power is used in a particular organization.

Activity 5.3

The following questions are designed to help identify the routines and rituals and other symbols prevalent in an organization and who uses them for their own purposes.

Think of your own organization or one you are familiar with.

1 *Which routines and rituals are most emphasized? Who enforces these?*

2 *What kind of language do the organization's leaders use to motivate employees and gain their loyalty? What does this tell you about which topics could be debated and which not? Which people appear to be able to 'go against the grain' – and why do you think this is acceptable for them but not others?*

3 *Who, in the organization, has the most impressive 'trappings' of office (office, furnishings, car, expense account etc.)? What kind of power do they symbolize?*

4 *Give examples of two different people who use the skills of 'gamesmanship' to get their own way: (a) one who does so through aggressive means; and (b) one who does so through operating craftily and with an apparently low profile. Consider just what it is they are manipulating in these processes.*

Individual power

The characteristics of power discussed earlier derive from sources associated with how an organization is structured and the roles played by those working within it. Buchanan and Huczynski (2004, p. 829) refer to Pfeffer (1992), who adds another source of power – that which derives from the personal characteristics of those wielding power. These include the following:

- energy, endurance and physical stamina;
- ability to focus energy and to avoid wasteful effort;
- sensitivity and an ability to read and understand others;
- flexibility and selecting varied means to achieve goals;
- personal toughness; willingness to engage in conflict and confrontation;
- able to 'play the subordinate' and 'team member' to enlist the support of others.

Thompson and McHugh (2002) also refer to Pfeffer, who was interviewed by *Business Magazine*. Illustration 5.8 is an extract from this interview.

Illustration 5.8

Interview with Jeffrey Pfeffer

'Getting things done requires power. The problem is that we would prefer to see the world as a kind of grand morality play with the good guys and the bad ones easily identified. ... In corporations, public agencies, universities and government, the problem is how to move forward, how to solve the many problems facing organizations of all sizes and types. Developing and exercising power requires both will and skill. It is the will that often seems to be missing. To manage with power, means recognizing that in almost every organization there are varying interests. It means figuring out what point of view those various individuals and sub units have on issues of concern to you ... and thus it is imperative to understand where power comes from and how sources of power can be developed. Finally, managing with power means understanding the strategies and tactics through which power is developed and used in organizations.'

Source: Business Magazine in Thompson, P. and McHugh, D. (2002) *Work Organizations* (New York, Palgrave, p. 117).

It is interesting, when considering Pfeffer's views together with the list of personal characteristics identified earlier, that power derived from these sources is potentially available to anyone given its non-dependence on position, status or control of knowledge or resources. However, the use of power is unlikely to succeed unless used in conjunction with these. This leads to the issue of those who lack power – in other words the issue of powerlessness.

The politics of powerlessness

If there is one thing that symbols of power are intended to do, it is to make others who do not control these symbols feel their own lack of power. Conversely, many people are relatively powerless because of the way particular organizational factors affect them. In addition, some groups of people, for instance women and those from some ethnic minority groupings, appear powerless in relation to, on the one hand, men and, on the other, the majority groupings. People with physical disabilities may be excluded from positions of status and decision making because of prejudice or simply a lack of physical access to the places where the exercise of power takes place.

Women's lack of power

A number of writers (Kanter, 1979; Gordon, 1993; Handy, 1993; Morgan, 1997) have discussed the position of women in relation to their perceived powerlessness compared to men. For instance, Morgan (1997) argues that formal organizations typically mirror what, in the West, has been (and to a large extent still is) a patriarchal society. Thus those jobs that involve strategic decision making and the control of finances, as well as those which relate to machines and technology, are generally done by men. Jobs that involve caring, supporting others (e.g. secretaries), helping others (e.g. receptionists) tend to be done mainly by women.

Wilson (1995) has compiled a comprehensive summary of statistics showing that women earn less than men on average, that they occupy a much greater proportion of jobs at the lower levels of organizations relative to their overall numbers, and that they make up the vast majority of part-time workers (frequently doing more than one part-time job), thus having little employment protection, sickness benefits and, if they become unemployed, unemployment benefit. The Department for Education and Employment publication (2000) *Labour Market and Skills Trends 2000* reports that in 1999 80 per cent of part-time employees in the UK were women. The same report shows that jobs held by women are disproportionately (compared to men) concentrated in a narrow range of industries and occupations, for instance in clerical and secretarial occupations and in public administration, education and health. In 2004 the Equal Opportunities Commission (EOC) reported that this had only marginally improved. In its 2005 annual report 'Sex and power: Who runs Britain' the EOC confirmed that top roles in British public life were still unrepresentative of society as a whole, even though 2005 marked the 30th anniversary of the Sex Discrimination Act.

In the year 2000 Maitland (2000a) reported that, although women held a 54 per cent share of banking, finance and insurance jobs, they by no means occupied higher level jobs in the City of London (Britain's financial centre). A 'macho culture of long hours and big bucks' was said to discriminate against women becoming managers. In the same report, Helena Dennison, Chair of the City Women's Network, was quoted as saying: 'The City is about ten years behind business. ... There's a lot of open discrimination, but there's also a lot of covert and very subtle discrimination, in running down women's confidence. *We're not talking about sexual issues but about power*' [author's emphasis]. At the end of 2004, just 1 per cent more women were occupying senior positions in business, the police force and judiciary than a year previously. Women accounted for 11 per cent of director-level positions in the private sector and 21 per cent in the public and voluntary sectors. In terms of female Members of Parliament, the UK ranks 14th out of the 25 European member states news (BBC news website, 2004).

The metaphor of the 'glass ceiling' has become well known in discussions of the lack of any significant number of women in middle to top management jobs. Wilson (1995, p. 153) features a cartoon by Amanda Martin that says: 'Girls, DO NOT shatter the glass ceiling – it hurts.' It goes on to give advice about the elaborate precautions that need to be taken in order to dismantle this kind of ceiling. Illustration 5.9 demonstrates the slow progress made by women entering the higher levels of management.

There are a number of explanations of why women occupy jobs characterized by low skills and low pay and, if they have achieved professional status, still do not rise in any significant numbers to the higher levels in their profession or the

Illustration 5.9

The north–south divide in Europe Inc.

FT

There is a new north–south divide in Europe reflected in the make-up of the boardrooms of big business. In the far north, women directors are starting to make their presence felt, occupying 22 per cent of board seats in the largest companies in Norway and 20 per cent in Sweden. Top boards in Spain and Italy, however, remain almost exclusively male. The split is revealed by a survey indicating that: Europe wide, women hold just 8 per cent of the 3,600 directorships in the top 200 companies (by sales). Between the extremes of Norway and Italy are Germany and the UK, where women have 10 per cent of the boards' seats, the Netherlands with 7 per cent and France, with 6 per cent.

Female faces are even rarer in senior management, with women representing 5 per cent of the upper echelons from which board directors are typically recruited. Given these figures, a key question posed is: Is there a case for quotas? However, whilst in Norway and Sweden the governments' threats to enforce female quotas have been one factor behind the growing numbers of women in the biggest boardrooms in recent years, Eivind Reiten, chief executive of Norsk Hydro, says that most businesses oppose enforced positive discrimination. ... In Italy, Carmine Di Noia, deputy director-general of Assonime, the association of limited companies, dismisses quotas as a way of redressing the under-representation of women on boards. He says this is a social and cultural issue that is not peculiar to business but is evident in other areas such as politics.

Others are more critical of Italian business, where the few prominent women tend to be members of powerful families. 'The top circles of Italy's powerful business and political elite always consisted predominantly of men, and the tradition persists', says Valerie Ryder, coordinator of the European Professional Women's Network in Italy.

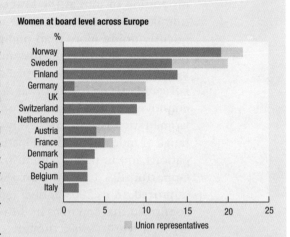

Women at board level across Europe

Union representatives

Note: the survey covered about 2,700 directors on supervisory boards and nearly 900 on unitary boards in 13 countries.
• Companies with at least one woman on board: 62%.
• Companies with more than one woman on the board: 28%.
Source: EPWN European BoardWomen Monitor

Research published by Catalyst, a US company organisation that works for women's advancement in business, suggests investors should be worried about the situation. In assessing the gender make-up of top management and the financial performance of 353 Fortune 500 companies between 1996 and 2000, it found that, on average, the quartile with the largest proportion of women had a return on equity 35.1 per cent higher, and a total return to shareholders 34 per cent higher, than the quartile with the lowest female representation. The link worked the other way too: on average, top-performing companies had more women in their leadership teams. .... Some companies have clearly decided there is a strong business case for having more women at the top. But today's survey shows how mistaken it is to assume that women are making progress across the board.

*Source: Alison Maitland, 'The north–south divide in Europe Inc.',
Financial Times, 14 June 2004.*

higher levels of management and thus, gain at least position power. One is reflected in the comment on the BBC news website (2005) that states: 'Women are being held back in the workplace by inflexible practices and outdated attitudes to family responsibilities.' Another is that, because of the need to absent themselves for childbearing, women are not perceived to be committed to their work and employer. However, although it is clear that this belief about women prevails in the minds of many recruiters and senior managers, the evidence shows this to be a myth (Wilson, 1995). Women who commit themselves to a job and career do so in no way differently to men. A more complex reason that is put forward by a number of writers (e.g. Kanter, 1979; Morgan, 1997) is that the prevailing structures and power balances in organizations, which are predominantly based on a male model of what organization and management is about, conspire indirectly to reduce the power sources of women. More recently, McKenna (1997) (as discussed in Buchanan and Badham, 1999, p. 123) refers to the world of male politics in which: 'Sitting back and hoping for recognition is seen as passivity, a lack of fire, guts and ambition. Essential for success is self-promotion, and conformity to the "unwritten rules of success".' McKenna (1997, p. 51) says: '[Success is about] maintaining silence in the face of politics and backstabbing. … It has little to do with performing good work or being productive and everything to do with pecking order and egos.'

Illustration 5.9 considered the progress of women in employment across Europe. Figure 5.1, overleaf, shows the top and bottom ten rankings of countries across the world in terms of gender balance. Based on the World Economic Forum (WEF) statistics, 'gender balance' was calculated according to factors such as: equal pay, equal access to jobs, representation of women in decision-making structures, equal access to education and access to reproductive healthcare. The survey covered all 30 industrialized countries in the Paris-based Organization for Economic Development (OECD), plus 28 emerging market countries.

These statistics show several of the most populous nations in the world (India, Pakistan, Turkey and Egypt) at the lower end of the table. 'Their rankings reflect disparities between men and women on all five areas of the index,' the WEF said in its report, with the only bright spot being India's high score for political empowerment of women. Several Latin American countries (Venezuela, Brazil and Mexico) do not fare much better, with the problem (according to the WEF) being: 'not lack of opportunity once they have entered the workforce, but rather in giving them access to the educational training and basic rights, such as healthcare and political empowerment, that enables them to join the workforce'.

By contrast Sweden, Norway, Iceland, Denmark and Finland 'provide a 'workable model' for the rest of the world'. According to the WEF chief economist Augusto Lopez-Claros, 'These societies seem to have understood the economic incentive behind empowering women'.

In line with comments in the article featured in Illustration 5.9, Italy (and Greece) have the worst rankings in the European Union at 45 and 50 respectively, mainly because of women's lack of decision-making power and poor

Bottom 10 countries for gender equality	Top 10 countries for gender equality
49. Venezuela	**1.** Sweden
50. Greece	**2.** Norway
51. Brazil	**3.** Iceland
52. Mexico	**4.** Denmark
53. India	**5.** Finland
54. South Korea	**6.** New Zealand
55. Jordan	**7.** Canada
56. Pakistan	**8.** United Kingdom
57. Turkey	**9.** Germany
58. Egypt	**10.** Australia

Figure 5.1 Bottom and top 10 states for gender equality

Source: World Economic Forum Gender Gap Index, story from BBC News: http://newsvote.bbc.co.uk 16/05/05

career prospects. In Asia, China was the highest-rated country at number 33 with Japan at 38 a few places behind. Finally, the United States, the world's largest economy, came 17th in the WEF's equality table. According to the report: 'It ranks poorly on the specific dimensions of economic opportunity and health and well-being, compromised by meager maternity leave, the lack of maternity benefits and limited government-provided childcare.'

Given these measures, there are some positive signs that the power balance might be shifting. Maitland (2000b) says: 'Headhunters argue that it is only a matter of time before women join the board in larger numbers. Some companies are explicitly asking for "balanced shortlists" of candidates.' She also reports on a (UK) Institute of Management survey which found that women account for 22 per cent of all British managers, compared with just 8 per cent a decade ago. A Canadian newspaper, *Financial Post*, gives a more upbeat report on the increased number of women going into senior positions, to a large extent because of the 'flood tide of women over the course of the past 20 years who have worked their way up within organizations' (*Financial Post*, 2000). In other parts of the world such as the Middle East a 'bigger role for ... women in business [is] recommended' (Avancena and Saeed, 2000). PR Newswire (2000) also reports on a US Department of Commerce Women in Business Development Trade Mission to Cairo, Egypt; Nairobi, Kenya; and Johannesburg, South Africa. One part of the article quoted from in Illustration 5.9 describes the pharmaceutical group AstraZeneca's efforts to put programmes in place three to four years ago to promote diversity. The company has ('unusually') four women non-executive directors on its 12-strong board, although there are no women in the senior executive team. Women account for about half the employees and 18 per cent of the top 115 managers below the executive team. The company says it has a better record than the industry average for giving women international assignments. Programmes that have helped it win external recognition include flexible hours and a variety of 'life-style-friendly leave' options.

If, as suggested here, the projections about increases in the numbers of women in management and senior management positions in traditionally male-dominated occupations comes to pass, then this is predicted to alter the culture within which business is done. What is in general called the 'feminization' of business (see for instance McKenna, 1997; Gratton, 2000) could very well alter the current view of organizational politics and power. What is not yet tested is whether the numbers of women opting out of 'large business' to start up their own companies (Gracie, 1998 reports this to be almost one-third of all new UK businesses in 1997) will be tempted to remain. Neither is it certain that feminization of the workplace will make a difference to the endemic organizational issues of power imbalances and organizational politics, particularly when change implies redundancies and/or redesignation and redesign of jobs.

Activity 5.4

Think of someone whom you consider does their job very well, but has been passed over for advancement . Assuming there is no reason why this person could not do the higher-level job (given time and training if necessary), why do you think they have not progressed?

In your analysis, draw on the concepts of power discussed in the preceding sections and any explanations related to the possible lack of power of the person concerned.

Powerlessness because of cultural differences

The previous chapter discussed how national cultural differences can influence many aspects of organizational life. Care must be taken, therefore, not to assume that practices in one culture can be transferred, without question, to another. For instance, it would be unwise to assume that factors that motivate some groups of people will, similarly, motivate others; a leadership style which works well in organizations where a westernized culture prevails may not be popular in countries where the power distance between levels in an organization is much greater.

The implications of these cultural differences for a discussion of power and powerlessness hinge on the very issue of difference. For instance, as the previous chapter showed, there are definite differences in the behaviour of people from different cultures but, more importantly – because they are so difficult to change

– in the values and attitudes they bring to the workplace. Therefore people from cultures scoring high on Hofstede's (1981) high power distance cultural dimension will expect managers to make all major decisions (and even some minor ones). However, in western cultures, which characteristically score low on the power distance cultural dimension, these expectations can frequently be interpreted as a lack of ambition and unwillingness to take responsibility for actions. This, in turn, does not train these people to gain power sources such as 'control of decision processes' and 'formal authority', two of the sources of power given by Morgan (1997). Morgan also cites 'ability to cope with uncertainty' as another source of power. This relates directly to another of Hofstede's cultural dimensions – uncertainty avoidance. Consequently, if a minority group's cultural upbringing is one where ambiguity must be controlled, they will not be prepared to demonstrate attitudes and behaviour, which will gain them power in this direction.

A final example is the difference in orientation towards others that is found between different cultural groupings. The perspective of power in western society is based mainly on the power of the individual, yet in many other societies (particularly in East Asian countries) people are expected to show loyalty to their group. It is the performance of the group that matters. Power is linked to the power of the group. Yuet-Ha (1996) points this out in her discussion of the differences between western and East Asian work-related values and their relationship to work-related competencies. Her findings suggest that, for people from an East Asian culture, it is relatively easy to implement teamworking and shared responsibility and support. However, it is relatively difficult to implement such things as open communication, participation, decisiveness, empowerment, delegation of authority and responsibility, taking responsibility in leadership, and sharing information. Given that most of these competencies are ones favoured in western societies, people from ethnic minority groups that favour other competencies are unlikely to progress when working in UK, US and some European countries, unless they can change others' perceptions of their differences. As Morgan points out with one of his sources of power, their lack of power in the first place makes this difficult to achieve. This too can be supported by findings discussed in the previous section.

Positions of powerlessness

The discussion thus far demonstrates the relationship between powerful and powerless groups that mirrors the areas selected for legislation as attempts have been made to provide more equality of opportunity in an organizational world where power has, traditionally, gravitated to white men. Legislation has certainly helped to eliminate the more overt prejudices that have prevented women and people from ethnic minority groups from enjoying the benefits given to others, even if certain organizational and covert processes still contrive to reduce their access to power sources and forms of influence. However, there are other groups of people who do not have the benefit of legislation – because no particular prejudice is shown against them – yet still find themselves relatively powerless. These groups are not, as might be expected, those working at the lowest levels of the organization. They are powerless because of the particular positions they occupy. It has been over 25 years since Kanter (1979) singled out, among others, first-line supervisors and staff professionals as examples of people lacking power.

According to Kanter, power comes from access to resources, information and support to get a task done; as well as the cooperation of others in doing what is necessary. She maintains that both of these capacities derive not from leadership style and skill but from a person's location in the formal and informal systems of the organization. This includes both the way the job is defined and the types of connections to other important people in the organization. Three 'lines' of organizational power are defined: (1) lines of supply; (2) lines of information; (3) lines of support. These have been discussed already as being basically related to resource and position power. Of additional relevance here is the power that comes from *connections* with other parts of the organizational system. Kanter identifies this as deriving from two sources – job activities and political alliances. She says (pp. 65–6):

1 Power is most easily accumulated when one has a job that is designed and located to allow *discretion* (nonroutinized action permitting flexible, adaptive, and creative contributions), *recognition* (visibility and notice), and *relevance* (being central to pressing organizational problems).
2 Power also comes when one has relatively close contact with *sponsors* (high level people who confer approval, prestige, or backing), *peer networks* (circles of acquaintanceship that provide reputation and information, the grapevine often being faster than formal communication channels), and *subordinates* (who can be developed to relieve managers of some of the burdens and to represent the manager's point of view).

When people are in situations where they have strong lines of supply, information and support, their job allows them discretion and their work is recognized as being relevant to the organization's purposes, they can more easily let go of control downwards and, thereby, develop their staff more effectively. In contrast to this situation, Kanter (1979, p. 67) says:

> The powerless live in a different world. Lacking the supplies, information, or support to make things happen easily, they may turn instead to the ultimate weapon of those who lack productive power – oppressive power: holding others back and punishing with whatever threats they can muster.

This situation is quite frequently that of the first-line supervisor. Illustration 5.10 shows how multiple causes combine to influence the attitudes and behaviour of first-line supervisors and people in similar positions and increase their feelings of powerlessness.

Kanter also discusses the position of staff professionals, that is, those people who act as 'advisers behind the scenes'. These are people who must 'sell' their

Illustration 5.10

First-line supervisors and powerlessness

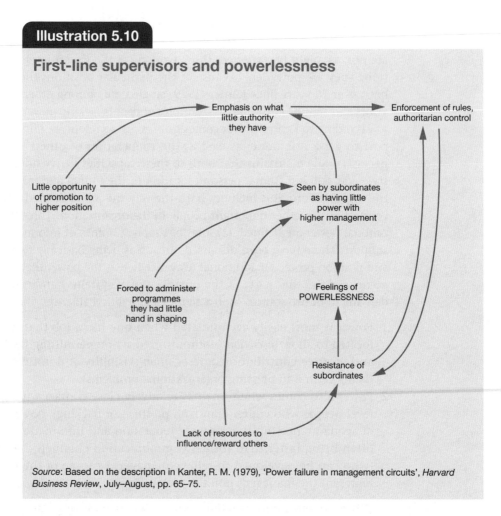

Source: Based on the description in Kanter, R. M. (1979), 'Power failure in management circuits', *Harvard Business Review*, July–August, pp. 65–75.

knowledge and expertise and bargain for resources, but who, quite often, do not have power to bargain with – they have few favours to offer in exchange. Experience of many organizations shows that people working in human resource departments are frequently in this situation. They often have little line experience and, therefore, are not involved in the mainstream organizational power networks. Being specialists, their ability to cross functions or undertake general management positions is restricted. They are, therefore, likely to get 'stuck' in a limited career structure. Having little power themselves, they cannot pass it on to others. In addition, they are prey to having their work contracted to agencies or consultants outside the organization. The effect of this relative powerlessness is that they tend to become 'turf-minded', protecting their patches, drawing strict boundaries between themselves and other functional managers. These various aspects of powerlessness, collectively, lead to conservative attitudes that are resistant to change. Activity 5.5 asks you to assess a job in terms of its capacity to generate power for its occupant.

Activity 5.5

The following is a list of factors that contribute to power or powerlessness. For your own job, or one you know well, take each factor in turn and tick the middle or last column as appropriate.

Factor	Generates power when factor is:	Generates powerlessness when factor is:
Rules in the job	☐ Few	☐ Many
Predecessors in the job	☐ Few	☐ Many
Established routines	☐ Few	☐ Many
Centralized resources	☐ Few	☐ Many
Communications	☐ Extensive	☐ Limited
Task variety	☐ High	☐ Low
Physical location	☐ Central	☐ Distant
Relation of tasks to current problem areas	☐ Central	☐ Peripheral
Competitive pressures	☐ High	☐ Low
Net-forming opportunities	☐ High	☐ Low
Contact with senior management	☐ High	☐ Low
Advancement prospects of subordinates	☐ High	☐ Low
Authority/discretion in decision making	☐ High	☐ Low
Meaningful goals/tasks	☐ High	☐ Low
Participation in programmes, meetings, conferences	☐ High	☐ Low

Consider the overall picture obtained of the job. How powerful might the person occupying it be?

Source: Based on factors suggested by Kanter, R. M. (1979), 'Power failure in management circuits', *Harvard Business Review*, July–August, pp. 65–75; and Gordon, J. R. (1993), *A Diagnostic Approach to Organizational Behavior*, Allyn & Bacon, p. 425.

●●●● The link between politics, power and conflict

In the first section of this chapter politics was described as the use of power. However, as Robbins (2005, p. 400) points out, political behaviour, although defined as those activities undertaken to influence others, is particularly relevant to those activities that are not part of someone's formal organizational role. In an ideal organizational world there would probably be no need to behave other than in accordance with one's formal role. However, because the organizational world is made up of human beings, each of whom has his or her own set of values, interests and beliefs, there are bound to be differences of opinion as to the very many issues that pervade everyday organizational life, let alone those prevailing in conditions of change. Even in organizations which apparently have a strong dominant culture, the experience of that culture will vary for individuals and groups who carry with them their own sub-cultures. What is more, a dominant culture will not solve one of the perennial issues in all organizations – the existence of scarce resources, which are never sufficient for everyone to have all they want.

As the previous section discussed, the control of resources is an important source of power in organizations and, as resources (of whatever kind) are almost always scarcer than most people would like, additional resource power is frequently being sought. This, in its turn, results in individuals and groups seeking to gather more power to themselves. In other words, they will compete for power. The issue then becomes one of whether this type of competition is helpful to the achievement of organizational performance or whether it becomes dysfunctional. Handy (1993, p. 298) appears in no doubt about this when he says, 'competition for power nearly always turns to conflict', with the implication that, while competition is not necessarily undesirable, conflict is. However, whereas Handy's discussion of conflict implies some disapproval, Morgan (1997) takes a more pragmatic view indicating that conflict is a familiar feature of life in an organizational society. His argument rests on the assumption that, because organizations are designed as systems which, at the same time, promote competition as well as cooperation, one of their outputs will, inevitably, be conflict.

This view emphasizes the plural nature of interests, conflicts and sources of power and has become known as the 'pluralist' frame of reference (Morgan, 1997, p. 199). This stands in contrast to the 'unitary' frame of reference that emphasizes the philosophy that organizations have goals to which all organizational members subscribe, with all working towards their attainment. Whereas managers holding a pluralist view of the way organizations should operate stress the idea of a coalition of divergent interests that will sometimes result in conflict, managers subscribing to a unitary philosophy consider conflict as an aberration from the normal state of affairs which recognizes only formal authority as the legitimate source of power. Thus, from a unitary frame of reference, managers are considered as the only people with the 'right to manage' while others are expected to subordinate their own personal interests to the good of the organization. From this point of view, the only type of power recognized is formal position power. Expert power might be recognized but, in the main, only as a facet of position power.

Robbins (2005, p. 423) prefers the term 'traditional' to describe this view which assumes that all conflicts are bad. He says: 'The traditional approach treats conflict synonymously with such terms as violence, destruction, and irrationality. Consonant with this perspective, one of management's major responsibilities is to try to ensure that conflicts don't arise and, if they do, to act quickly to resolve them.' The ideas of Taylor (1911) and his principles of scientific management are examples of a unitary approach to managing. The idea, still current in many places, that all industrial action by workers is wrong stems from this view. The difficulty in accepting a unitary view of organizational life, as the human relations theorists showed (e.g. Mayo, 1933; Barnard, 1938; McGregor, 1960), is that it leaves no room for dealing with the multiplicity of interests which are now accepted as part of a democratic way of doing things; hence the formulation of the concept of 'pluralism'. Illustration 5.11 summarizes these two different views.

A consideration of the unitary frame of reference, as portrayed in Illustration 5.11, shows that organizational politics, in the well-ordered world of the unitarist, should not exist. However, this view sits uncomfortably not only with the notion of a pluralist society, but also with the comments reported in Chapter 2 about the seemingly increasingly chaotic circumstances that are being predicted for organizations now and in the future. In such times political behaviour is to be expected, with its associated tendency to generate both competition and cooperation (of which conflict is a part). To ignore the role of conflict as a positive force as well as a negative force in the context of organizations and change is to ignore the realities of human living. Therefore a more detailed understanding of the nature and sources of conflict and how to manage in situations of conflict is important for anyone involved in organizational change.

Illustration 5.11

The unitary and pluralist views of interests, conflict and power

	The unitary view	The pluralist view
Interests	Places emphasis upon the achievement of common objectives. The organization is viewed as being united under the umbrella of common goals, and striving towards their achievement in the manner of a well-integrated team.	Places emphasis upon the individual and group interests. The organization is regarded as a loose coalition that has but a remote interest in the formal goals of the organization.
Conflict	Regards conflict as a rare and transient phenomenon that can be removed through appropriate managerial action. Where it does arise it is usually attributed to the activities of deviants and troublemakers.	Regards conflict as an inherent and ineradicable characteristic of organizational affairs and stresses its potentially positive and functional aspects.
Power	Largely ignores the role of power in organizational life. Concepts such as authority, leadership and control tend to be preferred means of describing the managerial prerogative of guiding the organization towards the achievement of common interests.	Regards power as a variable crucial to the understanding of the activities of an organization. Power is the medium through which conflicts of interest are alleviated and resolved. The organization is viewed as a plurality of power holders drawing their power from a plurality of sources.

Source: Burrell, G. and Morgan, G. (1979), *Sociological Paradigms and Organisational Analysis* (London, Heinemann Educational Books Ltd, p. 204).

● ● ● ● Conflict in organizations

The previous section established a link between power, politics and conflict. However, the concept of conflict itself is by no means uncontentious. What one person calls conflict, another might call 'hard bargaining'. A number of definitions of conflict can be found in the organizational behaviour literature. Examples of these follows.

> We can define conflict … as a process that begins when one party perceives that another party has negatively affected, or is about to negatively affect, something that the first party cares about.
> (Robbins, 2005, p. 422)

> For our purpose we can see conflict as: behaviour intended to obstruct the achievement of some other person's goals.
> (Mullins, 2005, p. 904)

> Conflict is the result of incongruent or incompatible potential influence relationships between and within individuals, groups or organizations.
> (Gordon, 1993, p. 448)

> Conflict can be a disagreement, the presence of tension, or some other difficulty between two or more parties. … Conflict is often related to interference or opposition between the parties involved. The parties in conflict usually see each other as frustrating or about to frustrate, their needs or goals.
> (Tosi, Rizzo and Carroll, 1994, p. 436)

These definitions, collectively, include the following aspects of conflict. First, it must be perceived by the parties to it, otherwise it does not exist. Second, one party to the conflict must be perceived as about to do, or actually be doing, something that the other party (or parties) do not want – in other words there must be opposition. Third, some kind of interaction must take place. In addition, almost all accounts of conflict agree that it can take place at a number of levels: between individuals, between groups or between organizations. Gordon (1993) also points out that an individual may experience conflict within themselves; that is, they may experience internal conflict. This might be because of the incompatibility of goals set for them or a confusion over the roles they are asked to play. Conflict, however, is not a unidimensional concept. It comes in different guises according to its degree of seriousness and capacity to disrupt or, in some cases, improve a difficult situation. Thus a further definition that encapsulates the possibilities of conflict is offered by Martin (2005, p. 746):

> Conflict can be considered as something that disrupts the normal and desirable states of stability and harmony within an organization. Under this definition it is something to be avoided and if possible eliminated from the operation. However, it is also possible to consider conflict as an inevitable feature of human interaction and perhaps something that if managed constructively could offer positive value in ensuring an effective performance within the organization.

The nature of conflict

Organizational conflict can be thought of as occurring in 'layers' (Open University, 1985) as shown in Illustration 5.12.

The identification of 'layers' of conflict is useful in demonstrating that not all conflict is of the 'do or die' variety; it depends on what has caused the conflict. Handy (1993) argues that all conflicts start from two types of difference. These are, first, differing goals and ideologies, which relate most nearly to the level of differences in values. The second cause is differences about territory, which relate most closely to the level of differences of interest. Other writers (e.g. Pfeffer, 1981; Tosi *et al.*, 1994; Mullins, 2005; Robbins, 2005), between them, offer the following list of sources of organizational conflict.

Illustration 5.12

The 'layers' in organizational conflict

Misunderstandings
These are 'getting the wrong end of the stick' – genuine misconceptions about what was said or done.

Differences of values
These are the other end of the scale, as it were, from misunderstandings. Conflicting values lead to the most serious disagreements. The values involved may be based on ethical considerations such as whether to take bribes (e.g. sales commissions) or not; the level at which safety should be set; whether to deal with regimes that condone particular ways of behaving (e.g. imprisoning those who disagree with them) which would not be acceptable in the home country. Differences of values may also involve disagreements about the purpose of the organization, that is, the ends for which it exists. Thus differences of values are almost always about ends or goals or objectives.

Differences of viewpoint
Different parties may share the same values but have differences of view on how particular goals or purposes should be attained. Thus differences of viewpoint are disagreements on the means by which particular ends should be achieved. For example, two parties may agree on the goal to increase profitability but disagree on how to do this. One may argue for increasing price, the other may argue for keeping price stable and cutting costs.

Differences of interest
Status, resources, advancement and so on are all desirable 'goods' that most people want and, if they have them, they want to keep hold of them. The distribution of these goods is not a once and for all process; it is constantly being adjusted through budget setting, organizational restructuring, strategic planning and so on. Therefore, competition between individuals and, particularly, departments is ever present.

Interpersonal differences
These are what most people would refer to as 'personality clashes'. For whatever reason, some people find it difficult to get on with others. This might be because of differences of temperament, style or ways of behaving. Care should be taken, however, not to mistake other types of differences for personality clashes. Accounting for conflict under this heading is often used as an excuse for not facing up to differences that might be occurring for other reasons.

Source: Based on Open University (1985), Units 9–10 'Conflict' course T244, *Managing in Organizations* (Milton Keynes, Open University, p. 57).

Interdependence

Different organizational groupings depend upon each other to a smaller or larger extent. Sometimes the dependence relationship is mutual. For instance, the marketing department is dependent on the production department to produce the goods said to be desired by the customer. Production is dependent on sales and marketing for gaining customers who want the products and thus keep the production workers in jobs. At other times, the dependence is more one-way. The direction of dependence is related to power balances between groupings. Robbins (2005) draws attention to the fact that nearly all line-staff relations are based on one-way task dependence.

Organizational structures

Conflict is likely because of the power imbalances that prevail in hierarchical structures. This sort of conflict, of course, overlaps with the concept of dependence. However, horizontal differentiation brings its own problems. Both Robbins (1990) and Tosi *et al.* (1994) refer to research by Lawrence and Lorsch (1969) that demonstrated how research, sales and production departments all had different orientations towards formality of structure, interpersonal relationships and timescales. They both argue that increased differentiation between departments, with each becoming more specialized in its activities, will lead to increased potential for conflict between them. Tosi *et al.* describe the value differences between mechanistic and organic organizational forms.

Rules and regulations

Robbins (2005), in particular, mentions the role of rules and regulations in reducing conflict by minimizing ambiguity. For Mullins (2005) this impacts on the clarity of definition of the roles people are expected to play. Robbins maintains that where there is high formalization (i.e. standardized ways for people and units to interact with each other) there are fewer opportunities for disputes about who does what and when. Conversely, where there is low formalization, the degree of ambiguity is such that the potential for jurisdictional disputes increases. Robbins maintains that conflict is more likely to be less subversive in highly formalized situations. In situations where the rules are vague, the opportunities to jockey for resources and other power bases increases. What is more, these activities can take place as easily through covert as through overt means. In contrast to this, Tosi *et al.* warn that rules and procedures do not necessarily guarantee an absence of conflict. In situations of over-regulation, people can become frustrated by their lack of autonomy and a perceived lack of trust of them by their superiors.

Limited resources

One of the sources of power in organizations is access to resources and the ability to bestow desired rewards on others. In good times, when resources are plentiful, the potential for conflict through competing for resources is reduced. In conditions of reducing profits or revenues or when redundancies are occurring, the potential for conflict over reduced resources rises. In addition, in economically hard times, gaining resources and extra rewards for subordinates is much more difficult, with the attendant potential for increased dissatisfaction among the workforce.

Cultural differences

The previous chapter identified a number of ways in which people from different nationalities and societies differ. Therefore conflict can arise through misunderstandings or through inappropriate behaviour on the part of those with one set of cultural characteristics towards those with other characteristics. In addition, it would not be surprising to find cross-cultural differences in relation to resolution of conflicts. For instance, people who come from a collectivist culture, such as Japan, are more likely to avoid outright confrontation than people who come from more individualistic cultures such as the United States. People from cultures scoring high on Hofstede's (1981) power distance dimension are more likely to appeal to a higher authority and use bureaucratic rules and regulations to resolve conflict than people from cultures that score low on the power distance dimension.

Environmental change

Mullins (2005) lists this as one of his sources of conflict. He mentions shifts in demand, increased competition, government intervention, new technology and changing social values as possible causes of conflict. At the time of writing, the UK government is threatening to withdraw subsidy from the further and adult education sector for the training of sports coaches. This has resulted in articles and letters in newspapers as well as items on news programmes. If the subsidy is withdrawn it is likely to affect the number of people enrolling on these courses and, therefore, the employment of the tutors concerned.

The identification of different sources of conflict is helpful in understanding more about organizational conflict but is not as straightforward as it looks. The relationship of sources of conflict to the layers of conflict identified earlier is complex. Many situations involve more than one layer of conflict. For instance, almost all types of conflict will include elements of misunderstanding, and differences of values are often entwined with interpersonal differences. In addition, differences of viewpoint are closely linked to differences of interest. For example, the means thought appropriate to gain particular goals (for instance the formulation of rules and procedures) are intimately related to issues about control, status, resources and so on. The Open University material referred to in Illustration 5.12 makes a useful comment on the relationship between interests and views, as follows:

Interests are not only shaped by our views, they are also masked by them. The pursuit of personal or departmental advantage is a largely covert affair. Interests are modest to the point of prudishness; they do not walk naked through the corridors of organizations but go heavily clothed, preferably in a fashionable attire woven from the latest ideas about the best way to achieve organizational goals.

(1985, p. 59)

This quotation shows how conflict is not necessarily expressed in loud arguments or fights. It also shows how political behaviour is frequently the outcome of differences resulting in conflict. However, conflict resolution does not necessarily imply political behaviour as defined by Robbins at the beginning of the chapter – that is, activities outside the formal organizational role requirements – as some of the strategies for resolving conflict show.

Approaches to conflict

Strategies for managing conflict will vary according to the frame of reference of an organization's management. The orientation of managers subscribing to a unitary philosophy of organization will be to suppress conflict whenever possible. Conflict is likely to be seen as the work of agitators and the dominant strategy will, therefore, be one of denigrating those thought to be the cause or dismissing them from the organization. The paradox is, however, that, in a democratic society, this strategy will either cause further, more extreme conflict behaviour or drive the expression of conflict underground. The suppression of conflict within a unitary frame of reference will be successful so long as those without power fear the consequences of conflict (e.g. lockouts, dismissal, unemployment) sufficiently to avoid it. However, as soon as acceptable alternatives to the prevailing situation are available (e.g. alternative employment, successful industrial action), then conflict will again manifest itself, thus reinforcing the view that organizations cannot, in general, be managed as unitary wholes. Recognition of their pluralist characteristics is required if conflict is to be managed successfully.

Most writers on the subject of organizational conflict offer advice on how to manage conflict. Schelling (1960) suggests that parties to a conflict can act in three different ways. The first is to compete, in which case one party wins and the other loses. The second is to cooperate, in which case both parties win. The third is a mixture of these two where the parties both compete and cooperate, with both winning something but not all they had hoped. A more comprehensive model of conflict resolution behaviours is Thomas's (1976) conflict-handling styles (see Figure 5.2).

Reference to Figure 5.2 shows that Thomas identifies five styles for handling conflict: competing; collaborating; avoiding; accommodating; compromising. Each style is positioned on two axes representing two different concerns. The vertical axis represents a concern to satisfy one's own needs. The horizontal axis represents a concern to satisfy the other party's needs. Illustration 5.13 identifies the situations when it would be most appropriate to use each conflict-handling style.

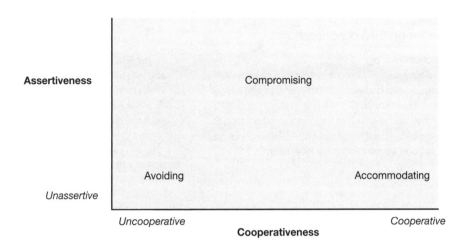

Figure 5.2 A model of conflict-handling styles

Source: Adapted from Thomas, K. W. (1976), 'Conflict and conflict management', in Dunnette, M. D. (ed.) *Handbook of Industrial and Organizational Psychology* (Chicago, Rand McNally, p. 900).

Illustration 5.13

Situations in which to use the five conflict-handling styles

Competing

1 When quick, decisive action is vital – e.g. emergencies.
2 On important issues where unpopular actions need implementing – e.g. cost cutting, enforcing unpopular rules, discipline.
3 On issues vital to company welfare when you know you are right.
4 Against people who take advantage of non-competitive behaviour.

Collaborating

1 To find an integrative solution when both sets of concerns are too important to be compromised.
2 When your objective is to learn.
3 To merge insights from people with different perspectives.
4 To gain commitment by incorporating concerns into a consensus.
5 To work through feelings that have interfered with a relationship.

Compromising

1 When goals are important, but not worth the effort or potential disruption of more assertive modes.

2 When opponents with equal power are committed to mutually exclusive goals.
3 To achieve temporary settlements of complex issues.
4 To arrive at expedient solutions to complex issues.
5 As a back-up when collaboration or competition is unsuccessful.

Avoiding

1 When an issue is trivial, or more important issues are pressing.
2 When you perceive no chance of satisfying your concerns.
3 When potential disruption outweighs the benefits of resolution.
4 To let people cool down and regain perspective.
5 When gathering information supersedes immediate decision.
6 When others can resolve the conflict more effectively.
7 When issues seem tangential or symptomatic of other issues.

Illustration 5.13 *continued*

Accommodating

1 When you find you are wrong – to allow a better position to be heard, to learn and to show your reasonableness.
2 When issues are more important to others than to yourself – to satisfy others and maintain cooperation.
3 To build social credits for later issues.

4 To minimize loss when you are outmatched and losing.
5 When harmony and stability are especially important.
6 To allow subordinates to develop by learning from mistakes.

Source: Thomas, K. W. (1977), 'Toward multi-dimensional values in teaching: the example of conflict behaviors', *Academy of Management Review*, vol. 12, p. 487.

Each conflict-handling style has an outcome in terms of its capacity to tackle the content of the conflict and the relationship with the other party as follows:

1 *Competing.* This creates a win/lose situation, therefore the conflict will be resolved to suit one of the parties only. The win/lose situation can lead to negative feelings on the part of the loser and damage the relationship.
2 *Collaborating.* This creates a win/win outcome, where both parties gain. It frequently brings a high quality solution through the results of the inputs of both parties. Win/win outcomes result in both sides being reasonably satisfied. They require openness and trust and a flexibility of approach.
3 *Compromising.* The needs of both parties are partially satisfied. It requires a trading of resources. Openness and trust may not be as great as for collaboration but compromise might set up a relationship that, in the future, could move to collaboration.
4 *Avoiding.* This does not tackle the problem. It creates a no-win situation. It does, however, allow a cooling-off period and allows the parties to (perhaps) gather more information to begin negotiations afresh or decide there is no conflict after all. It can give rise to frustration on one side if they think the issue is important while the other side do not.
5 *Accommodating.* This can create a lose/win situation, but retains a good relationship between the parties. It involves recognizing when the other party might have a better solution than oneself. It is used when relationships are more important than the problem. It builds goodwill.

Activity 5.6

Analyze a conflict from your own organizational experience to identify which one or more of the layers of conflict described in Illustration 5.12 apply to it.

If it has already been resolved, which of Thomas's approaches identified in Illustration 5.13 were used?

If it is still happening, which of Thomas's approaches do you think is most appropriate to its resolution?

Sometimes, however, as Morgan (1997) has pointed out, conflict is of a different kind altogether. Rather than having a philosophy of pluralism, some organizations are 'radicalized' to the extent that divisions between managers and other employees are almost irreconcilable. Thus the radical frame of reference that characterizes these organizations derives from a view of society as comprising antagonistic class interests which will only be reconciled when the differences between the owners of production and the workers have disappeared. Based on a Marxist perspective, this view does not usually prevail in the West to the extent that behaviour in conflict situations goes so far as to cause the downfall of organizations and the social structures that support them. While occasionally, as a result of industrial action on the part of workers and management, organizations may close down, in the long run the power of the owners tends to prevail.

Activity 5.7

Read the following story.

Raheel and Veronica both worked at the same level in the sales department of Keen Machine, a large motorcycle agency that held the sole rights to sell one of the leading brands of motorcycle. They each managed a team of salespeople. Each team was responsible for a different geographical area. Although the teams operated independently of each other, they shared the services of two administrators who dealt with orders, invoicing etc. The administrators also carried out typing and other administrative work for Raheel and Veronica. This work was done by whoever was available at a particular time.

Every year, all the salespeople had to undergo performance appraisals, which were performed by their manager (either Raheel or Veronica). However, it seemed that the administrators had somehow been 'missed out' from this process. The sales director decided therefore that they also should be appraised and, to be fair to both, by the same person (either Raheel or Veronica).

Raheel's sales team had faced some difficulties on their 'patch' recently and Raheel was having to work hard to recoup their previous good performance. The sales director, not wanting to distract Raheel from this task, asked Veronica to carry out the administrative staff appraisals.

Up to this time, Raheel had always had a good relationship with both administrators and had no complaint about their work for him. However, recently he began to notice that, if both he and Veronica gave work to the administrators at the same time, Veronica's work seemed to get done first – this was in spite of the fact that he had always thought he had a better relationship with them than Veronica. He complained to the administrators, who both declared they did not show any 'favouritism' to either himself or Veronica. He was still not satisfied but could think of no reason why their behaviour towards him should have changed.

Attempt to explain this situation using concepts and ideas related to issues of power and conflict.

Most people will have a preferred conflict-handling style, depending on their personality, culture, socialization and organizational experiences. However, effective management of conflict requires the use of any of these styles, depending on the circumstances.

Power and conflict in times of change

The discussion so far shows that power, politics and conflict are indisputable aspects of social and organizational life. They are, therefore, of crucial importance to the issue of organizations and change. On the issue of power, French and Bell (1990, p. 280) take a positive view, saying: 'The phenomenon of power is ubiquitous. Without influence (power) there would be no cooperation and no society.' Others (e.g. Robbins, 2005) speak of the 'functional' role of conflict. Yet, as some of the preceding discussion shows, power and conflict, turned into politics, can be used to negative effect. The issue for managers of organizational change, therefore, is to use power and conflict in positive ways to enhance the change process and reduce unnecessary resistance. However this is, as they say, easier said than done.

The two faces of power

The idea that power has two faces was put forward by McClelland (1970) to explain its positive and negative aspects. In their discussion of McClelland's theories, French and Bell (1990, p. 280) say: 'The negative face of power is characterized by a primitive, unsocialized need to have dominance over submissive others.' Positive power derives from a more socialized need to initiate, influence and lead. Therefore positive power recognizes other people's needs to achieve their own goals as well as those of management and the organization. Negative power is about domination and control of others; positive power seeks to empower, not only the self, but also others.

The terms 'constructive and destructive' can also be used in relation to different types of conflict and are clearly linked to the concepts of positive and negative power. The use of negative power almost inevitably results in destructive conflict, with the attendant breakdown in communications and unwillingness to contemplate any view but one's own. Discontent such as this tends to multiply in conditions of uncertainty that are an inherent part of situations of change. It is in such situations that power balances are upset and disagreements that might, normally, have been settled by compromise, escalate into destructive win–lose situations. Organizations facing conditions of change are, in many respects, at their most vulnerable to the political actions of those who stand to gain from the change as well as those who stand to lose.

The problems of change

It could be argued that some types of change are less problematic than others and, clearly, radical, frame-breaking change is more likely to bring the greatest conditions of uncertainty and fear of what the future may bring. Even so, small-scale, incremental change can upset the balance of power through small but significant redistributions of resources or changes in structure that make some people's skills or experience more desirable than those of others. However, regardless of the content of any change, most writers would agree that it is the process through which the organization must go to get from one state to another that brings the most problems. Nadler (1988) suggests three major problems associated with this transition process. The first of these is the problem of resistance to change; the second the problem of organizational control and the third is the problem of power. Figure 5.3 builds on these ideas to illustrate some interconnections between power, conflict, change and political action.

Figure 5.3 shows some possible implications for people's attitudes and behaviour during periods of organizational change. Thus the transition process from the current organizational state to the desired one, rather than being merely a series of mechanistically designed steps, is fraught with possibilities of conflict and political action.

Figure 5.3 illustrates the role of power and conflict during periods of organizational change. 'Behind' each of the elements are many of the concepts discussed in relation to power, conflict and their expressions in political action. For instance, some types of change will challenge some people's values and beliefs

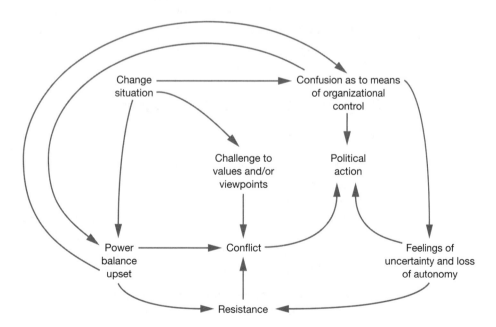

Figure 5.3 The problems of change

and so induce an internal state of conflict that, in turn, means they are likely to resist the change. In addition, because values and beliefs are involved, this resistance will have a moral imperative attached to it. Confusion about the means of organizational control – that is, who and what is being monitored and how – is closely associated with disturbances in the power balance which will most frequently be linked to position and resource power. During times of confusion such as this, opportunities present themselves for taking political action using invisible sources of power. In this context conflict, viewed as a problem, is likely to be resolved, if at all, by the use of win–lose strategies.

The role of symbolic action in the management of strategic change is discussed by Johnson (1990) and this will be considered further in the next chapter. Of interest here, however, is the fact that during periods of relative stability in organizations, symbols, such as stories and myths, rituals and routines and the more physical manifestations of status and power, play a major part in sustaining that stability. Consequently, in periods of organizational change, these same symbols (and their relationship with symbolic power) can be used in the process of resisting change. What is more, this argument holds whether the change is incremental or concerned with a shift in the organizational paradigm that was discussed in Chapter 4 as the cultural web. In addition resistance, as a general term, to other than marginal changes incurs what was described in Chapter 2 as 'strategic drift' (Johnson et al., 2005). Thus the process of strategic drift, if allowed to continue without check, leads to confusion as to organizational goals and the means of achieving them. This in turn lays down the conditions for conflict and political action.

The problems of change sometimes appear overwhelming. However, as McClelland (1970) said, there is a positive face to power as well as a negative one. There is, equally, a positive face to conflict and political action in the context of organizational change.

The positive use of conflict and power

Robbins (2005) and the Open University (1985) use the terms functional or dysfunctional, and constructive or destructive conflict respectively. Indeed, with respect to functional conflict, Robbins refers to the interactionist approach to conflict which views it as not only a positive force, but also one that is absolutely necessary for a group to perform effectively. In support of this contention he argues that too low a level of conflict is just as dysfunctional as too high a level. Thus there is a level of conflict – an optimal level of conflict – that engenders self-criticism and innovation to increase unit performance. Robbins (2005, p. 424) says about this:

> When conflict is at an optimal level, complacency and apathy should be minimized, motivation should be enhanced through the creation of a challenging and questioning environment with a vitality that makes work interesting.

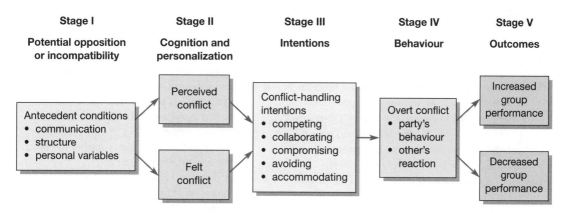

Figure 5.4 The conflict process
Source: Robbins, S. P. (2005) *Organizational Behavior, Concepts, Controversies, Applications*, 11th edn, Prentice Hall, p. 424.

Figure 5.4 illustrates this. It depicts a five-stage process of moving from an initial conflict situation through to alternative positive or negative outcomes. Note stage III 'Intentions' uses Thomas's (1976) model of conflict-handling styles shown in Figure 5.2.

The Open University draws attention to the fact that conflict acts to draw those on the same 'side' together in solidarity, but it can also create solidarity among those who are on different sides. This is because, as each side puts its point of view forward (even though in argument), information is revealed and shared and awareness of each other's goals and views is enhanced. Therefore, conflicts can result in *integrative* effects, but only if attempts to work through the conflict are non-coercive and use methods of openness and honesty.

Mills and Murgatroyd (1991, p. 159) talk about conflict and consent 'being in tension'. Most members of organizations will not revolt if they perceive that the methods of control used to achieve organizational purposes are based on some shared view of how these methods will be applied. For instance, Hofstede's (1981) concept of power distance as one of the dimensions of culture is useful in explaining why people from some cultures will accept a more authoritarian type of decision making and control than will people from other cultures. If an organization's workforce is culturally inclined to risk taking and the tolerance of uncertainty, it will not be as comfortable with strict rules and regulations as one that, in Hofstede's terms, has high uncertainty avoidance.

Furze and Gale (1996) take an optimistic view of conflict in entitling their chapter on this 'Making conflict useful'. Illustration 5.14 lists a number of guidelines given by Furze and Gale for dealing with conflict. (The comments are not necessarily those of Furze and Gale.)

The guidelines for dealing with conflict (Illustration 5.14) are general ones and, if adhered to, may result in what Thomas (see Figure 5.2) called collaboration, where both parties stood to win. These same guidelines are also useful in

Illustration 5.14

Guidelines for dealing with conflict

1 *Encourage openness*. This refers to the need to explore objectives, facts, views and the assumptions that surround the issues. Openness requires statements of who benefits and how. It assumes that conflicts cannot be resolved if issues associated with them remain hidden.

2 *Model appropriate responses*. The issue here is one of role modelling. If one party is prepared to make positive responses to contention, rather than being defensive or dismissive, this acts to encourage the other party to do likewise.

3 *Provide summaries and restatements of the position*. Doing this helps to keep communication going and is a helpful slowing down of the process when it becomes heated and points that are made are in danger of being ignored and lost.

4 *Bring in people who are not directly involved*. These outsiders can act as additional fact providers or take on the more process-oriented role of mediator or arbitrator. A mediator can facilitate a negotiated solution while an arbitrator can dictate one. Other possibilities are conciliators who act as communicators between the two parties (particularly if they will not communicate directly) and consultants. Instead of putting forward specific solutions, the consultant tries to help the parties learn to understand and work with each other.

5 *Encourage people to take time to think and reassess*. This means building in time for reflection and space apart. It may mean 'shelving' the problem for a short while but not as a means of avoiding it.

6 *Use the strengths of the group*. This refers to taking advantage of opportunities to use non-combative members of the group to which the combatants belong. Doing this brings others into the conflict, not to take sides but to play a positive and creative role.

7 *Focus on shared goals*. Rather than concentrating from the start on differences, seek instead to identify where agreements exist – even if these are very small and, apparently, insignificant. These form a useful base on which to move outwards to assess just where differences exist. Parties to a conflict are often surprised at the amount of agreement present but of which they were unaware.

8 *Use directions and interests to develop areas of new gain*. Concentrating on other people's ideas can identify areas of potential gains. Then using guideline 2, summarize these in order to move forward.

9 *Try to build objectivity into the process*. Objectivity can be encouraged by asking those involved to express both the strengths and weaknesses of their position. What must be recognized, however, is that objectivity will always be tempered by people's value systems.

10 *Adopt an enquiring approach to managing*. This means probing through what appear to be the symptoms of conflict to understand the actual causes. Unless the fundamental cause is identified, the conflict will continue to flare up at regular intervals.

Source: Based on Furze, D. and Gale, C. (1996), *Interpreting Management. Exploring Change and Complexity* (London, Thompson International Press, pp. 312–17).

the context of organizational change and are even more desirable in view of the increased potential for conflict at these times.

Care must be taken, however, to recognize the inevitability of shifting power balances, yet as Illustration 5.15 shows, the use of power in situations of change can be beneficial.

However, as the account of change in Illustration 5.15 shows, one result of the use of power by Brian Davies was to the detriment of the people who lost their jobs. Even so, because the basis on which people were chosen for the new-style company was seen to be open and fair – not based on politics or tribal allegiances – the changes appear to have been accepted and new confidence instilled in the employees. As far as can be gained from this account, the use of power has been put to positive effect.

Illustration 5.15

Flight to revival

Joel Kibazo reports on Kenya Airways' turbulent path to privatization

When Brian Davies became managing director of soon-to-be privatized Kenya Airways, he realized he would have to draw on more than just experience to transform the African loss-making state carrier.

A former general manager at British Airways, Davies, together with Malcolm Naylor, the finance director, and Des Hetherington, who has since left the airline, had been part of Speedwing, the British Airways consultancy that carried out a 1992 study of the airline and recommended plans for its revival.

The consultancy team had found an airline on the verge of collapse. There was little cost control, which had contributed to the growing losses which hit $50m (£33m) in 1992. And senior management posts were awarded on the basis of political affiliation and tribal loyalty, with the result that the management hierarchy not only mirrored that of the Kenyan civil service but could have been a case study of the country's social structure.

The board of the company, chaired by the late Philip Ndegwa, a former governor of the central bank of Kenya, subsequently asked the Speedwing team to take over the running of the company and prepare it for privatization.

Looking back over the last four years, Davies, who prides himself on having a direct but firm management style, says it has been a turbulent but interesting flight. As expatriates they have had to face the additional problem of a press campaign that labelled them 'white colonialists'.

One of the first things Davies had been warned about was the local custom of never doing anything on time. Arriving an hour late is not always considered rude.

'I have a personal fetish about time and I was warned that you can't do things on time in Africa.'

Having decided on times of meetings, he would lock the doors to the meeting room and start without the latecomers. Initially this led to meetings with only about half the number of senior management staff but, as he says, 'the latecomers were soon embarrassed. It worked.'

Management's new promptness clearly percolated through to operations, where the airline's poor record of flight departures was a central issue. 'Today,' he says with pride, 'around 90 per cent of flights leave on schedule and around 85 per cent within 15 minutes of the set departure time. This made me determined to show that other things could also be tackled.'

Another target was staffing. The new team arrived after some 900 people had already been laid off, easing the burden of the staff reorganization. Yet given the tribal traditions it still proved to be one of the most sensitive operations. The management asked employees to resign and reapply for their jobs.

The reorganization was complicated by the company's six-tier management structure. Naylor remembers: 'I could not ask for a file without the message having to be passed down a chain of six people. It was crazy but that is how things had always been done here. You have to understand that in this culture position and seniority are very important.'

Following the review, the management was streamlined to three tiers, with each manager given specific tasks and budget responsibilities together with spending targets. Nine managers, said to have owed their positions to political or tribal affiliation, were sacked. But Davies says the review brought a new confidence to the staff. 'Everyone was able to see we had not based this on tribe or politics.'

Over the last four years the staff has fallen by a further 400 to 2,300 through a voluntary redundancy

▶

Illustration 5.15 *continued*

scheme, the first such scheme in a Kenyan state-owned company. Losses were reduced to $30m in 1993 and in 1994 the airline recorded its first profit, $7m, which rose to $17m last year. In 1994, the government assumed responsibility for all the airline's external debt arrears of about $82m and converted $33m owed to it into equity. Profits this year are expected to be ahead of the $22m expected by analysts.

Most of the changes in the first year were carried out against a background of a local press campaign against the new management. As the management came from the UK a commonly held view was that it was simply preparing the carrier for sale to British Airways. The more enterprising reporters published the management's hotel bills. Davies admits that at times he wondered what he had let himself in for. 'But in the end I knew we had a job to do and I wanted to see it through.' He says a Time Manager International (TMI) course early on in his career at British Airways, which emphasized putting people first, had been useful.

He moved to introduce some elements of TMI into courses he organized at Kenya Airways. 'If you show you value the employees then they too will treat the customer with the same care and attention.' While arranging a course he discovered that 75 per cent of his staff had never been on an aircraft. 'This meant that they simply had no idea of what we were about.' A lunch aboard an old Boeing 707 aircraft was quickly arranged.

It would have been difficult to usher in so many changes without friction and Davies does admit to a number of misgivings. 'People misunderstood our open management style. We called each other by our first names and openly argued about a point. Here, they observe niceties and people were offended by our way of discussing things. It was an Anglo-Saxon way of doing things.' It took a word from the then chairman to highlight the error of the new team's ways.

Davies also says he underestimated the effects of tribal allegiances. 'We would say we are only interested in the Kenya Airways tribe. But in fact we were ignoring reality. Tribe is a powerful aspect that cannot be ignored. For example, people find it difficult to discipline someone from their own tribe. Things are getting better but we have had to learn to live with that factor.'

Last year, the Kenyan government invited international carriers to take a stake in the airline. In January KLM, the Dutch national carrier, announced it had taken a 26 per cent stake. The management is now engaged in a series of briefings for international and local investors ahead of next week's flotation of 48 per cent of the company's shares, to be quoted on the Nairobi stock exchange. The government will retain a 23 per cent holding while 3 per cent of the shares will be used for an employee share ownership scheme.

Those expecting Davies to bow out of the company he has transformed have been wrong footed. He and Naylor have just accepted a two-year extension to their contracts. 'The last three years have been challenging. The next two years will be ones of fun as we enter the growth stage.'

Source: Kibazo, J. (1996), 'Flight to revival', *Financial Times*, 22 March, p. 12.

Action on power, conflict and change

The story of Brian Davies and his management of change at Kenya Airways (Illustration 5.15) appears to have followed (though not deliberately as far as is known) the four action steps that Nadler (1988) proposes for shaping the political dynamics of change. These actions are proposed in response to what Nadler perceives as one of the problems of change mentioned earlier in the chapter – the problem of power. The first of these is to ensure or develop the support of key power groups. This involves identifying those individuals and groups who have the power either to assist change or to block it. As Nadler says, not all

Activity 5.8

Based on earlier work, Robbins (2005, p. 431) developed traditional and non-traditional techniques for use in conflict management and resolution. The table below identifies these techniques and describes what they mean in relation to the management or resolution of conflict.

Table 5.1 Robbins's conflict-management techniques

Conflict-resolution techniques	
Problem solving	Face-to-face meeting of the conflicting parties for the purpose of identifying the problem and resolving it through open discussion.
Superordinate goals etc.	Creating a shared goal that cannot be attained without the cooperation of each of the conflicting parties.
Expansion of resources can	When a conflict is caused by the scarcity of a resource – say, money, promotion opportunities, office space – expansion of the resource can create a win–win soloution.
Avoidance	Withdrawal from, or suppression of, the conflict.
Smoothing	Playing down differences while emphasizing common interests between the conflicting parties.
Compromise	Each party to the conflict gives up something of value.
Authoritative commmand	Management uses its formal authority to resolve the conflict and then communicates its desires to the parties involved.
Altering the human variable	Using behavioural change techniques such as human relations training to alter attitudes and behaviours that cause conflict.
Altering the structural variables	Changing the formal organization structure and the interaction patterns of conflicting parties through job redesign, transfers, creation of coordinating postions, and the like.

Conflict-stimulation techniques	
Commmunication	Using ambiguous or threatening messages to increase conflict levels.
Bringing in outsiders	Adding employees to a group whose backgrounds, values, attitudes, or managerial styles differ from those of present members.
Restructing the organization	Realigning work groups, altering rules and regulations, increasing interdependence, and making similar structural changes to disrupt the status quo.
Appointing a devil's advocate	Designing a critic to purposely argue against the majority positions held by the group.

Source: Based on original work of Robbins (1974). *Managing Organizational Conflict: A Nontraditional Approach*. Prentice Hall, Upper Saddle River, New Jersey, pp. 59–89]

Read again the account of Kenya Airways in Illustration 5.15.

To what extent do you think Brian Davies's actions reflected the conflict-management techniques suggested by Robbins?

power groups have to be intimately involved in the change. However, some groups will need to be included in the planning of any change to guard against their ultimately blocking it, not because it might affect them adversely, but because they had been ignored.

The second of Nadler's action steps is using leader behaviour to generate energy in support of the change. The guidelines for dealing with conflict, listed in Illustration 5.14, could very well be guiding principles here. In addition, sets of leaders working in coordination can significantly influence the informal aspects of organizational life. The third action step is using symbols and language to create energy. This has already been discussed in reference to the use of symbolic power and, in particular, Johnson's (1990) discussion of the role of symbolic action in managing strategic change. Finally, the fourth action step for shaping the political dynamics of change is the need to build in stability. This is the use of power to ensure some things remain the same. These might be physical locations, group members, even hours of work. It is helpful to provide sources of stability such as these to provide 'anchors' for people to hold on to during the turbulence of change. In addition, there is a need to let people know what will remain stable and what is likely to change.

The discussion in this chapter set out to show the importance of power and conflict as elements in the politics of change. Managers who, in times of change, can reasonably assess who has what power and the way in which it will be used – with possible consequences for potential and actual conflict – have a good chance of implementing the change they seek. The chapter concludes, therefore, with a description of one way of analyzing the potential for action of individuals and groups according to: (a) their power to block change and (b) their motivation to do so.

The first step in analyzing the potential for action, in favour of or against change, is to identify who holds sufficient power to assist change or, alternatively, to work against it – that is, to carry out a 'power audit'. This can be done by using a questionnaire such as is shown in Figure 5.5. This is based on the descriptions of the characteristics and sources of power discussed earlier in the chapter.

The questionnaire in Figure 5.5 should be used for each individual or group that is considered to be significant for the success or otherwise of any change process.

The second step is to compare the power of any individual or group to block change with their desire or motivation to do so. Assessing motivation to block change is not straightforward. It can be gauged, however, by considering whether the changes proposed will alter the degree of power held. As a general rule, if this is likely to be lowered, then resistance to change can be expected and vice versa. Figure 5.6 allows any individual or group to be categorized according to their power to block change and their motivation to do so.

Indicators of power to help or hinder change	Individual Group A*	Individual Group B*	Individual Group C*
Position 1 Status to hierarchy/formal authority 2 Power to change organizational structure, rules and regulations 3 Control of strategic decision processes 4 Control of operational decision processes			
Resources 5 Control of scarce resources 6 Control of budgets 7 Control of technology 8 Ability to reward or punish staff			
Personal characteristics 9 Involvement in interpersonal alliances and networks, with links to the informal organization 10 Able to exert 'charismatic' leadership to get others to follow 11 Able to cope with uncertainty			
Knowledge and expertise 12 Information specific to the change situation 13 Skills specific to the change situation 14 Knowledge and expertise unique to situation concerned			
Symbols 15 Quality of accommodation 16 Use of expenses budget 17 Membership of high-level decision-making committees 18 Receipt of company 'perks' 19 Unchallenged right to deal with those outside the organization 20 Access to the 'ear' of top management			

* Indicate against each indicator, the degree of power for each individual or group, according to whether it is high (H), medium (M) or low (L).

Figure 5.5 Assessing power

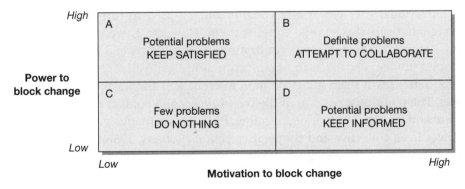

Figure 5.6 The power and motivation to block changes

Each cell of the matrix shown in Figure 5.6 represents a different situation and strategy to deal with it. Thus, if an individual or group has little power to block change and, in addition, little motivation to do so (as represented by cell C), no immediate action needs to be taken. However, if there is both power to block change and the motivation to do so (cell B) this represents a serious situation in terms of the need to negotiate with those concerned and, if possible, to reach a collaborative agreement.

A potential danger to any change is represented by those who fall into cell A of the matrix – those with a high degree of power but little motivation to do anything about the change. This is because, if the situation itself changes, their interest could be increased and this might then move them into cell B. A strategy towards these people, therefore, should be one of 'keeping them satisfied'. This means maintaining their awareness of how the change might benefit them.

Cell D of the matrix represents a different kind of problem. It might be tempting to ignore these people but, because change situations are dynamic – particularly situations of incremental change – the people categorized into cell D might begin to gain power and thus move into the more contentious group represented by cell B. Consequently, these people should be kept informed of change developments, with some effort being made to persuade them that the change might bring them benefits. However, it must be recognized that these people may be the ones who, in any radical restructuring or change in systems, lose their jobs. Containment in the short term might, therefore, be the most appropriate strategy.

The axes of the matrix in Figure 5.6 are presented in negative terms in relation to organizational change. It is equally possible to label the axes 'power to facilitate change' and 'motivation to facilitate change'. The categorization of individuals and groups according to this framework would not necessarily be the converse of that used in Figure 5.6. Therefore, it is worth completing two matrices for a fuller analysis of power, conflict and change.

The capacity for organizations to change, both incrementally and radically, depends on the multiplicity of different interests and values that are part of organizational life. Power and conflict can be used to further the aims of change, but can also be used to resist them. However, there is some evidence (e.g. Roberts, 1986) that most organizations, both publicly and privately owned, adopt a 'mixed' approach to organizational life generally. Thus, members of organizations will share some common interests and also have some conflicting ones. The traditional concept of the use of power and conflict as 'weapons' represents only a small part of organizational life. An alternative view is that power derives from collective and cooperative action (Roberts, 1986). Care should be taken, however, as the exercise of power and the management of conflict may differ cross-culturally, as is evident from the discussion in Chapter 4.

Finally, the style and function of leadership in the sharing or withholding of power and the management of conflict are crucial for organizational life generally but, particularly, in times of change, and in particular the function of leadership. The next chapter completes Part Two of the book by addressing the role of leadership in organizations and change.

Comment and conclusions

Power and politics in organizations are analogous to modes of political rule. In countries where a western-type democracy prevails, the dominant form of organization has been based on the notion of rational–legal authority in the form of bureaucracies. Much of what is written today, however, urges organizational management to adopt more organic forms of organization where rules are more fluid and coordination and cooperation are seen as the way forward.

A workforce operating on cooperative lines is likely to be more innovative and productive than one where individuals and groups are in constant conflict with each other.

However, as the discussion in this chapter shows, some individuals and groups have larger and more varied sources of power than others and, in the nature of a competitive society and environment, will choose to use them to influence others in desired directions. In addition, some groups are relatively powerless, not because of their diminished abilities, but as a reflection of the position occupied in the wider society. The discussion also referred to perspectives on conflict which say that some level of conflict can be constructive by contrast to other levels and types of conflict being destructive. A characterization of power proposed by Buchanan and Badham (1999, p. 56) is helpful, as a shorthand, in remembering what power encompasses:

1 Power is a *property of individuals*, defined across a number of identifiable power sources or bases, some structural, some individual, and exercised in attempts to influence others.
2 Power is a *property of relationships* between members of an organization, identified by the extent to which some individuals believe, or do not believe, that others possess particular power bases.
3 Power is an *embedded property* of the structures, regulations, relationships and norms of the organization, perpetuating existing routines and power inequalities.

Issues of changing power balances and the accompanying increase in conflict levels almost inevitably come to the fore in situations of organizational change. Figure 5.5 brings together statements representing many elements that contribute to the degree of power held by individuals and groups. It might be thought somewhat tedious to have to answer questionnaires, such as the ones in Figure 5.5, when the excitement or the fear of change approaches. However, without some form of analysis of power distribution and the propensity for political behaviour and conflict, change managers or change agents will find themselves facing the problems of change depicted in Figure 5.3.

Power, political activity and opportunities for conflict exist within organizations at all levels. These are heightened in times of change. Consequently, changing strategies, structures and cultures, as discussed in Chapters 3 and 4, will almost certainly bring with them changing power balances and bring out the propensity for people to act politically to get the best 'deal' for themselves and their close associates. Consequently, managers and others working with change ignore the politics of change at their peril.

Discussion questions and assignments

1 Drawing on the types of power suggested by different writers and researchers, give examples of each based on your organizational experiences.

2 Discuss the idea that power and powerlessness are simply two sides of the same coin.

3 Discuss the proposition: 'In times of change, conflict between individuals and groups is inevitable.'

4 Discuss the following statement: 'Conflict can add substantial value to creating an effective organization.'

Case example ●●●

Testing the rhetoric of empowerment

Everyone says they are in favour of delegating, but truly effective proponents of the art, being creative, are rare.

For decades, management gurus have preached the benefits of pushing decisions down the line, allowing those doing the work to say how resources should be used. This has been given various names – delegation, empowerment, involvement, commitment. And the logic is irrefutable. More can be achieved, people will be motivated, managers are free to think about strategy, and so on. Yet every day I am struck by the number of minor decisions blocked by head-office diktat.

As a group, managers are not good at delegating. In surveys, 70 per cent of managers rate it one of

their weakest skills. And they get worse at delegating once they reach their late forties, say their staff.

Of the 30 per cent who think they are effective delegators, only one in three are thought to be good by their subordinates. The rest are rated as 'dumpers' who believe delegation means clearing their desk by dumping accumulated trivia on to everyone else.

In the past week alone, I encountered three examples of poor delegation. The first was a large European business with annual sales of £56m and

5,000 staff. One 45-year-old divisional head has worked for the company for 25 years. He is totally trustworthy and very experienced but he has no control over the salaries he pays his people.

A global financial services company I visited is little better. In the past financial year, one employee, a 36-year-old woman, generated a fee income of £2m for her employer. Yet she has to seek approval from her boss in New York before hiring an assistant.

And on Monday, I attended the morning meeting of partners in a firm of accountants. The senior partner monopolized the entire meeting, while his supposed 'colleagues' sat in total silence.

I have learnt five things about delegation. First, 'empowerment' is more about rhetoric than sharing power. Second, other centralizing forces, such as information systems, minimize the impact of that movement. Third, work organizations remain the least democratic and centralized power structures in most western societies. Fourth, those who criticize bosses for not delegating are usually guilty of the offence themselves. And fifth, the poor record of delegation often reflects a mutually convenient arrangement between bosses and their direct reports.

When you observe people's career progress, it soon becomes clear why delegation is such a difficult issue. Managers in their twenties know little about delegation. Childhood hardly encourages it: schools are familiar with the practice of a pupil delegating maths homework to a friend. It is called cheating.

However, young managers are eager to control the decisions that affect them. They are usually highly critical of their boss's unwillingness to delegate.

During these early years, managers do learn something: that delegation is much easier in theory than in practice. That is partly because the effect of decisions can be dramatically different from what they anticipated. To commit a serious cock-up is a relatively simple – and frighteningly public – achievement. Because delegation is a political process, understanding its politics is essential.

Armed with these insights, managers move into their thirties and middle management. At that moment, they realize that it becomes clear to a majority that preserving the status quo is more attractive than foisting revolution. Delegation is all

very well, but exposes them to uncomfortable scrutiny. Before long, these middle managers tend to look for havens where they can sit on resources and watch for threats.

Do not misunderstand me: many are brilliant managers of the status quo. Routine services are their forte. They centralize control, minimize delegation and insist that others follow their systems. And it works – until the all-powerful central figure leaves or retires.

Among these middle managers are some real delegators. These people get rid of what they are doing now and badger their bosses for more power and excitement. There are notable exceptions, but most are in their thirties or early forties and will not rest. They learnt in their twenties that their future depended on delegating. They are risk takers who delegate courageously and expect others to deliver.

But even among this small number of high-flyers, time will eventually tell. Younger managers leave to create their own excitement. Older managers become less willing to take risks. The head office tightens its grip.

Can people who are poor delegators learn to do better? Surveys by London Business School's Interpersonal Skills Programmes suggest it is not easy. We can reiterate the logic that others develop when tasks are delegated, but most managers know this already.

They ignore the advice, because it suits them and their direct reports. The bosses can continue under the illusion that they are indispensable. Their subordinates are guaranteed an easier life – after all, everyone seeks some stability. It is a mutually beneficial arrangement that kills most attempts to improve delegation.

Delegation is an individual choice that requires effort. You have to want to change the way you manage. If you do want to improve, then begin by asking some basic questions: Why do you end up with all the work? What sort of impression are you giving others about your capability for bigger things?

Learn to say 'No'. Be especially wary of 'dumpers'. After any transaction ask: 'Who ended up with the work?' There is no prize for being everyone's workhorse; it is not an admired role in work organizations.

Source: Professor John W. Hunt, *Financial Times*, 13 October 2000.

Case exercise   Analysing the causes of change

1 How easy is it to delegate? John Hunt, the author of the piece above, asks these questions. Can you answer them? And what do the answers tell you about adopting a participative style of leadership?

2 If your experience in delegation has been disappointing, examine how you went about it. Was the task clear? Did you agree to a schedule? Was the person capable or did they need training? Did you delegate or abdicate? Did you regularly monitor the work and coach the person so that they knew exactly what you wanted, by when and in what format? In short, were you, in your own way, one of the 'dumpers'?

●●●● Indicative resources

Brooks, I. (2003) *Organizational Behaviour* (2nd edn), Harlow: Pearson Education Limited. This text is an introduction to organizational behaviour and focuses on the interactions of indidividuals and groups within an organizational setting and then relates the interactions to theory and practice. Brooks's chapter on power, politics and conflict is a useful introduction to this topic area and creates a good foundation for our chapter that ultimately leads to these issues in relation to change management.

Fisher, S., Ibrahim Abdi, D., Ludin, J., Smith, R., Williams, S. and Williams, S. (2000) *Working with Conflict: Skills and Strategies for Action*, Zed Books, USA. A toolkit of strategies for managing conflict within the workplace. The book is broken down into four sections: initial analysis, strategy, action and learning. This will be useful for students and new managers.

Robbins, S. P. (2005) *Organizational Behaviour* (11th edn), Englewood Cliffs, NJ: Prentice Hall. This text, although focusing on behaviour in the workplace, has an excellent section relating to conflict and negotiation. It focuses mostly on these topics in relation to the organization, groups and teams.

●●●● Useful websites

www.bambooweb.com This is a site that has been supported by the Open Content Encyclopedia. It is specifically designed to offer support in relation to conflict and negotiation. It includes help guides and articles and links you to other relevant sites depending on the area of interest relating to conflict.

www.pearsoned.co.uk This is an excellent site to get information on books related to this topic area. Many of the books published by Pearson have supporting links to book-related activities. Just log on to e-learning or information related to authors.

To click straight to these links and for other resources go to
www.pearsoned.co.uk/senior

 References

Avancena, J. and Saeed, A. (2000) 'Bigger role for gulf women in business recommended', *Saudi Gazette*, Middle East Newsfile, 26 May.

Barnard, C. I. (1938) *The Functions of the Executive*, Cambridge, MA: Harvard University Press.

bbc.co.uk/news – *Gender Gap Biggest in Egypt*, 16 May 2005.

bbc.co.uk/news – *Women Still Face Glass Ceiling*, 3 December 2004.

Brooks, I. (2003) *Organizational Behaviour* (2nd edn), Harlow: Pearson Education.

Buchanan, D. and Badham, R. (1999) *Power, Politics and Organizational Change*, London: Sage.

Buchanan, D. and Huczynski, A. (2004) *Organizational Behaviour – An Introductory Text* (5th edn), Harlow: Financial Times Prentice Hall.

Burrell, G. and Morgan, G. (1979) *Sociological Paradigms and Organisational Analysis*, London: Heinemann Educational.

Department for Education and Employment (2000) *Labour Market and Skills Trends 2000*, London: Department for Education and Employment.

Equal Opportunities Commission (2004) 'Sex and power: who runs Britain', bbc.co.uk

Financial Post (2000) 'Cracking the glass ceiling: a new girls' network of top women takes its place in Canada's business firmament: power and influence: it's no longer lonely at the top for women in business', *Financial Post*, Canada, 4 March.

Fisher, S., Ibrahim Abdi, D., Ludin, J., Smith, R., Williams, S. and Williams, S. (2000) *Working with Conflict: Skills and Strategies for Action*, Zed Books.

French, W. L. and Bell, C. H. (1990) *Organization Development: Behavioral Science Interventions for Organization Improvement*, Englewood Cliffs, NJ: Prentice-Hall.

Furze, D. and Gale, C. (1996) *Interpreting Management: Exploring Change and Complexity*, London: Thompson International.

Gordon, J. R. (1993) *A Diagnostic Approach to Organizational Behavior*, Needham Heights, MA: Allyn & Bacon.

Gracie, S. (1998) 'In the company of women', *Management Today*, June.

Gratton, L. (2000) *Living Strategy: Putting People at the Heart of Corporate Purpose*, Hemel Hempstead: Prentice Hall.

Handy, C. (1993) *Understanding Organizations*, Harmondsworth: Penguin.

Hardy, C. (1994) *Managing Strategic Action: Mobilizing Change, Concepts, Readings and Cases*, London: Sage.

Hofstede, G. (1981) 'Culture and organizations', *International Studies of Management and Organizations*, vol. X, no. 4, pp. 15–41.

Hunt, J. W. (2000) 'Testing the rhetoric of empowerment', *Financial Times*, 13 October.

Johnson, G. (1990) 'Managing strategic change; the role of symbolic action', *British Journal of Management*, vol. 1, pp. 183–200.

Johnson, G., Scholes, K. and Whittington, R. (2005) *Exploring Corporate Strategy: Text and Cases* (7th edn), Harlow: Financial Times Prentice Hall.

Kanter, R. M. (1979) 'Power failure in management circuits', *Harvard Business Review*, July–August, pp. 65–75.

Kibazo, J. (1996) 'Flight to revival', *Financial Times*, 22 March, p. 12.

Lawrence, P. R. and Lorsch, J. W. (1969) *Organization and Environment: Managing Differentiation and Integration*, Homewood, IL: R. D. Irwin.

McClelland, D. C. (1970) 'The two faces of power', *Journal of International Affairs*, vol. 24, no. 1, pp. 29–47.

McGregor, D. (1960) *The Human Side of Enterprise*, New York: McGraw-Hill.

McKenna, E. P. (1997) *When Work Doesn't Work Anymore: Women, Work and Identity*, New York: Hodder & Stoughton.

Maitland, A. (2000a) 'Sexual incrimination: Management women in the city: the macho culture of long hours and big bucks has been highlighted by two bankers' discrimination cases, but there are signs of change', *Financial Times*, 20 January.

Maitland, A. (2000b) 'Wanted: more uppity women: Boardroom appointments: Alison Maitland looks at the reasons why only 5 per cent of the directors of FTSE 100 companies are female', *Financial Times*, 7 November.

Maitland, A (2004) 'The north–south divide in Europe Inc.', *Financial Times*, 14 June 2004, p. 9.

Martin, J. (2005) *Organizational Behaviour and Management* (3rd edn), London: Thomson.

Mayo, E. (1933) *The Human Problems of Industrial Civilization*, New York: Macmillan.

Mills, A. J. and Murgatroyd, S. J. (1991) *Organizational Rules: A Framework for Understanding Organizational Action*, Milton Keynes: Open University.

Morgan, G. (1997) *Images of Organizations*, London: Sage.

Mullins, L. J. (2005) *Management and Organizational Behaviour* (7th edn), Harlow: Pearson Education Limited.

Nadler, D. A. (1988) 'Concepts for the management of organizational change', in Tushman, M. L. and Moore, W. L. (eds) *Readings in the Management of Innovation* (7th edn), New York: Ballinger, pp. 718–32.

Open University (1985) Units 9–10, 'Conflict', Course T244, *Managing in Organizations*, Milton Keynes: Open University.

Paton, R. (1994) 'Power in organizations', in Arson, R. and Paton, R., *Organizations, Cases, Issues, Concepts*, London: PCP.

Pfeffer, J. (1981) *Power in Organizations*, Marchfield, MA: Pitman.

Pfeffer, J. (1992), *Managing with Power: Politics and Influence in Organization*, Boston, MA: Harvard Business Press.

Pfeffer, J. (1993) 'Understanding power in organizations', in Mabey, C. and Mayon-White, B. (eds) *Managing Change* (2nd edn), London: PCP.

PR Newswire (2000) 'Department of Commerce Acting Assistant Secretary and Director General to lead women in business development trade mission to Egypt, Kenya, South Africa', 1 October.

Robbins, S. P. (1974) *Managing Organizational Conflict: A Nontraditional Approach*, Upper Saddle River, NJ: Prentice-Hall.

Robbins, S. P. (1990) *Organization Theory: Structure, Design and Applications*, Englewood Cliffs, NJ: Prentice-Hall.

Robbins, S. P. (2005), *Organizational Behavior* (11th edn), Englewood Cliffs, NJ: Prentice-Hall.

Roberts, N. C. (1986) 'Organizational power styles: collective and competitive power under varying organizational conditions', *Journal of Applied Behavioral Science*, vol. 22, no. 4, pp. 443–58.

Ryle, J. (1996) 'Soft silverware', the *Guardian*, 26 July, p. 3.

Schelling, T. C. (1960) *The Strategy of Conflict*, Cambridge, MA: Harvard University Press.

Stacey, R. (1996) *Strategic Management and Organisational Dynamics*, London: Pitman.

Taylor, F. W. (1911) *Principles of Scientific Management*, New York: Harper & Row.

Thomas, K. W. (1976) 'Conflict and conflict management', in Dunnette, M. D. (ed.) *Handbook of Industrial and Organizational Psychology*, Chicago, IL: Rand McNally, pp. 889–935.

Thomas, K. W. (1977) 'Toward multi-dimensional values in teaching: the example of conflict behaviors', *Academy of Management Review*, vol. 12, pp. 484–90.

Thompson, P. and McHugh, D. (2002) *Work Organisations* (3rd edn), London: Palgrave.

Tosi, H. L., Rizzo, J. R. and Carroll, S. J. (1994) *Managing Organizational Behavior*, Oxford: Blackwell.

Weber, M. (1947) *The Theory of Social and Economic Organization*, London: Oxford University Press.

Wilson, D. C. (1992) *A Strategy of Change*, London: Routledge.

Wilson, F. M. (1995) *Organizational Behaviour and Gender*, Maidenhead: McGraw-Hill.

Yuet-Ha, M. (1996) 'Orientating values with Eastern ways', *People Management*, 25 July, pp. 28–30.

Chapter 6

Chapter 6

The leadership of change

One of the major debates concerning organizational change relates to the role of those who lead it. This chapter addresses the issue of leading change. It includes a discussion of whether there is one style of leadership best suited to managing change or whether different styles of leadership are required according to different change situations. Issues regarding resistance to change and the identification of strategies for managing it are also recognized.

Learning objectives

By the end of this chapter, you will be able to:

- identify those characteristics which distinguish leadership from management;

- discuss whether there is 'one best way' of leading or whether leadership style and behaviour should vary according to the circumstances;

- evaluate the possible relationship between organizational life cycle theories and different leadership styles and behaviours;

- assess the compatibility of different leadership approaches with different types of change situations;

- critically review the issue of resistance to change in terms of its implications for leading the processes of planning and implementing change.

●●●● Management and leadership

The issue of leading change links strongly to everything already discussed – both in Part One and in the three preceding chapters. For instance, the management and leadership of organizations is played out through formal organizational structures with their accompanying rules and regulations – as discussed in Chapter 3 – yet the practice of both management and leadership influences is also influenced by, an organization's culture, the way power is distributed and the approach taken to conflicts. Thus management and leadership are both parts of the formal and informal aspects of organizational life, as Illustration 6.1 shows.

Illustration 6.1

Tesco chief

Tesco's (a leading UK supermarket) chief executive, Sir Terry Leahy (49 years old) is so ordinary; it makes him extraordinary among his peers. Unlike many other people in senior executive positions, he does not have a chauffeur-driven car, he does not sit on any other companies or boards and he shuns networking in favour of talking to staff and customers on the shopfloor.

To Sir Terry, the customer must come first, and it appears to be more of a religion than a rule. Every Friday, he walks the floor of one of his stores, and he is also a regular visitor to those owned by the competition. He takes pride in knowing what different jobs entail and what customers buy, and he is always keen to hear what people want.

Sir Terry was knighted in 2003, and is less keen to talk about himself – except in the context of Tesco's business. Tesco has grown under his stewardship and has become the third largest grocer in the world after Wal-Mart of the US and Carrefour of France. Tesco controls about a quarter of the UK market. Approximately £1 from £8 spent ends up on one of the Tesco services. Tesco's international expansion has resulted in a portfolio of 2,300 stores in 12 countries worldwide.

'The only personality I believe in is Tesco', he says, according to the magazine *Management Today*. But despite being intensely private, Sir Terry likes to point to his background as a man of the people. He grew up in Liverpool, the son of a greyhound trainer who worked as caretaker on the council-owned farm where they lived.

As the only one of four children who received a university education, he gained a business science degree from Manchester University. After university, he worked at the Co-op for a year and a half, then quit to move to London with his wife.

At age 23 he joined Tesco stacking shelves and initially working on a casual basis. Before he turned 30 he became Tesco's marketing director at a time when it was little more than a troubled supermarket chain struggling to keep up with the UK supermarket chain, Sainsbury's. Eight years later, in 1992, he was appointed to Tesco's board of directors, and by the time he was 40, in 1997, he had worked his way up to become chief executive. By then he had helped turn things around, having spotted Tesco's fundamental flaw, namely its long-standing desire to copy Sainsbury's .

During the early years, Sir Terry became obsessed with all things Tesco. The obsession has lasted, but he has replaced his formerly aggressive management style with an impassioned and some say humourless directness. His friends insist that behind the tough guy exterior there is a deadpan Liverpudlian humour. His detractors, on the other hand, believe Sir Terry is incapable of small talk and describe him as dour. He is more at home discussing football in a Liverpool pub than among London's glitzy set, and this is the root of his rapport with

Tesco's customers and staff. His down-to-earth approach to life is reflected everywhere in the way he runs the business. Unlike some competitors, Tesco's headquarters, on an industrial estate in Hertfordshire, are devoid of anything lavish.

Source: Jorn Madslien 12/04/05 BBC – profile: Tesco chief Sir Terry Leahy. bbc.co.uk

Stars of Europe – a hands-on retailer
Tesco has managed to successfully expand beyond Britain into eastern Europe and even into parts of Asia. The architect of this transformation is Sir Terry

Leahy, the company's unassuming chief executive. A Tesco veteran who took over in 1997, the 49-year-old Leahy is viewed by his own management team and his rivals as a creative leader who is willing to take risks on new products, store formats and lines of business. ...

Tesco is considered the Wal-Mart of Europe ... despite Leahy's willingness to take some risks to feed Tesco's rapid growth, he isn't quite ready to go up against the formidable Wal-Mart on its home turf.

Source: Cohn, L. (2005) 'A Hands-on Retailer', *Business Week*, 30 May 2005, pp. 50–1.

A distinction can, however, be made that places management rather more firmly in the context of the formal organization with leadership more naturally associated with the informal aspects of organizations. This chapter is mainly about the role of leadership as part of organizational life and, in particular, its relationship to organizational change. However, it is useful to be clear about the relationship between management and leadership before discussing leadership in more detail.

Management can be thought of as a function that is part of an organization's formal structure. This is evident in Mullins's (2005, p. 190) statement that he regards management as:

- taking place within a structured organizational setting and with prescribed roles;
- directed towards the attainment of aims and objectives;
- achieved through the efforts of other people; and
- using systems and procedures.

He goes on to say:

> It is through the process of management that the efforts of members of the organization are co-ordinated, directed and guided towards the achievement of organizational goals. Management is therefore the cornerstone of organizational effectiveness, and is concerned with arrangements for the carrying out of organizational processes and the execution of work.

This definition draws on the idea that management is a particular function, which is embedded in the organizational structure and involves a number of different kinds of activities that are, nevertheless, associated with each other. Thus Fayol (1949) proposed five elements of management – planning, organizing, commanding, coordinating and controlling – which can be seen to relate to formal organizational systems. Naylor (2004), also distinguishes between the two:

> Management is the process of achieving organizational objectives, within a changing environment, by balancing efficiency, effectiveness and equity, obtaining the most from limited resources, and working with and through people. (p. 6)

Leadership is the process of influencing people towards achievement of organizational goals. (p. 354)

Other writers and researchers have concentrated more on the roles that managers play, that is, what managers do. For instance, Illustration 6.2 describes the ten roles that Mintzberg (1979) suggested as a result of his study of chief executive officers in both small and large organizations.

Mintzberg (1979) grouped managerial roles into three sets: interpersonal roles (figurehead, leader, liaison); informational roles (monitor, disseminator, spokesman); decisional roles (entrepreneur, disturbance handler, resource alloca-

---

Illustration 6.2

Mintzberg's managerial roles

Figurehead
In the figurehead role, the manager acts as the representative or symbol of the organization. Examples of this role are attending meetings on behalf of the organization, giving out long-service awards or appearing on 'platforms' as a representative of local business.

Leader
The manager, as leader, is concerned with interpersonal relationships, what motivates his or her staff and what needs they might have.

Liaison
The liaison role emphasizes the network of contacts with others in and outside the organization. Liaising with others allows the manager to collect useful information. In the liaison role, a manager might belong to a professional institution.

Monitor
Monitoring the environment to keep informed of competitors' activities, new legislation, changes in the market, and so on, are all examples of a manager's monitoring role.

Disseminator
The role of disseminator includes keeping staff and others within the organization informed. This could be done in a variety of written and spoken forms and may be on a one-to-one basis or through group meetings.

Spokesperson
As spokesperson, the manager gives information to others outside the organization. He or she speaks on behalf of the organization, for instance on the organization's policies and activities.

Entrepreneur
The role of entrepreneur is associated with innovation and change. It includes the design and implementation of different types of change, from small-scale job redesign to large-scale organizational restructuring depending on the level of the manager concerned.

Disturbance handler
The manager in this role acts to solve problems that arise, often unexpectedly. Managing to intervene in a conflict situation or find a solution to a machine breakdown are examples of this role.

Resource allocator
The majority of managers control some kind of resource (e.g. money, labour, time) that they can use, or allocate, at their discretion. Allocating money according to budgets is one aspect of this role. Other possibilities are the scheduling of subordinates' work and allocating equipment.

Negotiator
All managers have to play the role of negotiator when they debate who will do some things and who will do others. Coming to agreements on the scope of people's jobs and their pay are examples of negotiating.

Source: Based on Mintzberg, H. (1979), *The Nature of Managerial Work* (Englewood Cliffs, NJ, Prentice Hall).

tor, negotiator). An examination of these categories and the roles within them highlights the ambiguity of the relationship between management and leadership. As this framework shows, leadership is just one aspect of a manager's job, a view that is echoed by Handy's (1993) contention that leading (which he takes to include the roles of figurehead, leader and liaison) is mostly concerned with the interpersonal aspects of a manager's activities. Consequently, although a manager must also be a leader, a leader does not always have to be a manager. Kotter (1990), as shown in Illustration 6.3, gives a useful summary of the differences between leading and managing.

Both Mintzberg's and Kotter's distinctions between leadership and management agree with Mullins's (2005) conclusion that management is concerned with activities within the formal structure and goals of the organization, while leadership focuses more on interpersonal behaviour in a broader context. His

Illustration 6.3

Comparing management and leadership

	Management	Leadership
Creating an agenda	Planning and Budgeting – establishing detailed steps and timetables for achieving needed results, and then allocating the resources necessary to make that happen	Establishing Direction – developing a vision of the future, often the distant future, and strategies for producing the changes needed to achieve that vision
Developing a human network for achieving the agenda	Organizing and Staffing – establishing some structure for accomplishing plan requirements, staffing that structure with individuals, delegating responsibility and authority for carrying out the plan, providing policies and procedures to help guide people, and creating methods or systems to monitor implementation	Aligning People – communicating the direction by words and deeds to all those whose cooperation may be needed so as to influence the creation of teams and coalitions that understand the vision and strategies, and accept their validity
Execution	Controlling and Problem Solving – monitoring results vs. plan in some detail, identifying deviations, and then planning and organizing to solve these problems	Motivating and Inspiring – energizing people to overcome major political, bureaucratic, and resource barriers to change by satisfying very basic, but often unfulfilled, human needs
Outcomes	Produces a degree of predictability and order, and has the potential of consistently producing key results expected by various stakeholders (e.g. for customers, always being on time; for stakeholders, being on budget)	Produces change, often to a dramatic degree, and has the potential of producing extremely useful change (e.g. new products that customers want, new approaches to labor relations that help make a firm more competitive)

Source: Adapted with the permission of The Free Press, a division of Simon & Schuster Adult Publishing Group, from *A Force for Change: How Leadership Differs from Management* by John P. Kotter. Copyright © 1990 by John P. Kotter Inc. All rights reserved.

statement (p. 284) that 'leadership does not necessarily take place within the hierarchical structure of the organization' typifies this view. To support this contention, he refers to Watson's (1983) 7-S organizational framework of: strategy, structure, systems, style, staff, skills and superordinate (or shared) goals.

Based on this, Watson maintains that management is more concerned with strategy, structure and systems, while leadership is more concerned with what he calls the 'soft' Ss of: style, staff, skills and shared goals. Leadership, then, is concerned with establishing shared visions and goals; with interpersonal relationships and communication; and with motivation and getting the best out of people. Utimately, leadership is about influencing others in pursuit of the achievement of organizational goals.

However, as Smith (1991) points out, rather than being about absolute influence, leadership is about relative influence, in that 'a leader is someone who has more influence over others than they have over him or her' (p. 207). This introduces the idea of the leader and the *group*, thus implying the importance of *followers*. The discussion which follows shows that other factors also influence people's perception of what constitutes 'good leadership'. It will become evident also that there is no universally agreed view as to what this is. There are, however, a number of approaches that offer ways to understanding leadership and its relationship to organizational performance and organizational change.

Approaches to leadership

There is a range of theories purporting to explain what makes a person a good and effective leader. These can be put into two broad categories. The first includes those theories which contend that there is 'one best way' of exercising leadership and, therefore, that there is a particular set of characteristics which 'good' leaders should possess. The second category challenges this and suggests that there is no one best way, but a range of leadership styles that should be applied differentially according to the situation in which leadership is required. Fitting somewhere between these two is the concept of 'the team as leader', or what has more recently become known as 'distributed leadership'.

The 'one best way' to lead

Traits of leadership

The first of the approaches to leadership under this heading is not really a theory of *how* to lead. It is more a theory of what leaders should be like, in other words what traits (e.g. physical and personality characteristics, skills and abilities and social factors such as interpersonal skills, sociability and socio-economic position) are indicative of a successful leader. However, a survey of the research on this issue shows that there is a degree of confusion as to whether there are certain personality and other characteristics which, when present, 'fit' a person to be a leader. Early research (Stodgill, 1948; Mann, 1959) came to the conclusion that there were few relationships between the traits possessed by leaders and their performance. The notion of 'born to lead' did not hold up under scrutiny. However, more recent studies reveal stronger evidence of an identifiable set of personality and cognitive traits that are said to characterize successful leaders.

The first of these is a *meta-analysis* (one that surveys and brings together the results of other studies) carried out by Lord, De Vader and Alliger in 1986 which concluded that there could be six traits which distinguish successful leaders from others:

1 intelligence
2 having an extrovert personality
3 dominance
4 masculinity
5 conservatism
6 being better adjusted than non-leaders.

A few years later, Kirkpatrick and Locke (1991) also surveyed existing leadership studies and suggested their own list of six leadership traits:

1 drive (achievement, ambition, energy, tenacity, initiative)
2 leadership motivation (personalized or socialized)
3 honesty and integrity
4 self-confidence (including emotional stability)
5 cognitive ability (the ability to marshal and interpret a wide variety of information)
6 knowledge of the business.

In 1996 Dulewicz and Herbert reported on their original research on a sample of 72 managers who, on the basis of several indicators of success, could be identified as either 'high-flyers or low-flyers'. What these two researchers did was to administer two different personality tests to these managers to determine what characteristics differentiated the high-flyers. The results showed that the high-flyers scored higher than the low-flyers on the following:

- risk-taking
- assertiveness and decisiveness
- achievement
- motivation
- competitiveness.

They also showed exceptional managerial skills:

- planning and organizing
- managing staff
- motivating others.

Activity 6.1

Read Illustration 6.1 again. Which of the leadership traits do you think Terry Leahy possesses? Do you think the description 'not networking' and 'aggressive management style' have positive or negative connotations in this context? Justify your conclusions.

Look in newspapers and magazines such as Management Today, Business Week *and* People Management *for articles on top managers and leaders in the public or private sectors or in the business of sport. See if you can construct your own list of leadership traits that, according to what is said in the accounts, indicate a successful leader.*

What may be helpful to you is to identify two or three well-known people, research their profiles and identify what specific traits or managerial preferences they have. How does your list compare with those of Lord and his colleagues, Kirkpatrick and Locke, and Dulewicz and Herbert? How far are you convinced that your or others' lists are valid in this respect? How might you design a piece of research to test trait theories of leadership?

It is interesting to compare and contrast these three lists. For instance, the trait of intelligence comes up in the first two studies mentioned and this is given further confirmation in Fiedler's (1989) *Cognitive Resource Utilisation Theory* (CRUT). This says that, under normal circumstances, a leader's intelligence will add crucially to his or her success as a leader. Consequently, a leader's intelligence is an important resource for any group. However, as Fiedler points out, there are some situations that can prevent leaders using the intelligence they possess – such as poor relations with their boss, poor interpersonal relationships and a non-directive style. Therefore intelligence on its own is not sufficient to guarantee a successful leader. The characteristics of dominance (Lord *et al.*, 1986), drive and self-confidence (Kirkpatrick and Locke, 1991) and almost all the characteristics listed by Dulewicz and Herbert (1996, p. 16) are required to support the use of a leader's cognitive capacities. What is particularly relevant about Dulewicz and Herbert's list, in comparison to the other two, is the addition of the characteristic of risk taking that is probably most relevant in times of organizational change. Two statements from their article make this point:

> Our most successful general managers are also willing to take risks rather than seek comfort in familiar situations; are determined to see things through to completion; set stretching targets for themselves and others; and are highly competitive and poor losers. ...
>
> The competencies required of high-flyers will tend to concentrate on the ability to cope with change and uncertainty and the promotion of innovation.

The concept of 'innovation' associated as it is with 'creative thinking' (see Henry, 2001 and Henry and Mayle, 2002), which appears in the latter statement, brings in a leadership trait that does not appear in the three lists mentioned earlier. Innovation is a process that finds expression in much of the literature relating to organizational behaviour in environments responding to strong triggers for change. It implies a set of leadership characteristics, which are related more to what is commonly known as 'right-brain' thinking as opposed to 'left-brain' thinking; that is, a preference for thinking and decision making which uses intuition in addition to, and just as much as, reason and logic. Lank and Lank (1995, p. 19) define intuition as follows:

> a brain skill; operating largely from the right hemisphere; capable of entering awareness at physical, emotional and mental levels; whose sources are the subconscious, unconscious and/or superconscious; and which enters consciousness without rational thought or careful analysis and quantitative calculation.

Bennett III (1998, p. 590) links intuition to tacit knowledge that he conceptualizes as:

> idiosyncratic, subjective, highly individualized store of knowledge and practical know-how gathered through years of experience and direct interaction within a domain.

All three of these writers contrast intuition (or intuitive processing) and decision making with analytical, rational, logical thinking and decision making. They argue that, particularly in situations of uncertainty and turbulence (that is situations which in Chapter 2 were characterized as ill-structured, messy or soft), intuition is just as important for decision making as more explicit decision-making processes based on the collection of 'facts' and logical reasoning. However, both Lank and Lank's and Bennett III's articles are theoretical rather than empirically based.

By contrast, Andersen (2000) offers a good argument based on an empirical study of 33 managers working in an organization in the service sector in Sweden. Although a small study, one interesting aspect of Andersen's research is the method of identification of the managers' decision-making styles. For this he used Keegan's Type Indicator (KTI) (Keegan 1980, 1984) which measures preferences in terms of the way issues and problems are perceived and the way decisions about them are made. Based on the theories of Jung (1976), individuals use either *sensing* (respect for facts and information) or *intuition* (respect for possibilities and tacit knowledge and reasoning) for perceiving issues associated with problems and either *thinking* (respect for analysis, particularity, precision and logic) or *feeling* (based on their own values, but with respect for other people's feelings and emotions) for making judgements about what to do. Completion of the KTI identifies an individual as preferring *either* sensing *or* intuition *and* thinking *or* feeling to guide their behaviour in terms of decision making. What is more, within each pair of preferences (sensing and thinking; sensing and feeling; intuition and thinking; intuition and feeling) one will be 'dominant' and the other 'auxiliary'.

Using a fairly robust method of measuring leadership effectiveness – what the company termed 'gross profit margin' – Andersen found that the managers with dominant intuition combined with auxiliary thinking decision-making styles (what they term a 'creative-innovative' decision-making style) were the more effective ones. He concludes:

> This study suggests that intuition as the dominant decision-making function is related to organizational effectiveness. The focus on future opportunities and threats as well as actions to preserve flexibility and handle uncertainty appears to be the reason why intuition in managers is effective.

This conclusion must remain a possibility only, given the limited nature of this research. However, other writers, not only academics (see Bunting's (2000) newspaper article 'Rewiring our brains' and the website of the Institute of Personnel Development's magazine *People Management* at www.peoplemanagement.co.uk/women.htm), have coined the phrase 'the feminization of business leadership' to extol the virtues of intuition as expressed more in the way female managers operate compared to what is seen as the more traditionalist 'command and control' styles of male managers. Pollock (2000, p. 19) describes how: 'Companies are turning to music, storytelling, visual art and even comedy in order to develop their people, engender creativity in the workplace and enhance their corporate image.' She quotes Nicholas Janni, teacher at the Royal Academy of Dramatic Art and visiting fellow at the Cranfield School of Management, in saying:

> The old style of management – control, protect and know everything – is no longer effective. That's a very masculine thing, which is not wrong, but it has big limitations. Arts-based learning is about using different parts of your brain. ... we're talking about using your imagination. This relates to what could be, as opposed to knowledge, which is limited to what is.

In spite of these contentions, the 'feminization of business' does not seem to have reached top management in terms of women's representation. The reality (Hoar, 2004) is that only one female is a chief executive among the FTSE 100 companies. Therefore there is clearly more work and research to do in this area in relation to its effectiveness.

This discussion of the perceived need for managers to use intuition, as well as the more deliberately applied cognitive skills of reasoning and logic, can be compared to another trait that is being discussed as necessary for leaders to be successful. According to Goleman (1998, p. 93), who is reckoned to have developed the concept, '*Emotional intelligence* is the sine qua non of leadership' [author's italics]. On the basis of an examination of competency models in 188, mostly large, global companies, Goleman claims to have found which personal capabilities drove outstanding performance in these organizations. He grouped the capabilities into three categories: purely technical skills, cognitive abilities and competencies demonstrating emotional intelligence, which he defines as having the five components of: self-awareness; self-regulation; motivation; empathy; social skills. While not decrying the need for leaders to have technical skills (such as accounting and business planning) and cognitive capabilities (such as analytical reasoning), he claims these are 'threshold capabilities'; that is, while being *necessary* to successful leadership they are not *sufficient* without the addition of emotional intelligence.

An examination of the components of emotional intelligence, however, might suggest that there is little new in these in terms of the psychological and social characteristics of individuals defined by psychologists throughout the ages. As evidence of this is a closely argued article by Woodruffe (2000), who draws on other people's work, as well as his own detailed arguments, to rebut the claim that emotional intelligence adds anything more to what is already known about the behaviours and competencies of leaders and others. What Woodruffe does concede is that EI (as it is now known) has popularized the need for leaders to exhibit these capabilities in the service of bringing greater effectiveness to their management of people and the tasks they are involved in. This view is reflected in the work of Higgs and Dulewicz (2004, p. 175), who suggest that EI is concerned with achieving one's goals through the capabilities to: (1) manage one's own feelings and emotions; (2) be sensitive to the needs of others and influence key people; and (3) balance one's own motives and drives with conscientious and ethical behaviour.

All this may be no bad thing if it encourages managers and leaders at all levels in organizations to pay attention to the need to use what Beer and Nohria (2000) call 'soft' *as well as* 'hard' approaches to leading organizational change. In addition, looking over the lists of leadership traits identified earlier in the chapter, only one of the components of emotional intelligence appears there.

The results from doing Activity 6.2 (see overleaf) are only an indication of the applicability of trait theories of leadership – after all, if you did this on your own, you have a sample of only two leaders! These theories do, however, appear to offer something in relation to the type of person best suited to lead others.

This idea certainly appears to find favour in the many descriptions of supposed leaders of change – what Reich (1991) calls 'the entrepreneurial hero'. This notion that there are some people who are, characteristically, leadership material is supported by implication when Kanter (1991, p. 54) says: 'I discovered the skills of change masters [by which she means those successfully bringing about change] by researching hundreds of managers across more than a half-dozen industries. I put change-master skills in two categories: first, the personal or individual skills and second, the interpersonal ones, how the person manages others.' She goes on to identify what she calls 'kaleidoscope thinking' as well as the ability to communicate visions, and be persistent. Coalition building and working through teams are aspects of her second category of skills. Other researchers have come to similar conclusions about the nature of leadership. For instance, Westley and Mintzberg (1989) claim to have identified a range of what they term 'salient capacities' of five well-known leaders (Edwin Land, Steven Jobs, Rene Levesque, Lee Iacocca, Jan Carlzon). The capacities of imagination, sagacity and foresight are prominent among them.

Yet Reich (1991) warns against the idea of the leader as hero with some set of hero-like characteristics. The concept of successful leadership is seen as more complex than this, as is evident in the title of Reich's chapter, 'The team as hero'. In support of Reich is the argument of Landrum, Howell and Paris (2000)

Activity 6.2

Think of two leaders you know, or have known, well. One should be a person whom you judged to be successful as a leader and the other quite the opposite – that is, unsuccessful. On the following scales, indicate the extent to which each person possesses that particular trait.

If possible, ask some other colleagues to carry out the same activity.

	Very high	High	Average	Low	Very low
Need to achieve					
Need for power					
Leadership motivation					
Self-confidence					
Honesty and integrity					
Intelligence					
Knowledge of the business					
Assertiveness and decisiveness					
Competitiveness					
Emotional stability					
Extrovert personality					
Willingness to take risks					
Intuition and use of tacit knowledge					
Self-awareness					
Self-regulation					
Empathy					
Social skills					

From your results, what conclusions can you form as to whether successful leaders possess some traits that others do not? Compare your results with those discussed in the literature and with other people's views. From further discussions and comparisons with others, what key conclusions can be drawn from this activity?

that, while many writers claim that 'strong' (by which they generally mean charismatic) leadership is what is required for strategic and 'turnaround' change, there is also a 'dark side' to charismatic leaders. These writers comment that charismatic leaders can lead followers in directions unhelpful to the organization. They also point out a possible propensity for narcissism and quote the words of Post (1986, p. 679) who stated that the charismatic leader: 'Requires a continuing flow of admiration from his audience in order to nourish his famished self. Central to his ability to elicit that admiration is his ability to convey a sense of grandeur, omnipotence, and strength.' Landrum *et al.* (2000) refer to *unethical* charismatic leaders who are controlling, manipulative and self-promoting – characteristics that can jeopardize and even sabotage the turn-around efforts of the organization. To mitigate these possibilities and overcome the difficulties of leaders being all things to all people and situations, Landrum *et al.* argue for a team approach to designing and implementing strategic change, which incidentally is not unusual in more 'collective' societies (see Chapter 5), such as are found in the Far East.

Having said this, western thinking is still more likely to veer towards the idea that there is one best way to lead. However, instead of trying to find a set of characteristics to describe *what* a successful leader is, these ideas concentrate more on *how* a leader ought to *behave* in order to be successful.

Leadership behaviour

Bass (1990) lists no fewer than 29 different systems for classifying leadership behaviour. However, Wright (1996), in commenting on this, maintains that many of the concepts are so similar that four main leadership styles of behaviour can be identified. These are (p. 36):

1 *Concern for task.* The extent to which the leader emphasizes high levels of productivity, organizes and defines group activities in relation to the group's task objectives and so on. (Also called concern for production, production-centred, task-oriented and task-centred leadership.)
2 *Concern for people.* The extent to which the leader is concerned about his or her subordinates as people – their needs, interests, problems, development, etc. – rather than simply treating them as units of production. (Also called person-centred, person-oriented and employee-centred leadership.)
3 *Directive leadership.* The extent to which the leader makes all the decisions concerning group activities him- or herself and expects subordinates simply to follow instructions. (Also called authoritarian or autocratic leadership.)
4 *Participative leadership.* The extent to which the leader shares decision making concerning group activities with subordinates. (Also called democratic leadership.)

Given this classification of leadership style, it might be supposed that there are differences in the effects of using one style rather than another. However, Wright's review of a range of studies attempting to link leadership style with high performance and subordinate satisfaction found little evidence of a single style. Consequently, no one style seemed to emerge as the most appropriate in all situations and where, for instance, a participative leadership style was related to high performance and satisfaction of subordinates, it was not clear whether the leader's style was the causal variable or vice versa. Given this, it is interesting to note that two famous studies of leadership (Stodgill and Coons, 1957; Likert, 1961), known respectively as the University of Michigan studies and the Ohio State studies, separately identified two independent dimensions of leadership which were, in essence, a combination of the four types of behaviour described earlier. The Ohio researchers named these 'consideration' and 'initiating structure'.

Consideration is the degree to which a leader builds trust and mutual respect with subordinates, shows respect for their ideas and concern for their well-being. This dimension is linked to a participative, human relations approach to leadership. It therefore combines the 'concern for people' and 'participative leadership' styles identified by Wright.

Initiating structure is the degree to which a leader defines and structures his or her own role and the interactions within the group towards the attainment of formal goals. It has elements of both the 'directive leadership' and 'concern for tasks' styles described earlier.

The University of Michigan researchers used the terms employee-centred and production-centred leadership for these dimensions but they were virtually the same in description to those of the Ohio researchers. The main point about these dimensions is that, because they are deemed to be independent of each other, a leader's behaviour can be categorized in four different ways. Thus, leaders can be:

- high on consideration and high on initiating structure
- high on consideration and low on initiating structure
- low on consideration and low on initiating structure
- low on consideration and high on initiating structure.

The relationship of these two-dimensional theories to the idea of a 'one best way' of leading manifests itself most clearly in the way Blake and Mouton (1964) built on these concepts to propose that the most effective leadership style is one which is high on both dimensions. Figure 6.1 gives the positions of five different leadership styles on a later version of Blake and Mouton's managerial grid – now called the 'Leadership Grid®' (Blake and McCanse, 1991).

The different combinations of concern for people and concern for production set out in Figure 6.1 result in different combinations of leadership characteristics as follows.

The 9,1 Authority–Compliance leader has a high concern for the task and little concern for people, emphasizing efficiency and the organization's needs at the expense of the needs of people. There is a belief that production can only be achieved if people are closely supervised and controlled. According to Blake and McCanse (1991, p. 55): 'A Grid style like 9,1 is unlikely to elicit the cooperation, involvement, or commitment of those who are expected to complete the task.'

The 1,9 Country Club leadership style is based on the assumption that productivity will follow if the needs of people are satisfied. These leaders believe that people cannot be pressured into doing things – they need to be well treated to get them to perform well. According to Blake and McCanse, however, this leadership style, although encouraging friendly and pleasant relationships, produces results where productivity suffers. Creativity and innovation are undermined because of the possible conflict that might surface as a result of challenges to existing ways of doing things.

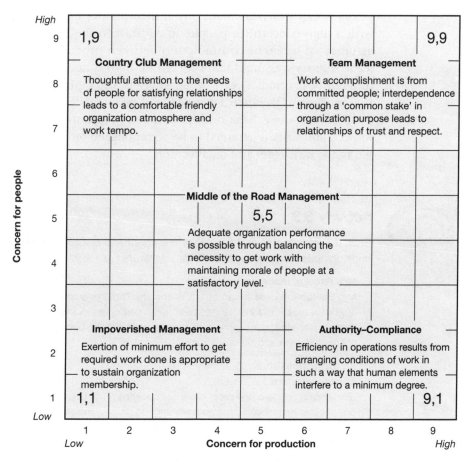

Figure 6.1 The Leadership Grid®

The 1,1 Impoverished Management or laissez-faire leadership style is characterized by minimum concern for both production and the needs of people. The 1,1 leader's desire is to remain as uninvolved as possible with other people, compatible with fulfilling the requirements of the job and sustaining organization membership. Conflict is deliberately avoided by remaining neutral on most contentious issues.

The 5,5 Middle of the Road leadership style is concerned with moderate rather than high performance. This results from a desire to balance the contradiction between production and people's needs through compromising in the face of conflict. It includes a willingness to yield on some points in order to gain on others. This is a team-oriented style, but because negativity is not tolerated complacency can set in and the team can lose sight of reality.

The 9,9 style of Team Management incorporates high concern for production with a high concern for people. In contrast to the 5,5 leadership style, which assumes an inherent contradiction between production and people, the 9,9 leadership style assumes that concern for both is necessary and that they do not inherently contradict each other. There is an emphasis on working as a team that recognizes the interdependence of people with each other, together with the task to be done. Relationships between people are based on mutual trust and respect, and work is assumed to be accomplished only if employees are committed to the task, team and organization.

Activity 6.3

Read the following extract from an article about Mrs Isabella Beeton, famous for her book on household management that was written in 1859.

Mrs Beeton: management guru

Mrs Beeton's approach can be summarized in three principles, which would certainly appear in most modern management texts: setting an example and giving clear guidance to staff; controlling the finances; applying the benefits of order and method in all management activities.

An example to staff
(In her own words.)
'Early rising is one of the most essential qualities … as it is not only the parent of health but of other innumerable advantages. Indeed when a mistress is an early riser, it is almost certain that her house will be orderly and well managed. On the contrary, if she remain in bed till a late hour, then the domestics, who … invariably partake somewhat of their mistress's character, will surely become sluggards.'

'Good Temper should be cultivated. … Every head of a household should strive to be cheerful, and should never fail to show a deep interest in all that appertains to the well-being of those who claim the protection of her roof.'

'The Treatment of Servants is of the highest possible moment. … If they perceive that the mistress's conduct is regulated by high and correct principles, they will not fail to respect her. If, also, a benevolent desire is shown to promote their comfort, at the same time that a steady performance of their duty is enacted, then their respect will not be unmingled with affection, and they will be still more solicitous to continue to deserve her favour.'

Source: Wensley, R. (1996), 'Mrs Beeton: management guru', *Financial Times,* 26 April, p. 15.

The article continues to quote from Mrs Beeton's book on the need to keep 'a housekeeping account-book … punctually and precisely'. On the issue of order and method she says: 'Cleanliness, punctuality, order and method are essentials in the character of a good housekeeper.'

Can you place Mrs Beeton on the Leadership Grid® of Blake and McCanse? Support your positioning.

The Leadership Grid® assumes that there is one best style of leadership, that of the 9,9 'Team Management' style – regardless of the situation.

The Leadership Grid® is a simplified way of categorizing different aspects of leadership behaviour. There are, however, other categories of leadership behaviour that overlap with these, but which are more detailed in their descriptions; for instance, the 'powers of the person' discussed in an article by Useem (1996) who says that these kinds of behaviours transcend those of particular value to particular situations. These are as follows:

- challenging the process
- searching for opportunities
- experimenting
- inspiring a shared vision
- envisioning a future
- enlisting others
- enabling others to act
- strengthening others
- fostering collaboration
- modelling the way
- setting an example
- celebrating accomplishments
- recognizing contributions.

In addition to these Useem, drawing on a study of 48 firms among the Fortune 500 largest US manufacturers, gives the following behaviours as characterizing the most successful chief executive officers:

- being visionary;
- showing strong confidence in self and others;
- communicating high-performance expectations and standards;
- personally exemplifying the firm's vision, values and standards;
- demonstrating personal sacrifice, determination, persistence and courage.

These five characteristics are not dissimilar to the type of leadership Robbins and Coulter (2005, pp. 433–6) refer to as 'charismatic-visionary' leadership. This focuses on the personality of the leader and the influence he/she has to get others to behave in certain ways. They suggest that this form of leadership offers clear and compelling imagery that taps into people's emotions and inspires enthusiasm to pursue the organization's goals. Charismatic-visionary leaders exhibit the following:

- the ability to explain the vision to others;
- the ability to express the vision, not just verbally, but through behaviour that reinforces the vision;
- the ability to extend or apply the vision to different leadership contexts.

This is yet another study which implies that there are certain desirable leadership qualities whatever the situation. What is important about these last two lists, however, is that these are behaviours which can be likened to those actions said to be characteristic of *transformational* leadership as compared to the less visionary styles of leadership associated with *transactional* leadership (see Illustration 6.4) and, therefore, more likely to be effective in times of change.

Illustration 6.4 compares and contrasts transactional and transformational leadership. The essential differences have been neatly summarized by Tichy and Ulrich (1984, p. 60) as follows:

> Where transactional managers make only minor adjustments in the organization's mission, structure, and human resource management, transformational leaders not only make major changes in these three areas but they also evoke fundamental changes in the basic political and cultural systems of the organization. The revamping of the political and cultural systems is what most distinguishes the transformational leader from the transactional one.

According to Bass (1990), transactional leaders are those who initiate structure and are considerate to employees – they might, therefore, be considered to be 9,9 leaders. However, transformational leadership goes beyond this, as confirmed by Robbins (2005, p. 367) who says: 'Transformational leadership is built *on top of* transactional leadership – it produces levels of subordinate effort and performance that go beyond what would occur with a transactional approach alone.' The relationship between transformational leadership and team and organizational performance is discussed by Tichy and Ulrich (1984) through reference to some well-known leaders of US corporations, the conclusion being that transformational leaders are those most likely to 'revitalize organizations ... transform the organizations and head them down new tracks' (p. 60). Robbins (2005) quotes evi-

---

Illustration 6.4

Transactional and transformational leaders

Transactional leader
- *Contingent reward*: contracts exchange of rewards for effort, promises rewards for good performance, recognizes accomplishments.
- *Management by exception (active)*: watches and searches for deviations from rules and standards, takes corrective action.
- *Management by exception (passive)*: intervenes only if standards are not met.
- *Laissez-faire*: abdicates responsibilities, avoids making decisions.

Transformational leader
- *Charisma*: provides vision and sense of mission, instils pride, gains respect and trust.
- *Inspiration*: communicates high expectations, uses symbols to focus efforts, expresses important purposes in simple ways.
- *Intellectual stimulation*: promotes intelligence, rationality and careful problem solving.
- *Individualized consideration*: gives personal attention, treats each employee individually, coaches, advises.

Source: Bass, B. M. (1990), 'From transactional to transformational leadership: learning to share the vision', *Organizational Dynamics*, Winter, p. 22.

dence from studies with US, Canadian and German military officers as well as managers at Federal Express to support the superiority of transformational leadership over transactional leadership in terms of being correlated with lower turnover rates, higher productivity and higher employee satisfaction.

What is more, the effect of transformational leadership on subordinates is confirmed in Behling and McFillen's (1996) model of charismatic/transformational leadership where the leader's behaviour is said to give rise to inspiration, awe and empowerment in the followers, resulting in exceptionally high effort, exceptionally high commitment and willingness to take risks. Figure 6.2 is a model of transformational leadership that includes not only the leader's characteristics, attitudes and behaviour but also the reactions of those who are led.

It would appear that transformational leadership behaviours add to the two dimensions of leadership identified in both the Ohio State and Michigan University studies. This view is supported by the results of work by researchers in Finland and Sweden (Ekvall and Arvonen, 1991; Lindell and Rosenqvist, 1992a, 1992b), which shows early evidence of a third dimension related to development-oriented leader behaviour – in other words, behaviour related specifically to leadership in an organizational change context. What is not clear is whether transformational leadership is the most recent leadership behaviour to be recommended whatever the circumstances or whether it is simply an additional leadership behaviour to be used in situations of radical change. Tichy and Ulrich

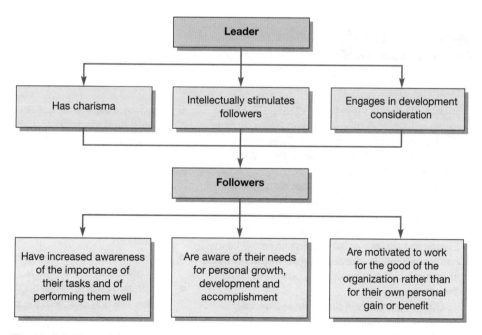

Figure 6.2 Transformational leadership

Source: Adapted from Bass, B.M. (1990) by J George and G Jones – *Understanding and Managing Organizational Behaviour*, 4th edn, p. 394.

(1984) and Bass (1990) seem to argue that transformational leadership is the best way to lead whatever the circumstances. Indeed, Bass (1990, p. 20) goes so far as to say that transactional leadership is, in many instances, 'a prescription for mediocrity', arguing that only transformational leadership can make a difference in an organization's performance at all levels. By contrast, Ekvall and Arvonen and Lindell and Rosenqvist seem to suggest that behaviours approaching transformational leadership may be most appropriate in conditions of change.

Activity 6.4

Read the account in Illustration 6.5 of the leadership profile of the head of Ryanair.

Assess Micheal O'Leary's leadership style in terms of the discussion above on transactional and transformational leadership and the model of transformational leadership in Figure 6.2.

In the context of the account in Illustration 6.5, compare your own or someone else's experiences of travelling with Ryanair to what you might expect from Mike O'Leary's attitude to his business.

In the context of the discussions so far on the 'one best way' to lead, research reports in the press on the experiences of Ryanair's employees.

Illustration 6.5

Leadership profile

Micheal O'Leary is the most successful CEO in the airline industry in Europe (*Observer*, 2002a, b, c). In 2004 his estimated net worth was £224 million, making him the 19th richest man in the United Kingdom (*Sunday Times*, 2004).

As CEO of Ryanair, O'Leary has employed a business model that was based on Southwest Airlines (a low-cost US airline company). He felt that he should be able to copy the model to use in Europe and achieve equal success. In fact O'Leary has pushed the boundaries of what seemed possible in cutting costs and maintaining profitability within the company.

O'Leary's strategy is simple, based on the Southwest business model, he says, 'Our strategy is like Wal-Mart: we pile it high and sell it cheap' (*Business Week*, 2004). That means using small

airports, where planes can get back in the air in just 20 minutes. Free meals? Forget about it: even a bottle of water sets customers back €3. Under the leadership of Micheal O'Leary, cost cutting has become the prime objective:

- Online bookings – Ryanair secures 97 per cent of their bookings online, eliminating travel agents and others who might otherwise gain commission.
- One-class travel – all passengers fly the same class offered by the company.
- Ticketless boarding – Ryainair does not issue tickets. The only cost is to the customer when they print their own ticket from the Internet.
- Unallocated seats – first come first served only, which speeds up the boarding process.

- Flying to secondary airports – this lowers operating expenses when Ryanair flies to cheaper, quieter locations, where airport taxes are lower and landing fees usually reduced.
- Point-to-point flying – one-way tickets are booked, therefore the company takes no responsibility for flight connections
- In-house marketing – by eliminating advertising agencies, the strategy is to spend as little as possible on marketing and benefit as much as possible from free publicity (good or bad).
- No refund policy – unless the flight has been cancelled before the date of travel, there is no circumstance where you would expect a refund.
- Corporate partnerships – Ryanair has negotiated various corporate partnerships including car hire, hotel bookings, insurance, loans and credit cards to name a few, which enables these companies to advertise on the Ryanair website.
- Additional charges – for changing a booking, overweight luggage, in-flight service.

From this overview of the company practice, the developments in the Ryanair strategy led by O'Leary are clear. He has no problem with attacking competitor companies through the use of the media; there is no union recognition within the company, therefore staff relations have been strained to say the least at times.

His leadership trademarks are varied, clearly he portrays for the media a brash, controversial, larger than life character. He rushes around in a rugby shirt and a pair of jeans as he has disregarded the old O'Leary look of a formal accountant. He is passionate about his role and rarely apologetic for his behaviour and decisions – a no-nonsense manager.

Several prominent people have made comments on his leadership:

'He is almost certainly one of the most successful leaders in the industry, with a unique business model, discipline and an extraordinary level of confidence'
(Sir Micheal Bishop, Chairman, BMI British Midland, cited *Observer*, 2002b)

'He is deified within the organization. He is a genius. Every meeting is like a business master class.'
(Business Associate, cited *Observer*, 2002b).

'He would sell his granny to make a bob. He has a massive ego. People have a sneaking regard for his success, but he has no morals whatsoever. Staff don't like him, but he has made a fortune for shareholders.'
(Retired airport source, cited *Observer*, 2002c)

It is fair to say that no one – not shareholders, customers, staff or competitors really knew what no-frills meant until O'Leary's approach to leadership came along. The strategy is being the lowest-cost airline in Europe. O'Leary has confidence that the cost is what will get customers coming back, not the quality of service they receive once they use the service.

The leadership issues, which vary, are important to assess. If you read the articles that have been written online (www.ryan-be-fair.org) penny pinching seems to be even worse for the employees. Their mobile phone chargers have been banned from the workplace recently to save money, staff are apparently paying for their own training, they pay for their own uniforms and are not paid any sick leave when on probationary period for the company.

Micheal O'Leary may have to reassess his strategy in the future if his money-saving plans go too far ... while the profits are high, he is deemed to be a success!

Source: www.ryanair.com; *Observer* (2002a, b, and c); Cohn (2005); *Sunday Times* (2004).

Micheal O'Leary (see Illustration 6.5) appears to have a well-defined leadership style. A question remains as to whether one particular way of leading can be appropriate regardless of the stage of development of an organization, the environment in which it exists or the people who work in it; or whether different leadership styles and behaviours are required according to the different situations prevailing as organizations' environments change, along with associated changes in strategy and functioning. Before moving into a discussion of this, it is useful to consider the degree to which leadership should be concentrated in the individual leader, as trait and behaviour theories suggest, or whether a more team-based and distributive form of leadership is possible and even desirable.

Team and distributed leadership

In recent years the focus on teamwork in organizations has become increasingly important. Reich's (1991) warning against the idea of the leader as hero has already been mentioned, with Landrum, Howell and Paris (2000) arguing for a team approach to designing and implementing change. Robbins and Coulter (2005, p. 435) echo this view in their suggestion that one of the cutting-edge approaches to leadership is team leadership. They maintain that the attributes of leaders discussed in much of the literature need to be adapted when managing in a team setting. For instance: 'they (leaders) have to learn skills such as having the patience to share information, being able to trust others and to give up authority, and understanding when to intervene.' These authors propose four key areas that distinguish team leadership from the leader as an individual:

1 the ability to act as a liaison with people and departments external to the team;
2 the ability to act as troubleshooters to try and resolve issues/problems at team level;
3 the ability to resolve conflicts at team level;
4 the ability to act as coach, thus ensuring that all team members develop to their full potential.

These abilities go some way to meeting some of what Kotter (1996, p. 172) says twenty-first-century organizations need compared to twentieth-century ones – that is:

- fewer bureaucratic structures with fewer rules and employees;
- fewer hierarchical levels;
- management training and support systems for many people, not just for senior people;
- a culture that is externally oriented, empowering, quick to make decisions, open and candid, more risk tolerant.

Having said this, the move from operating bureaucratically to a team-based structure is not straightforward as Illustration 6.6 shows.

Discussions of what teamworking means emphasize concepts such as interacting or coordinating (Baker and Salas, 1997, p. 332), shared leadership roles, individual and mutual accountability, collective work products and decisions by consensus (Katzenbach and Smith, 1993, p. 113). Much of this reflects the discussion in the previous section on democratic or participative leadership. However, these models of leadership continue to focus on the leader as an

Illustration 6.6

From bureaucracy to teamwork

By means of a questionnaire survey of a sample of 346 employees of a large public sector social services-type organization, McHugh and Bennett (1999) examined the feasibility of carrying out a large-scale transformational change in its structure, from one that was based on strict bureaucratic principles to one which favoured self-managed teamworking. The proposed change was in response to government initiatives to make such organizations more market-oriented, responsive to clients, flexible in the way staff worked and generally to act more like a commercial company. They questioned the staff on: the degree to which they interacted with others in their day-to-day job; whether they considered themselves as working in teams; and what they thought was meant by teamworking. Having established that most (96 per cent) respondents could define teamworking (albeit using what might be a standard textbook definition); that the majority (89 per cent) indicated their job required them to work as part of a team; but that only 66 per cent preferred to work together with others (31 per cent preferring to work independently), they examined a range of attitudes towards teamworking in the light of management's known views that this was the way forward.

The results showed a sizeable percentage (between 35 and 42 per cent) believing that management within the organization did not understand the meaning of teamwork and that managers would find it difficult to give up their control, in order to encourage workforce democracy and empower others to make decisions. In spite of this, a large majority thought that the organization should move towards teamworking, but only, it seemed, because top management had decreed it, even though the infrastructure required to make it work had not been given sufficient attention.

From the research, a number of factors emerged that would either facilitate or impede teamworking. Facilitating factors included: having managers and staff committed to communication; the freedom to make decisions; greater staff enthusiasm; training people to help them understand the concept of teamworking; and having team rewards. Impeding factors included: low staff motivation; lack of management and staff commitment; a reward system that supports competition rather than cooperation; no management and staff understanding of the concept; no acceptance of devolved responsibility; bureaucratic management styles; and adherence by management to the old ways of doing things.

What was evident was that a number of 'trip wires', as defined by Hackman (1994), existed within the organization that highlighted the strength of the impeding factors against the weakness of the facilitating factors in terms of the changes required for teamworking to become established as the preferred way of working.

The article goes on to elaborate on the trip wires.

Source: Based on McHugh, M. and Bennett, H. (1999), 'Introducing teamwork within a bureaucratic maze', *The Leadership and Organization Development Journal*, vol. 20, no. 2, pp. 81–93.

Activity 6.5

Based on your knowledge, through either working in or being a customer of, organizations in the public sector, list the trip wires you can see in changing such organizations to permit: 'enhanced delegation, empowerment of staff and, among those who occupy managerial roles, a commitment to the concept of team player as opposed to manager'.

Prepare a plan to help overcome the trip wires. In what order would you put each element of your plan? Make an estimate of the time required to implement each element of your plan.

individual. An alternative view is that of 'distributive' leadership. This is expressed by Yukl (2002, p. 432) as follows:

> An alternative perspective (to the heroic single leader), that is slowly gaining more adherents, is to define leadership as a shared purpose of enhancing the individual and collective capacity of people to accomplish their work effectively. ... Instead of a heroic leader who can perform all essential leadership functions, the functions are distributed among different members of the team or organization.

Yukl's definition is intended to apply to organizations in general. It is interesting, though, to compare this to one that, although formulated to apply specifically to school leadership, is also applicable to most small and medium sized enterprises.

> This (distributive leadership) sees leadership as a function which is widely dispersed through the organization rather than as a responsibility vested in an individual, and succeeds in creating a more collegial perception of the organization than more charismatic leadership models typically do. It assumes that there is an underlying values consensus that enables staff to work harmoniously towards shared purposes and to agree on the bases by which the effectiveness of the organization can be judged.
>
> (Anderson, L., Bennett, N., Carwright, M., Newton, W., Preedy, M. and Wise, C., 2003, p. 21).

Both these definitions draw attention to leadership being much more than the formal property of particular individuals and allow the distinction between formal and informal leadership to be made. According to Anderson *et al.* (p. 29) this places 'leadership in the context of participative, shared decision making, which stimulates and leads to more effective organizational change'.

According to Storey (2004, p. 253) benefits of distributed leadership to senior management and others are:

- avoiding the overloading of senior staff;
- offering growth and development opportunities for multiple individuals;
- allowing for decision taking and execution by individuals and groups with the most appropriate capabilities;
- carrying motivational potential and building commitment to the whole enterprise.

She goes on to say: 'Another argument is that, as the environment becomes more complex, uncertain and subject to rapid change, so must organizations adapt. This is usually inferred as requiring leaders at every level, and most notably perhaps in "customer-facing" roles where responsiveness is at a premium.'

All this can be referred to, in the opinion of Bottery (2004, p. 20), as 'exciting stuff' with the appeal and attraction of distributed leadership appearing self-evident. Nevertheless, as the account in Illustration 6.6 and Bottery's further discussion indicates, a number of caveats must be made. First, visions of distributed leadership must take account of the asymmetry of power, particularly the accumulation of resources power attaching to some formal positions. Senior managers and others might not wish to share the status and symbols that attach to their positions. However egalitarian an organization is, power and influence in decision taking are hardly ever shared equally. Second, not everyone will subscribe to the idea of being a leader, even if this is an informal one. As Storey (2004, p. 254) says: 'some organizational members may in reality be rather attached to the relative comfort and lack of exposure that may derive from operating under the dominant leader mode'. Third, is distributive leadership concerned only with matters internal to an organization or is it something that extends beyond? How will customers, shareholders, external policy makers react to dealing with what might appear to be 'weak' senior managers and multiple points of decision making?

These concerns are not intended to deny the real possibilities that even partial moves to a distributed form of leadership could bring. This should be kept in mind as the discussion in the next section moves to considering whether and how approaches to leadership can be tailored to the specific organizational circumstances prevailing at any one time.

Contingency approaches to leadership

From the discussion so far, it is clear that trait and simple behavioural theories of leadership have some support. However, as Figure 6.3 shows, there are many things that can influence organizational outcomes in addition to those associated with a leader's qualities and behaviour.

Figure 6.3 Situational influences on leadership effectiveness

Therefore, in contrast to theories of leadership which argue for a universal view of what traits and/or behaviours leaders should have, other theories maintain that a leader's behaviour should be contingent upon the organizational situation prevailing.

Behaviour along a continuum

One of the best-known theories of leadership, which takes into account situational factors, is that of Tannenbaum and Schmidt (1973), which arranges leadership behaviour along a continuum not dissimilar to the 'directive' and 'participative' leadership styles that contribute to the dimensions of the Ohio State and Michigan studies discussed previously.

At the 'boss-centred leadership' extreme, which assumes a high level of leader power, leaders *tell* subordinates what to do. At the other, 'subordinate-centred leadership' extreme, leaders and subordinates *jointly* make decisions. Moving along the continuum between these two positions, from the area of greatest freedom for leaders to the area of greatest freedom for subordinates, the leadership style becomes increasingly less authoritative and more participative. To this extent, the styles of leadership suggested are little different from those identified by the Ohio State and Michigan University studies, except in the degree of independence of the dimensions. What is different from the 'one best way' theories is that Tannenbaum and Schmidt do not support one preferred leadership style. On the contrary, they suggest that a leader should move along the continuum, selecting the style that is most appropriate to the situation prevailing, for which they use a threefold categorization according to the 'forces' that they say should determine the style of leadership to use. These three forces are in the manager, in the subordinate and in the situation.

- *Forces in the manager.* Each manager will have his or her own combination of personality characteristics, skills and knowledge, values and attitudes that predisposes the adoption of one particular style of leadership or another.
- *Forces in the subordinate.* Subordinates vary in their characteristics such as the degree of support needed, experience in and knowledge of the work, commitment to organizational goals, expectations as to how leaders will behave, previous experience of different leadership styles. As Smith (1991, p. 212) says: 'Inexperienced, immature and uncommitted subordinates may force even the most participative manager to adopt an autocratic, telling, style.'
- *Forces in the situation.* These divide into two categories: first, the nature of the task or problem itself and, second, the general context in which the leadership activity takes place. This can include the time available to make a decision, the organizational culture and power balances between the different participants in the situation and general opportunities and constraints arising from organizational structures and processes as well as environmental and societal influences. A simple example is that should a fire break out (a well-defined problem with an objective criterion of success), an appropriate leadership style would *not* be to call a meeting to discuss what should be

done. A more relevant example is the case of new government regulations that must be adhered to and over which there is little opportunity for flexibility in implementation. In some cases changes in the organizational environment are so sudden and severe that a more authoritative leadership style is the only one relevant to the situation. In other cases, the prevailing organizational structure and culture may force a more participative style of leadership. Illustration 6.7 is an example of the application of these concepts to leadership in a situation facing the Beautiful Buildings Company in one of its ventures to build luxury apartments in Japan.

Illustration 6.7

Little room to manoeuvre

Jayne was pleased that she had been put in charge of BB Company's latest building venture, the second of its kind in Japan. She had limited experience of working in this country but had spent some time talking to staff working on the other Japanese site about how to approach the management of those employed on the building works. She knew, therefore, that there were a number of factors she would need to take into account when deciding on her own leadership approach.

The diagram illustrates the situation Jayne faced.

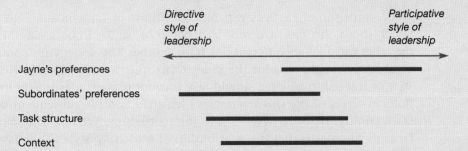

The length of rules on the diagram indicate the degrees of freedom available to Jayne in the situation facing her. The line indicating her own leadership style shows her preferences were for a more consultative/participative style that she had been accustomed to using with staff in Britain. However, most of the Japanese employees were accustomed to a more formal management–subordinate relationship and were likely to work in this type of relationship, given the fact that Jayne was a woman. The task of building the apartments was complex but, in many ways, defined. Much of what was required had been worked out beforehand. However, as with all building works, unknown factors such as the weather and possible unexpected problems with the ground, let alone any industrial relations problems that could arise, contributed to there being certain unstructured elements to the situation. If any two of these factors combined, some extensive negotiations might need to be held between management and workers or their representatives. The BB Company prided itself on its care for its workers, so the organizational context was one that veered more towards a human relations type of approach than an authoritarian one. Even so, profit was profit and the industry was a very competitive one. The organization did not want anything to go wrong.

What the diagram shows is that Jayne has not much room for manoeuvre in deciding what approach to take as a leader in this situation. The overlap between all the forces is not large. If she cannot influence any of the factors associated with the subordinates, the task and the context, she must make sure to adopt a leadership style that tends towards the directive end of her preferences.

Fiedler's contingency model of leadership

The task-oriented/people-oriented continuum of leadership styles is also the centrepiece of Fiedler's (1967) contingency theory of leadership. In this case, however, the three situational variables said to determine the style of leadership to be adopted are:

- *Leader–member relations:* the extent to which a leader has the support of her or his group members. To determine this, questions might be asked about the willingness of group members to do what the leader tells them, the degree of trust existing between the leader and the followers and the extent to which followers will support the leader's decisions.
- *Task structure:* the extent to which the task or purpose of a group is well defined and the outcomes can be seen clearly to be a success or failure. To determine this, questions about the measurability of the outcomes might be asked. In other words, is it possible to judge 'success' objectively or might there be different views on how the outcomes should be assessed?
- *Position power:* the amount of power (particularly reward power) the leader can use to accomplish his or her, and the group's, purposes. The issue here is whether leaders have the support of higher management for the way they deal with subordinates.

A comparison of Fiedler's variables with those of Tannenbaum and Schmidt (1973) shows the 'task structure' variable to be similar in both cases. However, the other variables are different one from another. The underlying 'contingency' argument, though, remains the same. Consequently, according to Fiedler, the style of leadership adopted should take account of particular situational conditions in terms of the three variables identified and the subsequent degree of favourability, or otherwise, of the total situation. What is different about Fiedler's findings is that the relationship of leadership style to the favourableness/unfavourableness of the situation is a curvilinear one. In other words, when the situation is very favourable or very unfavourable, the most effective leadership style is said to be a task-oriented, more directive one, rather than a person-oriented one.

When the situation is of moderate favourability to the leader, the style recommended is a person-oriented one. Table 6.1 illustrates this in a simplified form. Of course, in reality, the relationship is not as simple as this. However, the argument that a more consultative and participative style is necessary in situations of confusion and maybe suspicion seems logical. When the situation is very favourable to the leader, he or she can probably take a more directive style, given the trust and support to be expected from group members. In very unfavourable situations the leader must emphasize the need for task accomplishment in order to push the group towards its goals. This requirement, in turn, dictates a more directive, task-oriented approach.

Implicit in Fiedler's contingency theory is that leaders can adapt their leadership styles to the prevailing situation. However, Fiedler believes this to be

Table 6.1 Fiedler's contingency theory of leadership

	Leader–member relationships	Task structure	Position power	Leadership style
1	Good	Structured	High	Task-oriented
2	Good	Structured	Low	style recommended
3	Good	Unstructured	High	
4	Good	Unstructured	Low	Person-oriented
5	Poor	Structured	High	style recommended
6	Poor	Structured	Low	
7	Poor	Unstructured	High	Task-oriented
8	Poor	Unstructured	High	style recommended

difficult and, therefore, suggests either that leaders should be chosen so that their management style fits the situation or that elements of the situation need to be modified. However, neither strategy seems easy, thus confirming the existence of certain difficulties in 'matching' leaders and leadership situations.

Hersey and Blanchard's situational theory

Another difficulty with contingency theories is the question of how much importance should be attached to each contingency factor. Clearly the task and the amount of power held by the leader are important, but it seems logical that the characteristics and expectations of group members or subordinates are more important in deciding what style of leadership to adopt – after all, it is these people who must carry out the task.

This would appear to be the case with Hersey and Blanchard's (1993) situational leadership theory, which puts greatest stress on one major situational factor – the readiness of what they term the leader's 'followers'. According to this theory, a leader's behaviour should depend on the readiness of followers to accept responsibility and to be willing to make their own decisions. As with the other theories already discussed, the leadership behaviour is defined by Hersey and Blanchard in terms similar to those used for the initiating structure and consideration behaviours identified by the Ohio State researchers. The theory agrees with these researchers that these two behaviours are independent of one another. Therefore a leader could be low on both task and relationship behaviour, high on both or high on one and low on another. As a result any leader's behaviour may fall into one of four quadrants – which go from 'telling' through 'selling' and 'participating' to 'delegating'. The readiness of followers also falls into four categories, each of which, in an ideal world, should trigger one of the four types of leadership behaviour. Gordon (1999, pp. 234–6) refers to this theory as a 'life-cycle' model of leadership, presumably because the followers move from being both unable and unwilling (or too insecure) to take on responsibility for their own actions, to being either unable but willing (or confident) or willing but unable, to the highest state of readiness where they are both able and willing to take responsibility for decisions and actions.

Figure 6.4 shows how a leader's behaviour should change according to the quadrant into which the followers' readiness falls. An examination of Figure 6.4 shows the similarity of the four quadrants to the four corners of Blake and McCanse's (1991) Leadership Grid®. This is not surprising given the two leader-

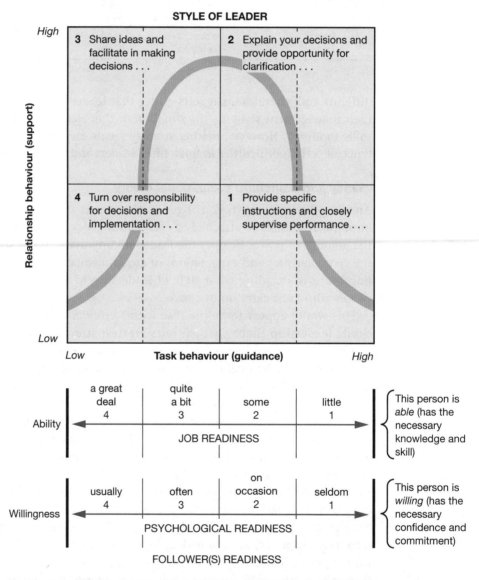

Figure 6.4 Hersey and Blanchard's theory of situational leadership

Source: Hersey, P. and Blanchard, K. H. (1993), *Management of Organizational Behavior: Utilizing Human Resources*, 6th edn (Englewood Cliffs, NJ, Prentice Hall, p. 197).

ship styles and the combinations available. However, while Blake and McCanse argue for a 'one best way' of leader (the 9,9 way) for all occasions, Hersey and Blanchard argue that a leader's style should be contingent upon the characteristics and attitudes of those who are led. In contrast to, for instance, Fiedler's views, both theories assume a leader's style is flexible enough to change according to the prevailing situation and, in Hersey and Blanchard's case, that it can presumably change in the presence of different groups and as the followers 'mature' through the cycle referred to by Gordon (1999). Illustration 6.8 is an account of the leadership situation at the World Bank just after James Wolfensohn joined it. At the time of writing, he has just completed his time there, so the account was written some time ago. However, it is a very good example of how forces in the leader, the subordinates and the situation could be said to influence the leadership style to be adopted.

Activity 6.6

Using any of the theories already discussed, carry out an analysis of the situation facing James Wolfensohn in his role at the World Bank.

If you were James Wolfensohn, what leadership style would you adopt to help gain the objectives he mentions? Justify your views.

Illustration 6.8

World Bank chief's cry from the heart

Michael Holman and Patti Waldmeir on Wolfensohn's passionate appeal to senior management

Seldom if ever can a World Bank president have made a speech as impassioned and as critical as the one Mr James Wolfensohn made to senior management at a meeting in Washington on 12 March.

It was a cry from the heart of a man who seeks to inspire as much as to lead, but who has seen that inspiration blocked by cynicism and distrust. For 90 minutes before 300 senior colleagues, Mr Wolfensohn fought that cynicism with the rhetorical weapons he uses so well: frankness, sincerity, passion and hyperbole.

He concluded on a high note, adopting the tone of enthusiasm he hopes will infect the work of his subordinates around the world: 'I am ... talking about a new atmosphere of change and a new atmosphere of hope and a new dream ... where we

can say we are affecting the lives of people in the world (more) positively than anyone else, and we are doing it brilliantly.'

He spoke of a 'humanized' Bank, of a future when 'we can say that we care, that we can cry about poverty, that we can laugh when people have a good time, that we can embrace our clients, that we can feel part of them, where we can tell our kids we made a difference'. He had even invited two of his own children to earlier inspirational sessions, 'because I want them to be proud of me, I want them to think that what I am doing is different'.

But these comments came at the end of an extraordinarily critical session in which the new Bank chief, reviewing progress after nine months as head, alternately cajoled, chastized, implored and berated

Illustration 6.8 *continued*

his listeners. Participants say the atmosphere was by turns subdued, and electric.

The issues were wide-ranging. But again and again, Mr Wolfensohn hammered home one central message with a vivid metaphor: there was a 'glass wall' which was standing in the way of his efforts to ensure that the Bank was more efficient as a development agency.

The Bank chief's frustration was palpable: he has staked his reputation on revolutionizing the internal culture of the organization, as an essential prerequisite to improving the Bank's ability to deliver development worldwide.

Among other things, Mr Wolfensohn wants success in the Bank to be judged by the performance of projects rather than the number of loans approved.

At times, his tone bordered on despair: 'I don't know what else we can do, in terms of standard or even non-standard approaches, to try to bring change in the institution. I just don't know what else to do.

'How can we get a new basis for working inside the bank? How can we change the atmosphere? How can we move from cynicism, distrust and distance, to risk-taking and involvement? ... [T]here is so much baggage. There is a need, somehow, to break through this glass wall, this unseen glass wall, to get enthusiasm, change and commitment,' he said.

'I cannot have a situation where we as a group don't have that sense of excitement, commitment, and trust. I don't expect it overnight, but I have to tell you we have got to change this, and I don't know how to do it. I just don't know how to do it.'

Bank insiders say his comments were partly designed to shock his audience – the managers whose past performance has inspired widespread distrust among the staff. They say Mr Wolfensohn does not believe his experiment in more effective management is in peril.

But the evidence from internal Bank studies of personnel, cited by him in the meeting, is grim. Results of Bank 'focus' (study) groups 'undeniably show that there is a lack of trust in management, a huge sense of cynicism and there is some distance which I cannot get my hands on between expressed desire to move forward for change, and commitment in the organization ... there is a palpable reservation in the air.'

The distrust is hampering efforts to restructure the organization. Mr Wolfensohn is keen to improve the Bank's relationships with its clients by creating posts for 'country managers' who would be the main point of contact for governments. These country managers would then draw on specialist skills within the Bank through an internal market.

Senior officials say that staff support the principle of this plan, but fear that it will be exploited by the chosen managers, who will exercise favouritism and patronage in the way they use resources elsewhere in the organization.

This sometimes operates among people of the same nationality and sometimes under 'fiefdoms' which have developed over time, officials say.

The studies show that 40 per cent of Bank employees do not trust management. Bank insiders believe this is partly the result of past personnel policies: 'When good people don't always get promoted and those promoted are not always good, then the management responsible for that does not engender trust,' said one participant in the meeting.

Such a personnel issue was high on the agenda at the meeting: senior staff were unhappy about alleged favouritism on the part of Mr Wolfensohn and his top aides in the choice of individuals for a new training initiative. But questioners soon moved on to other issues. One senior manager took the opportunity to complain: 'Up to now, I've had the impression that you thought you had all the answers, and that the message was "get on board, or get off the ship".'

Others spoke of a 'culture of approval, a culture where people don't express their opinions forthrightly' for fear of jeopardizing career prospects. For his part, Mr Wolfensohn said he was astonished at 'the lack of interpersonal generosity (and) the lack of a team, a sense of team'.

He appealed to his colleagues to do their own independent thinking about change: 'I do not have a monopoly on the ideas ... I am enfranchising every one of you ... to come up with some ideas of how we can bring about the change,' he said, adding, 'there is just something here which the surveys show, and which I can feel, which is inhibiting us ... and I just beg you to think about it.'

Source: Holman, M. and Waldmeir, P. (1996), *Financial Times*, 29 March, p. 4.

Path–goal theory of leadership

The assumption of a flexible style of leadership in Hersey and Blanchard's (1993) theory is also true of what has come to be called the 'path–goal' theory of leadership, which also argues that leadership style (directive, supportive, participative or achievement-oriented) is contingent upon various situational factors. Originally developed by House (1971), path–goal theory maintains that the leader should use the style of leadership that is most effective in influencing subordinates' perceptions of the goals they need to achieve and the way (or path) in which they should be achieved. The theory relates directly to expectancy theories of motivation in that a leader will be judged successful if she or he can help subordinates reach their goals. In other words effective leadership will help subordinates turn effort into appropriate and high-level performance.

Two dominant situational factors are relevant to this theory. These are, first, the characteristics of the team or group members, that is the subordinates; and, second, the nature of the task or job and the immediate context in which it takes place. The task of the leader is, therefore, to use a style that is congruent with the skills, motivation and expectations of subordinates and with the goals to be achieved, the design of the jobs and the resources and time available. Figure 6.5 is a generalized diagram of these factors that are presumed to intervene between the effort put into doing a job and the subsequent performance.

The subordinate characteristic of 'locus of control' in Figure 6.5 is of interest as it has not appeared in any of the other main leadership theories considered so far. In the same way as leaders may, characteristically, veer towards one style more than another, subordinates also have preferences for the way they are managed and this is influenced by their locus of control, that is, their beliefs

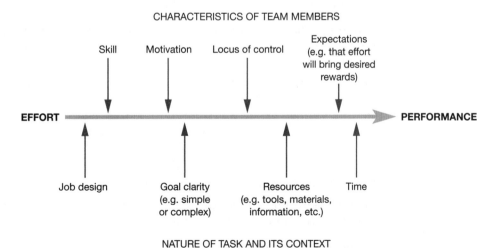

Figure 6.5 Factors intervening between effort and performance

about who controls their lives. Smith (1991, p. 220) describes the concept of locus of control as follows:

> The locus of control concerns a person's beliefs about who controls their life. People with an internal locus of control believe that they control their own lives. People with an external locus of control believe other people control their lives. According to path–goal theory of leadership non-directive styles of leadership should be used with 'internals' and a directive style should be used with externals. Internals like to be asked, externals like to be told.

Robbins (2005, p. 346) gives the following hypotheses connecting leadership style with path–goal theory situational factors:

> Directive leadership leads to greater satisfaction when tasks are ambiguous or stressful than when they are highly structured and well laid out.

> Supportive leadership results in high employee performance and satisfaction when subordinates are performing structured tasks.

> Directive leadership is likely to be perceived as redundant among subordinates with high perceived ability and with considerable experience.

> The more clear and bureaucratic the formal authority relationships, the more leaders should exhibit supportive behaviour and de-emphasize directive behaviour.

> Directive leadership will lead to higher employee satisfaction when there is substantive conflict within a work group.

> Subordinates with an internal locus of control (those who believe they control their own destiny) will be more satisfied with a participative style.

> Subordinates with an external locus of control will be more satisfied with a directive style.

> Achievement-oriented leadership will increase subordinates' expectations that effort will lead to high performance when tasks are ambiguously structured.

Robbins (2005) refers to the work of Keller (1989) and Woffard and Liska (1993) as examples of support for path–goal theory, saying (p. 325): 'The research evidence generally supports the logic underlying the path–goal theory. That is, employee performance and satisfaction are likely to be positively influenced when the leader compensates for things lacking in either the employee or the work setting.' While this is likely to be true, effective leaders are also those who can match their leadership approach to the strategic focus and values of the organization in which they operate.

Matching organizational models and leadership roles

The discussion thus far has identified a number of situational variables, which might be said to influence the style and behaviour of leaders:

- leaders' predispositions to one style rather than another;
- the strength of their power base to deliver rewards to their followers;

- the expectations and skills of the followers and their preparedness for different degrees of autonomy in their own actions;
- the nature of the task to be achieved;
- the many factors (e.g. organizational structure, culture, time and resources available) that make up the organizational context in which leadership operates.

With respect to the latter, it could be argued that an organization's strategic focus together with preferred forms of control will determine many of the other factors and, therefore, the particular leadership style adopted. Two different pieces of research pick up on these ideas to suggest links between different organizational models and different approaches to leadership.

The first of these is that of Quinn (1988), who proposes four organizational models distinguished on the basis of two bipolar dimensions (see Table 6.2). These are:

(a) the adaptability and flexibility of the way organizations operate as opposed to the desire for stability and control;

(b) whether organizations are outward looking (towards the environment and the competition) or internally focused towards the maintenance of systems and procedures.

Table 6.2 summarizes the different characteristics of the four organizational models that result from combining these four different organizational orientations. (Figure 6.6 shows these in diagrammatic form.) Quinn uses the terms 'the

Table 6.2 Summary of Quinn's four organizational models

Human relations model (adaptable and internally focused)	Open systems model (adaptable and externally focused)	Rational goal model (stable and externally focused)	Internal process model (stable and internally focused)
Towards: • Flexibility • Decentralization • Differentiation • Maintenance of the socio-technical system	Towards: • Flexibility • Decentralization • Differentiation • Expansion • Competitive position of overall system	Towards: • Centralization • Integration • Maximizing output • Competitive position of overall system	Towards: • Centralization • Integration • Consolidation • Continuity • Maintenance of socio-technical systems
Values: • Human resources • Training • Cohesion • Morale	Values: • Adaptability • Readiness • Growth/acquisition • External support	Values: • Productivity • Efficiency • Planning • Goal setting	Values: • Information • Management • Communication • Stability • Control
THE TEAM	THE ADHOCRACY	THE FIRM	THE HIERARCHY

Source: Based on Quinn, R. E. (1988), *Beyond Rational Management: Mastering the Paradoxes and Competing Demands of High Performance* (San Francisco, Jossey-Bass, p. 48).

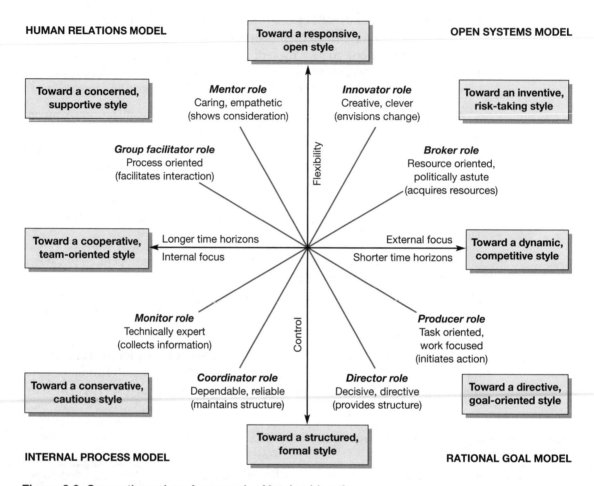

Figure 6.6 Competing values framework of leadership roles

Source: Quinn, R. E. (1988), *Beyond Rational Management: Mastering the Paradoxes and Competing Demands of High Performance* (San Francisco, Jossey-Bass, p. 86).

hierarchy', 'the firm', 'the adhocracy' and 'the team' as a shorthand way of describing the internal process, rational goal, open systems and human relations organizational models respectively.

What is interesting about the framework illustrated in Figure 6.6 is Quinn's linking of different dimensional positions with leadership style and the roles leaders should play. An examination of Figure 6.6 shows leadership styles positioned around the outer edge of the framework with the leadership roles inside them. From this it can be seen that different leadership styles and behaviour 'fit' different organizational models.

A second piece of research, by Farkas and Wetlaufer (1996), came to similar conclusions to Quinn about the dependence of leadership style and behaviour on the needs of the organization and the business situation at hand. On the basis of interviews with 160 chief executives around the world, these researchers found five distinctive approaches to leadership, each of which was associated with different emphases in terms of strategic planning, research and development (R&D), recruitment and selection practices, matters internal to the organization or matters external to it and with whom, and how, they spent their time. According to Farkas and Wetlaufer (p. 111) the leadership approach to be adopted depends on answering questions such as: 'Is the industry growing explosively or is it mature? How many competitors exist and how strong are they? Does technology matter and, if so, where is it going? What are the organization's capital and human assets? What constitutes sustainable competitive advantage and how close is the organization to achieving it?' To these questions one could also add: 'What kind of changes is the organization facing and what do these mean for the role of leadership?'

Leadership in times of change

The discussion so far suggests a number of conclusions, not all compatible, about leadership in times of organizational change. The first, which relates to the 'one best way' of leading, is that most of the characteristics presumed necessary for successful leadership by the trait theorists appear relevant to leaders of change. However, Kirkpatrick and Locke's (1991) identification of drive, leadership motivation, honesty and integrity, self-confidence, cognitive ability and knowledge of the business seem most relevant – along with the trait of general intelligence and the recognition that intuitive decision making is not out of place or 'second class' to other decision-making processes based on rationality and logic. The second is that, given these characteristics, there might be a particular type of leadership behaviour which is most appropriate to leading change. This is the development-oriented behaviour that the researchers Ekvall and Arvonen (1991) and Lindell and Rosenqvist (1992a, 1992b) claim to have found. The third is that transformational leadership seems almost tailor-made for leading change. For instance, in their book entitled *The Transformational Leader* Tichy and Devanna (1990) put forward a dramatic analogy of transformational leadership when they propose triggers for change emerging from what they call 'the prologue' of the new global playing field. Acts I (Recognizing the need for revitalization), II (Creating a new vision) and III (Institutionalizing change) all follow on from this prologue. The 'epilogue' of 'History repeating itself' serves to emphasize the continuous nature of change and, therefore, the necessity for continuous transformation of organizations and the people in organizations having the continuing need for transformational leadership.

If these conclusions are accepted, the search for leaders of change could stop here. However, as the contingency theories of leadership show, leadership style and behaviour can vary according to the different characteristics of different organizational situations. In addition to those described, these situations also include an organization's stage of development, the nature of the change process itself and the forces for or against any change, including individuals' and groups' resistance to change.

Leadership and the organizational life cycle

The stages through which an organization goes as it forms, develops and matures (and maybe disappears) were discussed in Chapter 2 with particular reference to the work of Greiner (1972). However Greiner, as well as identifying these phases in an organization's evolution, also sets out the different organizational practices required during each evolutionary phase. One of these practices is the style top management should adopt according to an organization's growth phase (see Table 6.3).

Table 6.3 Matching top management style to organizational growth phases

Organizational growth phases	Phase 1 Growth through CREATIVITY	Phase 2 Growth through DIRECTION	Phase 3 Growth through DELEGATION	Phase 4 Growth through COORDINATION	Phase 5 Growth through ELABORATION
Top management style	Individualistic and entrepreneurial	Directive	Delegative	Watchdog	Participative

Clarke (1994, p. 12) elaborated on the phases and styles propounded by Greiner to suggest the following management styles:

- *Phase 1*: individualistic, creative, entrepreneurial, ownership
- *Phase 2*: strong directive
- *Phase 3*: full delegation and autonomy
- *Phase 4*: watchdog
- *Phase 5*: team oriented, interpersonal skills at a premium, innovative, educational bias.

Greiner's suggestions are helpful in drawing attention to the need for change in the management style of top management and other organizational leaders as organizations evolve and mature. This need is supported by suggestions by Clarke and Pratt (1985) who identify four different styles of managerial leadership required at different stages in the life of an organization:

1 the *champion* to fight for and defend the new business;
2 the *tank commander* to take the business into its next stage of growth, someone to develop a robust team and direct the business into exploitable parts of the market;
3 the *housekeeper* to keep the business on an even keel as it enters the mature stage to provide efficiency as well as effectiveness;
4 the *lemon squeezer* to get the most out of the business as it is in danger of decline.

The idea that organizations at different stages of growth need different leadership approaches has also been taken up by Quinn (1988) whose work has already been discussed (see Table 6.2 and Figure 6.6). For instance, Quinn argues that an organization will start its life cycle positioned predominantly in the open systems (the 'adhocracy') quadrant of the framework (see Figure 6.6). As it grows and develops, it will include the elements of the human relations model (the 'team') and a focus on productivity and accomplishment from the rational goal model (the 'firm'). As it reaches the stage of formalization, it will become less oriented to the open systems and human relations models and will take on more of the characteristics of the internal process model (the 'hierarchy'). Finally, in its elaboration of structure stage, it will use elements of all the organizational models, but will refocus, in particular, back to the open systems model. The implications of this life cycle for any organization's management and its leadership approach are shown in Table 6.3. This implies that an inventive risk-taking style – typified by innovative, broker-type behaviour – is most appropriate in the early stages of an organization's development. As the organization develops towards an established collectivity, this should be tempered with a style more supportive of employees and more group-oriented – in other words leaders should behave as mentors and group facilitators. As growth and development continue and the organization enters a more formalized stage, a more conservative, cautious style is suggested and so the roles of monitor and coordinator become most important. Finally, in an organization's most elaborated stage, leadership styles are required that are flexible enough to change orientation according to the complex, changing situations within the organization itself, but with an emphasis on resource acquisition and innovation in anticipation of further change.

Activity 6.7

Compare and contrast the leadership styles and behaviours described by Greiner, Clarke and Quinn in terms of their relationship to, and usefulness for, managerial leadership during the different phases or stages of an organization's development.

How do these leadership styles and behaviours accord with your own experience of effective and ineffective leadership at different organizational growth stages?

The results of completing Activity 6.7 may reveal some differences in the three classifications of leadership styles and behaviours surveyed. However, an issue which arises from all three descriptions is that of whether the same leaders can take the organization through all these phases. Theories such as those of Hersey and Blanchard (1993) and path–goal theory (House, 1971) would say 'yes'. However, Fiedler (1967), in his exposition of a contingency theory of leadership, would advise caution in this respect. This is also the view of Clarke and Pratt (1985) and is further supported by evidence that, because different people have different thinking styles (Kirton, 1976) and preferred behavioural roles

(Belbin, 1993), they will have different preferences for the way they interpret and cope with change. Care should be taken, therefore, not to assume that the same leader can be 'all things to all situations'. In addition, it may be that one style of leadership may be appropriate to a particular type of change while another may be appropriate to a different type of change.

Leadership and the nature of change

In Chapter 2 a range of different ways of defining change were reviewed. Table 6.4 is a reproduction of Table 2.2 in Chapter 2 that shows how different typologies of change might relate one to another and to the environmental conditions giving rise to them.

Table 6.4 Environmental conditions and types of change

Environmental forces for change			Types of change				
Ansoff and McDonnell (1990)	Strebel (1996a)	Stacey (1996)	Tushman et al. (1988)	Dunphy and Stace (1993)	Balogun and Hope Hailey (2004)	Grundy (1993)	Stacey (1996)
Predictable	Weak	Close to certainty	Converging (fine-tuning)	Fine-tuning	Adaptation	Smooth incremental	Closed
Forecastable by extrapolation	Moderate	Close to certainty	Converging (incremental)	Incremental adjustment	Evolution		Contained
Predictable threats and opportunities				Modular transformation	Reconstruction	Bumpy incremental	
Partially predictable opportunities	Strong			Corporate transformation	Revolution		
Unpredictable surprises		Far from certainty	Discontinuous or frame breaking			Discontinuous	Open ended

There is little in the literature to suggest which leadership styles and behaviours are most associated with each type of change. Two exceptions stand out. The first is the assumption that transformational leadership is associated with transformational or frame-breaking change. The second is the work of Dunphy and Stace (1993) who have, specifically, linked styles of leadership to types of change. Figure 6.7 shows the results of these linkings.

An examination of Figure 6.7 shows that any style of management can be used with any type of change. However, Dunphy and Stace's research with 13 service sector organizations which had gone through large-scale environmental change indicates that, for transformational change at the corporate level, a directive/coercive style of leadership is likely to be most successful. What is interesting, however, is Dunphy and Stace's (p. 917) statement that: 'Once this basis for organizational renewal is in place, there is a choice to be made at the

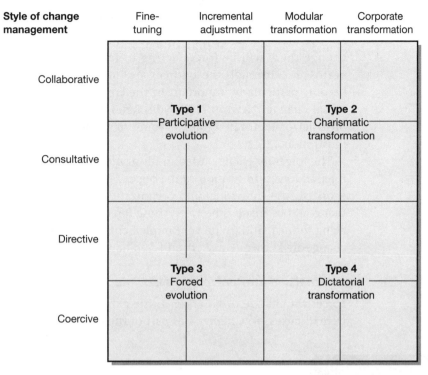

Figure 6.7 The Dunphy and Stace change matrix

Source: Reprinted by permission of Sage Publications Ltd from Dunphy, D. and Stace, D. (1993), 'The strategic management of corporate change', *Human Relations*, vol. 46, no. 8, p. 908. Copyright (© The Tavistock Institute, 1993).

corporate level as to the mix of directive and consultative strategies needed to keep the momentum of change.' With regard to accompanying change at the business (operational) level, they suggest a more consultative style to win commitment of employees at that level.

Logic suggests that a more consultative style of management is more appropriate to converging, incremental types of change that are, in turn, likely to be associated with environmental forces for change which are predictable and of moderate strength, as shown in Table 6.4. However, Strebel (1996a) proposes a model that not only links leadership style and approach to environmental forces for change, but also links these to the degree to which an organization is open to change initiatives. Consequently, any discussion of the leadership of change must take account of the capability and willingness of any organization to remain either closed or open to the prospects of change. Leading change, therefore, will almost certainly be concerned with overcoming resistance to change.

Obstructing and facilitating processes for change

For the management of any organization that is reacting to, or planning for, change there will be forces acting to facilitate the change and forces acting against it. Although these forces are important for any type of change, they become particularly important in the context of frame-breaking or transformational change. Newton (1993) discusses a number of processes that, she says, obstruct or facilitate change. Some of these factors and others are given in Illustration 6.9.

The forces *for* change listed in Illustration 6.9 are categorized into external and internal forces (in relation to the organization). The forces *against* change are categorized into individual and organizational responses. Yet another distinction that could be made is between those forces which: (a) prevent a new perspective being formed, and (b) prevent implementation of change once the intentions for change are known (Ginsberg and Abrahamson, 1991).

External and internal forces associated with change

Forces for change originating in the external environment of an organization were discussed in Chapter 1 as part of the PEST description of the organizational

---

Illustration 6.9

Forces for and against change

Driving forces for change

1 *External forces*:
- role of the state
- social pressures
- changing technology
- constraints from suppliers
- stakeholder demands
- competitor behaviour
- customer needs.

2 *Internal forces*:
- organizational growth
- pressures for increased performance
- managerial aspirations
- political coalitions
- redesign of jobs
- restructuring.

Driving forces against change

1 *Individual resistance*:
- fear of the unknown
- dislike of the uncertainty and ambiguity
- surrounding change
- potential loss of power base
- potential loss of rewards
- perceived lack of skills for new situation
- potential loss of current skills.

2 *Organizational resistance*:
- inertial forces deriving from the systemic nature of organizations
- interlocking aspects of structure, control systems, rituals and routines, signs and symbols
- inertial forces deriving from group norms
- potential loss of group power bases
- entrenched interests of stakeholders
- lack of organizational capability
- lack of resources
- threat to resource allocations.

environment. These, together with internal forces, such as the need for new product development or restructuring to accommodate new technological processes, are likely to facilitate change in that they are the triggers for change. However, these forces may be counteracted by other forces that resist change; for instance those listed in Illustration 6.9 which, themselves, may be externally or internally generated. However, the role of leading change is more likely to be concerned with resistance from inside the organization (which can be from individuals or be organizationally generated), this being the type of resistance most immediately manageable.

It is clear from an inspection of the factors listed in Illustration 6.9 that, for specific change situations, some forces will be stronger than others. One technique for depicting the range and strength of forces for and against change is that of *force field analysis*. Developed in the 1960s, force field analysis is based on the idea that, in any change situation, there are forces supporting change and forces opposing it. The theory, upon which the technique is based, implies that when the balance of the two sets of forces is equal, no change will occur. Thus it is argued that, if change is desired, the forces supporting change need to be strengthened and those opposing change weakened. Figure 6.8 is a generic representation of a force field diagram, while Illustration 6.10 (drawing on the advice of Carnall (2003) and Buchanan and Huczynski (2004)) outlines the steps necessary for carrying it out.

Paton and McCalman (2000) suggest that force field analysis, as well as operating as a technique in its own right, can be incorporated into other change situation analyses such as the TROPICS test discussed in Chapter 2. The results of such analyses help in deciding the extent to which an organization is open or closed to change. In this respect also, Strebel (1992, p. 67) offers the following advice:

1 Look for closed attitudes by examining what processes are in place for bringing new ideas into the industry, company or business unit, especially at the highest levels; and by probing whether management is aware of the change forces.
2 Look for an entrenched culture by examining what processes are in place for reflecting on values and improving behaviour and skills; and by enquiring to what extent behaviour and skills are adapted to the forces of change.

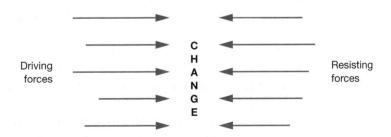

Figure 6.8 A force field diagram

Illustration 6.10

Force field analysis

Step 1: Define the problem in terms of the present situation, with its strengths and weaknesses, and the situation you would wish to achieve. Define the target situation as precisely and unambiguously as possible.

Step 2: List the forces working for and against the desired changes. These can be based on people, resources, time, external factors, corporate culture.

Step 3: Rate each of the forces for and against change in terms of strength: high, medium or low. Give the strength ratings numerical values: 5 for high, 3 for medium, and 1 for low; this allows totals for driving and resisting forces to be calculated.

Step 4: Using a diagram such as that in Figure 6.8, draw lines of different lengths to indicate the different strengths of the forces.

Step 5: Label each line to indicate whether that force is very important (VI), important (I) or not important (NI).

Step 6: For each very important (VI) and important (I) force supporting the change, indicate how you would attempt to strengthen the force. Then do the same for those forces opposing the change, but in this case indicate how you would weaken the force.

Step 7: Agree on those actions that appear most likely to help solve the problem of achieving change.

Step 8: Identify the resources that will be needed to take the agreed actions and how these resources may be obtained.

Step 9: Make a practical action plan designed to achieve the target situation, which should include:
- timing of events
- specified milestones and deadlines
- specific responsibilities – who does what.

3 Look for rigid structures and systems, by examining when the organization, business system, the stakeholder resource base and the industry last changed significantly; and by enquiring to what extent the structures and systems are capable of accommodating the forces of change.

4 Look for counterproductive change dynamics by examining whether historical forces of change are driving the business; and by enquiring to what extent the historical forces of change have become the new force of resistance.

5 Assess the strength of the overall resistance to change by examining to what extent the various forces of resistance are correlated with one another; and by describing the resistance threshold in terms of power and resources needed to deal with the resistance.

Assuming assessments such as these can be done, Strebel's (1996) juxtaposition of the level of intensity of forces for change (which he designates as weak, moderate or strong and which could be calculated from use of force field analysis) with the degree of resistance expected (that is, whether an organization is closed to change, can be opened to change, or is open to change) is useful for determining the leadership behaviour and overall management approach to implementing change (see Figure 6.9).

The role of leadership in Strebel's model is most clearly spelt out in the case of weak environmental change forces in an organizational situation of being closed to change. Of this situation, Strebel says that weak change forces imply

Resistance	PROACTIVE	REACTIVE	RAPID	
Closed to change	Radical leadership	Organisational realignment	Downsizing and restructuring	Discontinuous paths
Can be opened to change	Top-down experimentation	Process re-engineering	Autonomous restructuring	Mixed paths
Open to change	Bottom-up experimentation	Goal cascading	Rapid adaptation	Continuous paths
	Weak	Moderate	Strong	Change force

Figure 6.9 Contrasting change paths

Source: Strebel, P. (1996a), 'Choosing the right change path', *Mastering Management*, Part 14, *Financial Times*, p. 17.

proactive change; in an organization unused to and closed to change, this implies radical leadership. By this Strebel means an approach that will break the dominant culture of resistance by starting with top management and continuing through a process of shaking up others in the organization. The proposed behaviour of change leaders (or, as Strebel refers to them, change agents) in this and the other situations shown in Figure 6.9 is summarized by Strebel as follows (1996, p. 6):

> It is useful to distinguish between the different levels of 'change-force' intensity. Weak change forces are difficult to discern and require skill in communications and in identifying the value creating idea – but there is time for experimentation. Moderate change forces are those which have started to affect performance but do not threaten survival: getting people's attention is easier and multi-disciplinary teams should be employed.
>
> Those organizations with high resistance have very few 'change agents' and require a radical approach to break the dominant culture. The process should start with resistors at the top, can benefit from headstrong leadership (though can equally end in a disastrous ego trip), and requires some form of reorganization. In organizations that can be opened to change, management has to help the change agents, and top-down experimentation is desirable. In organizations that are already open to change there is usually little risk in leaving the resistors until last. Bottom-up experimentation and goal cascading should be possible.

Strebel's model of paths to change is quite complex and, as this discussion is focused on leadership, the paths to change identified in the final column are only tangentially relevant – they are discussed further in Part Three. What is important, here, is to note Strebel's comment (p. 5) that: 'Change leaders cannot afford the risk of blindly applying a standard recipe and hoping it will work. Successful change takes place on a path that is appropriate to the specific situation.'

Responding to resistance to change

Leadership can be conceptualized in terms of its three main functions within a group or organization (Open University, 1996, p. 38):

1 the *strategic* function: developing a sense of direction in the group or organization;
2 the *tactical* function: defining the tasks necessary to achieve the group's or the organization's goals and making sure that these tasks are carried out effectively;
3 the *interpersonal* function: maintaining the morale, cohesion and commitment of the group or organization.

It is important to note that these functions do not, necessarily, divide themselves among leaders at the top, middle and other parts of organizations. All the functions are carried out by all leaders whatever their status. However, it is reasonable to suggest that the strategic and tactical functions will feature more prominently in the planning and early stages of change, with the tactical and interpersonal functions featuring more prominently during the change process and when the change is in place.

Reducing or overcoming resistance to change depends on identifying the sources of resistance, as discussed earlier. It also depends on a leader's ability to be task oriented (both strategically and tactically) when the time requires it, but also relationship oriented to address the more individualized resistances to change. A first step is to recognize the conclusions of a number of writers (e.g. Rashford and Coghlan, 1989; Clarke, 1994; Nortier, 1995;) that individuals faced with change often go through a traumatic process of shock and denial before they come to acknowledge and adapt to it. What must not be forgotten, however, is that change can be exciting and can bring new and positive opportunities for all. The notion of a vision and communicating that vision is important in this context, as exemplified by Clarke (1994, p. 124) when she says: 'It is a vision of a new future which provides the pull-through and momentum for change.' This view is reinforced by two articles (Beer, Eisenstat and Spector, 1990; Kotter, 1995) in the *Harvard Business Review*, both of which refer to the need for a vision to guide the change. This is, however, clearly not sufficient, as the other points of advice from these authors show (see Illustrations 6.11 and 6.12).

The advice on what to do given by Beer *et al.* (1990) and on what *not* to do given by Kotter (1995) clearly overlap in content and intent and each element of advice is offered as relevant for all situations. By contrast, an earlier article by Kotter and Schlesinger (1979) is more circumspect in detailing a range of different approaches for dealing with resistance to change:

- education and communication
- participation and involvement
- facilitation and support
- negotiation and agreement
- manipulation and cooptation
- explicit and implicit coercion.

Illustration 6.11

Six steps to effective change

1 Mobilize commitment to change through joint diagnosis of business problems.

2 Develop a shared vision of how to organize and manage for competitiveness.

3 Foster consensus for the new vision, competence to enact it and cohesion to move it along.

4 Spread revitalization to all departments without pushing it from the top.

5 Institutionalize revitalization through formal policies, systems and structures.

6 Monitor and adjust strategies in response to problems in the revitalization process.

Source: Beer, M., Eisenstat, R. A. and Spector, B. (1990), 'Why change programmes do not produce change', *Harvard Business Review*, November–December, vol. 68, no. 6, pp. 158–66.

Illustration 6.12

Why transformation efforts fail

According to Kotter (1995), transforming organizations fail through:

1 not establishing a great enough sense of urgency;

2 not creating a powerful enough coalition;

3 lacking a vision;

4 undercommunicating by a factor of ten;

5 not removing obstacles to the new vision;

6 not systematically planning for and creating short-term wins;

7 declaring victory too soon;

8 not anchoring changes in the corporation's culture.

Source: Kotter, J. P. (1995) 'Leading change: why transformation efforts fail', *Harvard Business Review*, March–April, vol. 73, no. 2, pp. 59–67.

In detailing the advantages and disadvantages of each method, Kotter and Schlesinger explain the particular set of circumstances where each approach might be used. For instance, if the change initiators possess considerable power, and change must come quickly, some form of coercion would be appropriate. By contrast, an approach associated with negotiation (or more collaboratively, participation) is more likely to succeed where the change initiators do not have complete information and where others have power to resist.

The value of Kotter and Schlesinger's (1979) analysis lies in the way it can help managers understand specific instances of opposition to change in order to work out an approach relevant to a particular situation. This, together with Illustrations 6.11 and 6.12, bring this chapter's discussion back to the beginning, when the question was posed as to what leadership approach works best in situations of organizational change. Taken together, these illustrations show how leaders of change need to have certain attitudes and behaviours which are of benefit regardless of the prevailing situation, but they also need to understand that some behaviours are more effective in some situations and other behaviours more effective in other situations.

Comment and conclusions

Leadership theories vary from those which maintain that there are a set of characteristics that leaders must have if they are to gain success in what they do to those which argue that no single leader can be successful regardless of their own preferences and the situation they find themselves in.

Regardless of which set of theories gain attention at any time, agreement is becoming evident that leading change requires more than the command and control behaviours fashionable in times when organizations operated in stable predictable environments. The replacement of repetitive work with machines, the increasing emphasis on knowledge and the need to innovate to survive and prosper have brought a recognition that, for people to be creative, while working in situations of uncertainty requires leaders who are able to harness the skills of others through working in collaborative rather than hierarchical ways.

This does not imply an emphasis on 'soft' approaches to leadership in neglect of hard decisions to be made in some circumstances. This view can be summarized in terms of Beer and Nohria's (2000) 'E' and 'O' change strategies. An E approach to change is based on economic value while an O approach is based on organizational capability. Thus, in an E approach to change (which the authors term a 'hard' approach), shareholder value is the only legitimate measure of corporate success. This implies heavy use of economic incentives, layoffs, downsizing and restructuring. Leaders who subscribe to an O approach (which can be termed a 'soft' approach) believe that they should aim to develop corporate culture and human capability through individual and organizational learning in a process of collaboration with others at all levels of the organization.

Operating E and O approaches to change simultaneously is very difficult for most leaders of change. Combining the two could bring the worst of each and the benefits of neither. For instance, doubling or trebling shareholder returns through subscribing to an E approach could fail to build the commitment, cooperation and creativity necessary for sustained competitive advantage. Embracing an O approach could make it difficult to take tough decisions in times of economic downturn and the need to survive. Beer and Nohria advise that, unless organizations can find leaders who, exceptionally, have the will, skill and wisdom to work with both approaches, the way to proceed is to sequence them, with an E approach preceding an O approach. What is more, in the light of the doubts expressed earlier in the chapter, that one person can adopt different styles of leadership according to circumstances, there is a case for two leaders of change chosen for their contrasting traits and styles. Alternatively or additionally, the idea of team leadership is not unreasonable if the team is small with the members agreed on the vision and goals.

Leadership, together with the other aspects of organizational life discussed in this part of the book, comprise the context in which change takes place. With the description of this context now completed, we can proceed to the more practical considerations of how to design, plan and implement change, discussed in Part Three.

Discussion questions and assignments

1 Drawing on your own experience of organizational change, describe:

   (a) a situation where, in Reich's (1991) terms, someone acted as 'hero';

   (b) a situation where the notion of the leader as hero was less evident than Reich's concept of the 'team as hero'.

2 What were the advantages and disadvantages of these two different leadership situations? Justify your answer.

3 In the context of the discussion of different types of change posed in Chapter 2, and the idea that organizations must be alert to their ever-changing environments, debate the advisability of seeking managers at all levels who can act as transformational leaders.

4 Examine the concept of 'leaders of change' as it might apply across different societies and organizations.

5 If you wanted to identify and develop your own leadership skills/style, from the reading and research provided, how might you begin to do this?

Case example ●●●

Managers may excel at operational tasks, yet still stumble during the transition to a more senior role: tough lessons on the road to leadership

That our organizations need better leadership if they are to survive and prosper in these turbulent times has become a truism. Simply stated, leaders are people who: establish new direction, gain the support, cooperation and commitment of those they need to move in that new direction and motivate them to overcome obstacles in the way of the company's goals. We also agree on what leadership is

not. Leadership differs from management, an equally valuable but different set of activities.

Leadership development is not a smooth, continuous or incremental process, but is punctuated by inflection points. These key junctures, which Herminia Ibarra (2004) calls leadership transitions, are the points in a person's career at which they either learn how to lead or become derailed. A

Case example *continued*

transition is a move into a new role – whether formal assignment, a project, or a role imposed by an unexpected event such as a crisis – which is so fundamentally different that the old ways of operating are no longer valid or effective.

Consider the experience of Anne – After a steady rise through the functional ranks in logistics and distribution, Anne found herself blind-sided by a proposal for a radical reorganization that came from outside her division. Accustomed to planning for annual improvements in her basic business strategy, she failed to notice shifting priorities in the wider market. Although she had built a loyal, high-performing team, she had few networks outside her group to help her anticipate the new imperatives. Worse, she was assessed by her boss as lacking the broader business picture. Frustrated, Anne contemplated leaving. Anne's predicament is not unusual. The most common learning challenges for aspirational leaders are the following:

learning to see, not just produce good ideas

communicating clear messages that have emotional impact

delegating and involving others

improving social skills, such as empathy, listening and coaching.

Consider the experience of Jeff – he is a general manager of a consumer product subsidiary, and was praised by his company for his turnaround skills. But after three or four successful assignments he found himself in trouble at all levels. His relationship with an older, more conservative colleague in marketing suffered from miscommunication and mutual lack of trust. At each point of disagreement Jeff had taken over, at times doing his colleague's job. After this, he received his first poor performance review. His manager questioned his ability to delegate and to communicate laterally with other groups within the company. He sought and gained the motivation, practice and feedback that ultimately broadened his leadership style.

These examples suggest that the leadership transition can provoke deep self-questioning: Who am I? What do I want to become? What do I like to do? Do I have what it takes to learn a different way of operating? Is it me? Is it worth it?

Ibarra suggests that there are three things in particular that can help support leaders to change; motivation, practice and feedback, and coaching.

If we consider Anne and Jeff's transitions, in each case the most important changes to be made involved not skills but values … with greater attention to the leadership transition as a personal passage, organizations will better prepare promising managers for leading roles in the business.

Source: Ibarra, H. (2004), 'Tough lessons on the road to leadership', *Financial Times*, 5 August, 2004, p. 11.

Case exercise

1   From definitions and discussion at the beginning of the chapter and key points raised in this illustration, what do you consider to be the main differences between management and leadership? Share your response with others to assess whether there is a general consensus.

2   The illustration suggests that leadership development 'is not a smooth, continuous or incremental process, but is punctuated by inflection points'. Do you agree or disagree with this statement? Support your arguments with theoretical frameworks and examples you may have from your own experience or through examples you have researched in the general business domain.

3   In relation to the 'management of change', is there anything that Anne and Jeff could have done in relation to their roles to have assessed their environment more effectively and help them better prepare for the changes within their organizations?

4   From areas discussed in this chapter, is there anything the organization could have done to better prepare Anne and Jeff for the changes in their roles?

●●●● Indicative resources

Armstrong, M. and Stephens, T. (2005) *A Handbook of Management and Leadership*, London: Kogan Page. This text provides information on key theories and best practice related to management and leadership. Included in this is the issue of delivering change and case examples that support management, leadership and change.

Harvard Business Review (2004) *Leadership in a Changed World*, Boston, MA: Harvard Business School Press. This book (not a text) is part of a series of books published by Harvard Business School to compile key writers' ideas in relation to different business areas. This particular part of the series offers eight 'leading thinkers' on leadership and the impact of leadership in a changing environment. The key thinking with this book is leadership and globalization and the future of leadership in an ever-changing global economy.

Kotter, J. P. (1996) *Leading Change*, Boston, MA: Harvard Business School Press. A considerable amount of writing in the area of leadership was undertaken by Kotter throughout the 1990s. His contribution to leadership and change has been substantial. This particular book has been built on various previous articles and books and focuses specifically on leadership and change. It incorporates management as well and identifies that the success of business cannot be relied on management techniques alone leadership skills and behaviour needs to also be considered.

●●●● Useful websites

www.dti.gov.uk The Department of Trade and Industry has expanded its website and has now included helpful information for businesses of all sizes. What is particularly useful, and supports key areas offered in this chapter, is the section on 'achieving best practice'. It includes work that has focused on inspirational leadership; some testimonials and case studies are also included.

www.on-leadership.com This site provides articles and case studies in relation to leadership in organizations, and has information on education materials, publications and online resources.

> To click straight to these links and for other resources go to
> www.pearsoned.co.uk/senior

●●●● References

Andersen, J. A. (2000) 'Intuition in managers: are intuitive managers more effective?', *Journal of Managerial Psychology*, vol. 15, no. 1, pp. 46–67.

Anderson, L., Bennet, N., Cartwright, M., Newton, W., Preedy, M. and Wise, C. (2003) Study Guide, *Leading and Managing for Effective Education*, Milton Keynes: Open University Press.

Ansoff, I. H. and McDonnell, E. J. (1990) *Implanting Strategic Management*, Englewood Cliffs, NJ: Prentice-Hall.

Armstrong, M. and Stephens, T. (2005) *A Handbook of Management and Leadership*, London: Kogan Page.

Baker, D. P. and Salas, E. (1997) *Team Climate Inventory Manual and User's Guide*, Windsor: ASE Press.

Bass, B. M. (1990) 'From transactional to transformational leadership: learning to share the vision', *Organizational Dynamics*, Winter, pp. 19–31.

Beer, M., Eisenstat, R. A. and Spector, B. (1990) 'Why change programmes do not produce change', *Harvard Business Review*, November–December, vol. 68, no. 6, pp. 158–66

Beer, M. and Nohria, N. (2000) 'Cracking the code of change', *Harvard Business Review*, May–June, pp. 133–41.

Behling, O. and McFillen, J. (1996) 'A syncretical model of charismatic/transformational leadership', *Group & Organization Management*, vol. 21, no. 2, June, pp. 163–91.

Belbin, M. (1993) *Team Roles at Work*, Oxford: Butterworth Heinemann.

Bennet III, R. H. (1998), 'The importance of tacit knowledge in strategic deliberations and decisions', *Management Decision*, vol. 36, no. 9, pp. 589–97.

Blake, R. R. and McCanse, A. A. (1991) *Leadership Dilemmas: Grid Solutions*, Houston, TX: Gulf Publishing.

Blake, R. R. and Mouton, J. S. (1964) *The Managerial Grid*, Houston, TX: Gulf Publishing.

Bottery, M. (2004) *The Challenges of Educational Leadership*, London: PCP.

Buchanan, D. and Huczynski, A. (2004) *Organizational Behaviour* (5th edn), Harlow: Pearson Education Limited.

Bunting, M. (2000) 'Rewiring our brains', the *Guardian*, 13 November.

Carnall, C. A. (2003) *Managing Change in Organizations* (4th edn), Harlow: Pearson Education Limited.

Clarke, C. and Pratt, S. (1985) 'Leadership's four-part progress', *Management Today*, March, pp. 84–6.

Clarke, L. (1994) *The Essence of Change*, Hemel Hempstead: Prentice Hall.

Cohn, L. (2005) 'Hands-on retailer', *Business Week*, McGraw-Hill Companies, 30 May, pp. 50–1.

Dulewicz, V. and Herbert, P. (1996) 'Leaders of tomorrow: how to spot the high-flyers', *Financial Times*, 20 September, p. 16.

Dunphy, D. and Stace, D. (1993) 'The strategic management of corporate change', *Human Relations*, vol. 46, no. 8, pp. 905–20.

Ekvall, G. and Arvonen, J. (1991) 'Change-centred leadership: an extension of the two-dimensional model', *Scandinavian Journal of Management*, vol. 7, no. 1, pp. 17–26.

Farkas, C. M. and Wetlaufer, S. (1996) 'The ways chief executive officers lead', *Harvard Business Review*, May–June, pp. 110–22.

Fayol, H. (1949) *General and Industrial Management*, London: Pitman.

Fiedler, F. E. (1967) *A Theory of Leadership Effectiveness*, New York: McGraw-Hill.

Fiedler, F. E. (1989) 'The effective utilisation of intellectual abilities and job relevant knowledge in group performance: cognitive resource theory and an agenda for the future', *Applied Psychology: An International Review*, vol. 38, no. 3, pp. 289–304.

Fiedler, F. E. and Chemers, M. M. (1974) *Leadership and Effective Management*, Glenview, IL: Scott Foresman.

Fiedler, F. E. and Chemers, M. M. (1984) *Improving Leadership Effectiveness: The Leaders Match Concept*, New York: John Wiley.

George, J. and Jones, G. (2005) *Understanding and Managing Organizational Behaviour* (4th edn), Harlow: Pearson Prentice Hall.

Ginsberg, A. and Abrahamson, E. (1991) 'Champions of change and strategic shifts: the role of internal and external change advocates', *Journal of Management Studies*, vol. 28, no. 2, pp. 173–90.

Goleman, D. (1998) 'What makes a leader? IQ and technical skills are important, but emotional intelligence is the sine qua non of leadership', *Harvard Business Review*, November–December, pp. 93–104.

Gordon, J. R. (1999) *A Diagnostic Approach to Organizational Behaviour* (6th edn), Englewood Cliffs, NJ: Prentice-Hall.

Grundy, T. (1993) *Managing Strategic Change*, London: Kogan Page.

Hackman, R. (1994) 'Tripwires in designing and leading workgroups', *The Occupational Psychologist*, vol. 23, pp. 3–8.

Handy, C. (1993) *Understanding Organizations*, Harmondsworth: Penguin.

Harvard Business Review (2004) *Leadership in a Changed World*, Boston, MA: Harvard Business School Press.

Henry, J. (2001) *Creativity and Perception in Management*, London: Sage.

Henry, J. and Mayle, D. (2002) *Managing Innovation and Change*, London: Sage.

Hersey, P. and Blanchard, K. H. (1993) *Management of Organizational Behavior: Utilizing Human Resources* (6th edn), Englewood Cliffs, NJ: Prentice-Hall.

Higgs, M. and Dulewicz, V. (2004) 'The emotionally intelligent leader', in Rees, D. and McBain, R. (eds) *People Management: Challenges and Opportunities*, London: Palgrave-MacMillan.

Hoar, R. (2004) '50 most powerful women: the definitive list, *Management Today*, July, pp. 38–45.

Holman, M. and Waldmeir, P. (1996) 'World Bank chief's cry from the heart', *Financial Times*, 29 March, p. 4.

House, R. J. (1971) 'A path–goal theory of leader effectiveness', *Administrative Science Quarterly*, September, pp. 321–38.

Ibarra, H. (2004) 'Tough lessons on the road to leadership', *Financial Times*, 5 August, p. 11.

Jung, C. G. (1976) *TYPOLOGI. Till fragan om de psykologiska typerna, Typologie – Zur Frage der psychologischen Typen*, Olten, Walter-Verlag AG, 1972 (translated from the German), Stockholm: Berghs Forlag.

Kanter, R. M. (1991) 'Change-motor skills: what it takes to be creative', in Henry, J. and Walker, D. (eds) *Managing Innovation*, London: Sage.

Katzenbach, J.R. and Smith, K. (1993) *Wisdom of Teams: Creating the High-performance Organization*, Boston, MA: Harvard Business School Press.

Keegan, W. J. (1980) *How to use the Keegan Type Indicator (KTI) and the Keegan Information Processing Indicator (KIPI)* New York: Warren Keegan Associates Press.

Keegan, W. J. (1984) *Judgements, Choices and Decisions*, New York: Wiley.

Keller, R. T. (1989) 'A test of the path–goal theory of leadership with need for clarity as a moderator in research and development organizations', *Journal of Applied Psychology*, April, pp. 208–12.

Kirkpatrick, S. A. and Locke, E. A. (1991) 'Leadership: do traits matter?', *Academy of Management Executive*, May, pp. 48–60.

Kirton, M. J. (1976) 'Adaptors and innovators: a description and a measure', *Journal of Applied Psychology*, vol. 61, pp. 622–9.

Kotter, J. P. (1990) *A Force for Change: How Leadership Differs from Management*, New York: Free Press.

Kotter, J. P. (1995) 'Leading change: why transformation efforts fail', *Harvard Business Review*, March–April, vol. 73, no. 2, pp. 59–67.

Kotter, J. P. (1996) *Leading Change*, Boston, MA: Harvard Business School Press.

Kotter, J. P. and Schlesinger, L. A. (1979) 'Choosing strategies for change', *Harvard Business Review*, March–April, vol. 57, no. 2, pp. 106–14.

Landrum, N. E., Howell, J. P. and Paris, L. (2000) 'Leadership for strategic change', *Leadership and Organization Development Journal*, vol. 21, no. 3, pp. 150–6.

Lank, A. G. and Lank, E. A. (1995) 'Legitimizing the gut feel: the role of intuition in business', *Journal of Managerial Psychology*, vol. 10, no. 5, pp. 18–23.

Likert, R. (1961) *New Patterns of Management*, New York: McGraw-Hill.

Lindell, M. and Rosenqvist, G. (1992a) 'Is there a third management style?' *Finnish Journal of Business Economics*, vol. 3, pp. 171–98.

Lindell, M. and Rosenqvist, G. (1992b) 'Management behavior dimensions and development orientation', *Leadership Quarterly*, Winter, pp. 355–77.

Lord, R. G., De Vader, C. L. and Alliger, G. M. (1986) 'A meta-analysis of the relation between personality traits and leadership perceptions: an application of validity generalization procedures', *Journal of Applied Psychology*, vol. 71, pp. 402–10.

McHugh, M. and Bennett, H. (1999) 'Introducing teamwork within a bureaucratic maze', *The Leadership and Organization Development Journal*, vol. 20, no. 2, pp. 81–93.

Madslien, J. (2005) BBC profile: Tesco chief Sir Terry Leahy, bbc.co.uk, 12 April.

Mann, R. D. (1959) 'A review of the relationship between personality and performance in small groups', *Psychological Bulletin*, vol. 56, no. 4, pp. 241–70.

Mintzberg, H. (1979) *The Nature of Managerial Work*, Englewood Cliffs, NJ: Prentice-Hall.

Mullins, L. J. (2005) *Management and Organisational Behaviour* (7th edn), Harlow: Financial Times Prentice Hall.

Naylor, J. (2004) *Management* (2nd edn), Harlow: Pearson Education.

Newton, J. (1993) 'Obstructing and facilitating processes in strategic change: a research approach', Proceedings of the British Academy of Management Conference, 20–2 September.

Nortier, F. (1995) 'A new angle on coping with change: managing transition', *Journal of Management Development*, vol. 14, no. 4, pp. 32–46.

Observer (2002a) 'Cost cutting Ryanair flies above the storm', *The Observer*, 3 February.

Observer (2002b) 'Micheal O'Leary: a real businessman', *The Observer*, 16 June.

Observer (2002c) 'The life of Ryan', *The Observer*, 16 June.

Open University (1996) Book 6. 'Managing people: a wider view', MBA Course, Milton Keynes: Open University.

Paton, R. A. and McCalman, J. (2000) *Change Management: A Guide to Effective Implementation*, London: Sage.

Pollock, L. (2000) 'That's infotainment', *People Management*, 28 December, pp. 18–23.

Post, J. M. (1986) 'Narcissism and the charismatic leader–follower relationship', *Political Psychology*, vol. 7, no. 4, pp. 675–88.

Quinn, R. E. (1988) *Beyond Rational Management: Mastering the Paradoxes and Competing Demands of High Performance*, San Francisco, CA: Jossey-Bass.

Rashford, N. S. and Coghlan, D. (1989) 'Phases and levels of organisational change', *Journal of Managerial Psychology*, vol. 4, no. 3, pp. 17–22.

Reich, R. B. (1991) 'The team as hero', in Henry, J. and Walker, D. (eds) *Managing Innovation*, London: Sage.

Robbins, S. (2005) *Organizational Behaviour, International Edition* (11th edn), Upper Saddle River, NJ: Pearson Education Limited.

Robbins, S. P. and Coulter, M. (2005) *Management* (8th edn), Englewood Cliffs, NJ: Prentice-Hall.

Smith, M. (1991) 'Leadership and supervision', in Smith, M. (ed.) *Analysing Organizational Behaviour*, New York: Macmillan.

Stacey, R. (1996) *Strategic Management and Organisational Dynamics*, London: Pitman.

Stodgill, R. M. (1948) 'Personal factors associated with leadership: a survey of the literature', *Journal of Psychology*, vol. 25, pp. 35–71.

Stodgill, R. M. and Coons, A. E. (1957) *Leader Behavior: Its Description and Measurement*, Columbus, OH: Ohio State University Bureau of Business Research.

Storey, A. (2004) 'The problem of distributed leadership', *School Leadership & Management*, vol. 24, no. 3, August, pp. 251–65.

Strebel, P. (1992) *Breakpoints: How Managers Exploit Radical Business Change*, Cambridge, MA: Harvard Business School Press.

Strebel, P. (1996) 'Choosing the right path', *Mastering Management*, Part 14, *Financial Times*, pp. 5–7.

Tannenbaum, R. and Schmidt, W. H. (1973) 'How to choose a leadership pattern', *Harvard Business Review*, vol. 51, May–June, pp. 162–80.

Tichy, N. M. and Devanna, M. A. (1990) *The Transformational Leader* (2nd edn), New York: Wiley.

Tichy, N. M. and Ulrich, D. O. (1984) 'The leadership challenge – a call for the transformational leader', *Sloan Management Review*, Fall, pp. 59–68.

Tushman, M. L., Newman, W. H. and Romanelli, E. (1988) 'Convergence and upheaval: managing the unsteady pace of organizational evolution', in Tushman, M. L. and Moore, W. L. (eds) *Readings in the Management of Innovation*, New York: Ballinger.

Useem, M. (1996) 'Do leaders make a difference?' *Mastering Management*, Part 18, *Financial Times*, pp. 5–6.

Watson, C. M. (1983) 'Leadership, management and the seven keys', *Business Horizons*, March–April, pp. 8–13.

Wensley, R. (1996) 'Mrs Beeton, management guru,' *Financial Times*, 26 April, p. 15.

Westley, F. and Mintzberg, H. (1989) 'Visionary leadership and strategic management', *Strategic Management Journal*, vol. 10, pp. 17–32.

Woffard, J. C. and Liska, L. Z. (1993) 'Path–goal theories of leadership: a meta-analysis', *Journal of Management*, Winter, pp. 857–76.

Woodruffe, C. (2000) 'Emotional intelligence: time for a time-out', *Selection and Development Review*, vol. 16, no. 4, pp. 3–9.

Wright, P. (1996) *Managerial Leadership*, London: Routledge.

Yukl, G. (2002) *Leadership in Organizations* (5th edn), Englewood Cliffs, NJ: Prentice-Hall.

Orange, a study of change: part 2

What business is the mobile phone industry now in?

A key issue for any organization in any industry is to ask what business it is in. As was suggested in the first part of this Case Study, Orange moved the focus of its core business from the product, the cell phone, to the customer benefit received, the aspiration for personal communication capability. To understand how fast the basic handset is changing, one has only to watch a sample of the globally successful New York-based TV soap drama *Friends*. Before the change in fashion is noticed, before the change in consumer electronics in their living rooms and offices catches the eye, the enormous bricks the actors put to their ears to make a phone call shouts: 'This programme belongs to an earlier age.' This change in design of the handset is a visible embodiment of the vast changes afoot in the industry; changes that are less perceptible to the eye.

The technological advances of mobile telephony have resulted in the mobile phone being an effective point of convergence for three formerly distinct technologies: communications, computing and consumer electronics. This makes demands on the design and production of goods and services in mobile telephony; it also changes the competitive sphere.

Fragmentation and specialization in the industry

As the technologies converge, and competitors change, so the opportunity for new companies increases; many in the same emerging economies as mentioned above. Nokia, despite its claims to the contrary, cannot claim learning curve advantage when the game is constantly new. More nimble operators, with lower costs, most notably in the Far East, have sprung up offering new combinations of deliverables. This is yet another factor that has enabled the value in the chain to move towards the network operators. The learning from developing new technology was passed from the original players, such as Nokia and Motorola, to groups of electronics manufacturing services, in order to cut manufacturing costs. These groups then held the cutting-edge developments in their firms – and are effectively selling them on to branded network operators. 'A flourishing ecosystem has sprung up of small firms specialising in areas such as handset design, chip design, testing and software' (Economist, 2004).

Orange has been a leader as a network operator, due to its connections with the consumers, and has been able to create competitive advantage from selling the products from these specialist firms as own-brand handsets. It has, for example, been able to use its brand to sell an unknown Taiwanese company's Smart phones.

Emerging markets

Emerging markets are another dynamic feature in this global industry. At the Cannes exhibition in 2005 India, China and Brazil were highlighted as regions that would drive growth in the future. Jay Naidoo, Chairman of the Development Bank of Southern Africa, noted that these areas were not the only emerging areas: 'There are a billion people in Africa, but only 51 million using cellphones; by 2006 we could see a quarter of Africa's billion people using them' (BBC, 2005a). Orange is well placed globally to take advantage of these emerging markets (see Case Study Part One for locations), but can it make money in them? Sunil Bharti Mittal, Chairman and Group Managing Director of Bharti Enterprises, which runs a large Indian mobile service, said India should add another 150 million subscribers by 2010 and he urged Africa to lower rates, following his model for India. 'You can do this in countries with big populations and still make money' (BBC, 2005a).

A changing competitive environment

Nokia became the number one player in the design and manufacture of cell phones without competing against the might of Japan. Sony formed a strategic alliance with one of Nokia's key competitors, Ericsson and, subsequently, Sony Ericsson has become a major force in the industry. Perhaps in retaliation, the latest offering from Nokia is, effectively, a games console, taking head-on Sony's supremacy in gaming. Meanwhile, for the consumer, the cell phone in the hand has increasingly become the palm computer. Internet connection and Microsoft Office application availability have taken the place of the PCN. T-Mobile launched it's a new 'Pocket office' in February 2005, with a set self-selecting the fastest network available. The Microsoft mobile phone, with two cameras and a 'Qwerty' keyboard, is another response to converging technologies. The questions are: Will PCN firms fight back? Could Texas International become a player in this emerging industry? Texas International makes computer chips for more than half the world's mobile phones (BBC, 2005b) and is keen to make multimedia functions more affordable. 'We're going to drive them down into meat-and-potatoes phones that have the largest market share', says Doug Rasor, a marketing vice-president at Texas.

Network operation, which is the area of the industry where Orange competes, is an increasingly powerful part of this convergence. They have the direct contact with end consumers that, in the right organizational setting, is one that is in touch with consumers and has a flexible, adaptable and learning-oriented culture. However, Orange has a good track record here and can provide the edge in understanding morphing consumer demand.

Operators also feel the first failures on the technological front, as grumbles about handsets not delivering come first to them. As *The Economist* noted in 2004, network operators are not as tempted towards vertical integration as manufacturers, as they like to have someone to blame when things go wrong. As the technological demands become more complex, they hold more power if they have a range of companies and geographical locations from which to source the handsets.

Issues requiring change management skills for Orange

Technical focus

In February 2005 Orange outlined its vision of mobile broadband and discussed first steps in the delivery of converged services. Orange Group CEO, Sanjiv Ahuja, commented:

> This is the year when mobile broadband will come of age – when we expect to see significant numbers of our customers begin to explore next generation services, enabled by mobile broadband. As a mobile operator, we are in a unique position as part of the France Télécom group to provide our customers with solutions to connect every aspect of their personal and professional lives through offering simple, innovative communication solutions. Across the France Télécom Group, we share a philosophy that strives to put the customer at the centre of everything we do.

Vivek Badrinath, Executive Vice-President of Products, Technology and Innovation, added:

> Orange as a company has always been about innovation and that's exactly what we're doing with mobile broadband for our customers – we're innovating with new technologies, smart devices and converged solutions in a way that other operators just aren't equipped to do. Our strength lies in being part of the France Télécom group, Europe's largest fixed, Internet and mobile company. This gives us access to excellence in R&D, infrastructure, support and, most important of all, a shared belief in the importance of putting customer needs at the heart of what we do. The future's bright, the future's Orange.

It is a challenge to change continuously and innovate. For example, Nokia has a culture of engineering innovation and yet has fallen prey to the complacency that is a key danger to the number one player in any market. This is despite what has been described as Finnish adaptability and its own self-belief. 'In ten years' time I would like to be dubbed as the company that brought mobility and the Internet together. It's not going to be easy, but this organization loves discontinuity, we can jump on it and adapt. Finns live in a cold climate: we have to be adaptable to survive' (Chief Executive Mr Ollilla, Economist, 2000). Nevertheless, despite these brave words, by 2004 the jury was out on whether this would be enough for Nokia. Instead Mr Brian Modoff, an analyst at the Deutsche Bank, considered that Nokia's strategy would have to change. 'They will be more of a brand, a design shop, rather than building everything', he says.

As the network operator Orange stands to gain from this. Since the issue is now less one of vertical integration back to the manufacturers, the focus moves forward to the interface with the consumer. Orange's strategy has been to build on the brand image by forming alliances with whichever manufacturer has the more technically relevant phone.

Ever newer technologies

More of a threat, in the light of the heavy investment made in third generation (3G) licences, sold by the governments of Europe at optimistically high prices, and even before 3G could be fully realized with consumers, there appeared on the edge of the market in 2005 the technology after 3G – Wimax. This wireless technology can boost data transmission speeds and may pave the way for rural high-speed access in particular. Its suitability for this was successfully trialled in rural Kent in the United Kingdom in early 2005.

The analyst firm Telecom View was predicting that Wimax would steal a large piece of market share from 3G and become the clear winner (BBC, 2005c). The better return on investment offered by technologies such as Wimax could thereby dent the possible returns of 3G networks. At the same time, just as the volume of mobile calls overtook fixed landline calls, BT announced a move to link the two via a new technology named Bluephone. This service revolved around a hybrid device that uses mobile networks when the customer is out and about, but uses the fixed line when the same customer is operating from home.

This will also have application in rural settings, as it can provide mobile signals for the 11 per cent of the United Kingdom currently unable to be reached by mobile technology. Only one model of handset is to be available initially, bringing predictions that this is a fatal flaw. Dave Williams, the Chief Technical Officer at O_2, said,'The number one reason people have for picking a phone service is the handset they can get with it. If you are limited to a choice of one phone it is a lot more risky' (*Independent,* 2005). On top of this, before the 3G phones begin to take off, 'super 3G' is being developed by an alliance between NTTDoCoMo and Vodafone, which is intended to be 10 times faster than 3G. The first stage of development is to be completed by 2007, with no date yet fixed for a commercial launch.

Orange has always been more of a brand than a cell phone seller. Tom Lynch, President of the Motorola handset business, commenting on his own organization, says: 'We are trying to think more broadly about it, which is why we call it 'the device formerly known as the cell phone' (Economist, 2004). Orange was there years earlier. Can it retain its first mover advantage, or will it begin to lose it, as has Nokia in the manufacturing side of this industry?

Personalization

Orange has strong values in the brand about enabling *personal* communication (see Part One of the Case Study). The departing Marketing Vice-President Richard Brennan noted in July 2004 his belief that:

> Orange will continue to grow, innovate, and break down barriers, just as it always has done. With all the great people within the company, and the passion and ambition that they display, I can honestly say I believe now more than ever, that the future's bright, the future's Orange.

The challenge for Orange is to build on these company values in the context of significant turbulence with respect to the market, the competition and technological innovation. Orange, as always, is in a situation of managing change.

Orange's advertising copy continues to focus on what is cool and leading edge. It featured strongly at the 2005 Cannes trade exhibition. The company's theme at Cannes was 'Orange Everywhere', which was about giving customers what they needed, whenever and wherever they needed it. It focused on giving customers access to the people, places and information that mattered to them – music, games, movies, news, contacts, email, photos or their favourite football team.

One means Orange has used to connect this message to its customers is film. 'Orange Wednesday' links Orange to the latest showing at everyone's local cinema, thus becoming the differentiating benefit on offer at the time. One issue is to maintain this constant focusing on changing customer needs and interests. To do this is partly a question of framing its basic business proposition. Didier Quillot, Executive Vice-President, Orange France, commented on the website in 2005:

> Orange is passionate about delivering a better future today by offering the most simple and intuitive personal communication experience to as many of our customers as possible. The

launch of 3G services in France in 2004 was an important first step in mobile broadband and we will be widening that experience this year, with the deployment of EDGE technology. Orange believes that continuing success demands the continuing personal touch to technology.

Increasingly customer-focused competition

The latest development is that a more consumer-focused competitor has entered this market – and a new question is raised for Orange's leaders: 'Can Orange compete on the customer service front with EasyMobile?' Part One of this Case Study noted that Orange holds the record for customer satisfaction in what has never been a very customer-friendly business. Now the gap in the market has been spotted by the serial entrepreneur, Stelios Haji-Ioannou, and potentially plugged by his alliance with a successful Danish mobile service. The customer facing alliance has been branded easyMobile. Frank Rasmussen, the CEO, promises 'The impact of easyMobile's entry into the market will be profound and with the customers as the big winners' (press release, 2005). He continues: 'British mobile users are treated badly compared with other mobile users in Europe', and boasted of his UK competitors that 'in future they need only follow the lead of easyMobile.com to improve their services.'

What is more, not only does easyMobile appear to share the customer focus of Orange, but it claims also to make a difference:

> We will not only operate with respect towards our customers, but also show our gratitude to the research to change the world for the better … 'we make the difference'.

Orange launched a court case to protect the colour orange (remember, it patented the use of a particular Pantone orange for its marketing communications); but the question remains: 'Can they respond offensively as well as defensively to this new entrant into the market?'

Integrating technologies and customer demand

Orange management is bullish on its website: 'This is an era when exciting innovations like mobile broadband and fixed-line convergence are transforming possibilities for the customer and Orange will be at the forefront of these developments.' Yet, in the face of all this change, can Orange remain competitive? What skills and competences can it rely on to build its brand and its profits in the face of such industry-level turbulence? As the *Financial Times* noted (2004) 'Operators, however, are engaged in a deadly guessing game: which are the applications which will tempt users to spend a little more each month, so jacking up the all-important arpu [added rate per user]?'. How relevant is the established model of adoption of new products (see Figure 1) to such a fast-moving marketplace? It may well be advisable for organizations competing in this industry to subdivide this market by sets of benefits sought by customers.

Do consumers want Smart phones or cheap talk?

Hindsight is a less precious commodity than foresight. Yet, with hindsight it is easy to see that the industry overvalued the 3G technology and unnecessarily furnished the coffers of governments licensing this new technology at the turn of the millennium. Confident predictions in 2000 that within a couple of years 3G would be rolled out and declining profits in

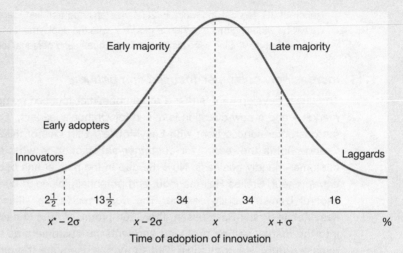

Time of adoption of innovation

*x = mean time for adoption

Figure 1 New product adoption segments

the industry would be restored by customers paying for the added-value services available have proved hollow. In 2005 sales finally began to accelerate from an admittedly low base. New competitors into the market, such as Hutchinson's 3, however, proved that such increase in market share could only come at the sacrifice of predicted profit. Lower prices attracted customers rather than more sophisticated applications.

In December 2004 Orange became the third entrant into the UK market for 3G services. And yet the retailer Carphone Warehouse accused Orange of failing to put its marketing weight behind the move. Orange has not done so because the predicted profits have proved elusive. Indeed Orange was forced into a 'buy one, get one free' offer. Nevertheless, predictions of take-off continued: 'If you want my personal opinion I think 3G will go mad in the second half of the year' commented Dunstone, Chief Executive of Carphone Warehouse (*Guardian* 2005).

Given this belief that '2005 is going to be the year that 3G phones become inescapable' (BBC, 2005c), it is worth noting that this event is being couched in terms of a bonanza for the consumer. The new competitor, 3, offered cut-price rates and signalled market acceptance that customers wanted to use voice services, and to use them cheaply. But this shift in technology, enabling faster voice services, combined with the low cost of voice calls, means that the industry is not reaping the rewards of its heavy investment in the technology. 'Show me an operator that believes their voice business can sustain them, and I'll write their obituary', said Ransom, Chief Technology Officer at Alcatel (BBC, 2005c). And so the marketing effort for Orange must be around video messaging and other multimedia capabilities.

Satellite navigation, maps on the handset for pedestrians, the phone as credit card, waved over the point-of-sale system at the store checkout, all these represent potential high added-value uses for consumers, available with the technology. The question is whether customers will pay for them. A 2004 CapGemini report suggested that while phone manufacturers add complexity to compete with each other, users simply want a cheap phone that works well and reliably.

What does it take to manage change in this environment?

Given this turbulent environment, does Orange have the organizational capacity to respond successfully to these challenges? Hewlett-Packard was renowned for its commitment to its employees, for its low-key 'management by wandering about', and yet its performance suffered when the rate of change in its industry quickened in the 1980s with the advent of PCs. A number of questions arise for Orange at this time:

- Is there a contract between Orange and its employees that can be harnessed and developed to increase profits in this market; and what does it look like? Where is value to be added in this industry?
- How can the organizational leaders in Orange keep the value and continue to create value in its brand?
- How can it have an identity to which graduates can be attracted while it remains very flexible?
- How can it respond to the challenge in its core product – the relevance of the somewhat perplexing question: 'So what do you want your phone to be today?' (Financial Times, 2004).

Case exercises   Orange (part 2)

1 Use the organizational iceberg (see Figure 4.1) to examine how the formal organizational elements of Orange might be impacted by the changes outlined in this case study.

2 Given the clear changes in products and services matched by changes in strategy and financial resources, how might the goals be changed, the structures altered and systems, procedures and management be aligned?

3 Consider the informal organizational elements in Figure 4.1 and discuss how these will change in the light of the changes highlighted in the case.

4 Consider your experience of mobile phone use, visit an Orange store, and supplement your reading of this case by further resources such as the business press and websites. Using all these sources, construct a cultural web for Orange (see Illustration 4.3).

5 What sources of power do you think Orange's chief executive has? How well do Quinn's four organizational models (see Table 6.2) fit the Orange case? Place Orange on the framework provided at Figure 6.6. How should the leadership at Orange respond to the changes outlined in this case? Use Figure 6.7 to frame your discussion. Does Orange model continuous change (see Figure 6.9)?

6 Obtain a copy of Beer and Nohria's article, referred to in Chapter 6, and analyze the change scenario at Orange in terms of the E and O approaches suggested there.

7 How relevant is the established model of adoption of new products (see Figure 1) to such a fast-moving marketplace? Is the failure of Orange to accurately predict consumer take-up of 3G services a hint that Orange is stumbling, or is this merely a short-term block as the innovators make way for the early adopters with a fairly certain early majority to follow?

●●●● References

All direct quotations from Orange executives regarding figures, recruitment advertising, future plans, etc. are taken from the Orange website: orange.co.uk

BBC (2005a) 'Emerging markets key to mobile future', 16 February; http://news.bbc.co.uk/1/hi/business/4270681.stm.

BBC (2005b) 'Cheaper chip for powerful mobiles', 15 February; http://news.bbc.co.uk/1/hi/technology/4266725.stm.

BBC (2005c) 'The future in your pocket',1 March; http://newsvote.bbc.co.uk/mpapps/pagetools/print/news.bbx.co.uk/1/hi/technology/4110555.stm

Economist (2000) 'A Finnish fable', *The Economist*, 14 October, pp. 131–4.

Economist (2004) 'Battling for the palm of your hand', *The Economist*, 1 May, pp. 79–81.

Financial Times (2004) 'Creative business: is extra intelligence a dumb plan?' *Financial Times*, 19 October, p. 13.

Guardian (2005) 'Carphone boss says 3G "will go mad"', the *Guardian* 15 April http://www.guardian, .co.uk/mobile/article/0,2763,1460310,00.html

Independent (2005) 'BT pins hopes on Bluephone to rescue its position in voice calls', *Independent*, 22 February, p. 39.

Press release (2005) 'easyMobile.com offers spare computer processing capacity to World Community Grid', 28 February; https://www.easymobile.com/selfcare/emcontent/press/news2.html

Part Three

STRATEGIES FOR MANAGING CHANGE

Two major themes have emerged from the discussions in Parts One and Two of the book that have a bearing on the practical issues of preparing for, designing and implementing change in organizations. These can be grouped broadly into the categories of the content of change and the context in which it happens. Part One concentrated on the context of organizational change and what causes it, while Part Two explored the formal and informal aspects of organizational life that influence the process of change and within which change happens.

This part of the book turns to the practicalities of *doing* change in the sense of designing, planning and implementing change – in other words concentrating on the processes through which change comes about. Two different approaches to managing change processes, each encompassing various methodologies, are discussed respectively in Chapters 7 and 8. These approaches relate directly back to the types of change discussed in Chapter 2, in particular, the concepts of hard and soft problems, that is, difficulties and messes. Consequently, Chapter 7 concentrates on change approaches that are based on rational–logical models of change which are most appropriate for situations of hard complexity where the 'people' issues are low. In contrast, Chapter 8 recognizes that many change situations involve issues of organizational politics, culture and leadership (as discussed in Part Two) that dictate an approach to change which can deal more easily with situations characterized by soft complexity.

Finally, Chapter 9 considers issues that will affect changes in the future for organizations, both in terms of what future organizations might look like and the attitudes and behaviour of those working in them as they might impact on future organizational change.

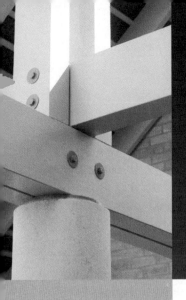

Chapter 7

Hard systems models of change

There are a number of models for handling change in situations of hard complexity. This chapter describes one and, in order to demonstrate its use, applies it to a particular change situation. The limitations of this type of model are discussed.

Learning objectives

By the end of this chapter you will be able to:

- recognize change situations (problems/opportunities) characterized mainly by hard complexity, where the use of hard systems methodologies are appropriate;

- describe the main features of hard systems methodologies for defining, planning and implementing change;

- explain the hard systems model of change (HSMC) as representative of hard systems methodologies of change;

- discuss the limitations of hard systems methodologies of change and, therefore, the need for other change methodologies more suited to situations of soft complexity.

●●●● Situations of change

In Chapter 2 a number of different ways of categorizing organizational change were discussed. These ranged from changes that happen incrementally, and which may affect only one part of an organization, to the more radical, frame-breaking or discontinuous changes, which pervade almost every aspect of an organization's functioning. As Chapter 2 also showed, expectations with respect to the ease with which change happens vary according to its perceived complexity. Consequently, change in situations that are characterized by hard complexity is more likely to be enacted easily and speedily than change in situations which show soft complexity, that is, where issues are contentious and there is a high level of emotional involvement on the part of those likely to implement the change and those who will be affected by it.

There are many approaches to planning and implementing change. Some are more appropriate to situations of hard complexity – which Chapter 2 also described as 'difficulties' – while others are more appropriate to situations of soft complexity or, as Chapter 2 characterized them, 'messy' situations. Flood and Jackson (1991), using a systems perspective, classify various methodologies in a similar way but use the terms 'simple system' and 'complex system' instead of difficulties and messes. What is of more interest, though, is that Flood and Jackson also classify these methodologies according to their appropriateness of use in situations characterized by different ideological viewpoints. Three ideological viewpoints, representing three types of relationships between people, are defined. Two of these (the unitary and pluralist viewpoints) have been discussed already in Chapter 5 (see Illustration 5.11); all three are described in Illustration 7.1.

Using an extensive list of different methodologies for problem solving and change, Flood and Jackson suggest which ones are most appropriate in situations characterized as simple or complex systems but modified by whether relationships between people tend to be of a unitarist, pluralist or coercive nature. It is not the purpose here to consider all the possibilities. What is important, for this discussion, is to note that different logics dominate each possibility in terms of suggesting a particular approach to change. Consequently, in situations of hard complexity (e.g. where simple systems and a unitarist ideology of relationships prevails), a particular type of change approach will be appropriate, whereas in situations of soft complexity (e.g. where complex systems and a pluralist ideology of relationships prevails), a different type of change approach should be used. This chapter concentrates on the first of these situations, to describe an approach to change that is representative of those approaches which are best applied in the relatively bounded situations described variously as difficulties, simple/unitarist systems or, in more straightforward terms, 'hard' situations.

Illustration 7.1

Characteristics of unitary, pluralist and coercive relationships

Unitary
People relating to each other from a unitary perspective:
- share common interests
- have values and beliefs that are highly compatible
- largely agree upon ends and means
- all participate in decision making
- act in accordance with agreed objectives.

Pluralist
People relating to each other from a pluralist perspective:
- have a basic compatibility of interest
- have values and beliefs that diverge to some extent
- do not necessarily agree upon ends and means, but compromise is possible
- all participate in decision making
- act in accordance with agreed objectives.

Coercive
People relating to each other from a coercive perspective:
- do not share common interests
- have values and beliefs that are likely to conflict
- do not agree upon ends and means and 'genuine' compromise is not possible
- coerce others to accept decisions.

Source: Based on Flood, R. L. and Jackson, M. C. (1991), *Creative Problem Solving: Total Systems Intervention* (Chichester, Wiley, pp. 34–5).

Systematic approaches to change

Most people have the capacity to think logically and rationally. Indeed, some would say this is the only way to approach problem solving or respond to opportunities and, therefore, there can be one basic way of planning and implementing change. It is upon this premise that the more systematic approaches to managing change are based. Derived from earlier methods of problem solving and decision making such as systems engineering methods and operational research (Mayon-White, 1993), these 'hard' approaches rely on the assumption that clear change objectives can be identified in order to work out the best way of achieving them. What is more, a strict application of these approaches dictates that these objectives should be such that it is possible to quantify them, or at least be sufficiently concrete that one can know when they have been achieved. For instance, consider the situation described in Illustration 7.2.

Illustration 7.2 provides an example of what appears to be a difficulty about which most people could agree – it appears to have fairly defined boundaries. There are clearly some problems with the way IT faults are reported to the IT support

Illustration 7.2

Dissatisfaction with the system for providing IT support services

Susan, a member of staff of the Faculty of Art and Design at Northshire University, was making a telephone call to the office of the IT support service to report that the computer link from her office to the resource centre was not working. As usual, there was no one there – she supposed the staff employed in the office were somewhere in the Faculty seeing to someone else's computer. She decided, therefore, to send an email but knew that, because of the time it took to respond to individuals, it would not be dealt with by the IT support team before the next day. Even then, from past experience, she suspected that when it was received she would not get a response without at least one reminder and perhaps two. Overall she took a particularly dim view of the quality of IT support service provided and was sure that, if she were responsible for this service, she could improve its effectiveness without too much effort and resources.

service and the way they are responded to when they are received. It is also clear that some quantitative indices could be devised on which to judge the system and that might give evidence of improvement if this were to take place. What follows is, first, a generalized description of a model of change which is most suited to situations such as that described in Illustration 7.2 – that is, in situations which are more of a difficulty than a mess and, second, a more fully worked-out example of its use to plan and implement change in the Beautiful Buildings Company.

The hard systems model of change

Some of the clearest expositions of methods for planning and implementing change in 'hard' situations are those found in Open University course materials (1984, 1994, 2000) and the writings of Flood and Jackson (1991) and Paton and McCalman (2000). The methodology for change described here draws on all these sources. To avoid confusion with the Open University's model, the 'systems intervention strategy' (SIS), and Paton and McCalman's 'intervention strategy model' (ISM), the approach described here is referred to simply as the 'hard systems model of change'.

Change in three phases

The HSMC is a method that has been developed for designing and managing change. Its roots lie in methods of analysis and change associated with systems engineering, operational research and project management, that is, where there is an emphasis on means and ends – in other words, on the means with which particular set goals are to be achieved. The HSMC is especially useful when dealing with situations that lie towards the 'hard' end of the hard–soft continuum of change situations. It provides a rigorous and systematic way of determining objectives (or goals) for change; this is followed by the generation of a range of options for action; the last step is testing those options against a set of explicit criteria. The method is also useful where quantitative criteria can be used to test options for change. However, it is also possible to use qualitative criteria – a possibility that is discussed later in the chapter. The process can be thought of as falling into three overlapping phases:

1. the *description* phase (describing and diagnosing the situation, understanding what is involved, setting the objectives for the change);
2. the *options* phase (generating options for change, selecting the most appropriate option, thinking about what might be done);
3. the *implementation* phase (putting feasible plans into practice and monitoring the results).

Within these three phases a number of stages can also be identified. These are shown in Illustration 7.3. What follows describes the stages in more detail.

Illustration 7.3

Stages within the hard systems methodology of change

Phases	Stages	Actions appropriate for each stage
Description	1 Situation summary	• Recognize need for change either to solve a problem or take advantage of an opportunity • Test out others' views on the need for change • Using appropriate diagnostic techniques, confirm the presence of hard complexity and a difficulty rather than a mess
	2 Identify objectives and constraints	• Set up objectives for systems of interest • Identify constraints on the achievement of the objectives
	3 Identify performance measures	• Decide how the achievement of the objectives can be measured
Options	4 Generate options	• Develop ideas for change into clear options for achievement of the objectives • Consider a range of possibilities
	5 Edit options and detail selected options	• Describe the most promising options in some detail • Decide, for each option, what is involved, who is involved and how it will work
	6 Evaluate options against measures	• Evaluate the performance of the chosen options against the performance criteria identified in Stage 3
Implementation	7 Develop implementation strategies	• Select preferred option(s) and plan how to implement
	8 Carry out the planned changes	• Involve all concerned • Allocate responsibilities • Monitor progress

The stages

Illustration 7.3 shows how the stages relate to the phases and provides an indication of likely actions at each stage. An important point to note, however, is that, although Illustration 7.3 presents the phases and stages as a series of sequential steps that follow logically on, one from another, this rarely happens so neatly in reality; nor is it desirable, as Paton and McCalman (2000, p. 84) make clear when they say of their version of this approach: 'Iterations will be required at any point, within or between phases, owing to developing environmental factors.' There will, therefore, be times when there is a need for iteration or 'backtracking', from one stage/phase to earlier stages/phases, as insights generated at later stages reveal the requirement for modifications to previous ones.

Phase 1: Description

Stage 1: Situation summary

The basic idea in Stage 1 is to start by describing the system within which change is going to be made. This is an important stage in the change process and should not be rushed. People who are centrally concerned with the change (those sponsoring it and those who will carry it out) should be consulted. Unless the specification of the problem and description of the situation are done carefully, the subsequent change objectives and process will be flawed.

This stage includes the following:

- Stating the commitment to the analysis and the reason for doing it. For example, statements such as the following might be made:

  A commitment to ensuring the current product range is maintained after the takeover.

  A commitment to developing new markets while maintaining market share for existing services.

  A commitment to reducing the amount of floor space occupied by merchandise not achieving at least a 25 per cent profit margin.

  A commitment to moving to another site or offices.

- Describing, in words and with diagrams, the situation within which changes will be set.

At the end of this stage the scope of the study will be defined, as will the range of problems and issues to be addressed. Try to defer, until Stage 4, thinking about *how* the change(s) will be brought about.

Stage 2: Identification of objectives and constraints

In the context of Stage 2, an objective can be defined as something that is desired; a constraint is something which inhibits or prevents achievement of an

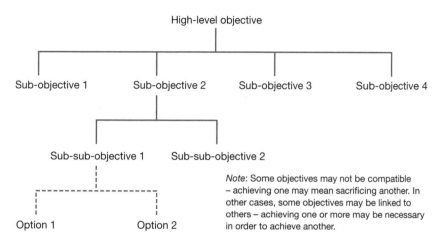

Figure 7.1 The structure of an objectives tree

objective. In reality, objectives are likely to be things over which members of organizations may have some control. Constraints are frequently things in an organization's environment (whether this is internal or external to the organization) over which it has little control. This stage addresses both objectives and constraints. It involves being clear about where the decision makers want to go and which ways might be impassable or perhaps temporarily blocked. This stage involves the following:

- Listing objectives that are consistent with the themes which emerged from the diagnostic stage.
- Arranging the objectives into a hierarchy of objectives – an objectives tree. An example of a generalized objectives tree is shown in Figure 7.1. This shows how the high-level objective comes at the top, with lower-level objectives (sub-objectives) arranged in descending order. Lower-level objectives 'lead to' or help the achievement of higher-level objectives.
- Listing constraints in terms of those that (a) are inviolable and (b) may be modified.

Stage 3: Identification of performance measures

The question to be answered in identifying performance measures is: 'How will I know whether or not I have achieved my objective?' If at all possible, use quantifiable measures, e.g. costs (in monetary terms), savings (in monetary terms), time (years, days, hours), amount of labour, volume etc. This stage includes the following:

- Formulating measures of performance, which can be put against the objectives on the objectives tree.

It is possible that some objectives cannot be quantified. In this case, some form of rating or ranking can be used as a measure of performance. Figure 7.2 is an example of an objectives hierarchy for improving the effectiveness of an organization's

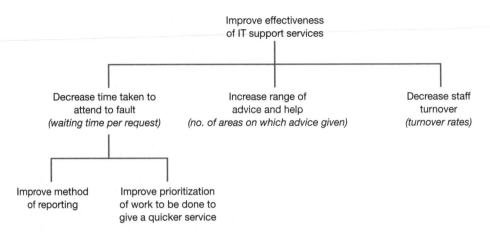

Figure 7.2 An objectives tree for improving the IT support services

information technology support service. The measures of performance for each of the main objectives are in brackets.

Phase 2: Options

Stage 4: Generation of options (routes to objectives)

The setting up of objectives to be achieved is based on the concept of *what* needs to be done to bring about change. By contrast, the generation of options stage is the stage of finding out *how* to achieve the objectives. If the objectives tree is well developed, as Figure 7.1 shows, some of the lower-level objectives may actually be options. There will, however, almost certainly be more. In addition, therefore, to any options that 'creep into' the objectives tree, this stage involves the following:

● Drawing up a list of options. This can be done by making use of any number of creative thinking techniques such as:
  – brainstorming
  – ideas writing
  – questioning others
  – focus groups
  – interviews
  – research
  – meetings
  – organizational comparisons/benchmarking
  – gap analysis

At the end of this stage a set of specific ideas should have been generated which will help the problem or opportunity – in the sense that they will further the achievement of the objective(s), rather than that they will break the constraints, and lead to beneficial changes to the situation described in Stage 1. Figure 7.3 gives a list of options for the sub-sub-objective of 'improve prioritization of

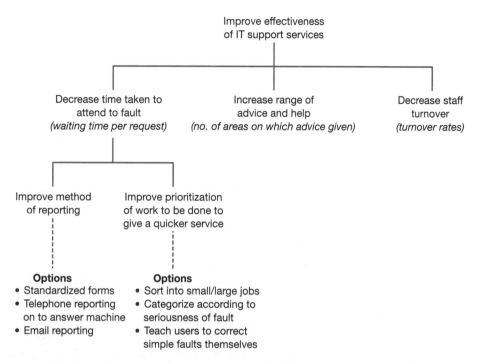

Figure 7.3 An objectives tree for improving the IT support services, with options generated for the two sub-sub-objectives

work to be done to give a quicker service' – which is one of the objectives in an objectives hierarchy for improving the effectiveness of the service given by an organization's IT department in support of those who use computer-based programs to help with their work.

Stage 5: Editing and detailing selected options

At the stage of editing and detailing some options, it may be necessary to sort the options, in terms of those that are likely to be feasible given the particular situation described in Stage 1 and the constraints identified in Stage 2. The selected options should then be described in more detail – or 'modelled' – in terms of what is involved, who is involved and how it will work. It may be that some options cluster together and are better considered as a group. Other options will stand independently and must, therefore, be considered in their own right. There are many ways of testing how an option might work. The following are some possibilities drawn from a comprehensive list produced by the Open University (1994, pp. 35–6).

(a) Physical models (architectural models, wind-tunnel test pieces, etc.).
(b) Mock-ups (make mock-ups of new products – sewing machines, aircraft, clothes dryers, etc.).
(c) Computer simulation models (for complex production systems, financial systems, etc.).

(d) Cashflow models (either manually produced or computer driven).

(e) Experimental production lines, or laboratory-scale plant.

(f) Scale plans and drawings (alternative office layouts, organizational structures, etc.).

(g) Cost/benefit analyses (as models of the likely trade-offs that would take place if a particular option were exercised; can be qualitative as well as quantitative).

(h) Corporate plans or strategies (any one plan or proposal represents a 'model' of how the corporation or organization could develop its activities in the future).

(i) Organization structure plans and proposals (for example, a chart of a new organization structure would show how the formal communication links or reporting channels would work if the structure were adopted).

(j) Organizational culture analyses (methods of describing organizational cultures as the means of identifying effects of different options on the culture of the organization).

Clearly, some of these processes can be time consuming and expensive. However, many options can be described or modelled through the use of diagrams (e.g. of different organizational structures, of input–output processes) or some form of cost-benefit analysis.

It is at this stage of the HSMC that each of the options generated for the objectives in Figure 7.3 would be explored in more detail, using the questions listed earlier about who would be involved, how it would work and what financial and other resources would be required for it to work. Some form of cost-benefit analysis could be used with costs and benefits being those of time as well as money.

Stage 6: Evaluating options against measures

The evaluation stage of the change process is a decision area. It allows choices of options to be made against the criteria identified in Stage 3. Figure 7.4 shows a generalized evaluation matrix that compares one option against another on the basis of the measures set during Stage 3.

Objectives and related measures of performance	Option A	Option A	Option A	Option A
Objective 1, measure 1				
Objective 2, measure 3				
Objective 3, measure 4				

Figure 7.4 An evaluation matrix

Before making your recommendation, you should complete the following:

- Check that the model you have used is an accurate representation of the system.
- Consider whether the model seems to contain any bias or mistaken assumptions.
- Evaluate each option, or combination of options, according to how well it meets the performance measures. Rating the options overall on a scale (say of 1 for very good and 5 for very bad) is a useful guide.

Figure 7.5 is a rough estimate of the desirability of some of the options generated from the objectives in Figure 7.3.

A more detailed examination of each option in Figure 7.5 would show more precisely the impact, in terms of the performance criteria, on each objective listed. For the purposes of this example, however, an estimate has been made. On the basis of these, it is clear from the evaluation matrix in Figure 7.5 that some of these options could be combined. For instance, the best method of reporting should be combined with the best method for prioritizing work to be done. On this basis, option 2 combined with option 3 seem to contribute most to the main objective. However, if an email standard format of reporting were to be used, this would also help speed and accuracy in reporting faults. It could also include space for indicating urgency in terms of lack of access to the particular program affected. The only problem with an email solution is it relies on this function not being the one at fault! If this is the case, written or telephone communication must be resorted to.

Objectives and related measures of performance	Options			
	Telephone reporting on to answer machine	Email reporting	Categorization according to seriousness of fault	Use of written standardized reporting form
Sub-objective Decrease time taken to attend to fault *(waiting time per request)*	Low cut in waiting time	Medium cut in waiting time	High cut in time for serious faults; low cut for simple faults	Low cut in time – delays through need to post
Sub-sub-objective Improve method of reporting *(fault reporting received more quickly and accurately)*	High increase in speed of reporting	High increase in speed and some increase in accuracy of reporting	No effect	High increase in accuracy of reporting
Sub-sub-objective Improve prioritization of work to be done *(serious faults dealt with first)*	Difficult to estimate	Small improvement	Great improvement	Some improvement

Figure 7.5 An evaluation matrix for some options to improve the effectiveness of the IT support services

Phase 3: The implementation phase

Stage 7: Implementation

In problems of a definite 'hard' nature, implementation will rarely be a problem. With problems tending towards 'softness', implementation will be a test of how much people involved in the change have participated in its design.

There are three strategies for implementation:

1 pilot studies leading to eventual change
2 parallel running
3 big bang.

Pilot studies help sort out any problems before more extensive change is instituted, but they can cause delay – a factor that is particularly important in a fast-moving, dynamic situation.

Parallel running applies most frequently to the implementation of new computer systems, but can be applied to other kinds of change. The new system is run, for a time, alongside the old system, until confidence is gained that the new system is reliable and effective.

Big bang implementation maximizes the speed of change, but can generate the greatest resistance. Big bang implementations carry a high risk of failure unless planned very carefully.

Implementation often involves a blend of all three strategies.

Stage 8: Consolidation – 'carry through'

It takes time for new systems to 'bed in'. It is at this stage that there tends to be a decline in concentration on the need to support the change, and nurture both it and the people involved. Yet this is one of the most crucial stages if the change is to be accepted and successful. Even after the implementation process further changes can be forced on the situation at any time if the imbalance between the system and the environment becomes too great. There is no justification for 'sitting back'.

●●●● Using the hard systems model of change

Illustration 7.4 describes concerns about the way large plant and machinery is acquired and maintained for use on the building sites of the Beautiful Buildings Company. What follows is a description of the process Gerry Howcroft went through to identify a number of options for improving this situation to put before the senior managers' meeting. The description takes the form of notes made by Gerry, interspersed with comments on the method he used.

Illustration 7.4

Financial savings on the provision and maintenance of plant for use on building sites

'The next item on the agenda is the issue of the increasing costs of providing and maintaining major items of plant on the UK building sites. At our last meeting we saw an earlier draft of this paper. We must now come to some decision as to which option to follow and how it will be implemented.'

So spoke Gillian Lambeth, the Managing Director of the Beautiful Buildings Company, at one of its regular senior managers' meetings. The next item on the agenda was the increasing costs of purchasing and maintaining large items of plant (such as cranes, diggers and earth-moving equipment) used on the various UK building sites. The item had come to the fore because of the latest rises in the cost of purchasing and maintaining some of these large items of plant, which were necessary components in any building project. What was more, in the case of plant breakdowns, getting the specialist maintenance services to effect speedy repairs was always problematical.

Gerry Howcroft, who was responsible for overseeing management of all the UK sites, had prepared a number of options for change that he believed would reduce these costs and improve the maintenance problems. These had already been discussed in rough form at a previous meeting. He had now gained more information on the costs, etc. of following the different options and had distributed the latest version of these to the managers before the meeting. The meeting now settled down to discuss what to do.

Change at the BB Company

> ### Gerry Howcroft's Note 1   21 May
>
> Need to think back to that course on managing change.
>
> Is this a difficulty or a mess?
>
> Application of criteria discussed in the book they gave us (Senior, 'Organizational Change' – Chapter 2 – Illustrations 2.7 and 2.8) ... situation is: bounded in terms of problem definition, people involved, timescale and resources available.
>
> Plus – situation is like Stacey's conditions of 'close to certainty' rather than conditions of 'far from certainty' (also mentioned in Senior's book – Chapter 2).
>
> Think, therefore, that this is more of a difficulty than a mess.
>
> So – think will have a go at using the HSMC.

Stage 1: Summarizing the BB Company's concerns

As overall sites manager, Gerry was responsible for the acquisition and maintenance of plant and equipment deemed necessary for carrying out the complex activities that take place on any building site. In this role, he had to make sure that large plant such as cranes and diggers were fit to carry out the required work. This entailed his finding the best suppliers in terms of cost and service back-up and ensuring proper maintenance of the plant. Recently, however, the costs of maintaining two large cranes and a digger, which were currently being used on two different sites, had begun to escalate and it seemed as if costs generally for using plant such as this were rising. Gerry wondered whether the equipment had been ill-used or not well maintained or whether it was simply beginning to wear out. As part of the first stage of applying the HSMC he decided to visit the sites in question and talk to the site manager and any others who had views about the provision, use and maintenance of this type of plant. On his return he summarized his findings in another note (see Note 2).

> ### Gerry Howcroft's Note 2   19 May
>
> Visited Karen (site manager) at the Three Towers site. She said cranes such as these should last 'forever' if looked after. Think this far-fetched given the way the guys use them. Didn't seem to be anyone personally responsible for servicing and maintaining them – one of the men got some overtime each week to hose them down – if they broke down and the operator couldn't fix it, the service agent was sent for. On the other hand, Jed (who operated the crane all the time at the Riverside site) said his crane was just so old that, in spite of good maintenance it had 'had its day' – this in spite of Jed's obvious feelings of 'ownership' towards the crane!
>
> Think there are many contributions to rising costs – a couple of diagrams might help – see Note 3.

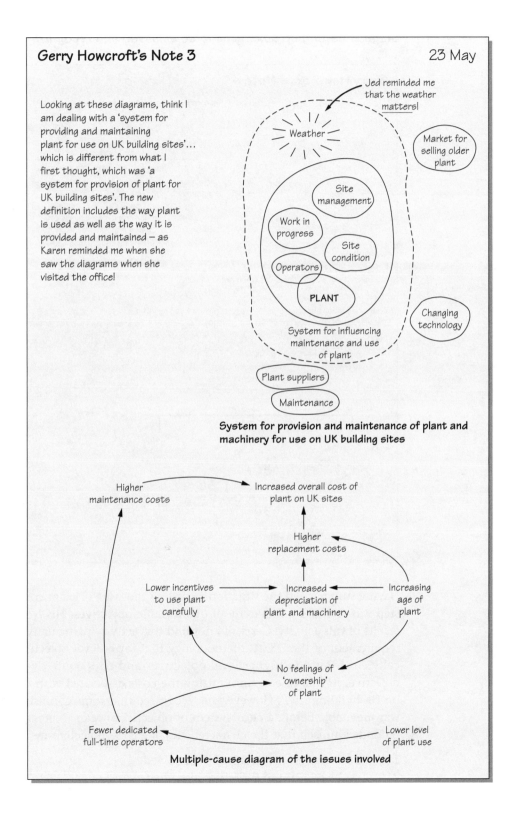

Gerry Howcroft's Note 3   23 May

Looking at these diagrams, think I am dealing with a 'system for providing and maintaining plant for use on UK building sites'... which is different from what I first thought, which was 'a system for provision of plant for UK building sites'. The new definition includes the way plant is used as well as the way it is provided and maintained – as Karen reminded me when she saw the diagrams when she visited the office!

Jed reminded me that the weather matters!

Weather

Market for selling older plant

Site management

Work in progress

Site condition

Operators

PLANT

Changing technology

System for influencing maintenance and use of plant

Plant suppliers

Maintenance

System for provision and maintenance of plant and machinery for use on UK building sites

Higher maintenance costs

Increased overall cost of plant on UK sites

Higher replacement costs

Lower incentives to use plant carefully

Increased depreciation of plant and machinery

Increasing age of plant

No feelings of 'ownership' of plant

Fewer dedicated full-time operators

Lower level of plant use

Multiple-cause diagram of the issues involved

Stage 2: Setting up objectives to be achieved and recognizing constraints

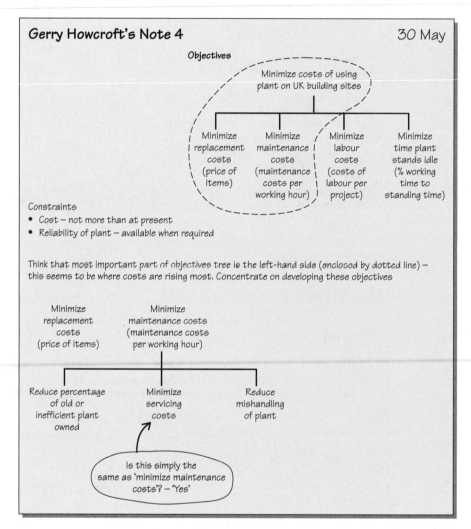

Having summarized the situation regarding the issue of plant costs, Gerry's next step was to build a hierarchy of quantifiable objectives. His Note 4 shows the results of this activity. Gerry did not find this activity particularly easy, given the requirement of the HSMC methodology that lower-level objectives should logically contribute to higher-level objectives and contribute overall to the top objective, in this case of 'minimizing the costs associated with the use of plant on UK building sites'. However, he recognized that some confusion of objectives was inevitable before a clear system of objectives began to emerge. Even so, he reminded himself that the characteristics of a good objective are as follows:

1 It should address the problem to be solved.
2 It must be relevant to the issues identified.

3 It should provide a guide on what needs to be done to make the change from the current situation to the desired situation.

4 It must be something that can feasibly be acted upon.

It can be seen from Gerry's Note 4 that he did not develop all the higher-level objectives into more detailed sets of sub-objectives. Given his knowledge of his management colleagues and their way of thinking, he made a decision to concentrate on the objective 'Minimize maintenance costs' to develop sub-objectives for further consideration, but also to consider the objective 'Minimize replacement costs'. With regard to the objectives 'Minimize labour costs' and 'Minimize time plant stands idle', he kept these 'in reserve' in case of need for further exploration of the issue.

Having developed his objectives hierarchy as far as he could in a direction thought feasible and achievable, the next step for Gerry was to develop further the measures of performance for the objectives identified (encircled) in Note 4.

Stage 3: Identify performance measures

Gerry Howcroft's Note 5	2 June
Objective	**Measure**
1. Minimize replacement costs	Cost of replacing item of plant over a specified period of time averaged out per year (assume cost of new plant for now).
2. Minimize maintenance costs	Cost of maintenance (includes servicing and repair) averaged out on a working hourly basis – i.e. does not include time standing idle.
3. Reduce percentage of old/ inefficient plant	Say no plant to be more than eight years old.
4. Reduce mishandling of plant	Difficult to measure. May have a look at training given – assuming training improves standard of plant handling. Another measure might be cost of maintenance per operator – easier to do when operator full time on plant. For now using a scale of 1 (low) to 5 (high) according to effect on plant might be okay.

Note 5 shows the table Gerry compiled to ensure he had some idea of how he would tell if and when an objective had been achieved. From Gerry's Note 5, it can be seen that some objectives are more difficult to quantify in *practice*, even if, theoretically, measures can be put upon them. In addition, the simple measure of 'price of items' for the objective 'Minimize replacement costs' was not sufficient. The cost needed to be expressed for a certain period of time, which could be related either to (say) a number of years or the period of a particular project. The measure for reducing mishandling of plant could, perhaps, have been formulated in monetary terms but, for the present, Gerry decided to use a scale to judge the likely effects of any option on this objective.

Stage 4: Generate options for change

Gerry Howcroft's Note 6   6 June

Options for change

Objective:	Minimize replacement costs
Options:	Find cheapest supplier
	Stop buying plant
	Increase replacement time
	Get someone else to replace the plant
	Hire not buy
	Lengthen life of plant
	Buy second-hand
Objective:	Reduce percentage of old/inefficient plant owned
Options:	Sell everything over a certain number of years old
	Sell everything not used on a regular basis and hire occasionally as required
	Replace old plant with new plant more frequently
	Don't own any plant
	Borrow plant from others
Objective:	Minimize servicing costs
Options:	Reduce number of services per period of time (say operating hours)
	Obtain cheaper provision of services
	Don't service at all
	Operators do all servicing rather than just basics
	Use other people's plant, which they service
	Contract out servicing to lowest bidder
Objective:	Reduce mishandling of plant
Options:	Train operators in plant handling
	Institute operator gradings (linked to pay) based on handling performance
	Contract out operating to operators employed by specialist agencies

---

Having set up some objectives to be achieved – hopefully, to improve the situation – Gerry's next step was to generate a range of options that would enable the objectives to be achieved. He did this by asking Kerry, one of the site managers, and the accounts manager to help in 'brainstorming' ideas for change. The results of this brainstorm are shown in Note 6.

Stage 5: Edit options and detail selected options

Gerry Howcroft's Note 7   9 June

Themes emerging from options list

- Finding a cheaper source for buying plant (either new or second-hand)
- Don't buy plant – hire or borrow
- Use only plant which is less than eight years old (or whatever period seems appropriate considering rise in repair and maintenance as age increases)
- Increase the period of time before replacement
- Service plant less frequently than at present
- Train operators to do all servicing and maintenance
- Contract out operating to specialist firms
- Offer incentives for better operating practices

Comments

Some of these options contradict each other, so if one is taken up another might be automatically cancelled – e.g. 'Increase time before replacement' conflicts with 'Use plant eight years old or younger'.

Given the importance the MD attaches to safety on sites, I am going to go for options that are in line with her concerns and which meet the constraint of 'reliability of plant'.

For the time being, therefore, I am going to turn an objective into a constraint and work to have plant that is no older than eight years.

Within these constraints, the following seem worthy of further consideration.

1 Continue buying own plant (search for cheapest deals) with maintenance outsourced.
2 Continue buying own plant with maintenance done by own staff.
3 Continue buying plant that is used continuously and hire other for occasional use: maintenance of own plant done by own staff.
4 Continue buying plant that is used continuously and hire otherwise but outsource maintenance of own plant.
5 Hire all plant with maintenance as part of the deal.
6 Offer incentives for good performance in plant handling.

I guess there are more permutations but, depending on how the costings come out on these, we can look at those later.

Gerry considered all these options in the light of the constraint of maintaining a high level of reliability of plant. It seemed that the options might reduce to a few main themes. At this point Gerry decided to try out the options list on a couple of colleagues (one of whom was the company accountant) to see which they thought might be feasible. He also used his own judgement. He eventually arrived at a list that included some options as they stood, amalgamated others, and eliminated yet others (see Note 7).

As Note 7 indicates the options available seemed to range from, at the one extreme, the BB Company's owning and maintaining all plant to, at the other extreme, hiring (or leasing) plant that was maintained entirely by the suppliers. A number of possibilities were clearly possible between these two. The options listed as 1 to 5 are a mix of these. What is evident from the range of possible options is that some quite detailed information is required before one option can be evaluated against another. In addition, option 6 might only be relevant if one of options 1 to 4 were chosen. If option 5 were chosen, incentives to operate the plant well might not be thought relevant if all maintenance costs were included in the hire contract.

Stage 6: Evaluate options against measures

The method of evaluating options against the measures of performance associated with each of the objectives to be reached varies according to the type of options generated. For example, if the options are different production systems,

---

Gerry Howcroft's Note 8   16 June

Objectives and related measures of performance	Options					
	1 Continue buying own plant with maintenance outsourced	**2** Continue buying own plant with maintenance by own staff	**3** Continue buying continuously used plant and hire plant that is used only occasionally: maintenance of own plant done by own staff	**4** Continue buying continuously used plant and hire otherwise: outsource maintenance of own plant	**5** Hire all plant with maintenance as part of the deal	**6** Offer incentives for good plant-handling performance
Minimize replacement costs (£ per year)	High cost	Medium cost	Medium cost	Medium cost	Medium cost	Low cost
Minimize maintenance costs (£ per working hour)	High cost	Medium cost	Medium cost	Medium–high cost	Medium cost	Low cost
Reduce mishandling of plant (scale of 1 to 5 – 1 being least effective, 5 being most effective)	1	3	2	1	1	4

Need to give some information on this to the senior managers' meeting on 23 June – only a week away!
Have got only limited information on options – still, can make some guesses at this point and will take the views of colleagues as to which options to pursue – then must get better information on hiring etc.

not only would these have to be evaluated on cost measures, but they might also involve evaluation through building some simulations of the different systems. These could, of course, be physical models but they could also be computer models. For Gerry's purposes, it was possible to construct an evaluation matrix that allowed comparison of options one against another in terms of the measures of performance for the defined objectives. Note 8 is a record of Gerry's first attempt, on very limited information, at an evaluation matrix.

Gerry took copies of the first draft of the evaluation matrix to the senior managers' meeting. The outcome of the discussion of what he had prepared was that he should get more information on options 3, 4 and 5, which involved different levels of hiring plant instead of purchasing it. What Gerry had to do, in effect, was to go back to Stage 5 to get more detail about these options before preparing a final evaluation matrix. This took some time, what with getting information from the finance department (only to discover that it was not kept in a 'user-friendly' form!) and from companies that hired out plant and equipment. Eventually, however, having gathered as much information as he could, he prepared a final evaluation matrix for discussion at the meeting referred to in Illustration 7.4.

The outcome of that discussion is recorded in Gerry's Note 9.

Gerry Howcroft's Note 9   5 August

What a long discussion, which went round and round in circles – difficult to decide between one option and another – the evaluation matrix was very helpful but then decisions are not always perfectly logical!

Eventually, decided on the hiring option with maintenance all-in – however we could not change overnight to this from where we are at present – just purchased a new digger on the Blackton site.

Will need to do a thorough survey of the state of plant on all the sites to determine when to make the changeover to hiring.

Interesting that the meeting decided to retain our own operators for now (even though could get an agency to supply these) – so will start talks with Personnel as to how we might give extra training and/or offer incentives to improve operator performance – after all, the maintenance costs part of the hiring contract is dependent on the amount of maintenance needed – large repairs will incur extra cost.

Seems an implementation strategy is required!

Stage 7: Develop implementation strategy

Gerry realized that the 'big bang' strategy for implementing change was not viable for his situation. Some of the plant had only recently been purchased, while other items were some years old. Overall, plant on the various sites was in different states of repair. Gerry therefore decided to go for the 'parallel running' implementation strategy where older and/or poorly maintained plant was replaced first. This would also offer the opportunity of monitoring the costs of hiring against owning *in reality* as against the theoretical case that the options had presented. If, after all, the savings proved negligible or negative, another evaluation of options could be done.

One good thing about retaining the company's own operators was that there were likely to be few problems from the workforce on the changeover. What might happen, however, was the occasional hiring of plant plus operator when it was required for a limited, short period. This would give a chance to see how such hirings were received generally.

Stage 8: Carrying out the planned changes

For Gerry and the other senior managers the changes, when implemented, will need monitoring. Changing from purchasing plant to hiring it may not mean much change in the way plant is operated on the building sites. However, the changes in the way maintenance and repairs are done will require operators and site managers to learn a new system of reporting and getting these done.

One of the benefits of going through the processes involved in applying the HSMC methodology was that Gerry realized how little monitoring of the costs of plant usage had been done up to the change. When trying to obtain the costs of the different ways of providing and maintaining plant, he became very much aware of the diffuse nature of much of the information he wanted. From now on, he was going to make sure that the finance department arranged its systems so that monitoring of large expenditure such as this could be monitored. This would, of course, mean yet more change, but in a different part of the organization.

Further uses for the hard systems model of change

The HSMC has been posed as a methodology for change that is most appropriately used in situations of hard complexity, or what have been termed difficulties. The case study involving Gerry Howcroft and the BB Company illustrates this use. In Gerry Howcroft's case, there is reason to believe that resistance to the planned changes will not be high. However, this is not always the case, as the discussion in Chapter 6 showed. Whenever and wherever possible, therefore, those people who are likely to be affected by the change should be consulted as early as possible. In addition, support from senior management is essential for any but the most localized, operational types of change.

It was clear that, in Gerry's case, the information he needed to construct an informative evaluation matrix was not easily obtainable – particularly with regard to that which he required from his own organization. This stage of the methodology can, therefore, be quite long if a realistic evaluation of options is to be done. By the same token, it is possible to go through the stages of the methodology quite quickly to address key factors associated with the change situation. A small group of people could quickly drive a way through this methodology to suggest at least a tentative solution in a situation requiring change. In addition, as Paton and McCalman (2000, pp. 94–5) point out:

> A Q & D (quick and dirty) analysis can be a useful starting point for the change agents tackling a more complex problem. It will indicate key factors and potential barriers to change, it will highlight the principal players and give an indication of resource requirements. Such an analysis will at an early stage set the scene for things to come and provide the change agents with a valuable insight into the complexities of the transition process.

An example of using the HSMC in this 'quick and dirty' way, that is as a starting point to an analysis of more messy situations, is given in Illustration 7.5 and Figures 7.6 and 7.7 (overleaf). These demonstrate the early stages in considering how to expand the provision and delivery of open and resource-based learning in the further education colleges run by the local education authority of 'Shire County'.

Illustration 7.5

Change in the further education colleges of Shire County

This state of affairs brought forth the following commitment statement:

> In an environment of decreasing numbers of 16–19 year olds and limited numbers of adults
> participating in further education, the aim for the future is to make it possible for more
> people to participate in education and training through the expansion of open and resource-
> based learning (O&RBL) both as an integral part of mainstream provision as well as an
> alternative but equally credible way of facilitating and accrediting learning.

A causal-loop diagram (see Figure 7.6) was constructed to provide further information
about the forces operating for and against the desire to expand O&RBL. From this a range
of objectives were formulated, together with a list of possible measures of performance.

An initial attempt at an objectives hierarchy is shown in Figure 7.7.

Possible measures of performance (not particularly attached to specific objectives):

- Establish O&RBL centres by ? (date).
- Extend availability of provision to 48 weeks per year by ? (date).
- Achieve x % of open and resource-based learners by ? (date).
- ? (number) of companies using O&RBL by ? (date).
- ? (number) of staff trained in the delivery of O&RBL by ? (date).
- ? (number) of students gaining qualifications through O&RBL by ? (date).
- Complete changeover to providing mathematics instruction in modules by ? (date).
- ? % increase in use of O&RBL in all mainstream provision by ? (date).

Existing state of affairs

- Falling numbers of 16–19 year olds coming into further education (FE)
- Only small percentage of adults participating in FE
- Current FE provision not always accessible to needs of adults in terms of content, qualifications and mode of delivery

GAP

Desired state of affairs

- Increase proportion of 16–19 year olds in FE
- Significant increase in number of adults in FE
- Improve accessibility for all learners, but for adults in particular, i.e. greater choice of content, qualifications and mode of delivery relevant to educational and training needs

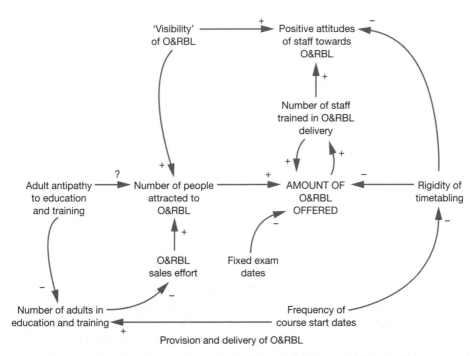

Note: The + signs denote a causal relationship in the same direction. The – signs denote a causal relationship in opposite directions

Figure 7.6 Causal-loop diagram of the situation facing Shire County further education services

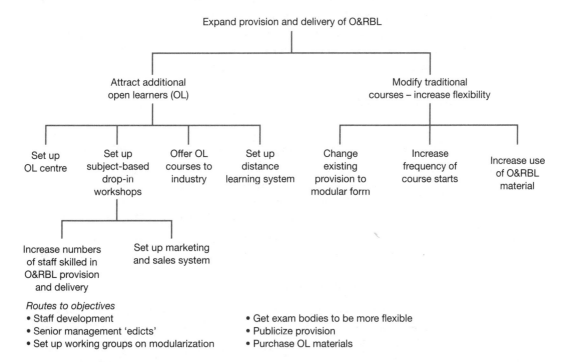

Figure 7.7 Hierarchy of objectives for expanding O&RBL provision in Shire County

● ● ● ● Comment and conclusions

The hard systems model for change provides a practical approach to change that has been designed to be applied to situations – such as the Beautiful Buildings Company example – of low to medium complexity (difficulties). It is particularly useful when an area of the organization may need to be changed but may not infringe on other areas and when choices based on rational decision making can be made (see March's 1984 theories of choice and decision making).

The HSMC can also be effective to begin to diagnose a change situation (see Illustration 7.5) before categorizing it into more simple or more complex change. For instance, using the HSMC in the case of Shire County was useful for setting out the commitment to change, carrying out (with the help of diagrams) a situational analysis of the forces for and against the change and formulating some objectives and measures of performance in preparation for planning and implementing the change. What this methodology was less good at doing was identifying the political and moral issues surrounding the implementation of radical change of this kind. In addition, current organizational, professional and institutional cultures were clearly going to work to make changes of this kind difficult to achieve.

This was a case where the changes desired were going to take some time to come to fruition and these would involve changes not only to the buildings and teaching areas (i.e. physical changes) but also in people's attitudes and behaviours – changes that would include both staff and students (present and potential students). The changes being proposed here were more in line with what has been described as 'organizational development', that is, change that is ongoing, which involves most parts of the organization and most of its members and that will not succeed without the involvement of all concerned at all stages in the change process. The next chapter describes in more detail a change process more relevant to situations of soft complexity – in other terms, situations known as messes.

Discussion questions and assignments

1 Can you think of a time at work when a change, that would be considered 'hard' or 'difficult' was not implemented as effectively as planned? If you were to apply the HSMC approach could you identify where things went wrong?

2 Can you think of change situations within your organization that are more difficult than messy, where the HSMC would be both appropriate and effective? What factors would you need to consider in order to ensure effective planning, decision making, implementation and review?

3 Through issues raised in this chapter, under what circumstances might the HSMC not be appropriate, and why? Could some of these issues be overcome so as to be able to use this phased approach?

Indicative resources

March, J.G. (1984) 'Theories of choice and making decisions', in Paton, R., Brown, R., Spear, R., Chapman, J., Floyd, M. and Hamwee, J. (eds) *Organisations: Cases, Issues, Concept*s: London, Harper & Row. This text offers a critique of models for change which assumes that the process of choice is a rational one, based on having complete, or almost complete, knowledge of the alternatives which are generated. They argue that choices frequently involve moral as well as cognitive issues and that decisions about action, once made, are then overtaken by events which make implementation difficult if not impossible.

Open University (2000) *Managing Complexity: A Systems Approach*, Course T306, Milton Keynes: Open University. http://www3.open.ac.uk/courses/bin/p12.dll?C01T306. This is an Open University course that draws on and extends a range of approaches to managing complexity which have been developed by internationally recognized systems practitioners. They include the soft systems method, the viable systems model and the hard systems method. Of particular relevance to the material in this chapter is Block 2, which discusses the hard systems approach.

Paton, R. A. and McCalman, J. (2000) *Change Management: A Guide to Effective Implementation* (2nd edn), Sage: London. This text does what it says in the title. It is useful in reinforcing the approach to change discussed in this chapter (see Chapter 4) and also discusses two more change approaches – 'Total project management' and 'The organization development model' (the latter of which is the subject of the next chapter). Particularly, helpful is Chapter 3, 'Mapping change', which 'teaches' how to use diagrams effectively in diagnosing and implementing change.

Useful websites

www.open.ac.uk This is the Open University website. There are links from here to information about all the courses it offers.

http://www.ukss.org.uk/ The UK Systems Society website. The UK Systems Society (UKSS) is a non-profit-making, professional society registered as an educational charity. The Society is committed to the development and promotion of 'systems' philosophy, theory, models, concepts and methodologies for improving decision making and problem solving for the benefit of organizations and the wider society. The UKSS hosts a major conference every year with keynote speakers and the opportunity to offer or hear papers on all aspects of systems thinking, processes and applications.

To click straight to these links and for other resources go to
www.pearsoned.co.uk/senior

 References

Flood, R. L. and Jackson, M. C. (1991) *Creative Problem Solving: Total Systems Intervention*, Chichester: Wiley.

Mayon-White, B. (1993) 'Problem-solving in small groups: team members as agents of change', in Mabey, C. and Mayon-White, B. (eds) *Managing Change* (2nd edn), London: PCP.

Open University (1984) Block III, 'The hard systems approach', Course T301, *Complexity, Management and Change: Applying a Systems Approach*, Milton Keynes: Open University Press.

Open University (1994) 'Managing the change process', Course B751, *Managing Development and Change*, Milton Keynes: Open University Press.

Open University (2000) *Managing Complexity: A Systems Approach*, Milton Keynes: Open University Press.

March, J.G. (1984) 'Theories of choice and making decisions', in Paton, R., Brown, R., Spear, R., Chapman, J., Floyd, M. , and Hamwee, J. (eds) *Organisations: Cases, Issues, Concepts*: London: Harper & Row.

Paton, R. A. and McCalman, J. (2000) *Change Management: A Guide to Effective Implementation* (2nd edn), London: Sage.

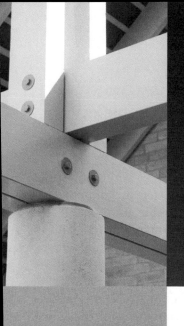

Chapter 8

Soft systems models for change

Through a revision of the concept of soft complexity, this chapter begins by challenging the notion of rationality as applied to organizational change. This is followed by a short description of Lewin's three-phase model of change as a prelude to a more detailed description and discussion of organizational development as an approach to change. Some limitations of organizational development (OD) as a change philosophy and as a change approach are discussed.

Learning objectives

By the end of this chapter, you will be able to:

- recognize that some change situations (problems/opportunities), by nature of their complexity and particular characteristics, require soft rather than hard systems approaches to change;

- consider the philosophy, value orientation and theoretical underpinnings of organization development as a generalized example of soft systems models for change;

- outline and describe the processes and practices that comprise most OD approaches to designing and implementing organizational change;

- critically review the limitations of OD approaches to managing change.

●●●● **Managing change in situations of soft complexity**

The previous chapter ended with an example of the need for change for which the HSMC had limited applicability. This was because the situation that gave rise to the requirement to expand open and resource-based learning in further education colleges in Shire County was characterized by elements of both hard and soft complexity. As Chapter 7 highlighted, it was possible, using the HSMC, to build an objectives hierarchy with measurable performance criteria and to generate some options for bringing about the necessary changes. However, while this was fine in theory, other factors – the organizational culture, entrenched power bases and established leadership styles, as well as the simultaneous reorganization of the county education service that was driving the change – combined to make the process of change much more complex, diffuse and confused than it appeared at first sight. In summary, what faced those charged with bringing about the changes was much more of a mess than a difficulty, implying that a different approach to planning and implementing change was required.

In a chapter aptly named 'The art and science of mess management' Ackoff (1993) identifies three different 'kinds of things' that can be done about problems. He says (p. 47): 'They can be *resolved, solved or dissolved.*'

According to Ackoff, 'to resolve a problem is to select a course of action that yields an outcome that is good enough, that *satisfices* (satisfies and suffices)'. This is an approach that relies on common sense, based on previous experience as to what might work or not and, to some extent, on trial and error. People who use this approach (and Ackoff says most managers are problem resolvers) do not pretend to be objective in their decision making. They use little specially collected data, either of a quantitative or qualitative nature, justifying their conclusions by citing lack of time or lack of information or too complex a situation for anything other than minimizing risk and maximizing the likelihood of survival. Ackoff calls this the 'clinical' approach to dealing with messes, a metaphor that emphasizes different people preoccupied with different aspects of the problem situation, but coming together to reach some consensus on how to proceed with resolving the problem. However, while this approach is likely to keep most people satisfied and 'on board' with the change, a major criticism is that, because of its commitment solely to qualitative-type thinking based on past experience and hunch, it lacks analytical rigour in its formulation of objectives and the means of evaluating their attainment. Therefore it is never quite clear how far the objectives of the change have been met.

This criticism can certainly not be levelled at the 'solvers' of problems. By contrast with resolvers of problems, rather than using simple common sense and what might have been successful in the past, solvers of problems use approaches to problems that are much more heavily reliant on research-based scientific methods, techniques and tools. This means they eschew qualitative models in favour of quantitative models in their aspirations to be completely objective. Ackoff calls this the 'research' approach to mess management. It is much more likely to be used by management scientists and technologically oriented managers. This approach is akin to hard systems models of change in its emphasis on quantitative methods of analysis, objective setting and generation of options for change as demonstrated in the description of the HSMC in the previous chapter. However, while addressing the lack of 'hard' data in the clinical approach to mess management, the research approach is limited in that its techniques are more applicable to mechanistic systems (which lend themselves to performance definition and measurement) than to purposeful human behaviour (which includes many unmeasurable elements). In addition, given that a mess is not just one problem but a complex of problems interacting one with another, decomposing the mess to deal with one problem at a time (as this approach would suggest) loses the essential properties of the larger more complex whole. This is summarized well by Ackoff when he says (p. 51):

> Therefore, when a research-orientated planner decomposes a mess by analysis, he loses its essential properties. ... As a consequence, what he perceives as the hard facts of the mess are really soft fictions of his imagination, abstractions only loosely related to reality.

From this it seems that both resolvers, with their clinical approaches to bringing about change, and solvers of problems, with their research approaches to change, are limited in their capacity to plan and implement change in unbounded soft situations characterized as messes. Consequently Ackoff suggests a third approach, based on the concept of *dissolving* problems. Of this approach to problem solving he says (p. 48):

> To *dissolve* a problem is to change the nature, and/or the environment, of the entity in which it is embedded so as to remove the problem. Problem dissolvers *idealize* rather than satisfice or optimize because their objective is to change the system involved or its environment in such a way as to bring it closer to an ultimately desired state, one in which the problem cannot or does not arise.

He calls this approach the 'design' approach in that problem dissolvers, in addition to using the methods and techniques of problem resolvers and problem solvers, seek to redesign the characteristics of the larger system containing the problem (for instance changing the organizational culture, structure, systems and/or processes). Thus they look for dissolution of the problem in the wider containing system rather than looking for solutions in the contained parts. Ackoff (p. 48) maintains that only a minority of managers use this approach and they are those 'whose principal organizational objective is *development* rather than growth or survival, and who know the difference'. Of the concept of development he says (pp. 48–9):

> To develop is to increase and desire to improve one's quality of life and that of others. Development and growth are not the same and are not even necessarily related.

As an example of this he refers to the fact that a heap of rubbish can grow without developing and a person can develop without growing.

As the situation for change unfolded in the further education system in Shire County it became evident that this was not a problem to be resolved or solved, but a complex set of problems that was likely to require the wider system containing it to be redesigned, if progress was to be made towards achieving the stated objectives. These objectives themselves were, incidentally, somewhat unclear and by no means shared by all.

It is not usual to find reference to 'dissolving' problems in the literature on change. Yet most of the change models associated with 'soft' situations and systems (i.e. those characterized by soft complexity) imply a need for redesigning systems at many levels of the organization. These include issues associated with individuals and the groupings they form, as well as with organizational strategy, structure and processes. This means not only an emphasis on the *content* and *control* of change (as the hard systems models of change dictate), but also an emphasis on the *process* by which change comes about, or as Buchanan and Boddy (1992, p. 27) maintain, a need for 'backstaging' as well as 'public performance'. In other words, there is a need to be concerned with what Buchanan and Boddy (p. 27) call 'the exercise of "power skills", with "intervening in political and cultural systems", with influencing negotiating and selling, and with "managing meaning".'

The consequences of this are that designing change in messy situations must also include attention to issues such as problem ownership, the role of communication and the participation and commitment of the people involved in the change process itself. It also means, as evidenced in the following section, challenging the notion that planning and implementing change can be wholly rational, a notion that the majority of hard systems models of change assume.

The challenge to rationality

For some time the literature on corporate strategy and strategic change (see, for instance, Johnson, 1990; Kirkbride, Durcan and Obeng, 1994; Carnall, 2003; Stacey, 2003) has put forward arguments challenging the idea that people make decisions and choices according to some rational model of decision making. For example, Johnson (1993) argues strongly that rational models of change, with their associated scientific management techniques, overlook the significance of the cultural, political and cognitive dimensions of organizational life. The discussion, in Chapter 4, of Johnson *et al.* (2005) of the cultural web is a strong indictment of the contention that managers and implementers of change always (or even frequently) act according to some abstract formulation of what is rational in any particular situation.

This is not to say, however, that people do not act rationally. It is to say (Carnall 2003, p. 99) that they act according to their own view of what is rational for them. Carnall uses the example of 'clinical' rationality in healthcare, where rationality is apparent in the decisions of doctors that govern the pattern of care provided and the use of resources. This, however, does not mean that all doctors have the same views, beliefs or attitudes or that they would argue for the same vision of healthcare. This will include their particular perspective of the causes, consequences and need for change, moulded by their values, culture, attitudes and political position within the organization. Any case for change will not, therefore, be accepted according to some (supposedly) objective rational analysis. Change, in this scenario, will only be possible and effective if it is accompanied by processes that address, in particular, the feelings, needs and aspirations of individuals, the group processes that bind them together and the structures and systems that are forces for stability rather than change. Added to these are the cultural, political and symbolic processes that act to maintain the current organizational paradigm, or 'the way things are done around here'.

Given all this, it appears that hard systems models of change, although necessary in some defined and agreed situations, are not sufficient to explain organizational messes and are extremely limited in providing a model for planning and implementing change in these situations. For instance, hard systems approaches to change require the setting of quantifiable objectives against which criteria for their attainment can be set. This assumes that there is little argument about *what* the change objectives are. These approaches are useful in situations where change is sought to the *means* whereby things are done and where a problem can be *solved* in the terms discussed by Ackoff in the previous section. By contrast, as the discussion in Chapter 2 showed, one of the distinguishing features of organizational messes is that there is no agreement on what constitutes the problem, let alone what changes are required. Consequently it is more likely that those involved in these types of situations are looking to challenge not just the *means* of doing things, but also the *purposes* and *why* things are done as they are *at all*. In other words, they are searching for ways to *dissolve* rather than just *solve* problems, in the terms discussed by Ackoff. In summary, therefore, what this latest discussion leads to is an argument for an approach to change that can cope more effectively with situations of soft complexity – in other words some type of soft systems model for change.

There is neither the space nor the necessity to illustrate here all the different variants of models for bringing about change in soft, messy situations. What follows, therefore, is a generalized description of 'organizational development' (more commonly known as the OD approach) – an umbrella term for a set of values and assumptions about organizations and the people within them that, together with a range of concepts and techniques, are thought useful for bringing about long-term, organization-wide change; that is, change which is more likely to dissolve problems than resolve or solve them.

●●●● Organizational development – philosophy and underlying assumptions

According to French and Bell (1999, pp. 25–6), in their book *Organization Development: Behavioral Science Interventions for Organizational Improvement*, organization development is:

> a long term effort, led and supported by top management, to improve an organization's visioning, empowerment, learning and problem-solving processes, through an ongoing, collaborative management of organization culture – with special emphasis on the culture of intact work teams and other team configurations – using the consultant–facilitator role and the theory and technology of applied behavioral science, including action research.

Cummings and Worley (2005, p. 1), in their book *Organization Development and Change*, say organization development is:

> A process that applies behavioural science knowledge and practices to help organizations build the capacity to change and achieve greater effectiveness, including increased financial performance and improved quality of work life. OD differs from other planned change efforts, such as technological innovation or new product development, because the focus is on building the organization's ability to assess its current functioning and to achieve its goals. Moreover, OD is oriented to improving the total system – the organization and its parts in the context of the larger environment that affects them.

More succinctly, they offer the following (Cummings and Worley, 2005, p. 1):

> Organizational development is a systematic application and transfer of behavioural science knowledge to the planned development, improvement, and reinforcement of the strategies, structures and processes that lead to organizational effectiveness.

An examination of these definitions confirms some distinguishing characteristics of the OD approach to change:

1 It emphasizes goals and processes but with a particular emphasis on processes – the notion of organizational learning (Senge, 1990; Pedler, Boydell and Burgoyne, 1991; Argyris and Schon, 1996) as a means of improving an organization's capacity to change is implicit in OD approaches.
2 It deals with change over the medium to long term, that is, change that needs to be sustained over a significant period of time.
3 It involves the organization as a whole as well as its parts.
4 It is participative, drawing on the theory and practices of the behavioural sciences.
5 It has top management support and involvement.
6 It involves a facilitator who takes on the role of a change agent (Buchanan and Boddy, 1992 and French and Bell, 1999).
7 It concentrates on planned change but as a process that can adapt to a changing situation rather than as a rigid blueprint of how change should be done.

In addition, French and Bell (1999, p. 29) give the following ten OD principles:

1 OD focuses on culture and processes.
2 OD encourages collaboration between organization leaders and members in managing culture and processes.
3 Teams of all kinds are particularly important for accomplishing tasks and are targets for OD activities.
4 OD focuses on the human and social side of the organization and in so doing also intervenes in the technological and structural sides.
5 Participation and involvement in problem solving and decision making by all levels of the organization are hallmarks of OD.
6 OD focuses on total system change and views organizations as complex social systems.
7 OD practitioners are facilitators, collaborators, and co-learners with the client system.
8 An overarching goal is to make the client system able to solve its problems on its own by teaching the skills and knowledge of continuous learning through self-analytical methods. OD views organization improvement as an ongoing process in the context of a constantly changing environment.
9 OD relies on an action research model with extensive participation by client system members.
10 OD takes a developmental view that seeks the betterment of both individuals and the organization. Attempting to create 'win–win' solutions is standard practice in OD programmes.

The discussion that follows develops these definitions and underlying philosophy and assumptions.

The significance of people in organizations

The OD approach to change is, above all, an approach that cares about people and which believes that people at all levels throughout an organiszation are, individually and collectively, both the drivers and the engines of change. Consequently one underlying assumption is that people are most productive when they have a high quality of working life. In addition there is an assumption that, in many cases (and perhaps the majority), workers are under-utilized and are capable, if given the opportunity, of taking on more responsibility for the work they do and of contributing further to the achievement of organizational goals.

Paton and McCalman (2000, p. 121) offer three 'fundamental' concepts with respect to the management of people and gaining their commitment to their work and organization:

1 Organizations are about people.
2 Management assumptions about people often lead to ineffective design of organizations and this hinders performance.
3 People are the most important asset and their commitment goes a long way in determining effective organization design and development.

These assumptions are not new. Even so, many managers continue to believe in Taylorism and scientific management – which in Matsushita's (1988) words means: 'executives on one side and workers on the other, on one side men [sic] who think and on the other men [sic] who can only work'. Yet Matsushita, drawing on his experience as head of the Sony organization, went on to say:

> We are beyond the Taylor model; business, we know, is so complex and difficult, the survival of firms so hazardous in an environment increasingly so unpredictable, competitive and fraught with danger, that their continued existence depends on the day-to-day mobilization of every ounce of intelligence.

The OD approach to change is entirely in line with these sentiments. What is more, these sentiments extend to a number of assumptions regarding people in groups. The first of these is that people are in general *social* beings. They will, therefore, form groups – whether these are legitimized by the organization in terms of formal work teams or whether they are the more 'informal' groupings that form part of every organization's functioning. French and Bell (1999, p. 68) reinforce this assumption by saying that: 'One of the most psychologically relevant reference groups for most people is the work group, including peers and boss.' Consequently the work group becomes increasingly important in any attempt at change. Yet in many cases work groups do not utilize effectively resources for collaboration. For instance, the formal leader of any group cannot perform all the leadership functions at all times and in all situations. Thus, for a group to become effective, all group members must share in problem solving and in working to satisfy *both* task and group members' needs. If work groups are managed in such a way as to engender a climate of mistrust and competition between participants, then any change will be seen as a threat rather than an opportunity and all the negative aspects of group functioning will come to the fore to work against the change. OD approaches to change assume, therefore, that work groups and teams are an essential element in the process of designing and implementing change. However, as individuals interact to form groups and other collective working relationships, so do groups interact and overlap to form larger organizational systems that, in their turn, influence an organization's capacity to learn and change.

The significance of organizations as systems

One of the characteristics of OD approaches to change mentioned earlier in the chapter is that it involves the organization as a whole as well as its parts – a characteristic exemplified by Pugh (1993, p. 109) when he refers to organizations as 'coalitions of interest groups in tension'. Chapter 1 introduced the idea that organizations are systems of interconnected and interrelated sub-systems and components that include more formal organizational structures and processes, as well as the more informal aspects of organizational life such as culture, politics and styles of leadership which are closely bound up with the values and attitudes people bring to their workplaces.

This idea is one of the most important assumptions of OD as a process of facilitating change. This is because, first, it reinforces the systemic nature of organizational life and the fact that changes in one part of the organization will inevitably impact on operations in another part. For instance, the multiple-cause diagrams used in previous chapters to depict a number of different change situations are good illustrations of the *interconnectedness* of causes and consequences of complex messy situations.

Second, and related to this, it challenges the assumption that a single important cause of change with clear effects can be found, as well as the assumption that any cause and its effects are necessarily closely related in space and time. This is most clearly stated by Carnall (2003, p. 104) when he says:

> [The] causes of a problem may be complex, may actually lie in some remote part of the system, or may lie in the distant past. What appears to be cause and effect may actually be 'coincidental' symptoms.

Third, any organization is a balance of forces built up and refined over a period of time. Consequently, proposed change of any significance will inevitably change this balance and will, therefore, almost certainly encounter resistance, particularly of the type that was categorized as 'organizational' resistance to change mentioned in Chapter 6 (see Illustration 6.9). Consequently, OD approaches assume that no single person or group can act in isolation from any other. For instance, if win–lose strategies are common to the behaviour of management, this way of dealing with conflict will permeate other workers' attitudes to settling disputes and disagreements. By way of contrast, if managers openly discuss problems and take views on how these might be addressed, then this culture of trust and cooperation will reach into other parts of the organization's functioning – hence the belief that OD activities need to be led by top management if they are to succeed in bringing about successful change.

Fourth, because organization development as a concept is assumed to operate throughout an organization, the OD process is most definitely not a 'quick fix' to the latest management problem. This is articulated by French and Bell (1999, p. 75), who say that change 'takes time and patience, and the key movers in an OD effort need to have a relatively long-term perspective'.

Finally, OD approaches to change are essentially processes of facilitating *planned* change. Consequently, an effective manager of change:

> *anticipates* the need for change as opposed to reacting after the event to the emergency; *diagnoses* the nature of the change that is required and carefully considers a number of alternatives that might improve organizational functioning, as opposed to taking the fastest way to escape the problem; and *manages* the change process over a period of time so that it is effective and accepted as opposed to lurching from crisis to crisis.   (Pugh, 1993, p. 109)

The significance of organizations as learning organizations

The ideas in the previous two sections (the significance of people in organizations and the significance of organizations as systems) come together in the assumptions that, for organizations operating in increasingly complex and turbulent environments, the only way to survive and prosper is to be a *learning organization*.

The concept of a learning organization and the associated concept of *organizational learning* were discussed briefly in Chapter 4 in the context of the broader discussion of organizational cultures. The concept of a learning organization is built upon the proposition that there is more than one type of learning. In support of this proposition are writers such as Argyris (1964, 1992) and Argyris and Schon (1996) who distinguish between *single-loop* and *double-loop* learning or, as Senge (1990) terms them, *adaptive* and *generative* learning. The concepts of single- and double-loop learning can be explained in terms of systems for change that are either goal oriented or process oriented (Open University, 1985). In brief, a goal-oriented approach to change is directed towards changing the means by which goals are achieved. By contrast, those who subscribe to a process-oriented approach to change, while still concerned with goals, focus more on fostering a change process that enables the goals to be challenged. In other words, goal-oriented approaches are concerned with doing things better, while process-oriented approaches are concerned with doing the right things.

With a goal-oriented approach, the problem or issue is likely to be seen as an interesting, though possibly substantial *difficulty*; that is it is perceived primarily as a technical and financial matter with a specific time horizon and hence fairly well bounded. The main focus is on increased efficiency of goal achievement. Management of this type of change is frequently done through a project team led by more senior managers concerned primarily with cost-benefit aspects (goals and constraints). A goal-oriented approach is analogous to thermostatically controlling the temperature of a heating system. The temperature is predetermined and the thermostat merely alters the means through which the temperature is maintained. In essence, what is not questioned is the initial setting of the goal. It is not difficult to see that goal-oriented approaches to problems, issues and change are basically congruent with hard systems models of change. Once the objective is identified, then the issue that remains is to establish the most efficient means of achieving it – hence the function of objectives trees as described in the previous chapter.

By contrast, within a process-oriented approach the problem is likely to be seen as distinctly *messy*. The changes might have long-term and, as yet, unforeseen ramifications, which make the formulation of goals and constraints problematic. The problem is much more concerned with changing the behaviour of people and the structures and cultures within which they work. A process-oriented approach starts by identifying who must be involved in the process, what sort of issues should be addressed and how all this can be facilitated. The phases of the project are by no means as clearly defined as in a goal-oriented approach. It may take some time before the problem itself is agreed, which will most likely challenge the goal itself. In these situations single-loop learning is necessary as a means of monitoring the performance of organizational systems and subsystems in relation to the objectives set for them. However, single-loop or adaptive learning, which depends mainly on individualistic learning, is not sufficient in situations that require creative thinking to develop new visions and ways of doing things.

Elkjaar (1999, pp. 86–7), writing in a book edited by Easterby-Smith, *et al.*, entitled *Organizational Learning and the Learning Organization*, speaks of 'social learning' and that it is necessary to participate and be engaged in organizational projects. In a good exposition and critique of the learning organization, Paton and McCalman (2000, p. 218) summarize the views of double-loop or generative learning as expressed by the main writers on learning organizations/organizational learning as follows:

> They emphasize a collaborative, participative approach centred on team processes. They demonstrate a commitment to the creation of a shared vision of the future direction of the company and the necessary steps, structural and behavioural, to achieve that vision. They stress a proactive approach to learning, creating new experiences, continuous experimentation and risk-taking. Finally, they each emphasize the role of leaders to facilitate the change process and to foster a commitment to learning.

This quotation indicates that process-oriented/double-loop/generative learning involves issues associated with organizational structures, cultures and styles of leadership in terms of the capacity of these aspects of organizational life to support and facilitate this type of learning. It certainly draws attention to many of the issues discussed in Part Two, the importance of people and the concepts associated with organizations as collections of subsystems interacting and reflecting the organizational system as a whole – concepts that are wholly in line with the organizational development approach to change.

Figure 8.1, overleaf, summarizes the philosophy and underlying assumptions of OD as a process for facilitating organizational change. The remainder of this chapter attempts to spell out in more detail the nature of the OD process itself.

● ● ● ● The OD process

OD is at heart a process of facilitation of organizational change and renewal. It operates at all levels of the organization – individual, group and organizational. It is a relatively long-term process for initiating and implementing planned change. It takes into account the messy nature of many organizational problems, which involve unclear goals and differing perspectives on what constitutes the problems, let alone how to solve them. It recognizes organizations as social entities where political as well as intellectual responses to change can be

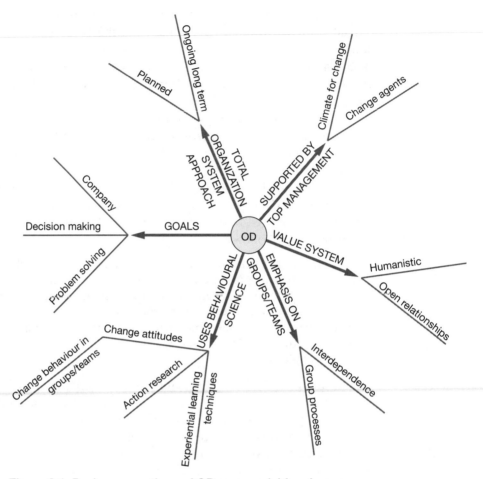

Figure 8.1 Basic assumptions of OD as a model for change

expected. It agrees with Benjamin and Mabey's (1993, p. 181) statement that: 'While the primary stimulus for change in organizations remains those forces in the external environment, the primary motivator for *how* change is accomplished resides with the people in the organization.'

On the basis of these assumptions, organization development as a process for instigating and implementing change has two important characteristics. The first is that it is a process of change which has a framework of recognizable phases that take the organization from its current state to a new more desired future state. Second, within and across these steps, the OD process can be perceived to be a collection of activities and techniques that, selectively or accumulatively, help the organization and/or its parts to move through these phases. The idea of phases can be most clearly demonstrated through a consideration of Lewin's (1951) three-phase model of change. This is followed by a more detailed description of OD as it has developed in more recent times.

Lewin's three-phase model of change

As already mentioned, most OD models of change consist of a series of phases (or steps/stages, depending on nomenclature). One of the earlier and most influential models of planned change that is still referred to extensively in the literature on change is Lewin's (1951) model of the change process. This consists of the three phases of *unfreezing, moving* and *refreezing*.

Unfreezing

The first of these phases – unfreezing – concerns the 'shaking up' of people's habitual modes of thinking and behaviour to heighten their awareness of the need for change. According to Cummings and Worley (2005, p. 22), this implies disturbing the status quo by either strengthening the forces that could *push* for change and/or weakening the forces which are maintaining the situation. This is likely to include the introduction of information showing discrepancies between desirable goals and modes of operating and what is currently happening. According to Goodstein and Burke (1993), it might even include selectively promoting employees or terminating their employment. For instance, in the case of the largest college, Pitford College, in Shire County (see Chapter 7, Illustration 7.5), a member of staff was promoted to be Director of Open and Resource-based Learning (O&RBL). Other staff had their responsibilities changed to include 'tutoring' (rather than teaching) students working mainly in a self-service type of learning environment. All staff received news that a new O&RBL centre was to be built and that the timetables of all full-time students would be altered so that at least 20 per cent of their time would be spent learning in the new centre, using multimedia materials on a 'pick and mix' basis according to their needs. Part of this unfreezing process was the extensive consultation with heads of departments and other decision makers to discuss the new developments – which were seen as challenging the prevailing wisdom of how education and training in the further education sector should happen.

Moving

The second phase of Lewin's change process – moving – is essentially the process of making the actual changes that will move the organization to the new state. As well as involving new types of behaviour by individuals, this includes the establishment of new strategies and structures, with associated systems to help secure the new ways of doing things. In Shire County this involved a number of different activities. First, a series of staff seminars on the concept and operation of O&RBL were carried out. As a result staff were concerned with redesigning their courses to include at least 20 per cent delivery of learning on O&RBL principles. In fact, some staff planned to deliver certain learning programmes as *predominantly* O&RBL programmes.

In addition, in Pitford College and one of the other two colleges in Shire County, large new O&RBL centres were built with multimedia teaching and learning facilities. Dignitaries representing education, industry and commerce were invited to the opening ceremonies, which were used as a symbol for change as well as advertising the facilities to those who might support them. The inclusion of local employers' representatives emphasized the importance of providing for the needs of adult learners as well as those of the youngsters who had, traditionally, been the main 'customers' of these colleges. What is more, in the redefinition of teaching as 'facilitating learning' it was recognized that the managers of these new O&RBL centres did not necessarily have to be academics. This was further reinforced by associating the new centres very closely with existing library and computer services whose staff were not classed as academics.

Refreezing

Lewin's final phase in the change process – refreezing – involves stabilizing or institutionalizing the changes. This requires securing the changes against 'back-sliding' and may include recruitment of new staff who are 'untainted' by the old habits. The continuing involvement and support of top management is crucial to this step. All of the elements of Johnson et al.'s (2005) cultural web (see Chapter 4) are important in establishing new ways of doing things. Once strategy, structure and systems have been changed it is equally important to reinforce the changes through symbolic actions and signs such as a change of logo, forms of dress, buildings design and ways of grouping people to get work done. The use of continuous data collection and feedback is essential to keep track of how the change is progressing and to monitor for further change in the light of environmental changes.

As an example of Lewin's three-phase change process, Goodstein and Burke (1993) make reference to the change British Airways (BA) made, from being a government-owned enterprise to being a privately owned one – a change that involved moving from what was basically a bureaucratic and militaristic culture to a service-oriented and market-driven one. Regarding the refreezing step, they mention how the continued involvement and commitment of top management helped ensure that the changes were 'fixed' in the way BA did business. Promotion was given to those employees who displayed commitment to the new values with a 'Top Flight Academy' being established to train senior management according to the new way of doing things. In addition, Goodstein and Burke (pp. 169–70) say: 'Attention was paid to BA's symbols as well – new, upscale uniforms; refurbished aircraft; and a new corporate coat of arms with the motto "We fly to serve".'

In the case of the colleges in Shire County, although the move to a culture of open and resource-based learning continued to some degree, it was constrained by a slackening off of commitment from top management as the environment in which the colleges operated changed yet again and brought new imperatives. Included in this were changes in the economic environment that brought changes in the political environment. These were increasing unemployment rates among young people and, as a result, a commitment on the part of government to increase training opportunities through funding further education provision for the 16–19 age group. In addition, there was an increase in training opportunities for adults. These opportunities operated outside the further education system, thereby, perhaps, lessening the requirement for more flexible provision within the further education colleges themselves. Consequently the phase of 'moving' the current situation to the desired future one was never fully completed and the follow-through of refreezing – absorbing the change into the culture of the organization – was put in jeopardy.

Lewin's three-phase model of organizational change can be criticized mainly for its concept of refreezing, that is, the idea of cementing the changes into place to create a new organizational reality. While this aim to prevent the backsliding mentioned earlier is laudable, it tends to ignore the increasingly turbulent environment within which many modern organizations operate and the need for *continuous* change. In addition, Burnes (2004, p. 997), in his critique of the model, said that it assumed organizations operate in a stable state, it was only suitable for small-scale change projects, it ignored organizational power and politics, and was top-down management driven.

This should not, however, detract from the debt that current OD approaches owe to the work of Lewin and his colleagues. This debt is summarized by French and Bell (1999, p. 44) when they say: 'Lewin's field theory and his conceptualizing about group dynamics, change processes, and action research were of profound influence on the people who were associated with the various stems of OD.' This remains the case today.

Lewin's concept of organizational change as a *process* dominates much of OD theory, a view supported by Burnes (2004) in his recognition of Lewin's contribution to understanding group behaviour and the roles groups play in organizations and society. In addition there is widespread recognition that organizations must carry out an assessment of where they are now, where they want to be in the future and how to manage the transition from the one state to the other. Where current theories of OD are leading, however, is to a realization that change is a process that is not linear and which is itself complex and messy, including many loops back and forth from one stage in the process to another. The following description tries to capture the essence of this. However, because of the limitations of the written word to describe something that is so dynamic in action, the process may appear more mechanistic than it is in reality. It should be remembered that what is being proposed is only a framework within which many variations may occur.

OD – an action–research-based model of change

According to Paton and McCalman (2000, p. 169), 'change is a continuous process of confrontation, identification, evaluation and action'. They go on to say that the key to this is what OD proponents refer to as an action–research model. French and Bell (1999) and Cummings and Worley (2005) give detailed descriptions of action research. Succinctly, it is a *collaborative* effort between leaders and facilitators of any change and those who have to enact it. In simplified form, it involves the following steps.

1 management perception of problem(s)
2 consultation with a behavioural science expert
3 data gathering and preliminary diagnosis by consultant
4 feedback to key client or group
5 joint agreement of the problem(s)
6 joint action planning
7 implementation
8 reinforcement and assessment of the change.

Therefore action research is, as its name suggests, a combination of research and action. This means collecting data relevant to the situation of interest, feeding back the results to those who must take action, collaboratively discussing the data to formulate an action plan and, finally, taking the necessary action.

A number of elements distinguish this approach from the hard systems model of change discussed in Chapter 7. First, it is not a 'one-off' event, which ends when a change has been completed. In their article describing the application of OD in an American electricity utility, Alpander and Lee (1995) illustrate this by saying: 'Organizations which are successful in maintaining their competitiveness have learned to view change not as a one-time event, but an ongoing process necessary to remain on the cutting edge in meeting customer needs.' This includes the ideas within the concept of a learning organization discussed earlier. Second, it is an iterative or cyclical process that is continuous and which, if OD is taken as part of an organization's philosophy of action, continues as part of everyday organizational life. Third, each of the components of the model (diagnosis, data gathering, feedback to the client group, data discussion and work by the client group, action planning and action) may be used to form each of the phases that make up a typical OD process. Furthermore, these components may, collectively, form cycles of activity *within* each stage of the OD process. Finally, the OD approach to change is firmly embedded in the assumption that all who are or who might be involved in any change should be part of the decision-making process to decide what that change might be and to bring it about. It is not, as some hard systems models of change suggest, a project planned and implemented by senior managers or some designated project manager, with the assumption that other workers in the organization will automatically go along with it.

Building on the concept of action research, Figure 8.2 shows the major stages of the OD model. These are now described in more detail. It is important to note that change on the scale involved in most OD efforts does not succeed without some established facilitation function. Hence the emphasis on the role of the consultant, or as termed here the *change agent*, as evidenced by positioning this person or group in the centre of the diagram. The role of the facilitator or

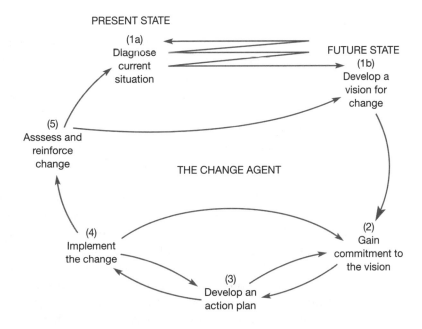

Figure 8.2 The OD model for change

change agent is discussed later in the chapter. What follows first is a more detailed description of the stages that make up the OD model itself.

Stages 1a and 1b: The present and the future

An examination of Figure 8.2 shows two stages strongly linked together in a symbiotic relationship. Hence the labelling of them as 1a and 1b – that is, two processes that are, in effect, intertwined and which could be regarded as one. The reason for this is that it is never clear whether a change process should start with the development of a vision for change (that is, where the organization wants to be), followed by a diagnosis of where the organization is at present; or whether a start should be made with diagnosing 'what is', followed by statements about 'what could be'. For instance, Buchanan and McCalman (1989), in their four-step model of perpetual transition management, pose the 'trigger layer' (which examines environmental opportunities and threats) before the 'vision layer' (which defines the future). By contrast, Mabey and Pugh (1995) put as the first stage the process of agreeing the organization's purpose/mission. This is followed by an assessment of the organization's external and internal environments.

In reality, as the zigzag arrow in Figure 8.2 shows, these two processes act in parallel, with each process feeding the other as it proceeds until some idea of a future direction is achieved. However, for ease of description, Stages 1a and 1b are discussed separately.

Stage 1a: Diagnose current situation

This stage is where the concept of PEST (political, economic, technological and socio-cultural factors) and the metaphor 'winds of change' (see Chapter 1) are useful as tools for diagnosing triggers for change that emanate from the external environment of the organization. In addition the temporal and internal environments must be assessed. In an ideal world this would be done on an ongoing basis: (a) to detect strategic drift (see Chapter 2) and (b) to gather data on the organization's capacity to respond to a change in direction or ways of operating. However, sometimes it takes a crisis to trigger this type of diagnosis. For instance, individuals in a newly created UK university (previously a polytechnic) had been pressing for several years for an increase in research activity supported by appropriate resources. It was only when the university lost valued government grant money that senior managers declared that 'something must be done' and a major investigation was instigated to ascertain what this might be and how it could happen.

Diagnostic processes such as these clearly call upon the data-gathering component of the action–research aspects of the OD model and the feedback of the results for discussion and verification by those concerned with, and involved in, the subsequent change. As mentioned earlier, in addition to data gathering about the organization's external environment, there is also a need for a more detailed examination of such things as:

- organizational purposes and goals
- organizational structure and culture
- prevailing leadership approaches and styles
- recruitment practices, career paths and opportunities
- reward structures and practices
- individuals' motivation and commitment to their work and organization
- employee training and development provision
- intra- and inter-group relationships.

The diagnostic stage forms the foundation for the *intervening*. It is the beginning of the data collection process that will continue throughout the intervention. It should provide information about the 'total system'. Data gathering, therefore, is done at the individual, group and organizational levels and should include those things that form barriers to organizational performance as well as those which contribute to organizational success. Table 8.1 provides a comparison of different methods of data collection.

Activity 8.1

Consider your own organization or one with which you are familiar.

If you were appointed as a change consultant to this organization, what data would you want to collect and how would you go about doing this – without alienating the people concerned from the process?

Table 8.1 Comparison of different methods of data collection

Method	Major advantages	Potential problems
Questionnaires	1 Responses can be quantified and easily summarized 2 Easy to use with large samples 3 Relatively inexpensive 4 Can obtain a large volume of data	1 No empathy 2 Predetermined questions/ missing issues 3 Over-interpretation of data 4 Response bias
Interviews	1 Adaptive – allows data collection on a range of possible subjects 2 Source of 'rich' data 3 Empathic 4 Process of interviewing can build rapport	1 Expense 2 Bias in interviewer responses 3 Coding and interpretation difficulties 4 Self-report bias
Observations	1 Collects data on behaviour, rather than reports of behaviour 2 Real time, not retrospective 3 Adaptive	1 Coding and interpretation difficulties 2 Sampling inconsistencies 3 Observer bias and questionable reliability 4 Expense
Unobtrusive measures	1 Non-reactive – no response bias 2 High face validity 3 Easily quantified	1 Access and retrieval difficulties 2 Validity concerns 3 Coding and interpretation difficulties

Source: Nadler, D. (1977) *Feedback and Organization Development; Using Data-based Methods*. Reading, Mass Addison Wesley 156–8. Reprinted in Cummings and Worley (2005, p. 117) by permission – Pearson Education, Inc., Englewood Cliffs, NJ.

Methods of collecting data include questionnaires, individual and 'focus-group' interviews, observation and examination of organizational documents, which are considered to be 'unobtrusive measures'. Price (1987) suggests collecting data on what people *think*, *feel* and *do* in terms of the *tasks* they perform, their *ways of working* and the *relationships* they have with each other. Many of the illustrations and activities in the chapters in Part Two are useful diagnostic tools for use at this stage in the change process.

Activity 8.2

Go back to Part Two of the book and list those illustrations and activities you think might be useful for the process of carrying out a diagnosis of the current state of your organization or one with which you are familiar.

It is clear that data collection and analysis are crucial to this stage in the OD process. It is important to note, however, the necessity for giving feedback on the findings to those from whom the data came, for further discussion and verification – a process particularly important in the case of data gained from the administration of questionnaires and through observation, where there is little interaction between questioner and questioned. This feedback process also serves the purpose of developing a vision for change – that is, where the organization wants to be in the future.

Stage 1b: Develop a vision for change

An organization's sense of what needs to change comes out of the process of organizational diagnosis and creative thinking. However, as we have already seen, this does not happen only when the diagnosis is complete. As the diagnosis proceeds and problem and success areas emerge, theories of what should be changed begin to form. These, in turn, bring demands for new information that will eventually move the process towards some definition of what the future should look like.

One way of looking at this stage of activity is to perceive it as a *creative* phase, in the sense that 'something new' is being looked for. This might imply a different strategy in terms of products, services or markets. It might also imply a change in structure and culture – including the way people are managed and led. Flood and Jackson (1991) suggest the use of metaphors as organizing structures to help people think about their organizations. The examples given are: organizations as machines, organisms, brains, cultures, teams, coalitions and prisons. Thus, Stage 1a would be concerned with identifying what metaphor most matched the current organization and Stage 1b would identify a metaphor to which its members might aspire.

Cummings and Worley (2005 pp. 160–1) say that:

> The vision that an organization has describes the core values and purposes that guide the organization as well as an envisioned future toward which change is directed. It provides a valued direction for the designing, implementing, and assessing of organizational changes.

They also suggest that a vision can energize commitment as people will be working towards a common goal. And as the discussion in the previous chapter shows, vision plays a key role in effective leadership.

Burnside (1991, p. 193) says:

> A vision can be described as a living picture of a future, desirable state. It is living because it exists in the thoughts and actions of people, not just in a written document. It is a picture because it is composed not of abstractions but of images.

On the concept of 'images', Burnside quotes Lievegoed (1983, p. 75) as saying: 'Images are more meaningful than abstract definitions. Images always have a thought content, an emotional value, and a moral symbolic value' and goes on to say: 'A vision is thus integrative because it brings these dimensions together.' According to Burnside there are two main aspects to visions – the strategic picture, which he calls the 'head' side, and the relational picture, which he calls the 'heart' side.

The charter and mission statements of the Body Shop reflect closely the views and ideals of its owners. In addition, considerable effort is put into spreading the messages they contain to everyone operating in 50 countries with over 1,900 outlets spanning 25 languages and 12 time zones (as at June 2005). Indeed the development of an extended Body Shop Charter was achieved through groups of employees from all levels of the organization meeting off site at intervals for many months (see Activity 8.3).

Activity 8.3

How far do you think the following statements made by The Body Shop go towards meeting the definitions of a vision given above?

THE BODY SHOP'S TRADING CHARTER

We aim to achieve commercial success by meeting our customers' needs through the provision of high quality, good value products with exceptional service and relevant information which enables customers to make informed and responsible choices.

Our trading relationships of every kind – with customers, franchisees and suppliers – will be commercially viable, mutually beneficial and based on trust and respect.

THE BODY SHOP'S MISSION STATEMENT – OUR REASON FOR BEING

- To dedicate our business to the pursuit of social and environmental change.
- To CREATIVELY balance the financial and human NEEDS of our stakeholders: employees, customers, franchisees, suppliers and shareholders.
- To COURAGEOUSLY ensure that OUR business is ecologically sustainable, meeting the needs of the present without compromising the future.
- To MEANINGFULLY contribute to local, national and international communities in which we trade, by adopting a code of conduct which ensures care, honesty, fairness and respect.
- To PASSIONATELY campaign for the protection of the environment and human and civil rights, and against animal testing within the cosmetics and toiletries industry.
- To TIRELESSLY work to narrow the gap between principle and practice, while making fun, passion and care part of our daily lives.

In 1976 the first Body Shop opened for business in Brighton, England, selling 25 hand-mixed products. Due to franchising, those people who had bought into Anita Roddick's vision were able to be a part of this success story.

The journey continues – for the 'people' who are now part of Roddick's management team, they have a few thoughts for the future of the company: 'Activism has been part of the DNA of The Body Shop. The past has been a testament to an extraordinary partnership with millions of men, women and children all over the globe'. And what about the future? The unique blend of product, passion and partnership that characterizes the story will continue to evolve. It is a shared vision. So the great experiment goes on.

Source: The Body Shop www.thebodyshop.co.uk

This example of employee involvement in the development of an organization's vision underlines the close linking of Stages 1a and 1b and their combined outputs in identifying an organization's present and desired states in terms of two aspects of its functioning. These outputs are: first, the gap that represents the difference between an organization's current strategy and goals and those to which it must aspire in order to respond to the forces and circumstances of the external environment; second, the gap between what Benjamin and Mabey (1993, p. 182) call: 'the core values as related internally to the ethos of the organization'.

Stage 2: Gain commitment to the vision and the need for change

It is at the second stage of the process that feedback from the results of Stages 1a and 1b is most important. Unless those concerned and involved with the change have been consulted and have participated in the process to this point, there will be little incentive for them to 'buy into' the new vision and the change process that will follow it.

Illustration 8.1

Pugh's principles and rules for understanding and managing organizational change

Principle 1: Organizations are organisms
This means the organization is not a machine and change must be approached carefully, with the implications for various groupings thought out. Participants need to be persuaded of the need for change and be given time to 'digest' the changes after implementation.

Principle 2: Organizations are occupational and political systems as well as rational resource-allocation ones
This means that thought must be given to how changes affect people's jobs, career prospects, motivation and so on. It also means paying attention to how change will affect people's status, power and the prestige of different groups.

Principle 3: All members of an organization operate simultaneously in the rational, occupational and political systems
This means that all types of arguments for change must be taken seriously. It is not sufficient merely to explain away different points of view. Rational arguments for change are as important as those which involve changes in occupational and political systems.

Principle 4: Change is most likely to be acceptable with people who are successful and have confidence in their ability and the motivation to change
This means ensuring an appropriate place (or set of people) from which to start the change and to ensure the methods used are relevant to those who are 'first in line' in accepting the change.

Source: Based on Pugh, D. S. (1993), 'Understanding and managing change', in Mabey, C. and Mayon-White, B. (eds) *Managing Change*, 2nd edn (London, PCP), pp. 109–10.

This stage is akin to the 'conversion layer' of Buchanan and McCalman's (1989) model of perpetual transition management – the one that follows the trigger and vision layers which were mentioned earlier. However, gaining recruits for the change is not easy, as Pugh's (1993) four principles for understanding the process of organizational change show (see Illustration 8.1 and Activity 8.4). These principles in turn draw attention to the need for managers to use many different and interacting ways to gain the commitment and involvement of all concerned in the change programme.

Activity 8.4

Identify a major change in an organization with which you are familiar – preferably one in which you have been involved.

Consider each of Pugh's principles and make notes regarding the following in terms of gaining people's commitment to the need for a new vision and associated change.

Principle 1
- *Were the implications for different groupings thought out?*
- *What (if any) methods were used to persuade people of the need for change?*

Principle 2
- *Was thought given to how the changes might impact on people's:*
  - *positions and prospects?*
  - *status?*
  - *power?*

Principle 3
- *Were the comments (supportive or otherwise) of different people and groups taken seriously and acted upon?*

Principle 4
- *How much effort was made to increase people's confidence in the new vision?*
- *How much effort was made to identify those people and groups who were most likely to 'spearhead' the change?*

Pugh's four principles draw attention to the need for, not just two-way, but many-way communication as part of the process of gaining commitment to the vision and the need for change. This is one of the reasons why most descriptions of OD-type models of change emphasize the importance of managing resistance through discussion, negotiation and active participation of those likely to have to make the changes. Established work groups and teams become particularly important at this stage, as is evidenced by French and Bell's (1999, p. 155) statement that:

Collaborative management of the work team culture is a fundamental emphasis of organization development programmes. This reflects the assumption that in today's organizations much of the work is accomplished directly or indirectly through teams. This also reflects the assumption that the work team culture exerts a significant influence on the individual's behaviour. ... Teams and work groups are thus considered to be fundamental units of organizations and also key leverage points for improving the functioning of the organization.

Consequently the process of gaining commitment to change must include working at the group level of the organization and recognizing the strength of influence of both formal and informal group leaders. In addition, it is more efficient of time and effort to communicate with individuals as groups than with them solely as individuals – even though this should not be the only means of communicating with them. It is not, however, sufficient merely to inform people of the vision and the necessity for change. This is because visions for change are rarely so clearly structured that information from all levels of the organization can be ignored. As Smith (1995, p. 19), writing on the realities of involvement in managing change, says: 'No top manager can know at the outset [of any change] exactly what needs doing, what information is needed, or where it is located.'

Jones (1994, p. 49), a colleague in the same consultancy practice as Smith, talks of 'listening to the organization'. Reporting research with top management on the reasons why large-scale programmes of change often fail, Smith (1995) says that nearly all the managers interviewed reported on how much they had underestimated the importance of communication. However, as Jones says, this is not simply a question of senior management shouting louder from the top. This will not identify and bring to the surface the doubts that people have and their fears of what change might mean for them. Neither will it bring to the surface any problems with implementing the vision that top management may not be able to see for themselves.

Far from shouting from the top, the action–research cycle of collecting and analyzing data and feeding back the results should be maintained here, as in the previous stages, so as to avoid widespread alienation of the workforce from the need to change and the vision to which it relates. Lloyd and Feigen (1997, p. 37) neatly summarize the dangers of not doing this when they say: 'Vision statements only work when the needs of those at the bottom of the organization are integrated upwards with the needs of the market.' Accomplishing this means being sensitive, not only to people's worries about the way tasks and structures may be affected by the change, but also to what Mabey and Pugh (1995, p. 36) term the 'emotional readiness for change, the quality of existing relationships and the latent commitment to new ways of working'. Otherwise, any plan for action has little chance of being successfully implemented.

Stage 3: Develop an action plan

The development of an action plan can be thought of as beginning the phase of managing the transition from an organization's current state to its desired future state, as shown by the 'JOURNEY TO THE FUTURE' label in Figure 8.2. However, it also continues the process of gaining commitment to the vision but with a somewhat changed emphasis on *how* that vision can come about.

A number of issues are important in this stage of the OD process. One is the issue of *who* is to guide the planning and, later, the implementation of the change. Another is the issue of precisely *what* needs to change to achieve the vision, while a third is *where* any intervention should take place. The following explores these issues in more detail.

The role of a change agent

The success of using an OD approach to facilitate change rests on the qualities and capabilities of those who act as the facilitators of change. Moving organizations from current to future changed states is not easy and requires knowledge and skills that some managers do not possess. In addition, many managers are so close to the day-to-day issues and problems of managing that they are unable to stand back from the current situation to take a long look at how things might be different. For these and other reasons, such as a need for managers themselves to learn how to manage change, the use of a change agent is usually deemed desirable in most OD approaches to change. However, the change agent as facilitator of change does not necessarily have to be from outside the organization – he or she might very well come from another part of the organization, not the one that is the focus of the change. Indeed some large organizations have departments or divisions that are specifically set up to act as OD consultants to the rest of the organization. What should also be borne in mind is that all the skills and competencies required of a change agent might not reside in one indiviual. It might, therefore, be preferable to use more than one person or, in the case of large-scale change, a team of people.

Buchanan and Boddy (1992) devote a complete book to the subject of the change agent. In it they give a helpful list of the competencies of effective change agents, based on research on how managers deal with change (see Illustration 8.2, overleaf).

The list in Illustration 8.2 is a useful one and is reminiscent of the characteristics of 'transformational' leaders discussed in Chapter 6. However, this list must be considered in the context of how it came about. The evidence for constructing the list came mainly from questioning project managers – that is *internal* change agents who were concerned with changes in their own project areas. Perhaps, because of this, it emphasizes more the *content* of the change and how to get ideas accepted, rather than the *process* skills of consultation and

Illustration 8.2

Competencies of an effective change agent

Goals

1 Sensitivity to changes in key personnel, top management perceptions and market conditions, and to the way in which these impact the goals of the project in hand.
2 Clarity in specifying goals, in defining the achievable.
3 Flexibility in responding to changes outwith the control of the project manager, perhaps requiring major shifts in project goals and management style and risk taking.

Roles

4 Team-building activities, to bring together key stakeholders and establish effective working groups and clearly to define and delegate respective responsibilities.
5 Networking skills in establishing and maintaining appropriate contacts within and outside the organization.
6 Tolerance of ambiguity, to be able to function comfortably, patiently and effectively in an uncertain environment.

Communication

7 Communication skills to transmit effectively to colleagues and subordinates the need for changes in project goals and in individual tasks and responsibilities.

8 Interpersonal skills, across the range, including selection, listening, collecting appropriate information, identifying the concerns of others and managing meetings.
9 Personal enthusiasm, in expressing plans and ideas.
10 Stimulating motivation and commitment in others involved.

Negotiation

11 Selling plans and ideas to others, by creating a desirable and challenging vision of the future.
12 Negotiating with key players for resources or for changes in procedures and to resolve conflict.

Managing up

13 Political awareness, in identifying potential coalitions and in balancing conflicting goals and perceptions.
14 Influencing skills, to gain commitment to project plans and ideas from potential sceptics and resisters.
15 Helicopter perspective, to stand back from the immediate project and take a broader view of priorities.

Source: Buchanan, D. and Boddy, D. (1992), *The Expertise of the Change Agent* (Hemel Hempstead, Prentice Hall, pp. 92–3).

participation which form an essential part of the facilitation role. In this respect it can be compared with Paton and McCalman's list of the roles taken on by effective change agents:

1 to help the organization define the problem by asking for a definition of what it is;
2 to help the organization examine what causes the problem and diagnose how this can be overcome;
3 to assist in getting the organization to offer alternative solutions;
4 to provide direction in the implementation of alternative solutions;
5 to transmit the learning process that allows the client to deal with change on an ongoing basis by itself in the future. (Paton and McCalman, 2000, p. 182)

In contrast to the concept of a change agent, Kotter (1996) uses the concept of a 'guiding coalition' and suggests four key characteristics as being essential for it to be effective:

1 Position power: Are enough key players on board, especially the main line managers, so that those left out cannot easily block progress?
2 Expertise: Are the various points of view – in terms of discipline, work experience, nationality, etc. – relevant to the task at hand adequately represented so that informed, intelligent decisions will be made?
3 Credibility: Does the group have enough people with good reputations in the firm so that its pronouncements will be taken seriously by other employees?
4 Leadership: Does the group include enough proven leaders to be able to drive the change process? (Kotter, 1996, p. 57)

It is clear, however, that the guiding coalition cannot, by itself, cause widespread change to happen. What it can do is to set targets for change that, collectively, will move the organization and its members much closer to realizing the vision which was developed in Stage 1b and further refined in Stage 2. Having done this, the issue becomes: 'Who is to do what, with what kind of involvement by others?'

Responsibility charting

Beckhard and Harris (1987, pp. 104–8) have developed a technique called 'responsibility charting' that assesses the alternative behaviours for each person or persons involved in a series of actions designed to bring about change. They describe the making of a responsibility chart as follows:

> Responsibility charting clarifies behaviour that is required to implement important change tasks, actions, or decisions. It helps reduce ambiguity, wasted energy, and adverse emotional reactions between individuals or groups whose interrelationship is affected by change. The basic process is as follows:

> Two or more people whose roles interrelate or who manage interdependent groups formulate a list of actions, decisions, or activities that affect their relationship (such as developing budgets, allocating resources, and deciding on the use of capital) and record the list on the vertical axis of a responsibility chart [see Figure 8.3, overleaf]. They then identify the people involved in each action or decision and list these 'actors' on the horizontal axis of the form.

The actors identified can include:

R = the person who has the *responsibility* to initiate the action and who is charged with ensuring it is carried out.
A = those whose *approval* is required or who have the power to veto the decision. This could be the responsible person's superiors.
S = those who can provide *support* and resources to help the action to take place.
I = those who merely need to be *informed* or consulted but who cannot veto the action.

Key:
R = Responsibility (not necessarily authority)
A = Approval (right to veto)
S = Support (put resources towards)
I = Inform (to be consulted before action but with no right of veto)

Figure 8.3 Example of a responsibility chart

Certain ground rules are set out when making a responsibility chart. French and Bell (1999, pp. 172–3) summarize these as follows:

> First, assign responsibility to only one person. That person initiates and then is responsible and accountable for the action. Second, avoid having too many people with an approval–veto function on an item. That will slow down task accomplishment or will negate it altogether. Third, if one person has approval–veto involvement on most decisions, that person could become a bottleneck for getting things done. Fourth, the support function is critical. A person with a support role has to expand resources or produce something that is then used by the person responsible for the action. This support role and its specific demands must be clarified and clearly assigned. And, finally, the assignment of functions (letters) to persons at times becomes difficult. For example, a person may want A–V (approval–veto) on an item, but not really need it; a person may not want S (support) responsibility on an item, but should have it; or two persons each want R (responsibility) on a particular item, but only one can have it.

This discussion of responsibility charting illustrates the 'chicken and egg' nature of planning organizational change. While it is right to consider who will lead and participate in implementing change, this has to be done in conjunction with what it is that needs to change.

Activity 8.5

Identify a change initiative in which you have been involved (or one with which you are familiar). You may find it helpful to use the example identified in completing Activity 8.4.

To give you practice in using a responsibility chart, list some of the actions associated with that change and assign the people involved according to their responsibility role(s).

Consider whether Beckhard and Harris's ground rules for assigning roles were adhered to. If not, did this cause confusion of responsibilities and/or impede action?

The what and where of change

Pugh (1986) has devised a matrix of possible change initiatives based on the different issues that can hamper change and the level at which they occur. Figure 8.4 (see overleaf) is a reproduction of what has become known as the 'Pugh OD matrix'.

The matrix reproduced in Figure 8.4 can be used to help with action planning (as represented by the initiatives listed in italics) about: (a) the type of intervention required to facilitate change in line with the organization's vision (represented by the columns), and (b) the level at which it should take place (represented by the rows). For instance, at the level of the individual, problems may be occurring because there are few opportunities for promotion from the job of factory floor supervisor to higher levels of management, salespeople see no reason to change given their current bonus plan and many middle managers have made their jobs to suit their own needs rather than those of the organization. Problems at the inter-group level might include marketing and production arguing about the feasibility of setting up a new production line to satisfy what the marketing staff consider to be a market opportunity. Intervention is frequently required at the organizational level when an organization's structure prevents the emergence of, let alone action upon, initiatives that could be beneficial to the organization as a whole.

Beckhard and Harris (1987, p. 73) suggest the following organizational subsystems – any of which can be considered as a starting point for change:

- *Top management:* the top of the system.
- *Management-ready systems:* those groups or organizations known to be ready for change.
- *'Hurting' systems:* a special class of ready systems in which current conditions have created acute discomfort.
- *New teams or systems:* units without a history and whose tasks require a departure from old ways of operating.
- *Staff:* subsystems that will be required to assist in the implementation of later interventions.
- *Temporary project systems:* ad hoc systems whose existence and tenure are specifically defined by the change plan.

	Behaviour (What is happening now?)	Structure (What is the required system?)	Context (What is the setting?)
Organizational level	General climate of poor morale, pressure, anxiety, suspicion, lack of awareness of, or response to, environmental changes *Survey feedback, organizational mirroring*	Systems goals – poorly defined or inappropriate and misunderstood; organization structure inappropriate – centralization, divisionalization or standardization; inadequacy of environmental monitoring – mechanisms *Change the structure*	Geographical setting, market pressures, labour market, physical condition, basic technology *Change strategy, location, physical condition, basic technology*
Inter-group level	Lack of effective cooperation between sub-units, conflict, excessive competition, limited war, failure to confront differences in priorities, unresolved feelings *Inter-group confrontation (with third-party consultant), role negotiation*	Lack of integrated task perspective; sub-unit optimization, required interaction difficult to achieve *Redefine responsibilities, change reporting relationships, improve coordination and liaison mechanism*	Different sub-units' values, lifestyle; physical distance *Reduce psychological and physical distance; exchange roles, attachments, cross-functional groups*
Group level	Inappropriate working relationships, atmosphere, participation, poor understanding and acceptance of goals, avoidance, inappropriate leadership style, leader not trusted, respected; leader in conflict with peers and superiors *Process consultation, team building*	Task requirements poorly defined; role relationships unclear or inappropriate; leader's role overloaded, inappropriate reporting procedures *Redesign work relationships (socio-technical systems), self-directed working groups*	Insufficient resources, poor group composition for cohesion, inadequate physical set-up, personality clashes *Change technology, layout, group composition*
Individual level	Failure to fulfil individual's needs; frustration responses; unwillingness to consider change, little chance for learning and development *Counselling, role analysis, career planning*	Poor job definition, task too easy or too difficult *Job restructuring/modification, redesign, enrichment, agree on key competencies*	Poor match of individual with job, poor selection or promotion, inadequate preparation and training, recognition and remuneration at variance with objectives *Personnel changes, improved selection and promotion procedures, improved training and education, bring recognition and remuneration in line with objectives*

Figure 8.4 The Pugh OD matrix

Source: From Course P679 Planning and Managing Change, Block 4, Section 6. Copyright © The Open University.

Activity 8.6

What similarities and differences can be found between Pugh's levels of analytical focus and Beckhard and Harris's list of subsystems for intervention?

In addition to the issue of where change interventions might take place, the planning of OD interventions must also take account of the degree of change needed, that is, the scope of the change activities. In terms of the Pugh OD matrix, this means considering whether: (a) people's *behaviour* needs to change, and/or (b) the *organization's structure and systems* need to change and/or (c) the *context or the setting* needs to change. According to Mabey and Pugh (1995, pp. 40–1):

> The first (left-hand) column is concerned with current behaviour symptoms which can be tackled directly. Since it suggests methods and changes which address the symptoms without intervening into the required system or setting, this column comprises the least radical of the development strategies. Indeed in some cases the results may not be recognized as change at all – merely as overcoming some difficulties in the proper workings of the current system. Thus in one application, as the result of a team-building exercise with a Ward Sister and her staff, the functioning of the ward, the morale of staff, and the standard of patient care all improved. The Hospital Management Committee regarded this process not as a change, but one of getting the organization to work properly.
>
> But it may be that this degree of intervention is not sufficient to achieve the required aims. It could be that, however improved the group atmosphere and leadership style, the group will not function well because it is not clear what the organization requires of it, adequate information to carry out the group task is not available at the appropriate time, and the tasks are inappropriately divided and poorly allocated to the members of the group. In these circumstances, the second column, concerned with organizing the required system, is the appropriate degree of intervention. This is a greater degree of intervention because it may require change in the structure, systems, information flows, job design, etc., which inevitably affects a much wider range of the 'organizational environment' of the particular group.
>
> Even this degree of intervention may be insufficient. The problems may lie in the contextual setting (changing market pressures, physical distance, poor group composition, poor promotion procedures, etc.). Then the degree of intervention in the third (right-hand) column is appropriate. This is a still greater degree of intervention requiring strategy changes, considerable expenditure of resources (both financial and human), and carrying with it greater likelihood of disruption with its attendant costs. It is not, therefore, to be undertaken lightly.

Mabey and Pugh go on to say that, as action moves from the left through to the right-hand column, a greater degree of intervention and commitment is required. Consequently, they suggest starting at the left column of the matrix and moving towards the right only as it becomes necessary because of the dictates of the problem. Activity 8.7 offers an opportunity to become more familiar with the content of the matrix and how it might be used in planning change.

Activity 8.7

The best way to understand the Pugh OD matrix is to apply its different 'cells' to a real organizational example.

Choose a situation from your own experience where a need for change has been established.

Go through the matrix and note which cells are appropriate for starting interventions that will help in the change process.

If you find this too difficult to start with, look at the following list of organizational problems and activities and note in which of the Pugh matrix cell(s) you would place them.

1 *The accounts department who 'lived' on the top floor always seemed to be at loggerheads with the research and development team who were 'housed' in an outside annex.*

2 *Since the redundancies, which were mentioned wherever you went in the organization, people were moaning about the amount of work they had to do and the lack of recognition of this by senior management.*

3 *The staff in the post room appeared bored with their jobs. Admittedly, the work was rather repetitive.*

4 *It took too long to get an answer to queries, because the boss had always to be informed.*

5 *The members of the project group felt abandoned and without leadership.*

As stated earlier, the process of developing an action plan for change should be done through consultation and collaboration with those who will implement the change, thus reinforcing commitment to change. Beckhard and Harris's (1987, p. 72) concept of the action plan being a 'road map' for the change effort is a useful one. In addition, they say that an effective action plan should have the following characteristics:

- *Relevance:* activities are clearly linked to the change goals and priorities.
- *Specificity:* activities are clearly identified rather than broadly generalized.
- *Integration:* the parts are closely connected.
- *Chronology:* there is a logical sequence of events.
- *Adaptability:* there are contingency plans for adjusting to unexpected forces.

The last of these characteristics is particularly important. As anyone knows, it is all well and good setting out on a journey with the route well defined beforehand. However, because of the many things that exist to thwart the best-laid plans (in the case of the journey: traffic, passenger sickness, road works, accidents and so on), the plan must be flexible enough to adapt to the changing circumstances of not only *what* needs to change, but also possible changes in the transition process itself. Consequently, as Figure 8.2 shows, the development of an action plan must always be linked closely to its subsequent implementation.

Stage 4: Implement the change

Any text dealing specifically with organization development as a change methodology contains details of different techniques and methods for initiating and implementing change (see, for instance, French and Bell, 1999; Cummings and Worley, 2005). For the present purposes, the activities in italics in the Pugh OD matrix in Figure 8.4 can be used to illustrate ways of initiating organizational change. As the matrix illustrates, these relate to the different levels of analytical focus and the scope of the change activities. The following gives additional details of those activities that require further explanation. It should be noted however that, because these activities are mainly concerned with the behaviour column of the matrix, it *does not mean* that they are, necessarily, any more important than the activities concerned with structure and context. They are selected for further explanation simply because they may not be as familiar as some of the others.

Survey feedback

Surveys can be used to assess the attitudes and morale of people across the organization and are used at different stages in the OD process. At the implementation stage they are important for the effective management of the change. Feedback from these surveys to those involved in the change activities helps stimulate discussion of what is working and what is not and should result in modifications to the action plan or the way it is being implemented or, sometimes, to a reorientation of the vision.

For example, in 1994 Lloyd's of London, one of the City's prestigious financial institutions, carried out an employee opinion survey on the progress of a large-scale change programme, the results of which were fed back to the staff involved for further discussion and appropriate action. Clarke, Hooper and Nicholson (1997, p. 29), writing about this, say:

> The process was designed to demonstrate to people that the corporation was not just saying: 'Your views are important', but that it actually meant it. Not only was the management team prepared to listen; it would also distribute the results openly and honestly. More importantly it would act on the views expressed. Sophisticated timetabling, communications, objective-setting and measurement ensured that this happened.

The survey was repeated 18 months later to identify progress on actions resulting from the first survey.

Organizational mirroring

'The organization mirror is a set of activities in which a particular organizational group, the host group, gets feedback from representatives from several other organizational groups about how it is perceived and regarded' (French and Bell, 1999, p. 186). Organizational mirroring is different from interventions at the inter-group level, being concerned with relationships between three or more groups. It is a technique that benefits from the services of a change consultant who is not connected with any of the groups involved in the process. A 'fish-bowl' technique is frequently used as part of organizational mirroring. This is where the group asking for feedback (the host group) first sits and listens to what the other group representatives have to say (without interruption). The representatives of the host group and the other group then exchange places to allow the host group to have their say (ask for clarification, information, etc.) without interruption. Finally, the representatives of both groups are divided into small sets to work together on problems that emerge before all coming together to devise action plans, assign people to tasks and set target dates for improvements to be completed.

The techniques of survey feedback are most frequently associated with gaining information on people's attitudes and behaviour. It should not be forgotten, however, that other types of information gathering will be just as important – for instance with regard to progress against financial and other quantifiable measures of organizational performance.

Inter-group confrontation (with third-party assistance)

Although a technique of 'confrontation' sounds alarming it enables two groups, which have their unique specialties, to confront organizational issues that go beyond their particular expertise. Mabey and Pugh suggest that an exercise such as this might require two days of work away from distractions and be helped by a 'neutral' facilitator. The objective is to help the members of the two groups increase their awareness of the importance of each other's activities to the overall organizational performance and thus reduce a sense of 'them and us'.

French and Bell and Mabey and Pugh suggest a process where each group is asked to produce two lists. The first is the complaints 'we' have against 'them'. The second is the complaints that 'we' think 'they' would have about 'us'. Lists are then shared between the two groups. According to Mabey and Pugh, two characteristics usually emerge. First, some of the complaints can be dissolved fairly quickly, being the result of simple misunderstandings or lack of communication. Second, the lists of both groups show a surprising degree of congruency; in other words 'we' know what they think about 'us' and 'they' know what we think about 'them'. The lists form the basis for further discussion and exploration of how conflict can be resolved and more positive working relationships established.

Role negotiation

Role negotiation is a technique developed by Harrison (1972). Basically it involves individuals or groups negotiating to 'contract' to change their behaviour on a *quid pro quo* basis. In general it requires the help of a facilitator and (typically) during a day's workshop session, each set of participants is asked to say what they want the others to *do more of, do less of or maintain unchanged*. A follow-up meeting a month or so later assesses progress and, if necessary, renews or sets up new contracts. It is important to note that this *does not* involve probing people's likes and dislikes about each other. It concentrates solely on the roles they play and their behaviour as part of these.

Process consultation

This is rather more than a technique in that Schein (1987) has written a book entitled *Process Consultation*. From Schein's point of view process consultation is a central part of organizational development. According to French and Bell (1999, p. 164): 'The crux of this approach is that a skilled third party (consultant) works with individuals and groups to help them learn about human and social processes and learn to solve problems that stem from process events.' The kinds of interventions that are part of process consultation are: agenda-setting; feedback of observational data; coaching and counselling of individuals and suggestions about group membership; communication and interaction patterns; allocation of work, responsibilities and lines of authority. French and Bell say (p. 163):

> The process consultation model is similar to team-building interventions and intergroup team-building interventions except that in PC greater emphasis is placed on diagnosing and understanding process events. Furthermore there is more emphasis on the consultant being more nondirective and questioning as he or she gets the groups to solve their own problems.

Team building

Team building is an essential part of the OD process. Individuals working together do so in many different ways – not all of which contribute to team effectiveness. Consequently issues such as the overall size of the team, the characteristics of its members, the focus and direction of the team and its role within the organization are important. In situations of change any or all of these might also need to change. Team changing and team building techniques can help in this.

Team-building techniques can be used for established long-term groups as well as for special, shorter-term, project groups. Processes included in team building are: (a) diagnosis of the task together with individuals' and group needs; (b) diagnosis and negotiation of roles; (c) responsibility charting; (d) understanding and managing group processes and culture. Usually a change agent or independent consultant/facilitator is used to help in team building.

Life and career planning

There are a number of exercises that can help in career planning, which is part of life planning. One is to draw a lifeline representing the past, present and future. Past events are positioned according to important things that have happened in life, including things done well and things done not so well – 'ups' as well as 'downs'. Future desired events are also recorded on the line, and some indication is given of time of achievement. Another exercise is to write one's obituary as if death were to occur now and then as if death was some years in the future. The last exercise is intended to give some idea of what is hoped for in the near and far future. The use of a life coach or mentor can be helpful in the application of these techniques.

Activity 8.8

Think back to the change which you identified for Activity 8.5. Which of the techniques (at any level or scope) in Pugh's OD matrix were used as the change was implemented? Were they appropriate?

The role of short-term wins

Implementing change that will ultimately transform an organization is a *long-term process* and it is understandable if commitment to the vision becomes somewhat weakened on the way. Consequently the achievement of 'short-term wins' (Kotter, 1996) is important, both as a motivating factor and as a mechanism for tracking the progress towards the longer-term goals. However, Kotter goes further than this in identifying six ways in which short-term wins can help organizational transformations. These are:

- *Provide evidence that sacrifices are worth it:* Wins greatly help justify the short-term costs involved.
- *Reward change agents with a pat on the back:* After a lot of hard work, positive feedback builds morale and motivation.
- *Help fine-tune vision and strategies:* Short-term wins give the guiding coalition concrete data on the viability of their ideas.
- *Undermine cynics and self-serving resisters:* Clear improvements in performance make it difficult for people to block needed change.
- *Keep bosses on board:* Provides those higher in the hierarchy with evidence that the transformation is on track.
- *Build momentum:* Turns neutrals into supporters, reluctant supporters into active helpers etc.   (Kotter, 1996, p. 123)

Short-term wins do not, however, happen automatically as part of the change process. They have to be planned *deliberately* so that they become much more probabilities than possibilities. According to Kotter (pp. 121–2), a short-term win has three characteristics:

1 It is visible: large numbers of people can see for themselves whether the result is real or just hype.
2 It is unambiguous: there can be little argument over the call.
3 It is clearly related to the change effort.

An example of a short-term win is when a company reduces delivery time on one of its ten main products by a predetermined percentage in a predetermined time; or when the number of customer complaints reduces by (say) 50 per cent during the first half of the year; or when the jobs of a group of employees become easier to do because they are getting more relevant information in a more timely way. Short-term wins are not those of the type: 'We expect to increase our sales in the next couple of months'; neither is the fact that two previously sworn enemies are now talking pleasantly to each other a short-term win, unless the outcome is some further improvement in morale and organizational performance.

The setting and assessment of short-term wins links the implementation stage of the OD process to the more all-embracing assessment of the organization's progress towards its vision and the continuing reinforcement of the change process itself.

Stage 5: Assess and reinforce the change

Assessing change

In organizational situations of hard complexity it is relatively easy to assess the extent to which change has been achieved. The setting of 'hard' objectives and quantifiable performance measures makes this a more straightforward process. However, in the softer, more 'messy' situations where change methodologies of the OD type tend to be used, change is an evolving process concerned not only with changes in quantifiable performance objectives, but more frequently with changes in attitudes, behaviours and cultural norms where measurement is bound to be less precise. Even so, measurement of these things is possible. It is also desirable in terms of its role in providing positive feedback that the change process is 'working' and in testing how far the organization has moved towards achievement of its vision.

A number of ways are available for measuring the softer issues associated with change:

1 *A survey or cultural audit*, which can potentially cover all staff. Its results can be quantified and quickly disseminated. The audit can be done at regular intervals to provide repeated snapshot measures of an organization's progress towards its change objectives. The Nationwide Building Society is an example of an organization that uses such a system as part of its commitment to continuous improvement.

2 *Interviews with individuals or focus groups*, which allow the collection of more qualitative, in-depth information. An example of testing what a company's vision and values statement meant to staff was the exercise carried out by The Body Shop just after a public challenge to its integrity regarding its stance of being socially responsible in its policies and practices. The Body Shop called it 'gazing into the mirror'. It consisted of 44 meetings, each with 20 different

staff and managers from all parts of the organization. All the meetings were attended by a board member and a moderator who later summarized the discussions to produce a report of the main themes arising and subsequent recommendations for action.

3 *An examination of turnover and absenteeism rates* as an indication of general morale and well-being.

4 *An analysis (through observation or questionnaire) of group performance* in terms of task achievement, but also in terms of the quality of meetings (including number of meetings and length) and leader performance.

5 *'Picturing the organization'*, that is, asking staff to present their perception of the organization in graphical or image terms rather than in words. This might include the use of metaphors in line with those suggested by Morgan (1986) in Chapter 4 or Flood and Jackson (1991) (see Stage 1b earlier in this chapter).

Alternatively, it might be in the form of a 'Rich Picture' (Checkland, 1981), that is, a collage of images represented by drawings and symbols connected by other symbols depicting the relationships between them. Figure 8.5 is an example of a rich picture depicting a situation of change from a centrally run service for people with learning disabilities. This meant a change from mainly hospital-based provision to provision which was in line with a 'care in the community' concept – that is, devolving care to a myriad of much smaller units, the management of which had to 'sell' their services (in competition with others) to the national health authority which was charged with 'buying' them on behalf of the users.

When the rich pictures about an organization start to resemble images closely related to the vision, management can have some confidence that the change has been successful in respect of how employees feel about it.

Reinforcing and consolidating change

Farquhar, Evans and Tawadey (1989, p. 49) say: 'A real danger in the process of organizational change is the failure to carry it through sufficiently far. Companies may be tempted to relax when the immediate crisis recedes while they still have not addressed the deeper organizational problems which generated the crisis.' The lesson from this is that the new order resulting from any change needs to be institutionalized. This is well put by Mabey and Pugh (1995, p. 50) when they say:

> Individuals need to be held personally accountable for prescribed initiatives; new working relationships and boundaries between different working groups need to be negotiated; ways of recognizing and rewarding desirable behaviours and attitudes need to be devised to demonstrate that the organization is serious about the change strategies that have been set.

It is pointless expecting people's behaviour to change if this is not reinforced by concomitant changes in personnel policies and practices, including appraisal, career development and reward systems. In addition, staff training

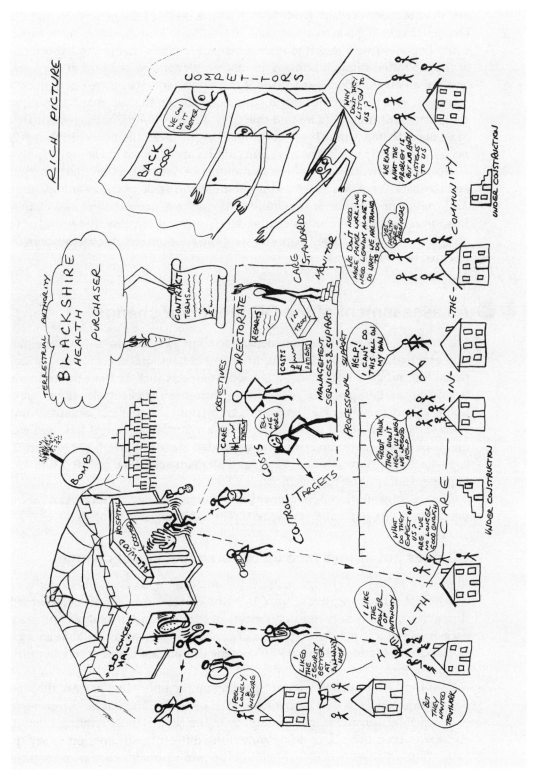

Figure 8.5 Rich picture of changes in the organization of services for people with learning disabilities

and development needs to reorient itself to the needs of the new vision and the changes that help guide its attainment. According to Farquhar *et al.* this is particularly important with regard to middle managers. While change can happen fast at the top (often through bringing in new people) and be accepted at the lower levels of an organization (particularly if the rewards for change are clear), middle managers, who perform the bridging function between the two, may be slower to accept new cultures, policies and practices. Yet it is middle management that must make change work. They must, therefore, be given the new skills they will need – particularly when structures and cultures are expected to change.

More generally, the action–research model of data collection, data analysis and feedback for action is just as important at this stage of OD as at any other. Any change programme is stressful, but if employees continue to *own* change this stress will become not negative stress but, rather, positive pressure to accept that change can be the norm, with the adoption of innovative, change-oriented behaviour.

An assessment of the OD model for change

The model of OD presented here departs to some extent from early OD models that emphasized mainly the attitudinal and behavioural aspects of organizational life and gave insufficient attention to aspects such as strategy, structure, technology and, in particular, the needs of customers or clients, let alone shareholders, and the financial environment within which most organizations operate. Not only has it drawn from these earlier models, but it has used elements of other, more directive change models such as Kotter's (1996, Part 2) eight-stage change process and Paton and McCalman's (2000, pp. 10–13) model of perpetual transition management.

Even so, organization development as a philosophy and a process can be critiqued according to a number of criteria. The following are examples.

OD does not always face up to harsh realities of change

Almost all models of change include, in one form or another, the underlying concept of unfreezing. From an OD point of view this would be achieved through a typical action–research process of data collection, analysis and feedback as part of a participatory process of education for change. Yet authors such as Clarke (1994) and Johnson (1990) describe this process of unfreezing in much harsher terms.

Thus Clarke (pp. 147–8) talks of 'speeding up the unfreezing process' through *destabilizing* people to detach them from the old order. She quotes the example of Centraal Beheer, an insurance company in the Netherlands, 'creating an anxiety greater than the risk of doing something different'. She goes on to say (p. 149): 'Pent-up anger and discontent are the motivators for change; no significant change is possible without them.' Clarke talks the language of crisis and even of engineering a crisis in order to speed up the unfreezing process.

Johnson (p. 190) goes further than Clarke with his talk of 'symbolic acts of questioning or destruction' to start the unfreezing process. He gives examples of John de Lorean trying to change his division of General Motors by promulgating stories to ridicule the dominant culture and of Lee Iacocca firing 33 out of 35 vice-presidents within three years of taking over at Chrysler. Johnson continues this line of thinking by saying (p. 190): 'As conflict and debate grows, managers may actually foster it by symbolic acts of conflict, destruction and degradation.'

However, care must be taken that crisis is not seen merely as a threat and, as Ferlie and Bennett (1993) point out, paradoxically reduces energy, creativity and flexibility. From an OD point of view crisis would be seen as an opportunity that, in Ferlie and Bennett's (p. 270) words, 'forces awkward issues up the agendas [when] we are likely to see continuing pressure from pioneers, the formation of special groups who evangelize the rest of the organization, high energy and commitment levels, and a period of organizational plasticity in which anything seems plausible'.

Alternatively, as Farquhar et al. (1989, p. 37) point out: 'Not all companies see crisis as a prerequisite for major organizational change. The World Bank, for example, believes that a trigger of another kind may be sufficient. This could range from the aspirations of top management, through anxiety about an uncertain future, to a downturn in results.' Monitoring the internal and external organizational environments on a regular basis can detect potential crises in their early and most treatable phases. What needs to be recognized is that change without crisis is most frequently incremental and time is needed to build the momentum for larger-scale, more radical change.

OD is limited when change situations are 'constrained'

OD has been promoted as a change model for coping with situations of soft complexity where goals and also the means of achieving them are unclear. However, there are situations which have many of the characteristics of soft complexity yet are constrained in the sense that the goals are predetermined and the means of achieving them are to some extent set. In other words change is dictated by top management or the precise requirements of some part of the organization's external environment. For instance, healthcare is proscribed by the need to safeguard the public against malpractice and legislation regarding the use of treatments and drugs. Setting up a new doctor's practice must adhere to many different forms of regulatory requirement. Franchisees must often run their businesses according to the dictates of the franchiser.

It may be, of course, that, when change is desirable, a hard systems model of change is most appropriate. However, 'dictated' change is likely to bring resistance from those who must implement it. Therefore, although the earlier stages of the OD model may not be applicable, there is still the requirement to develop an action plan, implement, assess and reinforce change. In addition, gaining commitment to, and participation in, this part of the change process by those who must make the change is of the utmost importance. Consequently, even in highly constrained situations of change, implementation must be as carefully executed as in any other OD process.

OD in the public sector

Chapter 3 discussed the work of Burns and Stalker (1961) and illustrated the differences between mechanistic and organic organizational structures. A consideration of these shows how an organic structure, rather than a mechanistic structure, is more suited to organizations embracing an OD model of change. Consequently the application of OD in the mechanistically structured, bureaucratic organizations that are typical of governmental and publicly accountable organizations is a difficult undertaking. Writing on organizational development in the public sector, McConkie (1993, pp. 634–42), from a North American perspective but one that applies generally, discusses a number of reasons why the application of OD in public sector organizations is likely to give rise to problems. These, together with others, are the following:

1 The basic philosophical differences between the assumptions and values of OD and those of the bureaucratic model (which is typical of most public sector organizations) are significant because public sector organizations typically reflect strong adherence to bureaucratic norms and behaviour patterns – forms and patterns foreign to those of OD – therefore making OD application difficult and sensitive, though not impossible.

2 Public sector organizations have multiple authoritative decision makers and multilevel accountability and reporting relationships. They are also 'supervised' by many interests, such as the general public, other government agencies, interest groups, the media and so on. All these make it difficult, first, to get support and gain approvals for an OD initiative and, second, to guide OD designs to fruition because so many people and interests 'get in the way'.

3 Financial support is difficult to obtain for OD work in public sector organizations. This is because, first, funding for consultancy (i.e. external change agents) is limited compared with that available in the private sector and, second, so many different people have to agree to the spending of funds.

4 In public sector organizations, the large variety of different and frequently conflicting interests, different political allegiances, reward structures and values make OD, as a system-wide effort, difficult to apply. OD interventions are, therefore, more likely to be of a small-scale nature in single departments or work groups.

5 McConkie (p. 640), on the writings of Golembiewski (1989), says: 'Five aspects of the public "habit background" ... make it an inhospitable host for OD: public patterns of delegation, the legal habit, the need for security, the procedural regularity and caution, and the slowly developing image of the "professional manager".'

6 Decision making in public sector organizations tends to be pushed upwards towards the top. This contrasts with OD objectives that seek to increase self-control and self-direction of organization members, something which is difficult if decisions must always be passed to upper levels of management. What is more, deciding where the 'top' is can be confusing. It might be the highest level of the administration, but it may be necessary also to take account of elected and appointed political interests – which may be at both local and national level. The generally accepted assumption that OD-type interventions should have the support of top management and, frequently, should be led by them, sits uneasily with the realization that, in some instances, for political reasons the top may not want to be seen to be involved.

These points paint a depressing picture for the likelihood that any OD model for change could succeed in public sector organizations. However, as the public sector (in the United Kingdom, for example, the health service, local authorities, some government departments) has become more privatized in its outlook and with regard to outcomes, the OD model for change becomes more realistic and easier to apply. Indeed, because of the extreme complexity of these organizations and the massive changes they are having to face, change models that do not take account of the soft, messy situations they face have little likelihood of succeeding. Illustration 8.4 is an extract from the 'Employers' Organisation for local government' website, where it makes the case for the use of OD in the context of the large-scale changes faced by institutions of local government in the United Kingdom.

Illustration 8.3

Making sense of change – saying goodbye to 'initiative fatigue'

Why should we be interested in Organisation Development?

Councils are facing unrelenting pressure to provide better quality services at a time when they are under unprecedented scrutiny. The introduction of the corporate governance and capacity assessment presents a further challenge, not least because it comes on top of other government initiatives, such as best value.

Change initiatives often fail because organisations try to implement a number of activities too quickly and without proper coordination or thought about the implications for people management. This leads to 'initiative fatigue' where staff become disillusioned and more resistant to change.

Many authorities are beginning to consider the importance of Organisation Development as part of

preparing for e-government. So far, there has generally been more emphasis on ICT, systems and the use of technical experts, yet more than 50 per cent of ICT projects fail because of cultural or organisational problems. E-government will demand support at the top and people with organisational development expertise helping to plan and implement ICT and related changes strategically throughout the local authority.

During recent years 'Organisation Development' (OD) has re-emerged as a key element in the strategic management of change, providing a focus for the cultural and organisational change needed for continuous improvement, aligning systems, culture and activities to the achievement of organisational goals. It enables better use of financial, human and technological resources, fosters a greater sense of

Illustration 8.3 continued

organisational purpose and it is therefore more likely to deliver the required performance improvement.

What is Organisation Development?
OD is about moving the organisation on by taking deliberate, planned steps to create an environment that will enable staff to understand and deliver the council's objectives. Responding to and working with key stakeholders forms an essential part of this process.

OD involves both 'hard' and 'soft' issues. The 'hard' issues for OD are strategies and policies, structures and systems. The 'softer' issues in the main are developing appropriate skills, behaviours and attitudes, culture and a style of leadership that will enable the organisation to achieve optimum performance. Both the 'harder' and 'softer' issues of OD need to be addressed to avoid conflict between goals and needs.

What sorts of activities are integral to Organisation Development?
Many activities contribute to a favourable 'climate' for progress. A clear sense of direction, strong leadership and a focus on people management issues including the management of performance and the promotion of learning, creativity and innovation are essential. Feedback, sharing ideas across the organisation and the community and evaluating progress are also key.

In this way OD can be widely accepted and integrated within the culture of the organisation as a whole to ensure maximum strategic benefit. This requires authorities to identify the skills they need to build organisational capacity and plan how these will be developed or acquired. Each authority will make its own decisions but there are ranges of activities

that will need to be brought together if OD is to deliver significant performance improvement.

These include linking OD with council objectives, finding and developing staff with the right skills to help champion OD throughout the organisation and encouraging wide participation and ownership of the continuous improvement process among staff and elected members. Building in this perspective at the beginning will mean that changes are grounded and sustainable, with people management considerations integrated into the process.

Where is Organisation Development located within local authorities?
In principle OD can be located anywhere in an authority structure, though recent research shows that where posts are located within the Chief Executives' Department there is closer liaison and a more flexible organisational response to wide-ranging demands. But wherever the function is located there are a wide range of behaviours, skills and knowledge that will be needed across the organisation.

Taking it forward – What next for you?
● Have you got commitment and involvement at the top of the organisation?
● Is there someone in your organisation who is coordinating OD activities?
● Have you got a 'map' of the OD activities happening in your organisation?

Source: Employers' Organisation for local government website: http://www.lg-employers.gov.uk/od/index.html

The EO has produced practical tools to support councils to manage organisational development and change. For example, we have produced a checklist of skills and capacity building requirements for successful organisational change

OD in different cultures

The discussion in Chapter 4 identified issues associated with differences between people from different societal cultures. It also touched upon diversity of gender and race within national groupings. It is not difficult to find many organizations, large and small, that operate across the globe.

This chapter and the previous one have described at least three ways of designing and implementing organizational change. In addition, ways of dealing with resistance and conflict have been addressed. What must be recognized, however, is the predominantly western bias of much that is written about organizations and change. Consequently, writers such as Jaegar (1986) and more recently Adler (1997) do well to warn that not all change methods and techniques are transportable across national boundaries to other parts of the world or even to different ethnic groupings within single countries. This is particularly the case with the range of techniques associated with OD as a philosophy and a methodology for bringing about change.

In an extensive discussion of organizational development and national culture, Jaegar links typical OD values with each of Hofstede's (1980) dimensions of culture and concludes that they have a low correspondence with high power distance, high uncertainty avoidance, high masculinity and moderate individualism. Consequently, some OD-type interventions are unlikely to gain easy acceptance in societies that score high on these dimensions. This is confirmed by Cummings and Worley (1997), who give an example of people from Scandinavian countries as being sympathetic to OD change methods, which is in line with their scores on Hofstede's dimensions. They contrast this with people from Latin American countries (who score high on power distance, uncertainty avoidance and masculinity), who are unlikely to be comfortable with some of the OD ways of effecting change.

The OD philosophy of people-centred leadership and employee participation in the change process is unlikely to find favour in countries such as France and Italy where managers subscribe to ideals of hierarchy and formalized organizational systems (see Laurent, 1983). The title of Jack's (1997) article in the *Financial Times* – 'Caste in stone' and his comment, 'Challenge French corporate hierarchies at your peril' – say much of French managers' attitudes to the participative styles of leadership that are typical of OD approaches to change.

One consequence of these reservations about the degree to which OD approaches can be used wherever change occurs is that there is a need for OD-type techniques to vary according to whether an organization operates in what Keegan (1989) terms an *ethnocentric* or *geocentric* way. Organizations with an ethnocentric orientation are those that tend to offer a standard product across the world and operate with centralized decision making from the home country base. Managers, wherever they are located, are usually chosen from the home country nationals on the basis that operations and ways of managing 'abroad' should mirror those in the home base.

By contrast, organizations with a geocentric orientation accept that things might be done differently in different countries. Consequently, although there is still a degree of overall centralized coordination of activities, products, operations and methods of management are tailored to the different conditions in each country. In this type of organization, instead of managers being 'sent out' (e.g. as expatriates) from the home country, the organization trains and develops host country managers to operate in a decentralized, mainly autonomous way.

The consequences of this distinction are that similar approaches to change are more likely to be used in ethnocentrically operated organizations than those that organize on geocentric principles where approaches to change are more likely to be tailored to the cultures in which they are being used.

Having said that, there remain many OD techniques that can be used in spite of there existing less than propitious attitudes and beliefs on the part of those involved. Citing Harrison (1972), French and Bell (1990) use the concept of 'depth of intervention' to distinguish those techniques that interact mainly with the more formalized organizational systems (such as job enrichment, management by objectives, role analysis and attitude surveys) and those which go deeper into exploring the informal and more personal organizational systems – for instance team building, encounter groups and interpersonal relationship explorations. Depth of intervention is a useful concept for deciding how 'deep' to go in the use of OD-type interventions as part of the process of change that involves people from different cultures. It is particularly relevant for those organizations that operate outside their home country environment.

Comment and conclusions

Soft systems models for change, of which OD is a well-known example, contrast with hard systems in being able to address the issues of soft complexity inherent in the type of 'messy' situations described in Chapter 2. Soft systems approaches to change emphasize not just the content and control of change but also the *process* by which change comes about. They require consideration of the cultural and political aspects of organizations as much as the structure and systems. 'Change agents' facilitating change using these approaches require influencing skills and the skills of negotiation. Because different individuals respond to their different *perceptions* of events, which will differ one from another, change agents need to understand the aspirations and feelings of those working in change situations as well as the group processes that bind them together.

Soft systems models of change are, essentially, *planned* approaches to change. This does not mean, however, that they cannot account for unexpected and surprising events. Indeed the requirement to iterate frequently around and across the different phases and stages of the model takes account of the probability that there will be 'changes within changes' occurring. Taken together, hard and soft systems models of change offer those working with change ways of addressing issues in their simplicity and complexity to enhance the work or organizations and the lives of those working in them.

Discussion questions and assignments

1 Debate the pros and cons of using external change agents compared to internal ones.

2 Compare and contrast the HSMC and OD approaches to change. Give examples of types of change situations where each may be appropriate.

3 Draw a rich picture of life as experienced by you in your organization.

4 If your manager is looking for a 'quick fix' to manage a change process, how might you justify using an OD approach to change?

Indicative resources

Cummings, T. and Worley, C. (2005) *Organization Development and Change* (8th edn), Mason, OH: Thomson South-Western. This text also focuses on OD. However, a part of the book is dedicated to the effective implementation of this process and how it can be used in both public and private sectors. There are numerous case studies as examples of issues associated with OD and applications of it in a variety of organizations.

French, W. L. and Bell, C. H. (1999) *Organization Development* (6th edn), Upper Saddler River, NJ; Prentice-Hall. French and Bell have dedicated much of their time to promoting and educating in the field of OD. This text offers a good introduction to OD and guidance in using this approach.

Whitney, D. and Trosten-Bloom, A. (2003) *The Power of Appreciative Inquiry*, San Francisco, CA: Berrett-Koehler. These two authors are testimonials to achieving change through innovative and creative ways in partnerships with organizations. Based on the principles of OD (people and their potential), it is an interesting book in relation to work with individuals, groups and organizations. In particular, it supports the ideas and concepts associated with learning organizations.

Useful websites

www.lg-employers.gov.uk/od/ This site provides support for students, managers and organizations in relation to the OD process. It identifies key OD concepts, provides examples of making a case for OD, managing the process, key tasks and responsibilities and also provides useful case studies of the process in action.

www.actionlearningassociates.co.uk This site is helpful for those who have further interest in action learning. It provides a working definition, offers examples of how action learning can be used, how the groups operate and how to use 'in-house' sets for the purposes of OD.

www.ifal.org.uk This is the UK's official action learning site.

To click straight to these links and for other resources go to
www.pearsoned.co.uk/senior

 References

Ackoff, R. L. (1993) 'The art and science of mess management', in Mabey, C. and Mayon-White, B. (eds) *Managing Change*, London: PCP.

Adler, N. J. (1997) *International Dimensions of Organizational Behavior* (3rd edn), Cincinnati, OH: South-Western College Publishing, ITP.

Alpander, G. G. and Lee, C. R. (1995) 'Culture, strategy and teamwork: the keys to organizational change', *Journal of Management Development,* vol. 14, no. 8, pp. 4–18.

Argyris, C. (1964) *Integrating the Individual and the Organization*, New York: Wiley.

Argyris, C. (1992) *On Organizational Learning*, Oxford: Blackwell.

Argyris, C. and Schon, D. A. (1996) *Organizational Learning II*, Reading, MA: Addison-Wesley.

Beckhard, R. and Harris, R. T. (1987) *Organizational Transitions: Managing Complex Change* (2nd edn), Reading, MA: Addison-Wesley.

Benjamin, G. and Mabey, C. (1993) 'Facilitating radical change: a case of organization transformation', in Mabey, C. and Mayon-White, B. (eds) *Managing Change* (2nd edn), London: PCP.

Buchanan, D. and Boddy, D. (1992) *The Expertise of the Change Agent: Public Performance and Backstage Activity*, Hemel Hempstead: Prentice Hall.

Buchanan, D. and McCalman, J. (1989) *High Performance Work Systems: The Digital Experience*, London: Routledge.

Burnes, B. (2004) *Managaing Change: A Strategic Approach to Organisational Dynamics* (4th edn), Harlow: Financial Times Prentice Hall.

Burns, T. and Stalker, G. M. (1961) *The Management of Innovation*, London: Tavistock.

Burnside, R. M. (1991) 'Visioning: building pictures of the future', in Henry, J. and Walker, D. (eds) *Managing Innovation*: London: Sage.

Carnall, C. (2003) *Managing Change in Organizations* (4th edn), Harlow: Pearson Education.

Checkland, P. (1981) *Systems Thinking, Systems Practice*, Chichester: Wiley.

Clarke, J., Hooper, C. and Nicholson, J. (1997) 'Reversal of fortune', *People Management*, 20 March, pp. 22–6, 29.

Clarke, L. (1994) *The Essence of Change*, Hemel Hempstead: Prentice Hall.

Cummings, T. G. and Worley, C. G. (1997), *Organization Development and Change* (6th edn), Cincinnati, OH: South-Western College Publishing.

Cummings, T. G. and Worley, C. G. (2005) *Organization Development and Change* (8th edn), Mason, OH: South-Western, p. 117.

Elkjaar, B. (1999) 'In search of a social learning theory', in Easterby-Smith, M., Burgoyne, J. and Araujo, L. (eds) *Organizational Learning and the Learning Organization: Development in Theory and Practice*, London: Sage, pp. 75–91.

Farquhar, A., Evans, P. and Tawadey, K. (1989) 'Lessons from practice in managing organizational change', in Evans, P., Doz, E. and Laurent, A. (eds) *Human Resource Management in International Firms: Change, Globalization, Innovation*, London: Macmillan.

Ferlie, E. and Bennett, C. (1993) 'Patterns of strategic change in health care: district health authorities respond to AIDS', in Hendry, J., Johnson, G. and Newton, J. (eds) *Strategic Thinking, Leadership and the Management of Change*, Chichester: Wiley.

Flood, R. L. and Jackson, M. C. (1991) *Creative Problem Solving: Total Systems Intervention*, Chichester: Wiley.

French, W. L. and Bell, C. H., Jr (1990) *Organization Development: Behavioral Science Interventions for Organization Improvement*, Englewood Cliffs, NJ: Prentice-Hall.

French, W. L. and Bell, C. H. (1999) *Organization Development: Behavioural Science Interventions for Oragnizational Improvement* (6th edn), Upper Saddle River, NJ: Prentice-Hall.

Golembiewski, R.T. (1989) *Organizational Development: Ideas and Issues*, New Brunswick: Transaction Publishers.

Goodstein, L. D. and Burke, W. W. (1993) 'Creating successful organization change', in Mabey, C. and Mayon-White, B. (eds) *Managing Change*, London: PCP.

Harrison, R. (1972) 'When power conflicts trigger team spirit', *European Business*, Spring, pp. 27–65.

Hofstede, G. (1980) *Culture's Consequences: International Differences in Work-related Values*, London and Beverley Hills, CA: Sage.

Jack, A. (1997) 'Caste in stone: challenge to French corporate hierarchies at your peril', *Financial Times* 10 April.

Jaegar, A. M. (1986) 'Organization development and national culture: where's the fit?' *Academy of Management Review*, vol. 11, no. 1, pp. 178–90.

Johnson, G. (1990) 'Managing strategic change: the role of symbolic action', *British Journal of Management*, vol. 1. pp. 183–200.

Johnson, G. (1993) 'Processes of managing strategic change', in Mabey, C. and Mayon-White, B. (eds) *Managing Change* (2nd edn), London: PCP.

Johnson, G., Scholes, K. and Whittington, R. (2005) *Exploring Corporate Strategy* (7th edn), Harlow: Pearson Education.

Jones, P. (1994) 'Which lever do I pull now?: the role of "emergent planning" in managing change', *Organisations & People*, vol. 1, no. 1, January, pp. 46–9.

Keegan, W. J. (1989) 'International-multinational-global marketing: a typology', Chapter 1 in Keegan, W. J. (ed.) *Global Marketing Management* (4th edn), Englewood Cliffs, NJ: Prentice-Hall.

Kirkbride, P. S., Durcan, J. and Obeng, E. D. A. (1994) 'Change in a chaotic post-modern world', *Journal of Strategic Change*, vol. 3, pp. 151–63.

Kotter, J. P. (1996), *Leading Change*, Boston, MA: Harvard Business School Press.

Laurent, A. (1983) 'The cultural diversity of Western conceptions of management', *International Studies of Management and Organisations*, vol. XIII, nos 1–2, pp. 78–96.

Lewin, K. (1951) *Field Theory in Social Science*, New York: Harper & Row.

Lievegoed, B. (1983) *Man on the Threshold*, Driebergen: Hawthorne Press.

Lloyd, B. and Feigen, M. (1997) 'Real change leaders: the key challenge to management today', *Leadership & Organization Development Journal*, vol. 18, no. 1, pp. 37–40.

McConkie, M. L. (1993) 'Organization development in the public sector', in Cummings, T. G. and Worley, C. G., *Organization Development and Change* (5th edn), St. Paul, MN: West.

Mabey, C. and Pugh, D. (1995) Unit 10, 'Strategies for managing complex change', Course B751, *Managing Development and Change*, Milton Keynes: Open University Press.

Matsushita, K. (1988) 'The secret is shared', *Manufacturing Engineering*, March, pp. 78–84.

Morgan, G. (1986) *Images of Organization*, London: Sage.

Open University (1985) Unit 8, 'Process', Course T244, *Managing in Organizations*, Milton Keynes: Open University Press.

Paton, R. A. and McCalman, J. (2000) *Change Management: A Guide to Effective Implementation*, London: Sage.

Pedler, M., Boydell, T. and Burgoyne, J. (1991) *The Learning Company*, London: McGraw-Hill.

Price, C. (1987) 'Culture change: the tricky bit', *Training and Development*, October, pp. 20–2.

Pugh, D. (1986) Block 4, 'Planning and managing change', *Organizational Development*, Milton Keynes: Open University Press.

Pugh, D. (1993) 'Understanding and managing change', in Mabey, C. and Mayon-White, B. (eds) *Managing Change* (2nd edn), London: PCP, pp. 108–12.

Schein, E. (1987) *Process Consultation Volume II: Lessons for Managers and Consultants*, Reading, MA: Addison-Wesley.

Senge, P. (1990) *The Fifth Discipline: The Art and Practice of the Learning Organization*, New York: Doubleday Currency.

Smith, B. (1995) 'Not in front of the children: the realities of "involvement" in managing change', *Organisations & People*, vol. 2, no. 2, pp. 17–20.

Stacey, R. (2003) *Strategic Management and Organisational Dynamics: The Challenge of Complexity* (4th edn), Harlow: Financial Times Prentice Hall.

Whitney, D. and Trosten-Bloom, A. (2003) *The Power of Appreciative Inquiry*, San Francisco, CA: Berrett-Koehler.

www.lg-employers.gov.uk/od/how/index.html.

www.thebodyshop.co.uk

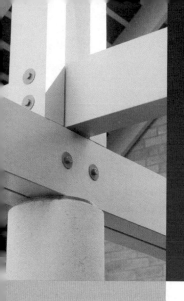

Chapter 9

A changing future – factors for effective change

The material in this chapter builds on what has already been discussed in the book, but takes a more 'futuristic' focus. It is, therefore, to some extent speculative. However it is hoped that the material will provide an impetus for considering two aspects of organizational change. The first is what organizations of the future might look like. The second is to speculate on the impact that more wide-ranging changes in society will have on people and their attitudes to work. The possible conflicts between the two are addressed with suggestions on some factors that might help to make organizational change a success. There is also the opportunity, through examples, to demonstrate that for most organizations planned change can aid in managing change. It is also an opportunity to show that organizations also have to respond to unplanned environmental triggers, that demonstrates the reality of having to manage 'unpredictable' elements.

Learning objectives

By the end of this chapter, you will be able to:

- identify trends in business organizations and areas that may need to be addressed in the future to manage change more effectively;

- recognize that planning for change can be influenced by internal and external factors that make 'predictability' difficult at times;

- provide examples of planned change and unpredictable change being part of organizational life;

- begin to apply the principles discussed in previous chapters to identify and plan for change successfully using a 'factors for success' planning tool.

●●●● Introduction

The two chapters in Part One examined the way organizations and the context in which they operate have changed throughout time and discussed the way political, economic, social and technological changes impact on the way organizations operate today. The concept of organizational change was shown to be heterogeneous, in that there are many types of change occurring both sequentially and simultaneously, sometimes predicted and sometimes coming as a 'surprise'.

This picture was elaborated in Part Two by addressing aspects of organizational life that intervene to influence change outcomes in one direction or another. During this discussion a variety of contrasting ideas on the nature of change and how it should be responded to and managed were advanced. Finally, in Part Three, two major methodologies of change were described. Given all this, it would be ideal if the overall outcome were an all-embracing, widely accepted theory of change with agreed guidelines on 'how to do it'. Unfortunately this is not the case. This is particularly so when organizational managers and others working with organizational change attempt to look into the future in the hope of predicting when and how their organizations, in whole or part, should prepare for what lies ahead.

The purpose of this final chapter is, therefore, to examine some of the ideas that have been put forward – particularly as the millennium came and went – regarding what the future holds. It addresses issues associated with the way changing demographics, households and families, occupations and employment, education, lifestyles, communities, government and state are likely to influence and change the nature of organizational life, directly or indirectly, in the next decade and beyond. In doing this, and within the conventions of the systems approach described in Chapter 1, it provides a feedback loop and reiteration of what was said there but, in the case of the discussion here, takes a somewhat wider and more speculative perspective.

What is said here may be controversial; it may provoke agreement or disagreement, even though it is grounded in a variety of people's theories, research and opinions. It may lead to frustration in that the issues cannot be dealt with one by one, but interact in a systemic way one with another. In this it mirrors the soft complexity of much organizational life. It is hoped, however, that it will lead to an improved process of debating the future of organizations and the way they operate, within an ever-changing, only partially predictable and, of itself, 'messy' organizational environment.

●●●● Some general trends

In August 1999 the Department of Trade and Industry (DTI) in the United Kingdom published a report entitled *Britain Towards 2010: The Changing Business Environment* (see Scase, 1999). It is recommended for anyone interested in and working with organizational change and can be ordered free from the DTI Department of Trade and Industry, 1 Victoria Street, London, SW1H OET. A scenario called 'Foresight 2015' can also be accessed through the Foresight website (www.foresight.org.uk).

The year of this report might make it appear dated. However, the DTI has not published anything so comprehensive since, and the trends are still paramount in influencing current and future changes in organizational life. More recent publications (see for example, Arnold, Silvester, Patterson, Robertson, Cooper and Burnes, 2005) confirm many of these predictions in addition to adding to them. The DTI report starts with a list of some major trends that are likely to affect industry, lifestyles and social structures and which, in turn, will affect organizations – their strategies, structures, how they are led, employment practices and the need to work with change. Eleven trends are mentioned:

1 *Individuality*: a decline in traditional family forms.
2 *Choice*: an increase in choice of home, work, leisure.
3 *Mobility*: an increase in the mobility of individuals regarding residence, working, and personal relationships.
4 *Identity*: increased 'fluidity' in personal identities because of increased mobility and more transient working arrangements, personal relations and leisure.
5 *Independence*: increased freedom from traditional obligations leads to more self-centredness, self-indulgence and hedonistic psychologies.
6 *Anxiety and risk*: a more rootless society giving rise to feelings of insecurity; society perceived as perhaps high risk and threatening or exciting and challenging.
7 *Creativity*: increased focus on self-interest and individuality will encourage personal creativity generating a more innovative society.
8 *Globalization*: increase in the international division of labour with greater global segregation between the developed and underdeveloped economies: Islamic and Christian societies, Russia, central Europe and euroland; the challenge to Britain is to become a leading-edge information economy.
9 *Information and communication technologies (ICTs)*: increasing capabilities of ICTs leading to the decline in traditional forms of organization including large public sector as well as commercial and voluntary organizations.
10 *Bio-technologies*: genetic engineering; increased ability to control patterns of reproduction, not just sex of babies; technologies to improve health, both physical and psychological.
11 *Socio-economic inequalities*: increased polarization in cultural, educational and material living standards.

Illustration 9.1 lists the key changes between 1971 and 2002 (the latest UK government statistics) in the demographic, social and economic characteristics of households, families and people in Great Britain.

At the more micro-level of the organization, Arnold *et al.* (2005, pp. 521–2) suggest features that will affect the 'people' aspect of changes and issues relating

Illustration 9.1

Key changes in the demographic, social and economic characteristics of households, families and people in Great Britain between 1971 and 2002

- A decline in household size and changes in household composition
- A growth in the proportion of lone-parent familes
- An increase in the proportion of people living alone
- An increase in the proportion of people who are cohabiting
- An increase in home ownership and a decline in the proportion of households living in social housing
- An increase in the household availability of consumer durables
- An increase in the prevalence of self-reported longstanding illness or disability
- A decline in the prevalence of smoking
- A decrease in the proportion of working men belonging to an occupational pension scheme
- An increase in the proportion of working women belonging to an occupational pension scheme.

Source: www.statistics.gov.uk; Living in Britain No 31, Results from the 2002 General Household Survey.

to how organizations may manage employees in the United Kingdom and other western countries. Most relevant for this discussion are the following:

- *Structural changes*: elimination of layers of management; reduction in numbers of people employed together with moves to increased teamworking; pressures for individuals to work harder and longer.
- *Working patterns*: increased use of short-term contracts; part-time working (predominantly women), with many people having two or more jobs; working at or from home – currently around 3–5 per cent of those in employment.
- *Workforce characteristics*: decreasing birth rates (in the West) and increased longevity leading to rise in the average age of people in work; patterns of immigration leading to more diverse workforce in terms of ethnicity, values and gender.
- *Workforce skills*: increased requirement for workers to learn new skills in line with changing technologies and the competitive environment.
- *Employment choices*: increasing self-employment and working in small organizations – nearly 50 per cent of people in the United Kingdom are self-employed or work in organizations employing fewer than 20 employees.
- *Pension schemes*: ageing population and more mobility between occupations and organizations leading to increasing pressure on occupational and employer-based pension schemes.

Some of these changes have already begun to happen, however the extent to which they will influence future work remains to be seen. It is not intended to discuss all these in detail but to explore those of particular relevance to, and that have implications for, organizational change.

 **Demographic changes**

UK increase in proportion of older people

In the context of predictions of total population increase (see Illustration 9.2), it is well known that Britain has an ageing population. In 2001 Kandola predicted that there would soon be 40 per cent of people over 50 years of age with only 5 per cent in the 15–19 age group. Two years later, Cannon (2003) predicted that the proportion of the UK population over 65 would rise from 15 to 23 per cent by 2050. These demographic changes appear to be 'relatively' slow, however there is evidence that current profiles are realistic as life expectancy increases and fertility rates fall within western societies. Over the next 20 years these trends will bring a fall in the proportion of people under 25 and a large increase in adults aged 50 to 65+.

Illustration 9.2

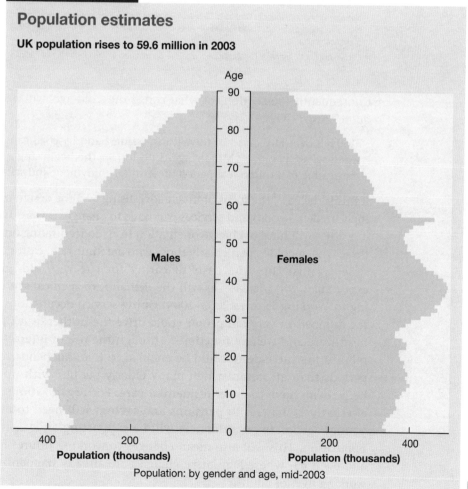

Population estimates

UK population rises to 59.6 million in 2003

Population: by gender and age, mid-2003

Illustration 9.2 continued

In mid-2003 the United Kingdom was home to 59.6 million people. The average age was 38.4 years, an increase on 1971 when it was 34.1 years. In mid-2003 one in five people in the United Kingdom was aged under 16 and one in six was aged 65 or over.

The United Kingdom has a growing population. It grew by 232,100 people in the year to mid-2003, and the growth was 0.4 per cent in each of the years since mid-2001. The United Kingdom population has increased by 6.5 per cent in the last 30 years or so, from 55.9 million in mid-1971. Growth has been faster in more recent years. Between mid-1991 and mid-2003 the population grew by an annual rate of 0.3 per cent.

The United Kingdom has an ageing population. This is the result of declines both in fertility rates and in the mortality rate. This has led to a declining proportion of the population aged under 16 and an increasing proportion aged 65 and over.

In every year since 1901, with the exception of 1976, there were more births than deaths in the United Kingdom and the population has grown due to natural change. Until the mid-1990s this natural increase was the main driver of population growth. Since the late 1990s there has still been natural increase but net international migration into the United Kingdom from abroad has been an increasingly important factor in population change.

Source: Office for National Statistics, General Register Office for Scotland (www.gro-scotland.gov.uk), Northern Ireland Statistics and Research Agency(www.nisra.gov.uk), 9 September 2004; http://www.statistics.gov.uk

Crown copyright material is reproduced with the permission of the Controller of HMSO.

Consequently, perceptions of what constitutes 'old age' will need to change. To quote Scase (1999):

> Today's over 50s – clad in their jeans, trainers and baseball caps – no longer view themselves as old. ... Middle age is no longer the beginning of the end but the beginning of a thirty-year period of personal enjoyment and self-indulgence.

If this is the case, the focus of much advertising and the design of wanted – rather than needed – goods and services will have to change. Leisure and entertainment industries will have to change orientation from concentrating on the under-35s to those who are older, particularly those who are 'time rich, cash rich'.

Set against this, the costs of caring for the very old, given longer life expectancy, will increase, as will the demand for medical services and (according to Working Futures 2003–2004) caring service occupations. The increase in the numbers of very old people could drive the further development of ICTs in healthcare and welfare functions. Through the use of interactive, audio-visual monitoring the elderly could be enabled to live independent lives for longer periods than at present when many elderly people, with no one close by to help them, have to enter residential care. For organizations this means that alternatives/changes to pensions and savings will need to materialize as the younger generations ultimately will be supporting an ever-increasing 'older' population. This will also mean changes to working futures for those over 60 and even 65, where legislative changes are already happening to extend the working lives of adults.

Household composition

Associated with these changes is the less-known trend in the increasing number of single person households, the increase coming particularly from younger middle-aged people not yet engaged in 'live-in' partnerships, and especially women in the 15–44 age group as well as older widows, given the propensity for men to die at a younger age than women. The institution of marriage in Britain has been losing popularity since 1981 – the Government Actuary's Department (GAD) (2005) predicts that this trend will continue and that, by 2011, 33 per cent of women and 40 per cent of men will never have been married. By 2021, the prediction rises to 36 per cent of women and 43 per cent of men. The news release from the GAD (2005) says:

> The recent steep fall in marriage rates at ages under 30 will, in time, have an impact at older ages. So there will be marked falls in the married population, and increases in the never-married population at ages 30 to 64 in the period to 2031.

This does not mean that all these people live alone – cohabiting will gain in popularity. Even so, the number of households in England and Wales is projected to increase by 7 per cent (1.60 million) between 2001 (the latest comparison year given by the Department of the Environment, Farming and Rural Affairs (DEFRA)) and 2011 and 14 per cent (3.15 million) between 2001 and 2021. Part of this increase in housing need will result from people living longer and the predicted increase in single person households (by 2010, 49 per cent of all households).

Fewer births and early retirements

Illustration 9.3 reflects the concern in Europe about the changing balance in the ages of working people compared to retired people. For instance, in the United Kingdom: 'Average completed family size has now levelled off, from a peak of nearly 2.45 children for women born in the mid-1930s to 1.74 children for women born after 1985. In 2003 there were 3.34 persons of working age for every person of pensionable age. By 2010, this demographic support ratio will decline to 3.11. … Longer-term projections suggest the support ratio will briefly stabilize around 2.30 in the 2040s, declining slightly further to around 2.15 in the 2060s' (Government Actuary's Department, 2004).

Illustration 9.3

An endangered species: fewer births make old Europe fear for its future

Many governments concerned by slow population growth are hoping for a new baby boom. But policies to bring about social changes are expensive and controversial. In eastern Europe, they are attempting to buck the trend. Hospitals in Estonia are braced for a baby boom. New maternity wards are being carved out of space allocated to other departments as the tiny Baltic state prepares itself for Europe's biggest surge in births in decades.

Since the 1970s birth rates have been falling in Europe, North America and Japan, as the generation of people born in the post-1945 baby boom took

Illustration 9.3 *continued*

advantage of the spread of contraception to have fewer children than their parents. At first this produced big economic gains as more women went to work, helping to boost the labour force. But as the baby boomers move towards retirement a smaller generation will take their place.

Today there are 30 people of pensionable age for every 100 working age adults in the developed world. By 2040 there will be 70, according to projections based on United Nations data.

The population issue is creeping on to the European agenda. Italy last year published a ground-breaking White Paper on the welfare state, giving priority to managing the demographic transition and placing the family at the centre of political action.

In the United Kingdom, France and Scandinavia, birth rates have fallen relatively little. In Britain, a big contributor is a high rate of teenage pregnancy, which stems population decline, but brings social problems and is something that the government wants to reduce. In France, birth rates have been held up by pro-family policies going back decades. In the last 20 years Scandinavian states, led by Sweden, have boosted their fertility to French levels by adopting some of the French policies.

Meanwhile, as older people retire, a bigger economic burden falls on the remaining workers, which reduces productivity growth and limits the economy's capacity to finance welfare spending. Employers have aggravated the position by pushing for early retirement schemes. In France, just 38.5 per cent of men aged 55–64 worked in 2000, compared with 65.3 per cent in 1980.

Source: Wagstyl, S. (2004) 'An endangered species: fewer births make old Europe fear for its future', *Financial Times*, June 11, 2004, p. 17.

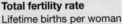

Total fertility rate
Lifetime births per woman

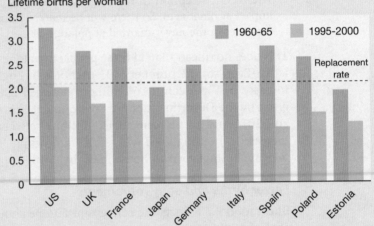

Participation of women in the labour force
Rate, % (prime-age women between 25–54)

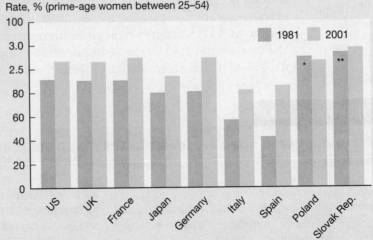

* 1992 figures ** 1994 figures

Alongside these changes, and coupled with the increasing emphasis on occupational and private pensions, there is likely to be a continued rise in the trend towards early retirement, even though in the United Kingdom, women retiring from now on will not draw their state pensions until they are 65 – as men do now. What is more, while there are still retired people who have only their state pension to live on, there are a significant number of others who have good levels of spending power, helped by the fact that, while younger people face high mortgage charges, many retired people have paid for their homes. European businesses of the future must consider how to adapt their products and services to satisfy the needs and wants of increasing younger populations in the east, while also attending to the needs and wants of the older people who are 'cash rich and time rich'.

Changing lifestyles

Demand for housing

Many of these trends, including increasing migration in Europe (through a recently expanded European Union), longer life expectancy and greater frequency of divorce and 'split-ups' among those living together, combine to suggest the need for at least 3 million additional homes by 2015 (DEFRA, 2005). If elderly people are enabled to live longer in their own homes this trend will add to the projected increase in the number of homes needed by single people and other groups just mentioned. Given the limitations on building in country areas, new or refurbished homes are likely to be built on 'brown sites' or in cities and towns, leading to urban regeneration with the possibilities of reversing the current decline in inner city life and business. The provision of apartments, both up market and for low-income single people may be a significant part of this development. Whatever and wherever this building takes place, it is good news for the construction industry.

Leisure and sport

There are sharp differences in lifestyles between single men and single women. For instance, women are likely to enjoy more intensive and broader social networks and to be more actively involved in leisure, recreation, education and cultural activities than men. By contrast men are more likely than women to participate in sport or other physical activity. The General Household Survey (2002) reports that 41 per cent of men and 31 per cent of women belong to some type of sports club, with women sports participants more likely to receive tuition.

Illustration 9.4 details plans to increase participation of all people in both sporting activities and the arts. All this suggests the need for organizations to practise gender and minority groups-based market segmentation with market intelligence taking more account of these categories of consumers for marketing and retailing purposes.

Illustration 9.4

Leisure activities in Britain

Taking part in the arts, sport and recreation are perceived to have beneficial social, economic and health impacts. In December 2002 the Prime Minister's Strategy Unit and DCMS jointly published a report called Game Plan. It has a target of 1 per cent growth per year in regular sports participation for people aged 16 or over (with a view to achieving at least 50 per cent participation in 2020).

As stated in its Corporate Plan 2003–2006, Arts Council England aims to increase the number of people who engage in the arts. It is trying to ensure that there is a growth in participation among black and minority groups, disabled people and socially excluded groups.

Source: http://www.statistics.gov.uk; Richards, L., Fox, K., Roberts, C., Fletcher, L. and Goddard, E. (2004) 'Living in Britain: Results from the 2002 General Household Survey'.

Living alone

Businesses, perhaps small to medium in size, associated with the personal, more individualized requirements of people living on their own (for instance, a decrease in the demand for mass-produced clothes and other goods and corresponding increase in branded 'limited edition' fashion and 'state-of-the-art' household objects) will increase. Fear of crime and the demands for personal security systems will lead to greater demand for interactive communication technologies and household security products such as video surveillance systems.

Men and women

The past two decades have begun to see changes in the roles of men and women, with regard to employment and domestic and child responsibilities. The *Working Futures (2003–04) National Report* says:

> Between 2002 and 2012, the total level of employment in the UK labour market is projected to grow by almost 1.5 million jobs. ... [T]he majority of the additional jobs are expected to be taken up by women ... the increase in the number of part-time jobs alone almost accounts for the entire increase.   (Wilson *et al.*, 2004)

However, as Illustration 9.5 indicates, although gender roles, (particularly regarding household tasks) are likely to change, with more sharing of domestic duties, any shift in this direction should not be exaggerated. Scase (1999) drawing on data from The British Social Attitudes Survey and the ESRC British Household Panel Study suggests that changes of this kind in the past have not been pronounced and, on this basis, are unlikely to be dramatic in the future. In addition, the burden of household responsibilities will continue to be heaviest on working-class women, sometimes as a result of 'serial' personal relationships. Men will continue to be able to avoid their domestic obligations. Where families can look after their longer-living elderly relatives, it is women on whom the

Illustration 9.5

Dads shun nappy changing for work

New fathers won the right to two weeks leave in April 2003. Statutory Paternity Pay (SPP) when first introduced was paid at £100 per week, rising to £102 in the financial year beginning in April 2004. This amount could be claimed back by employers from the government. Some employers also allow extra time off and more money for fathers in addition to SPP.

Only one-fifth of working fathers have taken up their right to paid paternity leave. As many as 400,000 fathers could be eligible for time off each year, and take-up was expected to be about 70 per cent when the benefit was launched, however the Inland Revenue estimates that only 79,210 fathers have taken time off.

These figures mirror the take-up figures for new flexible working rights, which show 31 per cent take-up among women and only 10 per cent among men.

The reality is that the SPP payment is a very small proportion of the amount men bring into the home per week, and having a substantially reduced salary over this time is not an option for most families. Through comments from the public, fathers are taking some time off, but choosing to use annual leave, which means full pay for the time away from work.

There is also pressure for men to remain at work as they fear losing their jobs. Malcolm Bruce, the Liberal Democrats' trade and industry spokesman, said, 'The right to paid paternity leave will remain an empty victory for fathers as long as the cultural norms dictate that duty to their jobs overrides that to their families.'

Source: Based on information at BBC News: www.bbc.co.uk, 26 July 2004.

majority of this care will fall. Middle-class women are more likely to be able to afford the emerging ICT systems of surveillance and use the Internet to order food deliveries for their elderly relatives than those from low-income families. Single low-income people will not be able to afford to buy and maintain their own home, having to rely on house sharing or low-cost rented accommodation.

The discussion on flexible working below serves to emphasize the continuing requirement for organizations to move in this direction if women, in particular, are to be brought further into the workforce, and not just in lower-paid, part-time work.

Other parts of the world

Many of these trends – positive and negative – contrast, of course, with those in some other, particularly non-European countries, where marriage with children is still the expected and perhaps preferred form of household and where elderly people are looked after by their families. In some countries the expected lifespan for many people does not run into 70 years and over. Parker (1998) reports World Bank statistics showing that the number of men and women aged between 15 and 64 years of age in the global workforce increased by 100 per cent over the years from 1965 to 1995. The total number was 2.5 billion in 1995, of whom only 380 million lived in high-income countries. Daniels and Radebaugh (2001, p. 764) say: 'Demographers are nearly unanimous in projecting that populations will grow much faster in emerging economies (China being the exception) than in industrial countries, at least up to the year 2030.'

●●●● Occupational changes

Illustration 1.4 in Chapter 1 shows the Institute for Employment Research's (2004) predictions regarding the net employment requirements for 2012 among the major employment groups. Table 9.1 gives similar information, with statistics from 1982 through to predictions for 2007 and 2012. This suggests an increase in numbers employed in the managerial and professional occupations related to a decline in those associated with administrative, secretarial, skilled and semi-skilled manual and clerical tasks.

Two decades ago the largest proportion of all UK jobs (30 per cent) was to be found in the manufacturing sector. As the millennium approached, this reduced to 17 per cent. The agricultural sector has decreased its share of the labour market over this period from 5 to 2 per cent. Sectors that have increased their hold on the labour market are distribution, hotels and restaurants (18 to 23 per cent); banking, finance and insurance (11 to 19 per cent); and, to a lesser extent, public administration, education, health and other services (24 to 28 per cent) (see *Labour Market and Skills Trends*, February 2000, available free from the UK

Table 9.1 Occupational changes 2007–12, United Kingdom: all industry sectors

Employment levels (000s)	1982	1992	2002	2007	2012
1 Managers and senior officials	2,698	3,336	4,349	4,580	4,934
2 Professional occupations	2,003	2,501	3,305	3,650	4,008
3 Associate professional and technical occupations	2,406	3,025	4,121	4,500	4,895
4 Administrative, clerical and secretarial occupations	3,895	4,205	3,857	3,603	3,434
5 Skilled trades occupations	4,289	3,901	3,341	3,062	2,801
6 Personal service occupations	925	1,310	2,147	2,449	2,894
7 Sales and customer service occupations	1,527	1,784	2,334	2,518	2,732
8 Transport and machine operative	2,981	2,591	2,473	2,316	2,225
9 Elementary occupations	4,463	3,989	3,409	3,094	2,735
Total	25,186	26,639	29,336	29,772	30,658

Percentage shares	1982	1992	2002	2007	2012
1 Managers and senior officials	10.7	12.6	14.9	15.4	16.2
2 Professional occupations	8.0	9.4	11.3	12.2	12.9
3 Associate professional and technical occupations	9.6	11.3	14.0	15.1	16.0
4 Administrative, clerical and secretarial occupations	15.5	15.8	13.2	12.2	11.4
5 Skilled trades occupations	17.0	14.6	11.4	10.2	9.1
6 Personal service occupations	3.7	4.9	7.3	8.2	9.4
7 Sales and customer service occupations	6.1	6.7	7.9	8.5	9.0
8 Transport and machine operatives	11.8	9.7	8.4	7.7	7.2
9 Elementary occupations	17.7	15.0	11.6	10.4	8.9
Total	100.0	100.0	100.0	100.0	100.0

Source: From *Working Futures: New Projections of Employment by Sector 2002–2012*, vol. 1, The Sector Skills Development Agency (Wilson, R., Homenidou, K. and Dickerson, A. 2004). The Sector Skills Development Agency (SSDA) commissioned the Institute for Employment Research (IER) at the University of Warwick and Cambridge Econometrics to produce *Working Futures*. This comprises a series of reports presenting projections of UK employment (2002–2012) by occupation, sector, UK country and English region. The reports are available from SSDA's website: www.ssda.org.uk. Updated projections of employment (*Working Futures*, 2004–2014) are to be published by the SSDA in autumn 2005. A network of UK-wide Sector Skills Councils (SSCs) has been charged to lead the skills and productivity drive in industry or business sectors recognized by employers. The SSDA has been established to underpin the SSC network and promote effective working between sectors.

Department for Education and Employment (Department for Education and Skills, Sanctuary Buildings, Great Smith Street, London, SW1P 3BT)). Looking to the future, the Institute for Employment Research (IER), 2004, p. 3) says that between 2002 and 2012 the largest employment gains will be in the service sector (see Figure 9.1). It says:

> Business services along with computing and related industries are expected to generate the most jobs. Health, retailing and education are all expected to show significant expansion over the coming decade. At the other end of the spectrum, the manufacturing sector is expected to show a net decrease in the number of workers employed. In particular, the engineering industry, transport equipment and heavy manufacturing such as metals and chemicals are expected to require fewer workers.

Figure 9.1 details the projected percentage change in UK employment by industrial sector between the years 2002 and 2012.

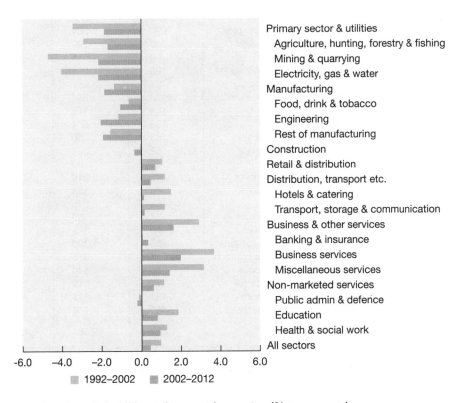

Figure 9.1 Trends in UK employment by sector (% per annun)

Source: From *Working Futures: New Projections of Employment by Sector 2002–2012*, vol. 1, The Sector Skills Development Agency (Wilson, R., Homenidou, K. and Dickerson, A. 2004). The Sector Skills Development Agency (SSDA) commissioned the Institute for Employment Research (IER) at the University of Warwick and Cambridge Econometrics to produce *Working Futures*. This comprises a series of reports presenting projections of UK employment (2002–2012) by occupation, sector, UK country and English region. The reports are available from SSDA's website: www.ssda.org.uk. Updated projections of employment (*Working Futures*, 2004–2014) are to be published by the SSDA in autumn 2005. A network of UK-wide Sector Skills Councils (SSCs) has been charged to lead the skills and productivity drive in industry or business sectors recognized by employers. The SSDA has been established to underpin the SSC network and promote effective working between sectors.

An examination of statistics for specific occupations (see Figure 9.2) shows that expanding occupational groups include caring service occupations, corporate managers and most professional occupations (for example in teaching, health and science). In contrast, employment demand in other occupations, such as elementary clerical occupations or in skilled trades associated with metal, plant and machinery, are in structural decline. The IER report concludes, however, that with significant numbers of workers needing to be replaced and, overall, the creation of additional jobs, there will need to be an even greater emphasis on training and retraining.

Occupation	Change in demand 2002–12		
	Expansion	Replacement	Net
Caring personal service occs	703	633	1,336
Corporate managers	662	1,321	1,983
Teaching/research prof.	273	552	825
Bus./public serv. assoc. prof.	225	604	829
Science/tech professionals	203	299	502
Sales occupations	202	755	957
Customer service occupations	196	211	407
Culture/media/sport occs	193	252	445
Business/public service prof.	178	244	422
Science associate prof.	144	178	322
Health associate prof.	130	514	644
Protective service occs	83	230	313
Transport drivers and ops	62	421	483
Health professionals	50	93	143
Leisure/oth pers serv occs	45	214	259
Skilled agricultural trades	10	123	133
Other skilled trades	−54	248	194
Managers and proprietors	−77	469	392
Skilled construct. trades	−90	342	252
Admin. & clerical occupations	−180	1,309	1,129
Elementary: trades/plant/mach.	−213	376	163
Secretarial & related occs	−244	540	296
Transport & mach. ops	−311	519	208
Skilled metal/elec. trades	−408	627	219
Elementary: clerical/services	−460	1,108	648
All occupations	1,322	12,181	13,503

Figure 9.2 Expansion, replacement and net change in employment by occupational group (000s), 2002–12

Source: From *Working Futures: New Projections of Employment by Sector 2002–2012*, vol. 1, The Sector Skills Development Agency (Wilson, R., Homenidou, K. and Dickerson, A. 2004). The Sector Skills Development Agency (SSDA) commissioned the Institute for Employment Research (IER) at the University of Warwick and Cambridge Econometrics to produce *Working Futures*. This comprises a series of reports presenting projections of UK employment (2002–2012) by occupation, sector, UK country and English region. The reports are available from SSDA's website: www.ssda.org.uk. Updated projections of employment (*Working Futures*, 2004–2014) are to be published by the SSDA in autumn 2005. A network of UK-wide Sector Skills Councils (SSCs) has been charged to lead the skills and productivity drive in industry or business sectors recognized by employers. The SSDA has been established to underpin the SSC network and promote effective working between sectors.

These changes will impact not only on the employment practices of organizations, but also on education and training systems in terms of the learning programmes they offer. This in turn implies changing government policies and the focus of the trades unions.

These statistics relate to organizations in the United Kingdom. By contrast, the World Development Indicators (World Bank, 2005) for developing country regions show that, though agriculture is still overwhelmingly the dominant occupation for workers in low-income regions (e.g. south Asia), it is a declining industry in Europe and Central Asia (e.g. Russia is producing only 92 per cent of the food that it produced a decade ago and livestock production has fallen by 25 per cent). The World Bank statistics indicate that, with 1.9 billion people, East Asia and the Pacific is the fastest growing region in the world, with high-technology exports (aerospace, computers, pharmaceuticals and scientific instruments) amounting to 33 per cent of manufactured products. This region is on track to achieve the development goals set by the World Bank in terms of 'Education for All'. The high completion rates (97 per cent) for those enrolled for primary school education, with the opportunity to continue to higher levels, is without doubt contributing to the move from the production of low-cost, low-value-added goods to the production of higher-value goods and services now being seen.

Yet another developing region is that of Latin America and the Caribbean. The World Bank says: '[It] has the highest gross national income (GNI) per capita of all developing country regions.' At 66 per cent of GDP in 2003, it had the highest level of services of any developing region. It has the highest life expectancy at birth, 71 years, and the lowest under-5 mortality rate. Perhaps by coincidence it has the lowest military spending among developing regions. By contrast, the Middle East and North African region has the highest military spending in the developing world, almost double the spending of the next highest region (Europe and Central Asia).

The situation for women across all the developing regions varies widely. For instance, compared to South Asia, where women are doing better (e.g. girls on track to achieve universal education by 2015; 43 per cent of women's employment in non-agricultural sectors; and the highest female representation in parliament – 10 per cent – almost on a par with high income countries (21 per cent)), the situation for women and children in South Asia is bleak on all indicators.

Overall (in terms of their economies, industries, occupations, education and health) the six developing regions for which the World Bank produces statistics show significant variations in stages of development. These variations have, in turn, implications for organizations working across national and regional boundaries and even for those organizations that trade outside of their domestic market. As the discussions in Part Two of the book in particular demonstrated, there is no single way of organizing across national and cultural boundaries. Planning internationally but delivering locally is easier in some regions than others, given the variable rates of meeting goals for education and health. However, the picture in some regions shows significant industry occupational changes that are not going to stop.

At the time of writing (2005) discussions among the 'G8' group of countries on 'Making Poverty History' will hopefully lead to actions to address the needs of the least developed regions for water, power and housing, as well as educational and health services. Organizations working to help these countries will themselves see changes in the way they work with these peoples to enable them to become more independent of aid.

Changing employment policies and practices

Workforce diversity

Robbins (2005, p. 17) says:

> One of the most important and broad based challenges currently facing organizations is adapting to people who are different – workforce diversity. While globalization focuses on differences between people from different countries, workforce diversity addresses differences among people within given countries.
>
> Workforce diversity means organizations are becoming more heterogeneous in terms of gender, race and ethnicity. ... Managers in Canada and Australia, for instance, are having to adjust to large influxes of Asian workers. The 'new' South Africa is increasingly characterized by blacks holding important technical and managerial jobs. Women, long confined to low-paying temporary jobs in Japan, are moving into managerial positions. And the European Union co-operative trade arrangement, which opened up borders throughout much of Western Europe, has increased workforce diversity in organizations that operate in countries such as Germany, Portugal, Italy and France.

He goes on to identify broad categories in business and work that will affect the future success of businesses coping with the environment in which they operate and expands on some of these key areas:

- *Responding to globalization* – increased numbers of people travelling, increased numbers of employees working around the world, in and with other cultures.
- *Managing workforce diversity* – not only considering a variety of cultural backgrounds working together, but managing the legislation and policies relating to work and flexible working and integrating it into the business.
- *Improving quality and productivity* – to some extent many businesses and the markets in which they operate may be reaching saturation point. Consumers tend to want more for less, and all of this within the context of corporate responsibility (Robbins, 2005, pp. 15–26).

With respect to Britain, Figure 9.3 gives the projected changes in economic activity rates for men and women over the period 2002 to 2012.

> For men the largest employment increases are expected in the professional and associate professional occupations, where around 200,000 and 300,000 new jobs respectively are projected between 2002 and 2012.
>
> For women the projected largest number of new jobs are in the associate professional and technical occupations (with a projected increase of almost 800,00) and personal service occupations (projected to rise by over 700,000). (Wilson *et al.* 2004)

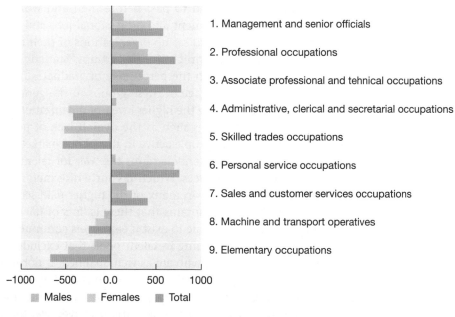

1. Management and senior officials

2. Professional occupations

3. Associate professional and tehnical occupations

4. Administrative, clerical and secretarial occupations

5. Skilled trades occupations

6. Personal service occupations

7. Sales and customer services occupations

8. Machine and transport operatives

9. Elementary occupations

−1000   −500   0.0   500   1000

■ Males   ■ Females   ■ Total

Figure 9.3 Occupational change by gender, 2002–2012

Source: From *Working Futures: New Projections of Employment by Sector 2002–2012*, vol. 1, The Sector Skills Development Agency (Wilson, R., Homenidou, K. and Dickerson, A. 2004). The Sector Skills Development Agency (SSDA) commissioned the Institute for Employment Research (IER) at the University of Warwick and Cambridge Econometrics to produce *Working Futures*. This comprises a series of reports presenting projections of UK employment (2002–2012) by occupation, sector, UK country and English region. The reports are available from SSDA's website: www.ssda.org.uk. Updated projections of employment (*Working Futures*, 2004–2014) are to be published by the SSDA in autumn 2005. A network of UK-wide Sector Skills Councils (SSCs) has been charged to lead the skills and productivity drive in industry or business sectors recognized by employers. The SSDA has been established to underpin the SSC network and promote effective working between sectors.

Women are expected to lose significant numbers of administrative, clerical and secretarial jobs as well as those in elementary occupations (for the latter a loss of 700,000 jobs). Men are forecast to lose around 500,000 jobs in the skilled trades occupations.

Overall, though, as mentioned above, female employment is expected to increase by around four times as much as the increase in male employment, taken across all occupations.

Since 1970 an increasing proportion of women have obtained academic, professional and managerial qualifications and more and more are entering the medical, legal and management professions. However, Maitland (2000a) points out that only 5 per cent of directors of FTSE 100 companies are women. A *Financial Times* article of 20 January 2000 says: 'Women are still alien beings in certain parts of the City of London.' Even in the United States, where almost half of middle management is female, only 13 per cent of women are offered foreign postings (see Maitland, 2000b). By contrast, the National Management Salary Survey (1998) reports a rising trend in the percentage of managers who are women – although the slope of the graphs is less steep as the level of management responsibility rises. The issue is the length of time that will need to pass before men and women are represented equally in high-level management and professional jobs and whether women will decide 'enough is enough' and set up organizations of their own. This is a similar situation for people from ethnic minority groups. Statistics quoted by Kandola (2001) indicate that although the percentage of graduates from ethnic minority groups is double the percentage of these groups in the general population their chances, currently, of reaching the higher levels of organizations are low.

All this is in spite of issues such as the overall lack of population growth in Britain, coupled with fewer people active in the labour market, which are perceived by some as leading to what Kandola terms the 'war for talent'. In response to this concern, employment practices, which favour white men in middle and upper management roles, as well as in many of the higher-paid sectors of industry, will need to change. Kandola maintains that there is 'lots of talent out there' and the war for talent will only continue to exist if employers continue to 'fish in fished out waters'. By this he means fishing in talent pools that exclude women and people from ethnic minority groups who are as well qualified, if not more so (54 per cent women and 13 per cent ethnic minorities, which is double the number of people of ethnic minority origins in the general population) than white men. As many other European countries are also likely to face the perceived war for talent the pressure will be on to encourage emigration from developing countries – although only those 'chosen' for their particular skills and abilities are likely to be welcomed. By contrast, jobs can be exported to developing countries where there is an ample supply of labour, a policy that has the advantage of being able to hire workers (frequently well qualified) at lower wages. Alternatively, or additionally, the push to adopting robotics and other labour-saving devices will strengthen.

If employers and managers are to meet the increasing demands for knowledge workers and strive towards operating learning organizations, as discussed in earlier chapters, they will need to change their employment policies and practices not only to attract but also to retain women and employees from minority groups. Difference among employees is something to be welcomed rather than something that is a matter for suspicion. People feel comfortable with other people who are like themselves in looks and attitude. However, homogeneity among employees is not a recipe for high organizational performance now or in the future, given that creativity and innovation are keys to organizational success. Organizations will need to change to ensure they employ people of varied talents and skills and living/behaviour patterns if they are to meet the changing needs of the new sets of customers that demographic and lifestyle changes will bring. This in turn is likely to require modified ways of managing personnel and perhaps offering more flexible ways of working to suit the needs of those groups who cannot or do not want to take up full-time, five days a week working out of the home. In other words, offering a variety of patterns of employment.

What is becoming more significant is the challenge of recruitment in particular sectors of work. The Chartered Institute of Personnel and Development has amalgamated two reports in relation to recruitment, retention and turnover (2004a) and has suggested there are key challenges for employers at present and in the future.

Among the top challenges for businesses (from all sectors) are skills shortages/locating specialist skills, little room for progression in an organization, the competitive market and selecting and attracting the right people (CIPD, 2004b, p. 35).

Further findings from this report suggested there are only a 'minority of organizations who have reported reviewing the organization of work, training up internal candidates, redefining job content, recruiting overseas or even offering more flexible patterns of hours' (p. 36).

Changing patterns of employment

Patterns of employment and types of work relationship in the twenty-first century are increasingly diverse. This reflects both the changing business and organizational needs of employers, and the demands from workers themselves for a wider range of employment patterns. With respect to the growth in full-time, part-time and self-employment, earlier predictions (Institute of Employment Research, 1997/8) suggested that the percentage of all employment taken up by part-time work and self-employment would increase respectively by 25 per cent to 30 per cent and from 12 per cent to 15 per cent over the ten years to 2006. In agreement with this, the results of a survey done by Bacon and Woodrow (Bakhshi, 1999) showed that the number of people in manual occupations becoming self-employed increased by more than 450 per cent between 1997 and 1998 and, over the same period, self-employment among managerial and professional workers grew by almost 300 per cent. Small firms made up 93 per cent of all enterprises in the European Union – almost one-third of the workforce.

This reflection still holds true with recent published statistics (Linday and MacCauley 2004). However, while the Working Futures National Report (Wilson *et al.*, 2004, section 2) confirms the predictions on part-time working, it foresees a small fall in self-employment. Even so, as Illustration 9.8 shows (see pages 407–8), some rural areas are focusing on growing their own businesses.

According to LexusNexis, organizers of industrial relations seminars, the trend by employers and employees for more flexible ways of working has led to a major increase in the use of temporary and fixed-term appointments, part-time work, 'zero-hours' and annualized hours contracts. In addition, employers are increasingly turning to external sources to meet temporary needs or specialist requirements, by using agency staff, contractors, and freelance workers. The increased focus on effective equal opportunities policies has also been a driving force behind more flexible working arrangements.

Flexible working

It is not easy to define 'flexible working'. For this discussion it is probably sufficient to define it fairly loosely as patterns of employment that do not conform to the standard full-time working week of 40 hours or so carried out over typically five-day periods away from the home. More specifically, the Department of Trade and Industry (2005) in their second report on 'working flexibly' refer to employees' rights to request a change to the hours they work, a change to the times when they are required to work, or to work from home. This covers working patterns such as annualized hours, compressed hours, flexitime, homeworking, job sharing, self-rostering, shift working, staggered hours and term-time working (p. 18). This report found that awareness of the right to request flexible working has increased, with almost two-thirds of employees aware of the right to request flexible working, which was introduced in April 2003.

There are advantages and disadvantages for both employers and employees in working more flexibly. From the employer's viewpoint, it offers flexibility in managing workforce requirements as the demand for products and services varies over the year and day to day. From the employees' viewpoint, non-standard working offers flexibility of working to fit in with family and other commitments. Given the continuing reliance on women to carry out domestic duties, including the care of children and elderly dependants, women, in particular, welcome the opportunities offered by flexible working to fit work into other aspects of their lives.

Men also seem to want more flexible working arrangements, in this case, working from home. An article in the *Financial Times* entitled 'Men outnumber women in working from home' Bennett (2000) reports on a UK government survey from the Skills and Enterprise Executive (2001) into work–life balance which shows that of the 7,500 employees questioned 24 per cent of those allowed to work from home were men and 16 per cent women. When the respondents were asked if they would like to work more at home, 38 per cent of

Illustration 9.6

Managers still fight flexible working

Flexible working has boomed in UK workplaces over the past three years but its growth is still hampered by many managers' resistance to change, according to a survey out today. Research by the Chartered Institute of Personnel and development (CIPD) reveals almost two-thirds of employers quizzed have seen an average 20 per cent expansion in practices including part-time work or changed hours or place of work.

However, the survey also found that, while the great majority of employers believe flexible working schemes help with staff retention and motivation, most say they face difficulties in putting the changes into practice. Over three-quarters of the organizations said they were constrained by 'operational pressures' when implementing flexible working, such as concerns about ensuring continued productivity and levels of customer service. The study found that, in practice, both productivity and customer service had benefited from flexible working in most organizations, probably as a result of careful planning.

Most of the 585 employers surveyed who offer flexible working also reported difficulties with implementing changes because line managers were not good at managing employees working flexibly and did not always support the option ... evidence of the growth of flexible working, now used by just over a quarter of employees, according to the survey, comes as Labour prepares to publish a paper to pave the way for extended rights to flexibility. The CIPD found that four in ten organizations already extended the right to flexibility beyond the legal requirement.

Source: Ward, L. (2005) 'Managers still fight flexible working', the *Guardian*, 23 February 2005. www.guardian.co.uk

men and 33 per cent of women said they would. By contrast employers did not, overwhelmingly, appear to favour homeworking in that, of the 2,500 companies surveyed, only 22 per cent allow staff to work from home (see Illustration 9.6).

Since this time, the introduction of the right to request flexible working appears to have changed the situation. Since the legislation was introduced in 2003, the DTI reports that there is much more awareness of the choices for employees and that a considerable number of requests each year are supported by the host organization (DTI, 2005). What is more, the DTI reports that, from their survey, 19 per cent of women requested flexible working compared to 10 per cent of men. Interestingly, men and women without dependent children request flexible working in almost equal proportions compared to much larger percentages of women than men with dependent children requesting flexible working. Across different occupational groups, the number of requests was highest among employees working in sales and customer service occupations and administrative and secretarial occupations (19 per cent). Requests were lowest among managers and senior officials and skilled trade occupations (19 per cent).

One of the downsides of flexible working is that it does not always attract good pay rates, and opportunities for career advancement are variable even if pay is good. Commitment to an organization by its employees is still frequently evidenced by long working hours and 'visibility' at the workplace, even though the employees themselves do not see flexible working arrangements for others as particularly unfair (Bennett, 2000). Non-standard working can offer personal liberation. However, the pessimistic view is that some of these arrangements will simply lead to a greater proportion of low-paid jobs undertaken mainly by women, school leavers, students and older, pre-retired men. For instance, the decline in the number of small shops in favour of large supermarkets and 'out of town shopping', the increase in call centres and the growing need for care assistants to care for an ageing population have all combined to introduce replacement but still part-time, low-paid jobs.

Cooper (2001), has carried out substantial research in this area, and in an article entitled 'Careers, work and life: ways of finding a better balance', argues that the defining characteristics of the 1990s were a short-term contract culture, with outsourcing, downsizing and *long working hours*. More flexible working, then, does not necessarily mean shorter working time. This is evidenced by the government survey discussed by Bennett, which indicated that the most commonly cited reason for wanting to work from home was 'to get more work done' rather than to fit work more easily around other responsibilities. Cooper argues forcibly that long working hours adversely affect the health and well-being of workers and their families. What is more, some types of flexible working (e.g. short-term contracts, seasonal working, and working on an outsourced basis) engender high levels of job insecurity. In spite of this, Cooper (2001) sets out a variety of ways in which flexible working, rather than exploitation, can help employees to address their work–life balance issues at the same time as helping organizations to recruit and retain people of talent, whichever gender, social or ethnic grouping they come from.

A quotation from Scase (1999, p. 55) is an example of how some local government authorities have responded to their communities and provided work opportunities to meet the needs of their employees:

> New demands from communities will have implications for local government. The use of ICTs will encourage the adoption of new employment and work practices. Some local authorities are already ahead of many private sector organizations in adopting new management philosophies. They have embarked on strategic outsourcing and sub-contract many of their activities. Many have adopted 'family friendly' employment policies encouraging part-time and flexi-work, as well as job sharing. Some already operate as 'network' organizations, with a small core of purchasers negotiating quality control with external providers. They are also encouraging homeworking, allowing employees to operate in virtual teams.

The challenge to employers and organizations is to find ways of meeting the varied needs of employees while continuing to meet the customers, frequently on a 24-hour, seven-day-week basis.

An entrepreneurial economy

> There is a close relationship between the economy and small businesses. Small businesses create 75 per cent of the new jobs in our economy and make up more than 99.7 per cent of all employers so we are a major contributor to the American economy. As a consequence, however, other forces that affect the economy either positively or negatively have a major effect on small businesses.   (Kautz, J., 2005, Small Business Notes – entrepreneurship beyond 2000; http://www.smalbusinessnotes.com/aboutsb.html)

This quotation comes from a US website that specializes in writing about and giving information and advice to small businesses. According to this site, a Global Entrepreneurship Monitor (GEM) ten-country study (including the United Kingdom) conducted by researchers from Babson College, London School of Business, and the Kauffman Foundation found a: 'wide and potentially growing disparity in entrepreneurial business activity within several of the world's developed countries' that contributed to a significant gap in economic growth. For instance, the number of people who start up in business ranged from more than 1 in 12 in the United States to fewer than 1 in every 67 people in Finland.

Entrepreneurship, however, is not limited to commercial business. Ashoka is an independently funded organization founded by Bill Drayton, a former McKinsey & Co. consultant and assistant administrator at the Environment Protection Agency in the United States. Ashoka exists to promote 'social entrepreneurship'. According to this organization's website:

> The job of a social entrepreneur is to recognize when a part of a society is stuck and to provide new ways to get it unstuck. He or she finds what is not working and solves the problem by changing the system, spreading the solution and persuading entire societies to take new leaps. (Ashoka: www.ashoka.org)

The differences between business and social entrepreneurs might seem great but, as the Illustrations 9.7 and 9.8 show, the spirit and motivation to set up organizations and plan how things are done are not so far apart.

Illustration 9.7

Healthcare in South Africa

Ashoka Fellow Veronica Khosa was frustrated with the system of healthcare in South Africa. A nurse by trade, she saw sick people getting sicker, elderly people unable to get to a doctor and hospitals with empty beds that would not admit patients with HIV. So Veronica stated Tateni Home Care Nursing Services and instituted the concept of home care in her country. Beginning with practically nothing, her team took to the streets providing care to people in a way they had never received it – in the comfort and security of their homes. Just years later, the government had adopted her plan and through the recognition of leading health organizations the idea is spreading beyond South Africa. Social entrepreneurs such as Veronica redefine their field and go on to solve systemic social problems on a larger scale.

Source: Ashoka: Innovators for the Public, 1700 North Moore Street, Suite 2000, Arlington, VA 22209, USA http://www.ashoka.org/fellows/social_entrepreneur.cfm

Illustration 9.8

Sink or swim for rural business

The speed of change in Northern Ireland's rural economy is presenting communities with starkly different scenarios

While many towns struggle to come to terms with factory closures, others are embracing the robotic age amidst labour shortages. The Lakeland county of Fermanagh depends heavily on tourist spending, which helps boost a fragile rural economy. Jobs are vital to the economic life of towns throughout Fermanagh and neighbouring Tyrone. But Northern Ireland communities have faced some dark days and a string of factory closures. Irvinestown, Enniskillen and Lisnaskea have all experienced the cold draught of global economic pressures and are trying to recover from the departure of major employers. When Irvinestown saw its two major employers – both textile factories – depart, many questioned whether the town had a future. The Daintyfit bra factory closed with the loss of 80 jobs, while another 180 went when the Desmonds textile factory ceased production.

Economic void

But three years on, the green shoots of recovery are beginning to emerge. The former bra factory is headquarters to a local action group that aims to reverse job losses and economic decline. The Fermanagh Local Action Group aims to help revive the local economy by encouraging small rural businesses. Natasha McGrath said they aimed to create up to 100 jobs by seeing if small businesses could fill the economic void. 'We are hoping to run three new programmes that should commit another £600,000 and this is what it is all about – getting money on the ground to people who need it,' she said.

Secret recipe

Viola Burns has the recipe for just such a business. As a girl, she baked buns for her father's bread van. She now employs eight bakers in a building behind her bungalow near Enniskillen, producing up to 2,000 boiled fruit cakes every week. Viola uses an old Fermanagh recipe and insists on the fruit being soaked in sherry the night before baking.

Illustration 9.8 *continued*

'The next day the bakers blend our secret recipe of spices and then bake the cakes slowly', says Viola.

Endless market

In town after town, Ulster's proud textiles tradition is unwinding. One by one the factories have succumbed to low-priced Far Eastern imports. Norman Lyons worked for over 20 years in the Desmonds factory in Omagh. When the doors eventually closed, Norman faced competing with hundreds of others for any available job. Investing his redundancy money in a computerized embroidery machine, Norman has picked up the threads of his career. Working from his converted garage, his micro-business provides a living for himself and his wife.

'I got some funny looks when I said I was going into embroidery but the market is endless, be it schools or clubs or shops,' said Norman.

Robot workers

But while small business may be beautiful for some, in places such as Cookstown they are thinking big. The demise of the Irish pig industry is a sorry tale. From a thriving industry with over 1,800 farms, fewer than 500 pig units remain. But Cookstown, where they have been slicing bacon and making sausages since 1938,

is now seeing evidence of a renaissance. Grampian Country Pork has modernized the Cookstown factory and the workforce has expanded to almost 600, making it Britain's biggest pig processing plant. And robots may soon be employed to help boost output. Managing Director Bob Copsey said: 'We need to remove some of the extremely heavy jobs and dirtiest tasks, and the technology and innovations are there on the continent.' Meanwhile in nearby Dungannon some of the United Kingdom's most modern food processing factories are expanding as fast as they can find new workers.

Hope for the future

But the contrast in fortunes with some smaller towns further west is stark. Family ties, schools and low pay mean it is unrealistic for many to move, or even commute. It is hoped the growth of small indigenous businesses will bring opportunities for some at least. It has been a painful time in Northern Ireland's economic history, but the combination of micro-business and new, super-sized food companies offers hope for a more stable future.

Source: M. Cassidy (2004). BBC Northern Ireland's rural affairs correspondent, BBC News, 10 November 2004.
http://news.bbc.co.uk/go/pr/fr/-/1/northern _ireland/3540008.stm

In the light of the discussion thus far on the changes brought through shifting demographics and lifestyles as well as the desire for different kinds of working arrangements, if industries and business or social communities and the organizations within them fail to respond to: (a) the expectations of increasingly educated workforces, many of whom are single persons who may wish to make work their central life interest; (b) couples who are interested in balancing work and home; and (c) individual and groups who want a totally different focus to their work, then many people will be encouraged to set up their own business. As evidence that this may already be happening, an article in *Management Today* (see Gracie, 1998) reports that women founded almost one-third of all new businesses in the United Kingdom in 1997. Further evidence of this might not appear in official statistics, but Illustration 9.8 indicates that the entrepreneurial spirit is present in Fermanagh. In addition, in farming areas, farmers and their families have been to the fore in diversifying, whether it is offering holiday accommodation, making additional products on the farm or taking over the retailing of their products themselves.

A reasonable projection from the Bacon and Woodrow (1999) survey (see 'Changing patterns of employment' earlier in this chapter) is that this trend will continue but with significant differences across economic sectors. According to Scase (1999, p. 26): 'The numbers of self-employed will be greatest in the media and entertainment industries, hotel, catering and leisure, and in the financial services sector.' On the other hand, there are numerous examples of individuals or small groups setting up businesses or practices in the caring services, architecture, design, and small-scale production.

In line with the desire for more flexible forms of employment, many of these self-employed people will be on fixed-term, performance-related contracts – probably spending much of their time *as if* employed but responsible for their own employment costs. People such as this will be responsible for their own financial planning and pension costs, thus relieving the organizations they work for of 'overhead' costs and their administration. The development of ICTs has assisted people to set up their own business and will continue to be a significant aspect of this. Current disadvantages of being a particular sex or age, coming from an ethnic minority origin or being physically challenged can, for some jobs, be overcome with the assistance of ICTs, allowing homeworking and communications regardless of distance.

The desire for people to set up their own businesses and organizations, for whatever purpose, has implications for governments, financial institutions, and education and training organizations. Some or all of these organizations might have to adapt and change to support an entrepreneurial culture.

Small businesses, as with much larger organizations, have to plan (strategically), find effective ways of structuring, decide what type of leadership they will operate and remain alert to their market environment in order to survive and prosper. Many small organizations will remain small but will still need to adapt and change according to changing political, economic, social and technological environments. Perhaps the most significant forms of support for entrepreneurs are the policies and help that can be given by national and local government, together with those organizations that can help with resources, but also the encouragement of a culture that includes taking risks. In what is becoming known in the West as the 'knowledge-based organization', as the next section shows, organizations do not necessarily have to be 'seen to be seen'!

● ● ● ● Operating virtually

The discussion in the previous section indicates a trend towards an entrepreneurial economy in Britain and other countries. The discussion in Chapter 3 of a move in some sectors to organizing 'virtually' reflects the increasing emphasis on the need for workers whose value lies in their knowledge and ability to innovate in an increasingly global economy. A thoughtful article by Ridderstrale (2000) entitled 'Business moves beyond bureaucracy' argues that organizations

need new structures as the requirement for greater creative thinking and knowledge spreads. Ridderstrale refers to a study by McKinsey, which found that some
20 per cent of world output is open to global competition. The forecast is that in
30 years the percentage will be 80 per cent. He goes on to say: 'It is in Bangalore,
India, where 140,000 IT engineers are challenging the hegemony of the West'
(p. 14). The rise of ICT companies shows how conventional attitudes to employment and promotion of non-white males have been bypassed. In Silicon Valley,
the home of so many telecommunications companies, employment of women,
immigrants and people below 35 years of age is greater than employment of
these groups in traditional US companies.

In the future, hierarchical management structures will be less evident. As
some businesses move through the stages of development from the domestic
stage to the international stage and finally the global stage, the management of
intellectual capital will require skills that nurture creativity and innovation in
workforces rather than compliance as in the past. The regimes of control and
command will no longer suffice. In a world of outsourcing and contract working, managers will need skills to plan and coordinate 'associates' who are
working in different parts of the world.

There is now considerable time being spent on research relating to the effectiveness of working virtually. This supports the notion that the concepts of the
'virtual organization' and 'virtual teams' are continuing to grow. Most examples
relate to a network of individuals who are joined together by advanced technology. There are fewer case examples from the small business sector.

It is clear, however, that organizations are rapidly moving towards a more dispersed workforce that is using technology to link workers and their functions
together, and it will ultimately alter the nature of work. David Skyrme,
Managing Editor of I^3 (an Internet-based publication focusing on the 'net-
worked knowledge economy') has been reviewing issues related to virtual
working since the late 1990s. He writes:

> Companies need flexibility and access to the best talent, wherever it is; organiza-
> tions enter strategic alliances and need access to experts; and if they can be
> effective through working virtually while avoiding cost of relocation, they will.
> They will create multi-function, multi-location teams to assemble their best talent
> worldwide. Project teams will come and go as needs dictate.
>   (http://www.skyrme.com/updates/u11.htm, 1997 and 2005 updated).

Ridderstrale (2000, pp. 14–15) suggests four ways that organizations can depart
from the bureaucratic model. The first is to *flatten* the organization, not by removing the middle management layers but by flattening from middle management up
and down. The second way is to introduce *flexibility* in structures. This means
moving away from vertically structured organizations to ones structured in such a
way that people can move across functional and geographical borders. Third,
managers and others need to know who can do what, where and how. This is reminiscent of organizations being learning organizations. It means 'the development
of an inventory of core competences and "core competents", the people who

make the competences happen'. Finally, Ridderstrale talks about the need for organizations to be more *tribal*. This means that information is held among all members of the organization. The organization as a tribe shares values, vision, attitudes, culture and norms but lets individuals and groups find best ways of achieving the vision. Ridderstrale maintains that this starts by hiring people with the 'right' attitudes. Interestingly, the byline for another article by Kehoe (2000, p. 20) asserts: 'In the new economy (i.e. the "Internet economy"), changing your attitude is more important than changing your software.'

Scase (1999, p. 27) says: 'Organizations of the future will be heavily dependent on information management. Supply chains will be characterized by co-operative relations between companies through joint ventures, strategic alliances and partnerships.' Employees of, and contractors to, virtual organizations will not work 'at the organization', so smaller premises will be required. Organizations will make considerable cost savings in this way, but will have to provide the means for workers to come together at regular periods to socialize and to reinforce organizational cultures and values. All this, however, implies a change in the contract of commitment between organizations and those they employ – whether directly or indirectly in a plethora of different ways.

The changing psychological contract

It has become evident that with all of the changes in organizational functioning there has been a change in the psychological contract between employers and employees. The phrase was first coined in the early 1960s, and became more popular during the economic downturn of the 1990s (Chartered Institute of Personnel and Development, 2004b, p. 36). The CIPD suggests that the psychological contract 'offers a valid and helpful framework for thinking about the employment relationship against the background of a changing labour market'.

Arnold *et al.* (2005) suggest that the term psychological contract is proving a useful one to describe or explain people's responses to the changing context of careers. It is also helpful in identifying changes in organizations' and employees' expectations.

Scase (1999, p. 29) says:

In the workplace of the future, employees will have very different psychological expectations. Most employees will consider their organizational commitment to be temporary. They will have few expectations of long-term careers and will tend to regard employment contracts as short-term negotiated arrangements.

Sparrow (2000, p. 202), in line with this view, says, in the abstract to an article about the future of work:

It is argued that we shall witness fundamental transitions in forms of work organization. Initially, this will not compensate for the deterioration in the psychological contract that has been experienced by those who have lived through an era of downsizing. However, it will raise the need to develop new competencies to cope with the changes in work design.

The main issues to consider for the future here are the levels of engagement in relation to trust, commitment and involvement, fairness, and recognition that present and future employers and employees have with each other.

Not everyone would agree with statements such as these about the changing workplace. However, discussions throughout the book and evidence from a number of 'future thinkers' appear to be sufficient to warrant a closer look at what this means in more detail, both for organizations and the way they operate and the people who work within and with them. Therefore, as this discussion begins to draw to a close, the thoughts of a number of eminent academics and researchers have been chosen to represent much of what is being said and to form the basis for speculation as to where organizations and those who work with them go from here.

The first of these articles is by Miles *et al.* (2000). They start their article with a quotation from William E. Coyne, Senior Vice-President for Research and Development at 3M:

> Most modern companies now recognize that the best way to increase corporate earnings is through top-line growth, and the best route to top-line growth is through innovation.

The basic message of Miles *et al.* is that in the currently emerging era of continuous innovation, knowledge is the key asset whose exploitation will determine the success of many organizations. The issue which challenges them is, however, that they perceive no existing organizational model which is sufficiently worked out to ensure the facilitation of innovation. For example, they say (p. 301): 'Innovation cannot be managed hierarchically because it depends on knowledge being offered voluntarily rather than on command.' Furthermore, they maintain that approaches to facilitating innovation require investments that often appear to be unjustified within current organizational accounting systems.

Their argument is that models of organizing that involve standardization and, more recently, customization, which have required, respectively, 'meta-capabilities' of coordination and delegation, are no longer sufficient for innovation to flourish. This is because organizations of the future need not just knowledge but knowledge generation and transfer, which in their turn require social interaction and exchange between organizational members. The logical outcome of this, they argue, is that *collaboration* is the key to innovation – what Miles *et al.* call the new 'meta-capability'. Acknowledging that collaboration is not entirely natural in many of today's organizational cultures, they suggest three conditions for collaboration to happen:

1 People need *time* to discuss ideas, reflect, listen and engage in a host of activities that might produce fresh ideas.
2 They need to develop strong bonds of *trust* between each other – a willingness to expose one's views without the fear of being exploited and to probe more deeply for new insights and perspectives.
3 People need a sense of *territory*, that is a 'stake' (marking one's place) in the outcomes of the collaborative process. These visible stakes might be stock ownership, stock options, visible awards, collegial recognition and so on.

In organizational terms, they also maintain that the organizational model of the future will go beyond the functional, divisional, matrix and network organizations (such as those discussed in Chapter 3) and will involve alliances, spin-offs and federations – that is, organizations operating more in virtual structures, with large degrees of self-management and self-directing teams.

Other writers have argued in similar ways to Miles *et al.* and many of them are discussed in Chapters 3 and 4. However, much of the tenor of the article by Miles *et al.* assumes a style of leadership that is participative, caring of followers, and which recognizes the role of everyone in the efforts to make any organization successful. This is exemplified in Bennis's (2000) article: 'The end of leadership: exemplary leadership is impossible without the full inclusion, initiatives and cooperation of followers' and in McGill and Slocum's (1998) article: 'A *little* leadership please?' All these writers argue for the demise of 'top-down' leadership. Bennis (p. 73) says: 'The most urgent projects require the coordinated contributions of many talented people working together' and (p. 74): 'No change can occur without willing and committed followers.' He maintains that it is only in the solving of relatively simple technical problems that top-down leadership is effective. For the resolution of 'adaptive', complex, messy problems many people at all levels of the organization must be involved and mobilized. A couple of further quotations (p. 76) will suffice to give the flavour of what Bennis has to say:

> Post-bureaucratic organization requires a new kind of alliance between leaders and the led. Today's organizations are evolving into federations, networks, clusters, cross-functional teams, temporary systems, ad hoc tasks, lattices, modules, matrices – almost anything but pyramids with their obsolete TOPdown leadership.

And:

> The new reality is that intellectual capital, brain power, know-how, human imagination have supplanted capital as the critical success factor and leaders will have to learn an entirely new set of skills.

It is sufficient to note that McGill and Slocum express their view of leadership in the title of their article 'A *little* leadership, please?' They argue for models of leadership that are 'non-positional, team-based, or empowering' (p. 40). It is not intended to go into the details of the full content of McGill and Slocum's discussion here. It is certainly worth reading, however, in the hope of providing a counterbalance to the many articles lauding the 'hero' leader who, as it happens, is in most cases male and, in western countries, white.

A paradox

A look back at the list of general trends for the future posed at the beginning of this chapter and a summary of the discussion so far paints the following scenario. On the one hand there is a picture of people becoming more individualistic, independent, hedonistic, living for some of their adult lives alone, communicating increasingly through ICTs and with more choice in respect of their lifestyle. This attitude to life and work is reinforced by the increase in 'non-standard' working that is frequently insecure and which does not engender organizational commitment. On the other hand there are business 'philosophers' and academics and, to a much smaller extent, managers arguing for more organic, network and virtual organizations that require collaborative attitudes and behaviour on the part of their workforce, so that innovation – which is seen as essential for organizations to survive and prosper – can flourish. This implies a commitment to the principles of empowerment of subordinate staff.

However, in spite of the emphasis put on empowering employees to work in organic, network and virtual forms of organizations, many large organizations continue to conform to hierarchical principles of structure and accountability as described in Chapter 3. The skills that managers need to be successful in this type of organization are not those which comfortably agree with the principles of empowering subordinate levels of staff. Even if empowering abilities are developed, they are unlikely to be rewarded or acknowledged. Behaving in empowering ways does not support the culture and processes that make these managers successful. Many of the characteristics – such as showing determination, drive/energy, leading from the front, objective decision making and personal achievement – are not among the key empowering characteristics.

Chapters 4 and 8 discussed the concepts of the learning organization and organizational learning. Schein (1999), in an article entitled 'Empowerment, coercive persuasion and organizational learning: do they connect?', notes how these concepts, together with those of 'generative' or double-loop learning, require employees to develop new thinking skills, new concepts and points of view and cognitively to redefine old categories and change standards of judgement. Such changes increase individuals' capacity to deal with situations in new ways and lay the basis for developing radically new skills.

By comparison with single-loop learning, which socializes individuals into specific attitudes, double-loop learning requires collaboration, but also a change in values and assumptions about how the world operates and what is good and what is bad. According to Schein, however, requiring individuals to learn to think and behave in these kinds of ways is essentially asking them to put themselves through transformational culture change – coming as they frequently have from organizational cultures suited more to traditional bureaucratic norms of command and control – not least because these types of systems discourage creativity and innovation. He goes on to say (p. 7): 'But paradoxically, when we speak of "culture change" in organizations we are typically demanding levels of cognitive redefinition that can probably only be achieved by some version of coercive persuasion.' This is because these individuals are being asked to *disconfirm* what they have believed is *right* – what they have been used to doing for much of their organizational life.

This seems a worrying scenario if there is a belief, as Miles *et al.*, Bennis and others assert, in alternative, more satisfying and effective ways of running organizations. However, throughout this book, no one has argued that change is easy. The final section, therefore, draws together some threads in the hope that change can be seen as something that can and should be welcomed and which makes for an interesting life.

The multiple paths to change

In May 1996 the journal *Human Relations* brought out a special issue entitled 'Organizational change in corporate settings' that is recommended reading for anyone interested in investigating further different theories of change and their relationship to each other. What is interesting in the context of the present discussion is that all the articles, taken together, suggest there are many ways of understanding and managing change.

This is a view that has surfaced throughout the book and particular reference was made to it in Chapters 2 and 6 in the discussion of the work of Dunphy and Stace (1993) and Strebel (1996), who argue that different change contexts require different change policies and practices. In a later article, Stace (1996) refers to organizational contingencies and paths to change, concepts that chime with Strebel's advice on how to choose the right path to change, depending on the change context. Thus, for these scholars and others, provided the various contingent factors can be identified, choosing a path to change becomes uncontentious.

However, the idea of *choice* may not be what it seems. This is because contingency approaches to change assume, in the main, that change can be *planned*. However, as the discussion of Quinn's (1980) and Wilson's (1992) work in Chapter 2 shows, this is not always the case, as change emerges in ways that are frequently unexpected. In addition, even if one particular path has been chosen, a multitude of influences can arise to deflect both its end point and the means of getting there. What is more, the issue of planned change does not necessarily include the issue of whether change should progress incrementally or take place through more radical transformational means. Much depends on whether the world is seen as reasonably predictable, unpredictable or verging on chaos – in other words, whether the world is seen through the eyes of what Kirkbride, Durcan and Obeng (1994) term the modernist, sophisticated modernist or postmodernist view of change.

Briefly, a *modernist* view of the world would see change as incremental, evolutionary, constantly developing, following a linear path and worked out according to a known recipe about what should change and how. Thus modernists tend to believe in change models based on simple cause and effect: if the right levers are pulled in relation to desired outcomes, those outcomes should surely follow.

A *sophisticated modernist* view of the world would see change as transformational, revolutionary, periodic, following a circular path (i.e. 'moving in a complex and dynamic fashion from emerging strategy to deliberate strategy and back again' (Kirkbride *et al.*, p. 157)) and one where the end point can change as the change process unfolds. As a result, this view recognizes that the world does not stand still for long, hence the requirement for an approach to change that, according to Mintzberg (1990), creates change in response to emerging strategy.

The *postmodernist view* of change is best summed up in the words of Kirkbride *et al.* (pp. 158–9):

> The post-modern world can ... be seen as one characterized by randomness and chaos, by a lack of certainty, by a plethora of competing views and voices, by complex temporalities, and where organizations are unable to produce recipes for dealing with the unstable environment.

Others write similarly:

> In essence, the post-modernist approach rejects the notions of progress, linearity and regular patterning. Change can occur in any direction at any time, which itself could be conceived of in new ways such as 'spiral time'.
>
> (Burrell, 1992; Filicove and Filipec, 1986)

A cursory examination of some of today's organizations, and those in the future, will show that there is 'truth' in all these views of change – the 'trick' is to know when and where one or the other is current. For instance, in limited, constrained situations, a modernist view of change, may be most appropriate and might loosely be linked to the hard systems model of change, which implies transition rather than transformation and planned rather than emergent change.

The version of an OD model of change presented in the previous chapter is more congruent with a sophisticated modernist view of the world – provided the presence of continuous feedback loops is stressed and it is recognized that the vision and its associated change goals are not fixed – in the sense that the change process is never complete.

The postmodernist view of change does not easily attach itself to any recognizable model of change. What it does point towards, however, is a model of organization that is organic, flexible, niche market-oriented, where jobs are highly de-differentiated, de-demarcated and multi-skilled in a context of employment relationships based on subcontracting and networking (see Clegg, 1990 and the discussion of network and virtual organizations in Chapter 3). Change, in this context, could take on any number of faces and forms. Table 9.2 summarizes the issues raised in this chapter and briefly points the way for the organizations of the future.

Table 9.2 Paths to change

Considerations for the future	Implications for organizations
Demographic changes	• In western societies, service and product shift to meet the needs of adults 50+. In developing countries, cognizance taken of improving birth survival rates and increased longevity of life. • Changes in the expectations of women and members of minority groups in the workplace.
Changing lifestyles	• Issues associated with housing, transport, IT and environmental issues. • Increased expectations of health systems in relieving illness and contributing to longer lives.
Occupational changes	• Moves away from agrarian economies (in developing countries) and manufacturing (in western countries) towards a knowledge economy.
Changing employment policies and practices	• Changing nature of the psychological contract, increased demand for flexible working, social and corporate responsibility.
Operating virtually	• 24-hour 'opening', the influence of working across continents. • Increasing mobility of employees.

Comment and conclusions

Given what this chapter has said, successful change is more likely to take place effectively if the following happens:

- First, there is the need for continuous surveillance of the internal and external organizational environments as well as the temporal environment because, as pointed out in Chapter 1, time itself is a cause for change.
- Second, there is the need for change managers and facilitators to understand the characteristics of situations giving rise to change and be familiar with the different presenting characteristics so as not to think incremental change is appropriate when nothing but transformational change will do and vice versa.
- Finally, planning is all well and good, but success is more likely when plans remain flexible even to the extent of contemplating changes of vision, mission or purpose as time unfolds.

Although change can be planned, it quite frequently simply emerges. Whether planned or emergent, it takes a number of different forms, each of which requires a different type of action. While there is no one best way to achieve successful organizational change, making efforts to understand the wide variety of change situations and to be familiar with the different characteristics of change itself will help organizations and their members negotiate appropriate paths to change and, therefore, face the future with some degree of confidence. There are key areas that should be considered in relation to the diagnosis, implementation and review of change situations:

1 *Multiple paths to change*
- Continuous environmental scanning (internal and external) in order to get early warning of change demands.
- Understanding of the different types of change.
- Adopting a contingency approach to developing plans for managing change based on your understanding of the change scenario being faced.
- Building flexible plans.

2 *The challenge of diversity*
- Regarding differences between people as something to be valued.
- Recognizing that interacting with people across different cultures is essential to effective organizational effectiveness.

3 *Empowerment and control*
- Change is more likely to be a success if those it affects are willing collaborators.
- The effective collaboration of employees/stakeholders is more likely if they are involved at all stages of the change process and not just its implementation.
- Behaviours relevant to empowerment should be reinforced through appropriate reward mechanisms.

4 *Creativity and innovation*
- Creative and innovative approaches to change are more likely to flow from a diverse workforce.
- Creativity and innovation require a creative organizational climate if they are to flourish.
- The organization and its managers need to foster structures and processes that facilitate creativity.

Change is about nothing if it is not about persistence. This means persisting in the face of an ultra-unstable environment; persisting in the face of systems that are built for stability rather than change; persisting in the face of plans which are out of date as soon as they are formed. It means applying the same principles to people as are applied to 'things' – that is, the knowledge that nothing is perfect. This means recognizing that people will act in infuriating and annoying ways but that, when necessary, will bring the genius of their humanity to solve apparently insoluble problems. For organizations, it is learning that change is necessary, and often very effective even 'when business is good'. Change is not easy but it can be interesting. It is certainly worth the journey even if the place of arrival is surprising.

Discussion questions and assignments

1 How might using information gained from statistical trends help plan for change in organizations?

2 What do you think the future holds for your organization or one that interests you? How can you plan for this?

Indicative resources

Arnold, J. with, Silvester, J., Patterson, F., Robertson, I., Cooper, G. and Burnes, B. (2005) *Work Psychology* (4th edn), Harlow: Pearson Education. This book is extremely useful when focusing on trends that employers and managers face today and in the future. Chapters 7–15 focus on behaviour in the workplace and change. All of this is useful if you are managing people in the context of change management. Also useful for those interested in behaviour and change management.

Capon, C. (2004) *Understanding Organisational Context: Inside and Outside Organisations* (2nd edn), Harlow: Pearson Education Limited. This text has an introductory flavour of all areas associated with business. This is useful for students and managers who would like to set the scene for other areas of organizations, for example marketing, operations management and the competitive environment. It creates a useful context to which concepts in *Organizational Change* have further developed in relation to change management.

Useful websites

www.dti.gov.uk This is useful for statistics in relation to business and the economy in general. It also provides guidelines on policies and best practice within an organizational context.

www.inc.com/magazine The reader can find articles from many of the categories on offer, such as business, financial investment and education and reference. It focuses on research and current/future trends in the areas outlined above.

www.futurestudies.co.uk An independent 'think tank', specializing in advising how to understand and plan for possible/probable futures. Some useful discussion sites, i.e. the future of the European Union.

> To click straight to these links and for other resources go to
> **www.pearsoned.co.uk/senior**

References

Arnold, J, Silvester, J. Patterson, F., Robertson, I., Cooper, C. and Burnes, B. (2005) *Work Psychology: Understanding Human Behaviour in the Workplace*, Harlow: Pearson Education.

Ashoka: Innovators for the Public, 1700 North Moore Street, Suite 2000, Arlington, VA 22209; http://www.ashoka.org/fellows/social_entrepreneur.cfm

Bakshi, V. (1999) 'Financial products "must fit flexible work patterns"', *Financial Times*, 10 February, p. 9.

BBC News, 'Dads shun nappy changing for work', BBC News, www.bbc.co.uk, 26 July.

Bennett, R. (2000) 'Men outnumber women in working from home', *Financial Times*, 30 October.

Bennis, W. (2000) 'The end of leadership: exemplary leadership is impossible without the full inclusion, initiatives, and cooperation of followers', *Organizational Dynamics*, pp. 71–80.

Burrell, G. (1992) 'Back to the future: time and organization', in Reed, M. and Hughes, M. (eds) *Rethinking Organization: New Directions in Organization Theory and Analysis*, London: Sage.

Capon, C. (2004) *Understanding Organisational Context: Inside and Outside Organisations* (2nd edn), Harlow: Pearson Education Limited.

Cassidy, M. (2004) BBC News, 10 November; http://news.bbc.co.uk/go/pr/fr/-/northern-ireland/354008.stm

Chartered Institute of Personnel and Development (2004a) *Managing the Psychological Contract*, December, London: CIPD.

Chartered Institute of Personnel and Development (2004b) Report: *Recruitment, Retention and Turnover*, December, London: CIPD.

Clegg, S. R. (1990) *Modern Organization: Organization Studies in the Postmodern World*, London: Sage.

Cooper, C. (2001) 'Careers, work and life: ways of finding a better balance', *Financial Times Mastering Management*, 8 January, pp. 12–13.

Daniels, J. D. and Radebaugh, L. H. (2001) *International Business: Environments and Operations* (9th edn), Upper Saddle River, NJ: Prentice-Hall.

DEFRA *Household estimates and projections: 1971–2021.* www.defra.gov.uk; accessed 10 May 2005.

Department of Trade and Industry (2005) 'Results from the second flexible working survey', *Employment Relations Research Series No 39*, London: DTI; http://www.dti.gov.uk/bestpractice/people/flexible-working.htm

Dunphy, D. and Stace, D. (1993) 'The strategic management of corporate change', *Human Relations*, vol. 46, no. 8, pp. 905–20.

Filicove, B. and Filipec, J. (1986) 'Society and concepts of time', *International Social Sciences Journal*, vol. 107, pp. 19–32.

Government Actuary's Department (2004) 'United Kingdom population set to pass 60 million next year', News Release, GAD, Finiaison House, 15–17 Furnival Street, London EC4A 1AB; http://www.gad.gov.uk

Government Actuary's Department (2005) 'Marital status projections', 1991–2031, News Release 2005/1, 10 March. GAD, New King's Beam House, 22 Upper Ground, London SE1 9RJ; http://www.gad.gov.uk

Gracie, S. (1998) 'In the company of women', *Management Today*, June, pp. 66–9.

Institute for Employment Research (1997/8) Review of the Economy and Employment, University of Warwick.

Institute for Employment Research (2004) Bulletin Number 73, University of Warwick; http:ww2.warwick.ac.uk/ fac/soc/ier/publications/bulletins

Kandola, B. (2001) 'The future of diversity', British Psychological Annual Conference, Glasgow, 28 March–1 April.

Kautz, J. (2005) 'Small business notes: entrepreneurship beyond 2000'; http://www.smallbusinessnotes.com/aboutsb/beyond2000.html

Kehoe, L. (2000), 'Silicon power with added value', *Financial Times*, 8 November, p. 20.

Kirkbride, P. S., Durcan, J. and Obeng, E. D. A. (1994) 'Change in a chaotic world', *Journal of Strategic Change*, vol. 3, pp. 151–63.

Linday, C. and MacCauley, C. (2004) 'Growth in Self-employment in the UK', *Labour Market Division*, October. Office for National Statistics.

McGill, M. E. and Slocum, J. W., Jr (1998) 'A little leadership, please?', *Organizational Dynamics*, vol. 26, no. 3, pp. 39–49.

Maitland, A. (2000a) 'Women plan change of make-up in boardrooms: only 5 per cent of FTSE 100 directors are female, but campaigners seek to eliminate all-male culture', *Financial Times*, 7 November.

Maitland, A. (2000b) 'America's gender gap travels abroad', *Financial Times*, 20 October.

Miles, R. E., Snow, C. and Miles, G. (2000) 'The Future.org', *Long Range Planning*, 33, pp. 300–21.

Mintzberg, H. (1990) 'Strategy formation: schools of thought', in Frederickson, J. (ed.) *Perspectives on Strategic Management*, New York: Harper Business, pp. 105–235.

Office for National Statistics, 1 Drummon Gate, London, SW1V 2QQ; http://www.statistics.gov.uk/

Parker, B. (1998) *Globalization and Business Practice Managing Across Boundaries*, London: Sage.

Quinn, J. B. (1980) 'Managing strategic change', *Sloan Management Review*, vol. 21, no. 4, pp. 3–20.

Richards, L., Fox, K., Roberts, C., Fletcher, L. and Goddard, E. (2004) 'Living in Britain: Results from the 2002 General Household Survey'; www.statistics.gov.uk

Ridderstrale, J. (2000) 'Business moves beyond bureaucracy', *Financial Times Mastering Management*, 6 November, pp. 14–15.

Robbins, S. P. (2005), *Organizational Behavior* (11 edn), Upper Saddle River, NJ: Prentice-Hall.

Scase, R. (1999) *Britain Towards 2010: The Changing Business Environment*, Department of Trade and Industry, August.

Schein, E. (1999) 'Empowerment, coercive persuasion and organizational learning: do they connect?' *The Learning Organization*, vol. 6, no. 4, pp. 1–11.

Skills and Enterprise Executive (2001), 'Get a life, get a work life balance', London: Department of Education and Employment, 5EN 399.

Skyrme, D. (0000) http://www.skyrme.com/updates/ull.htm

Sparrow, P. R. (2000) 'New employee behaviours, work designs and forms of work organization: what is in store for the future of work?', *Journal of Managerial Psychology*, vol. 15, no. 3, pp. 202–18.

Stace, D. (1996) 'Dominant ideologies, strategic change, and sustained performance', *Human Relations*, vol. 49, no. 5, pp. 553–70.

Strebel, P. (1996) 'Choosing the right path', *Mastering Management*, Part 14, *Financial Times*.

Wagstyl, S. (2004) 'An endangered species: fewer births make old Europe fear for its future', *Financial Times*, 11 June p. 17.

Ward, L. (2005) 'Managers still fight flexible working', the *Guardian* 23 February; www.guardian.co.uk

Wilson, D. (1992) *A Strategy of Change, Concepts and Controversies in the Management of Change*, London: Routledge.

Wilson, R., Homenidou, K. and Dickerson, A. (2004) *Working Futures 2003–04: New Projections of Occupational Employment by Sector and Region, 2002–2012*, vol. 1, *National Report*, University of Warwick, Institute of Employment Research.

World Bank (2005) www.worldbank.org/datadataby-topic/reg-wdi.pdf.

Author index

(Please note that the page numbers in brackets indicate end of chapter reference pages)

Subject index